Plurality and Perspective in Psychoanalysis

Plurality and Perspective in Psychoanalysis

Adam Rosen-Carole

LEXINGTON BOOKS
Lanham • Boulder • New York • Toronto • Plymouth, UK

Published by Lexington Books
A wholly owned subsidiary of The Rowman & Littlefield Publishing Group, Inc.
4501 Forbes Boulevard, Suite 200, Lanham, Maryland 20706
www.rowman.com

10 Thornbury Road, Plymouth PL6 7PP, United Kingdom

British Library Cataloguing in Publication Information Available

Library of Congress Cataloging-in-Publication Data

Rosen-Carole, Adam, 1979-
Plurality and perspective in psychoanalysis / Adam Rosen-Carole.
p. cm.
Includes bibliographical references and index.
ISBN 978-0-7391-6951-3 (cloth : alk. paper)
1. Psychoanalysis. I. Title.
BF173.R648 2013
150.19'5--dc23

2012050316

The paper used in this publication meets the minimum requirements of American National Standard for Information Sciences Permanence of Paper for Printed Library Materials, ANSI/NISO Z39.48-1992.

Printed in the United States of America

Contents

Chapter One

Questions of Commitment

> The need to lend a voice to suffering is a condition of all truth.
>
> —T.W. Adorno, *Negative Dialectics*

THE AUTHORITY OF PRAXIS

What does it mean to be committed to psychoanalysis today? What is the nature of its claim, its authority? Why is psychoanalysis so compelling, indeed engrossing for some and yet so repulsive to or simply negligible for others? Most discussions of such questions rush headlong into the longstanding, largely stagnant debate about the *validity*, i.e., scientific credibility, of psychoanalytic knowledge or therapy. I would rather urge patience and suggest another, more circuitous path.

To be committed to psychoanalysis is at once a matter of seduction and rational conviction. On the one hand, psychoanalysis is incorrigibly seductive: strikingly adept at drawing out patterns of significance from what had seemed but brute facticity, extraordinarily helpful in making sense of what was otherwise obdurately obscure (perhaps all too familiar yet insufficiently understood), at their best, analytic interpretations are poignant, incisive, and practically orienting. Anyone with a predilection for detective stories, mysteries, or biographies (generally, for narrative) knows very well the force of this seduction — it is mesmerizing. From Freud's day to the present, psychoanalysis cannot but risk appearing as if a skeleton key capable of unlocking any and all mysteries, whether personal, cultural, or political: a universal solvent, an expository discourse of unlimited value and validity, yet another metaphysics. And precisely in virtue of the enthusiasm it may elicit, psychoanalysis risks impeding inquiry and instituting obscurity there where it yields provocative insight.[1] On the other hand, psychoanalysis is superbly convincing: in virtue of the scope, depth, and detail of the insights it affords, its therapeutic efficacy, and its partial corroboration by extra-clinical means, psychoanalysis solicits rational assent.

To be committed to psychoanalysis is to experience oneself and others through the insights and forms of attention learned from and through this type of research or encounter: it is a matter of conversion. In part, the authority of psychoanalysis is the authority of a form of life, which means that whether one comes to psychoanalysis as a patient, a practitioner, an academic, or altogether otherwise, its authority is encouraged by the various successes and discoveries — the flourishing — of the life of which it is a part. More precisely, this means that, in part, the authority of psychoanalysis emerges in and through the *sensibility* that one's life would be wanting in integrity, orientation, and fullness without the forms of attention, the insights, the questions and capacities it enables or encourages. *The authority of psychoanalysis is ineluctably, although not exclusively, first-personal.*

To say that the authority of psychoanalysis is in part first-personal is to say that its authority is elaborated but not simply grounded in the reasons we can share in support of our commitments to it, that its claim on us is irreducible to discursive reason. As with any conversion experience, there will always be a remainder of a discursively or thematically irrecuperable element, a persistent elusiveness of that which claims us, and thus an unsettledness of the claim itself. Call this the signature of the event. Consequently, when called upon for an account, accounting for the meaning and binding force of one's commitments involves not only showing that psychoanalytic theories or particular psychoanalytic interpretations are coherent, comprehensive, therapeutically effective, and/or confluent with evidence from various sectors of credible scientific research. Accounting for the authority of one's commitments to psychoanalysis is not just a matter of debunking or defusing skeptical claims that psychoanalytic knowledge is but wild speculation. Although this is important in its time and place, an adequate assessment of commitments to psychoanalysis involves an appreciation of psychoanalysis as a modern form of practical reason *(phronesis*). Only so understood can the character of commitments to psychoanalysis be appropriately elaborated and assessed.

As a form of practical reason, psychoanalysis is not just a doctrine or set of theoretical statements and principles that can be externally applied to various life-contexts. To apply theory from afar is to be as if out of touch with the world, insulated from the liabilities of experience, unable to undergo the unfolding of life as suggesting or compelling a certain perspective (or range of perspectives) on it and on oneself as involved in it. Thus, paradoxically, such efforts of application yield self-estrangement by means of a fantasy of interpretive sovereignty; lose the world in the pursuit of unfettered access to it; forfeit whatever rational authority they might claim as they become absorbed in a fantasy of the inviolable integrity of a surveying rational consciousness. To be committed to psychoanalysis, on the contrary, is to undergo a sort of suggestibility or compulsion, to suffer a passion or even madness that yields insight, and in the name of a more robust dispensation of reason to resist the rational anxiety that ensues.[2]

To be sure, a certain detachment from and thus disorientation in the world, call it the insuperability of practical skepticism or the fact of autonomy, is inevitable; it is our nature. Modern social conditions that foster moral isolation, ruthless self-interest, and other manners of social abstraction may make this condition more conspicuous, but they do not on their own account for it. We are doubly displaced: from nature, of which we are certainly a part, yet which cannot fully guide or direct us; and from culture, which as our "second nature" cannot but condition and orient us, though forever incompletely. And under conditions of expansionist social rationalization — conditions wherein, increasingly, forms of social reproduction are externally imposed, bereft of sensuously compelling and reflectively endorsable claims, unresponsive or insufficiently responsive to our needs and desires, i.e., coercively *in force* irrespective of whether or not they organize a world hospitable to the flourishing of the various beings subject to them — our displacement is exacerbated, often unbearably so. The affective corollary of social reification — forms of social reproduction the motivations for and mechanism of which are insistently obscure, even self-obscuring, thus largely unimpactable by those caught up in them — is a paradoxical sense of displacement, a sense of being dominated yet detached, immured yet adrift. Or at least anxious investments in ossified social life, as much as resistances to it, suggest as much.

But that we are not wholly governed by nature or culture — that, as Hegel suggests, the right of subjectivity is indeed infinite — obviously does not mean that we are untouched by them, that we are estranged to the point that all we can do is assume this alienation, either by cynically reveling in it[3] or by plaintively lamenting our loss.[4] Assuming a detached perspective from which to apply theoretical principles to various life-contexts is both cause and effect of a nihilism that psychoanalysis, as a modern form of *phronesis*, and so an attempt to sustain significant passivity, continually resists. Such a perspective is the false sovereignty made all the more tempting in a world in which we feel constrained and controlled yet insufficiently supported, hemmed in yet abandoned and disoriented. It is the perspective on ourselves that we feel the world has taken: one which we cannot abide, and yet, anxiously, feel compelled to assume. It is a self-infliction and naturalization of the social injury we suffer that carries with it a seductive, however thin, aura of agency. It is masochism parading as agency, compulsive repetition as reason.

In an increasingly socially engineered world whose touch is often too rough and rigid, yet in whose intrusive embrace we nonetheless feel isolated, it is tempting, all too tempting, to attempt to assume a position of detachment and thereby disclaim the often discomfiting touch of the world as no connection at all. (Or conversely, we might attempt to assume our immersion in the world in a largely unreflective and uncomplicated way, bury ourselves in routines, lifestyles, domestic pursuits and disputes, etc., but the anxious impulsion to social immersion bears traces of the reflective disquietude it seeks to deny; and in any case this would be just the flipside of the same.) Fantasmatically fashioning ourselves as self-enclosed spectators who survey and select our life paths from afar, seeking to abstract ourselves from the residual, however opaque, claims of nature and the complicated cultural and political inheritances (tradition, "prejudice,"[5] etc.) by which we are permeated and in-formed, we become the alienated consumers and effective bureaucrats we are meant to be: ideologically ensnared in the world from which we presume a fundamental detachment.

Does not the hasty, anxious assumption of such detachment bespeak an overwhelming, unnegotiated connection, a wordliness that is its persistent condition? Does not even the attempted assumption of such detachment bespeak its inherence in a world that might be inhabited fundamentally otherwise?

To begin to appreciate the compelling character of psychoanalysis as a modern form of *phronesis* is to appreciate the posture of applying theory from afar, of spectatorial abstraction and uncommitted engagement, as an attempted leave-taking from a scene of life from which it forever fails to fully extract itself: today, a socially enforced fantasy of independence. To apply theory to various life-contexts is to presumptuously excuse oneself from a social gathering from which one has already been ejected, and at once to disavow the interrelatedness and interdependency of the lifeworld in which we are always already enveloped. It is to indulge a hubristic and defensive desire to secure a posture of self-subsistence as a condition for connection to and conviction in the world — in effect, blackmail. Does not the attempt to achieve such sovereign independence, especially given the vigor with which it is pursued in the face of its obvious paradoxes and impasses, look like a defensive retreat from an insistent permeability, an ongoing exposure to the oftentimes confusing and disorienting unfurling of events, from the flux of life in general and our reified social world in particular? As much as this stance may contribute to certain scientific and technological developments that are not to be underestimated, *as a fundamental stance* such autonomy is an indemnification purchased at too high a price: the price of stillness, of coldness to the movements of life. This so-called autonomy is our mortification. Evasion of unseemly complexity and indeterminateness, of the insistence of the object, cannot but culminate in paralysis.

This is by no means to decry reflective distance. Such detachment may amount to a provisional respite from the inordinate intricacies of experience, a contemplative refuge in which to take shelter from the oftentimes overwhelming complexity of events. At its best, such a stance is a provisional resting point from which we seek more adequate perspectives on events for which our habits of understanding and practical response have proven inadequate, a pole of an unending dialectical oscillation, the other end of which is (remediated) exposure to and immersion in the flow of life in its indefinite becoming, its excess of anticipation.[6] However, disintricated from this dialectic and assumed as a fundamental stance, such autonomy forever fails to orient us *in* the world; it broadens the gap between self and world in the very effort to bridge it. From such a perspective, the world becomes merely a grid of information to be drawn upon, indifferently available to the classifications and calculations of our self-initiated projects, dead to us because invested with significance only by us. And in turn, we become dead to the world: unresponsive to its claims on us (and in us), insulated from its subtle and not so subtle insistences, condemned to a false freedom. Such a perspective is solitary confinement masquerading as engaged life.

But, to be sure, deadness is a fate of the living. Such detachment can never achieve the emancipation from the flux of life desired, is never quite as immune from the lifeworld's touch as it presumes. Sustaining this stance proceeds through the perpetual disavowal of dependency, the incessant repudiation of the touch of the world, the continual deadening of sensitivities to that by which we are claimed and captivated, and to ourselves as so claimed. Such detachment feeds on our worldliness, preying on and surreptitiously elaborating the touch of the world it would deny. That we are fundamentally unresponsive to the world's claims on us and in us is little more than presumption: a fantasy of sovereign stillness. Such presumption condemns those under its spell to responsive dispositions to which they will tend to remain oblivious or prone to disavow: the pursuit of freedom becoming the everlasting occasion for self-restriction; the pursuit of unfettered rationality becoming a practice of studied ignorance.

To apply theory from afar is an assault on the essential exposedness of the human — indeed, both an assault on this exposure and an effect of it. It is an assault on the human as unavoidably open to and propelled by that which cannot be brought back to its decisions and decrees, on that which traverses the human, situating decision and decree — broadly, cognitive and practical self-determination — as indelibly belated, an *affirmation* of that which is already in motion. To be sure, to affirm in this sense is not simply to accommodate oneself retrospectively to what is already the case; it is not to confuse facticity with intractable fate. Rather, affirming — which is to say, committing to — that by which we are captivated, claimed, or moved is an opening onto, perhaps an inflecting appropriation, of what will have been[7] our determinate possibilities for understanding and intervening in the world. It is an opening onto involvements that exceed our powers of legislation and appropriation out of which arise our capacities to spark developments in the flux of becoming, to inflect life in its unfolding and renew its comprehension. Affirmation is ambivalent, undecided: inextricably related to beginning, innovating, ushering in the unanticipated, as much as to receptivity, inheritance, even the undergoing of the immutable. It is the drama of experience: a dialectic of freedom and necessity. Affirmation, here a cipher for the temporality of praxis, cannot be thought as either (1) simply a *retrospective* accommodation to what is given or (2) simply a *projective*, voluntaristic willfulness. To affirm is to attune to, to commit ourselves to, the unfolding of life in its (in)determinate — highly conditioned yet persistently enigmatic and open-ended — possibilities, to life and to ourselves as developing into what it and we may yet be. It is to open onto the futurities latent within the development of life, which means, simultaneously, to open onto one's concrete possibilities for understanding, intervening, and self-actualization: for understanding and influencing the development of phenomena from within and thereby learning how to become oneself. It is a matter of living the interval.

Practical reason is a form of affirmation or commitment that involves embracing and avowing our exposure to life, adhering both to its determinate and determining articulations and to its mutability, its incessant becoming, its extra-rational insistence, in order to orient ourselves *within* it. This involves an unrelenting attention to phenomena unfolding from what they manifestly are into what they are yet-to-be (including but not limited to what they are yet-to-be-seen-as), a steadfast attention to and reckoning with futurities latent in the present, indeed fracturing the present, preventing it from collapsing and congealing into a closed, (de)finite givenness. This involves unremitting attention to life in its concreteness, which is to say, its imperfectly legible blend of determinacy (manifestness) and indeterminacy (potentiality), and so resolute attention to ourselves as the loci of certain possibilities for the world's development otherwise.

As a form of practical reason, psychoanalysis is a cultivated and compelling form of perception (not simply nature, not simply culture — pressing for a reworking of that old dichotomy), a manner of inhabiting the world through which otherwise illegible features of experience are interpreted and otherwise unnoticed features of experience are illuminated in ways that guide but do program our responses to them. Practical reason is a wellspring of heteronomous impulsions, that is, affectively weighty inclinations to respond to phenomena in specific sorts of ways: the medium of a certain manner of objectivity. Against the Kantian urge to condemn psychoanalysis on this ground, i.e., as "impure" practical reason, it is important to underscore that it is precisely the impulsions yielded by our commitments and convictions, by our exposure to that which touches and moves us, and so by the priority of the object or the other, that opens the space of agency.[8] Wanting for such exposure, the pursuit of autonomy would be paralyzed because empty.

If it is a modern form of *phronesis*, our commitments to psychoanalysis cannot be thought apart from the successes and failures they yield in practice, e.g., their felicity in attuning us to various features of experience as significant and advantageous orienting of our responses to them. Such responses may take various forms: from puzzlement and reflective reverie, to sustained inquiry, to specific sorts of action, to abiding in and yielding to the affective textures of experience, to various ways of acknowledging the distortions, fractures, and allusiveness of experience, to name only a few. What is important to underscore is that commitments to psychoanalysis are to be evaluated in terms of their success in keeping us *in touch* with others and with ourselves (oftentimes as utterly elusive, to be sure), in terms of their ability to mediate a world within which our forms of perception, reflection, and response are *sensible*, that is, meaningful, experientially weighty, and sensible within the context of our aims and constraints.[9] Along with Kristeva, we can now say that one of the key tasks of psychoanalysis is to promote a tendential reintegration of the semiotic and the symbolic: resistance to nihilism.

It is one thing to conclude as a result of a certain demonstration that psychoanalysis generally or a particular psychoanalytic interpretation is rationally defensible. It is quite another matter to be compelled or claimed by certain dimensions of experience to take a psychoanalytic perspective on them and respond accordingly (or more precisely, to affirm and commit to a perspective already obtaining), fully acceding to the vulnerability of and responsibility for such a commitment, responding in a way that would neither forget nor suppress the affective weight of what moved one to respond in the first place nor one's role in sustaining the space within which such pathos unfolds. The first-personal authority of psychoanalysis is a matter of the compelling force it accrues through the successes and discoveries of the life it conditions, indeed from which it becomes indissociable. This is to say, though, that the first-personal authority of psychoanalysis, as achieved through the flourishing of the life of which it is a part, is limited by social, economic, and suchlike forces that impede, diminish, or corrupt such flourishing. The compelling character of psychoanalysis, its authority, is conditioned by the shape of our world, indeed doubly so: (1) (to maximally compress the point) "wrong life cannot be lived rightly";[10] (2) in part, what makes psychoanalysis compelling in late capitalist modernity is its facilitation of a modicum of resistance against the tendential severance of subject and substance, i.e., the socially enforced compulsion to assume a stance of fundamental detachment and the consequent disorientation in a field awash with possibility. As the authority of psychoanalysis is attendant upon the success of attempts to forge patterns of conceptual entailment and material inference and incompatibility, and as such success must be social if the authority of psychoanalysis is to be sustainable and not just that of a neurotic mythology, the authority of psychoanalysis, even first-personally, cannot but be fraught in a context of expansionist social rationalization. The psychoanalytic aspiration is today near-utopian: at stake is nothing less than reactivating experience and tradition, thus community and history, in a way that would be subjectively satisfying, i.e., would respect the infinite right of subjectivity, and even more, would proceed through the unsealing of sensitivity from the protective encasement of its information-bombarded shell where, taking shelter from systematic manipulation, it withers. The authority of psychoanalysis is extremely frail in the face of the forces it is up against, which perhaps partially explains the tendency of many analysts to in-group, jargon-heavy parochialism.

Surely, though, first-personal experiences of the compelling character of psychoanalysis — the sense that it exposes dimensions of life that would otherwise remain concealed and encourages life-enhancing capabilities — are woefully insufficient to qualify psychoanalysis as a legitimate mode of self- and world-disclosure, especially to those inclined to disqualify all forms of knowing that do not neatly fall in with the protocols of the modern sciences. Social rationalization is the tendential evisceration of the media of exemplary authority. Even for those not so inclined to equate the full scope of knowledge with what can be yielded or verified by the protocols of the natural sciences, who are disposed to acknowledge authority arising from sources other than the valid application of scientific method, the practical authority of psychoanalysis, i.e., the first-personal authority it garners through experiences of the flourishing to which it is believed to contribute or reflective affirmations of the life of which it is a part, may nonetheless be insufficiently persuasive.

How then does one make psychoanalysis persuasive? How can one elaborate and support one's commitments to psychoanalysis in an age under the ascendancy of science? How to motivate the interest and credulity of those who do not share our convictions (including those parts of oneself that do not fully share one's psychoanalytic convictions)? How can commitments to psychoanalysis be authorized other than first-personally? Or can they? It is precisely the palpable power of psychoanalysis to claim and organize its adherents' attention, even indeed sometimes to inspire a certain zeal, that is bound to provoke questions about indoctrination and ideology, about psychoanalysis as a new religiosity[11] or mythology.[12] It is important to engage these questions, which also means engaging the various cultural conversations in which the theoretical and therapeutic claims of psychoanalysis are debated, tested, and thought through, not only in order to support the claims of psychoanalysis to cultural legitimacy (a condition of even its first-personal authority), but also to refine our sense of what we are committed to. Through such refinement, the quality of our judgments that would affirm—or deny—the influence of psychoanalysis may be significantly enhanced; and even if not, the yield of self-awareness would be hardly negligible.

Psychoanalysis has never been immune from stringent critique, and however much the vehemence of such critique may be responsible for confining the force, originality, and insight of psychoanalysis to somewhat isolated sectors of therapeutic work and the academy,[13] the barrage of criticism to which it has been continually subject is not to be lamented. The persuasiveness of psychoanalysis — its ability to claim us as a compelling form of knowledge and not just a compulsive habit of the imagination — is indissociable from the successes with which psychoanalytic insights and procedures have withstood various forms of critical scrutiny. To withstand is not necessarily to unequivocally triumph in the face of critical questions, let alone to lay skepticism to rest once and for all, but perhaps to find ways of abiding in and working through the problematics opened by critique, to negotiate such problems thoughtfully rather than combatively, to find some grace in the choreography of claim-making and critique. Psychoanalysis is and will remain problematic, never above suspicion, because, as we will see, its plurality generates an unavoidable, "internal" moment of skepticism (among other reasons). What is important to underscore for now is that explicitly critical discourses that seek to debunk psychoanalysis as a legitimate form of knowledge or therapy, as much as the weight of the world (problems, conflicts, sufferings) that challenges psychoanalytically-informed capacities to make sense of it or make our way through it with any measure of success, are, in a way, salutary.[14] Without such challenges as promptings to dialectical clarifications, our understanding of what we are committed to would be much less clear. And without a certain skepticism about psychoanalysis, both personally and culturally, and the various ways of testing its claims prompted by such skepticism, psychoanalysis would risk devolution into dogma, especially amongst those strongly committed to various partisan perspectives. The suggestion, then, is not just to accept the irrepressibility of skepticism but to appreciate its dialectical value. Otherwise, one can only despair of — i.e., hastily dismiss — that which is not fully immune from it, which is to say, everything.[15]

SUBJECTIVITY, OBJECTIVITY

In the course of exploring the question of what it means to be committed to psychoanalysis, Jonathan Lear has emphasized that such commitments are fostered through an unending reflexive return to the questions of what psychoanalysis is and what it is to be an analyst. Eloquently and with great insight, Lear underscores the never-ending nature of developing oneself as analyst: to be an analyst is to confront, time and again, the question of what it is to be an analyst, to sustain this question as a question, and so to continually develop oneself as an analyst through engaging this question. The paradigmatic question for Lear is: Is *this* analysis? Is *this* particular therapeutic relationship, in its uniqueness, a recognizable permutation of psychoanalysis even though its specific texture is different from any previous instance of psychoanalytic therapy? Even though Lear does not take the thought in this direction, one may infer that commitments to psychoanalysis among current or former analysands, or even in those who have never experienced clinical psychoanalysis, are likewise manifest not only in decisions to undertake or remain in psychoanalytic therapy but also in reflection in the service of refining the practices in which these commitments become meaningful. To be committed to psychoanalysis in these cases too implies putting the insights and forms of attention learned in the clinic (or elsewhere) to the test in everyday life. And the success of this life — measured by its passionate fullness; by the ability to bear tension, frustration, and anxiety; by felicitous reflection on and the ability to work toward the attainment of our various and varied desires; by the well-cultivated capacity to receive and respond to our desires and meanings as well as those of others — is simultaneously the measure and meaning of one's commitment to psychoanalysis. Lear puts the point in these concise terms: "Analysis has a termination, therapeutic action does not" (2004, 33). Therapeutic action names the ongoing employment of psychoanalysis in a life wherein the meaning of psychoanalysis, and so the meaning of one's commitments to it, are developed through discoveries and successes both within and beyond the clinic.

This sounds right, so far as it goes. However, Lear's account makes it seem as if the practical authority of psychoanalysis is its *only* measure and meaning. Are the reasons we can give to support our commitments to psychoanalysis as not just efficacious or life-enhancing but a genuine form of knowledge wholly irrelevant to the authority of psychoanalysis, either first- or third-personally? Mustn't it matter that psychoanalysis can stake a reasonable claim to genuine insight? In making the legitimacy of psychoanalysis exclusively a question of its therapeutic efficacy, or more broadly, practical authority, Lear forestalls the development of judgments about the validity of psychoanalytic knowledge, sidestepping a needed debate about the third-personal authority of psychoanalytic knowledge — a debate needed if psychoanalysis is to assume the cultural standing its adherents cannot but want for it and which its skeptical detractors are unwilling to admit so long as it comes up short before the standards of the exact sciences. What is missing from Lear's account is an inquiry into how engaging the question "What is psychoanalysis?" may lead not only to maintaining our commitments and transforming our understanding of that to which we are committed but also to developing persuasive accounts of psychoanalytic insights and forms of attention as genuinely disclosive.[16] Is not every experimental investigation of a psychoanalytic claim a way of asking "What is psychoanalysis?"

Psychoanalysis rightfully emerges from Lear's account as (1) underdetermined, that is, ever-available to re-signification within certain parameters, and (2) an ever-developing practice rather than a fixed set of skills or insights. As he concisely puts the point, "[p]sychoanalysis is, in part, constituted by an ongoing debate on what psychoanalysis is" (2004, 55). Although Lear's focus is on the development of the meaning of psychoanalysis from the point of view of the clinician, this formulation suggestively implies that the meaning of psychoanalysis is not determined exclusively by clinicians' self-understandings but also by a variety of others who have in various ways internalized psychoanalytic insights, forms of attention, and modes of research. And yet, while Lear masterfully brings out the *indeterminacy* and *variability* of what it means to be committed to psychoanalysis and establishes the internal connection between the indeterminacy of psychoanalysis and the task of continually developing oneself as an analyst, what is missing is an account of how we can *learn* about psychoanalysis from the concrete challenges that provoke reflection on its indeterminacy, specifically about the nature and status of its claims and concepts, and so about ourselves as committed to a cognitive-therapeutic practice of this type. To his credit, Lear will not go as far as Joseph Sandler in saying that "psychoanalysis is what is practiced by psychoanalysts," thus tacitly admitting absurd enterprises such as Reich's late work on "orgone energy" into the fold (1982, 44). But *why* such practices should not be regarded as psychoanalytic Lear does not, perhaps cannot say.

What Lear fails to emphasize is that one rarely if ever faces the questions "What is it to be a psychoanalyst?" or "What is psychoanalysis?" in the abstract, i.e., in solitary, speculative contemplation. Rather, one tends to raise and engage these questions when prompted by specific difficulties, challenges, or failures, the successful negotiations of which allow us to refine our understanding of the nature and status of psychoanalysis and so develop accounts of its compelling character in other than first-personal terms.[17] Thus, what needs to be underscored is that crises or aporias in psychoanalytic theories and practices ("practices" here understood in the broad sense of "life practices") afford not only opportunities for practical improvement and theoretical insight into the *indeterminacy* of psychoanalytic knowledge (although these are not to be underestimated), they also offer opportunities to develop and refine judgments about the nature and status of psychoanalytic claims, and so to enhance the rational force of our commitments to them and facilitate the development of persuasive accounts of their "validity."

And worse, Lear's account more or less ensures that psychoanalysis will never be acknowledged as cognitively and practically compelling in a culture under the sway of scientism,[18] while simultaneously insulating the cultural hegemony of Science from the provocations of psychoanalysis and sophisticated science. Within Lear's framework, it becomes wholly unintelligible why a culture such as ours would ever want, let alone need, to take the cognitive or practical potential of psychoanalysis seriously. In having psychoanalysis' claim to legitimacy mirror a limited self-conception of science wherein its authority is simply a matter of its instrumental efficacy, its ability to shape the world in accord with the prerogatives of privileged human desire (as if the authentic discoveries of science were irrelevant to its cultural authority), Lear opens the door to the charge that medicalized psychiatry or cognitive-behavioral therapy can achieve "results" more quickly and cost-effectively than psychoanalysis. Such a charge is of course true — pills can neutralize depression or anxiety much more quickly than psychoanalysis can, say, induce modifications in overburdened psychic structures — but beside the point.[19] The question is whether we want depression or anxiety *neutralized* or rather value other sorts of responses to our suffering: a question, ultimately, of who we take ourselves to be.

The claim of psychoanalysis to cultural authority cannot simply turn on the question of its "efficacy" if only because this criterion is too equivocal to serve as a pivot for the comparison of different therapies: psychoanalysis often has different aims (which are not necessarily outcomes; sometimes the goal is the path or the development of the science[20]) than other therapies, so its effectiveness in achieving its aims tells us little to nothing about how it is to be assessed vis-à-vis therapies with different aims.[21] Or if by "efficacy" one means the most adequate means to accomplish established ends, and these ends are defined by a culture that prizes accommodation and integration above all, e.g., return to love and work, then psychoanalysis will be forever found wanting. Given our cultural climate, the authority of psychoanalysis in the foreseeable future will stand or fall with the accounts we can develop to motivate acceptance of the rationality (the sensibleness, the specific objectivity) of psychoanalytic knowledge and esteem for the kinds of results — the forms of life — available through psychoanalytic practice.

In modeling the claims of psychoanalysis on a limited self-conception and criteriology of science — i.e., in shutting out the insights of sophisticated, self-reflective scientists and philosophers of science, namely, those who understand the authority of scientific practices to issue from factors other than their brute efficacy — and then collapsing the differences between psychoanalysis and science, Lear leaves no room for conversation *between* psychoanalysis and science, and dooms the defense of the former by implicitly conceding the framework of evaluation to the latter. Thus, to the extent that science is a placeholder for cultural authority, Lear's account blocks the development of the claims of psychoanalysis to cultural authority.

In order to make what is at stake in my misgivings about Lear's account more perspicuous, let us take a closer look at his argument. A psychoanalyst,

Lear contends, is one who "constitutes herself as a certain kind of subject by repeatedly and creatively bringing herself back to the project of becoming/being a psychoanalyst" (2004, 38). What it is to be an analyst is forever uncertain and unfinished, anything but a stable and secure accomplishment. To be an analyst, Lear explains, is a "subjective concept" in the sense that it requires the creative work of subjects who are perpetually learning to live with psychoanalysis. The meaning of the concept is coextensive with the ways we (analysts) develop to live with it or live it out: its meaning is coextensive with its use. Fortunately, albeit perhaps symptomatically, Lear does not leave the meaning of psychoanalysis wholly to the discretion of those who self-identify as analysts; its meaning cannot be simply posited, enacted by force of will. Psychoanalysis unfolds within certain limits. For instance, analysts must find ways of understanding and contributing to the self-understanding of analysands without imposing or even suggesting determinate paths to recovery.

> We avoid suggesting this or that outcome to our analysands, avoid moralizing, avoid telling them that they really will be happy if only they achieve this particular social goal. In that sense, we are not in the business of psyche-synthesis. At best, we try to facilitate a process in which the analysands can engage in psyche-synthesis for themselves. We help others come to better understand themselves, but how they go on with that better understanding is up to them. (2004, 60-61)

Thus, "when we can identify a certain form of human interaction as 'suggestion,' we are in a position to reject it as part of psychoanalytic technique" (2004, 35). The anonymous authority of the ban on "suggestion" is the inverse image of the open-ended concept.

The work of the analyst, Lear suggests, is similar to the work of love: "*Lover* is a subjective concept in the sense that someone who loves is constantly in the process of shaping herself into a person who loves. She is constantly in the process of becoming a certain kind of subject. This is an unending project. A person can dedicate her life to better understanding — and better living out — what it is to love others. There is no end to the ever-deepening complexity — or simplicity — of the project" (2004, 38). A lover is one who continually asks herself, "'What it is to love (this person or idea)?'" (2004, 38). Likewise, for Lear, an analyst is one who asks what it is to love, to be committed to, psychoanalysis through her ongoing efforts to eliminate all elements of suggestion from her practice. The eradication of suggestion aims to (1) help the analysand "understand himself better, and to help him understand the [analytic] relationship" (2004, 54), and (2) facilitate the analysand's freedom, which means "not influencing our analysands to pursue any particular end, but . . . helping them to develop their own capacities for self-understanding, for understanding of others, and for thinking through what they want to do based on a better understanding of who they are and what they want" (2004, 54).[22] Another parameter is set as Lear argues that an analyst must keep "present to her mind a vivid sense of what is involved in preserving and facilitating the analytic relationship . . . . by ever renewed questioning of what would be involved in betraying it . . . . [and] seeing the analysis through to the end" (2004, 56-7). To be a lover or an analyst is to concernfully contend with the inadequacies of habit, with the risk of infelicity (betrayal, monotony, injury) run by the extension of previously felicitous practices. It is to respond to the singular relationship as it unfolds — often in surprising, although usually not wholly unanticipatable ways — day after day. Each day, to love is to respond with passion and compassion to the needs, desires, strivings, and sufferings that are at once unique to this day and conditioned by the history of the beloved's wishes, hopes, dreams, fears, and frustrations. So too, to analyze is to respond afresh, day after day, albeit with somewhat different aims, means, and intentions.[23]

Similarly, Lear suggests, "I constitute myself as a scientist by keeping myself open to changing how I investigate the realm that matters to me, in light of better understandings of what it would be to yield knowledge in that realm. It is essential to being a scientist that I ever be engaged with the question of how to live as a scientist. What counts as scientific activity is the activity of a scientist who behaves appropriately as such" (2004, 44). This claim is echoed and reinforced as Lear later emphasizes that a

> scientist is someone who shapes herself as a subject by ever-renewed commitment to inquiring into a certain realm in appropriate ways. The true scientist, then, will not just be inquiring into a certain realm, she will also be inquiring into the best ways of inquiring into that realm. Indeed, I constitute myself as a scientist to some extent by keeping myself open to changing how I investigate a given realm, in light of better understandings of what it would be to yield knowledge in that realm. (2004, 63-4)

In part, this claim is compelling. The history of science suggests that there is no single, determinate method that will yield conclusive, fully satisfactory knowledge of a particular object-domain, and as will be discussed later, there are reasons logically independent of this history to believe that theory is always underdetermined by evidence; thus keeping oneself open to changing one's forms of investigation is and will remain crucial to developing oneself as a scientist. Changing the assumptions, procedures, and aims of investigation on the basis of new findings is no doubt central to the development of science. If precision is understood as an unflinching acknowledgement of the specific complexions of determinacy and indeterminacy, of insight and obscurity, yielded by particular investigative strategies, then scientific knowledge becomes increasingly precise as it develops ways to acknowledge its findings as conditioned (limited, and thereby enabled) by its strategies of inquiry, which is to say: enhanced precision and openness to further inquiry (or inquiry otherwise) go hand-in-hand. Science, like psychoanalysis, is interminable.

But is the relatively open and reflexive investigation of a "realm that matters to me" an adequate characterization of scientific pursuit? Surely not. The account is much too thin and one-sided. Certainly not all investigations of "the realm that matters to me" are "appropriately" termed scientific investigations. Would Lear corroborate Bion's flippant remark in *Learning From Experience* (1962) about "all investigation being ultimately scientific"? (14) Likely not. Not all methods of inquiry are scientific and not all phenomena can or should be investigated scientifically. Science devolves into idealist ideology, into scientism, when its methods are uncritically extended to phenomena for which they are inapposite, say, when passion is hypothetically reduced to neurochemical reactions or behavioral dispositions and investigated as such, or when political commitment is measured and interpreted by sheer ballot count. The natural sciences presume certain concepts of their objects — e.g., that they are inert matter whose intelligibility is given through the laws under which they fall, that they are reproducible under experimental conditions, that their relevant features are fully quantifiable and mathematizable — that may not be appropriate models for the phenomena under investigation, thus when uncritically extended may misconstrue and occlude various salient aspects of such phenomena. Science yields a qualified truth. That something is *living*, say, organically integrated and thus perhaps violated rather than simply reconfigured if torn apart or impeded rather than simply caused to move otherwise if prevented from developing in accord with the natural-historical tendencies of its species,[24] cannot be registered as significant by mathematical physics. Indeed, a wide array of qualitative and normative features of various phenomena cannot be registered *as significant* by the perspective of modern mechanics or chemistry. Although science becomes modern (anti-dogmatic) through its commitment to the authority of empirical observation, modern science — at least in its canonical articulation — founds itself by constitutively excluding experience, casting it as "mere subjectivity" and contraposing it to the anonymity of impartial observation. More precisely, what is excluded is experience (thus history, tradition, technique, etc.) as a *productive* cognitive medium, a contributor to rather than ideal register of cognitive content. Some dim acknowledgment of the limitations of his account of science is contained in Lear's "to some extent" ("Indeed, I constitute myself as a scientist to some extent by keeping myself open to changing how I investigate a given realm"), but the qualifying phrase is barely noticeable as it is swept up in his emphasis on the status of science as a subjective concept. What science is other than a subjective concept is left utterly opaque.[25]

In its opacity, Lear's account of science vacillates between a vague voluntarism and an equally vague institutionalism: science is either what I, a scientist, call science or what the institution of science calls science. Both get something right: there is a moment of (probative) voluntarism involved in the arguably endless, iconoclastic or less aggressive suspensions of prevailing paradigms and otherwise unprecedented and (partially) underivable displacements through which new paths are projected (an anti-authoritarian, anti-traditional, i.e., skeptical moment of science is irreducible); and absent institutional acceptation, i.e., conventionalization as research methods and agendas, innovative proposals are stranded as mere possibilities, tendentially empty and inert. But neither independently nor together do voluntarism and institutionalism make for a satisfying account of science. One indication of this inadequacy is that both fail to account in any informative way for practices that claim to be scientific but are found not to be so; they cannot explain why we would ever call or want to call an inquiry pseudoscience, or scientific only in a qualified sense, or ascientific (say, ethical or philosophical), or simply nonscientific. All that can be said is just: this is not the way I (or we) do it. Thus both fail to limit the meaning of science in a way that allows its determinacy — let alone the specific determinacies of the various sciences irreducible to a monolithic science — to come into view in such a way that we could account for what is distinctive and valuable about (the) science(s) (thus for "the best ways of inquiring into that realm," the pursuit of which characterizes the "true scientist"), where its (or their) limits lay, and what counts as violating these limits. What falls away is (1) any relevant, informative distinction between science and scientism, thus (2) the ability for science(s) to become self-knowing and self-limiting, i.e., increasingly precise. What would be a "betrayal" of (some) science on Lear's account other than failing to remain open to the question of how one ought to inquire into a domain of interest? And more to the point, what would be the success conditions for this criterion, i.e., what would count as fidelity as opposed to betrayal? If norms are criteria for achievements, and various forms of failing to satisfy such criteria do not clarify the nature and significance of the achievements at issue, then normative *learning* becomes impossible and norms tend to solidify into and stagnate as dogma.

In a voluntarist vein, Lear characterizes science as just another subjective concept, as if *scientific* investigation is coextensive with the reflexive return to the question of what it is to "investigate the realm that matters to me" on the part of those who identify as scientists. Perhaps disquieted by such lassitude, Lear stipulates that such reflexive return is motivated by the "light of better understandings of what it would be to yield knowledge in that realm." But the qualification "in light of better understandings of what it would be to yield knowledge in that realm," though certainly salutary, either gives the lie to the voluntarist frame or breaks the relay of scientist-lover-psychoanalyst as identically subjective concepts. Perhaps Lear's suggestion is that it is not just any reflexive return but one based on authentic discovery or genuine methodological advancement that characterizes an investigative practice as scientific. If so, the meaning of science is determined not by any old subjective recreation of oneself "as a scientist," but only by the ways of doing so that are guided by and so may yield genuine understanding. This qualification would be the equivalent to the constraints Lear establishes for what constitutes genuine psychoanalysis. But what constitutes "better understanding," let alone "the best ways of inquiring," is left woefully indeterminate. As much as the constraints Lear's places on "authentic" psychoanalysis are too restrictive and heavy-handed — why is any element of suggestion inadmissible? Is the elimination of suggestion possible even if desirable? — the parameters he sets for science are too flimsy and vague. Perhaps "better understandings" just means understandings that allow for greater instrumentalization of the natural world (the development of techniques and technologies); or perhaps it means an enhanced quantifiability and manipulability of the matter at hand; or perhaps it means understandings validated by findings in other sciences; or perhaps it means understandings that fit with various metascientific theories. The list could be lengthened extensively (as we will see in chapter 7), and quite significantly (as too will be seen in chapter 7), scientific claims that satisfy certain criteria quite well are often in conflict with competing claims that satisfy different criteria. These matters need not detain us here; the central point for now is just that there is a discussion to be had about what constitutes "better understanding of what it is to yield knowledge in [a] realm" — a discussion about criteria — and the stakes of this discussion are the meaning and value, and so the authority, of science itself. The identity of science cannot be simply a function of self-identification if this discussion is to make any sense: being a scientist requires taking a stand — usually implicitly — in debates about what counts as scientific knowledge or advancing science (this, I think, is the suppressed kernel of Lear's insight into science), not just asserting that any open-ended, critically reflexive investigation of the "realm that matters to me" is, as such, science (which is what his account tends to imply despite occasional flat assertions of there being "better" or "best" ways of investigating, or at least does not shut off strongly enough).

In an institutionalist vein, Lear characterizes "[w]hat counts as scientific activity" as "the activity of a scientist who behaves appropriately as such," which sends us back to the same problems with an added worry about authoritarian consensus-building and exclusions or occlusions of the heterodox. Or if "behav[ing] appropriately as such" just means remaining open to subjective recreations of oneself as a scientist, then the worry about orthodoxy is alleviated but we are sent back to the problems of voluntarism discussed above.

In understanding the work of science as *only* or at least *emphatically* the continual, creative reengagement with one's preferred object or domain of inquiry, Lear makes altogether obscure why science would be culturally authoritative other than as a result of its technological upshot and why the imperative of technological development is not the single criterion dominating the organization and assessment of scientific pursuits. Further, so framing the claim of science forecloses meaningful debate between psychoanalysis and the sciences about the cognitive credentials, and more broadly, the authority, of psychoanalytic knowledge. Distressingly, when science is so thoroughly deflated, the critical pressure that it can put on psychoanalysis, a pressure in response to which those committed to psychoanalysis may seek to refine their understandings of the nature and status of that to which they are committed in order to present it clearly and persuasively to others (and to themselves) dissipates. Foreclosing debate between psychoanalysis and the sciences, Lear risks encouraging the devolution of psychoanalysis into precisely what some of its most vituperative scientific critics claim it is — a dogma.

The problems with and stakes of Lear's understanding of science are magnified in his discussion of objectivity, which is where this engagement with his recent work will conclude. In Lear's account of objectivity, the emphasis on the subjective concept manifestly fails to account not only for significant features of science but also for important aspects of psychoanalysis and of our commitments to it.

With regard to the question of objectivity, Lear follows the lead of Loewald, who, noticing that "the subject, under the specific conditions of the analytic experiment, directs his activities toward the observer, and the observer communicates his findings directly to the subject with the goal of modifying these findings," plausibly suggests that "[t]he interaction itself . . . cannot be adequately represented by the model of [objective] scientific neutrality. It is [objectively] unscientific, based on faulty observation, to use this model" (2004, 42).[26] For Lear as for Loewald, the objectivity of psychoanalytic knowledge is not a matter of its experimental verification. At least some of what an analyst perceives and infers cannot be experimentally reproduced, thus cannot be corroborated by independent inquirers. And when analytic interpretations are addressed to analysands with the aim of inducing modifications to their self-understanding or psychic structure, as they often are, another impediment to external corroboration is imposed: the "data" is contaminated. The differential structures of address operative in psychoanalysis and the natural sciences, respectively, and which are responsive to their different interests (modifying what emerges in the course of an analysis as opposed to verifying the accuracy of observations, testing inferences, etc.), makes all the difference to what can count in these two fields as objectivity, Lear stresses. While in various scientific fields one might consider objective only that which impartial observers have verified in the setting of natural scientific experimentation; in psychoanalysis, certain findings are in principle *not* available to a neutral observer: being part of an emotionally charged and mutually influencing dyad is a condition for being a participant-observer in the "analytic experiment."[27] There is a distinctively intimate relation between *discovery and creation* in psychoanalysis, thus a distinctive conception of objectivity.

With this suggestive thought about the difference between objectivity in science and psychoanalysis in the background, Lear proceeds to collapse the distinction between science and psychoanalysis, deforming the understanding of both in the process and squandering this intriguing suggestion about psychoanalytic objectivity. Returning to his core concern with the subjective concept, Lear contends that "[e]ven in the sciences the concept of objectivity is subjective; as I shape myself as a scientist, I must ask, What are the norms of inquiry, discovery, and communication that make my research objective?" (2004, 44). While engaging such questions may yield important revisions to (the) scientific understanding(s) of objectivity, such questions may just as easily, all too easily, open onto a preset range of answers, e.g., the norms of inquiry, discovery, and communication that make my research objective are just those that eliminate the residual stains of subjectivity and so reduce my objects to their quantifiable core. This is a prevalent answer to such questions from Descartes' *Second Meditation* onwards. But this is not the answer that Lear provides. Lear's answer to the question of what constitutes objectivity (implicitly, in both science and psychoanalysis — despite the line from Loewald) is: "The idea that we are relating to objects with sufficient respect for their being objects. That is, we are relating objectively to objects when we recognize that they are to a certain extent self-standing, that they have certain claims to stand out from the environment in which they are located, certain claims to independence, certain claims to reality" (2004, 44). Notice the inversion of the classical scientific claim that objectivity means recognizing an object as absolutely mediated by its law-governed causal environment, as a fully fungible example of the laws through which its meaning is given — merely chronologically unique. If one reads this elaboration of objectivity as respect for the self-standing through Plato, Aristotle, or Heidegger, all of whom are significant influences on Lear, the suggestion seems to be that objectivity is a matter of acknowledging objects' claims on our embodied (tradition- and interest-informed) attention to stand out, to come into view as existentially distinct and integral: as neither reducible to nor fully independent of subjectivity.[28] The suggestion would be that objectivity is not yielded by manipulating objects under controlled and repeatable experimental conditions but just the converse: a letting-be of objects that insist themselves as out-standing, as standing out from their environmental moorings and mediations, as showing forth or shining forth as relatively independent, as somehow whole, and as such pressing for an acknowledgement of both our relationship to them and their independence from us. Objectivity would mean resolute attention to and concerned reckoning with that which gives itself as relatively discrete and independent, as always in relation to us but never simply because of us (and thus concernful attention to ourselves or to something in which we participate — say, *logos* or *Geist* — as the medium of the object's insistence: "object-"consciousness implies "self-"consciousness). Objectivity, most simply, would mean dis-closure to experience rather than the self-evacuation of the subject of experience.

At the core of Lear's interpretation of objectivity is the claim that objectivity is a matter of how we *relate to* objects ("The idea that we are relating to objects . . ."; "we are relating objectively to objects when . . ."). Objectivity so construed is a form of *recognition,* not just cognition; recognition of the claims of objects as relatively self-standing, developed through our manners of relation to them. Objectivity is a cognition-yielding practical relation. It requires the development of bearings toward objects that allow them to stand-out, to manifest as they are. How we manage to acknowledge this claim as it arises, the forms of respect we cultivate through which beings can emerge as they are (rather than as they are integratable into our various plans and strategies — perhaps including efforts to construct a systematically integrated, deductive-nomological account of nature), is the meaning of objectivity here. As much as this interpretation of objectivity may be a fecund starting point for recasting the dominant meaning of the term and reevaluating its stakes, as it stands, Lear's interpretation is insufficient. And it certainly won't work for the sciences.[29]

The insufficiency really comes through as Lear discusses what this conception of objectivity would mean in the context of psychoanalysis. The goal of analysis, Lear claims, is to "allow analysands to relate to objects in new sorts of ways — to relate to them as distinct persons, having their own points of view — that is, to relate to them objectively" (2004, 47). As induced in (while never "suggested" by?) analysis, objectivity would mean perceiving and relating to others as exceeding and complicating one's habitual, often self-serving, defensively animated, or otherwise appropriative forms of perception and relation, e.g., tendencies to perceive and relate to another as a domineering and invasive parental figure, or the source of one's humiliation, or the linchpin of the sustainability of one's world. It would mean ek-statically undergoing and sustaining the experience of the transcendence of the other, thus sustaining the tension and uncertainty of experience. Or in a more conventional idiom, it would mean achieving some degree of emancipation, for others and for ourselves, from transference. "Becoming objective in this sense opens up the possibility for true human intimacy. For previously one was not genuinely relating to another — or rather, insofar as one did relate to others, it was through the confusing fog of one's own wishes, hopes, and disappointments, which were regularly experienced as being in the other" (2004, 47-8). Objectivity here means relating to others as subjects, as loci of distinct points of view, as irreducible to — however inexcisable they may be from — the roles they have come to play or could come to play in our psychic lives. What this means concretely will have to be negotiated and renegotiated in specific relationships; hence objectivity is a subjective concept.

Lear's implicit suggestion in so construing "objectivity" seems to be that the authority of psychoanalysis concerns not the external validation of its interpretations but the values/ends it promotes. And this seems right, to an extent. But is concern with objectivity in the ordinary sense of "valid knowledge" simply irrelevant when assessing what transpires in analysis? Are the claims to validity (or something akin thereto) of psychoanalytic interpretations, or more broadly, psychoanalytic forms of attention, in no way implicated in the compelling quality of our commitments to psychoanalysis, thus irrelevant to attempts to make these commitments persuasive to others? Would we be committed to psychoanalysis if it was demonstrated to be efficacious yet invalid? Or how might the shape of our commitments change were we to come to appreciate psychoanalysis as genuinely disclosive yet, to a great extent, neither valid nor invalid?

The question that Lear sidesteps as he anxiously asserts the subjective concept view of objectivity is how to compare, assess the value, and establish the points of purchase of different conceptions of objectivity — objectivity as self-conscious relational attuning to objects as self-standing ek-stasies as against objectivity as having nothing whatsoever to do with our relations to objects, indeed as the effect of extracting all distinctively human forms of perception from the scene of inquiry such that all that remains is the object itself. In shorthand, we might say that there is an anthropocentric and an anti-anthropocentric view of objectivity. The problem is how to evaluate their respective values with regard to various objects and pursuits. As he asserts and advocates for the anthropocentric view of objectivity, Lear collapses the differences between objectivity as pursued in psychoanalysis and as pursued in the natural sciences; but if psychoanalysis and the natural sciences ask after different sorts of objects and have different sorts of goals, it makes sense that what counts as objectivity in each will be different, and these differences might be worth holding onto. Simultaneously, he simplifies both the "standard" and "subjective" concepts of objectivity, leaving no way to assess how, say, the anthropocentric conception of objectivity might be important in and to the sciences or how the anti-anthropocentric conception of objectivity might be important in and to psychoanalysis.

Because Lear "argues" by assertion, he is open to, even invites, counter-assertion. For instance, a proponent of the standard natural scientific concept of objectivity might simply assert that recognizing the self-standing of objects is just the first step in science, a matter of data gathering, a provisional moment on the way to the "true" objectivity yielded by experimental procedures that excise the idiosyncrasies of human perception and inference-drawing from inquiry. If the prevailing anti-anthropocentric conception of objectivity is to be effectively contested — complicated, qualified, or transfigured — which it must be if the nature and status of psychoanalysis is to be adequately assessed, one will need to do more than just assert a competing conception, especially in a culture such as ours. Facilitating a conversation between (the) science(s) and psychoanalysis on the meaning(s) of objectivity is a necessary starting point if the authority of psychoanalysis is to be elaborated in other than first-personal terms.

SCIENCE AND HERMENEUTICS

Most agree that psychoanalysis does not measure up to the standards for validation operative in the natural sciences.[30] Yet severe disagreement persists about whether the inassimilability of psychoanalysis to the protocols of the natural sciences means that it is a mystifying pseudoscience or something else altogether.[31] It is this we must explore. For to be committed to psychoanalysis in the sense that claims me and that I want to explore is not a matter of ignoring the (in)validity of psychoanalytic knowledge, but neither is it a matter of obstinate presumptiveness about the validity and value of such knowledge.[32] To be committed to psychoanalysis in the sense that I want to explore is not to be padlocked into dogmatism but to bear the weight of persuasion in its passionate force and eminent questionability, which means, in part, to expose the vulnerabilities of conviction through efforts to convey its compelling force.

Part of the difficulty of accounting for one's commitments to psychoanalysis and making them persuasive is a result of the ways in which the questionability of psychoanalytic knowledge has been taken up in the literature. Due to the failure of these conversations to address the meaning and stakes of the specific objectivity and value of psychoanalysis, commitments to psychoanalysis and the reasons one might share with others in support of these commitments are hardly as sophisticated as they could be.

There was once, not so long ago, a tremendous debate about the scientific standing of psychoanalysis.[33] It was believed that if psychoanalysis could be systematized (experience-near concepts distinguished from experience-far concepts, a hierarchical order of theoretical statements established, etc.), it would give rise to concrete predictions that could then be subject to experimental vindication.[34] Or it was believed that at least certain psychoanalytic insights or interpretations could withstand the pressure of scientific scrutiny, so a variety of experiments — sometimes intriguing, sometimes absurd —

were devised to prove just that. Or it was believed that various psychoanalytic claims could be confirmed or disconfirmed through appeal to scientific findings in other fields. Or, especially in the 1980s, it was believed that if only psychoanalysts would abandon their nostalgic adherence to outmoded metapsychologies and learn to embrace information theory-based or cybernetic models of psychic life, psychoanalysis could be developed as a natural science on a par with others (the basis for this belief being a conviction that psychoanalysis is perfectly confluent with findings from neurophysiology). Eventually, the debate came to an impasse and dried up. Pundits continue to publish their confirmatory studies while detractors continue to substantiate their skepticism, but the debate has become gridlocked. Indeed, the reasons the debate was important in the first place, the questions to which it was responding, seem to have been forgotten.[35] Today, the unexamined assumption motivating a great deal of research and experimentation is that neurobiological and other such findings can prove, or at least significantly support, various elements of psychoanalysis. Here one might ask, Does psychoanalysis need to measure up to scientific protocols in order to be rationally satisfying?

A certain resurgence of the debate about the status of psychoanalysis occurred as alternative models of assessment arose that claimed to be more adequate, or at least friendlier, than those of the exact sciences. Debating the hermeneutic credentials of psychoanalysis became the order of the day. Interestingly, proponents of psychoanalysis now frequently found themselves arguing *against* those who would present it as an explanatory natural science, for it was believed that this was the first step toward a falsely imminent critique. The hermeneutics vs. science debate began in the 1960s,[36] intensified in the 1970s,[37] and reached a fevered pitch in the 1980s.

For quite some time, many analysts were ambivalent about situating their practice as a hermeneutic enterprise. Gitelson (1973), for instance, argues that psychoanalysis "occupies a middle ground between the extreme scientific positions of physics and historical learning" (401). Though it is not an exact science, Gitelson contends, it is still a "basic science" (1973, 416). But pundits of the hermeneutic approach to psychoanalysis would soon grow bolder. Meltzer (1978), for one, repudiates all claims for the scientificity of psychoanalysis as inappropriate at best and regressive at worst.[38] A decade later, Sass and Woolfolk (1988) express extreme confidence that psychoanalysis can ground itself in hermeneutics. More recently, Bowman, a bit more moderate than his predecessors but basically in line with them, has suggested that "[m]ore than any other science, depth psychology is the science of analogy and metaphor. Exactness, in this field, does not mean leaving metaphor behind; it means striving always to improve our metaphors so that they are the clearest we can make them" (2002, 71). From the 1980s to about the turn of the century, science became the enemy of psychoanalysis and the humanities its humble and hospitable accomplices.[39] With such dogmatism on all sides of the debate, the path to skepticism was paved.[40] Thus, unsurprisingly, since about the turn of the century, efforts to scientifically validate various elements of psychoanalysis have been aggressively renewed.

While granting the assessment of psychoanalytic knowledge relative autonomy from the methodological and epistemic criteria of the natural sciences allowed certain advances to be made, the debate about the scientific or hermeneutic status of psychoanalysis has become arid. Why? One reason is that there was insufficient sensitivity to issues of concept construction and distinction on all sides. Reviewing the literature, one finds a widespread failure to distinguish between various sorts of concepts employed in psychoanalysis and very little attention to their internal diversity, i.e., subclasses and differential constructions. This resulted in a failure to appreciate the different functions of different sorts of concepts and thus a failure to assess them appropriately. There is a world of difference between the function, thus the validity, of diagnostic concepts, interpretive concepts, observational concepts, metapsychological concepts (e.g., energetic, topographic, constitutional/genetic, dynamic, and developmental concepts), speculative concepts (or speculative axes of various concepts), biological concepts, therapeutic-technical concepts, characterological and psychological concepts, psychoanalytically-inflected anthropological and ethnographic concepts, and so on. And there is often a world of difference between various analysts' constructions and usages of concepts that are nominally identical. Failure to appreciate the different values of different sorts of concepts and the variable grounds of their construction condemned the debate about the scientificity or hermeneutical character of psychoanalytic knowledge and practice to superficiality and thus to inevitable impasse.

In order to begin to appreciate the conceptual diversity of psychoanalysis, and so the difficulties of isolating claims for scientific scrutiny or hermeneutic defense, let us note the following:

1. Nominally identical concepts may have different objects, values, and scopes.
    a. Energetic concepts may be used (as a subclass of interpretive-clinical concepts) to convey something about a client's experience of, say, depression or mania, exhaustion or anxiety; or they may be used to explain (in a metapsychological register, and thus aiming at third-personal, general intelligibility) excessively intense or unaccountably bland ideas: accounts of phobias, fetishes, obsessional ideas and love objects, etc. often utilize the assumption of a displaceable, condensable quantity of energy capable of variable investment; or they may be used in a

theory of mind (which is not identical to a metapsychology) to elaborate the relation between the psychic and the somatic: the assumption of psychic energy is often built into the concept of the drive as a pure and undifferentiated force or striving (*Drang*), which is then used to articulate the status of psychical forms as representatives or delegates of inchoate somatic forces.

b. Interpretive concepts may be clinical or extraclinical, and they may intend to convey a general insight or concern only a particular analysand or cultural configuration.
c. Energetic concepts (seemingly a subclass of metapsychological concepts, but often used in the construction of interpretations) may concern, as in Freud's work from *The Project* onward, not laws but broad trends (principles), or they may seek to articulate invariable laws, as in the work of many of Freud's early disciples, or they may be cast as reducible to other sorts of concepts, as in the case of Gill's (1977) contention that energetic concepts are reducible to infantile residues (thus to psychosexual concepts, whatever *they* are): the concept of psychic energy, Gill claims, is "a derivative of infantile psychosexual fantasies in which the mind is equated with an organ that can ingest, retain, and excrete substances" (588). Or if, as Gedo and Goldberg (1973) claim, "[m]odels of the mind are summarizing conventions which represent the clinical theory of psychoanalysis," then ostensibly metapsychological concepts are to be evaluated only in terms of their clinical value (10).

2. A concept from one concept class may but need not include concepts from another class.

    a. Developmental concepts may incorporate energetic concepts (e.g., Freud's discussion of the dissolution of the Oedipus complex in boys is a developmental story told — sometimes — in economic/energetic terms: narcissistic investment in penis overwhelms object-love for mother), but certainly need not.

3. Phenomena may be cast by the same author in terms of one sort of concept and then in terms of another.

    a. In *New Introductory Lectures*, Freud stipulates that trauma is an "essentially 'economic' concept'" but hardly ever talks this way elsewhere.

4. Concepts may be employed literally or metaphorically.

a. One might use energetic concepts phenomenologically rather than metapsychologically, e.g., to describe the experience of propulsion, of being *driven* to work which one may not intend. In this example, the rhetoric of energetics is but a helpful way of discussing the work opaquely aimed at and accomplished in the experience of being driven, not a claim about the infrastructure of psychic life. Compare Brenner (1957): "No one has ever seen psychic energy and no one ever will, any more than anyone has ever seen any of the forms of physical energy. The concept of psychic energy, like the concept of physical energy, is a hypothesis which is intended to serve the purpose of simplifying and facilitating our understanding of the facts of mental life which we can observe" (19).
b. Famously, in "Two Principles of Mental Functioning," Freud refers to the pleasure principle as a "fiction."

5. Concepts may be used more or less tentatively and probatively depending on whether the systems they compose are thought to (or aim to) achieve limited or unconditional validity.

   a. Freud, for instance, was forthright in claiming that psychoanalysis "never claimed to provide a complete theory of human mentality in general" (SE 14: 50), that psychoanalytic theories are "bungled . . . reproductions . . . [that] wretchedly dissect the great art works of psychic nature" (Freud to Jung, June 30 1909), and he certainly developed probative concepts in his late work (*Ego and Id, Group Psychology,Beyond, Moses*), while for Glover (1956), psychoanalysis is a general psychology concerned with internal and external stimuli undergoing unconscious registration and processing, e.g., falling within the principle of tension discharge. In line with Glover, Fenichel (1941) claims that "The young science of psychoanalysis has as its object of study the totality of human mental phenomena" (1). And in a similar vein, as if willfully denying a number of crucial passages in Freud, Hartmann (1964) asserts that "Analysis is also, and has always been in Freud's work, a general psychology. Freud's aim, expressed as early as in the 90s (1887-1902), was to get insight into the entirety of mental functions and not only the pathology of neuroses" (104).

6. The use of the same concept may occur in contexts that differ concerning relations of conceptual implication, which effects the value of the concept employed; that is, the use of concepts from the same class

may differ in value insofar as they are presumed to imply or remain independent from concepts from other classes.

a. For instance, for many analysts, clinical theory is either derived from, a subclass of, or otherwise conceptually dependent on metapsychology, while for Waelder (1962), "metapsychology . . . is far less necessary [to clinical practice], and some of the best analysts I have known knew next to nothing about it" (620).

A related problem is that most parties in the debates about the scientific or hermeneutical standing of psychoanalysis assumed a fundamental commensurability, even a univocity of psychoanalysis, which is greatly misleading if not wholly disingenuous. For instance, there was a prevailing prejudice that if one could validate or invalidate *Freud*— as if this name were synonymous with psychoanalysis as such, as if there were psychoanalysis *as such* — one could successfully defend or defeat the whole psychoanalytic enterprise. Often, such hopes for a final reckoning were invested in discussions of a relatively small portion of the Freudian corpus (notoriously, the status of seduction). In such cases, it was believed that if only one could validate or invalidate a specific partisan interpretation or concept, at the very least, significant headway would be made into the question of the legitimacy of psychoanalysis as such. There was a terrible disarray of universalist ambitions aggressively asserted through particular studies, and a great rancorousness was unleashed. But this dried up in time.

This was bound to occur, for one of the most salient characteristics of the field is and has always been the great plurality of theories, interpretations, techniques, aims, and research programs; thus there was always counter-evidence, counter-examples, counter-assertions. On might even say that asking whether a particular concept or interpretation can be scientifically or hermeneutically corroborated conceals as much as it addresses the more broad and vexing question of the rational character of commitments to psychoanalysis. Of course, it is not that such corroboration is irrelevant, but when pursued in too narrow a fashion, when assumed to yield a decisive demonstration of the (in)validity of psychoanalysis, the stakes of the broader question are forgotten and inquiry becomes confused: evidence turns into information in want of a relation to the guiding question. Detached from the guiding question, discoveries become mere details or ammo for academic battles.

Nearly lost in the vociferousness of such debates, yet thankfully transmitted though them, were questions such as: What does it mean to be committed to psychoanalysis and what are the value of such commitments in an age of the epistemic hegemony of the natural sciences, the concomitant ascendancy of technocratic and bureaucratic expertise, and pervasive reactionary irrationalism? What does it mean for psychoanalysis to claim one as *authoritative*, as compulsory (involuntary, like love) yet warranted, in some manner rational and publicly defensible, in disenchanted, post-Enlightenment times like these? How are we to account for, and thus compare, the incomparable insights and various manner of flourishing to which psychoanalysis gives rise? Even if developmental studies confirm a certain Kleinian hypotheses, even if predictions about developments in a particular analysand's associations are confirmed, even if certain psychoanalytic techniques are demonstrated to diminish the frequency of transference projections, why claim that such evidence warrants our — or should warrant others' — conviction in the value and validity of psychoanalysis? Generally, what sorts of epistemic and therapeutic promises can psychoanalysis make and why are these promises compelling?

Insisting on the scientific or hermeneutic status of psychoanalysis will not adequately address such questions, and all the less so when psychoanalysis is treated as a monolith. Psychoanalysis has never been a unified field. Thus attempts to validate or invalidate, support or undermine partisan concepts and interpretations are inevitably inconclusive — whence the unseemly longevity, the persistent undeadness of these debates. A Freudian, Kleinian, Winnicottian, Lacanian, Loewaldian, intersubjectivist, ego psychologist, self psychologist, and relationalist may all offer *radically* different interpretations of the "same" material,[41] and even when interpretations are similar, techniques may differ significantly. There are manifest differences in metapsychologies, developmental theories, theories of pathology, orderings of therapeutic ends, and so on across the field of psychoanalysis. What's more, such differences are to be found within each "school." Those sharing a partisan affiliation may, and often do, offer interpretations (etc.) that are not only significantly distinct from but emphatically incommensurable with interpretations (etc.) offered by those with shared commitments.

And yet the plurality of psychoanalysis is not a mere agglomeration. There are significant conceptual and technical patterns, trends, and unities to be discerned. And there is certainly a shared object domain. Indeed, I will attempt to show that there is something that can be called psychoanalytic knowledge, the nature and status, i.e., specific objectivity of which can be assessed.

An immediate difficulty imposes itself. Does not such an ambition bespeak a specifically philosophical hubris, an overeager desire to unify and define an irreducibly diverse and dissonant field? Is the effort to arrange the vast multiplicity of psychoanalytic voices into a harmonious whole not a fundamentally false gesture? Would Adorno not be right to protest that "the whole is the untrue"? Given the many currents in the tumultuous sea of psychoanalytic research, the philosophical ambition to specify the nature and status of psychoanalytic knowledge would seem to entail the illicit substitution of an imaginative invention ("psychoanalytic knowledge" as a discrete and determinable entity) for the genuine plurality of incommensurable psychoanalytic discoveries, research projects, and so forth: yet another resurgence of idealism. The linguistic torsion involved in speaking of "psychoanalysis," as if this were a unified and univocal field, is not slight. Indeed, a most perspicuous feature of discussions within, about, and drawing on psychoanalysis is the vast polysemic range of the term. The temptation to disclaim pretensions to semantic stability and unique reference and speak of psychoanalys*es* in the emphatically plural is almost overwhelming. For how else can one acknowledge the evidently irreducible plurality of psychoanalytic discourses, the conflict-ridden character of the field, and the seemingly unlimited transformations that psychoanalytic thinking undergoes as it is exposed to and appropriated by a variety of extra-clinical discourses and practices?

Although it would register something of the diversity of the field, the rhetorical shift from "psychoanalysis" to "psychoanalyses" would risk eliding many important distinctions by foregrounding those between psychoanalytic schools or major figures. In speaking of "psychoanalyses" rather than "psychoanalysis," partisan differences — such as the differences between Freudians and Kleinians on matters of technique, interpretive emphasis, salient pathogenic features, developmental theory, and so forth — may achieve prominence at the cost of neglecting many crucial distinctions that traverse the field. The differences between clinical, developmental, metapsychological, technical, speculative, and other forms of psychoanalytic knowledge and their different relations to a variety of evidential bases are irreducible to, although operative in the background of, partisan differences. Familiarity with the pertinent differences between a Lacanian and a Winnicottian interpretation is not the same as familiarity with the relation between clinical claims and psychoanalytic theory Lacan or Winnicott (or in their eponymous camps).

Neither the language of "psychoanalysis" nor that of "psychoanalyses" is altogether satisfying. Blindness and insight seem inextricably intertwined. The problem is not one of language alone — the torsion of language registers important tensions in the object, providing a clue, perhaps, to the specific objectivity of psychoanalytic knowledge. To anticipate, both systematically and historically there is a tension between the universalizing ambitions of psychoanalytic research and the particularizing pull of its objects, between the aspirations of psychoanalytic theory and the demands of therapy. More precisely, such tension is manifest in the conflicts between the demands of psychoanalytic research and those of therapy as well as *within* psychoanalytic research and therapy. Aporetic to the core, psychoanalysis cannot but pursue universality while striving to sustain attention to emphatic singularity.

Coming to terms with this and other such constitutive tensions, with the insuperable questions provoked by psychoanalysis and the difficulties of its practice, with the questionable, however compelling, perpetually unsettled authority of its claims, thus with the questionability, the engaging incompletion, of psychoanalysis itself, would be to acknowledge psychoanalysis as a historical discourse of suffering and healing under conditions of modernity rather than a metaphysical discourse of universal truth.[42]

If the tension is in the object, thus the practices, and not only in language, clearly no semantic decision will resolve the difficulty. Faced with genuine *aporias*, we must find another way to proceed.

NOTES

1. Witness Freud: "If one succeeds in arranging the confused heap of fragments, each of which bears upon it an unintelligible piece of drawing, so that the picture acquires meaning, so that there is no gap anywhere in the design, and so that the whole fits into the frame — if all these conditions are fulfilled, then one knows that one has solved the puzzle and that there is no alternative solution" (SE 19: 116).

2. "Theoria is a true sharing, not something active, but something passive (*pathos*), namely being totally involved in and carried away by what one sees" (Gadamer 2003, p. 130).

3. The world abandoned us so we will return the favor by embracing our detachment, for instance, by attempting to carve out and hole up in private life, attending as much as possible to family matters and private interests, or by adopting an unremittingly instrumentalist attitude toward oneself and others through which one revels in one's estrangement from nature and culture. Notice here the unsuspected proximity between liberalism and aesthetic radicalism as forms of cynical detachment.

4. Which is perhaps a way of sustaining a fantasy of symbiotic unity, of disavowing our constitutive dislocations. Notice that nostalgic conservatism aligns with liberalism and aesthetic radicalism as forms of life fueled by the trauma of constitutive dislocation.

5. Cf. Gadamer (2003) *Truth and Method*, especially pp. 269-277.

6. Thus by no means do I want to deny Charles Taylor's (1992) contention that "[d]isengaged rationality seems to separate us from our own narrow, egoistic standpoint and make us capable of grasping the whole picture. It is what allows us to become 'impartial spectators' of the human scene. The growth of scientific rationality can therefore be experienced as a kind of victory over our egoism. We are no longer imprisoned in the self" (331). My suggestion is simply that, assumed as a fundamental stance, disengaged rationality is self-defeating.

7. What will have been: this phrase marks a problem that cannot be directly engaged here. The problem is this: affirmation is riven by an inexhaustible tension between the limited and the unlimited, the conditioned and the unconditional. Though affirmation is necessarily a realization of a possibility confluent with and intelligible within the framework of a prevailing state of affairs, it may also have been, simultaneously, an opening onto that which may fundamentally exceed its constituting conditions, onto that which will remain incommensurate with and unintelligible as a continuation of a prevailing state of affairs. Affirmation perhaps accedes to the incalculable within the calculable. The determinate possibilities onto which we open are concrete (in the sense specified above) rather than self-identical, fully present. Cf. Martin Hägglund (2008) *Radical Atheism* for an insightful discussion of this point.

8. Of course, nothing said here is incompatible with a Kantian understanding of agency on a certain interpretation. Cf. Barbara Herman (1996) *The Practice of Moral Judgment* and Christine Korsgaard (1996) *The Sources of Normativity* and (2009) *Self-Constitution: Agency, Identity, and Integrity*.

9. This is not to say that psychoanalysis is *sufficiently* orientative, that it can offer thick-enough orientation to dispel our sense of being adrift in reified culture. This is not to say, then, that the orientation afforded by psychoanalysis in any way detracts from the necessity of significant social and political transformations as conditions for flourishing life, for life that is not just survived but lived in an emphatic sense. Against the corroding effects of capitalism, its ability to dislodge us from established forms of connection with each other and with the world — say, those elaborated by tradition (local customs and practices), religion, and social-political authority — the orientation that psychoanalysis can offer is tantamount to a tattered road-map through an infinite desert. Likewise, set against the powerful coordinating effects of capitalism (e.g., the culture industry), psychoanalytically-inspired forms of world-orientation are frail indeed. But perhaps the forms of attention and insight afforded by psychoanalysis, the transformations of subjectivity and intersubjectivity it can incite or prepare, are also fragments, opaque articulations (premonitions) of life fundamentally otherwise.

10. Adorno, *Minima Moralia* (section 18). Cf. Bernstein (2001), pp. 40-74 and Rosen-Carole (2010) "Menu Cards in Time of Famine: On Psychoanalysis and Politics."

11. For instance, Lévi-Strauss' claim in *Structural Anthropology* is that psychoanalysis is but modern shamanism: "what is it that fundamentally differentiates analysis from those other isolated islands of religiosity, lost in our disenchanted word — mystical sects, secret societies, extremist political organizations — all, indeed, united around a symbolic pact set in concrete? These little 'hordes,' as Freud had already noted, are by all accounts no less effective than analysis — to which we need only add, perhaps, that they are scarcely any better, assailed as they are by a social entourage that constantly tends to destabilize them" (cited in Borch-Jacobson 1991, p. 165).

12. What I will later say about psychoanalytic theories as *perspectives* is meant to deflate this zealotry and thereby partially deflate the significance of the question. But the worry about zealotry is uncircumventable, especially today. On the latter point, it is worth recalling Ernest Gellner's (1985) proposal that part of the attraction of psychoanalysis is that its attention to the irrational feels like a form of liberation, of advanced humanism, in light of the indifferent-to-the-human structures of rationalized modernity.

13. Somewhat isolated, for we must not neglect the lives that emerge from out of these corridors, bearing the commitments fostered therein.

14. The challenges posed by everyday problems, conflicts, and sufferings or more severe difficulties might be considered, in analogy with modernist painting, as magnified moments of abstraction. As in certain modernist paintings, bracingly evident abstraction witnesses the progressive but yet incomplete destitution of sensuous significance and underlines the consequent disorientation and depletion, as well as the temptation to their evasion, in which its authority is still obliquely felt, in the interval between analysis and everyday life, the orientative authority of psychoanalytic sensibilities (forms of sensuously compelling attention, reflection, and response cultivated by psychoanalytic practice), because *manifestly* under duress, are revealed in their essential and socially exacerbated fragility and inadequacy, their mismatch vis-à-vis might of the world. In such moments of magnified abstraction, sensuous significance — in painting as in psychoanalysis, the plenipotentiary of shared, ordinary life keyed to the demands of sensuous happiness — is harassed into admitting its helplessness, becomes evident as impossible (or at least imperiled) yet insistent, i.e., dominated, and thereby levels a nearly mute demand for a radical recalibration of the social order — for conditions felicitous to its flourishing.

15. Cf. Stanley Cavell (1979) *The Claim of Reason* , (1987) *Disowning Knowledge*, and (1988) *In Quest of the Ordinary*.

16. To be sure, persuasion need not proceed only through "accounts," but other manners of persuasion such as exemplarity seem of limited efficacy in contemporary cultural conditions, especially with respect to psychoanalysis. At least initially, concessions must be made to status quo rationalism as we consider how to make psychoanalysis persuasive to ourselves and others.

17. This will be the strategy of chapter 7.

18. "'Scientism' means science's [unduly confident] belief in itself: that is, the conviction that we can no longer understand science as one form of possible knowledge, but rather must identify knowledge with science" (Habermas 1971, 4). On the dangers of scientism, cf. Haber-

mas (1973) "Dogmatism, Reason, and Decision: On Theory and Practice in Our Scientific Civilization" in *Theory and Practice* and Gadamer (1975) "Hermeneutics and Social Science."

19. However, that psychoanalysis may be on-balance cost effective is suggested by Dossman, Kutter, Heinzel, and Wurmser (1997) and de Matt, Philipszoon, Dekker, and De Jonghe (2007).

20. Cf. Dreher and Sandler (1993) *What do Psychoanalysts Want?* and Rosen-Carole (2010) "Menu Cards in Time of Famine."

21. And besides, as we will see, uniformity hardly prevails when it comes to the goals pursued by analysts of various stripes.

22. Though Lear's goal is to make psychoanalysis normatively inert, notice the overlap between the conception of analysis sketched here and Charles Taylor's elaboration of ethical self-reflection in *Sources of the Self.*

23. What resounds in Lear's analogy but not his analysis is the provocation to reflexive return by the concrete, daily challenges of love and analysis. Today, as a lover, I reinvent what it means to love — *this kiss* will define the meaning of a kiss, *these acts* of support, encouragement, enthusiasm, and care will redefine the meaning of what it is to be a committed partner — only because my partner, today, requires concrete acts of care, passion, tenderness, etc. The question, "What is it to be a lover?" will arise as a conceptually formulated question, if at all, only indirectly, that is, only as a result of a practical failure to develop a mutually satisfying, practical response to the question. Ordinarily, the question, "What is it to be a lover?" will arise in its explicitly conceptual formulation only when no adequate way to address the complex demands of the day-to-day can be found. Similarly, today, as an analyst, one must reinvent what it means to facilitate the self-understanding and freedom of *this* analysand only because today *this* analysand is at a specific juncture in therapy and requires forms of care and support that do not come easily. It is the concrete challenges and dilemmas of analysis, and not the abstract question "What is it to be an analyst?" that provokes transfigurations of the meaning of psychoanalysis.

24. Cf. Michael Thompson (2012) *Life and Action: Elementary Structures of Practice and Practical Thought.*

25. One may consider it unfair to make so much of a sin of omission. If Lear's aim is to emphasize the heretofore little noticed structure of science as a subjective concept in order to render his presentation of psychoanalysis as a subjective concept more plausible, the desire for a more robust account of science may be misplaced. Thus my commentary can be read as complementary to Lear's, as emphasizing dimensions and stakes of science that are suppressed by Lear's focus on the subjective concept. Perspective cannot but give rise to exaggeration and distortion, hence the need for dialectic, a mutually clarifying and mutually challenging encounter of perspectives. But perhaps this is not just a difference in perspective and subtending interests. Are we not both urging a renewal of the relation between science and psychoanalysis? It is not incidental that Lear develops his analysis of the subjective concept through the example of science. The effect of the example is to unite psychoanalysis, love, and science as instances of the subjective concept, to show a certain confluence of these terms that, ordinarily, are starkly opposed. Lear's analysis of the subjective concept *of science* does not tell us anything new about the nature of the subjective concept. Presumably, then, the discussion of science is not meant to augment our understanding of either psychoanalysis *qua subjective concept* or the subjective concept itself. Something else must be at stake. What seems to be at stake is the relation between science and psychoanalysis: my hunch is that Lear wants to minimize their differences in order to release some of the steam from the polemic about the scientific credentials of psychoanalysis. But this is naïve. In minimizing the differences between science and psychoanalysis, Lear glosses over what is distinctive about both science and psychoanalysis, what it is about each field that makes it cognitively and practically compelling, and thereby he collapses any space for conversation between them wherein their relationship could be reevaluated, complicated, and renewed. Despite Lear's underlining and advocacy of reflective judgment, his treatment of the subjective concept renders it a surreptitious medium of identity-thinking.

26. Bracketed terms are Lear's.

27. Lear's easy dismissal of the possibility of external scientific corroboration of analytic judgments can surely be contested, as will be discussed in chapter 7, but that is not terribly important in this context.

28. Although the possible influence of Hegel on Lear is questionable, and if there is such an influence, certainly less marked and less extensive, the characterization of objectivity as respect for the self-standing can clearly be given a Hegelian inflection. Cf. *PhG* ¶168ff.

29. For an equally vague and one-sided rendering of objectivity, cf. Marcia Cavell (1993): "If 'objectivity' describes what is in the public domain and intelligible according to norms that are also public, then human thought and behavior can be understood only on the assumption that they, together with our interpretations of them, are objective in this sense" (74).

30. Whether there is or need be agreement about these standards and their relative pertinence in various sciences are separate questions to which we will return.

31. The charge that psychoanalysis is but a mystifying pseudoscience has been leveled by innumerable critics. Here are but a few: Nagel (1959), Eysenck and Wilson (1973), Grünbaum (1977, 1979, 1984, 1993), Farrell (1981; particularly chapter 4), Crews (1986), Wilcocks (1994), Coiffi (1998), Macmillan (1991), Torrey (1992), Debray-Ritzen (1972). Interestingly, most of these authors focus on Freud, as if debunking the scientific standing of Freud were equivalent to undermining the scientific credibility of psychoanalysis as such. For an intra-psychoanalytic deployment of the charge of mystifying pseudoscience, cf. Rapaport in Erikson (1959), p. 11.

32. Cf. Mitchell 2000, p. 159. Hitchcock's Marnie (Tippi Hedren) rightly exposes and ridicules the chauvinist aggression behind the latter stance as she knowingly says to her husband/captor Mark Rutland (Sean Connery), "You Freud, me Jane." In response to his desire to "analyze" her, which she rightly reads as an invasive desire to Know her, to tame, manipulate, domesticate, and seduce her, Marnie's "You Freud, me Jane" pointedly elaborates the self-inflated presumptuousness behind Mark's efforts at armchair (actually, in the context of the scene, bedside) analysis. Marnie's citation is poignant and precise. Just as Jane's "radical" move (in the context of 1930s Hollywood cinema) is to identify herself as the site of language, culture, and agency (*you* [Tarzan] is the object of the statement, *me* [Jane] is the subject, a subject who is, moreover, the bearer of language/culture into which "you" [Tarzan] is initiated. The line is not, as popular memory often has it, "Me Tarzan, You Jane."), Marnie identifies with knowledge, language, and agency ("Oh, I know this trick! And I know how to thwart it." she implies) in order to expose the violence of, and so undermine the presumption of care behind, Mark's attempt to reduce her to the object of his language games, his Knowledge, and ultimately his sexual mastery.

33. Though it may well have been a concern earlier, we can provisionally mark the decade of 1942-1952 as the start of widespread interest in the scientific appraisal of psychoanalysis. Throughout the 40s and 50s, most of the effort went into showing that psychoanalysis *could be* scientific (cf. the work of Henry Murry, John Dollard, and Neal Miller; to some extent, but from a more critical angle, Gordon Allport was part of this conversation). Showing that psychoanalysis *is* scientific was, for the most part, not even attempted until the mid 60s. In 1943, Sears' *Survey of Objective Studies of Psychoanalytic Concepts* appeared, containing a review of about 150 studies. This was followed in 1952 by Hilgard's major review, *Psychoanalysis as Science.* Then no major review appeared until Kline's (1972) *Fact and Fantasy in the Freudian Tradition*, which evaluated 700 studies, following which a slew of reviews were published, including Eysenck and Wilson's (1973) *The Experimental Study of Freudian Theories*, Fisher and Greenberg's (1977) *The Scientific Credibility of Freud's Theories and Therapy*, which reviewed 1800 studies, Farrell's (1981) *The Standing of Psychoanalysis*, Masling's *Empirical Studies of Psychoanalytic Theories* series (1983, 1986, 1990), Dahl, Kächele, and Thomä's *Psychoanalytic Process Research Strategies*, Macmillan's (1991) *Freud Evaluated*, and then Fisher and Greenberg's (1996) *Freud Scientifically Reappraised*, which reviewed approximately 2500 studies. According to Hornstein (1992), since the 1940s there have been as many 2,000 controlled experiments designed to determine the validity of psychoanalytic concepts.

34. This is still very much a contemporary concern, indeed it is at the core of Wallerstein's efforts to disclose the "common ground" of psychoanalysis and shore up its validity. Cf. Wallerstein 1975, 1992, 1995, 1999, 2000, 2004.

35. This account of the significance of the debate about the scientific standing of psychoanalysis may be something of an idealization. Perhaps the debate was really more about the cultural clout of psychoanalysis, or simply that of those professing adherence to psychoanalysis, or about science's monopoly on cultural authority, than anything else. About this I remain uncertain.

36. Cf., for instance, Home (1966), Rycroft (1966), Habermas (1968), and Klauber (1968), all of whom claim that psychoanalysis should be considered a hermeneutic rather than scientific endeavor.

37. Cf., for instance, Gill (1976), Klein (1976), Schafer (1976), and Ricoeur (1977), all of whom acknowledge the hermeneutic specificity of psychoanalysis but still want to claim that although psychoanalysis is not a natural science, it is still a science of some sort. Also cf. Peterfreund (1971) and Rosenblatt and Thickstun (1977, 1984), who argue that psychoanalysis is not a natural science and certainly should not be claimed as such on the basis of mechanistic energy models and structural metapsychologies. Whether or not psychoanalysis is eventually deemed a science, these authors demand that psychoanalytic metapsychology be henceforth based on information-theoretical and cybernetic models in order to render it confluent with the impressive findings of (then) contemporary neurophysiology.

38. Later, in his contribution to *The Klein-Lacan Dialogues*, Meltzer modifies his position, claiming that although psychoanalysis is certainly not an explanatory science, it may be a descriptive science of sorts (1999, p. 182).

39. Institutionally, this began (in the U.S.) in the 1960s with the hospitability to psychoanalysis shown by the English Department at Columbia under Trilling and Van Doren, the Social Relations department at Harvard under Parsons, and the English Department at SUNY Buffalo with Norman Holland leading the Group for Applied Psychoanalysis.

A range of intermediary positions that developed toward the end of the century should be noted. In addition to the large number of analysts with explicit, indeed often stalwart hermeneutic commitments (cf. D. Stern 1997), there were some who appreciated the import of hermeneutics but found fault with the conception of psychoanalysis as hermeneutical "all the way down," e.g., Lawrence Friedman (2000), as well as some who tried to split the difference, e.g., Gill (1994), who describes psychoanalysis as a "hermeneutic science" concerned with meaning, but meaning connections that are in many cases causal.

40. As Hannah Arendt puts the point: "One's first reaction against this, triggered off by the inescapable experience of *many* dogmas, all of which claim to possess *the* truth, is skepticism: the conclusion that there is no such thing as truth, that therefore I may either arbitrarily choose some dogmatic doctrine (arbitrary with regard to truth: my choice may be promoted simply by various interests and be entirely pragmatic). Or I may simply shrug my shoulders about so profitless a business" (1989, p. 33). (For the dialectical counterpoint, cf. Hegel *PR* § 141 Addition: " A longing may therefore arise for an objective condition, a condition in which the human being gladly debases himself to servitude and total subjection simply in order to escape the torment of vacuity and negativity. If many Protestants have recently gone over to the Catholic Church, they have done so because they found that their inner life was impoverished, and they reached out for a fixed point, a support, an authority, even if what they gained was not exactly the stability of thought.")

41. Cf. Stern (1985), 264-5; Scharff (2001); and Hansel (2000).

42. This text means to ask: What would it mean for psychoanalysis to become secular? What would it mean for those who practice psychoanalysis in various forms to become what Freud suggested clinical analysts were, namely, "secular minister[s] of souls [*ein weltlicher Seelsorger*]"? (SE 20: 225).

Chapter Two

Plurality in Psychoanalysis

> Most bitterly irreconcilable is that which is similar but which feeds on different centers.
>
> —Adorno, "Charakteristik Walter Benjamin"

> Not one but several interpretations have to be integrated into reflection. Thus the hermeneutic conflict itself is what nourishes the process of reflection and governs the movement from abstract to concrete reflection. Is this possible without 'destroying' reflection?
>
> —Ricoeur, *Freud and Philosophy*

INTRODUCTION: REVOLUTION AND ALMOST ANARCHY

Interpretations issuing from partisans of various psychoanalytic schools are often manifestly incommensurable, sometimes even mutually exclusive, and even when interpretations are commensurable to a certain extent,[1] deep disagreements about fundamental matters persist. For instance, Kohut claims that traditional psychoanalysis and self psychology are in no way mutually exclusive, rather, he suggests, the drive conflicts with which Freudians tend to be concerned are epiphenomenal — resulting from the structural deficiencies of the self to which self psychology is emphatically attentive. Kohut's claim is not that Freudian and other traditional psychoanalytic accounts are simply wrong, just limited: the phenomena with which Freudians and ego psychologists are primarily concerned, e.g., aggression and sexuality, are derivative; if there were not a problem with the structure of the self, assertiveness would not turn into aggression and love would not turn into sexuality in the voracious and possessive Oedipal sense of the term. And yet, as compatible as may be Freudian, ego psychological, and self psychological theories of pathogenesis (from Kohut's perspective) or their respective clinical orientations — Kohut claims that analysts have been unwittingly acting as self psychologists for quite some time, thus that conversion to self psychology would only involve, for the most part, a different understanding of what analysts are doing anyway — there remain serious disagreements about fundamental matters such as the inevitability of drive-conflict, the ultimate opacity of the unconscious, the need for a metapsychology (specifically, for energetics), the plausibility of Kohut's belief in a drive to redevelopment and healing, the relation between developmental theory and clinical practice, the risks and advantages of certain forms of "corrective emotional experiences," other clinical issues such as the neutrality of the analyst, how to interpret transference, and so on.

As early as the first half of the 1950s, the researchers conducting an APA commissioned inquiry into psychoanalytic therapy as practiced by self-identified analysts were compelled to suspend their work, having become convinced of the impossibility of achieving consensus on a definition of psychoanalytic treatment (Gitelson 1973, 241). At about the same time, Edward Glover noted that there is "no effective control of conclusions based on interpretation" (1952, 405).[2] And not long thereafter, even David Rapaport expressed concern that "[t]here is [as yet] no established canon for the interpretation of clinical observations" (1960, 113). A few years later, the extent of psychoanalytic plurality and the difficulty this poses for empirical research was acknowledged by Philip Seitz in "The Consensus Problem in Psychoanalytic Research" (1966). By 1972 Anna Freud was compelled to describe psychoanalysis as in a state of "revolution and almost anarchy" — psychoanalytic perspectives had already proliferated to the point where hope for ultimate reconciliation was almost sapped (152).[3] Today such a hope is but a dream or a nightmare.[4]

In 1984 the APA's Board of Professional Standards again attempted to establish a consensus-based definition of the analytic process, and like the 1950 effort, it failed miserably. After meeting twice a year for five years, the eleven analysts involved abandoned the project. Although they reached a vague consensus that psychoanalysis must have something to do with transference, resistance, a dynamic unconscious, conflict, defense, infantile sexuality, co-conditioning change and insight, etc., they could only agree to disagree about the particulars. By 1987 the polysemy of psychoanalysis became so palpable and the conflicts over its determination so intense that the term "psychoanalysis" became, according to Samuel Abrams, "a Babel, a shibboleth, and a weapon" (411). By 2000 Thomä would speak of the "chaotic appearance" of modern psychoanalysis and a great deal of research would be devoted to the question of whether this appearance is reducible. Yet while the increasing pluralization has impressed (or distressed) many an analyst, the significance of such plurality has yet to attract the serious attention it deserves.

This and the following chapters aim to (1) familiarize the reader with the great diversity of psychoanalytic perspectives, (2) suggest in the strongest possible terms that reasons for commitment to a particular interpretation or analytic approach rather than another are wanting in demonstrative force, and (3) highlight and unpack the significance of the interminability of debates between and within analytic schools. By so doing, greater precision about the nature and status of psychoanalytic perspectives and the knowledge they yield will be attained, which will advance our understanding of what is implied in bearing psychoanalytic commitments (what such commitments *mean*) and how such commitments can be appropriately assessed.

This foray into psychoanalytic diversity and the significance thereof will begin with a question posed to a few major psychoanalytic schools, a question the responses to which, as we will see, are remarkably varied: What is essential to analysis? The schools considered will not be presented in chronological order so as not to insinuate a notion of linear progress in the field. Nor will they be presented in accordance with the author's preferences, as should be clear. Instead, the order of presentation will be largely arbitrary in order to make clear that the history of psychoanalysis proceeds not as linear progress toward better answers to persistent questions or toward decidedly better questions but rather via exemplary displacements and recasting of the fundamental meaning and modality of psychoanalytic work. Although, to be sure, a subsequent school will to some extent address itself in a different manner to problems engaged by its predecessors, succession regularly proceeds via repudiations of the clinical ambitions and concomitant theories of pathology (i.e., normative commitments) of predecessors. Though there is conceptual and technical continuity and development to be sure, the history of psychoanalysis is largely a history of mutual pathologization. Psychoanalysis does not have a linear, developmental history but is rather, to a much greater extent than is yet appreciated, a discontinuous series of episodes in which exemplary reconfigurations of analytic work give rise to partisan convictions that relate to one another in the mode of polemical self-assertion. A coherent, let alone progressive history of psychoanalysis would be a falsification. It should also be noted that the extent of reconstructive treatment to which each perspective is subject will be in inverse proportion to its assumed familiarity or adequate characterization in the extant literature. For instance, Freud, with whom I consider most readers to be generally familiar, will be treated much less extensively than Kohut, with whom I assume most readers will be much less familiar. Tarrying with a particular figure does not indicate preference but rather attempts to redress historical occlusion or prevalent misunderstanding.

In this chapter we will also begin to ask: What constitutes a particular school's perspective? What is its specific configuration of blindness and insight? Although I would like to explore the specific configurations of blindness and insight in more than just the few schools and in much greater detail even with respect to these schools, that would be a book length project unto itself — perhaps more than one. Thus for reasons of limited space and because the aims of this chapter are simply to underscore the vast and significant differences between psychoanalytic perspectives and to begin unpacking the nature of a psychoanalytic perspective in order to prepare the way for later concerns with the appropriate assessment of psychoanalytic claims and commitments, this discussion of blindness and insight will slowly develop as we turn from Freud to his numerous successors, provisionally culminating in a few thematic reflections on the nature and status of psychoanalytic knowledge as perspectival knowledge that will be further developed in subsequent chapters.

Chapter 3 will explore differences in perspective irreducible to, although often associated with, partisan differences. To this end, chapter 3 will provide an overview of a few controversial topics; for as various analysts weigh in on these controversies, the heterogeneity of each school will come into more fine relief. The chapter will conclude with further thematic reflections on the nature and status of psychoanalytic knowledge. Chapter 4 will then provide a protracted example of disagreement over how to interpret a particular clinical phenomenon — unusually strong anxiety in early stages of analysis — in order to better illuminate just how complex, weighty, and irresolvable are differences in perspectives. Only then, once the irreducibility of psychoanalytic plurality is suggested in the strongest possible terms and its significance unpacked (chapters 5 and 6), will the source of the temptation to turn to science to establish what is viable in and valuable about psychoanalysis and adjudicate between competing camps become clear, which will be the focus of chapter 7.

PSYCHOANALYSES: BLINDNESS AND INSIGHT

Note on Strategy

The strategy of the chapter is to attend to the relationship between theories of pathology and therapy in a range of psychoanalytic theorists in order to unlock the basic contours of their theories. Distinctive theories of pathology correspond to distinctive theories of technique. Generally, a psychoanalytic theory is composed of three elements that codetermine each other in a various ways depending on the theorist: a theory of suffering or pathology, a theory of therapeutic action, and a theory of end state (e.g., health or desirable transformation).[5]

Freud . . . transference and resistance

Of what must an analysis consist if it is really psychoanalysis? For Freud, analysis is the analysis of transference and resistance. As he famously comments to Groddeck, "[w]hoever recognizes that transference and resistance are the pivot of treatment belongs irrevocably to our 'savage horde'" (5 June 1917). Or as he puts it elsewhere, a treatment "only deserves the name [psychoanalysis] if the intensity of the transference has been utilized for the overcoming of resistances" (SE 12: 143). Recognition of transference and resistance as the *sine qua non* of analytic practice implies a commitment to the following "principal constituents of the theoretical structure of psychoanalysis": the unconscious, repression, "the etiological significance of sexual life, [and] the importance of infantile experiences" (SE 20: 40).

As Freud conceives them, infantile and pre-latency childhood sexuality are too much to bear. We are confronted by stimuli — needs, drives, wishes, object attachments — the intensity of which we are ill-equipped to metabolize, and so by which we are invariably overwhelmed. Since our capacities to metabolize — bind, organize, and discharge — these stimuli are underdeveloped, repression, the most basic, automatic defense mechanism, is bound to ensue. However, though repression is partially effective, it inevitably pales in comparison with the force of the return of the repressed.[6] Repression serves the pleasure principle, it aims to decrease or provide an acceptably constant level of tension. But because the pleasure principle is better served by the compromised satisfaction of inadmissible wishes than by their simple repression — wishes, however inadmissible, invariably exert a pressure for satisfaction and so will raise tension if not gratified in some way — repression is inevitably breached.[7] Symptoms are the compromise formations initiated by the return of the repressed and contribute to the maintenance of repression by disguising the wishes they partially gratify. Hysterics, as Freud famously puts it, suffer from reminiscences, from memories of satisfaction that persist in the unconscious as wishes — wishes ready to invest, indeed to hypercharge, conscious or preconscious wishes that bear some resemblance or associative connection to them. To eliminate a symptom, then, is to sap the force of repression by retrieving repressed wishes. If there is nothing to repress, if the wishes are conscious, then there is no need for compromise formations, i.e., symptoms.[8] Interpretation moots repression by confronting us time and again with our disavowed wishes until we establish a firm conviction that these wishes are ours.

But this is no simple task. Analysis works by reversing repression, but no mere conveyance of information about unconscious wishes will do. The structures of defense that keep wishes unconscious must be modified, and for this to occur resistances must be systematically confronted and dismantled.[9] Because certain resistances bear on infantile and childhood beliefs, expectations, wishes, and repressions, for Freud, analysis is not analysis if it fails to make its way through the depths: "only analyses that have penetrated so far [i.e., into the deepest and most primitive strata of mental development] deserve the name (SE 17:10). As he says elsewhere, "analytic work deserves to be recognized as genuine psycho-analysis only when it has succeeded in removing the amnesia which conceals from the adult his knowledge of his childhood from its beginning (that is, from about the second to fifth year)" (SE 17:183).[10] By eliciting transference and working through transference as a resistance to memory (or in certain cases, various resistances to transference), repression is overturned—or at least not so easy to maintain. As what was unconscious becomes conscious, it can be negotiated afresh. I assume that most readers are familiar with the details of classical Freudian therapy, so I will limit myself to describing only the bare essentials.[11]

In the Freudian schema, what we find exaggerated are (1) the persistence of libidinal history in the organization of present forms of life — specifically in patterns of attention and response — and in one's availability to the future, (2) the governing force of the pleasure principle, and (3) psychosexuality, ambivalence, conflict, defense, and compromise. Coextensively, what we find deflated are (1) the confidence in sovereign self-determination, freedom, spontaneity, etc. associated with the classical humanist subject, (2) the primacy of the social (economy, History, tradition, etc.) associated, for instance, with certain strands of Marxism and ethnography, and (3) our availability to being claimed and moved by concrete others in a manner that fundamentally exceeds our libidinally charged habits of perception, understanding, and response.

Lacan . . . the liberation of desire

Though Lacan disagrees with Freud about the necessity of removing amnesia via genetic reconstruction, and though he is less interested in interpreting repressed content than in confronting the analysand with provocative questions, his elaboration of the essentials of psychoanalysis seems to echo Freud's in many respects. In *Seminar XI*, Lacan insists that psychoanalysis, if it is truly psychoanalysis, involves recognition of and negotiation with four fundamental concepts: the unconscious, repetition, transference, and the drive. However, Lacan's elaborations of these concepts take him quite far from Freud. Although this is not the place to spell out the disagreements concerning these concepts in any great detail, such disagreements are implied in Lacan's distinctive conception of the aims of psychoanalysis, which will be our focus. In the most abbreviated manner, the aims of Lacanian analysis can be described as follows: Lacanian analysis aims at the revitalization and enhanced symbolic aptitude or creativity of analysands who are considered to be constrained by the mirages of autonomy and identity (aided and abetted by ego psychology) and by the fictive contours of interpersonal relationships (analyzed and supported by object relations theory). Against such illusory shackles, Lacanian analysis seeks the abdication of fantasies of self-mastery, of inviolable integrity, and of harmonious and fully satisfying relations with others, and therewith, the release of the analysand's desire. Lacan seeks the dis-integration and dissemination of the analysand as s/he discovers more and more profound connections with the transindividual unconscious, with the unconscious as intimate and anonymous, labile and rule-governed (as language is). And he seeks to induce the analysand to take responsibility for, to subjectivize or symbolize, that which fundamentally precedes and exceeds her.

Lacan's clinical sights are set on returning analysands' unintended and indelibly enigmatic meanings to them, not primarily to assist them in achieving a greater understanding of the meanings returned (though that too), but rather to facilitate the acknowledgment that speech and deeds are laden with polysemic valences, knotted with associations, and energized by investments that forever evade conscious discernment, let alone subjective appropriation. The aim is to insist into the foreground the experience of being irrevocably divided, surprising and strange, organized by nodal points that one would never expect and the significance and force of which will always remain in excess of cognitive, narcissistic mastery. The aim is to promote an accommodation to a notion of the subject as decentered, rent by drives, perturbed by the Real, and structured by fantasies that forever elude full and final discernment or subjective appropriation.

Anticipating Foucault, Lacan insists that the subject become a problem to herself. And like Foucault, he conceives becoming a problem to oneself as an impetus to practices of creative self-formation, the exercise of freedom (what Foucault calls "care of self"). But what we must not fail to note is that, for Foucault as for Lacan, subjectivity is intrinsically inimical to stabilization in univocal identity and is invested by forces that forever elude intentional mastery, thus practices of self-formation are necessarily ongoing and incomplete, yielding self-formations that are never quite what they were thought to be, always more and less than intended.

To the extent that Freudian analysis promotes integration and self-mastery, Lacanian analysis promotes subjective dispersion and abdication of pretenses to self-mastery: letting-be as a manner of individuation. To the extent that Freud promotes accommodation to what is operative yet unavowed and unnegotiated, Lacan promotes openness to the new and unanticipated, to the futurities toward which desire bears us and which become more expansive as central identifications, fundamental fantasies, and privileged forms of object attachment and relation are unsettled. In Lacanian parlance, the aim is the hystericization of desire.

Thus the Lacanian clinic works quite differently than the Freudian clinic. Freud was convinced that the unconscious is the storehouse of objectively present memory-traces and wishes striving for fulfillment but blocked by conflicts with other wishes, commitments to various self-images and the satisfactions they accrue (secondary gain), and anticipations of undesirable consequences.[12] Because unavowable wishes have become symptoms, the aim of analysis is avowal, the reversal of repression. To this end, analysis seeks to suspend the client's moral framework sufficiently for repressed contents to manifest themselves in transference, whence the client can be confronted with them time and again via interpretation, gain some clarity about her motives for defense, and thereby, hopefully, establish a firm conviction in the reality of her repressed wishes thus to some extent render repression inoperative.[13] The uncanny is revealed as the familiar; what once seemed foreign is found to be at the heart of the self, reappropriated.

In contrast, the Lacanian clinic aims not so much to expand awareness of repressed content, and surely not to promote its integration into the projects of a presumptively autonomous subject, but rather to counteract tendencies that limit or dampen desire and countervail the perpetual dislocations of subjectivity effected by desire.

Even when they engage in outwardly similar clinical practices, Lacan and Freud pursue fundamentally different aims; what seems to be a common method is anything but. For instance, Lacan, like Freud, seeks to reconnect thoughts and feelings in transference with their sources (persons, situations, relationships, deeply impacting phrases or images from the past, etc.), but for Lacan this is not in order to reverse repression and thereby disencumber the pleasure principle. As an astute reader of Freud, Lacan recognizes that the pleasure principle promotes de-differentiation, tension discharge, equilibrium. And since, for Lacan, analysis aims to foster a life lived on the crisp edge of desire, suffused with the tension of becoming, carried forth by the force of the negative, and outside the fantasy of wholeness or equilibrium, the point of reconnecting transferential thoughts and feelings with their historical sources cannot be to reverse repression and thereby facilitate the smooth operation of the pleasure principle. Rather, reconnecting thoughts and feelings in transference with their sources is part of a larger project of traversing the fantasy of fulfilling the desire of the Other (i.e., a primary caregiver or subsequent representative of authority) and thereby liberating desire. What Lacan eventually aims to reveal by this type of transference interpretation is that the analysand cares so much about the desire of the Other that she has organized her life in accordance with her perceptions of and fantasies about it (what it is, what it would take to satisfy it, specifically what one must do in order to satisfy it, etc.) and thereby inhibited her ownmost possibilities of desire, of becoming.

What, then, on Lacan's account, is an analyst to do? Analysis, if it is truly analysis, involves the following dimensions:

(1) Diagnosis. Diagnostic questions are posed to rule out perversion or psychosis. If these are found, a different sort of treatment will be offered than the one outlined here.[14]

(2) Refusal of demand. Lacan suggests that we tend to enter analysis when our symptoms, inhibitions, etc. have reached a crisis point, when they no longer yield an acceptable level of satisfaction. By entering analysis, a client demands, whether or not consciously (and usually not), that the analyst restore a workable level of satisfaction, that s/he correct the client's malfunctioning pleasure principle. Lacan will offer no such band-aid. Unlike Freud, he does not want the analyst to serve the pleasure principle if this means supporting a fantasy of and efforts to return to equilibrium or homeostasis. Stasis, equilibrium, wholeness, composure, integrity, and harmonious balance are, for Lacan, ultimately unrealizable and self-destructive lures — features of the Imaginary that are the sources of our suffering — investments in which inhibit the primary aims of analysis, namely, (1) affirmation of and accommodation to the truth of subjectivity, that is, the truth of lack, dissemination, destructuration, in(de)finite becoming; and (2) subjectivization, that is, taking responsibility for and making an effort to symbolize the Real,[15] which, to the extent that it remains unsymbolized (and it can never be fully symbolized), operates as an impediment or fixation point that limits the liberation of the analysand's desire, her potential for becoming otherwise. The analyst must be a paragon of the negative; s/he must refuse the demand for normalization, the demand to return the client to a pleasurable-enough functionality that presumably once obtained.

(3) Insistence on the fundamental rule. The implicit promise assumed to govern the analytic contract, namely, that by means of the analyst's expertise and care life will return to the *status quo ante*, is broken. It is broken by the analyst's refusal, especially in early stages of the analysis, to affirm *or* reject the analysand's self-interpretations, by the short session, and by the analyst's obscure and enigmatic speech and deeds. For instance, the analyst will sometimes refrain from commenting on the meaning of a particular dream in order to undermine, or at least bring to awareness, the assumption that the analyst Knows, especially when the dream seems to have been produced or recalled for the sake of analytic elucidation. The demand is continually refused, the promise broken, but the frustration bound to ensure cannot be endured. Dues must be paid to the pleasure principle; it will not tolerate systematic neglect. And besides, if the hope that the analyst will provide a cure is aggressively sapped, it is unlikely that the client will proceed with the analysis for a sufficient amount of time for its value to come into view. Consequently, the analyst offers a substitute satisfaction: her interest in the analysand's continuing the course of treatment. Via a blanket interest in the analysand following

the fundamental rule of free association, the analyst expresses a desire for the analysis to continue, and since the analysand is presumably yearning to satisfy the analyst's desire, she readily conforms to, and if the analysis is successful, eventually internalizes this desire (the *point* of Lacanian analysis is to render analysis interminable).[16] Interest in one's own analysis develops through or is significantly enhanced by mimetic internalization of the analyst's interest expressed through the insistence that the analysand follow the fundamental rule (and of course through interpretations and interventions). The satisfactions of sustained self-inquiry and "self-"awareness (i.e., awareness of one's self in its emphatic and unmasterable strangeness, its continual outstripping of narrative coherence) substitute for those to which the client expected to return upon the removal of her symptoms. The analyst's desire is here conceived as the motor of analysis, as its catalyst or "cause."[17] In Lacanese, the goal is to supplant the relation to Demand by the relation to *l'objet a.*

(4) Inducing the transference neurosis. Relatively vague anxieties, diffuse difficulties, a broad sense of disconsolation or depression, etc. are channeled through transference and transformed into the isolable symptoms of a transference neurosis.[18] Analysis of the transference neurosis aims to reveal and eventually unsettle the client's fundamental fantasy, her basic frame of self- and world-interpretation — at least insofar as it constrains her desire and conditions her suffering. The assumption is that the analysand is anxiously fleeing the freedom of subjectivity, evading the complexity, demandingness, and creativity of ongoing negotiations with the in(de)finite mobility of her and others' desirousness. S/he has become ensnared in a sacrificial fantasy wherein, if only s/he could correctly read and satisfy the concrete desires of the Other, the Other would be whole again, omniscient and omnipotent, thus able to satisfy her completely. The analysand has become a supplicant and has achieved a great deal of satisfaction thereby —indeed such supplication has provided the analysand with, minimally, the comforts of a relatively stable world-orientation — but at the cost of occluding the in(de)finite desirousness of both self and other, of neglecting and avoiding the incessant mobility of desire in both self and other and so of inhibiting the forms of self-realization and relation that would proceed on this basis. Because the fundamental fantasy falsifies desire, makes it seem contingent and ultimately eliminable, the strategies of appeasement that issue from and sustain it abrade against the truth of subjectivity, thus are not only limited and limiting but bound to run awry. However, no matter how many such failures and frustrations the analysand runs up against, the basic framework, the fantasy of Symbiotic Satisfaction, remains in place. Misfires become motivations to try harder to satisfy the Other, but no matter how conscientious and inventive the analysand is in this endeavor, her efforts will be unavailing. The work of analysis, then, is to interrogate and eventually unsettle this fantasy, and trans-

ference neurosis facilitates this by providing a forum in which the concretized demands of the Other are projected onto the analyst and so become subject to mutual exploration.

Since the aim of inducing a transference neurosis is to allow for the sacrifice of sacrifice, that is, the sacrifice of the sacrificial deference to the desire of the Other, the questions that guide the analysis of transference and resistance are as follows: What is the analysand's understanding of and relationship to the desire of the Other? What does the analysand believe the Other (ordinarily and paradigmatically, primary caregivers) wants? What desires of the Other is the analysand continually trying to satisfy, transgress, or provoke? How has the perception of the desire of the Other come to organize the analysand's fundamental fantasy, character structure, symptoms, etc.? Broadly, the aim of interpretation — a practice that for Lacan is composed more of pointed questions and emphases (especially at earlier stages of the analysis) than, as for Freud, disclosures and commentaries on the genetic precursors of current symptoms, inhibitions, and anxieties — in this context is fourfold: (1) to strengthen the analytic bond: the attribution of meaning to material that had been experienced as meaningless (dreams, parapraxes, word choice, symptoms, etc.) compels the client's interest, even if or partially because in other moments of the analysis the analyst will insist on the irreducible opacity or even nonsense of the material, (2) to facilitate transference: even if the analyst's interpretations foreground the enigmatic significance of the material rather than presume to decode its "true meaning," interpretation, especially in the context of a transference neurosis, positions the analyst as the one who Knows, akin to the omniscient and omnipotent figure from whom the analysand solicits satisfaction, making the analyst a viable object for transference projection, (3) to promote symbolization: interpretation of transference does not aim to reveal transference as resistance to memory, as with Freud, but to encourage the analysand's symbolization of the material projected in order to set into motion the dialectic of self-creation and discovery through which she will pursue the liberation of her desire, and (4) to facilitate separation-individuation: the analysand's relationship to the desire of the Other manifest in the transference neurosis is slowly unsettled through techniques we will discuss in a moment and thereby her desire is released into the free play of creative self-affirmation.

(5) Dialecticization of desire. Once the client is sufficiently invested in her own analysis and a transference neurosis has been established, the analysis can proceed to the dialecticization of desire. The goal here is twofold: (1) to shake up and revivify the client's desire, to release it from fixations in fantasy, object attachment, and self-image, and (2) to disintricate desire from entrenched patterns of interpretation. At stake is the de-rigidification of the fundamental fantasy. More concretely, the ambition is to loosen attachments to certain (broadly speaking, sexual) opinions and fantasies, interrupt patho-

logical opinions, and undermine the central identifications that constitute the ego, regulate desire, and function as impediments to free association, symbolization, and creative self-affirmation or relationality.

The client has come to experience her life as a set of problems for which she does not have the solution (e.g., what can I do for the Other? What would complete her?), but the presumption that there are solutions that would yield full and final satisfaction contributes to a neurotic fantasy in the grip of which the client finds herself forever wanting and consequently suffers. This gets to the heart of Lacan's theory of "pathology." Because she measures herself against an impossible ideal, the analysand depreciates the in(de)finite striving of desire, the satisfactions onto which it opens, and possibilities for relation to others as, likewise, in(de)finite desirous strivings. As much as the client's symptoms suggest that she is deeply committed to projects, ideals, and relationships that she cannot fully avow, she is a closet nihilist: subtending her incessant neurotic activity is a dark current of despair. The presumption of the attainability of full and final satisfaction, Lacan suggests, impedes the client from experiencing herself and others as subjects of the unconscious — in(de)finite surgings of desire, perpetual openings onto unsure horizons — and so forestalls the assumption of the complex, demanding, but ultimately emancipatory work of affirming and accommodating one's truth and learning to live outside the parameters of mastery. The goal, then, is to dismantle this problem-solution framework and the fantasies and patterns of interpretation with which it is associated. The client is overly integrated, her desire must be allowed more free reign.

To this end, the analyst seeks to broker another exchange: residual demands for specific improvements (e.g., the removal of symptoms) for the pleasurepain (*jouissance*) of revitalized, open-ended desire, of being borne by desire, fractured by futurity, on the cusp of horizons and relations that are but faintly beckoning. Sidestepping or refusing demands may allow desire to surge forth, but as the transference neurosis reveals, desire thus liberated will be largely channeled and constrained by the fundamental fantasy. Thus the goal is the cultivation of a new subjective position, namely, the experience of oneself and others as, essentially, singularly in(de)finite pulsations of desire, ever-enigmatic and radically incomplete. *Analysis aims to foster a generalized and sustained sense of wonder: the ability to live-in-question.* Here, simply insisting on the fundamental rule will be of limited efficacy. The risk of free association alone (a risk enhanced by interpretation) is that the client will believe that her associations are determined by unconscious principles, that they unfold according to a code to which the analyst has the key. This too quickly sparks seduction and defensive idealization of the analyst as the one who Knows: the expert and cure-all. Though the maintenance of the transference neurosis requires positioning the analyst as the *sujet supposé savoir*, and though the belief in unconscious determination may be in some respects well-warranted, against Freud's focus on repressed content, Lacan emphasizes the intransigently inscrutable dimensions of the unconscious, that which is at least partially other to the order of meaning. For Lacan, it is not simply repressed wishes that fester in the unconscious, but signifiers that bear no definite relation to signifieds.[19] Thus what is required is a specific analytic pedagogy, a habituation to the in(de)finite life of desire, to the nonsensical dimensions of subjectivity, and so to the in(de)finite possibilities of and insuperable limits to interpretation of both self and other.

Before we proceed to the next dimension, articulating a few details of this pedagogy will bring into more fine relief what, for Lacan, makes analysis truly analysis. The analyst habituates the client to the inevitability of nonreciprocity and misrecognition because the desire for and presumption of reciprocity and recognition are bound up with fantasies of harmony and completeness that must be divested if desire, creative self-exploration, and symbolization/subjectification (which, in a way, all name the same) are to flourish and make possible new forms of relationality. To this end, the analyst occasionally makes it clear that her attention is directed elsewhere, or expresses boredom or even exasperation, or expresses interest in and directs the client to topics, words, phrases, etc. that seem altogether irrelevant to the material unfolding in the session. Or she may act as if she fails to comprehend what the analysand expects she has understood full well, perhaps could not but. Or she refuses to interpret where interpretation is evidently expected or solicited, or in some other way surprises the analysand.[20] What is suggested thereby is that communication and mutual recognition are impossible ideals, as impossible as the unencumbered satisfaction the analysand unconsciously expects them to yield, and that these ideals and the practices to which they give rise should be critically investigated rather than unreflectively assumed.[21] The enigmas of the analyst provoke a questioning attitude.

More precisely, what is made clear is that the analyst's desire cannot be decoded, and that because it remains to no small extent intractably illegible, it cannot be satisfied. The analyst attempts to break the cycle of demand-compliance/transgression (the Oedipal configuration) by always being elsewhere, always wanting something else, always seeing things otherwise. The analyst figures the obdurate opacity of the Other, meaning to make the awareness of this opacity inescapable. The goal is to disrupt and subject to interrogation the analysand's propensity to act on the basis of perceived demands to the point where she will be able to notice herself constructing/concretizing these demands and then ask after her reasons for doing so and about what the value of not doing so may be. What compelling futures might life beyond the prevailing fundamental fantasy hold out? Why does one make oneself tendentially unavailable to possibilities of self-realization and relation that are ever abounding, if only in fledgling form?

Misunderstanding is not the sadistic, perverse mantra that some (e.g., André Green) accuse Lacan of promoting. If the enigmatic practice is successful, the client comes to sense the impossibility of satisfying the Other (initially, the analyst), and may begin to sense that in analysis as in life outside the clinic it is not the analyst's desire that is at stake, nor anyone else's — it is her own. At stake in the Lacanian clinic is the vivification of the client's desire and the liberation of her capacities for in(de)finite self-exploration, for self-exploration though a relational dialectic of self-creation and discovery *as an in(de)finite subject of desire.*

What the Lacanian clinic means to make inescapably clear is something we are highly motivated to forget: that misrecognition of the other and of oneself are not contingent because both are subjects of the unconscious. Learning to live with the intertwining of blindness and insight, with the fact that recognition reifies, thus misrecognizes, is, for Lacan, accommodation to the truth of subjectivity as in(de)finite lack, as always elsewhere and otherwise. By refusing to conform to the normative protocols of intersubjective communication, by being somewhat aloof and "on a different page" or just downright obtuse, the analyst induces the sense that what both she and the analysand says or does signifies in ways that cannot be fully comprehended, let alone controlled; and suggests that a certain freedom is to be found in releasement.

Thus the analyst will seek to attune the analysand to her unintended meanings and eventually to the indeterminacy, the spontaneity and surprise, of signification as such. For thereby, the analyst establishes the utter impossibility of uncompromised self-awareness and self-mastery, and implicitly, the impossibility of fully knowing and controlling the Other, thus by extension, the impossibility of final fulfillment by the Other. To this end, the analyst will draw attention to the complex blend of determinacy and indeterminacy, of meaning and nonsense, manifest in the analysand's dreams, fantasies, garbled speech, slips, parapraxes, hesitations, word choice, idiomatic quirks, obscure and fleeting impressions and thoughts, and out of context affect or thoughts. Of paramount value will be anything that surprises the analysand, catches her off guard and keeps her off balance. The material upon which Lacan focuses is thus somewhat different than that to which Freud is drawn. As much as Freud looks for hidden meaning in ill-attended consistencies and patterns, Lacan focuses on surprises and seeks points of obdurate obscurity — intermixtures of meaning and nonmeaning. His point in so doing is to induce a lasting sense of oneself and others as subjects of the unconscious, forever foreign to ourselves and each other, rather than reveal the unfamiliar as the familiar. Or through a particular interpretive practice called "scansion," the analyst emphasizes something surprising or puzzling that was quickly glossed over by or was insufficiently troubling to the analysand. Again the point is for the analysand to consider the emphasized material such that, after finding herself unable to discover a coherent and compelling narrative with which to account for its meaning — guided by the Lacanian analyst, s/he confronts more and more resonances of the material, never its ultimate meaning — s/he learns to live with her insuperable opacity,[22] with the simultaneity of sense and nonsense.[23]

So although the analyst may at times interpret in the classical Freudian sense, this will be counterbalanced by various insistences on the nonsensical, the insistently indeterminate and/or overdetermined, on those elements that are only partly intelligible to or altogether elude intelligibility. At their best, Lacanian interpretations will provide words for which the analysand is searching, words with which to make some sense of her difficulties and sufferings, while at once conveying the obstinate obscurity of the material productively phrased, indeed of the analysand herself. This is a tenuous balancing act to be sure, and because the analysand is a glutton for meaning, for clear and coherent narratives and the identity they underwrite, these sorts of interpretations are offered infrequently.

Indeed because the analysand so craves coherence, and because scansion and other such techniques are sometimes insufficient to break the analysand from her fantasy of fully satisfying mutual recognition, the Lacanian clinic has recourse to the short session and oracular interpretation.[24] With regard to the former, the analyst may "punctuate" the session by stopping it short in order to indicate that something has emerged that warrants consideration and has been all too quickly passed over by the analysand (like scansion). By ending the session on *that* note, with *that* turn of phrase, or in the middle of what seems well-worn ground, the analyst gives her client something to ponder, something with which to become preoccupied. As Bruce Fink explains,

> When the analyst suddenly ends a session, he or she may accentuate surprise the analysand has just been expressing, or introduce the element of surprise through scansion, leaving the analysand wondering what it was the analyst heard that he or she had not heard, wondering what unconscious thought had been manifesting itself. This element of surprise is important in ensuring that analysis does not become *routine*, such that, for example, the analysand goes in every day, recounts his or her dreams and fantasies forty-five or fifty minutes, and goes home, nothing being shaken up, nothing bothering or preoccupying him or her all day and night. Lacanian analysis seeks to keep the analysand off guard and off balance, so that any manifestation of the unconscious can have its full import. (1999, 18)

Shaking things up this way, the analyst forestalls the defense against analysis that routinization can be — a defense ever so difficult to disrupt once it is established because, to a certain extent, it looks exactly like a well functioning analysis.[25] Though it seems that the analysand is engaged to the utmost in introspective association and is working through difficult material throughout the session, the barrage of disclosures effectively insulate and conceal important material that emerges, if at all, only at the very end of the session. The idea is that the short session will not allow material pressing forth despite the enormity of countervailing defensive pressures to wait until that last moments of the session to come to the fore because the session can end at any moment.

The short session is also important, especially when it seems arbitrary, as part of a broader effort to interrupt the idealization of the analyst as the one who Knows and thus can cure. As much as interpreting or directing the analysand to topics the analyst is interested in may position the analyst as the *sujet supposé savoir*, the short session may contribute to undermining this position. Of course, calling a precipitous end to the session may accentuate the analyst's seductively authoritative mystique. But the short session may also intimate — depending upon how subsequent sessions are conducted — that the analyst knows no more, or at least little more, than that something significant has been said or done, something that warrants further consideration. Or it may show that even if the analyst does have a sense of what this material means, this is not all that is important, that what is equally if not more important than knowing what obscure material means is the capacity to continue the dialectic of self-creation and discovery promoted by analysis and the liberation of desire it effects.

(6) Interpretation. Lacanian interpretations temper clarification with an emphasis on the multiple meanings and ambiguous qualities of the material interpreted. By means of an oracular style, they tend to highlight the polyvalent and enigmatic dimensions of the analysand's speech and deeds, seeking to arouse curiosity, incite associations, and accustom the analysand to the irreducible opacity of self and other, the abrasiveness of the human to all strategies of mastery. Through oracular interpretation, the analyst figures the equivocity and enigma of the unconscious, seeking to habituate the analysand to accept and eventually affirm equivocity and enigma: at certain moments of the therapy, the analyst disappears as a concrete individual, not in the sense of fusing with the transference projection but rather in the sense of becoming "a more abstract other, the other that seems to speak inadvertently, in the slips and cracks in the analysand's discourse. In a word, he or she must stand in for . . . the Other [the unconscious] . . . that which the analysand considers to be radically foreign, strange, 'not me'" (Fink 1999, 31-2). This style of interpretation does not dictate the truth of the analysand's repressed wishes to her, for such clear communication of content, on Lacan's view, tends to generate either agreement or revolt (an Oedipal configuration), both of which might (1) be considered resistances, for instance, resistances to one's increasing independence from the desire of the Other as the fundamental reference point of one's world-orientation and thus resistances to the

difficulties of creative self-elaboration, and (2) shore up convictions in stable and univocal meaning associated with the standpoint of the ego, which analysis attempts to undermine.[26] Rather, it aims to resonate with the unconscious, to speak to multiple sectors of material, and thus to incite new material, new connections between topics already considered, new associations, or new projections, all of which facilitate the ongoing self-exploration of the analysand, who, by symbolizing heretofore unsymbolized material or symbolizing old material anew (in Lacanese, this is called metaphorization or subjectivization), engages in a practice of simultaneous self-discovery and -creation. To this end, as noted, Lacanian interpretation tends to be oracular — condensed and enigmatic, suggestive but obscure, something over which to puzzle, a provocation. For instance, an interpretation may incorporate words, sounds, or names that have been identified as important to the analysand in order to suggest connections or provoke associations and reflection, even if this means phrasing the interpretation in a way that is not on face illuminative and may even involve distortions of the material under consideration.[27]

Confronted by an oracular interpretation, one cannot but ask: What could *that* mean? Why would the analyst say *that*? The perplexing quality of such interpretations mitigates the formidable risk that the analysand will glean a sense of how the analyst perceives her from his/her interpretations and will attempt to adjust herself to this image in order to appease the desire of the Other. Tendentially, irrespective of whether the analysand consciously agrees or disagrees with the interpretation, she unconsciously affirms the images of herself projected through the interpretation as who she must become. This is assimilation as resistance, the object of the immanent critique operated by oracular interpretation.

Though oracular interpretations cannot but sound strange, when effective, they sound "right," or better, resound well at the level of the unconscious in the sense that they hit on something significant, mobilizing questions and associations. At best, such interpretations strike the Real, touch that around which the analysand's Symbolic and Imaginary life are turning and spark symbolizations and associations that were previously foreclosed. In order to do so, however, the ego must be circumvented, otherwise it may insist on the dismissal of the oracular interpretation as mere gibberish or "poetry." Hence the equivocity of the interpretation is crucial to its efficacy. Oracular interpretation is equivocal not only in the senses that it seeks to resonate in a variety of ways with multiple sectors of material and makes itself available to a number of interpretations by the analysand, but also in the sense that it allows the ego to catch the drift of one level of meaning so that another can slip by. Just like a joke — which can sometimes function as an interpretation. Oracular interpretations speak *through* resistances.

(7) Late stages. Toward very late stages of analysis, interpretations may become increasingly classical in the sense of univocal, specific, and knowing

because the position of the *sujet supposé savoir* has been largely debunked and divested. If the analysand is not so prone to idealize the analyst or conform to the images of herself projected by the analyst's interpretations, she can receive interpretations as suggestions to be reckoned with. In the late stages, having investigated a large quantity of material, the analytic pair will search for key signifiers ("master signifiers") out of which symptoms, relations to one's body, and fundamental fantasies are constructed. The goal is to allow alternative forms of life to emerge that are less dominated by these master signifiers. As always, the aim of analysis is the liberation of desire. To be sure, sustaining attunement to surprise, forever in jeopardy of being eclipsed by commitments to the forms of life one is developing, is never surpassed as an analytic ambition; thus in these late stages, scansion is used to highlight *jouissance* where it is least expected. The analysand is continually confronted with his or her disavowed *jouissance* and enjoined to take responsibility for it, to affirm it in his or her ongoing dialectic of (self-)creation and discovery.

In the Lacanian clinic, what we find exaggerated are (1) the focus and primacy placed on liberating the fracturing insurgence of desirousness in excess of any particular configuration of desire, (2) more specifically, the imperative to cultivate openness to the unanticipated, the new, to futurities and relational possibilities toward which desire may yet bear us, (3) the pathogenic status of the central identifications, fundamental fantasies, and forms of object attachment and relation associated with fantasies of mutual recognition, harmonious integration, and complete satisfaction, and (4) the emphasis on the intransigently inscrutable, utterly enigmatic, perhaps even flatly nonsensical dimensions of the unconscious. What we find deflated are (1) the urgency of social accommodation and self-integration, (2) the curative power of content-based self-awareness, and (3) concern with suffering, which Lacan tends to read as just neurotic frustration.

Ferenczi . . . exemplary trust and active sympathy

A very different conception of psychoanalytic therapy was developed by Sandor Ferenczi. For Ferenczi, analysis pursues two specific goals: the reactivation of traumatic loss of trust in the world and the subsequent reestablishment of basic trust. The clinical innovations through which these goals are pursued take their lead from his distinctive theory of pathology and his assessment of the limits of free association. For Ferenczi, lack of sympathy and trust in the early environment are the major pathogenic phenomena. In his words, "the systematic training of children to blind obedience and motiveless respect for their parents [which manifests a decided lack of sympathy and trust] . . . might also be called [the] artificial breeding of neuropaths and sexually impotent people" (1952, 32). This basic lack of sympathy and trust in child rearing, compounded by broader social forces of intimidation and authoritarianism (for instance, what Ferenczi describes as the authoritarian myth of genital maturity), generates large-scale inhibitions and conditions the development of symptoms. In order to address pathology so construed, Ferenczi develops a novel clinical program. In its final formulation, analysis must (1) heighten tension sufficiently for unconscious material — specifically, deeply repressed conflicts and material related to the breakdown of basic trust — to come to the fore,[28] (2) relax the analysand sufficiently for free association to flourish, and (3) generate an atmosphere of sympathy and trust that contributes to healing the wound, the rift in the personality, torn open by imperious techniques of child rearing that culminate in the breakdown of basic trust.

More precisely, the analyst must be continually sympathetically attuned to the analysand's general emotional predicament and current affective state, for, on Ferenczi's view, patients only react to "real sincere sympathy" (1955, 161). For instance, only in the context of ongoing sympathetic responsiveness will the client's traumas reemerge.[29] Thus he calls his practice a cure by love: "[p]sychoanalytic 'cure' is in direct proportion to the cherishing love given by the psychoanalyst to the patient; the love which the psychoneurotic *needs*, not necessarily the love which he thinks he needs and therefore demands" (attributed by de Forest 1954, 15). Appropriately administered, analysis, for Ferenczi, provides a secure, affirming though not unchallenging context in which traumas can be relived and, via the mediation of interpretations that expresses understanding and acceptance, proceeded through otherwise, i.e., worked through in a way that conduces to the self-acceptance and more felicitous negotiation with heretofore disorganizing content possible only in an atmosphere of honesty and genuineness.[30]

In addition to sustaining sympathy and making sure this sympathy is felt by the analysand, the analyst must performatively convey an experience of the world as largely hospitable, as amenable to the analysand's development and flourishing. Specifically, the analytic relationship must be a medium in which the analyst's hopefulness and trust in the world manifest in an exemplary way, shining forth with such radiance that the world becomes illuminated as trustable once more. "A contrast to the environment surrounding the traumatic situation — that is, sympathy, trust — must first be created before a new footing can be established: memory instead of repetition. Free association by itself, without these new foundations for an atmosphere of trust, will thus bring no real healing. The doctor must really be involved in the case, heart and soul, or honestly admit it when he is not, in total contrast with the behavior of adults toward children" (1985 [1932], 170).[31]

The problem with free association alone, Ferenczi suggests, is that analysands may associate indefinitely but never reach a breakthrough, and the suggestion to maintain faith in the method sounds like desperate piety.[32] In order to address this snare, and specifically to facilitate the expression of split-off aspects of the psyche that the ordinary psychoanalytic technique could not render conscious, Ferenczi developed the "active technique" — to which he stalwartly adhered in the early stages of his career (1919 onward), but later came to consider but an option for dealing with particularly difficult cases.[33] The active technique underwent a number of formulations and revisions. In its final elaboration, it was divided into three phases.

First, the analyst prohibits various forms of autoerotism in the clinic (beard stroking, thigh rubbing, etc.) and sometimes also prohibits sexual activity outside the clinic. The aim is to increase tension in the session and thereby bring unconscious material into the fore and into focus so that it can be symbolized and analyzed.[34] Ferenczi's concern is that free association and interpretation alone — Freud's technique — may make for a relatively superficial analysis; habitual ways of satisfying repressed wishes are not artificially put out of play, the analysis may never reach the depths Freud desired to plumb. Consequently, the active technique aims to inspire the enactment of deeply repressed unconscious conflicts, specifically as they pertain to breakdowns in basic trust and sympathy.

Second, by means of sustained empathy, the analyst relieves the suffering and anxiety enhanced by aforementioned prohibitions and diminishes inhibitions sufficiently for free association to flourish. Analytic empathy also helps counteract the pathogenic lack of sympathy in the client's early environment. Such empathy may manifest in the following forms: sympathetic attunement expressed through interpretations; various measure of affective support and nourishment calibrated to the specific needs of the analysand (especially useful for severely regressed patients); expressions of tenderness including soothing, relaxing touches (especially useful for those who, as a result of trauma, for instance shell shock, split off parts of their personalities and are thus, ordinarily, inaccessible to analysis). Or the analyst may recommend relaxation techniques (especially useful for those considered to suffer from early infantile trauma) with the aim of diminishing anxiety and inhibitions.[35]

Third, the analyst actively encourages symbolizations of anxiety-laden material. S/he may impose a limit on the duration of analysis in order to prevent free association going on indefinitely when no breakthroughs are evident[36] or insist on the analysand completing sentences if s/he habitually fails to do so.[37]

Ferenczi's concerns with the limits of free association are strikingly similar to Lacan's concerns with routine as a defense against analysis. But despite this convergence, and though both aim to liberate interest in and adeptness at experimentation with life-possibilities, there are at least three elements of Ferenczi's technique that would profoundly vex Lacan.

First, Ferenczian sympathy — along with his later (1929-1932) practice of mutual analysis — risks reinforcing a fantasy of symmetry, of mutual recognition and reciprocity, thus it risks supporting the neurotic fantasy of Completeness from which the client, on Lacan's account, suffers and which, arguably more importantly for Lacan, impedes the flourishing of her in(de)finite desire. The risk of colluding with or directly encouraging a fantasy of harmonious fulfillment, which for Lacan signals the death of desire, is enhanced by Ferenczi's promise of a "cure," which, even if suspended in quotation marks in his theoretical writings, seems an implicit promise in his practice.

A corollary concern might be expressed about Ferenczi's (later) theory of pathology and its clinical implications. In what he would come to call "confusion of tongues," Ferenczi sees evidence of the client in early childhood having interiorized adult desires inscribed with hate, guilt, and prohibition that are grafted onto and partially eclipse her heretofore fundamentally tender — though not unconflicted, thus not pathogen-free — self- and world-relation. Violently intruded upon by messages from the parental unconscious that she has no means to avoid or defend against, e.g., messages concerning conflict between family members, and especially if already anxious because subject to the seduction that inscribes guilt-ridden passion in comparatively tender relations, the child will introject the invading messages and repeat them indefinitely in her self- and world-relations, the relatively tender milieu of childhood being violently disrupted by the aggression, passion, and conflict of the adult world.[38] Further, shocked, frightened, and dismayed by these alien messages, and in the grip of the unlimited power of adults to captivate, especially if such captivation proceeds as seduction, the child may become overwhelmed by anxiety, thoroughly confused, and consequently prone to identify with the aggressor. "The . . . anxiety, however, if it reaches . . . a maximum, compels them to subordinate themselves like automata to the will of the aggressor, to divine and gratify each one of his desires; completely oblivious of themselves, they identify with the aggressor . . . The most important change, produced in the child's mind by anxiety and fear-ridden identification with the adult partner, is the introjection of the guilt feelings of the adult; this makes the hitherto harmless play appear as a punishable offense" (1955, 162). To be sure, a certain proximity to Lacan's concern with submission to the desire of the Other can be discerned — Ferenczi like Lacan certainly means to disencumber the client from her excessive, subjectivity-diminishing enamorment with and especially her efforts to fulfill the Other — but Lacan would surely be suspicious of Ferenczi's efforts to restore the relatively tender milieu of childhood. Although, for Ferenczi, pathogenic conflicts are incumbent to infancy and childhood, he insists that adult desire damages the child, sometimes quite severely; and his clinical ambition is to revive the tender child in the adult, to restore basic trust, sympathy, tenderness, etc. — which may look to Lacan like trading one source of submission for another and a denial of the truth of subjectivity.

Despite Ferenczi's persistent conviction in the potentially pathogenic passions, conflicts, etc. of early psychic life, might a Lacanian not wonder whether he nonetheless encourages a fantasy of symbiotic plentitude and thereby surreptitiously promotes submission and subjective depletion? For Lacan, the violence of adult desire that Ferenczi denounces (or something akin thereto) is constitutive of subjectivity. Such desire is a spur to subjectivity, more like a pulsating, enigmatic signifier in response to which self- and world-symbolization proceed than an external impediment the removal of which would restore anything remotely akin to a prelapsarian paradise of childhood tenderness. Or, for Lacan, the violence of adult desire may be better construed as a figure of the inevitable rift in or self-incommensurability of subjectivity (a figure of the paternal metaphor, the Symbolic, etc.), indeed as a figure of the unconscious as Other, which would suggest that Ferenczi's efforts to expel this violent intruder are, effectively, efforts to deny the unconscious.

Second, the analyst's exemplarity may induce solicit transference idealization that Ferenczi does not have the resources to systematically undermine, as Lacan claims one must. Because Ferenczi requires that the analyst's trust in the world manifest itself, beckon to and eventually becoming mimetically incorporated by the analysand, from Lacan's perspective, he assumes and implicitly advocates that the analyst figure a model, pattern, or prototype to which the analysand ought conform. If the analysand is, as Lacan suggests, anxiously seeking an image of herself that would be approved by the analyst in order to evade the challenges of exercising freedom and merge with an idealized Other who is presumed to hold the keys to the Kingdom of Heaven, it may not just be the analyst's trust in the world that is mimetically instilled. Ferenczian exemplarity may unintentionally invite an unreflective (specifically, unconscious) incorporation of the social norms, structures of sensibility, evaluative proclivities, etc. operative in the analyst, at which point analysis (1) would become an ideologically suspect supplement to faltering practices of socialization, a symptom of social crisis rather than a practice through which to negotiate and work through such a crisis, (2) props up the standpoint of the ego and supports an illusory sense of personal integrity and stable identity, both of which contribute to defenses against the fracturing upsurge of desire (for Lacan, the truth of subjectivity), regulating desire there where it might be liberated, and inhibit free association, thereby impeding the efficacy of analysis on both Ferenczi and Lacan's terms, and (3) supports a fantasy of sacrificial supplication to the analyst's ideals as a way of winning her good graces and the complete fulfillment they harbor. From Lacan's standpoint, along with a sense of trust, the analysand may mimetically incorporate the formal consistency, i.e., the aura of subjective integrity, figured by the analyst, and this would likely be counterproductive if the aim of analysis is to sap the analysand's desire for and pathogenic expectation of sovereign integrity and the utopian promises it augurs. It would be to occlude of the dimension of the Real, the irritating kernel that disrupts the consolidation of both subject and object and renders them forever excessive of the horizon of transparency and instrumental control — an ontological mistake.

What's more, Ferenczian exemplarity, along with the third element that Lacan would find distressing, the active technique, risks installing a habit of looking to the analyst for substantive guidance and concrete direction — and the client would be all the more susceptible to this to the extent that Ferenczi is right that s/he suffers from a breakdown of trust and sympathy, and thus, presumably, from normative disorientation — at which point not only does the risk of artificially manipulated associations, etc. in analysis become severe, the analysis risks further establishing the desire of the Other as the analysand's fundamental principle of self-relation and world-orientation. The vicious circle of her suffering will remain unbroken as the client fails to fully engage the dialectic of self-creation and -discovery, the accommodation to and, eventually, affirmation of her singularly in(de)finite desire, at which analysis, for Lacan, ought aim.

To be sure, Ferenczi was well aware of at least some of the risks courted by sympathy and the active technique — if not so much those involving exemplary trust. He knew, for instance, that sympathy could promote emotional dependency and thus contribute to defenses against analysis. This is why, for Ferenczi, the cure of "love" is a supplement to and not a replacement for the classical Freudian technique of insisting on and interpreting free association — as is made especially clear by Ferenczi's eventual characterization of the active technique as "elastic." Further, a few components of Ferenczi's technique may mitigate these risks. For instance, Ferenczi's contention that "[t]he doctor must really be involved in the case, heart and soul, or honestly admit it when he is not" suggests that he was and wanted other analysts to be, to a degree, willing to expose their faults and failures. "[I]n total contrast with the behavior of adults toward children," the analyst must explicitly admit not only her specific faults and failures, but (when appropriate) her lack of omniscience and omnipotence. This, along with his late advocacy of mutual analysis (circa 1930) and his version of refusing the analysand's demands — recall that the analyst supplies "the love which the psychoneurotic *needs*, not necessarily the love which he thinks he needs and therefore demands" — may go some way in diminishing the risk of transference idealization and all that follows from it.

It should also be noted that Ferenczi's stipulation that "[a] contrast to the environment surrounding the traumatic situation — that is, sympathy, trust — must *first* be created before a new footing can be established: memory instead of repetition" may imply that basic trust is a *condition* for free association, thus may be propedeutic to the experiences of subjective destructuration that free association yields (emphasis added). As a condition for free association, basic trust may be a condition for the liberation of Lacanian desire.

Even in view of these qualifications, and even though transference idealization could well be worked through at later stages of the therapy, Lacan's worry would still be that insofar as Ferenczi's practice relies on the efficacy of the analyst as exemplar, it will fail to induce the requisite accommodation to the perpetual destructuration — the abrasive, resistant, non-assumable irritant — of desirous subjectivity, hence will fail to appropriately encourage its ongoing, creative reanimation.[39] Lacan's worry would still be that as an alluring model of affective propriety for the analysand ("you, like me, should feel a basic trust in the world"), the analyst, hubristically and indeed counter-analytically, fails to promote the release of the analysand's desire from the models (self-images and attendant forms of object relation, or in Lacanian parlance, fundamental fantasies) to which it has been confined, and which, for Lacan, are elements of the pathogenic matrix. On Lacan's account, transference idealization is a deep temptation and a fundamental resistance to analysis, thus it can never be worried over enough.

Finally, from Lacan's perspective, Ferenczi's theory of pathology is suspiciously generic and abstract.[40] Are loss of trust and sympathy always the primary sources and fundamental mediators of pathology? On what grounds are these experiences established as the root causes and persistent stakes of suffering and developmental stultification? Are experiences of loss of trust and sympathy empirical or fantasmatic, and what difference might this make? Indeed, what *is* loss of trust in the world? For Lacan, much more so than for Ferenczi, trauma, thus pathology, is radically singular, untraceable to standard paradigms, irreducible to established formulas. For instance, Lacan would resist the assumption that agoraphobia has some generic etiology wherein, say, the sight of something outdoors triggers an unavowable desire or deeply distressing conflict that transforms into or provokes anxiety, which then broadens into signal anxiety and suffuses the public domain, eventuating in agoraphobia. And all the more so would he resist the claim that the relevant desire has become unavowable or the conflict overwhelmingly distressing because of some early experience of authoritarian rearing, seduction, or intimidation as a result of which the bonds of trust and sympathy were broken. Or to give another example, though there may be some loss of basic trust or sympathy involved in the development of claustrophobia, this need not be the case. For Lacan, claustrophobia may arise — and this may be overly simplifying matters, but that just furthers the point — from a fantasy or experience that involves, even quite peripherally, a closet or cabinet or pantry (think of little Hans) or images associated with them. Or it may arise from experiences or fantasies that involve, again even quite peripherally, the word "closet," "cabinet" or "pantry" or words with which these terms are associated in a singular unconscious. Or it might arise as a result of some trauma that is loosely connected with either a confined space — say, some variant of the primal scene is experienced or imagined from the point of view of a child hidden in a closet — or a space experienced as too open, public, or otherwise exposed or vulnerable, e.g., a subtle twist on the example of agoraphobia above. In any case, Lacan would insist on the singular constellations of psychic life, and so would be suspicious of the explanatory and therapeutic primacy Ferenczi places on the loss and recovery of basic trust and sympathy.

Of course, Ferenczi could rejoin that (1) it is equally suspicious that Lacan situates enamorment with the desire of the Other, the fundamental fantasy, and so on as the core of neurosis and the matrix within which it unfolds, and (2) it is equally plausible that what Lacan considers the primary pathogenic fantasy is a compensation for traumatic breakdowns in basic trust and sympathy: even if there is no formula according to which symptoms and inhibitions develop, it may well be that the symptoms of disavowed desire on which Lacan focuses are epiphenomenal, derivative of or at least extensively conditioned by the basic difficulties in character formation that result from and will remain in place if analysis fails to address a loss of basic trust and inadequate sympathy in early infantile or childhood experience. Of course, Lacan could respond in kind, and we quickly run into a deadlock.[41]

As much as Lacan's theory of technique can be formulated as a critique of Ferenczi's, it works the other way around as well. For instance, for Ferenczi, Lacan's emphasis on subjective dispersal may only exacerbate the client's want of trust in the world by failing to provide sufficient regularity and stability where they are expected and, worse, scoffing at the desire for it. Furthermore, it may aggravate the tension and anxiety from which the client suffers to the point where deeply repressed unconscious material will never surface. From Ferenczi's perspective, Lacan's failure to provision sympathy and reestablish basic trust may leave the client's core problems and consequent sufferings in place; his directives to shift the topic or express interest in material that seems unimportant to the analysand may promote blind obedience and reenact the authoritarian scenario at the root of the analysand's loss of basic trust; his oracular interpretations may invite an image of the analyst as a mystical authority who can only be blindly obeyed, again repeating elements of the analysand's traumatic childhood; and his technique may fail to heighten and relieve tension at the right moments and so will be unable to access a wealth of material.

The point is not to stage a debate between Ferenczi and Lacan in order to decide who is ultimately right. Rather, the point is to underscore (1) the vast and irreducible differences in psychoanalytic theories of technique, (2) the vastly different, often conflicting conceptions of pathology, of analytic aims, and of the unconscious and other basic concepts that are bound up with them, and (3) the want of demonstrative force for arguments that presume to adjudicate between competing perspectives.

Pressing this point further, from a critical Lacanian (e.g., Zizekian) perspective, Ferenczi's conception of treatment seems either to be a pursuit of ideological affirmation of the status quo in whatever form or liable to devastate analysands' capacities to get on in the liquid modern world; or worse, their mutually aggravating because mutually undermining conjunction. If the liquid modern world is neither hospitable (institutionally and intersubjectively sympathetic) to the flourishing of distinctive individuals nor safe and trustable (say, for all the reasons risk society theorists have detailed),[42] why, one might wonder, would analysts contribute to concealing its endemic risks, dangers, and inadequacies by inculcating or presuming to inculcate basic trust and generating expectation of widespread sympathy? Would not so doing lead to massive frustration and confusion as the expectations inculcated are systematically disappointed and conduce to ideological complicity with a highly destructive social order and to the production of docile, all too trusting subjects? And compounding the problem, would not inculcating trust in a highly unstable and largely unsympathetic (in both ways, untrustable) world conspire with the manipulations rampant therein and render analysands incapable of successfully navigating the ever-shifting terrain of late capitalist societies? To the extent that analysis fosters trust, does it not diminish analysands' capacities to navigate a world that is decidedly — though unevenly — unstable and unsympathetic, a world that — within certain limits, of course, e.g., the limits of profitability — is increasingly governed by the imperative of incessant self-revolution?[43]

From such a perspective, the risks incurred supporting the analysand's accommodation to — trust in and expectation of sympathy from — the status quo in whatever form it takes is that analysis (1) becomes a mechanism of social-ideological integration, a conduit of conformism through which, in a world such as our own, its aims to support interest in and the accomplishment of distinctive individuality or an integrated personality are undermined, or at the very least complicit with the shape of the world that, as Ferenczi notes, is partially responsible for the analysand's suffering in the first place, and (2) generates an illusory belief that the world is coherently patterned, stable and predictable, which would devastate our capacities to navigate the perpetual dislocations and permanent crises of the liquid modern world, likely leading to massive frustration, seemingly inexplicable anxiety, and consequent reactions. Guided by such a perspective, one might query, can a world that demands immediate, unconditional affirmation really be a world we can trust, or does trust in the world require the world's hospitability to critical reflection, resistance, and reshaping? Or, conversely, one might ask: Might the world's "hospitability" to — its establishment of terrible consequences for failing to engage in — continual critical reflection and permanent self-reshaping be how it sustains social-economic stratifications and forestalls transformation beyond a certain limit? Might the imperative to adapt to ever-changing social and economic conditions contribute to a sense of overarching dread, a fear of immanent obsolescence, and so to a massive if mobile conformism?[44] Is Ferenczi's practice informed by antiquated assumptions about the stability of the social order and sympathetic cohesiveness of community life that may never have been true to the shape of the world and are, today, but ideologically animated relics?

Ferenczi's rejoinder could well be that if his technique successfully treats neurosis and contributes to a sense of security and self-acceptance necessary for self-experimentation and growth, even, or perhaps especially, in highly unstable conditions, then even if it incurs a number of risks, this is no reason to reject it. As risky as Ferenczian therapy may be under contemporary conditions, how successfully can one navigate the tumultuous terrain of the liquid modern world and how critical of invidious social forces and ideological imperatives can one be, if, crippled by neurosis, one's self-confidence, agential aspirations, and hopefulness for future flourishing are utterly devastated? Further, Ferenczi could well ask, Isn't the inevitability of risk and danger part and parcel of the risk theory his critic deploys against him? Even if under contemporary socio-economic conditions Ferenczi's practice works in ways it does not intend, even if, as action always may, it initiates effects it cannot fully predict or control, even if, when practiced in conditions Ferenczi did not foresee, it gives rise to consequences that partially mitigate its desired results, should it for such reasons be rejected? Would it not be fair of Ferenczi to demand of such a critic that she either (1) demonstrate rather than just speculatively suggest that Ferenczian therapy makes matters worse on its own criteria or (2) show Ferenczian therapy to be demonstrably less successful in avoiding the dangers the critic outlines than alternative practices and that avoiding such dangers is more important than achieving the successes at which it aims?

At this point, the critical Lacanian would likely point to a certain version of Lacanian therapy as successfully avoiding a number of the dangers outlined and insist on its various other virtues, but what dangers and accomplishments are the really important ones still needs to be established. If, say, a certain version of Lacanian therapy avoids a great number of the risks and dangers attributed to Ferenczian therapy but fails to cure in the way Ferenczi advocates, then Ferenczi's theory of pathology becomes a critique of Lacanian theories of technique and therapeutic aims: without instituting basic trust and provisioning sympathy adequately for it to be expected broadly, or at least for it to be recognized and accepted when and where offered, the client will be locked into patterns of neurotic inhibition, supplication, and self-destruction that may partially undermine the ambitions of the Lacanian clinic, and even if not, are strikes against it. At this point, the critical Lacanian would likely appeal to Lacan's theory of pathology in order to indict Ferenczi's technique and aims and/or to the socio-political risks and dangers Ferenczi but perhaps not Lacan's clinic courts, but this would beg the question, What are the really important dangers and accomplishments? Debate via mutual pathologization seems inevitable and irresolvable — which does not necessarily mean fruitless. Immanent critique has some footing but fails to be decisive, especially because it can be pursued by both sides. What should be clear is that there are significant and irreducible differences in psychoanalytic theories of technique (and the theories of pathology and analytic aim bound up with them) and a conspicuous want of demonstrative force in arguments that presume to adjudicate between them. Psychoanalytic plurality is irreducible, thus partisan commitments are unavoidably normative affairs: not outside of the space of reasons, but beyond justification.

Finally, although there is much agreement between Ferenczi and Freud, there are significant points of disagreement. On the one hand, Freud and Ferenczi agree on the clinical need for abreaction and that analysis must proceed to the roots. Ferenczi's "active" prohibitions aim to evoke

> certain early infantile unconscious pathogenic psychic contents, which never were conscious (or preconscious) but which date from the period of 'uncoordinated gestures or magical behavior', [which] cannot be simply remembered at all, but can only be reproduced by reliving in the sense of Freud's repetition. In this, active technique only plays the part of the *agent provocateur*; its commands and prohibitions assist in obtaining of repetitions that must then be interpreted or reconstructed respectively into memory" (1927, 217)

On the other hand, from Freud's perspective, Ferenczi's "heart and soul" engagement with the analysand, his cure of love, may indicate unresolved and counterproductive countertransference. As Freud says to Binswanger: "A person is not free until he recognizes and overcomes each manifestation of his countertransference" (1962, 65). The thought here is that only if the analyst avoids being drawn in by the transference and embroiled in the murky matters underlying it will she be free to interpret the analysand's perceptions of and responses to her as projections, that is, interpret the transference as transference. This is the lesson Freud drew from his failure with "Dora." To the extent that the analyst is recalled to her own conflicts and difficulties by the transference, to the extent that her unconscious resonates with the analysand's conflicted wishes, exorbitant passions, and anxieties, her objectivity wanes. According to Freud's model of transference interpretation — a model that was never entirely practicable and that today increasingly many reject — "[t]he physician should be impenetrable to the patient, and like a mirror, reflect nothing but what is shown to him" (SE 12: 118). Only if the analyst successfully figures a blank slate and is acknowledged as such by the analysand will the latter learn that her experiences of the analyst are conditioned by repressed wishes, conflicts, fantasies, and the like; that what she undergoes is a reflection of her own projections. And only then may the analysand be inclined to explore why she experiences the analyst in such grossly contextually inappropriate ways. The Freudian analyst, to stick with Freud's metaphors, must be a surgeon, a mirror, a general — someone who provokes and directs the introspective journeying of the analysand, someone who strategically suggests insights or poses questions that are resisted by or otherwise unavailable to the analysand, not someone who puts himself "heart and soul" into the treatment and lets his patient know when he doesn't feel "into it," let alone involves herself in mutual analysis. To the extent that Ferenczi is "heart and soul" engaged with the analysand, Freud would be suspicious of his enthusiastic declaration that he is "a wonderful clairvoyant [*Wahrsager*], that is, a thought reader!", that "I read (in my free associations) the thoughts of my patients" (Ferenczi to Freud, 22 Nov. 1910).[45]

A Ferenczian would likely counter by appealing to Freud's late "Constructions in Analysis," where Freud recognizes that when an analyst admits to fault or failure, e.g., that an interpretation has proven incorrect, his authority is not necessarily undermined. On the contrary, Freud indicates, this gesture may suggest to the analysand that the analyst is scrupulous, able to discern when and where s/he has erred, and this may bolster the analyst's authority. However, for Freud, what is important about the explicit retraction of an interpretation is securing trust in the analyst's interpretative competence and thereby establishing the conditions for efficacious — read: authoritative — interpretation. The analyst must be possessed of authority ample enough for her interpretations to be taken seriously as guides for the analysand's introspection wherein they are confirmed, or to persuade the analysand of the psychic reality and significance of material interpretively elaborated if introspective corroboration is not forthcoming.[46] To be sure, this is a late development; for most of his career Freud advocated a much more austere practice (whether or not he followed his own advice is a separate question). Thus, for the brunt of his career, Freud would likely claim that Ferenczi is on the wrong side of the debate between Charcot and Bernheim. For Charcot, hysterical symptoms result from persistent, powerful reactions to trauma. Freud initially agreed, and thus sought to reintroduce unconscious thoughts — discovered by putting the client into a hypnotic trance — to the client either while she was in a hypnotic trance or subsequently. Freud revised his thinking as he became more convinced that festering traumatic memories are often fantasmatic. Encouraged by Jung's word association test, from 1907 onward he abandoned hypnosis for what would become the classical method of interpreting free associations. Ferenczi sided with Bernheim who maintained that the unconscious could be influenced by suggestion. Hence Ferenczi's penchant for prohibitions, recommendations, and so on. As noted, Freud moved closer to this position late in his career, though he certainly did not draw out its many significant implications. Trust, for Freud, is instrumental to interpretive efficacy, not an independent therapeutic goal. For Ferenczi, clinical success depends on (but not only on) appropriately administered experience: experiences of lack of trust and sympathy in the early care environment are offset by experiences of trust and sympathy in analysis without which classical Freudian therapy cannot succeed. For Freud, memory and other mediators of conviction are adequate for clinical success: experiences that establish trust in the analyst are useful only insofar as they lead to the retrieval of repressed memories or belief in the reality and significance of repressed wishes suggested by the analyst; memory or conviction supplant repetition. And furthermore, for Freud, Ferenczian technique is hardly an internal supplement to his practice, for to the extent that the analyst is "heart and soul" engaged with the client, her interpretive competence, thus authority, is diminished, and thereby the analysis is impeded.

In some ways, Freud and Ferenczi have widely disparate theories of pathology and cure, at least so far as their respective emphases are concerned. For Ferenczi, unmet infantile needs lead to, or at least extensively condition, pathology, just as adequate early childrearing establishes both the conditions for and the model of (certain aspects of) the cure. For Freud, unmet developmental needs are not *per se* pathogenic, drive-conflict is,[47] hence therapy cures not by or on the grounds of provisioning the sorts of experiences that reestablish basic trust but by sapping the force of repression, by making what were once repressed wishes inescapably conscious, and to do this, it models itself on archeological science: what is buried must be excavated; if it is corrupted, partially corroded, or as may be the case, only its faintest traces remain, it will be reconstructed. Though he does not underestimate them, Ferenczi has surely not recognized, as Freud demands, "that transference and resistance are the pivot of treatment," and so, from Freud's perspective, Ferenczi does not belong "irrevocably to our 'savage horde.'" However much Ferenczi may insist that establishing basic trust and sympathy are requisite for memory to replace repetition, Freud may remain skeptical, countering that Ferenczi's inclination to alter his technique and the clinical problems he ran into that motivated his revisions to Freud's theories of pathology and technique are symptoms of Ferenczi's inability or disinclination to overcome countertransference. Did Ferenczi identify and redress Freud's failure to consider the full impact of the early care environment and draw its implications or was he just an inept Freudian?

With Ferenczi, what we find exaggerated are (1) the need for and significance of basic trust and sympathy, both developmentally and clinically, (2) the role of early traumas and consequent trends in identification in psychopathology, (3) the pathogenic and therapeutic significance of empirical practices, specifically, childrearing practices, and (4) most broadly, the import of empirical experience, e.g., pathogenic experiences of the breakdown of trust and sympathy, reorientational experiences provided by therapy, and so on. What we find deflated are, to some extent, (1) the clinical role of memory, fantasy, and repression, (2) the demand for analytic objectivity, (3) Freud's mildly melancholic sentiment that the most analysis can do is transform neurosis into ordinary misery, and (4) the severity of Lacan's interest in individuation and outrage over its psychosocial debilitation.

Winnicott . . . the desire for liberation

For D.W. Winnicott, analysis has three primary tasks: (1) articulating and modifying the analysand's feelings and impulses, (2) providing forms of care that redress failures in the early care environment, and thereby (3) reinitiating stultified development. In contradistinction to the Freudian theory of pathology wherein libidinal and aggressive impulses accrue enormous strength and combine in complex ways consequent upon repression and thereby become pathogenic, Winnicott's theory of pathology, similar to Ferenczi's, attributes a great bulk of pathology and suffering to deficiencies in the early care environment. Following the path forged by Ferenczi, Winnicott suggests that "it will profit us to look at the needs of infants, and then to translate these needs into language that is appropriate for all ages" (1965, 69). He differs from Ferenczi, though, in detailing a wider set of developmental needs and concomitant types of pathogenic failures of care: pathology cannot be simply ascribed to lack of sympathy and loss of basic trust.

Freud's and Winnicott's theories of pathology diverge, and thus do their respective theories of therapy, largely on account of their different theories of development. The Freudian infant turns to the caretaker for the sake of satisfactions that cannot be attained through autoeroticism, belatedly and begrudgingly relinquishing a frame of reference wherein s/he is self-sufficient, indeed omnipotent.[48] However, the expectation of total satisfaction is retained (or emerges with the experience of frustration and is retroactively projected) and this leads to frustration, aggression, conflict, repression, and so on. The caretaker, for Freud, can never be good enough to satisfy such extravagant expectations, thus pathology is preordained. In contrast, the Winnicottian infant's needs and expectations are much more moderate: s/he will develop sufficiently if the caretaker responds well enough to a basic set of developmental needs. This is not to say that the infant will develop without conflict and repression even in the best caring environment. But for Winnicott, if a basic set of developmental needs are met, conflict and repression need not reach the pathological intensity that Freudians assume they will. Whereas classical Freudians emphasize sexuality, ambivalence, intolerance of frustration, and the compromise formations to which they give rise, Winnicott, as an exemplar of the object relations tradition, emphasizes the fate of human dependency. Since for Winnicott the infant is neither primarily ambivalent nor ill-equipped to negotiate with its ambivalence, pathogenic conflict and repression are not inevitable. Thus his clinical focus is not on learning to avow or repudiate, say, infantile wishes for absolute satisfaction from a figure one also wants to kill, or on progressively divesting the fantasy of total satisfaction of its residual strength. Further, because the infant is not primarily ambivalent, s/he is not primarily self-evasive. Thus Winnicott's clinical focus is less on the dynamic unconscious and the shrouded unknown and more on developmental needs that, pressing forth implacably, await adequate attending.[49] For Winnicott, pathology most often stems from and is always conditioned by interference with or neglect of a set of developmental needs that can, and often are, sufficiently met. Thus our prospects for flourishing are, for Winnicott, much greater than classical Freudians assume: we can do better than ordinary misery.

Though his theory of pathology inherits much from Klein, Winnicott manifestly departs from her influence in attributing a great deal of pathology to failures in the early care environment rather than intrinsic phantasies, the excessive character of the drives (especially the death drive), or paranoid/schizoid and depressive anxieties and defenses that arise irrespective of the quality of care. In contrast to both Freud and Klein, Winnicott emphasizes the *contingency* of suffering and pathology. Against Klein's stress on the inevitability of anguish consequent upon oscillation between paranoid/schizoid and depressive positions — though he does not exactly disagree with her on this point — Winnicott stresses the potential for reactivated development to yield genuine relief from contingent forms of suffering. While Klein, in opposition to what she perceived as the distressingly optimistic ethos of the increasingly prominent school of ego psychology, attended emphatically to the ineliminable anxieties, anguish, and impasses of the human condition — ego psychologists seemed to her overly enamored with the prospects for successful social adaptation and personality organization promised by their brand of therapy and, vexingly, were disinclined to say anything about the death drive other than occasional disparaging remarks about its status as a speculative construct — Winnicott, though he is surely not one to gloss over the depths of human suffering, endeavors to underscore the contingency of certain forms of suffering (those conditioned by stunted development), to foreground the relief and contentment yet available to us.

Winnicott's theory of pathology corresponds to a distinctive theory of technique. The analyst's task is not — at least not immediately — to sap the strength of repressed impulses or mitigate the force of pathological expectations by bringing them to consciousness. Neither is it to support the integration of traumatic or conflictual material into a coherent, avowable life-narrative — again, at least not immediately. Rather, the primary task is to identify and redress failures in the early care environment that inhibit the client's development and thereby condition her conflicts, symptoms, and anxieties.

Reopening developmental pathways takes priority over modifying structures of defense, lifting repression, and fostering depressive integration.

Winnicott, like Klein, aspires to cultivate analysands' capacities to experience (integrate), reflect upon, and negotiate maturely with affects and impulses that would be otherwise overwhelming, triggers for splitting and projective identification. Though Winnicott and Klein agree that, broadly, the aim of therapy is to reconfigure the analysand's character structure, that is, to restructure the manners in which the analysand tends to relate to internal and external reality, Winnicott parts ways with Klein when it comes to her emphasis on interpretation. For Winnicott, the therapeutic response to overwhelming affects and impulses should not be limited to the typical Kleinian measures of interpretive recovery and exploration of the phantasies with which such impulses and affects are bound up. Neither should it rest at the exploration of the reasons such affects, impulses, and phantasies are unbearable. In addition to the sorts of interpretive intervention Klein urges, Winnicott, like Ferenczi, advocates reactivating — amplifying and foregrounding — developmental needs and provisioning for them, which means not only successfully meeting these needs in the limited space of the clinic but generating a conviction that the world beyond the clinic is amenable to their continual satisfaction. The aim is to bring into view the hospitability of the world to one's needs when and where this is actually the case. The goodness of the world must be allowed to shine forth, and a procedure that one might call emotional reeducation is, for Winnicott, essential to that end.[50]

Opposing Klein's emphasis on clarifying and especially explanatory interpretation, Winnicott insists that, especially in the earlier stages of therapy, the client is not to be simply informed about the latent meaning of manifest material. Rather, the client must first be supported in the development of capacities to productively reflect on and negotiate with material that, later, may be interpretively clarified. Specifically, the client is to be gradually enticed to vividly (re)experience developmental needs that have been long suppressed, and to allow herself to experience these needs as met by the ministrations of the analyst, to experience the world, when and where this is the case, as adequately responsive to these persistent needs. Then and only then, once development has progressed to a sufficient point — tendencies to dissociation have diminished, confidence in the capacity to negotiate afresh with affectively complex and otherwise difficult material, even with fundamental forms of self- and world-relation, thus trust in oneself and the world, is established — can the analysand productively engage with pathogenic phantasies and the rest. And even then, in contrast with Klein, Winnicottian therapy tends more toward reassurance and clarification than explanation and confrontation. It is the focus on empirical failures of caregiving and consequent developmental impasses as opposed to structural difficulties that sets Winnicott most apart from Klein. For Klein, oscillation between paranoid/

schizoid and depressive positions is inevitable, while for Winnicott, though this may be true, (1) the intensity of paranoid and depressive anxieties may not be as great as Klein suggests, (2) the intensity and pathogenic effects of paranoid and depressive anxieties may be conditioned by failures of early care and to a significant extent ameliorated by later care, (3) the needs to which paranoid/schizoid and depressive defenses may respond and which may condition their strength and specific character may not be reactivated sufficiently by Kleinian treatment for the analysand to experience them as needs, (4) Kleinian treatment does not seem to have the resources to facilitate the analysand experiencing these needs as met when the adequate care abounds, thus (5) independent measures to reactivate and redress failures in the early care environment are necessary; without this, analysis will only proceed so far.

For Winnicott, not only is Klein's emphasis on interpretation insufficient, hasty or overabundant interpretation may be counterproductive. Perceived overeagerness to interpret may be taken as a signal of the analyst's anxiety, and it is a manifest lack of anxiety that is crucial, according to Winnicott, for therapeutic efficacy. Even if Klein is correct about the pervasiveness and depth of anxiety, Winnicott advocates as a countermeasure not just confrontational or clarifying interpretation but containment and holding along with transmuting interpretation — in order to induce a sense of personal integrity, which, on his account, is the basis for the capacity to bear the affective fullness of and negotiate with the difficult material encountered in the course of analysis. Of course, a Lacanian would be distressed by Winnicott's efforts to institute personal integrity, especially by means of containment and holding. The Lacanian induction to the truth of desire and the various measures designed to shake up the analysand's comfort and complicity with her ideal of personal and intersubjective cohesion are diametrically opposed to Winnicott's ambitions and procedures. In a perhaps exaggerated response to Klein's exaggeration of the primacy and persistence of the experience, fear, and endless phantasmatic elaboration of disintegration, Winnicott's clinic focuses on inducing a sense of personal integrity. And it is to such an end that a manifest lack of anxiety on the analyst's part is essential.

For Winnicott, as for Klein, the analyst will be a receptacle for the analysand's projections. With regard to projection, Winnicott contends, what is crucial is not just that the analyst is therewith afforded the resources for making more accurate interpretations via countertransference analysis, as Klein would have it. Rather, he suggests, if the analyst can contain the analysand's freighted impulses and affects without breaking down or retaliating; if s/he can return these affects and impulses in a more palatable form, that is, in a form sufficiently akin to the affects and impulses in their overwhelming state, thus recognizable as the impulses and affects from which the analysand suffers, but sufficiently transmuted to become objects of reflective exploration rather than triggers of splitting, projection, or other defense mechanisms; and, moreover, if s/he can induce in the analysand a sense of personal integrity through sympathetic attunement and various measures that connect impulses, affects, or parts of the personality that are split off and projected, then the analysand's anxiety may sufficiently abate for the material to be verbalized and the analysis to proceed. Only if the analyst is manifestly attuned to and clearly affected by the difficult material the analysand is undergoing, yet remains relatively calm and collected, and in exemplary fashion takes the experience of such difficult experiences as the occasion for reflection, may the analysand come to feel confident in her capacity to both bear and productively engage such material. Analytic exemplarity is a condition for both the hope and the internalization of the skills necessary for the treatment to proceed. Thus it must be altogether clear that the analyst does not share the analysand's pathological expectations, that the analyst does not expect that undergoing these affects and impulses will end in total catastrophe: the analyst must exhibit a manifest lack of anxiety. This is not to say that s/he will be untroubled by the material, just that s/he will consistently convey a sense that the material, though decidedly difficult to bear, can be not only survived without the defenses it ordinarily activates but can be productively reflected upon and negotiated with otherwise. It is the exemplarity of the analyst, an exemplarity enhanced by the context of positive transference, that by inducing mimesis of the analyst's containing, holding, and interpretive functions allows the analysis to proceed. To the extent that the analyst is perceived as anxious, e.g., as anxiously intellectualizing and interpreting, which is the risk that typical Kleinian practice runs, the analysis will be impeded.

But is it analysis? Although Winnicott's distinctive perspective would be obscured were one to fail to heed the primacy he places on questions of development, it would be a severe mischaracterization to say that Winnicott so stresses empirical failures to meet developmental needs and the empirical, intersubjective aspects of a therapy designed to reinitiate development that he neglects the conflicts and anxieties in which "fully developed" individuals are invariably entangled. To be sure, the dynamic unconscious is less important for Winnicott than for Freud, just as the vicissitudes of phantasy are less important for him than for Klein. However, it would be unfair to say that Winnicott simply focuses on redevelopment at the expense of sustained consideration of the unconscious. Transference analysis plays a significant role in his therapy; indeed his clinical sights are set on responding to developmental needs articulated in the transference. Moreover, his claim is not that pathology, let alone suffering, is wholly attributable to failures to meet a range of developmental needs. Though he surely emphasizes (re)development, this does not mean that he flatly ignores the unconscious as a principle of self-distortion and resistance and so assumes the total transparency and ultimate eliminability of the sources of our suffering. Rather, the unconscious structures that Freud and Klein explore in great detail are downplayed by Winnicott in order to (1) give questions of development the prominence he believes they are due, that is, to open up a new problem-domain and dimension of treatment, (2) call into question the extent and inevitability of suffering to which we are, for most of his psychoanalytic predecessors, condemned (might Freud and Klein confuse certain sufferings contingently conditioned by stunted development with structural and thus to some extent inevitable sufferings? Might this be, therapeutically, a self-fulfilling prophecy? Might this even amount to a defensive avoidance of genuinely available prospects for flourishing? If so, what might motivate such defensiveness?), and thus (3) develop a more accurate assessment of the demands upon and prospects of therapy as well as the criteria according to which analytic successes and failures should be judged. As even a cursory glance through his writings amply demonstrates, it is surely not the case that Winnicott fails to consider unconscious structures (phantasy, conflict, etc.) that contribute to pathological formations in an overzealous attempt to right all wrongs through provisioning appropriate care. Redevelopment is no panacea, it is the precarious prospect of rebeginning. Indeed, for Winnicott, the reinitiation of development is in most cases propedeutic to or a fundamental dimension of the analysis of unconscious conflicts, phantasies, and so on.

But this does not mean that Winnicott is merely supplementing rather than critically challenging Freud and Klein — his theory of technique situates theirs as, in various respects, insufficient or worse. For instance, Winnicott departs from Freud and Klein's tendency to immediately focus on unconscious material because he doubts that the technical principles of classical analysis — sustained non-gratification coupled with accurate interpretations and provocations to explore further — are sufficient to access such material. Rather, on Winnicott's account, holding, containment, and transmutation are often preconditions for such access. Furthermore, for Winnicott, in many cases the principles of classical analysis will be counterproductive. The neutral, objective mirroring that Freud advocates may, from Winnicott's perspective, repeat and retrench the dire consequences of faulty caregiving insofar as it conveys a lack of concerned attunement, affective nonpresence. Surely a Freudian may disagree, insisting that analysands will learn, once the positive results of this form of treatment are evident, that this *is* a way of caring for the analysand. But Winnicott's worry is that (1) Freudians underestimate analysands' sensitivities to affective presence and absence and the consequences thereof, (2) because analysands are more sensitive to failures of attunement than Freudians presume, the impact of their technique will be to inhibit appreciation of affectively disengaged mirroring as a form of care even when certain successes come, thus (3) therapeutic success on the Freudian model becomes less likely because analysands cannot see things as

Freudians would like them to. So, although Winnicott's focus on redevelopment is not simply an addendum or merely complementary to Freudian and Kleinian theories and therapies but a real challenge to them, the focus on redevelopment is not meant to trade-off with focus on the unconscious. Quite to the contrary, it is meant to contextualize and thus refine it.

Because Winnicott's version of therapy is clearly geared to redress developmental deficiencies arising from inadequate early care environments, one is tempted to speak of him as a sort of sophisticated, developmentally inclined behaviorist or even as anticipating a number of developments concerning the relation between psychoanalysis and information theory. In such a vein, one might suggest that he seeks to redress the inappropriate conditioning operative in the patient's early care environment through analytic reconditioning. The temptation is so strong because Winnicott gives off the distinct impression that his treatment aims, for instance, to induce a belief in the stability and permanence of a caring figure by repeatedly surviving the analysand's frustration and anger.[51] Or to give another example: by returning affects and impulses in a more palatable, transmuted form, the analyst conditions the patient to believe that she can withstand and productively negotiate with material that was previously inadmissible, overwhelming, felt to be the harbinger of total devastation. Eventually analysis conditions the analysand to respond to once unbearable, defensively repudiated affects and impulses with self-soothing techniques and transmuting self-interpretations. Though Winnicott is no behaviorist, there is a kernel of truth in this mischaracterization.

Developmental needs identified and addressed in the course of analysis are, for Winnicott, if not dynamically repressed, surely not simply waiting in the ready for the right sort of response. If they were, then given that the sorts of care provided in analysis are not ordinarily different in type but only in degree (and sometimes not even that) from those provided by family, friends, work, romantic relationships, etc., there would be no accounting for the persistence of developmental stultification (or there would be good reason to doubt the theory of developmental stultification). However, Winnicott does assume an impulse to (re)development.[52] The impulse to (re)development is, for Winnicott, extraordinarily resilient, perhaps even ineradicable, but one must be sure to note that the needs that must be experienced as sufficiently met for redevelopment to commence are quite often buried, affectively unavailable, thus unimpacted by the right sort of care even when it abounds. Without the regression and abreaction induced by analysis through which long suppressed developmental needs are reactivated, they remain, if not precisely unconscious, buried and all but forgotten.[53] Because the analysand fears that these needs will not or even cannot be satisfactorily met, because she has been conditioned by a faltering care environment to believe that the world is just not the sort of place where these needs will be welcomed and well-provisioned, s/he refuses the experience of these needs as needs. And with good reason, for thereby s/he defends against an aching, anguished vulnerability and against the potential catastrophe of their affectively loaded resurgence and nonsatisfaction. S/he feels that if s/he were to experience these needs as needs and they were yet again neglected or ill-provisioned, s/he may not survive it. So even when adequate responses to these needs abound, they are not sufficiently vivid, not affectively present enough for the analysand to feel that they have been met. Thus reconditioning alone will not do. No matter how many times their environments respond satisfactorily to various developmental needs, certain analysands never feel that these needs have been met and so remain ensnared in compensatory pathological formations. Even in a systematically controlled environment that eliminates intervening influences, the numerical repetition of positive responses will be insufficient to effect the desired outcome. What is required on Winnicott's conception is *the reactivation of need*, thus a profound vulnerability that behaviorist therapy is ill-equipped to provoke and sustain, a vulnerability that may require prolonged tarrying with unconscious material and modifications to defensive structures that keep this material at bay. It is in the context of questions of development that the unconscious becomes important for Winnicott.

In conformity with classical analysis, Winnicott promotes the detailed exploration of unconscious beliefs, fantasies, wishes, aggressive impulses, conflicts, inhibitions, and so on, but not because he believes, as do classical analysts, that modifying structures of defense and bringing the unconscious to consciousness is independently curative or propedeutic to the cure (in the sense that all the analysand needs to do once unconscious material has become conscious is avow or repudiate the material). So long as developmental deficits are still in place, unconscious material is explored for the sake of providing the analytic pair with clues to the character of the analysand's unmet developmental needs, to the manner of the unconscious or otherwise defensive metabolism of their nonsatisfaction, and so to what sort of care is required to reinitiate development. Only in the context of adequate development will interpretations be experienced as something other than repetitions of early injuries. If Freud's paradigm is that of the archeologist excavating the depths in order to unearth buried and distorted remnants of archaic desire and aggression that, once brought to light, will become the material out of which a new (personal) civilization is forged, Winnicott's paradigm is that of the dialectical materialist who looks to the past in order to discover the revolutionary opportunities (developmental transitions) that, because they were not taken up successfully, condition present suffering. The analogy only goes so far, though. Historical opportunities for revolution, once missed, are gone forever — we can make partial reparation for lost revolutionary opportunities by taking up what is left of the revolutionary impulse in our contemporary political struggles, but since the constellation of conditions that once allowed for a radical transformation is no longer available, this irreversible loss must be taken into account as we seek to extend the revolutionary principle. On the contrary, missed opportunities for the developments with which Winnicott is concerned can be wholly reforged by an appropriately structured care environment, e.g., the right sort of analysis.

Although he expresses great confidence in prospects for successfully reinitiating development, this does not mean that Winnicott is exuberantly optimistic. Winnicott surely downplays constitutive ambivalence and the frustrations and pathogenic conflicts that, on Freud's account, ensues therefrom, but he may not disagree with Freud in the least that conflicts with which we are able to negotiate in more mature and successful ways as a result of analysis remain conflicts nonetheless. Nor is it likely that Winnicott would disagree with Freud that civilization produces both intrinsic discontents and difficulties that, though socio-historically contingent, cannot be addressed by analytic means. However, at least concerning the possibility of redevelopment, Winnicott downplays the Freudian emphasis on our commitments to our suffering — the idea that symptoms and inhibitions are compromise formations, i.e., the best forms of gratification we can come up with — and emphasizes, against Freud, the impulse to redevelopment, to liberate ourselves from those forms of life that have inhibited our flourishing. Though in one respect this makes Winnicott more optimistic than Freud, the suggestion that Freud had yet to explore a dimension of psychic and intersubjective life out of which may arise and which may condition forms of suffering and pathology is not exactly sunny. Successful development may just get us to the point where we meet more "mature" conflicts and sufferings. But again, Winnicott is not just supplementing psychoanalysis as he inherits it; his crucial suggestion is that the sorts of suffering and pathology encountered once development is successfully reactivated are less terrible and more manageable than those met in the context of stunted development; thus that inattention to issues pertaining to development and its reactivation skews psychoanalytic theories of pathology, therapy, and end state.

Specifically with regard to therapy, Winnicott's focus is on providing the right sort of corrective emotional environment to reinitiate development rather than, as with Freud and Klein, on the immediate excavation of unconscious material if for no other reason than that, failing to develop in appropriate ways, analysands will be unable to successfully negotiate with the material brought to light, indeed the procedures through which such excavations are pursued may be dangerous and counterproductive if they are experienced as repeating injuries. But the reactivation of and provisioning for developmental needs may require sustained consideration of and engagement with unconscious structures and material.

With Winnicott, what we find exaggerated are (1) the significance of dependency, specifically, the import of caregiving environments to pathology and healing, (2) the contingency of suffering, (3) the drive to (re)development, and (4) the role of analytic exemplarity. What is deflated is the inevitability of pathology, whether as a result of constitutive ambivalence and the frustrations and pathogenic conflicts arising therefrom (Freud) or as a result of the death drive and paranoid/schizoid and depressive anxieties and defenses (Klein).[54]

Ego Psychology . . . the rising star of the technical imperative

Originating in pre-World War II Europe (especially Vienna) and inspired by Anna Freud's contributions, ego psychology quickly established a stronghold on American soil. Initially, ego psychologists took their lead from Anna Freud's stalwart adherence to Freudian drive theory and the conflict model of psychoneurosis; yet they recognized, along with her, that father Freud's exaggerated focus on the id is inadequate to orient clinical practice and developmental research. Classical Freudian therapy was found wanting insofar as (1) it proved to be ineffective for a number of patients,[55] and (2) it fails to address a range of problems and the corresponding analytic aims with which ego psychologists were intensely concerned: specifically, focusing predominantly on the id does not provide sufficient resources — nor does it incline analysts to research programs that would develop the resources — to enhance ego strengths and thereby relative autonomy from id impulses and the overly encumbering superego imperatives into which id impulses may be filtered; nor does focusing on the id provide resources sufficient to facilitate the client's adjustment to and thriving in whatever social conditions obtain, which is paramount to the therapeutic agenda of ego psychology.[56]

Concerning the limits of Freudian developmental theory, the problems are that (1) it does not adequately account for environmental influences on development,[57] a problem aggravated by Freud's meager concern with the environmental conditions of adult flourishing,[58] and (2) its scope is too limited: predominantly focused on psychosexual development, Freud's developmental theory cannot account for id-free or conflict-free psychic functioning, e.g., the psychogenesis of reason in its extra-libidinal dimensions.[59] And since a clinical priority of ego psychology is to enhance control over and diminish the relative force of id impulses (which may be channeled into a stern superego) and thereby promote advanced reality-testing, delayed gratification, and thus the greatest possible personal adaptability and likelihood of success in social achievement, this developmental theory will not do. Or in Mahler and Jacobson's case, what is needed is a developmental theory that can account for features of psychic life irreducible to and sometimes consolidated prior to libidinal development, such as identity formation, for these have a great bearing on suffering and its alleviation, as well as on the potential for autonomy and self-assertion of the adult. On the basis of these two sets of concerns, ego psychologists began to *circumscribe the import of drive-conflict, downplay the self- and world-distortions entailed by the unconscious, and deflate the status of the id.* This allowed them to expand their clinical practice in two major ways.

First, clinical interests broadened beyond retrieving id-infused content (wishes, beliefs, ideas, etc.) in the service of its avowal and integration. To be sure, classical analysis of transference and resistance, efforts to bring unconscious structures and content to consciousness, and so forth play an important role in ego psychological therapy. But by deflating the assumed urgency of integrating repressed material, i.e., of accepting and allowing room for the fundamentally asocial impulses seething underneath the thin veneer of civility, they could shift the therapeutic focus to (1) diminishing the force of the id, specifically its issuance in snap decisions and symptoms, and (2) enhancing the capacity of the ego to control the id and successfully test for reality[60] — all to the end of enhancing clients' aptitudes for reflection on and adjustment to their social conditions and thereby facilitating the achievement of the goals they set for themselves therein. "Where the id was, there the ego shall be" is ego psychology's call to arms.

Although they take their lead from Freud's (1923) *The Ego and the Id*, much more so than Freud, ego psychologists are concerned with the genesis, relative strength of, and relations between the id, ego, and superego. In Anna Freud's words, "It is the task of the analyst to bring into consciousness that which is unconscious, no matter to which psychic institution it belongs. He directs his attention equally and objectively to the unconscious elements in all three institutions . . . when he sets about the work of enlightenment, he takes his stand at a point equidistant from the id, the ego, and the super-ego" (1936, 28).[61] The id is assumed to be strong enough — for ego psychologists, analysis will make that abundantly clear. Only by redressing Freud's insufficient concern with the ego (specifically, the psychosocial genesis of rationality) and the superego (specifically, the *adaptive* defenses it promotes) will analysis enhance the often feeble functioning of these agencies and thereby facilitate more sophisticated and satisfying negotiations of id, ego, and superego demands. Thus, with Anna Freud, the new clinical aims are to achieve a better balance between the respective forces of the three agencies and encourage adaptive defenses — her work is guided by a remarkable depathologizing impulse, that is, by a desire to put a positive spin on defenses and the superego.[62] Or, with Hartmann and his cohorts, the new aim is to isolate and augment conflict-free potentials for autonomous and adaptive development.

From the perspective of ego psychology, Freud's insights into the id are conditioned by his myopia to the potential of the ego; his emphasis on the confluence of the bestial and the human is welcome, but exaggerated. As we have seen, Freud's clinical practice is focused on slackening defenses via insistence on the fundamental rule and interpretations of transference and resistance. It aims to release unconscious material that can then be avowed and integrated in new, less painful and conflicted ways, or if not, repudiated and mourned. Starting with Anna Freud, ego psychologists begin to worry that this approach fails to modify major structures of defense, that its "depth" and efficacy are purchased at the price of a problematic restriction of scope, which in turn implies that it neither goes as deep nor works as well as classical Freudians presume. Thus ego psychologists tend to frame classical Freudian therapy as somewhat dangerous, a band-aid that aids and abets the persistence of problematic character structures that are defensively composed by the unconscious work of the ego.[63] For ego psychologists, free association is of limited value — at best it is a long-term goal. Although following the fundamental rule may incite id-infused material to come to the fore, (1) it does not facilitate adequate insight into the ego and superego, thus into defenses (the presumption is that in free association the id will express itself to attain gratification but the ego and superego will not, for their efficacy, thus that of defenses, is often attendant upon their silent functioning), and (2) it fails to induce the ego and superego to slacken their defenses beyond a certain point. Here, even the most sophisticated analytic interventions are often of limited use. Interpretations of transference and resistance, ego psychologists contend, fail to clarify or adequately undermine deep seated defenses because such defenses are bound up with the client's character structure and thus with a great deal of secondary gain. This problem of defense-resiliency is compounded by the inability of free association to adequately expose the structures of defenses. Consequently, according to ego psychologists, what emerges in free association will be, in much greater measure than Freud was willing to admit, colored by unconscious compromises, suffused with resistances, and so unable to provide clear access to the "deepest" and perhaps most problematic currents of psychic life. Free association may mask, for instance, a defensive isolation of affect.

But as opposed to the vast variety of analysts who take up Freud's mandate to go to the roots but find his procedures for doing so inadequate or disagree about where the roots lie (Ferenczi contends that the roots of pathology lie in the breakdown basic trust and sympathy, Winnicott claims that such roots lie in the environmental conditions of stunted development, Klein suggests the death drive and originary anxiety-elaborating phantasies) and so propose revisions to Freud's archeological strategies, ego psychologists are not inclined to take up what they consider the near-impossible and therapeutically suspect task of unraveling deep seated defenses. Though they aim to do as best they can in the way of reversing repression and dismantling pathogenic defenses, they also consider what can be gained by enhancing the relative strength of the ego and supporting defenses useful for adaptation while cultivating clear-sightedness about themselves and the world, believing that so doing may moot non-adaptive defenses. A sort of prosthetic psychosocial Darwinism, ego psychology aims to support adaptive but faltering defenses and eliminate the rest in order to encourage the development of the ego to its greatest possible heights of adaptive autonomy. To be sure, like classical Freudians, ego psychologists employ nongratification and interpretive interventions to exhume unconscious wishes, fantasies, and the like in order to subject them to conscious scrutiny and reflective endorsement or repudiation. But unlike Freud, their aim is not, or at least not exclusively, to promote the exploration and integration or repudiation and mourning of repressed wishes and fantasies; and it is certainly not to promote accommodation to the inevitable distortions, the limits to mastery and transparency, entailed by the unconscious. Where Freud preaches tolerance for the repressed, ego psychology enjoins control over the drives. Its aim is to strengthen the ego's command of the impulses released through the classical Freudian procedure: an aim shared with Freud, but on which ego psychologists place much greater emphasis. For this, when coupled with the skills of self-observation, delay of gratification, and reality-testing cultivated by their unique brand of analysis, promotes more realistic and adaptive functioning and thereby autonomy rather than anarchy.

In addition, for the great many ego psychologists influenced by Hartmann, a primary aim is to sap the erotic and aggressive dimensions of the impulses released, a procedure that Hartmann calls neutralization. Here ego psychologists diverge from Freud substantially.[64]

Whether released impulses are neutralized or cultivated, for ego psychologists the basic aim is successful social integration: this is a dream (or nightmare) of total mobilization.[65] To the extent that Freud's aim is to diminish the severity of the superego in order to foster a more fluid relation between the id and the ego and thereby expand the client's range of possibilities for creative self-realization, the aim of ego psychology is to secure for the client a relative autonomy from the id and within the social.[66] For ego psychology, the id, as well as the superego to the extent that it serves the pleasure principle or the id, are, though not exactly pathological, to be rooted out or reigned in and put in the service of the client's socially adaptive projects. The basic aim is adaptive autonomy — what some would call the elementary gesture of ideology or a repudiation of the political.

As an illustration, take the clinical work of Lawrence Kubie. For Kubie, the primary aim of analysis is not so much discovering or creating more adequate means of tension discharge or rendering the ego maximally capacious as it is achieving basic social integration and satisfaction therewith. The problem on which he focuses is not a neurotic compromise that fails to reduce tension to a bearable level or rhythm (like Lacan, but for quite disparate reasons and to vastly different ends, ego psychologists hold that psychoanalysis is not to be in the service of the pleasure principle) or unnoticed characterological rigidity. Rather, the problem is more or less what the client thinks it is — an inability to succeed in love and work despite a desire to do so.[67] The demand is not refused. Accordingly, the aim of analysis becomes — or the exaggerated emphasis is on — adapting successfully to and finding a measure of autonomy within prevailing social conditions. As we will see, both clinically and in terms of their expanded developmental research — here again following Anna Freud's cue — ego psychologists focus on the development of realistic, adaptive, socially successful functioning.

Second, ego psychologists expand their focus beyond neurotic psychopathology and symptom formation — still considered drive-based and conflict-ridden — to two domains: (1) character style and normal functioning[68] and (2) severe psychopathology, i.e., psychoses. By downplaying neurotic psychopathology and conflict sufficiently to lend sustained attention to character style and normal functioning, ego psychologists opened a fruitful direction of research into the development and structure of perception, cognitive styles, and general forms of life-orientation, both insofar as these bear upon clients' manifest difficulties and generally.[69] At stake in such research is validating the study of the ego as an independent category of analysis and demonstrating the compatibility of psychoanalytic and psychological research. The ego studied by ego psychology is not the precipitate of abandoned object-cathexes, the projection of a bodily surface, or the overtaxed mediator of the competing demands of the id, reality, and the superego — in other words, it is not the Freudian ego. For ego psychologists, Freud failed to appreciate the extent to which the ego can become a conflict-free sphere by means of which we master internal and external nature. The ego is as studies and therapeutically enhanced by ego psychology is the seat of motility, cognition, and perception, a medium of access to reality, or (as in the Hartmann-Rapaport tradition) the precipitate of modified, desexualized id-impulses. Within this tradition, the ego is understood, to a much greater extent than Freud considered, as functionally independent of all other psychic agencies, impulses, and trends: though it is not insulated from the influences, neither is it reducible to them. So characterizing the ego, ego psychologists put themselves in a position to contribute to the investigation of various topics with which academic psychology is traditionally concerned: learning, year-to-year development (not just phase-to-phase or stage-to-stage development), and at a more individualized level, the uptake of education, e.g., how one acquires language, mathematical and scientific skills, etc. Quite importantly for ego psychologists, this conception of the ego also makes possible investigations of pragmatic, everyday achievements, specifically, investigations of what facilitates or impedes them.

By attending to severe psychopathology, ego psychologists such as Spitz, Mahler, and Jacobson made significant discoveries concerning the interarticulation of intrapsychic and environmental conditions for successful development, specifically, for the development of the ego.[70] This led to both a more nuanced theory of pathology — a wider range of developmental needs and thus sites of developmental impasse were correlated with a wider variety of later ailments — and an expanded view of transference. Now transference was understood to express not only dynamically distorted wishes but the turbulent history of attempted development. Like Ferenczi and Winnicott, developmentally inclined ego psychologists claimed to glean from transference the character of developmental needs, the difficulties confronted in fulfilling them, and the desire for their successful accomplishment; specifically, they sought to locate failed attempts to compose psychic structure and the adaptive, compensatory measures to which such failures gave rise. This in turn led to a revised conception of what the clinic can offer. Mahler, for instance, suggests that the analyst's provisioning of corrective experiences can redress inadequate parenting and thereby promote a sense of coherent identity, foster separation-individuation, and so on. Interestingly, like Ferenczi, Mahler specifically suggests that tactful dosing of libidinal gratification promotes developmental maturation. Conversely, Jacobson suggests that inducing frustration, thus aggression, can lead to important growth experiences.[71] Other ego psychologists suggest that verbalization can promote a sense of self-definition and -coherence. Through various routes, Freud's concern with the Oedipal is expanded into a concern with the interrelations of the Oedipal and the pre-Oedipal, as his concern with the intrapsychic is expanded into a concern with the interface of the psychic and the social.

Both in the clinic and in developmental research, ego psychology promotes the development and seeks the sources of (thus potential impediments to) what are deemed normal capacities (language acquisition, intellection, social skills, etc.) and states (e.g., coherent identity).[72] There is no concern with the question Freud poses in *Civilization and its Discontents*, namely, whether a whole culture might be pathological. Likewise, there is no concern with the questions Lacan continually poses, such as whether coherent identity or the aspiration thereto is a defense against the truth of subjectivity or whether and to what extent pursuing the acquisition of social skills involves one in a pathogenic fantasy of complete integration? Rather, ego psychologists are concerned with the psychogenesis of average, expectable social skills and the psychosocial conditions for successful separation-individuation or other such socially esteemed developmental milestones, for thereby, they seek to build bridges with academic psychology and expand the range of patients for whom psychoanalysis will be of service and the services on offer. In the tradition of ego psychology, psychoanalysis does not just concern itself with returning neurotics "to love and work" but also assists those with relatively minor impediments in these areas to advance beyond their current limitations and assists those with massively constricting developmental impediments to achieve what maturity they may. For many ego psychologists, there is no such thing as a patient contraindicated for analysis. Their beneficent urge is voracious.

To recap, the ambitions of ego psychology are to (1) provide more adequate therapy for those who continue to suffer or are expected to suffer after the completion of classical id-focused analysis, (2) develop therapeutic techniques appropriate for those who simply need some help in their efforts of self-improvement — or later with Mahler and Jacobson, for those whose basic sense of selfhood is foundering and are thus in need of "growth experiences" without which ordinary aptitudes and achievements are unattainable, and (3) refocus developmental theory and research on the acquisition of normal capacities and states, i.e., on individuals developing adaptively to their environment rather than according to the urgencies of psychic conflict or anxiety-ridden phantasy. The guiding question is no longer exclusively: What conflicting unconscious wishes are expressed in symptoms, inhibitions, and other defensive forms of life and language? At least equal emphasis is placed on questions of how the ego becomes sufficiently strong to fend off id and superego demands such that an individual can project and pursue a relatively autonomous life-course and how the ego and superego can become strong enough for successful integration into natural and social reality? If analysts can interpret defenses against the id, why not against reality? Most broadly, the leading question for ego psychology is: How do we become adequately socialized beings, i.e., relatively conflict-free, self-aware, possessed of robust reality-testing capabilities, thus, with any luck, successful in our chosen courses of life? With ego psychology, psychoanalysis became a social lubricant — as such, it was intoxicating: the number of patients seeking analysis increased exponentially.[73]

In contradistinction to Freud, who late in his career became increasingly enamored with deep trends in cultural history, discontents intrinsic to culture and humanization, troubling resonances of the primitive in the contemporary, and so questions concerning relations between phylogenesis and ontogenesis, ego psychologists focus much more on the here and now. Or, with developmentally inclined ego psychologists such as Mahler and Jacobson, the emphasis is on supporting the development of those for whom focus on the here and now, for the time being, means attending to developmental deficit, i.e., to why the here and now stagnates in the there and then. The concerns of the late Freud, as well as his characteristic emphases on the etiological significance of infantile experiences and their fantasmatic metabolism (generally, the sexual etiology of neurosis), the ineradicability of unconscious wishes and inevitable breaches of repression, the insuperability of conflict, the governing force of the pleasure principle, and so the need for analysis to pivot on transference and resistance, are downplayed and considered with an eye to what practical advances are available here and now. Of course, just as

Freud's phylogenetic considerations were partly in the service of his ambition to understand and ultimately redress the suffering of his patients (occasional remarks to Ferenczi not withstanding), for ego psychologists, the paths to advances in the here and now may be quite circuitous — again, ego psychology does not deviate *that much* from classical Freudian method; in fact its pundits often see themselves as working in a complementary vein to it. But it cannot be emphasized enough that the range of problems with which ego psychology is concerned differs significantly from those on which the classical Freudian tradition is centered. And its ambition to enhance the ego's maturity in dealing with id impulses released through analytic nongratification, though inherited from Freud, is, compared with Freud's efforts on this front, much more extreme. Often unconvinced by accounts of ontogenic and phylogenic residues of bestiality haunting the heart of the human, ego psychologists tend to believe that accommodation and adaptation can be remarkably successful and need not come at too high a price. They do not share Freud's taste for the secret, his concern with what lies hidden beneath the comforting appearance of sociability or is strictly unintelligible within its terms.

We have seen that, on the ego psychological conception, analysis should augment the client's self-observing, gratification-delaying, and reality-testing prowesses. But how so? More precisely, the question is: since psychoanalysis in any form habituates analysands to self-reflection, complex and nuanced analysis of emotionally tumultuous situations, and delayed gratification, what (if anything) specifically distinguishes ego psychological technique? Ego psychology is certainly no monolith. Certain strands are confrontational and intervention prone. Of course within such strands nongratification (e.g., not answering the analysand's questions) plays a role, but at the right moment analysts incite their clients to recognize the contradictions and problems staring them in the face and refuse to release them from their responsibility for finding more mature ways of engaging such contradictions and problems. Concrete proposals for resolving these contradictions and problems may be offered, but this is not always the case. However, in contradistinction to Klein, for whom interpreting at the point of deepest anxiety is necessary to assuage anxiety and thereby facilitate analysis, thus who is ill-inclined to withhold an interpretation, especially a deep one, even the more confrontational and intervention prone ego psychologists refrain from deep interpretations, considering them ineffective or dangerous, and instead focus on the here and now; interpretations are addressed to active resistances, those that have already surfaced, with the aim of creating an alliance with the client's observing ego. Other strands intervene sparingly and confine interpretations, when they are offered, "insofar as possible, to the patient's fantasies about the analyst's person and the analytic relationship" (Brody, 25). Thus what distinguishes ego psychology is more aim than technique: adaptability, enhanced self-scrutiny, and so on. To be sure, ego psychological technique can be distinguished from other techniques, and certain uniformities of technique do prevail. For instance, for most ego psychologists, in contradistinction to classical Freudians, the analysand is considered not simply the object of the analyst's interpretations but also an ally. S/he is enticed into a "working alliance"[74] wherein s/he is considered both a "native informant" and a cohort in the struggle to realize the goals she sets for herself but, despite her best efforts, cannot realize. But again, it is primarily agreement in aim that distinguishes ego psychology. And it is in regard to its characteristic aims, or more precisely, since these aims are hardly unique, it is in regard to its characteristic insistence on and inflection of its aims, that ego psychology became so attractive to many and so vehemently denounced by it critics.

There is, to be sure, a quasi-egalitarian ethos operative in ego psychology that is often underappreciated by its critics. As is the fact that, in part, delaying gratification is so important to ego psychologists because they seek to promote questioning of need interpretations: to open the space of self-reflection and habituate analysands to and support them in sustaining this space rather than precipitously leaping into action. But unlike, say, Lacanians, ego psychologists are not inclined to focus treatment on the question of why certain desires or more complex ambitions are pursued *unless they seem affectively overburdened (conflict harboring), implausible, self-destructive, or massively ill-adjusted to social norms*. Because ego psychology refrains from asking after the ideological dimensions of ostensibly personal choices, from a Lacanian perspective it would seem a form of malicious egalitarianism, an imperious demand for equal conformity to uninterrogated social norms, thus in the service of a culture of individuation without individuals — a thoroughly ideological praxis.

In order to better appreciate how deep the imperative to social conformity runs in ego psychology, let us briefly consider its distinctive take on why we value objects. Ego psychology's simultaneous and mutually supporting *deflation* of unconsciously conditioned nontransparency, overdetermination, and limits to self-determination and *inflation* of the need for and realizability of adaptation commits it to a very different view from Freud's of why objects are valued. Ego psychologists accept, in fact exaggerate, Freud's contention that objects are valued only contingently: this is the famous separation of aim and object thematized from *Three Essays on Sexuality* onward.[75] But they disagree with Freud's claim that the value of an object is only its ability to reduce tension, thus with his characterization of aims. For ego psychologists, the reality principle is not just a deferred version and ultimately in the service of the pleasure principle. Furthermore, they are deeply uncomfortable with the simultaneous relativism and determinism implied by Freud's claim about the discontinuity of aim and object, i.e., with the suggestion that any object can become valuable, but objects only become valuable because repressed infantile wishes incessantly striving for gratification latch onto them, thus, ultimately, because their pursuit serves the pleasure principle. In order to reign in what, from their perspective, are the outlandish implications of this claim, ego psychologists emphasize that although objects become valuable for an individual contingently in the sense that there is no inborn value radar by means of which we are directed to the objects we should value (as any analysis will make abundantly clear — transference means inappropriate appraisal) and a vast variety of objects are substitutable as satisfactions of basic aims, certain aims are inherently valuable, and not only because their accomplishment satisfies the pleasure principle. For instance, the value of success at love and work (well-adjusted social integration) is taken as a given, not an expression of or in any way reducible to infantile wishes or the imperative of tension reduction and/or constancy. Finding an object is not always refinding an object; valuing can be autonomous from unconscious conflicts, distortions, irrational impulses, and (ostensibly) governing principles. Investment in an object need not be a form of compromised gratification. Though there may be a tension between its commitments to value realism and value pluralism, push that problem to the side. The point here is just to underscore the extent to which ego psychology prizes successful adaptation to culture in (near about?) *whatever* state.

Whether this is considered to result from innate ego development or to require adequate — average and expectable — early nurturance, ego psychology emphasizes and clinically supports adaptive potential, the ability to comply with and thrive in variable environmental conditions. Downplaying Freud's emphases on the inevitability of ensnarement in conflict and compromise, proclivities to self-distortion, the unruliness and persistence of the drives, the porosity of psychical agencies, the relatively nontransparent and semi-autonomous logic of the unconscious, and so on, ego psychologists emphasize and support capacities to engage in social life *for reasons of its intrinsic value*.

Interestingly, this structure of emphases precisely mirrors the ideological position of its diasporic pundits. The emphasis, close to the hearts of those fleeing the Nazis and, at least initially, only marginally accepted by the medicalized American psychological orthodoxy,[76] is on wholehearted adaptation, on the ability of the individual to manifestly adjust to variable environmental conditions, which means thoroughly internalizing and successfully performing in terms of their associated values and ideals.[77] More precisely, the emphasis is on wholehearted adaptation to a culture that prizes love and work as opposed to anything more "ambitious." The limits of social integration (expressly) promoted by ego psychology are those of American (liberal-capitalist) ideology.[78] In short, the ideological aspirations of the early diasporic ego psychologists, their interests in integrating into a society where self-creation, on the one hand, and science and social utility (especially salability), on the other, were of paramount value[79] mirror and perhaps in part determine their theoretical and clinical foci.[80] At the very least, the relatively rapid, positive reception of ego psychology on American soil seems to some extent conditioned by its express interest in collaborating with credible academic psychology[81] and its specific therapeutic promise: self-improvement that in no way requires radical social change — basically, socially desirable self-reform.

Attending to the work of a major figure in the ego psychological tradition, namely, Heinz Hartmann, should bring the dominant characteristics of ego psychology into greater focus. From Hartmann's perspective, the manner in which Plato's *Timaeus* addresses the question, "What would our ideal city/psyche look like in motion?" would be extremely suspicious, for it does so by depicting the city/psyche at war.[82] Suspicious of conflating movement and life with the specific determination of movement called war, Hartmann calls into question what can be known of the psyche when it is conceived as fundamentally in a state of strife, when the psyche is elaborated as a battleground, an arena of conflict between competing agencies and impulses.[83] Seeking to supplement what, on his view, is a violent and one-sided exaggeration of conflict in the prevailing conception of psychic life, Hartmann focuses on conflict-free ego potentials, that is, on perception, object-comprehension, language, and thinking insofar as they are immune from sexual or aggressive (thus potentially conflict-generative) determinants.[84] For Hartmann — and here he stands closer to Kohut than Freud, Lacan, Winnicott, Klein, or Ferenczi — eros and aggression are *not* fundamental components of or all-pervasive in psychic life. Rather, they are innate potentials that may or may not be developed in various psychic sectors. Hartmann's ambition is to study and support *motivation* in excess of sexual and aggressive determinants. Not everything can be brought back to the Oedipus complex or antecedent component drives, Hartmann insists.[85] Conflict-free capacities are both innate[86] — although sparked and nurtured by adequate environmental conditions, to be sure — and producible through "neutralization," i.e., through the "purification" of energy for non-conflicted functioning, such as when impulses or beliefs are relieved (by the ego) of their sexual or aggressive characteristics and put in the service of the ego and its aspirations for social achievement. Neutralization is not just sublimation of eros and aggression into socially esteemed endeavors but a transformation of the nature of the drive, a sapping of its sexual or aggressive dimensions that releases the energy on which the conflict-free sectors of the ego thrive: in the idiom of ego psychology, not sublimation but "change in function." The idea of neutralization raises questions of whether there are developmental antecedents to drive neutralization, and if there are, of how they can be supported in child rearing and therapy.[87] Pursuing these questions, Hartmann came to emphasize the role of prevention and education in combating pathology, claiming ego psychology's contributions to these fronts as, in part, establishing its uniqueness and value in the world of psychoanalysis.

Following Anna Freud's lead, Hartmann also emphasizes the "secondary autonomy" of defenses and regressive traits, their ability to be turned toward culturally prized ends. For instance,

> Reaction formation . . . is a defense called into play to keep one consciously unaware of the continuing, socially unacceptable pleasures involved in bathroom activities; the toddler's original fascination with his bowel movements is transformed into a conscious attitude of disgust. Yet reaction formation, originating in conflict, may eventually serve a highly adaptive function in the overall personality as a genuine pleasure in good hygiene and tidiness and thus graduate into a role outside of conflict. (Mitchell and Black 1996, 37)

Again, this is not sublimation: neither aim nor object is altered. What changes, at least in part, is the motivation for the practice. In a strikingly Nietzschian-Foucaultian vein, Hartmann insists on the distinction between the motivational genesis of a practice and its subsequent motivational power. But unlike Nietzsche and Foucault, he does so in order to underscore the domesticating recruitability of the archaic into the civilized.

In his own way, Hartmann is something of a dialectican, articulating the transformation of adaptive and non-adaptive characteristics into their opposites: adaptive traits (the features of "primary autonomy") can be pressed into the service of non-adaptive forms of life (e.g., when language becomes a medium of neurotic self-exhibition, befuddled by slips, etc.), just as non-adaptive (conflicted, defensive, or regressive) traits can enter the service of social adaptation (becoming "secondarily autonomous," say, when paranoiac proclivities make one an appealing political candidate or when regression to less structured, pre-Oedipal states are "in the service of the ego" of the artist).[88] In both theoretical and clinical work, Hartmann's slant toward optimism and affirmative culture is so strong that he is occasionally inclined to affirm for their adaptive, compensatory qualities traits that some would consider pathological. His core belief is that maladaptive traits can be, for the most part, which means to a *much* greater extent than most analysts of his day considered possible, eliminated or put into the service of socially integrated flourishing. Calling into question the penchant of many analysts to blanketly pathologize defenses and regressive characteristics and trends, Hartmann asks after their potentially positive value, thereby encouraging, at the very least, the development of more sophisticated distinctions between defenses that require dismantling and those to be left alone or encouraged.

In Hartmann's work, eros and thanatos are literalized, figured as discrete substances that can be added to or subtracted from various forms of life. Correspondingly, an individual life is figured as an emphatically plastic substratum: amenable to more or less complete self-shaping once the individual is disencumbered — to the extent possible, and Hartmann is not *wildly* optimistic here[89] — from non-adaptive conflicts, defenses, and regressive proclivities. Ego psychology, as exemplified by Hartmann's work, tends toward a technological en-framing (*Gestell*) of psychic life wherein its various features are objectivized, figured as manipulable objects and grafted onto a frame that supports their regulation and management. Hartmann, like many ego psychologists, operates under the technical imperative — not in these sense of a mandate for hyper-sophisticated refinements to analytic technique, but rather in the sense of an injunction to get the job done because the ends are so essential. His work, like that of many ego psychologists, thus tends to emphasize the reflective recuperability of psychic life and therewith its availability to autonomous transformation.

The ruling impulse is to develop a theory that accounts for and a technique that supports self-transformation within the (somewhat negotiable) boundaries of social norms.

What is exaggerated in Hartmann's work as in much of ego psychology is the plasticity of the human — our potential for conformity to social norms and malleability to intentional self-fashioning. Although ego psychologists are certainly familiar with lasting suffering, recurrent blundering, and inexplicable errancy; although they never deny the unconscious; although Hartmann, for instance, suggests that sexual and sleep disturbances may result of an individual cannot temporarily suspend her higher ego functions (1964, 56), to appreciate the uniqueness of ego psychology is to appreciate its extreme deflation of impediments to self-shaping and social integration. Even regression, Kris contends, can be controlled by the ego. With ego psychology there is no irritating kernel of the Real condemning all acts to some degree of immanent failure, as certain Lacanians would have it. Nor is there much emphasis on the insuperable persistence of trauma or unconscious wishes and the limits to self-determination and social integration they imply, as with Freud. Rather, the emphasis is on brokering a new balance of power between the id, ego, and superego that will maximize ego hegemony. To this end, the emphasis is on sapping the strength of erotic and aggressive impulses (neutralization), learning to delay gratification and test for reality, transforming once defensive, conflicted functioning into culturally adaptive behavior (secondary autonomy), and enhancing and securing innate sectors of conflict free functioning (primary autonomy). Although we may start out predominantly drive-governed — Hartmann and his followers insist that we are never exclusively so — through adequate socialization, which may become more adequate once informed by ego psychology, and perhaps a bit of therapeutic assistance, we can become predominantly ego-governed, which is to say, socially successful. The desire for the social, which is at once a desire for rational autonomy (conflict free functioning), is the madness of ego psychology, its one-sided hypervigilance.

Though there is a great deal of emphasis on plasticity, this is not considered, in a Lacanian vein, as an indication of the desirously labile nature of the human. Desires may be many and far-ranging, but, in principle, they can be successfully subordinated to self-set, socially sanctioned projects, that is, to the ego.[90] As opposed to Laplanche's suggestion that stable, conscious identity is but a thin veneer over an over-teeming, indeed ever-expanding, and tension-ridden series of unconscious identifications, ego psychology maintains a firm conviction in our ability to secure a coherent, core identity. The subject for ego psychology is not, in essence, perpetually dislocated by the propulsion of desire, forever in the process of becoming otherwise, as with Lacan, but an individual who, given adequate upbringing, or lacking this, given the right sort of therapeutic guidance, makes mature concessions to the id and the superego and thereby achieves robust autonomy within the limits of the social. Even if Lacan is right that the ego is the locus of social normativity, for ego psychology, this is no cause for distress but rather reason to rejoice.[91]

Ego psychology prizes above all the reality principle and successful adaptation rather than, say, accommodation to the truth of in(de)finitely desirous subjectivity (Lacan), the reestablishment of basic trust (Ferenczi), depressive integration (Klein), or reinitiated development (Winnicott) — although it is closest to the last. Its emphasis is on adaptability, autonomy, and ultimately, social success, which are to be won by disencumbering the ego from the quasi-pathological forces of eros and aggression, from irrational habits and dispositions to snap decision-making (symptoms), indeed in a way from the unconscious, and by inculcating and enhancing aptitudes for self-observation, reality-testing, and delayed gratification. With and against Marx's thesis, elaborated by Freud in his own way, that we make the world but not in conditions of our own choosing,[92] ego psychology acknowledges the limits to self-transparency and self-determination — conflict is a permanent feature of human life — but deflates their scope and significance, attributing such limits to largely remediable failures of early parental provisioning or later socialization[93] rather than, say, to primary and persistent ambivalence or to social irrationality (as Marx would understand it).

What becomes deflated in ego psychology is the "call of the wild" that Freud and Klein always seek to uncover in symptoms as much as in ostensibly rational, self-interested practices, and over which culture, they claim, is but a thin veil, or more precisely, which for Freud makes of culture a compromise formation. The emphasis is on the ego rather than the drives, even though drive theory is never abandoned. The emphasis is on normal development, its environmental conditions, and the remedial options available when development falters, rather than the insistent unruliness of the drives or the everyday madness of wish and fantasy's unconscious metabolism. Though its aims are to be achieved via the hegemony of the ego, ego psychology focuses on balance, harmony, stability; and here Freud is left well behind (Klein was all but unmentionable during the Hartmann era). Expanding psychoanalysis beyond Freud's focus on the Oedipal, ego psychology turns to the pre-Oedipal to uncover the elementary sociopsychic conditions of adult autonomy and the various impediments to it, impediments framed as dangers to be systematically eliminated or cajoled into the service of culture, sublated. To this end, Freud's emphasis on local symptoms is deflated in order to attend to the defensive functioning of the entire character structure. The desire is not really to dig deeper but to explore defensive functioning more broadly than had Freud. Thus when ego psychologists do concern themselves with infantile conflict, they pay particular attention to its impact on routine functioning, not just on symptoms, parapraxes, and suchlike anomalous formations. The desire is to paint the full horizon of the human rather than, as with Freud, amplify a murky detail, and to see what its potential for life may be. While Freud's inheritance of Darwin inclined him to explore the stratified layers of the primitive seething beneath the not so calm surface of everyday practices and frothing forth in pathological formations, Hartmann's inheritance of Darwin inclined him to explore how it is that we are adapted to the world and can become even more so.

With ego psychology, what we find exaggerated are (1) interest in and esteem for the ego, reality testing, adaptive defenses, and ultimately, self-determined social integration, (2) ordinary development and its environmental and psychological conditions, (3) character structure rather than local symptoms, (4) belief in the plasticity of the human, and (5) interest in systematizing and scientifically corroborating psychoanalysis and in coordinating it with academic psychology.[94] Coextensively, what we find deflated are (1) the disquieting persistence of the infantile in the adult, (2) the unconscious as a source of self- and world-distortions, overdetermination, and other such limits to self-determination, (3) drive-conflict and compromise, (4) the id and especially its Oedipal organization, and (5) sexuality and the death drive.

Self psychology . . . selfobject needs and the drive to development

Ego psychologists such as Hartmann, Kris, Lowenstein, Spitz, Mahler, and Jacobson pursued a pioneering interest in questions of development beyond the orthodox oral-anal-phallic framework. Broadening their research interests beyond matters traditionally pertaining to psychosexual development, they sought to unfold in fine detail the psychosocial history of a wide array of ordinary characteristics, capacities, and concerns and on this basis enable analytic practice and pedagogy to support their sometimes faltering development. This emphatic interest in development and its social conditions is radicalized by self psychology, taken to the roots of the archaic self and its selfobject relations.

The neologism "selfobject" means to convey the indissociable intertwinement of self and object. The object's (e.g., caregiver's) empathic attunement and phase-appropriate provisioning for the self's (e.g., child's) needs builds self structure, thereby contributing to narcissistic development understood as the development of cohesion and harmony within the self and between the individual and her social environment. The self for self psychology is inexorably relational, though not, contra Freud, inherently antagonistic to the social order. Although never explicitly, perhaps even more emphatically than ego psychologists, Heinz Kohut, founder of self psychology, projects the possibility of civilization without intrinsic discontents. At the very least, like Winnicott, he is inclined to insist on the contingency of suffering others deem structural, and like Winnicott and ego psychologists, but much less emphatically than the latter, he deemphasizes conflict and thereby expands the purview of developmental research and the offerings of psychoanalytic therapy. For Kohut and the self psychological tradition, development proceeds not from dependency and narcissistic self-interest to autonomy and object attachment, but from archaic to mature object love. And throughout life, selfobjects are required to support and sustain mature self structure, wanting which the self falls prey to illness. Self-selfobject relations are as central to self psychology as are objects as targets of aggression and desire in the Freudian tradition or as supports for phantasmatic elaborations of anxiety in the Kleinian tradition.

Like ego psychology, self psychology turns to the pre-Oedipal and other-than-Oedipal in order to expand the Freudian vision; going to the roots is not only a matter of digging deeper but of broadening one's understanding of what the roots have — or should have — nourished and set in place. But for self psychology, ego psychology, like Freud, is beclouded by a moral mythology of drives. From Kohut's perspective, Freud and ego psychology's exorbitant privileging of the drives, their penchant to construe them as the Great Criminal, if also imbued with enormous productive potential, results in severe limitations to their respective theoretical and clinical foci.

As Kohut understands him, for Freud, just as the work of culture is essentially that of sublimation, of recasting the aim and/or object of the drives to accord with social norms, the clinic is largely concerned with — limited to — integrating the abrasive expressions of drive-life, specifically by undoing drive-based barriers to self-awareness. Similarly, for ego psychology, as Kohut understands it, the work of culture proceeds through the sublimation, neutralization, and defensive adaptation of the drives, just as the clinic is largely focused on — limited to — reigning in the drives and establishing or maximizing the hegemony of the ego. In both cases, although drive-life is appreciated as an essential or the essential medium of cultural development, there is a tendency to mythologize — exaggerate to terrifying dimensions, inflate the explanatory power of, and substantialize – drive-conflict or the drives themselves, specifically, to construe one or the other as the principle source of suffering and pathology, which gives rise to moral fervor in the clinic as analysts seek to undermine the subversive, self-distorting power of the drives or drive-conflict.[95] One exaggeration (in the theory of pathology) leads to or supports another (in the theory of technique) and a radical misunderstanding of the work of analysis takes hold: "the essence of the curative process is defined neither by reference to the expansion of the realm of awareness nor, at least not per se, by reference to the increased ability of the psychic apparatus to modify the drives . . . . [self psychology does] not see the essence of the curative process as lying primarily in the expansion of the domain of the ego" (1984, 64). The essence of analysis is neither expanding cognition (1984, 108) nor enhancing reality-testing and self-control (1984, 142), nor in any other way is it ultimately a cure through reason as, say, Strachey and (sometimes) Freud would hold. Rather, according to Kohut, the essence of the cure is located in those practices, performed by analysts from Freud onward but not yet thematized and so wanting in sophistication, that modulate the analysand's selfobject relations, provide for her developmental needs, and thereby secure her sense of self-cohesion and self-worth and her vital interest in the world.

Because ego psychology is dead-set on rooting out dangers to the ego and reinforcing its achievements, like all of psychoanalysis heretofore, it fails to discern "crucial attributes of the psyche as it moves toward health" (1984, 65). Absorbed by concern for the drives and the ego, psychoanalysis' great insights into these domains has come at the cost of blindness to the ways in which, in any decent analysis, empathic attunement and other means of fulfilling clients' developmental needs builds self structure and reinitiates development, which, for Kohut, is the movement toward health. Ironically, psychoanalysis is beleaguered by a want of self-consciousness.

When it comes to thinking the psyche, it is always a question of movement. For Hartmann, recall, psychoanalysis is limited by a conflation of movement with conflict, specifically drive-conflict. For Kohut, psychoanalysis has succumbed to overenamorment with the subterranean movements of repressed sexual or aggressive wishes which manifests clinically in overwrought attention to their surface effects (symptoms, etc.) and the therapeutic alleviation of their conflicts or intensity. The fascinated attention psychoanalysis has lavished on the accrual of force by and shifting shape of sexual and aggressive contents consequent upon repression and on the movements of the ego as it tames the drives is both a source of its great achievements and a vexing limit. Seeking to release psychoanalysis from its self-incurred blindness and consequent therapeutic limitations, self psychology focuses on the process of cure, specifically on what the cure means to the analysand and on the self structures it slowly sets in place. Its attention is keyed to the movements of the psyche as it approaches developmental completion and to these movements from basic ideals, through basic talents and skills, to successful self-realization that characterize the psyche in its mature functioning: movements described as smooth, linear, focused or well-regulated, wholesome, and harmonious.

At root, Kohut contends, we suffer from failures of our early childhood selfobject milieu to meet our developmental needs, and as a result of which we want for a basic sense of self-cohesion, self-esteem, and vital, agential world-involvement, that is, for meaningful connections to others and to our own life practices.[96] The basic question is how we come to feel both vital and secure in ourselves, in our relations to others, and with regard to the meaningfulness of our ambitions. The basic problem is the enfeebled self's proclivity to disintegration, depressive detachment, and the consequent defenses, not the drives and their vicissitudes. The experience of the drives as fragmentary and fragmenting on which psychoanalytic theories of pathology tend to focus is, for Kohut, epiphenomenal, a byproduct of the self-in-breakdown.[97] Thus the pervasive clinical focus on the drives fails to adequately address the persistent fragility and discomposure of the self that both extensively conditions and independently causes suffering and pathology. More precisely, Kohut acknowledges that the problems to which self psychology is emphatically addressed are also addressed through the empathic attunement developed in any decent analysis, no matter what the analyst's partisan commitments may be, but he maintains that because the core problems of self-structuration and their treatment have not been given sustained attention, our understanding of the former and the efficacy of the latter are not nearly as advanced as could be, and need be.

For Kohut, part of the problem with psychoanalysis as he inherits it is that both Freud and ego psychology, though the latter less than the former, (1) tend to view the individual as a monad, (2) fail to discern the basic needs of the self, and thus (3) are unable to provide for those needs, as a result of which significant strata of pathology are left intact after "successful" analyses. Recall that for Freud — at least at certain moments in his reflections — the individual becomes attached to others only at the behest of the pleasure principle, that is, only in order to reduce tension to an acceptable level or rhythm or to secure particular satisfactions that cannot otherwise be had: the primary relation is to the law (of tension reduction), attachments to others wax and wane according to its demands. Likewise, in his reflections on narcissism and psychosis, Freud suggests that in the face of difficulty, object-libido may be simply withdrawn, reverting to ego-libido (secondary narcissism). Investment in an intersubjective milieu may be in a certain sense psychologically necessary — we fall sick from want of love, Freud suggests in his reflections on melancholia — but it is at bottom largely contingent. In these strains of Freud's thinking, the individual is construed as essentially a monad. As he famously puts it, the individual is like an amoeba extending and retracting pseudopodia of interest in others according to its current needs.

On the contrary, for Kohut and his school, subjectivity presupposes recognitive relations, intersubjectivity. "[T]he self's autonomy is only relative . . . a self can never exist outside a matrix of selfobjects," for it is these relations that succor and sustain the self in its most elementary composition and more advanced achievements (1984, 61). As with Winnicott, the basic unit of analysis is not the infant but the infant/caretaker dyad, or in self psychological terms, the self-selfobject matrix. As with Fairbairn, Spitz, and Bowlby, the self essentially seeks relatedness; it is propelled by the drives, regulated by the pleasure principle, and so on, but not reducible to such internal principles of movement: attachment to others is a primary good, wanting which the self is placed in severe jeopardy. In Kohut's words, "What leads to the human's self-destruction . . . is its exposure to coldness, the indifference of the nonhuman, the nonempathically responding world" (1984, 18).[98] With and against Ferenczi, Kohut suggests, the matrix of pathology is not manipulation or imposition but nihilism: a want of basic trust and sympathy more radical than Ferenczi could imagine.

Though ego psychology more readily acknowledges the impact of the psychosocial environment on the development of character structure and the ego, it fails to consider what self structures condition the development of character and must be in place for the ego to attain ascendancy. So focused on the conditions under which the drives become dangers to the individual's prospects for socially productive self-realization, hypervigilant about the need for more advanced control of the drives, ego psychology neglects the development of basic functions such as self-soothing and other fundamental matters such as the development of a sense of personal continuity through time, a firm sense of self-worth, genuine interest in the world, and secure bonds with others — as well as the impact of selfobject relations on such developments. For Kohut, if self structure is insufficiently established, individuals are hardly likely to become agents whose aspirations to self-determination and social success can be enhanced by ego psychology. Or if self structure is sufficiently established for an individual to be amenable to the type of help ego psychology offers, because ego psychology fails to discern the selfobject needs rumbling beneath drive conflicts and inadequate ego aptitudes, its efficacy even on these fronts will be limited and it will not be able to see why.

Clinically, ego psychology is predominantly concerned with accurate "here and now" transference interpretations *except* in the cases of patients suffering from inadequate development of psychic structure, in which cases the transference provides "an opportunity for reworking early disruptions, for the patient to use the analyst to try to fill unmet developmental needs, for the patient now as an adult to verbalize and experience with the analyst early fears and terrors that had, in childhood, seemed overwhelming" (Mitchell and Black 1996, 57). In such *exceptional cases*, accurate interpretation is subordinated to the facilitation of corrective experiences and the pursuit of emotional resonance. For Kohut, what ego psychology considers exceptional may well be the rule. And it is not just in these ostensibly exceptional cases that corrective experience and emotional resonance are more important than the accuracy of interpretation; quite to the contrary, for Kohut, the accuracy of interpretation is often no more than a means to provide corrective experiences of mutual attunement and thereby reinitiate development.

Neglecting the accretion of self structure that takes place if one is raised in a good-enough selfobject environment, ego psychologists, so concerned with reverse engineering the maturely functioning ego, are fixated on the upshot of a good-enough selfobject environment or on the conditions and consequences of inadequate *ego* development: the force of the drives distorting our self-images, provoking symptoms, subverting our intentions, etc. But, Kohut wants to ask, what if even the more or less well-functioning adult is only superficially invested in the world, prone to depressive detachment or defensively exaggerated interest in social life or to narcissistic rages and manias for which the drive-conflict model fails to account and so are immune to ego psychological and other such drive-focused therapies?[99]

Kohut suggests that beneath drive-impelled pleasure seeking and the guilt to which this may give rise — or more broadly, beyond the pleasure principle — (Freud's focus), beneath seemingly well-functioning, creative and productive life practices (ego psychology's focus), often lurks depression, diffuse rage, and a horrified sense that the world is and will remain bracingly cold, profoundly inhospitable. Further, Kohut suggests, such difficulties cannot be accounted for, let alone adequately addressed, by traditional forms of analysis. Moreover, Kohut contends, beneath pursuits of unconscious wishes and the defenses to which they give rise, or somehow harbored in them, may be a striving for development, but because this too fails to register on the classical Freudian and ego psychological radars, it remains unthematized and insufficiently addressed.

Perhaps in part because such "quality of life" concerns (a sense of self-worth, of vitality and meaningfulness, of adequate separation and connection, etc.) are difficult to measure, perhaps in part because the patients to whom ego psychology's expansion of services appeals do not often manifest problems with basic self structure (at least not obviously), and perhaps in part because these elementary structures are not the typical concerns of the tradition of academic psychology with which ego psychology seeks to build bridges, these issues have yet to receive the attention they are due. Such factors may play a role in ego psychology's neglect of basic self structure and its environmental conditions, but for Kohut, equally essential to its myopia is that ego psychology simply has not yet *discovered* selfobject transference. As a result, it is not in a position to appreciate the significance of early self development or the ramifications of its incompletion. Kohut takes himself to have discovered a whole new dimension of transference, namely, selfobject transference in which are expressed the basic needs of the self and some sense of what it would take to meet these needs. On the basis of the discovery that transference reveals not only drive conflicts, phantasies, unavowed wishes, libidinally invested patterns of attachment, and so on, but the basic needs of the self and what the analysand imagines would fulfill these needs, Kohut focuses his practice on renewing and correcting disrupted developmental processes, specifically, narcissistic development. Renewing stultified development by various means of empathic attunement is what, for Kohut and his school, makes analysis truly analysis.[100]

To the extent that the ego becomes an independent category of analysis for ego psychology, indeed its preoccupation, narcissism becomes so for self psychology. At first, Kohut claimed that narcissistic disturbances are isolable, independent pathological formations. Later, he came to hold that all suffer from narcissistic disturbances to varying degrees and that narcissistic disturbances condition all forms of pathology. In his words, defining mental health in terms of narcissistic development

> is not only more meaningfully applicable to human life in general, but more specifically relevant to the psychic disturbances that are prevalent today than definitions which, following the traditional Freudian and Kleinian norms, equate mental health with the attainment of a specific psychological task of early development: the attainment of postoedipal genitality, of the capacity for post-paranoid-depressive object love, of object constancy, or of any other number of specific developmental successes that are deemed to be critical. (1984, 7)

What was once considered critical is but a part of the whole, the noncomprehension of which distorts our understanding of and responses to the various parts — this, as we will see, is Kohut's basic critical-hermeneutical gesture. Kohut certainly misrepresents the tradition: in no way is mental health simply equivalent to the attainment of postoedipal genitality for Freud or to post-paranoid-depressive object love for Klein. For Klein, oscillation between paranoid/schizoid and depressive positions is unavoidable, thus post-paranoid-depressive object love is not even an intelligible option, let alone her great clinical ambition. But to the extent that Kohut's misrepresentations establish foils that bring into more fine relief his revolutionary insights into the significance of narcissistic development and better signal his break with the tradition that he was otherwise disinclined to admit, their heuristic value is to be appreciated. What should be worried over, I will suggest, are not his reductive readings of Freud and Klein — these are easily corrected — nor his penchant to read Freud, Klein, and others as essentially developmental psychologists — this just reflects his preoccupations and brings his characteristic emphasis into focus — but his presumption to speak to and for the *whole*, his arrogation of the prerogative to define mental health once and for all, the all-comprehending closure of his vision.[101] Seeking to remedy the partiality of psychoanalysis and thereby enhance its efficacy by giving narcissism the prominence it is due, Kohut conflates his deeper and more encompassing vision of suffering and healing with the firm and final establishment of *the definition* of pathology and mental health and of *the* set of therapeutic practices through which to attain the latter.[102] This terminal impulse or foundationalism, as we will see, is manifest in and conditions his appeal to the rhetoric of "need." Though this rhetoric is not in itself objectionable, Kohut's use of it insulates his reflections from critical questions that he seems always on the verge of raising, but to which he never gives voice.[103]

A related problem is that Kohut's definitions of the essence of the self and of its developmental needs and his fervent commitment to them effectively insulate his reflections from the question of how to motivate commitments to his version of analysis as against others. These definitions function as if *per se* premises. Eschewing criteria for commitment such as empirical confirmation of central hypotheses or comparative therapeutic efficacy, Kohut claims that his commitment to self psychology follows from his *deduction* of a number of therapeutic and theoretical positions from his definition of the self and its needs. The theological orientation of this gesture is not exactly subtle. In an exemplary passage, Kohut asserts that "[t]he basis on which my therapeutic conclusions rest is not expediency, however laudable, in instances carefully selected by the seasoned clinician, but a new definition of the essence of the self and a new conceptualization of its structural development" (1984, 8). On the one hand, Kohut's keen awareness that, especially given the scant interest of the psychoanalytic community (of his day) in large-scale, methodologically scrupulous outcome studies, any school will be able to muster cases to "demonstrate" the validity of its claims and procedures is to be appreciated. A good dose of suspicion is often helpful in counteracting the impulse to affirmative zealotry sparked by encounters with the incredible insights and impressive therapeutic promise of various psychoanalytic perspectives, especially those with which one was not previously familiar. If nothing else, Kohut's skepticism regarding the credibility of efficacy claims in the extant literature is (in his context, and remains) a welcome provocation to serious scientific work. But on the other hand, Kohut too quickly succumbs to the easy cynicism and reactive dogmatism of which he is so critical in others. It is undeniably difficult to work in a field where the compelling reasons for commitment to diverse perspectives sometimes seem to cancel each other out, or at least conduce to an undercurrent of skepticism the draw of which may at times become severe; where there are no decision rules for issues large or small, thus no immunity from the challenge of authorizing commitment through exemplary acts of responsibility, the risking of gestures in the complex choreography of claim-making and critique whose felicity or foundering are dependent on others' willingness to follow, on their sustained attunement to one's movements (and vice versa); indeed where the contours and constitution of the space of reasons in which one operates, hence what is required to enter a consequential claim or assume an inheritance, are remarkably ill-defined, perhaps unusually so; and where, perhaps in response to these difficulties, "seasoned clinicians" are too often concerned with carefully selecting cases that confirm their partisan convictions and winning some ground in a "war of position" than with seriously considering the evidentiary support for their claims vis-à-vis others or the criteria with reference to which claims and commitments are assessed. But this is just where courage is needed: courage to engage in a serious discussion about what makes for better and worse criteria for assessing the relative worth of various psychoanalytic claims and commitments, about the axioms and inferences the community is willing to accept, and about the values it seeks to promote — ultimately, about the nature of psychoanalytic reason.

Kohut, as much as the "seasoned clinicians" he admonishes, seems to be overwhelmed by the cacophony of voices clamoring for attention on the contemporary psychoanalytic stage, put off by the *incoherence* of the field, *insecure* about how to articulate the compelling force of his convictions while still acknowledging the viability and value of other perspectives, *uncertain* about how to persuade others of the efficacy of his procedures and the import of his ambitions in want of argumentative procedures that would culminate in demonstrative certainty. Kohut, much like those he castigates, averse to the difficult and *interminable* nature of debates about axioms, standards, values, and so on, thus rather than debate, he asserts, defines, deduces. He cheats, abdicating responsibility for his claims and therewith his connections to others. And he thereby becomes a classic case of narcissistic pathology. Succumbing to the vice he denounces in others, Kohut is surreptitiously cynical about the possibilities for persuasion or fruitful conversation in a field that does not allow for apodictic certainty or otherwise final resolution, such cynicism manifesting in its apparent opposite: dogmatic assertions about the value and deductive certainty of his perspective. This cynicism is as apparent in his claims to define the self and on the basis of this definition deduce its needs and the proper means to address them as in his (seemingly contradictory) claim that others will be persuaded only if they give it a chance in practice: he won't even try to persuade, he just lays out his findings and pleas for consideration. Distress over repeated encounters with incoherence, instability, and aporias in the field of psychoanalysis, with its irreducible plurality, is converted into decisive insistences on the internal coherence, stability, and self-secure validity of one's own position, both in Kohut and more broadly.[104]

Perhaps Kohut is more a creature of his times than he is willing to admit. As he notes, our times are troubled by the want of clear and collectively corroborated, stable values and by the reactive adherence to dogma. Might the orientation toward and privileging of closure, completion, and harmonious self-integration evident in Kohut's relation to psychoanalytic theory and practice[105] as much as in his description of the healthy self signal a reactive repudiation — the unnegotiated impact — of the troubled social conditions he so keenly perceives?

Kohut's resolute establishment of the definitions of mental health and analytic practice is all the more peculiar given that at the core of his innovative recasting of psychoanalytic theory and practice is a sociological observation embedded in which is, presumably an implicit contention that the basic forms of suffering that psychoanalysis confronts shift with the shape of the times, as should, presumably, the basic features of therapy. Kohut observes that today we suffer much less than previously from the harsh taskmaster of perfectionist morality and suggests that this has an enormous impact on what is seen in the clinic. On Kohut's account, once we were beset by a stern morality that inclined us to repress aggressive and sexual impulses that, consequent upon repression, were prone to accrue enormous strength and reemerge in distorted forms (symptoms) that far exceeded our capacity for control. Or if we were not inclined to repression, we were inclined to consciously suppress aggressive and sexual impulses, but because this was so difficult, indeed ultimately impossible, we tended to become consumed, at once mobilized and enervated, by the demand to keep them under wraps or channeled into socially productive forms, thus prone to extreme self-loathing and various defenses such as projection whereby we sought to cleanse ourselves of impulses we could not abide.[106] Although the reign of moral perfectionism has not been wholly dismantled, its strength has greatly diminished, thus have the problems to which it tended to give rise.

Today, Kohut suggests, we have succumbed to nihilistic fragmentation; society tolerates much but actively promotes little, thus we tend to feel unrecognized and unconnected, fundamentally disoriented, forever on the verge of breaking apart. And so we become all too available to whatever forms of solidarity or pseudo-solidarity present themselves (romantic, commercial, religious, ideological, etc.). We suffer not from stern superegos or austere social regulations but from others' profound disinterest in our doings, indeed in our very being.[107] We suffer from unbearable disappointment in a culture that touts itself as, in an unparalleled fashion, amenable to unconstrained self-realization but does little to actively foster this, thus from frustration with and profound disappointment over our seemingly inexplicable inability to achieve much that is meaningful: we suffer not from guilt but from shame. We have projects and ambitions, and we find pleasure in their pursuit, yet we feel deeply unsatisfied, not truly passionate about our chosen courses of life, incessantly mobilized and yet somehow dead, inauthentic. All that seems left to us is rigid identification with or aggressive latching onto those with whom we have (or can become convinced we have) something, anything in common, or compulsive pleasure-seeking whereby we attain a minimal but wholly unsatisfying subjective consistency. To a great extent, we have become consumers, always on the hunt for the sense of social belonging promised by each new commodity, especially the trendy ones, and by the ritual of consumption itself, but never made good on. Our sense of connectedness with others, and so with ourselves, is threadbare; collectively and individually, we are on the verge of unraveling, thus deeply tempted by offers of connection even if their acceptance involves massive self-suppression. Increasingly, we find ourselves huddled together in overcrowded cities yet morally and existentially isolated. Wanting for a culture that supports robust and well-balanced forms of separation and connection, Kohut suggests, "[m]an of our time is the man of the precariously cohesive self, the man who craves the presence, the interest, the availability of the self-cohesion-maintaining selfobject" (1984, 61). Hence for "a large number of patients who *now* enter psychoanalytic treatment, the essence of psychopathology is the defective self (i.e. the self prone to states of fragmentation, weakness, or disharmony)" (1984, 70; emphasis added); consequently, analysis of defense-resistances are "less important today than they once were and should no longer be construed as centrally important to theory and practice" (1984, 115). What is now centrally important, Kohut contends, is the empathic modulation of selfobject relations that compose self structure and allow for more satisfying forms of separation and connection.[108]

Although such sociological musings seem to commit Kohut to the thesis that psychoanalysis is a historical discourse of suffering and healing under the changing conditions of modernity rather than a metaphysical discourse of universal truth — notice that in the passage from 1984, 70, Kohut elaborates the *essence* of pathology in terms of what *appears now* in the clinic, seeming to problematize and perhaps implicitly recast the notion of "essence" — he would be hard pressed to admit it. As he sees it, just because his definition of mental health and his elaboration of the practices that promote it are "more specifically relevant to the psychic disturbances that are prevalent today," their validity is nonetheless universal, trans- or ahistorical. For Kohut, the contemporary clinic *amplifies, accentuates, and enhances the perspicuity* of what has always been the case: the eternally present. Though what we see on the couch today are symptoms of a culture that is less and less capable of providing for the basic needs of the self, these needs are invariable. They have always been at the root of pathology, its essence; and responding to them has always been the essence of the cure. Thus we must ask, What are these basic needs and how can analysis better address them?

The basic needs are for mirroring, idealization, and community. Originally, the need for *mirroring* is expressed as a need for primitive merger. Without adequate symbiotic fusion with caregivers, intense, primitive forms of rage and lethargy ensue (1984, 6). Though these may be the seeds of, respectively, extreme sensitivity to narcissistic injury and crippling depression in later life, ordinarily, which is to say, as a result of good-enough caregiving, they become but haunting residues of the archaic dimly felt now and again, an undercurrent of anguish occasionally surging forth to suffuse ordinary, flexible functioning with the memory of oblivion. Primitive needs are never perfectly met — meeting them perfectly would be a catastrophic form of failing. Rather, optimal failure, i.e., temporary and quickly-enough redressed failure to provide for basic needs that are for the most part met, leads to transmuting internalization of the function sought in the archaic self object.

Later, the archaic need for merger becomes the child's need to be looked upon with joyful approval and admiration, to be confirmed in her "innate sense of vigor, greatness and perfection" (Kohut and Wolf 1978, 414). At this point, caretakers' approving responses to affection and enterprise prevent innate dispositions to affectionate, assertive initiative and joyful pride in achievement from decomposing into fragments of oedipal sexuality and hostility, their exaggerated and distorted doubles. If such approval is not consistently forthcoming, the self becomes overburdened, weak and disharmonious (1984, 24). If approval is consistently forthcoming, a robust sense of self-acceptance, self-worth, personal resiliency, and self-confidence is firmly installed. This "wholesome" self structure will need to be refreshed by approval from self objects throughout life, but its basic structure will be set securely in place.

The need for *idealization* is initially the need for an omniscient, omnipotent, and infallible being by whose presence we are both calmed and uplifted. Often, infants and young children are overburdened and fragmented by need and by the drives, given to worry that their feeble powers are no match for the might of their needs and of the world. Consequently, they are prone to disconsolate withdrawal; they cannot do without divinity. Here too difficulties are inevitable. Caretakers are all too human: vulnerable and prone to aggressive outbursts and defensive retreats. However, if the figure onto whom one latches is sufficiently idealizable, her calm confidence — something like Ferenczi's basic trust in the hospitability of the world — is transformed via transmuting internalization into self-soothing structure just as her approval establishes a sense of self-worth.[109] Likewise, her impressive, seemingly limitless competence becomes a vital source of hope, the germ of belief in not only the possibility of one's own greatness, but in the prospect of greatness in the world. Only in the radiant light of exemplary magnificence, however illusory, will we be energized to seek what slender margin of utopia is available to us.

Later, the need for idealization is expressed as a need for an ideal figure — whether this be a particular individual, a nation, or an idea — to confirm and approve our vitality and assertiveness as well as the ideals they serve. We need to believe that others believe: our belief is rooted in and routes through others; cynicism is objectivity in its death throes. Here what is needed is the attunement, specifically the approval of others whereby our ambitions come to seem genuinely meaningful, not just flights of fancy. Others' affirmative attunement is our indication that our ambitions are livable, socially intelligible thus socially supportable, in principle accomplishable, and what's more, desirable, not just desired, a source of connection, of shared conviction, thus accomplishable not just in principle. What is needed from constitutive others is a sense that we may be constitutive others, or at least contributors, participants in projects that elaborate our inner ambitions and thereby our social bonds. In addition to the ongoing need for ideals and their exemplars, throughout life we require figures of idealized strength and calmness to both sooth and uplift us, to sustain the capacity for self-affirmation such figures once implanted.

The need for *community* initially expresses itself as a need for closeness via perfect empathy.[110] Wanting this, there will be intense frustration and archaic defenses. Later, the need for perfect empathy develops into the need to be surrounded by the quietly sustaining presence of alter egos, those with whom we share basic interests and ideals, along with an understanding of what it means to pursue them, to succeed and to fail; with whom we share sensitivities and urgencies, prereflective but (to an extent) reflectively redeemable promptings and responsive dispositions; with whom "we say . . . when . . .," agree in judgments or criteria and forms of life — a sensus communis.[111] This is a need, not unlike later developments of the need idealization, and not incidentally so, for mutual recognition, for others who "get us" and who we "get," others with whom we may disagree but with whom we know how to disagree (how to sustain and signal mutual interest or affection amidst conflict) because we are similarly inclined in our responses to each other and to the world. More precisely, this is a need for open-ended belonging mediated by elastic mutual attunement (recalibrable triangulation), for shared structures of attention, understanding, and response in the hold of which individual distinctiveness and talents can emerge as commonly, and so personally, significant. It is a need to find one's bearings amongst others similarly borne — there being no other way. Only if we feel securely placed in a community of peers who share — enact — our basic attitudes and take an interest in manifestations of our distinctiveness as of exemplary value will we feel confident in our basic world-orientation and confident that expressions of distinctive individuality are not just idiocy or pathological aberration. If, as Kohut affirms, "[d]isintegration anxiety . . . . is the deepest anxiety man can experience" (which sounds rather Kleinian), and if this is understood, as he tends to understand it (contra Klein), as an anxiety over loss of humanity, psychological death — more like becoming an uncoordinated automaton, a machine deprived of its functional context, than a drive governed animal — then the need for community is a need for human kinship, for a sense that however different others may be, their differences are intelligible permutations of a changing same (1984, 16). The need for community is the need for separateness and connectedness, a need to feel at once part of a transcending whole and valued for one's distinctiveness.

If these basic needs are fulfilled, a sense of wholeness, harmony, strength, vitality, and integrity will be established (1984, 6, 52, 197). When the self feels welcomed and supported by selfobjects' empathic and phase-appropriate responses, warmth and joy are its primary affective states, or at least the consistent undercurrents of its affective alterations. But if caregivers' pathology or negligence prevents them from responding appropriately to these needs, a desolate coldness sets in, soon followed by defenses, symptoms, rages, and/or depression. Without the warm glow of togetherness, solidarity with oneself and with others, we are prone to depressive withdrawal and defensive efforts to sustain ourselves through *joyless pleasure seeking*. We become "specialists without spirit, sensualists without heart" (Weber 1904/1930, 182).

Kohut's theory is one of good mechanics and bad tending: inadequate development follows upon inadequate caretaking and generates a sense of compromised existence, a sense that life has gone terribly awry, that it is somehow failed. But buried beneath the rage and disconsolation to which such failure gives rise, Kohut suggests, lies hidden a *need or drive to development*.[112] Kohut speaks in this context of the "search of the damaged self for the development-enhancing responses of an appropriately empathic selfobject" (1984, 192). The impulse to development, as a drive or need, is ineradicable, Kohut suggests, perhaps even in the worst conditions.[113] In the clinic, he notes, "[t]he patient protects the defective self so that it will be ready to grow again in the future, to continue to develop from the point in time at which its development had been interrupted. And it is this recognition . . . that best prepares the soil for the developmental move forward that the stunted self of the analysand actively craves" (1984, 141). Notice that Kohut figures the need or drive to development in teleological, as if intentional terms: "[t]he patient protects the defective self *so that* it will be ready to grow again in the future." This need or drive is figured as if it were an evolutionary inheritance, as if there by design, perhaps even the intention of Nature itself. Elsewhere, Kohut suggests that "[j]ust as a tree will, within certain limits, be able to grow around an obstacle so that it can ultimately expose its leaves to the life-sustaining rays of the sun, so will the self in its developmental search abandon the effort to continue in one particular direction and try to move forward in another" (1984, 205).

Does Kohut's thinking harbor or might it even be animated by a teleological, or more precisely, providential impulse epitomized by certain strands of Hegelianism or Marxism with which Kohut was no doubt familiar?[114] If so, does this signal a regressive repudiation of the moment of skepticism inherent in psychoanalytic reason and thereby psychoanalysis's claim to modernism? Does it attest to a skeptical self-interpretation of the problem of skepticism, an interpretation according to which the specter of skepticism indifferently unsettles all claims to cognition and can be laid to rest, if ever, only upon the establishment of a certainty-conferring foundation? Like all modernist discourses/practices, psychoanalysis makes use of features of a classical skeptical argument: it suspends accepted patterns of material inference, allowing logical possibility to interrupt conviction in ordinary cognitive criteria and defuse arguments that seek to affirm or negate an antecedent by pointing to the discovery of or failure to identify a consequent with which it is connected in a conditional judgment or, conversely, efforts to unpack conceptual commitments by discovering the consequents in which an antecedent must issue in specified conditions;[115] suspends ordinary constraints on concept projection; and suspends routine forms of practical response (acknowledgment) through which semantic stability and inferential significance (status) are established.[116] A somewhat skeptical enterprise, psychoanalysis casts doubt on the obvious; like a classical skeptical argument, it may even invoke the thought that our best-case cognitive claims, or what we take to be such, are misguided or worse (e.g., delusional). And it must do so, must make use of skeptical features in order to pursue the region of idiosyncratic psychic reality with which it is concerned. Paradoxically, only by deactivating what ordinarily confers conceptual determinacy (elaborates the "space of reasons") can psychoanalysis pursue the "deeper" determinations with which it is concerned. Only by (partially) deactivating ordinary practices and criteria of concept projection, material inference, and practical acknowledgment, only because in analysis one needn't mean what one says (one way to phrase Freud's fundamental rule would be: "one mustn't mean what one says"), because what analyst and analysand say in that context do not imply the commitments/responsibilities they would elsewhere, can psychoanalysis address idiosyncratic forms of reasoning, track the development and facilitate the reelaboration of personal myth. But once the door to skepticism is opened, confidence in what one finds behind any door will never be absolute — the risk of infinite veils cannot be abated; the specter of skepticism will forever float on the periphery, waiting for welcome in a moment of despair or avoidance or overeagerness. Accepting this means living-in-question without allowing the questionability of one's convictions and commitments to become a burden that one imagines might be lifted (if the skeptical entertaining of logical possibility is an imaginative affair, relieving this burden would mean the death of imagination). It means refusing to repudiate cognitive and practical claims on the ground of their persistent, but not always pertinent questionability. It means refusing to repudiate finitude as if so doing were a step toward something else, as if finitude were a limit rather than an all-embracing (evolving) condition. Tactfully accepting its skeptical dimension, neither making too much of it (say, a reason to repudiate the discourse/practice or to anxiously and aggressively pursue its alignment with the methodological and cognitive criteria of the exact sciences) or too little (say, maintaining dogmatic, mutually disinterested or mutually pathologizing partisan convictions) is how psychoanalysis sustains its claim to modernism (how it stakes this claim, or *might* do so, is another matter). What then to make of a psychoanalytic discourse that, at bottom, seems to have a bottom — a preserve of need ever-striving for fulfillment? What to make of Kohut's Oedipus-like knowingness? His inspiring confidence in recovery? His reconciling urge to authoritatively integrate, speak the truth, and dictate the future of psychoanalysis? In order to begin addressing these questions (the former more directly than the latter), let us enumerate a few point of conjunction between Kohut's work and certain strands of providential Hegelianism or Marxism.

First, Kohut speaks of "the patient" in the abstract, not of this or that patient. He speaks of and perhaps to a general, indeed all-encompassing "we," an anonymous, universal subject whose development is at stake, much like Hegel, on a certain reading, speaks of and perhaps to *Geist* and its development,[117] or like certain orthodox Marxists speak of and to the proletariat as the privileged subject-object of History.

Second, like a certain Hegel or Marx, Kohut maintains that although the analysand "actively craves" the developmental move forward, ordinarily, this "activity" is not conscious (intentional), but rather evident only in symptoms and defenses, as if a ruse of reason (1984, 141). It is in light of this insistence that "the analysand actively craves" development (1984, 141) that we are to read Kohut's earlier comment that the search for development-fostering selfobject responses is "reactivated" in the clinic: its "activity," its *energia* (being-in-motion) was never absent, only dulled and inconspicuous (1984, 71).

Third, for Kohut as for a certain Hegel, it will take a fully developed individual, one who has wholly overcome developmental defect and structural deficiency, who can authorize this reading of development as surreptitious pursuit of totalizing rational integration, ideal satisfaction.[118] Along these lines, strictly inverting Freud's bold claim that countertransference can be entirely overcome and objectivity thereby won, Kohut speaks of the analyst's "ultimately successful . . . attempt to look into himself and remove the inner barriers that stand in the way of his empathic grasp of the patient," as if "science" developed through the progressive eradication of the stain of subjectivity, as if cognitive and practical success required the overcoming of subjectivity rather than, say, its exemplary mastering, as if human separateness were a failing and fully remediable (ironically, by means of turning inward), thus as if prospects for total transparency were grounded in unlimited and unwilled mutual exposure (1984, 182). Kohut figures himself as inhabiting a privileged interpretive position, as if a prophet in the Maimonidean tradition where ethical perfection — perfection of character — and cognitive perfection are mutually conditioning (1984, 182).[119]

Fourth, when Kohut speaks of the patient's readiness to "continue to develop from the point in time at which its development had been interrupted," he implies that development strives to attain a predefined terminus and completes itself only when the whole gamut has been run, viz. either when what seem to be contingent impediments to full development (archaic needs) reveal themselves as necessary crisis points that catalyze developmental progress or when real impediments to developmental completion (faulty caregiving and its repercussions) are dissolved. Elsewhere the rhetoric of "striving for completion is explicit: "the defective self of the patient with a narcissistic personality disturbance will mobilize its *striving to complete its development*" (1984, 4; emphasis added; also see 44). Kohut's conviction that development can be completed, fulfilled, finished is steadfast: "in the analysis of narcissistic personality disturbances *all* existing defects in the self become spontaneously mobilized as selfobject (narcissistic) transferences," following which, he later suggests, they can be fully resolved and surpassed (4; emphasis added). Lack can be filled, defect overcome; the self can become, at least "structurally" nondefective, whole, harmonious, equilibrated, a basically self-transparent and self-determining unity — a perfect organism. Is this not an image of the end of History (Marxist, Hegelian or theological)? What are we to make of Kohut's seeming *faith in finality*?

Fifth, like a certain Hegel or Marx, Kohut is a thinker of the development of the harmonious whole. He describes his "essential therapeutic conclusion" as follows: "it is the *defect* in the self that brings about and maintains a patient's selfobject (narcissistic transference), and it is the working through of this transference which, via transmuting internalization, that is via a *wholesome* psychic activity that has been thwarted in childhood, lays down the structures needed to *fill* the defect in the self" (1984, 4; emphasis added). Here as elsewhere, the wholesome is linked with healing and fulfillment, the fragmentary with suffering and pathology. And as in certain Hegelian, Marxist, or other such providential discourses, the accomplishment of a harmonious whole indicating full development signals *essential completion* — not a final point of rest, but a point after which there will be no structurally significant movement, no movement that contributes to something one could call *development*. Kohut declares that the aim of analysis is the development of "an uninterrupted tension arc from basic ambitions, via basic talents and skills, toward basic ideals" (1984, 4) and describes this tension arc as "the *dynamic essence* of the complete, nondefective self; it is a conceptualization of the structure whose establishment makes possible a creative-productive, fulfilling life" (1984, 4-5; emphases added). This "dynamic essence" is not so dynamic as to allow what is encountered in the pursuit of basic ideals to recursively impact their formulation or that of basic ambitions: the tension arc must be uninterrupted, linear. The *dynamis* or movement essentially elaborated must be structure-sustaining, change within the confines of an established same, otherwise it would be but pathological turbulence. With and against ego psychology, Kohut suggests that, wanting for completion, the self's seemingly "productive" efforts produce little of significance, will not give rise to a sense of fulfillment. (Kohut often seems remarkably proximate to ego psychology but for his emphasis on fulfillment rather than unobstructed functioning and social success, i.e., productivity for its own sake.) Only when development is complete will there be real creativity and productivity, which is to be understood on the model of promising rather than experimenting — as non-deviation from the trajectory articulated by "self-set" (need-constrained) norms, linear progress from goals to achievements mediated by standing talents. Kohut's notion of developmental completion, indeed of happiness, emphasizes self-regulation and -integration, self-consistency and -coherence, and most tellingly, self-centering: "We should speak of having achieved a cure when an energetic continuum in the *center* of the personality has been established and the unfolding of a *productive* life has thus become a realizable possibility" (1984, 7; emphases added).[120]

Sixth, like a certain Hegel and Marx, Kohut is oriented toward a notion of freedom with a prominent positive dimension. Kohut insists that analysis aims at freedom (1984, 42, 66, 77, and 210), which he understands as expressive freedom, freedom to pursue, indeed to hold oneself to, direct paths from talent- or skill-expressing goals to their realization. The basic problem with psychoses, narcissistic personality disturbances, as well as classical transference neuroses, Kohut underscores, is that "the functional freedom of the self is impaired." Unlike ego psychology, Kohut's emphasis is not on unlimited adaptability, the freedom to function productively in infinitely variable social contexts, but the freedom to put basic talents and skills in play in achieving basic ideals and ambitions (1984, 8). In both ego psychology and self psychology, though in diametrically opposed senses, what is at stake is freedom from history as a means of freedom for history: with ego psychology, freedom from historical sedimentation (e.g., hypercathected habits of object relation) is a means to freedom for ongoing, adaptive accommodation to contingent historical demands; with self psychology, freedom from historical contingency (e.g., faulty rearing and its ramifications) is a means to freedom for the unfolding of the nuclear self, for the fulfillment of need and the accomplishment of one's ownmost goals, freedom for the realization of necessity. The freedom at which analysis aims on Kohut's conception is freedom *from* excess, deviation, or chance interruption, one might say freedom from the turbulence and trials of passion or from the intrusive and shattering exposure to the Other, freedom from futurity, and therewith freedom *for* self expression. More precisely, the freedom at which analysis aims is freedom *from* energy-consuming captivation by Oedipal conflicts, *from* "the bondage that had formerly tied the archaic self to the archaic selfobject," and *from* rigid defenses, habits, activities, and character structures that were set in place to compensate for deficient provisioning for basic needs (1984, 66). Development, and so analysis, aims at the cultivation — or more precisely, the liberation — of mature empathic attunement through which one acquires baseline capacities such as the ability to *regulate* inner tensions and achieve a *consistent, secure* sense of self-esteem, i.e., necessary conditions for the projection and pursuit of any goal whatsoever: "a successful analysis is one in which the analysand's formerly archaic needs for the responses of archaic selfobjects are *superseded* by the experience of the availability of empathetic resonance, the major constituent of the sense of *security* in adult life" (1984, 77; emphasis added). The freedom at which analysis aims, like the freedom at which history aims on a certain Hegelian conception, is no panacea or ecstasy. Rather, such freedom amounts to the well-instituted availability of prospects for the pursuit of individual ambitions, or more precisely, institution-respecting, structure-preserving individuation. The aim of development, thus of analysis, its handmaiden, is a basically coherent and cohesive self, a self sufficiently strong to remain true to itself, to remain "in harmony with the [established, settled] patterns of his own nuclear self," in harmony with itself (itself basic needs, talents, and ambitions) and its social milieu, a well-centered, capable and confident self (1984, 210; brackets added). For Kohut, freedom means reconciliation with necessity. The aim of development, and so analysis, is freedom understood as *balanced* separation and connection wherein affectionate bonds with others harmonize with and support self-assertion and achievement. On Kohut's conception, freedom means that, where fundamentals are concerned, nothing is out of place, implacably disturbing, threatening prospects for secure self-integration, -mastery, and -expression — nothing like the unconscious can have a prominent place in a life of freedom. What development, thus analysis means to foster is the freedom to pursue a meaningful because expressive life, a creative but well-regulated mobility: say, success in love and work. Kohut is as little concerned with political freedom, the freedom to influence the institutions that condition the development of talents and ambitions, or most broadly, need-interpretations, as is ego psychology, and to similar effect: his faith in finality, like ego psychology's enthusiasm for adaptation and Hegel's (reputed) bedazzlement by the freedom afforded by modernity's major institutions (the family, civic society, and the state), crowds out concern with radical critique through which freedom from reigning self-conceptions might be pursued.

Seventh, time — the time of development, the time of analysis, and the time of expressive accomplishment — is figured as a linear course of rational necessity or a contingent deviation, an eminently reparable mistake; movement is either forward or stalled. In analysis, for example, "[e]ach optimal failure [to provide for the analysand's needs] will be followed by an increase in the patient's resilience vis-à-vis empathy failures both inside and outside the analytic situation; that is, after each, optimal new self structures will be acquired and existing ones will be firmed" (1984, 69). Analysis proceeds along a direct path from the surface (late developments, i.e., Oedipal matters) to the depths (archaic, originary needs), seeking to secure an "*uninterrupted tension arc* from basic ambitions, via basic talents and skills, toward basic ideals" (1984, 4; emphasis added).

Eighth, like certain Marxists and Hegelians, Kohut is ambiguous about whether or not recognition of the telos is a condition for its realization. Though like them, it seems that for the most part, Kohut thinks so. For instance, when Kohut asserts that "this recognition . . . best prepares the soil for the developmental move forward," it is unclear whether he means that only when the need for development becomes conscious can it be fulfilled or that though "this recognition . . . *best* prepares the soil," the developmental move forward is in some sense inevitable (1984, 141; emphasis added). Given the characterization of Kohut above, it is highly likely that he intends the former.

Ninth, Kohut figures the work and position of the analyst as akin to that of a certain Marxist *avant garde* or priest, that is, as the bearer of insight into a telos that, though pressing forth at every moment (this is what the "analysand actively craves" — "actively," because it does not mean "consciously," serves to rhetorically redouble the urgency of the craving), will not be fulfilled until it is seen aright, as our need of needs. It falls to the analyst/priest/*avant garde* to enlighten us: her exemplary faith becomes our own.

Akin to certain Hegelian, Marxist, and theological discourses, Kohut's work harbors and is perhaps animated by profound faith in progress — not in the sense of a blinding and empty conviction that whatever happens is for the best, but in the sense of a clinically supported conviction that subtending suffering and pathology is an ineradicable urge to heal, to develop, on which analysis can call as it moves us progressively toward recovery. Here we must be very careful. Although Kohut at times speaks as if the drive or need for development is simply ineradicable, for instance when he notes that "[i]t is the working-through processes mobilized by the analysis of this central selfobject transference that, as clinical experience has taught us, ultimately leads to the strengthening of that compensatory area of the self, insufficiently established in childhood, *but yet not* [rather than "not yet"] *hopelessly defec-*

tive, which brings about the analytic cure," he does occasionally qualify such claims (1984, 206; emphasis and brackets added). In these more temperate moments, usually in a rather strained and convoluted voice, an ambiguous turn of phrase, he admits that *in principle* the drive or need for development may be destroyed: "the analyzable patient [and what of the unanalyzable patient?] who suffers from a conflict neurosis or a narcissistic personality or behavior disorder is an individual whose self—or, to be more exact, a remnant of whose self—is still, *potentially at least*, in search of appropriately responsive selfobjects" (1984, 71; emphasis and brackets added). Likewise, claiming that "selfobject transferences arise . . . in consequence of the fact that certain developmental needs were not responded to adequately in childhood but, on the other hand, were not frustrated completely," he at least *allows for the possibility* that complete frustration would eradicate a developmental need, thus the drive for its fulfillment (what is meant by "need" if even fundamental needs are eradicable? The path this question projects is carefully guarded, like the door to the Law[121]) (1984, 201). However, Kohut never reports a case in which the drive to development is wholly inoperative: one wonders whether he *could* recognize one, so firm is his faith in this drive and its destination (complete development). One suspects that even were he to encounter a case in which this need or drive seemed altogether lacking, Kohut would attribute this apparent anomaly to his own failure of vision consequent upon faltering technique, would turn inward in order to remove barriers to empathy. Teleology is maintained on credit of faith (*credo*). Although Kohut is sufficiently scrupulous to admit that the need or drive for development may be destroyed, he sequesters this possibility to the defused domain of the merely logically possible, allowing himself to heed a powerful interpretive inclination to convert apparent exceptions into ultimately reassuring crises — trials of faith. What would unsettle his teleological convictions become demands to decipher the signs of development's silent surging or to undertake efforts of self-reform through which (what thereby become) contingent impediments to the reanimation of the drive to development are removed.

By means of this brief analogical excursion I want to give force to the following question: *might Kohut's faith in need, specifically, in the need for or drive to development, register and repudiate his leading sociological observation, and more broadly, the insistence of contingency?* The forms of suffering and pathology appearing in analysis today are, Kohut contends, quite different from those encountered previously. Why then insist that what appears now is but an accentuated, more perspicuous manifestation of that from which, at root, we have always suffered, thus that analysis requires not large scale revisions but simple recalibration? Whence Kohut's proclivity to privilege the continuous and unified over the discontinuous and divergent, his reticence to acknowledge the possibility of the categorically new or structurally reconfigured, generally, his aversion to the contingency of the human condition? For one as for all, might not the human experiment end in total failure, utter catastrophe? (Such a possibility was a powerful and pervasive worry in Kohut's day.) Or might it be endless — say, as endless as the evolution of need-interpretations? What is held at bay and what is harbored in Kohut's preemptory decision against the chance of chance, the possibility of possibility beyond anticipated horizons, thus beyond our capacity for technoscientific (e.g., therapeutic) control? Is psychoanalysis for Kohut humanity's last, best chance for discerning its *essential* structures and *securing* its developmental completion — metaphysical humanism? And would he be alone in transposing psychoanalysis into a transcendental setting? A condensed way of putting these questions would be: What work is the rhetoric of "need" doing in Kohut's writings[122] and whence his faith in the need for or drive to development?

These are crucial questions not just for Kohut but for psychoanalysis today. In part, what is at stake is psychoanalysis coming to terms with trends that promote so thorough an integration of the individual and the social that both collapse. Alienated from the media of social authority (the possibility of voice), deprived of the sense of significance, of substantiality conferred by mutual interest, the functionally integrated — objectively substitutable thus subjectively hyperself-conscious — individual becomes aggressively absorbed in her enforced privacy, having to fend off a sense of insignificance or its impending through unabashed and ever-unsatisfying conformity or uninterrupted efforts to achieve authentic self-expression, to forge a life she can call her own, but finding herself lost, adrift in her own efforts of self-elaboration — these feeling either false (merely conventional) or pathetic (unconventionalizable, unpursuable because unconstrained, irreal). Wanting for bonds of mutual interest and their institutional and intersubjective expression, self-abdication or self-invention become as necessary as they are impossible; forms of tragic collusion. Correspondingly, the social becomes but a collection of techniques for constructing and coordinating private interests, bereft of its dynamic essence — dissonant interventions that would halt the slide into conformist coagulation; that would audaciously assume the authority to articulate (some aspect of) the content or concept of community, to project for it another path that it may learn to call its own; that would undertake exemplary acts of responsibility, that even when they fail may reinvigorate the question of community, return those avoiding responsibility to it and thereby to themselves (for a moment). Though Kohut aims to underwrite and induce the efforts of those seeking to displace a monadic conception of subjectivity, he ultimately collapses the social into the psychic, allowing the latter to constrain and extensively explain the former. He clearly wants to give a balanced account of the social and the psychic, but what is not actually harmonious cannot be theoretically reconciled. *Kohut's self psychology unwittingly elaborates the self-conception of subjectivity — as forever striving for stable, baseline structure that will support personally meaningful modes of social integration; permanently at risk of oblivion yet inordinately optimistic — under social conditions that conduce to its collapse. The domination of the social is registered and repudiated as the primacy of the psychic; specifically, as the discourse of need.* "Need" converts nihilism into implacable striving for self-assertion. However much Kohut insists that the self is inexorably relational and urges the appreciation of the constitutive character of relationality, the significance of this suffers a severe scope restriction. Relations with others may be formative, indeed constitutive, but our exposure is limited: this is the meaning of "need." Structurally, relationality may do *no more* than catalyze the development of, sustain, or express self structure and *no less* or *no worse* than obstruct it: need is as persistent as nihilism. With self psychology subjectivity — specifically, impulses to autonomy and authenticity — reemerges from its collapse as psychologism, its theoretical preserve. Ever-insistent, basic needs and their developmental trajectory inherit the force of social fragmentation; along with basic talents, ambitions, and ideals, they are as well defined as the conditions for and consequences of their social elaboration are vague, as stable as the social is stagnant. Self psychology, one might say, is dialectical stagnation.

This gives a clue to Kohut's distinctive structure of blindness and insight. His exaggerated insistence on and great insights into basic needs are conditioned by a certain sort of blindness — one of the eyes wide shut variety — to the significance of social-historical trends, specifically to those that debilitate the efficacy of exemplary need-interpretations. The needs to which he attends are as static as the social, and as promising (a whirlwind at the level of content but structurally hyperstable); his faith in development as deep as contemporary despair; his attention to psychological mechanism and psychological reality as relentless, and as attractive, as the machinery of social standardization. Kohut's attention is riveted to structures that should support a creative, productive, meaningful life — perhaps in part because it doesn't. His attention is keyed to the social conditions of such structure, but as if squinting, he restricts the scope of his concern in order to achieve focus — perhaps unavoidably. (What would clinical work look like, would it be possible, without some such scope restriction?) Blind to the broader conditions, thus the true contents, of his fundamental insights, Kohut's focus is achieved as fixation. Perhaps Kohut retreats from the social conditions — not just catalysts or enhancers — of narcissistic failure in particular and the significance of the contemporary shape of suffering generally because to do otherwise would be to come to terms with simultaneous trends toward overdetermining schematization and relentless, though limited, transformation, with something structurally off-balance, contradictory, with complex admixtures of determinacy of indeterminacy that do not add up to a harmoniously integrated whole. Attracted to the secure, stable, integrated, and objectively present, to what is complete or always already on the way to completion, Kohut perhaps cannot tolerate what, guided by his fundamental concerns, he cannot fail to see.

For instance, when Kohut claims that "the girl's rejection of femininity, her feeling of being castrated and inferior, and her intense wish for a penis arise not because the male sex organs are psychobiologically more desirable than the female ones, but because the little girl's selfobjects failed to respond to her with appropriate mirroring, since either no idealizable female parental imago was available to her, or . . . no alter ego gave her support during the years when a profound feminine self should have established itself," whatever its limits, the counter-Freudian insistence on the contingency of female castration anxiety and inferiority feelings, generally, the depathologization of femininity, are to be appreciated (1984, 21). But how can he so confidently reduce "the rejection of femininity" to these specific selfobject failures, thus tacitly project its remission consequent upon appropriate corrections? Do not the anxieties, the sense of inferiority, and the various wishes under concern have a great many social determinants that will exert their influence even if adequate selfobject relations abound in the early caregiving or later clinical context?[123] Does Kohut not covertly privilege the childrearing — familial — context despite his adamant insistence on the need for adequate selfobject relations throughout life? Is his notion of the family and its formative influence not artificially insulated from the broader compass of the social? Is his claim that social relations are *ultimately* conditioned by or, even more strongly, derivative of familial relations? What to make of the implied optimism — if only things go right in early family life (or in the clinic, which Kohut seems to understand as likewise self-contained) . . . ? Why, though noting their import time and again, does Kohut never undertake an investigation of the social conditions that supervene upon, if they do not already inform, early selfobject provisioning or the therapy modeled on it? Whence his fascinated attraction to and repulsion by the social, his unwitting and unavoidable involvements with what he seeks to keep at bay? Might Kohut's discussion of an unavailable "*female* parental imago" and his claim that "a profound feminine self *should have* established itself" suggest a certain heteronormativity, thus the influence of broader social currents on what is presumably their basis? With this discussion of what seems to be gender-specific selfobject needs, are not the well-policed borders of essence (basic need) breached? And is some such breach, though not necessarily this one, unavoidable? If this is a selfobject need, might not need be much more permeable to collective need-interpretations and their material mediations than Kohut cares to admit? If *this* is a need, might we not want to ask how to unlearn or relearn our needs rather than simply satisfy them?

Does not Kohut's emphasis on need and his faith in finality reproduce the fundamental mistake for which he chastises Freud and all of psychoanalysis heretofore: confusing an effect with a cause, taking a part for the whole?[124] How do we know when we have hit bedrock or that there is bedrock to hit? The spade may turn at the end of explanation, but that does not necessarily mean that we have hit firm ground. How do we assess Kohut's insistence on the priority of selfobject needs against Freud's insistence on that of the pleasure principle, libido, and aggression or Klein's insistence on paranoid and depressive anxiety, phantasy, etc? Has there yet been, can there yet be, psychoanalysis without metaphysics?

To what extent can psychoanalysis come to terms with the relative and perhaps changing weight of the social and the endopsychic as they interface — are reproduced and perhaps transformed — at the site of, indeed as, the individual? To what extent can it come to terms with the possibility that its theories or practices are dated? And how far need it, especially if the clinical lore is correct that experienced analysts of all stripes, i.e., no matter how antiquated their commitments, achieve basically similar outcomes at similar rates? How can psychoanalysis proceed without faith in finality? Need it?

These questions will be addressed in detail at various points throughout this project. They are raised here not only by way of anticipation but because Kohut's failure to address them seems significant. Why does he never devote himself to the questions that hauntingly insist throughout his writings? One might say that he simply cannot tolerate his own insights; or that he is averse to the crisis character of late capitalism and/or confused by its alignment with hyper-integrating aspects of cultural commodification (while perhaps also enticed by both); or that such intolerance, aversion, confusion, and attraction are unavoidable in a world such as our own. So focused on undermining — digging deeper than and excavating the buried foundations of — a certain psychoanalytic doxa that he finds most pronounced in Freud and Klein, Kohut cannot, will not lift his head to raise such questions. Has he, like Oedipus, blinded himself? As with Oedipus, might such blindness manifest a terrible, unnegotiated guilt — unavowable desires (say, to usurp authority and all that is associated therewith) recirculated as the aggressive energy of their repudiation, leaving gaping holes in the field of vision that themselves recall what will not be seen? Might such self-imposed blindness manifest an unresolved Oedipal guilt about overthrowing the authority of father Freud and mother Klein and empathically merging with a field of experience that their stern and shortsighted protocols prohibit? This would be all the more unpalatable to Kohut as he is convinced that the Freudian tradition overplays the import of Oedipus, failing to discern the narcissistic disturbances with respect to which Oedipal concerns are epiphenomenal. Kohut everywhere denies that his innovations are more than "emendations." In an unswervingly conciliatory voice he insists that his proposals are strictly complementary to Freudian psychoanalysis. Doth the lady protest too much?[125] Or, subtending, alongside, or permeating such Oedipal blindness may be blindness of another sort, that brought on by narcissistic disturbances and manifesting as rigid adherence to and excessive theoretical and clinical privileging (i.e., defensive idealization) of stability, harmony, fully integrated closure, and security or their prospects? Might Kohut's clinical innovations provide the terms for a suspicion about their emphases and values?

Or, might Kohut's insistence on the need for or drive to development exhibit a powerful urge to express his uniqueness? In his terms, this insistence might well bespeak not Oedipal revolt but an insufficiently supportive community, inadequate affirmation of his unique talents and skills. Might his insistence on the ineradicability of the drive to development be, in his own terms, defensive?

When Kohut admonishes Freud for citing Adler's statement that he could not live under Freud's shadow forever as an illicit, underhanded appeal to personal matters in a theoretical debate, might this be a preemptive self-defense, an unconscious warning to his readers (himself included) not to indulge questions of psychobiography — even those his theoretical innovations make possible — in theory debates lest they be similarly chastised?

What should be clear by now are the pervasive symptoms of *intolerance* in Kohut's work; although how to interpret them remains a question. With regard to the psychoanalytic tradition as he inherits it, what Kohut particularly cannot abide are claims that we persistently seek archaic forms of gratification, as if infantile wishes were insuperable and infantile sexuality of primary clinical and theoretical significance, i.e., pleasure-seeking more pertinent than the drive to development: "the anxious clinging to the archaic selfobject and its functions was not due to a childish reluctance to give up old gratifications; instead, it was a welcome indicator that the striving to complete the development of the self had never been totally given up" (1984, 209). Where a Freudian or Kleinian may underscore anxiety, archaic expectations, and inhibited individuation (i.e., developmental stultification), generally, where the tradition would concern itself with pathogenesis, Kohut emphasizes signs of health, of resiliency. But in order to receive his patients' anxious clinging to archaic selfobjects as signs of grace, as soothing, longed for ("welcome") indications of the ineradicability of the drive for development, in order to maintain faith in the law of progress, remain receptive to the various signs that confirm his providential convictions, Kohut will have to close the gates, blind himself to specific alternative interpretations and perhaps to the abyss over which his interpretive commitments, like all others, hang: *the indeterminacy of the symptom or sign.*

What if, following Freud, Kohut were to acknowledge that early on we undergo satisfactions that are both indelibly inscribed and irreducibly indeterminate, satisfactions that become wishes and as such forever linger, repeating/recasting themselves indefinitely? What if he were to acknowledge that such wishes are both insuperable, insuperably indeterminate, and extraordinarily influential? And what if, further, he were to acknowledge along with Freud that, unavoidably, such wishes will become ambivalent and conflictual, never fully satisfiable individually or collectively? And what if, finally, he were to accept that we are driven to seek the satisfaction of such wishes irrespective of whether or not this contributes to the development of self structure? That, as far as self structure is concerned (and perhaps more broadly), we can be our own worst enemies? That, as Lacanians would put it, drives are "stupid," unconcerned with our well-being or sometimes even their own satisfaction? What wholeness, harmony, or security of self-cohesion and social integration would then be possible? Though he claims his contributions are strictly commensurate with the tradition, Kohut would not be able to follow Freud — or any other major analyst — very far without undergoing a crisis of faith: minimally, a reconsideration of the need for or drive to development; maximally, an unsettling of the hermeneutic confidence evident in psychoanalysis since Freud.

Kohut cannot abide Freud's specific articles of faith, all the less so the way he keeps seemingly incompatible commitments simultaneously in play. What Kohut cannot bear, for instance, is Freud's fervent conviction that an individual's fate is in no small part determined by the contingent undergoing of early satisfactions and her constitutional capacity to bind and organize — metabolize — them; yet this fate remains indeterminate (contingency compounded) because the *repetitive returns* to objects and arrangements that promise to satisfy the ineradicable wishes into which early satisfactions are converted proceed as an open-ended, somewhat idiosyncratic itinerary. Equally unbearable is Freud's conviction, conversely, that the sorts of satisfactions we seek are in no small part determined by a universal scheme of psychosexual development which both limits the formative force of empirical childrearing practices and unfolds irrespective of its ramifications on the development of self structure; yet though in a certain way we are developmentally driven, we forever fail to decisively develop, remain permeable to the influence of the archaic, develop semi-discrete strata rather than along a linear, completable course. Kohut cannot tolerate the tension Freud means to sustain between determinacy and indeterminacy, his efforts to simultaneously underscore our fatefully contingent undergoing of early satisfactions (too much and too consequential exposure to the empirical), our proneness to repeat, return, and change in a manner that cannot simply be called progress (too expansive or indeterminate a conception of the empirical), and our programming to develop in ways Kohut specifically contests (insufficient and incorrectly conceived exposure to the empirical).

Fated where we should be free; overly exposed to the empirical yet unable to tap its potential; separate, yet each pursuing a personal path, yet unwittingly involved in patterns not of our own design, hardly autonomous; unable to achieve clarity about whether we are merely repeating, renewing and revising, or running off course — what Kohut cannot abide is perhaps (or at least his aversion may be amplified by) the striking accord of Freud's vision with the complex contours, confusions, and convolutions of late modern capitalism. (If so, Kohut's aversive blindness may reveal something about Freud's work that he could not himself see).

Whatever their source(s), there are symptoms of intolerance everywhere. Kohut's vehemently insists that anxious clinging to archaic selfobjects and their functions expresses a striving to complete development.[126] Freud insists with equal fervor that this indicates a "reluctance to give up old gratifications." Kohut calls this reluctance "childish," defaming it and perhaps by implication Freud himself. Why such intolerance toward Freud's interpretive orientation? Is his any more firmly founded, any more therapeutically productive? Whence the vituperative tenor of Kohut's rejoinder — why go the extra step of calling this clinging "childish"? If Freud is aligned with the childish, does this suggest that Kohut has assumed the place of the father? Would not Freud suggest that such a rejection and usurpation of the authority of the father bespeaks an aggressive assault, and beneath this, a difficult love, i.e., ambivalence? Would Kohut not rejoin that Freud illicitly subsumes everything under the Oedipus complex and that ambivalence is a byproduct of narcissistic disturbances to which he is largely immune? Could not Freud then retort that Kohut's single-minded, mad drive to enthrone selfobject needs as the most archaic substratum, as the primary factor in both development and pathology, is equally subsumptive, unthinking, illicit?

Psychoanalysis has always been a *profession of faith*. With their clinical practices and research programs organized by zealous commitments to competing axioms, dogmas, and paradigms, its adherents have always been involved in something of a religious war. Might such mania be motivated, at least in part, by the equivocity of their objects? Might aversion to the irreducible ambiguity of the sign or symptom, thus to the nature of their practice, their common condition, manifest as extreme, intolerant interpretive self-assertion and closing of ranks? Might the temptation to firm and fixed belief register and repudiate haunting insecurities inherent to the "talking cure" (insecurities pertaining to interpretive indeterminacy and to who we are if our primary relation to each other and to the world is not as knowers) and perhaps amplified by social forces that bear on our simultaneous attractions to and repulsions by indeterminacy? Might — or when might? — indulgence in metaphysics, even if unavoidable, be a way of avoiding the question of who those involved in analysis *are*, what they mean to each other and why they are compelled to engage in such a practice?

Bracketing these concerns for the time being, let us press on with our exploration of Kohut's unique innovations. Kohut's theory of need gives rise to a distinctive theory of pathology. Developmental needs for narcissistic maturation are the template through which all forms of pathology are interpreted. However, Kohut underscores, though always conditioned by insufficiently empathic responses to developmental needs, pathology is not reducible to them.[127] Thus he claim, for instance, that "perversion is not caused by the existing pregenital sexual fixations but . . . is a manifestation of the need to fill a structural defect" (Kohut in Gedo and Pollock, 397). Drawing our attention to developmental depravation and its consequences, Kohut regularly speaks of the ways in which distant and understimulating parents tend to generate narcissistic personality disorders in their children. Or, conversely, he will speak of overstimulating, encroaching, smothering, or otherwise overproximate parents who tend to generate classical transference neuroses in their children.[128] For Kohut, *pathogenesis always corresponds to specific forms of selfobject failure that leave children's developmental needs unfulfilled.* E.g., nonsupport for infantile or childhood grandiosity and exhibitionism that express a need for affirmation or insufficiently affirmative (unambivalent) responses to a child's uniqueness and accomplishments give rise to too little or defensively inflated (false) self-esteem and perhaps manic perfectionism. "Self psychology is now attempting to demonstrate . . . that all forms of psychopathology are based either on defects in the structure of the self, on distortions of the self, or in weakness of the self . . . . [and] that all these flaws in the self are due to disturbances of self-selfobject relationships in childhood" (1984, 53). *But selfobject failures are not the sole causes of pathology, let alone suffering.* "[T]ransference neuroses in the classical sense . . . the classical hysterias, the phobias, and the phobic nucleus of compulsion neuroses" are not "only variants of narcissistic personality disturbance," thus are irreducible to selfobject failures (1984, 11).[129]

Pathology responds to the quality — or more precisely, the specific deficiencies — of selfobject (largely parental) empathy. It always involves an underlying sense of compromised existence, and Kohut wants to underscore this as both essential and insufficiently appreciated, but not to the point of ignoring various symptoms that seem to run in a different direction, e.g., "pathological oedipal fantasies . . . [are] a *symptomatic consequence* of the flawed selfobject response" (30; emphasis added). Not ignoring but decisively downplaying Oedipal and suchlike matters, Kohut tends to focus on and cast pathology in terms of insufficiently coherent, fragmentation-prone selves who are extremely sensitive to narcissistic slights, following which they tend to succumb to rage and/or withdrawal and seek compensatory archaic merger with an archaic selfobject, regressing from more mature forms of empathic bonding. Drive conflict and so forth plays its part in his theory of pathology, but Kohut's basic gesture is to deflate the import of classical pathogens (ambivalence, drives, conflict, etc.) in order to shed light on the selfobject conditions that are never absent from the scene of pathology — that *in some cases* are solely or at least predominantly responsible for pathology and *in all cases* determine its shape.

In sharp contrast to the Freudian tradition, Kohut contends that Oedipal configurations are derivative and contingent: "The pathogenic Oedipus complex is embedded in an oedipal self-selfobject disturbance . . . beneath lust and hostility there is a layer of depression and narcissistic rage" (1984, 5). Kohut does not want to dismiss or discount the import of the Oedipal phase or the Oedipal complex, but neither does he want to limit his research or clinical attention to them. Thus he insists that even when tackling Oedipal neuroses, the analyst must remain attentive to the role of the selfobject milieu and questions of development: "All properly conducted analyses of oedipal neuroses will eventually reveal a layer of depression and diffuse rage concerning failures of the selfobjects of the oedipal period" (1984, 5). In cases of Oedipal neurosis, the analyst is to attend to oedipal matters first, and then — or simultaneously and with increasing emphasis — turn to the consequences of selfobject failures, e.g., depression and rage. Explaining his position in greater detail, Kohut claims that

> behind the noisy manifestations of castration anxiety which lie near the psychological surface and are easily discerned, there is another deeper anxiety that is not so easily identified . . . behind the fear of castration which occurs only during a specific developmental period—albeit the oedipal period traditionally felt to play a crucial role in the pathogenesis of psychic disturbances—there is another more pervasive fear of the disintegration of the self. This latter fear is present during all stages of psychosexual development—including the oedipal stage—and it plays a vastly more significant role in the pathogenesis of psychic disturbances than the first type of anxiety. (1984, 21)

Kohut contests Freud's exaggerated focus on Oedipal phenomena, including his presumption that each analysis, if it is truly analysis, must make its way through Oedipal matters, just as he contests Klein's presumption that each analysis must address the "depression, suspicion, and rage" of earliest infancy (1984, 7). For Kohut, it is not just that we suffer from overwhelming experiences of desire or aggression or from ambivalence and drive-conflict. Rather, the very experience of desire and aggression as overwhelming or unbearably conflicted bespeaks an incompletely structured self: "the flawed selfobject matrix . . . is the breeding ground for the pathogenic Oedipus complex" (1984, 5). The Oedipus complex is a "disintegration product which assumes the presence of a noncohesive or at least enfeebled self" (1984, 10). "[C]onflict neuroses are always rooted in the soil of a damaged self . . . . selfobject failures of childhood are laid down in the deepest layers of the . . . unconscious . . . and are regarded as the ultimate genetic factor " (1984, 107).

If the self is well cared for, thus well-structured, if an individual feels confident in her value, coherent, secure in herself and (in part because) securely bonded with others, affirmed in her achievements and supported in her difficulties, the Oedipal stage may be entered joyfully; affection and assertiveness rather than lust and destructiveness will be its primary characteristics; there will be no Oedipus complex.

Pouncing in haste on what seemed so profound, first in himself, then in the clinical and cultural phenomena to which he devoted his attention, Freud, on Kohut's conception, is blinded by his insight. Evident everywhere once its basic structure is elucidated, the radiant brilliance of the Oedipal complex offers itself to Freud's equally brilliant theorization, but such brilliance is a lure to complacency, thus, paradoxically, the shadow of ignorance. The Oedipus must be given its due: "If a self has attained . . . nondefensive structural completeness but is still unable to enact its intrinsic program [i.e., secure its basic ideals and ambitions] because its energies are consumed by unresolved oedipal conflicts, then oedipal conflicts will be mobilized in the psychoanalytic situation, and an oedipal transference will offer itself to be worked through" (1984, 5; bracketed comments added). But this need not mean that analysis must concentrate as intensely on Oedipal matters as it has. Turning the tables on the tradition's melancholic disposition, insisting that we are inclined to affection and assertiveness given good-enough caregiving (rather than, say, only as sublimations), Kohut sees himself as something of an iconoclast vis-à-vis Freudian and Kleinian hegemony.[130] Because they are so obtrusively obvious and so problematic, lust and destructiveness have, on Kohut's account, unduly monopolized analytic attention; he seeks our liberation from traditional fixations.

At this point, a few more words can be said about the distinctive structure of Kohut's perspective, its unique amalgamation of blindness and insight, its inflationary and deflationary trends. By deflating Freudian, Kleinian, etc. claims about the all-pervasiveness of sexuality and aggression and the havoc they wreak, Kohut is able to insist upon the contingency, the essential reparability, of *all* pathological formations (Oedipal conflict neurosis, perversions, psychoses, etc.) and inflate both the pathogenic import and wholesome potential of self-selfobject relations. Perhaps even more so than ego psychologists, Kohut maintains a firm belief in the capacity of each individual, no matter what she has suffered, to develop to the point of nondefensive structural completion, thus to focus her energy and attention on realizing her core ambitions. Despite abandoning much of Freud's theory of energetics, Kohut's perspective is guided by a belief that, energetically, human life is a zero-sum game: either our energy is devoted to the realization of core ambitions or it is consumed by pathology. His confidence in our potential for self-determination is conditioned by what, from another perspective, may seem like a tranquilizing collusion with the ideology of individualism, or at least a self-imposed blindness to the persistence of the disruptive, destabilizing, anxiety-inducing influence of the unconscious, sexuality, aggression, and/or contemporary social conditions.

(1) Deflation of sexuality, aggression, excess. When it comes to average parents, Kohut claims, it is only "during periods of temporary self disturbance" that they will "respond with a degree of sexuality to their child's affection" (1984, 15). Likewise, "normal nonsexual affection and normal nonhostile, nondestructive assertiveness" will prevail in the child unless s/he is mistreated (1984, 24). What many — ranging from Ferenczi to Lacan — would consider an Edenic ideal is, for Kohut, the norm. Here the norm is not the empirically probable — Kohut acknowledges the demographic prevalence of narcissistic disturbances and Oedipal neuroses — but what can and should obtain. Tendentially refusing to read affection as sublimated sexuality or, say, strivings for independence and "creative-productive" efforts as sublimated aggression, blinding himself to the signs of sexuality and aggression that Freud and Klein detect everywhere, Kohut develops a secure conviction in his comparatively tame and rosy vision of familial relations and human motivation.[131] Specifically, this deflation of sexuality and aggression allows him to maintain faith in prospects for harmony and security both within ourselves and in our relations to others. Like Hartmann, Kohut assumes an essential integrability between self and world — his sights are set on prospects for assimilation with little to no remainder.

In affinity with the ego psychological tradition, Kohut is a great thinker of ordinary achievement. While Freud and Klein's attention are keyed to disturbance, distortion, aberration, and seemingly intractable difficulty, Kohut's is keyed to the creative, productive, self-realizing accomplishments of the well-enough cared for. He is captivated by moments of relatively smooth functioning, and thus to a degree blind to (or just not so concerned with) the excesses, out of place behaviors or affects, slips, exaggerated conflicts, unwanted but nonetheless undertaken or unintelligible patterns of behavior, etc. that Freud, Klein, and others read as signs of sexuality, aggression, phantasy, and anxiety.

By inflating questions of development — to a degree, like Hartmann, assuming a technological perspective on the human, but much more concerned with whether adaptive functioning is meaningful, personally fulfilling — and downplaying traditional concerns with drives, the unconscious, phantasies, and so forth, i.e., forces and structures that work in or through us, perhaps informing but irreducible to our intentions, Kohut's faith in our prospects for self-determination remains secure. Kohut's primary focus is not on the drives and their fates, but on the (formally constrained) impact of contingent, empirical self-selfobject relations; not on the passionate surging of mutually incompatible, ineradicable wishes by which we are thrown off-kilter, overwhelmed and overtaxed, propelled into complex acts of sublimation and compromise formation, and with which we have to constantly negotiate, but on the development of wholesome, harmonious, integral, and non-defensively complete self structure and relations to others. Given an adequate upbringing and good-enough selfobject relations throughout life, the self will be secure in her relations to others and to herself, predominantly focused on realizing her "basic program," her core ambitions. Kohut correctly perceives that sexuality, aggression, the unconscious, and phantasy are, for most of the psychoanalytic tradition, forces or sources of excess. From his perspective, their import has been much overplayed.

(2) Deflation of phantasy and anxiety. Likewise, Kohut will not corroborate the traditional thesis that we are inherently (Klein) or inevitably (Freud) given to overstimulating or terrifying (anxiety producing) phantasies. Rather, he insists, sexual or hostile phantasies and their incumbent anxieties are the contingent byproducts of faulty selfobject relations. Only when parental pathology interferes with provisioning for a child's basic selfobject needs will we find

> [i]nstead of the further development of a firmly cohesive self able to feel the glow of healthy pleasure in its affectionate and phase-appropriate sexual functioning and able to enjoy self-confident assertiveness in the pursuit of goals . . . a continuing propensity to experience fragments of love (sexual fantasies) rather than love and the fragments of assertiveness (hostile fantasies) rather than assertiveness and to respond to these experiences . . . . with anxiety. (1984, 25)

Fantasy is but a fragment, a shard of what should have been and may yet be whole.[132] Elsewhere, Kohut speaks of "[p]athogenic sexual fantasies *replacing* the former joyful warmth" (1984, 30; emphasis added). It is a tradeoff: either adequate care and joyful warmth *or* inadequate care and sexual and/or aggressive fantasy. Although Kohut primarily focuses on childhood when making such claims, presumably he would disagree with, say, Freud's conviction that ordinary misery is the most we can hope for, Klein's contention that oscillation between paranoid/schizoid and depressive anxieties is irreducible, or Adornoian worries that the coldness of life under conditions of late liberal capitalism (mutual disinterest and mutual instrumentalization) devastates what chances for joyful warmth and coherent self-assertion there may "objectively" be, making a mockery, indeed an ideology, of such natural possibilities.

(3) Righting all wrongs. As we have seen, in Kohut's estimation, "the healthy child of healthy parents enters the oedipal phase joyfully" rather than overridden by disturbing or pathogenic covetousness and death-wishes (1984, 14). "Only if . . . parents do not function appropriately as oedipal selfobjects will the child experience high degrees of anxiety" (1984, 14).[133] Given adequate rearing, the self will be strong and cohesive enough to expe-

rience the drives as elements of its core motivational system: "if the self is healthy, the drives are experienced not in an isolated fashion but as an immanent modality of this healthy self" (1984, 208); "in the presence of a firm self, conflict per se is by no means deleterious, not even the largely unconscious conflict to which traditional analysis assigns the causative role in the psychogenesis of psychopathology" (1984, 45). If the self is well structured, healthy, "*pathogenic* conflicts will not arise, however great our pain, however absorbing our struggles"; presumably, difficult relations with others will be experienced and engaged as temporary problems likely to be resolved (dissolved or at least brought to a pragmatic closure), and quickly (1984, 208). Though astutely attentive to the difficulty of breaking cycles of pathology (pathological parents have trouble meeting their children's basic needs and so tend to raise pathological children, who in turn tend to raise pathological children, and so on [cf. 1984, 24]) and (at least intermittently) aware of the social conditions that promote narcissistic disturbances, Kohut insists, contra Adorno, that damaged life *can* be lived rightly. Damage can be repaired, harmony and joy reclaimed. Undauntedly enthusiastic about our interlocking prospects for personal integrity and social harmony, for uncompromised happiness, Kohut, while not simply oblivious to the difficulties and dissonances we will inevitably face, renders them as resources for expressive self-assertion, or at worst, temporary trials likely to be passed through with grace. Conflicts and confusions become but catalysts for the reassertion of the healthy self, a self perpetually seeking and regularly achieving reconciliation, a self set upon what seems a providential path. All encompassing, Kohut's optimistic enthusiasm, his anti-tragic orientation, is so strong as to suggest mania, and thus, perhaps, melancholy.[134]

The question, now, is: how does analysis work, how does it cure? That is, what makes analysis truly analysis? In all likelihood, Kohut would contest the form of the question. His claim would likely be that asking how analysis cures is different from asking after what makes analysis truly analysis. Insisting that what he inherits from Freud, and what defines the field of psychoanalysis, is methodology, not doctrinal content or specific clinical techniques, Kohut contends that what makes analysis truly analysis is empathy and vicarious introspection. These are ingredients of the cure, but the cure is irreducible to them; how analysis cures is complex, but what makes analysis truly analysis is quite simple. In unmistakably blunt terms, Kohut claims: "empathy is the operation that defines the field of psychoanalysis" (1984, 174). Elsewhere he states that "empathic observation of the experiences of . . . analysands in the analytic situation" is "the fundamental context from which all explanations derive" (1984, 4) and even goes so far as to say that "[w]e designate phenomena as mental, psychic or psychological if our mode of observation includes introspection and empathy as an essential constituent" (Kohut 1959, 462). Empathy, for Kohut, is the methodological basis for all of his claims (indeed, for all valid claims) about early development, mental health, and the cure; presumably, it is the basis for Kohut's definition of the self and its needs from which, he claims, his theories and techniques are deduced (1984, 4). In relation to his specific therapeutic procedure, Kohut specifies that selfobjects are "observable only via introspection and empathy" (1984, 50).

Empathy, to be clear, is not the same as compassion. Thus Kohut differs from those such as Ferenczi who prioritize clinical expressions of sympathy. Making this contrast clear, Kohut underscores that empathy is a method for objective data-gathering (1971, 300; 1977, 304-5; 1980, 458-59; 1984, 158). However, in line with Ferenczi, he suggests that certain clients will experience neutrality as a repetition of early deprivation, thus in practice he is often far from reserved. Empathy is the cultivated double perspective wherein one "attempt[s] to . . . experience the inner life of another while simultaneously retaining the stance of an objective observer" (1984, 175).[135]

Certain of these comments seem to commit Kohut to psychoanalytic pluralism in a big way, even to the point of capaciousness so expansive as to become vacuous. If not only selfobject relations but all "mental, psychic, or psychological" phenomena are disclosed through observations that include "introspection and empathy as an essential constituent," and "empathy is the operation that defines the field of psychoanalysis," then it would seem that *any* investigation of mental, psychic, or psychological phenomena is, by definition, psychoanalysis, and disciplines that presume to treat of mental, psychic, or psychological phenomena but do not employ a mode of observation that "includes introspection and empathy as an essential constituent" (say, neuroscience or certain strands of epistemology or behaviorism) are categorically deluded, not really concerned with mental, psychic, or psychological phenomena. What a peculiar blend of tolerance and intolerance this would be. Only psychoanalysis investigates what is properly designated mental, psychic, or psychological; and anything psychoanalysis (properly conducted) investigates is properly designated mental, psychic, or psychological? Unlikely. Worries over what seem peculiar feats of definitional fiat will be allayed once, first, we note that when Kohut claims that "[w]e designate phenomena as mental, psychic, or psychological if our mode of observation includes introspection and empathy as an essential constituent," he likely means to state a sufficient but not necessary condition for such designation (he does not say "if and only if"), and second, we recall that Kohut holds that "empathic observation of the experiences of . . . analysands *in the analytic situation*" is "the fundamental context from which all explanations derive." Here, Kohut seems to be committing himself to the strong claim that psychoanalytic knowledge is medium-bound, irrevocably bonded to the clinical context; in which case not just any investigation that employs empathy and introspection as an essential constituent is genuinely psychoanalytic but only those that proceed within a properly maintained clinical setting (however this is understood) and refrain from appealing to data or reflections not directly emergent from it.

There is certainly something off-balance in Kohut's attempt to define analysis. His vision expands and contracts. He wavers between various forms of unrestricted openness and essentialism, constantly overcorrecting, thus returning to the difficulties he thought he had surmounted. I take it that Kohut does not mean to commit himself to the abovementioned absurdities and that he is not all that interested in forwarding the medium-bound thesis; he just means to foreground the primacy of empathy in psychoanalysis and clear away its doctrinal detritus. But if we ask what it means to acknowledge the primacy of empathy in psychoanalysis, what accepting empathy "as an essential constituent" of the practice concretely amounts to, we will find that, for Kohut, analysis is not just any investigation that employs empathy but a very specific and highly regulated therapeutic procedure. As we will see, Kohut's manifest commitments to psychoanalytic pluralism conceal a number of resolute convictions concerning what makes for genuine analysis. Though he may deny it, I take it that for Kohut there are a set of practices that make analysis truly analysis.

On Kohut's conception, analysis ought predominantly concern itself with establishing and maintaining an empathic bond between analyst and analysand. On this basis, the analyst will be able to intensify and bring to the analysand's awareness her selfobject needs, fulfill them to some degree, provoke transmuting internalization of the needed function, and thereby usher the development of self structure to its completion whereupon the client can focus on realizing her core ideals and ambitions.[136]

To put it most schematically, analysis must proceed through three steps: analysis of defenses, unfolding and interpretation of transference, and establishment of empathic attunement between self and selfobject on mature levels. Or formulated in more classical terms, analysis proceeds through two phases: understanding (experience-near data gathering) and explanation (experience-far genetic reconstruction).[137]

The distinctiveness of Kohutian therapy cannot be appreciated at this level of abstraction, so let us turn to the details. Transference, Kohut assumes, ordinarily repeats development in reverse, thus, first, if there are any surface conflicts (Oedipal neuroses, etc.), analysis is to focus on them and facilitate their working through in more or less the classical manner (defense analysis in the context of a general refraining from interpretation, especially deep interpretation, during the early stages of analysis with the aim of facilitating the unfolding of free associations; then increasingly frequent and wide-ranging interpretation and facilitation of the analysand's reintegration or renegotiation of defensively repudiated material; then genetic reconstruction). The only major differences between Kohut and Freud at this point are that (1)

Kohut *may* speak of phase-specific selfobject needs and their nonfulfillment in his interpretations of Oedipal neuroses; (2) he *may* emphasize the joy or warmth experienced prior to letdown by oedipal selfobjects in order to pave the way for its resurgence; (3) unlike Freud, Kohut considers the goal of Oedipal analysis to be the transformation of the fragmentary oedipal self (overridden by incestuous sexuality and destructiveness) into the integrated oedipal self (affectionate/bonded and assertive/individuated), thus he may conduct this stage of analysis somewhat differently than would Freud or at least be differently inclined with regard to what is considered an indication of its completion; and (4) he considers selfobject failures to be the "basic pathogen[s]," thus will press on with the analysis well past the resolution of Oedipal and suchlike conflicts, that is, until these failures and the narcissistic disturbances to which they have given rise have been remedied (1984, 5). While Freud aims to return his analysands to love *and* work, that is, to ordinary misery, Kohut means to press further, his efforts coming to an end only when his analysands are capable of *loving work*.

Once Oedipal conflicts and like matters are resolved — or sometimes as a component of the analysis of Oedipal conflicts slowly gaining in frequency and intensity — the analyst is to attend to underlying selfobject needs: "after working through repressive oedipal material, the beginnings of a joyfully entered oedipal stage can be discerned and the revival of the faulty responsive oedipal selfobjects of childhood become evident via the patient's transference experiences" (1984, 68). At this point, the first move is to remobilize developmental needs, or more precisely, to acknowledge the developmental needs yet pressing forth for fulfillment, however stealthily, and support their burgeoning intensity. Only when these needs are sufficiently intense and consistently interpreted as such will the analysand come to believe, as she must and in a certain way wants to, that these are in fact her *needs*, thereby becoming primed to seek their fulfillment. To this end, the analyst is to support the client's efforts to verbalize her needs, not just to name them but to acknowledge their urgency, however dampened, their centrality, however concealed, their overriding and objective import. As we saw earlier, Kohut firmly believes that "[t]he patient protects the defective self so that it will be ready to grow again in the future, to continue to develop from the point in time at which its development had been interrupted. And it is this recognition . . . that best prepares the soil for the developmental move forward that the stunted self of the analysand actively craves" (1984, 141). To be sure, the analysand's recognition of her urge (need or drive) to complete development takes awhile to prepare. In this early stage, the analysand may suffer from deficient self structure, thus may be prone to rage, withdrawal, and/or fragmentation. If so, her self structure will have to be supported if s/he is to feel secure enough to begin to come to terms with the weight, vulnerability, and urgency of *need*, which means with its parental disappointment (which is often, Kohut says, the consequence of parental pathology) and the consequent sense of self-diminishment or derealization. To this end, the analyst is to remain empathically attuned to the analysand, offering her the basic sense of security that goes along with feeling understood, emotionally accompanied. More precisely, as Modell puts it, "the analyst is constant and reliable; he responds to the patient's affect; he accepts the patient, and his judgment is less critical and more benign; he is there primarily for the patient's needs and not for his own; he does not retaliate; and he does at times have a better grasp of the patient's inner psychic reality than does the patient himself and therefore may clarify what is bewildering and confusing" (Modell 1976, 291; let it be noted that Modell is not a Kohutian). Only once a secure empathic bond is established, only when the client feels sufficiently safe and held, can the analyst focus on framing her function in the transference as the object of needed selfobject responses and thereby help the analysand accept her specific needs, her broad need for growth, and the failures of her caregivers to provide what was needed. Thus the analyst must maintain her empathic connection with the client and continue to validate the client's needs, for through these acts of empathy, as later through more frequent interpretations that make the analysand feel understood, held and connected, the analyst cultivates the analysand's conviction that the therapeutic space can contain her needs, that these needs can be experienced without breaking down or falling to pieces and that, eventually, these needs can be managed otherwise, even met. Through consistent empathy and validation, and later through interpretation, the analyst injects hope into a desolate and despairing self.

In the next stage, the analyst seeks to fulfill the client's developmental needs and thereby develop her self structure to the point where she will be receptive and appropriately responsive to interpretations of her needs and of the regressive aims and defensive functions of her fantasies and defenses, interpretations which mean to further facilitate the development of self structure. Kohut's explicit — though certainly partial — abandonment of the nongratification principle in favor of inhabiting the developmental role transferentially projected as the deficient source of now stunted development indicates that he is less concerned with orchestrating opportunities for insight (nongratification is often used to intensify conflicts and bring them to the foreground whereupon they may be more readily recognized; this may seem less imperative to Kohut due to his convictions that analysands actively crave development, needs are objective, and empathy is a valid method for their elucidation) than with the potential for analytic neutrality to retraumatize the patient and thereby suppress reactivated developmental needs.

Once needs are sufficiently amplified and defenses are sufficiently diminished, and once it is established that the analyst can and will consistently, however minimally, meet the client's needs through empathic responsiveness — empathy goes some way in fulfilling *all* basic needs — and perhaps through other measures such as affirming the analysand's accomplishments or expressing some joy in her presence, the analyst will set about *failing* to meet the client's needs in a very specific way. The analyst must fail optimally, that is, at just the right time and to just the right extent that the client will begin to internalize the needed function (transmuting internalization). "Each optimal failure will be followed by an increase in the patient's resilience vis-à-vis empathy failures both inside and outside the analytic situation; that is, after each, optimal new self structures will be acquired and existing ones will be firmed" (1984, 69). For instance, by temporarily failing to affirm the client's achievements in a generally affirmative atmosphere, the analyst promotes the client's efforts to develop and sustain self-esteem; or by mildly disappointing the client in the calm milieu of analytic empathy, the client is induced to develop self-soothing structure. By failing well, time and again, to meet the client's needs in the context of a well-established expectation that the analyst can and will (to some extent) provide for these needs, the analyst encourages the gradual accretion of self structure. At this stage of therapy, the analyst will often draw attention to her successes and failures in fostering development.[138]

Throughout the analysis, though with varying intensity, (1) empathic affirmation will be employed to secure the client's capacity for self-affirmation and sense of integrity (the coherent self is mirrored into being) and (2) transference and resistance will be interpreted. On Kohut's understanding, resistance is motivated not so much by early conflicts and hyper-cathected commitments to the early compromises into which they issue, or by anxiety over negotiating with wishes, fears, beliefs, and expectations or elements of oneself long held defensively at bay, but by the fear and often the experience of retraumatization via empathic failure. Resistances are particularly prevalent during the more interpretation-heavy phases of analysis and are received as signals of interpretive error. In a way, resistances are salutary signs inasmuch as they reveal what needs are pressing forth and the specific sorts of failures to which they have been subject: resistances, for Kohut, signal sensitivities to traumatic disappointments once experienced, providing a fairly clear picture of the analysand's past. Much like Winnicott, Kohut maintains that inaccurate, poorly timed, too blunt, or dogmatically rigid interpretations will be experienced as repetitions of failures in the early care environment, and because some such failures are inevitable, so are resistances. Unlike Winnicott, however, Kohut claims that resistances signal a retreat from more mature empathic connectedness and are often followed by regression — temporary reversion to archaic selfobject needs such as that for fusion with an ideal figure or idea, or for perfect mirroring. In order to bring the analysand back to her previously attained level of development, the analyst must acknowledge her interpretive mistake and then interpret the dynamics of retreat.

Kohut's conviction in the insuperability of our striving for development, thus his confidence in the possibility of successful analysis, is largely dependent on — or expressed in — his distinctive conception of transference. On this conception, inadequately fulfilled basic needs express themselves in three fundamental forms of transference: mirroring transference, idealizing transference, and twinship transference. In these transferences, needs are remobilized: when they are accepted, encouraged, and to some degree met by the analyst (optimal frustration), they can be acknowledged by the analysand *as needs*, following which they can be interpreted, their significance and that of their ill-provisioning eventually explained (genetic reconstruction). More precisely, engaging mirror transference means engaging (partially providing for and interpreting) the analysand's damaged ambitions and continuing attempts to elicit approving selfobject responses. Here, the analyst will focus on understanding and reflecting back to the analysand the latter's experience of herself, specifically, her excitements and disappointments. The intended effect is a sense of personal substantiality, of "feeling real." Engaging idealizing transference means engaging the analysand's damaged ideals, her need for a figure that will accept idealization and some degree of merger with his or her greatness, calmness, and strength. Rather than analyzing, in the sense of dissolving, the patient's experience of the analyst's magnificence and perfection (e.g., as positive transference or defensive idealization), s/he will accept it for some time (unless of course it becomes excessive, an impediment to therapeutic progress). Engaging twinship or alter ego transference means engaging the analysand's damaged talents and skills and her searching for reassuring experiences of essential alikeness.[139]

Transferentially expressed needs insist until they are adequately met and the function for which they express a need is sufficiently internalized; this, for Kohut, is the telltale signal that they are truly needs. Thus throughout the course of therapy, the analyst will again and again reactivate (intensify) basic needs, for this, coupled with their optimal frustration and transmuting internalization of the needed function(s), will secure the client's ability to sustain herself with the aid of selfobject resources available in an average, expectable environment. As self structure accretes as a result of properly conducted analysis, the client becomes better able to identify and more eager to seek out mirroring and idealizable selfobjects elsewhere. Only once relations with such selfobjects are secured outside of analysis will the analysand's defensive attitudes, fantasies, and character structures, along with maladaptive behavioral dispositions provoked by unfulfilled basic needs, tend to dissolve.

Finally, once sufficient self structure and its social support system is securely established and defenses are largely dissolved, the analyst will draw attention to the most archaic stratum, to "the lethargies, depressions, and rages of early life" manifest in transference, and analyze the traumatic self-

selfobject relationships that gave rise to them (1984, 5). This opens the way for genetic reconstruction and the gradual termination of the analysis.

Kohut is convinced that deviations from this particular protocol will limit the efficacy of analysis — especially with regard to its true aims, but also, likely, with regard to any aims whatsoever — because they will repeat pathogenic selfobject failures and retrench deficits of self structure. Implying a soft criticism of Freud, an oblique criticism of Klein, and a severe criticism of ego psychology, bent as it is on enhancing reality testing, Kohut claims that

> [t]o *hammer away* at the analysand's transference distortion brings no results; it only confirms the analysand's conviction that the analyst is as dogmatic, as utterly unsure of himself, as walled off in the self-righteousness of a *distorted view* as the pathogenic parents (or other selfobject) had been. Only the analyst's continuing sincere acceptance of the patient's reproaches as (psychologically) realistic, followed by a prolonged (and ultimately successful) attempt to look into himself and remove the inner barriers that stand in the way of his empathic grasp of the patient, ultimately have a chance to turn the tide. (1984, 182; emphases added)

Freudian insistence on Oedipal matters, Kleinian insistence on anxiety-infused paranoid phantasies and depressive object attachments, Adlerian insistence on birth trauma, Lacanian insistence on the liberation of desire from its Imaginary captivity, or, generally, *insistence of whatever kind* (except, presumably, on the fundamental significance of developmental needs and their faulty provisioning, but even this can be insisted on too strongly or at the wrong moment), will be experienced as a repetition of selfobject failures:

> By insisting that his analysand's disease conform to the specific mold that he holds to be universal and by insisting, furthermore, that the analysand submit to the particular procrustean therapeutic process that the analyst considers the sine qua non of true analysis — be it the resolution of the Oedipus complex, the reliving of the emotions of the paranoid-depressive position, the abreaction of the trauma of birth, the reexperiencing of an early injury to the self, or any other theory-limited panacea — the analyst who undertakes such an attempt puts obstacles in the patient's path to recovery. (1984, 45-6)

Elsewhere, Kohut expresses the same reservations about dogmatic rigidity and heavy-handed interpretations, urging open-minded listening and specifying that

> By listening open-mindedly, I mean that [the analyst] must resist the temptation to squeeze his understanding of the patient into the rigid mold of whatever theoretical preconceptions he may hold, be they Kleinian, Rankian, Jungian, Adlerian, classical-analytic, or yes, self-psychological, until he has more accurately grasped the essence of the patient's need [does this effectively amount

> to a disavowal of the previous self-implicating concession?] and can convey his understanding to the patient via a more correct interpretation. . . theories must be the helpmates of the observer, not the masters. (1984, 67)[140]

In a similar vein, Kohut iconoclastically announces that "*all* analysts, including Freud, may be said to have been beginners" (1984, 115). Notice again the ambivalence of Kohut's self-implication in his critique of dogmatism: "all analysts," including himself, "may be said" — ambivalence mounts — "to *have been* beginners" — disavowal accomplished. Elsewhere he seems to declare allegiance to psychoanalytic pluralism: "[t]he particular theories that Freud's ordering mind instituted are particular theories. He may be the Newton of psychoanalysis. He undoubtedly is. But this doesn't mean that there are not other ways of ordering data" (Kohut in Kirsner 1982, 492).

Such remarks are curious. On the one hand, in all but the first, Kohut clearly implicates his theory of pathology and clinical practice in his critique of monolithic interpretive aggression. Is not insisting on "the reexperiencing of an early injury to the self" exactly what Kohut has in mind? But on the other hand, it is only on the basis of self psychological commitments that Kohut can claim that various interpretive insistences will be experienced as repetitions of selfobject failures. And he claims to explain how *the* psychoanalytic cure works, not just self psychology's idiosyncratic ambitions, implying that analysts, if they are to help their patients to the best of their abilities, must conform to his clinical protocols and emphases.[141] With more than a little hubris, Kohut claims that anyone who has achieved "a degree of therapeutic mastery" will rarely look at drives, wishes, and the defenses against them; rather, they will provide empathic security through emotionally resonating interpretations and other measures (1984, 115). Though all analysts "have been beginners," those that follow self psychological procedures presumably can become *masters*. As Kohut understands it, his description of self psychological technique is an account of what analysis at its best, at root, or in its essence — in some sense, "proper analysis" — has been doing all along: "traditional psychoanalysis . . . has *always* achieved its success via the three-step process that I have laid out" (1984, 104). Likewise, he understands his theory of pathology as the one true theory that accounts for the successes and failures, accuracies and inaccuracies of all the others.

So, in one respect, Kohut is a profound pluralist, a pundit of particularity cautioning against the illicit — counterproductive and unthinking — subsumption of clinical material into formulas and protocols that are rigid and reductive, creativity- and sensitivity-stultifying, thus increasingly difficult to destabilize or even discern. Along these lines, but also expressing firm fidelity to the core commitments of self psychology, Kohut claims that often what is crucial in an interpretation is not its specific content, which may be phrased in a Freudian, Kleinian, or any other psychoanalytic idiom, but the essential message of empathic attunement, a message that analysts of all persuasions are regularly able to convey. The specific phrasing of the interpretation, its determinate content, is described as the "nonspecific carrier" of its essential message (1984, 94). Further deflating the import of interpretive content, Kohut claims that in many cases the essential message is conveyed transverbally — through a general sense that something of the patient's suffering has been understood, even if it is expressed in terms the patient would not choose. Thus, in another respect, Kohut is a staunch dogmatist: the essential message of any decent interpretation is, ultimately, its empathic attunement to selfobject needs and their deprivations. Analysts have been speaking in self psychological terms all along, just unawares, thus without sufficient refinement, or one might even say unconsciously if one suspects that Kohut is positioning himself as the analyst of analysis. In any case, his critique of subsumption conceals a higher order subsumption, his manifest pluralism the congenial emissary of a thinly veiled, conversion inclined essentialism.

These issues come to a head in an exemplary passage where Kohut claims that even though what should be at stake is not a name, "analytic" or "nonanalytic," there is reason to submit to what he describes as the "pressure" or what we might describe as the *temptation* to "leave science behind" and "affirm that it would be quite justifiable to reserve the name 'analytic' *only* for those emotive results that come about via the *complete* understanding-explaining sequence [as he understands it], that is, via *accurate* understanding followed by dynamic-genetic interpretation" (1984, 104; emphases and brackets added).

With the relation between Kohut's manifest pluralism and subtending dogmatism in view, his distinctive structure of attention and argumentative procedure can be further clarified. Kohut manifestly focuses on and prioritizes the structure and function rather than content — e.g., the functional aptitudes and deficiencies of the self rather than the content of drive-conflict or phantasy, the structure of the self delimited by the three fundamental forms of transference rather than the content of free associations, and the bearing of interpretations on self structure and function rather than their content. But in the end, he insists on the import of content. The analyst must "resist the temptation to squeeze his understanding of the patient into the rigid mold of whatever theoretical preconceptions he may hold . . . *until he has more accurately grasped the essence of the patient's need and can convey his understanding to the patient via a more correct interpretation.*" That is, via self psychological technique and only thereby, "essence" can be "grasped," at which point the analyst may cede to the temptation, which is no longer a temptation but a rational obligation, to slot clinical material into the "mold" of a particular "theoretical preconception," namely Kohut's; and because such a grasp of the essential facilitates or just amounts to "more correct interpretation," this slotting will not involve "squeezing" and the template into which clinical material smoothly slides will not be a mere theoretical preconception but a validated classificatory scheme. "[T]heories must be the helpmates of the observer, not the masters," but the discovery of the essence of need is the discovery of impersonal truths, our true masters. *Need is the stable referent against which interpretations can be measured.* Kohut's account of developmental need situates all other versions of psychoanalysis as concerned with mere parts of a whole he has finally discovered, as confusing the effects of ill-provisioned selfobject needs with the causes of pathology, as clinically focused on the superstructural symptoms of the *basic* needs of the self: "the old theories of the analytic cure, although correct within their respective frames of reference, were incomplete" (1984, 75). "*All* analysts, including Freud, may be said to *have been* beginners," and many still are only beginners, i.e., only implicitly and haphazardly following the correct procedure, but Kohut's innovations mark the final culmination of analytic development: following him, in principle, analysts are no longer beginners.

Everywhere in Kohut's work, what is at issue is the insistence of faith (matters may not be so different in other cases). When Kohut *insists* — as we have seen, he says much the same on a number of occasions — that "[b]y *insisting* that his analysand's disease conform to the specific mold that he holds to be universal and by *insisting*, furthermore, that the analysand submit to the particular procrustean therapeutic process that the analyst considers the sine qua non of true analysis . . . the analyst . . . puts obstacles in the patient's path to recovery," to what extent is dogmatic and dominating insistence at issue as opposed to incorrectness, the wrong sort of insistence? To be sure, Kohut's quiet but decisive insistence on his own therapeutic and hermeneutic protocols is motivated, at least in part, by the disconcerting impatience of analysts bent on confirming, or just reasserting, the propriety of their procedures and by the harm (relative infelicity of analysis or worse) inflicted on patients when they do so. These worries are well worth considering. But so too is the extent to which Kohut's *faith in need* insulates his reflections from the criticisms he levels at others and what the consequences of their reflexive (re)turn would be.

What if anything would interrupt Kohut's faith that because needs are needs, they will unfold in transference without the analyst having to insist on them much, if at all. So long as the analyst maintains and occasionally modulates the empathic bond in a nonthreatening atmosphere, Kohut insists, the specific shape of the analysand's basic needs will become apparent to both analyst and analysand — though for a long while more perspicuously to the former — and the analysand will soon feel sufficiently secure to reexperience the force of her needs and see their fulfillment in and beyond analysis. This is an automatic, a law of transference. Kohut takes himself to have discovered in narcissistic transferences a portal to the past which is at once a providential path to a healthy, harmonious future: through transference analysis, the analyst will expose exactly what the client needed, from whom, i.e., what the specific shape of development-stalling deprivation was, and what is needed to remedy this deficient self structure. His faith is as insistent and unswerving as the (properly tended) drive to development.

Kohut is aware that pathologizing other perspectives invites attempts to turn the tables but cannot consider such gestures in good faith; his response will be adamant self-assertion. Thus he claims, for instance, that "interpretations of infantile seductive and aggressive behavior . . . that fall back on a theory of the narcissistic transferences as defensive will be experienced by patients as subtly censorious and disapproving" (1984, 91). His claim is that analysts who treat narcissistic transferences as resistances to "the truth" of infantile sexuality and aggressiveness will cause their patients to feel once again admonished for their *real* needs — let down, abandoned, existentially insulted. Absent acknowledgement, validation, and some measure of gratification of the developmental needs at issue, analysis will be experienced as repeating the selfobject failures at the root of the client's suffering: "By failing to acknowledge the validity and legitimacy of the patient's demands for development-enhancing selfobject responses . . . the analyst fails the patient in the same way the parent had failed" (1984, 173). With and against Lacan,[142] Kohut insists that the analyst *must not refuse the (right) demand,* that when the analysand expresses interest in overcoming her developmental deficit, the analyst must acknowledge both the specific need-deprivation and the continuing need to complete development. *Only self psychology speaks the truth of analysis*, that is, articulates the essence of analysis, elaborates it in various ways while showing that its plurality bespeaks an essential underlying truth. Deviations risk collusion with pathology, thus heretics must be converted. But how is this to be undertaken?

If we do not share Kohut's faith that the needs upon which he alights are universal, sequential, and invariable, and that they are bound to manifest in transference, specifically, in the reverse order of their onset; if we are committed to or at least willing to entertain other conceptions of therapy, are compelled by other concerns and differently disposes in our emphases; if Kohut's hermeneutic and therapeutic protocols are not self-validating, as he presumes; if Kohut faith is not as contagious as he supposes, then what are we to do? What could we say to him, or he to us?

If there is never commitment without faith (credo, credit), the questions are: (1) how to inspire faith? and (2) how to engage those disposed differently in their faith? How is faith motivated and modulated? How to effect a conversion or reconversion? Ironically, for all its tendential aversion to religion, sustained engagement with questions of faith seems highly significant for psychoanalytic theory and practice. Minimally, engaging such questions will require rethinking the simplified dichotomy of science and practices of faith; it may even project a path to a future beyond the illusion of scientism.

Unfortunately, with regard to such questions and trajectories, Kohut is of little help. With regard to the question of how to motivate faith in his convictions, Kohut is particularly unhelpful. When, perhaps coming to feel reckless or unproductive, or just running out of steam, insistent self-assertion comes to a halt, Kohut claims that others will come to see the value and validity of his insights only if — but not necessarily if — they put them into practice in the clinic. He asks for a leap of faith — as if, at root, psychoanalytic commitments border on the ineffable. Especially in the latter sections of *How Does Analysis Cure?* Kohut explicitly affirms that the validity of his claims cannot be publicly/discursively demonstrated; the issue is to be decided only by analysts giving self psychological protocols a chance in their own practices. In the end, Kohut enters a Pascalian plea for consideration, nothing more. He knows that faith cannot be forced; it is either clinical credence or nothing. Though there is something instructive in his balking at the demand for discursive demonstration, here he goes too far, hastily closing the door on questions of how to make commitments to psychoanalysis culturally persuasive, how to support one's commitments to psychoanalysis in an age under the ascendancy of science, and how commitments to psychoanalysis can be authorized other than first-personally. In Kohut's estimation, all psychoanalysis can do is leave the social to itself and get to work. One certainly hopes for more.

With Kohutian self psychology, what we find inflated are (1) empirical developmental needs, (2) the significance and motivational force of developing personally meaningful, vital and authentic life practices, (3) the selfobject matrix, (4) the etiological and clinical significance of narcissism, (5) the efficacy of empathic attunement, (6) the urgency and significance of redevelopment, and (7) optimism about our prospects for interlocking personal and social integrity. Affirmative emphasis is placed on the strength of the self, that is, on a self in harmony with itself and its social milieu, a self secured by its self-esteem and social bonds, a centered self able to realize her basic program and express her distinctive talents. Negative emphasis is placed on insufficient self-coherence, that is, on fragmentation prone selves who are enormously sensitive to narcissistic slights following which they succumb to rage and/or inclinations to withdraw and seek compensatory archaic merger with archaic selfobjects, regressing from the more mature forms of empathetic bonding. Coextensively, what we find deflated are (1) drives and their vicissitudes, (2) phantasy, (3) the Oedipus complex, (4) lust and destructiveness, (5) the influence of socio-historical conditions on a want of meaning, value, and a sense of integration with oneself and others, (6) contingency, and (7) the typical problematics of the Kleinian infant.

GRIDLOCK

Given the emphatic plurality and frequent incommensurability of psychoanalytic perspectives, is it any wonder that interpartisan discussions regularly devolve into a gridlock of self-assertion and mutual pathologization? Absent agreement about how to weigh the significance of pertinent phenomena, or even about what phenomena are pertinent, how to understand and respond to, let alone best understand and respond to, phenomena considered pertinent, and how theories of pathology, technique, and end-state are to be coordinated, how are compelling claims to theoretical and/or therapeutic progress to be staked, let alone comparatively evaluated?

A frequent — evasive — response to psychoanalytic plurality is attempting to *subsume* the phenomena and concerns of one's cohorts into the privileged terms of one's own perspective. Such aggressive attempts at unmasking simply underline the problem and — unwittingly(?) tend to — exacerbate the polemical charge of interpartisan debates, especially when they involve pathologizing others' theories and techniques. Even Freud was aware — albeit dimly and intermittently — of the prospect that his claims would be countered by ascriptions of pathology. E.g., at the end of his analysis of Schreber's memoirs, Freud asks whether his analysis may be a delusion. For instance, Fairbairn claims to advance on the Kleinian understanding of the world of internal object relations by framing intense involvement in it as the outcome of inadequate parenting. On his account, adequate rearing will result in an outward oriented child able to engage in significant relations with others rather than one absorbed by an internal object world. For Fairbairn as for more than a few contemporary Kleinians, inadequate responses to dependency needs provokes a turn from external reality to inward fantasy objects and relations. What is a classical Kleinian to do, if indeed she cares to respond, but reassert her position, search — likely with little luck — for empirical evidence that bears on the dispute, and attempt to subsume her interlocutor's empirically/intersubjectively-inflected perspective within the terms of her own theory (based on the assumption of primary phantasy and constitutional aggression), i.e., situate its claiming and/or content as epiphenomenal and/or pathological? Likewise, what is a classical Freudian to do but stick to her guns, see if empirical research has anything remotely relevant to say, and express reservations about collusion with pathological formations when Freud's theory of the female castration complex is subsumed by (1) Karen Horney's theory that penis envy is product of patriarchal culture, itself based on womb envy[143] or (2) a theory that situates it as a son's fantasy that supports his — perhaps wavering — sense of grandiosity and defends against dependency, fear of abandonment and injury, and so forth. Certain object-relations theorists hold that castration anxiety is a displacement of archaic, newly unearthed anxieties over loss of love, annihilation, our aggression and rage against those who are dear to us, envy, and so on,[144] and further, some claim, the privileging of Oedipal matters, such as Freud's theory of castration anxiety, is a defensive denial of relatedness to and identifications with the mother. What is a classical Freudian to say in response? Just shrug? Characterize the competing theory as derivative? Certainly, speaking second is no measure of progress. But what is? And whence the tendency to theoreticism?[145] Might the phenomena be as diverse as interpretations, or at least more so than any one theory can comprehend?

Analysts are assumed to be sufficiently well-analyzed to avoid pointless or inciting, self-amplifying aggression and clear-headed enough to notice when a run of argument has no hope of convincing its purported addressee or cannot possibly support the claims it intends to underwrite. Thus it seems worthwhile to (1) document the prevalence of psychoanalysts' attempts to establish theoretical or therapeutic progress by unmasking competing theories and therapies as (often distorted) parts of a whole of which they are unaware and accusing them of pathology or collusion therewith; and (2) indicate on this basis how further such attempts might well proceed if analysts took each other more seriously. These illicit moves can be found all too frequently in debates concerning every facet of psychoanalytic theory and practice.

1. What Freud describes as the use of "unobjectionable positive transference" (transference based on childhood susceptibility to authority without which interpretations would not be taken as seriously as they need to be, especially in the face of forces of repression and resistance), Mitchell pathologizes as an abusive claim to authority that is therapeutically counterproductive and collusive with trends to abuse authority amongst corrupt politicians, lawyers, doctors, priests, and so on (2005, 37).

2. For Kohut, the guilty, Oedipal complex-ridden individual plagued by intrapsychic conflicts central to Freudian and Kleinian theories is but an epiphenomenal manifestation of and dangerously draws attention away from (masks) the empirical narcissistic disturbances of childhood that are the root cause of suffering and pathology. Absent such developmental disturbances, the Oedipal years (3-5) would be pleasurable rather than guilty. Freudians, Kleinians, or anyone else inclined to render childhood or its consequences in tragic terms will conspire with the sufferings they diagnose by hypostasizing them and pursuing therapies bound to be, at best, superficial. In return, Kohut's theoretical and practical protocols based on the primacy of early, unmet "needs" may be characterized by Freudians and Kleinians as forms of defensive retreat from Oedipal conflicts.

3. The notion of the subject as riven by desire that Lacanians uphold as the truth of the human condition to which we must accommodate on pain of pathology would be, for Winnicottians, itself pathological, a manifestation of a "false self" formation. Rather than seeking to liberate desire from the snare

of Imaginary fixation, as do Lacanians, Winnicottians confronted in the clinic with the incessant lability of desire at which Lacanian therapy aims would seek to stabilize it through appropriate forms of therapeutic care. The very terms in which Lacanians extol the virtues of desire — unsatisfiability, incessant mobilization and self-splitting, self-estrangement, etc. — are, in a Winnicottian framework, signals of suffering, specifically, of pathological self-alienation. What Lacanians consider a central goal of therapy, namely, the intensification and unshackling of desire from any particular aim and object, is for Winnicottians a consequence of inadequate rearing that can and should be therapeutically redressed.

4. In turn, analysts with Culturalist commitments or, as with certain Lacanians, a particular socio-critical orientation, would likely situate the Winnicottian theory of the false self — or at least certain of its applications — as a psychologistic displacement of emphatically social phenomena and on this basis suggest that Winnicottian proposals for its treatment are bound to misfire — are at best of limited efficacy, and because confused about the nature of their limits, prone to ongoing, ever-disappointing, piecemeal revisions that make matters worse; and at worst liable to aggravate the client's sense of derealization or annihilation, to force her further into hiding, by (tacitly) denying the social truth of her psychological predicament. Winnicott characterizes the false self as feeling that relationality threatens a loss of autonomy, even annihilation; as feeling dead, her life futile or unreal; as involved in rigidly maintained yet unsatisfactory relations with others, thus as feeling her world to be generally impoverished. It is not difficult to see why, at least in certain cases, what Winnicottians would call false self pathology others' would call relatively acute self-consciousness of life in late capitalist modernity. Might not the false self's tendential dissociation of intellection and affective, bodily experience and its pervasive sense of being an imposter — split between external functioning ("performing") and an inner world cut off from social expression — bespeak its social truth? And might not psychologistsic deflection of this truth — optimistic insistence on suffering's contingency — make even more unlikely its overturning? Illicitly privileging the endopsychic and pathologizing the social is a frequent charge (Though there are two separate charges here, they are often conjoined.) Stern, for instance, often levels the charge of overwrought attention to the endopsychic and needless pathologization of ordinary, expectable social developments. E.g., "During the formative phase of the domain of core-relatedness, an infant can readily present clinical problems. They are not signs or symptoms of any intrapsychic conflict within the infant, however. They are the accurate reflection of an ongoing interactive reality, manifestations of a problematic interpersonal exchange, not psychopathology of a dynamic nature" (1985, 202). Or, attempting to reduce a fundamental Kleinian claim to the terms of his psychosocial developmental perspective and thereby exemplify his broader

claim that what Klein and others overgeneralize as pathological tendencies inherent to endopsychic life are often empirical psychosocial phenomena, Stern claims that "[b]ecause the thresholds for external stimulation are set so low, it would look as though the anxiety attacks were spontaneous — that is, internally caused, as Klein (1982) suggests — when in fact they were simply promiscuously triggered by expectable, everyday stimulation arising from almost anywhere" (1985, 190). The rejoinder from a classical Kleinian would likely involve the claim that, even if true, Stern's suggestion would put the analyst off the track of psychic reality, where all the action is and where therapy should be focused. Even if Stern is right about the etiology, Kleinians — who would here find many allies, especially Lacanians — would wonder, What is the analyst to do but respond to its psychic significance? Stern would perhaps respond that if the real issue is a low threshold for external stimulation, any therapy that fails to address this (e.g., with medication, suggestions for lifestyle changes, or character-oriented therapy) is bound to be limited and may make matters worse by emboldening those prone to anxiety attacks to put themselves in situations that will exacerbate their suffering. To which Kleinians may respond that even if anxiety is thereby exacerbated, this may be therapeutically productive. And so on *ad infinitum*.

5. Balint (1968) argues that Kleinian "consistent interpretation" is a countertransferential enactment of the omniscient object, a pathological collusion. Similarly, Betty Joseph argues that the rapid and deep interpretations common in classical Kleinian practice may reflect the analyst's anxiety, specifically, her difficulty containing the analysand's anxieties, terrors, etc., and may collude with intellectualization that keeps deeper dreads unacknowledged and untouched. For Joseph, rapid and deep interpretations miss the chance to "make contact with the patient's experience of living in an incomprehensible world" which is often crucial for therapeutic success (1989, 158).

6. As Mitchell notes,

> There is a striking symmetry between [Kohut and Kernberg's] approaches to narcissistic illusion; from the point of view of each, the approach of the other borders on the lunatic. From Kohut's point of view, the kind of methodical interpretive approach to narcissistic transferences recommended by Kernberg is extremely counterproductive, suggesting a countertransferential acting out, involving a difficulty in tolerating the position in which the narcissistic transference places the analyst, arousing anxiety concerning his own grandiosity (in the idealizing transference) or envy of the patient's grandiosity (in the mirroring transference). Thus, Atwood and Stolorow (1984) feel that the oral rage Kernberg sees in 'borderline' patients is actually an iatrogenic consequence of his technical approach. Methodical interpretation of the transference is experienced by the narcissistically vulnerable patient as an assault, and generates intense narcissistic rage, which Kernberg then regards as basic and long-stand-

ing, requiring the very procedures which have created it in the first place. From the vantage point of self psychology, Kernberg is continually creating the monster he is perpetually slaying.

Similarly, from the more traditional point of view (both in terms of drive theory and interpersonal theory), the Winnicott/Kohut approach is an exercise in futility. An unquestioning acceptance of the patient's illusions with the assumption that they will eventually diminish of their own accord represents a collusion with the patient's defenses; the analytic process is thereby subverted, and the analyst never emerges as a figure who can meaningfully help the patient in any real way. From the traditional vantage point, the Winnicott/Kohut approach suggests what Loewald (1973) has termed a countertransferential 'over-identification with the patient's narcissistic needs' (p. 346). Loewald further suggests that Kohut's avoidance of any focus on 'an affirmation of the positive and enriching aspects of limitations' of self and others constitutes a 'subtle kind of seduction of the patient' (349). As Kernberg notes, unresolved narcissistic conflicts in the analyst may foster excessive acceptance as well as rejection of the patient's idealization . . . to accept the admiration seems to be an abandonment of a neutral position' (1975, p. 298) (1999, 164).[146]

7. Yet Mitchell's tendency to subsume and pathologize his predecessors in order to establish the credentials of his relational perspective is so ubiquitous (cf. Mitchell 2005) that one wonders how an analyst so sensitive to and critical of this tendency in others can fail to notice it in his own work. Perhaps Mitchell's myopia to the frequency with which he ascribes pathology to other perspectives in order to secure his position is conditioned by his conviction that psychoanalytic perspectives are resources to be drawn upon when and where needed — not deeply incommensurable after all but rather, on their own, distorted because one-sided, thus in need of context-sensitive reconciliation. In turn, his commitments to critical eclecticism may be motivated by his keen observations of the impasses generated by mutual accusations of pathology, but such commitments sidestep the issue, moot it artificially, thus perhaps prepare the way for a return of the repressed.

8. Mutual subsumption has a long legacy in psychoanalysis. In 1919 Havelock Ellis published an essay whose purpose was to frame Freudian theory as artistic production rather than scientific work. To this Freud replied with an accusation of pathology: "we cannot but regard this view as a fresh turn taken by resistance and as a repudiation of analysis, even though it is disguised in a friendly, indeed in too flattering a manner" (SE 18: 263).

9. The charge of "resistance" to the scientificity of psychoanalysis has been a staple of the literature, sometimes leveled with a great deal of sophistication, sometimes not. Marcus Bowman's (2002) *The Last Resistance: The Concept of Science as a Defense Against Psychoanalysis*, in which he relentlessly pathologizes the denial of the scientificity of psychoanalysis in lieu of defending its claim to scientificity, is an instructive example of the latter.

Bowman's core claims, like those of many analysts, are asserted and repeated rather than in any way supported or compellingly elaborated; and this causes him little trouble, convinced as he is that the denial of his position is profoundly pathological. Although Bowman is not an analyst but an enthusiast of analysis, his discursive maneuvers are unfortunately exemplary. The basic moves of *The Last Resistance* are (1) defining psychoanalysis as inquiry into conflict and self-determination, and (2) defining arguments contending that psychoanalysis is not scientific as defenses against the truth of (1). Assuming that psychoanalysis is authoritative only if scientific and that science is skeptical reason,[147] Bowman diagnoses arguments against the scientific status of psychoanalysis as unwitting expressions of anxiety about and defenses against the loss of stable identity and tradition, i.e., modernity. Arguments against psychoanalytic scientificity are, he claims, symptoms, rationalized avoidance of the imperative to autonomy and emotional self-governance conveyed by the science of psychoanalysis. Criticisms of the scientific status of psychoanalysis are unmasked as regressive means of avoiding conflict and the work of self-determination. Even if Bowman is onto something, vehement, pathology-ascribing assertion seems more likely to amplify resistances than reduce them. And his position is certainly open to accusations of sociologism, i.e., avoiding particularistic psychic reality.

10. Many contemporary analysts emphasize that each analysand, thus each analysis, is unique. On this widely and increasingly shared view, each analysis is an experience that cannot be fully comprehended by the theories transmitted by the tradition; its conduct requiring sensitivity so subtle, respect for particularity so acute, that theory — though it certainly abides — begins to look like theoreticism. As Shepherdson puts it, "the subject's sexuality will be fashioned in every case according to a distinctive organization, with particular modes of satisfaction, and this is why psychoanalysis, as a matter of methodical procedure, cannot take place in the classroom, or be transmitted like other forms of knowledge, but rather requires that each subject explore the singular discourse that defines each one alone" ("Lacan and Philosophy" 2003, 135). Or as Lacan himself formulates the point, "each analyst is forced . . . to reinvent psychoanalysis" (cited in Borch-Jacobson 1991, 158), and in order to do so must assume "an ever renewed ignorance that prevents anyone becoming a 'case'" (1982, 322). Some go so far as to suggest that when critical self-awareness of theory-mediated expectations lapses, analysis will potentially, even decidedly, take a wrong turn. "If . . . the analyst listens to the patient with the expectation of hearing a transference distortion and is not open to the likelihood *and necessity* of learning something new about himself or herself, then the analysis is more likely to become derailed or to continue on the basis of compliance and submission to authority" (Aaron 1999, 254; emphasis added). But again one can easily imagine the charge being reversed: even though "[i]n transference the analyst risks

the dissolution of his knowledge, that is, of what the patient presumes his knowledge to be and of the knowledge that he has brought to bear in other cases . . . [although] [e]ach analysis modifies — or should modify — *at least some* of the beliefs about psychodynamics that I held before hearing what the analysand had to say," hyperactive attention to singularity may mean gross blindness to eminently applicable insights suggested by the tradition (a repudiation of passivity? Resistance to analysis?), signal anxiety about or defense against some feature of an interpretation suggested by the tradition, or the nature of one's investment in tradition (say, one's suggestibility), or indicate some manner of revulsion at what is common (perhaps a shared natural or social condition?) (Kristeva 1988, 51).

Circulating within an orbit of idolatry and iconoclasm, interpartisan debate (when it occurs) is extraordinarily animated yet stagnant, gridlocked. How might it achieve emancipation from interlocking trends of stalwart self-confidence and polemical fervor? How might it cultivate its critical animus?

CONCLUSION: GAINING PERSPECTIVE

Each psychoanalytic school reflects and develops distinctive foci, singular sensitivities and urgencies, sometimes expressing different conceptions of the aims of analysis or the nature of pathology. These include different demands on clinical practice (sometimes resulting from different patient populations), different sensibilities about the major problems or tensions in the current state of psychoanalytic theory and about the need to address them, different degrees of concern with and understandings of the role of psychoanalysis in its socio-political climate or in relation to broader cultural currents, different standards of argumentation and validation and different degrees of concern with these standards, and so on. Less readily discernible, though everywhere palpable, are foci elaborated as differential distributions of emphasis, characteristic contours of attention and concern, that condition and are conditioned by the abovementioned differences. Certainly, substantive commitments demarcate the various schools — for instance, commitments concerning the nature of development, pathogenesis, appropriate end state(s), and the relations between them — but no less significant are differences in habits of attention and orientation. Each school reflects and develops a distinctive distribution of emphasis and neglect, exaggeration and deflation, an interlocking order of blindness and insight. A psychoanalytic school is irreducible to its doctrinal commitments and research programs: it is a perspective.[148]

Perspective proceeds from judgment and is itself a form of judgment. It proceeds from judgment in the sense that it arises from and recalibrates a prior organization of sensibility, opinion, insight, and concern, that is, an established arrangement of mutually supporting — though perhaps also conflicting — dispositions of attention to and neglect of various phenomena and strata of significance that urge, indeed are elaborated as, and are in turn emboldened by a number of insights and possibilities for intervention.[149] Perspectives are borne by — swept up in and emerge in their distinctiveness from out of — a stream of prior perspectives and the historical currents coursing through them.[150] As a perspective or convergence of perspectives, *psychoanalysis is a historical discourse of suffering and healing (or transformation) under conditions of modernity, not a metaphysical discourse of universal truth.*

Proceeding from judgment, perspective is to some extent indelibly beclouded, impelled by and elaborating impulses and insights that forever remain reflectively irrecuperable: the conditioned can acknowledge its conditioning only in (what perhaps thereby becomes or alters) its own terms; it can express or elaborate but not precisely thematize — reflectively disintricate itself from, and from a position of detached spectatorial surveillance, fully objectify — its conditioning. A perspective is certainly coherent or at least cohesive, but forever belated and beside itself, a lived (and as if living) ekstasy rather than an objectively present entity. Indeed, what a perspective affords or amounts to is more and other than knowledge. Or, one might say, perspective pursues objectivity otherwise.

As a form of judgment, perspective embodies/enacts privileged distinctions, patterns of attention and interpretation, and corresponding action-dispositions, an interinvolved, though perhaps not *systematically* integrated set of categorical and inferential commitments. As a form of judgment, a perspective is more than nomination (S is P) and its inferential deployment (e.g., if P then Q); it unfolds as certain questions, factors, aspects, and prospects come into focus, into the fore, or otherwise become of compelling concern, as others recede into the (thick) margins if attended at all. In fact, it is often precisely (certain of) those questions, factors, aspects, and prospects that have been of central, orienting significance to the tradition(s) out of which a perspective emerges (or prominent treatments of them) that become marginalized (or treated quite otherwise) in the constitution of the new perspective.[151] Though it may be via intense exaggeration, e.g., highly consequential reinterpretation or repositioning, of something relatively marginal to its background traditions that a new perspective emerges, an inflation and repositioning of certain questions, phenomena, or concerns that, whether or not knowingly, levels a claim against those who have failed to notice, downplayed, or inadequately articulated their significance, thus a claim to and in the name of a recalibrated community. Perspective is a searching assertion of exemplarity, akin to an act of conscience. Accordingly, not every redistribution of emphasis or pursuit of a novel question portends a new perspective — such atomism would be incoherent — and what might, though not wholly unprecedented such that we are bewildered every time a new perspective emerges, incapable of assembling a perspicuous overview of salient trends — again, that would be incoherent — is not subject to theoretical comprehension. Perspective is as uncertain — as context sensitive — in its emergence and consolidation as it is powerful — context determining, decisively discriminating — in its affordance of orientation.

Perspective necessarily involves exaggeration: hyperbolic inflations of certain matters and corresponding intensifications of certain dispositions coincide with immoderate deflations of others. Thus, hardly a system of denotation and its inferential deployment that might attain exclusive and exhaustive completion, yet in a certain way totalizing, the order of reasons a perspective elaborates, the world it enjoins, is without equipoise — dynamically integrated but because mobilized by and an articulation of exaggerations, unconsolidated and as if askew (perspective is an angle but not a part of a whole). Exaggerated, prejudicially animated, perspective is unable to square itself (repose in itself on the basis of its correspondence) with "the facts of the case"; hasty as decision but no simple volition, a sorting that remains out of sorts. Dynamically integrating what does not immediately present itself as integrable and smoothly slide into place; what would not be held together by merely logical connectors, thus that the integration of which involves the discovery (the acknowledgment) of new possibilities of form (of life and language; a perspective, like a grammar, is a profane/material logic); what remains irreducible to and perhaps sends a tremor through its integrating dynamic, a perspective is a tenuous though compelling accomplishment.[152]

The enabling excesses and deficiencies bound up with perspectival presentations reflect distinct ways of knowing, distinctive concerns and commitments, and distinctive objects; but a perspective is not a limited take on what would be more adequately if more comprehensively elucidated, as if a sampling of an underlying substance, reference to which would explain the attractions of and adjudicate between alternatives. Such a reference would either speak past or, becoming involved in, reconfigure a perspective, not measure it authoritatively from afar. There is nothing outside the purview of perspective,[153] no external measure of capaciousness or exactitude, though a perspective may be more or less capacious or exact with regard to the phenomena with which it is concerned, thus is susceptible to immanent critique and dialogical development.[154] At stake in gaining perspective is a certain loss of "the world." What perspective suggests — and can do no more than suggest, though there is nothing more that might be done[155] — is that "the world" is not one: an all-comprehending context of contexts, an essentially finished — self-subsistent or externally sutured — thing, a plenum that accommodates and may corroborate but outstrips finite representations, a monad that *is* one though seen, said, and otherwise inhabited in many ways — the given elaborated but lost in translation. Rather, perspective suggests, "the world" is — if it *is* — nonself-coincident, irreducibly plural: most fidelitously elaborated — as are its elaborators — as engaged in dialectics of inflation/deflation and creation/discovery.

Insightful to be sure, in part composed of and perhaps concerned with further attaining valid knowledge, a perspective is not at root (as if roots did not extend into earth) or in essence (as if essence — if there is any — is not dispersed across an evolving grammar) a medium of objectivity. Reflecting and developing distinctive interests and orientations, ways of knowing and acknowledging, perspectives demand recognition of the limits of demonstrative reason as a condition for cognitive self-consciousness (the progressive attainment of which may correspond with enhanced object-responsiveness and thereby substantial gains in self-articulation), thus have an ethical dimension and corresponding existential stake; they require a certain comportment or character (*ethos*), a bearing up under or bearing of tension, uncertainty, and irresolvable, unencapsulable complexity, the faltering of which introduces simultaneously ethical and cognitive dangers. We can begin to elaborate these dangers in the following terms:

(1) Succumbing to Cartesian anxiety in the grip of which we would attempt to eliminate from the field of inquiry all objects about which we cannot make self-evident or demonstratively certain statements (e.g., psychic phenomena, at least in a vast variety of circumstances), we would not only severely limit that field, but falsify the knowledge we do have or might claim, as well as our nature as knowers/claimers, hence the nature of our relations with others, in two primary ways. First, we would conceal the ways in which the phenomena about which we have or can come to have a certain range of demonstrably certain knowledge are the same phenomena that, engaged otherwise, are relatively indeterminate, opaque and open-ended, or more precisely, of shifting significance in altered contexts, undistillable into essence(s) or principle(s). Qua mathematized, an object may be ideally knowable, but phenomena so objectified, qua experienced, are not, indeed are not primarily or essentially objects of subject-independent-theoretical-knowledge, and the vehement insistence that phenomena *are* their mathematizable stratum conceals their other dimensions, thus our own. To give way to Cartesian anxiety would be to avoid genuine insights, further prospects thereof, and the expansive engagements from which these insights emerge and on which they bear for the sake of a small island of certainty which may not be as isolated as it seems if the impulsion to its eternal peripatetic traversal is sourced in anxiety that bears, while defensively holding at bay, the elusive but persistent pressure of all manners of cognitive and recognitive claims. Isolation and monofocal attention to that which can be known with certainty or as self-evident trades-off with attention to dimensions of phenomena and ourselves that are more elusive but nonetheless pertinent in various — indeed the vast preponderance of — contexts. Manifesting an encouraging an unrea-

sonably rational (i.e., theoretical) self-conception and world-relation, Cartesian anxiety is self- and world-distorting and at least self-stultifying, both cognitively and existentially: indeed, forsaking the claims of reason for the pristinity and security of rationality would mean abandoning the sphere of intersubjective claiming, thus an immense array of cognitive candidates and capacities along with the very possibility of self-constitutive responsibility. To repudiate that which is not demonstrable or self-evident would mean not just emaciating reason in the name of rigorous rationality but self-abdication, refusing the minimum necessary conditions for becoming a self, i.e., staking oneself on (or as) an articulated order of responses to objects and others' claims to various sorts of consideration.[156] Hypervigilant attention to the certain is as one with systematic neglect of the informatively uncertain or other than certain/uncertain — e.g., that which and that upon which certainty may bear (hence the content because the inferential consequences of certainties; again Cartesian anxiety is self-defeating). Second, demonstrative certainties are conditioned by axioms and evidentiary procedures about which we cannot be certain, i.e., which we may trust or not trust, but not on rational grounds: a foundation is either external and inert or question begging; method models cognitive satisfaction, thus may bear without being able to identify the interests as well as the imprint of circumstances and conduct that vitiate its confident generalization.

For instance, Cartesianism implies a very specific concept of an object: an object is inert matter (extended substance) governed by universal, systematically integrated, thus fully intelligible mechanical laws. Thus it implies a conception of subjectivity as primarily theoretical consciousness, either ideally satisfied by contemplative self-closure or, because beholden to the body that bears it, a site of unending even if not unpredictable wanting best served by the maximal domestication of nature by instrumental reason. Without interest in the axioms of (1) nature as metaphysically integrated and (2) the corresponding concept of an object, Cartesianism could not get off the ground, and even if their assumption eventually yields deductively integrated knowledge of nature so specified, they would not themselves be *demonstrated* true or become self-evident — such axioms could not be deemed true or valid (or their converse) in terms of the rationality they inspire, for they are not among the objects they delimit as candidates for rational scrutiny (their casting as such could only be tautological, hence empty, question-begging, or a category mistake). This is more or less Hegel's point in "Observing Reason." There, the claim is that the standpoint of observing reason — the cold, distant "neutrality" of modern science on the basis of which it claims objectivity, hence preeminent authority, exceeds science's claim to objective neutrality: it is a commitment, an undertaking, indeed a complex set of social practices that cannot be licensed or accounted for, in any way made sense of, by scientific reason. It is a deed, as much decision as discovery, its authority dependent on our claims for or on behalf of it — more precisely, on the capacity of the practices in which it is embodied/enacted to claim us, compel our interest and find articulation in our self-conception — thus squarely within the evolving space of reasons it means to definitively circumscribe. Hegel suggests that such an ascientific "ground" of scientific reason is much more historically involved and existentially freighted — more *meaningful and material* — than it can acknowledge within its own terms: it wants for self-consciousness. Aspiring to absolute certainty, those who hold themselves (and perhaps attempt to hold others) to such axioms and the regime of rationality they inspire actively — which does not mean independently in the sense of without influence, self-sufficiently — posit the conditions of rational intelligibility and then misrecognize their collective activity (the complex, perhaps irreducibly complex, variety of practices in which this activity is elaborated) as an external and absolute truth. "The certainty of Reason seeks its own self as an objective reality" (*PhG*, 208). Indeed, Hegel suggests, those who so aspire cannot make sense of their passions as a primary medium of their involvements with others, thus cannot make sense of themselves. As more of a placeholder for the collective narrative practices through which such sense could be made than a serious instance of it, Hegel claims that the pursuit of knowledge from the standpoint of observing reason surreptitiously gives expression to both a lingering desire for absolute knowledge and absolute power once named "God" and an iconoclastic secular impulse: that is, to vague conflict in need of much more precise terms if it is to be negotiated. Ironically, observing reason expresses an identification with the God science presumes to have left behind and perpetually reenacts is parturition — ritually re-claiming its independence as if it were uneasy about it, perhaps could not yet believe it or found some difficulty believing in it. Enraptured by its image of rationality, observing reason is as dead to the significance of its own practice as it purports objects to be. Longing for impersonal rules of reason, a secure connection with things as they must be, those who so aspire lose track of themselves (the practical/existential upshot of their essentially transitive rationality, which is perhaps a fantasmatic satisfaction or a nexus of such satisfactions), misrecognise the nature of their interarticulated self-, intersubjective, and world-relations, and thus forsake the self-conscious activity that would consist in elaborating and orienting themselves with reference to the probable influences and consequences of their commitments (i.e., engaging in collective self-narration).

(2) The conflation of genuine knowledge with demonstrative certainty implies discounting the individual and collective development that proceeds only by negotiating matters opinable, say, therapeutic, political, or moral ends (perhaps also concept application, or at least a great range of it). As a fundamental attitude, Cartesian asceticism invites conformism — or frames resistance to it as mere preference, beyond the bounds of reason. Either way,

the mutually constitutive bonds of self, world, and words come undone; subjectivity is expelled as surveying consciousness.

To articulate a perspective is not to contribute to a unifying discourse the systematic completion of which is the condition for genuine knowledge; all possible perspectives would not add up to a total state of affairs.[157] It is not to *wish* matters opinable into the horizon of demonstrative certainty, thus wish those who would opine silent or onto the sidelines. It is not to *will away* the perspectives of others that would present matters in a different light, say, that shed by different concerns and sensitivities, and thereby call one's own perspective into question, say, in terms of its reach or relevance. Rather, to articulate a perspective is to venture, sometimes to insist, irremediably partial and provisional insights concerning matters that can be known and acknowledged in many ways into a field of competing opinions. In this respect, analysis, including but not limited to psychoanalysis, is interminable.

To articulate a perspective is to yield and devote sustained reflective attention to certain features of phenomena and/or experience that allows them to stand out with the prominence they have been heretofore denied and which, one feels, they are due. Perspective is a gathering and sheltering of significance against the strong winds of historical oblivion. Thus, presenting a perspective involves an ethics of exaggeration, a practice of immoderation, indeed of injustice, in the name of justice and truth — which remain on the horizon.[158] Through the passionate insistence into the fore and freighted reinterpretation or repositioning of certain ill-attended features of the phenomena under consideration, those features take upon, albeit perhaps fleetingly, the stature they are due as they are wrested from the concealment — distortion, diminishment, or outright occlusion — imposed by dominant dispositions of cognition and recognition. Perspective is thus simultaneously hubris and concern for the Other: the non-identical, marginalized, or constitutively excluded. Perspectival exaggeration is, however subtle and tactful its presentation, a hyperbolic rejoinder to dominant regimes of intelligibility and value. Such exaggeration is the first moment of the dialectical development of insight, the furtherance of which will require the tempering of a perspective's exaggerations — thus if need be, its reorientation away from historical occlusions in need of rectification — as its claims come into conflict with those of competing perspectives — perhaps those responsible for the occlusions against which it takes a stand, but now engaged not just as agents of concealment but as competing perspectives — whence, perhaps, the claims of multiple perspectives are mutually clarified and developed.

By dialectical development of insight I do not mean a lawfully regulated progression that culminates in total transparency, absolute certainty, or all-comprehending, systematically integrated self-closure. Quite to the contrary, by dialectical development I mean the continual specification of the matters under consideration from indefinitely many points of view; specifically, an ongoing, interarticulated clarification of the nature and significance of the phenomena under consideration, the perspectives as which insight is elaborated, and the social practices and interests that inform and are developed by these perspectives. On this conception, insight is advanced as refined responsiveness to and reflective elaboration of (1) the specific properties or qualities, tendencies and capacities, and context sensitive but not context bound significance of the phenomena under consideration; and (2) the phenomena's specific forms or manners of opacity or indeterminacy vis-à-vis demands for thematization or theorization, i.e., their specific proneness to be and manners of being said or specified in many ways, their specific routes of withdrawal from comprehension;[159] (3) the specific dispositions of blindness and insight, inflation and deflation of which each perspective is composed, the sensitivities and urgencies they elaborate/enact, and their possibilities for development, i.e., thresholds of tolerance; and (4) the conceptions of flourishing or of the good life, in virtue of which, indeed as elaborations and pursuits of which, perspectives attain their distinctive significance — can bear the weight of a life by aligning it with others and a world of concern, such orientation affording a field of expressive possibilities on which a life can stake itself, come into its own as it gives singular expression to collective animating interests. At the far end of its reflective upsweep, object-consciousness becomes normative self-consciousness; upon taking this turn, the dialectical development of insight unfolds as a practical-political medium, as practices of normative self-inquiry and self-articulation. [160]

A perspective comes into its truth, avoids the self-betrayal and distortions that would be devolution into dogmatic, authoritarian assertion, only by addressing itself to viable competitors by which it will be critically challenged and evaluated and which it will critically challenge and evaluate in turn. It is only as engaged with viable alternative perspectives that a perspective can maintain its provisionality, its availability to complication or contestation as the matters with which it is concerned or the manners of its concern are evaluated otherwise. By addressing others, a perspective urges mutual reflection on the scope, standards, and interests of insight, thus on the resonance of perspectives with those who pursue them — whence they might be found stale and external, merely habitual, ready to give way; of much more vital significance than had been admitted; or compelling but confused, in need of exploration and perhaps supplementation or transformation — the phenomena they elaborate, and that in virtue of which they are pursued, as well as on the facilitating — i.e., sociopolitical — conditions of their pursuit. As addressed to others, a perspective must explicate — elaborate the attractions and take responsibility for the risks and promise of its wide-ranging implications. By addressing others, perspectives are recalled to themselves as media of interarticulated freedoms and responsibilities — modernist media, thus sites of mourning for the mythology of "the world." The mutual evaluation of perspectives, if at all serious, requires each forgoing authoritative reference to its privileged cases — resisting the temptation to totalizing metaphysics. That is, mutual evaluation requires each perspective exposing itself to the terms of another with which it is not perfectly aligned, to horizons in which it will undergo tremors and perhaps transformations consequent upon confrontation with phenomena that do not automatically assimilate themselves to its terms or patterns of emphasis which it may find deeply perplexing, not simply irresponsible and perhaps in some ways compelling or at least intriguing. Further, it requires forgoing authoritative reference to privileged criteria for viable and valuable insight, thus forgoing the fantasy that such criteria are impersonally dictated, as if from on high. It requires refusing to reply on — better: learning that on pain of self-deception and self-stultification, that is, on pain of self-loss, one cannot rely on — criteria as if their authority were self-evident; requires risking criteria through their exemplary elaboration — risking the discovery of suppressed doubts, difficulties, and partial disorientation, or the discovery of what one will say, where one might be drawn as one gives an account of one's commitments, and risking unreserved exposure to others, thus the possibility of misrecognition or lack of concern. But mutual evaluation also requires that such criteria are not so extrinsic or emaciated that they can be abandoned or will collapse upon challenge; such criteria must be sufficiently compelling and sufficiently similar — another weighting rather than another, altogether unfamiliar world — to raise mutual challenges. Mutual evaluation means mutual exposure, each perspective exposing itself to being read in another's terms, being claimed by another's concerns, thus requires the conversion of another's skepticism into one's susceptibility to transformation, the bearing of another's skepticism as dissonance in one's self-relation. If such dissonance is truly integrated rather than intellectualized, cordoned off, it will manifest in the manner of a perspective's pursuit, specifically, as availability to interruption and recalibration. Other perspectives, especially when but not only when directly heeded, even when only vaguely sensed as an obscure insistence, diminish the hyperbolic confidence a perspective cannot avoid — the reparative or restorative exaggerations which are demanded by the relative marginality or unappreciated significance of that to which its attention is devoted — but to which it need not give itself without reserve. Other perspectives may become the dark lining that brings into relief while at once putting some pressure on and perhaps inducing some hesitation over the constitutive exaggerations, the hubris, of perspective. A perspective that has come into its truth through internal reference to others unfolds in the crosscurrents of inflation and deflation, articulates itself in or as the tension between the two impulses, remains confident yet ill at ease with itself, unconsolidated, as it tends to privilege one impulse or the other, is unable to finally come to terms with itself; an adventure: exposed, searching, undefined. Sustaining exposure to what urgently demands recovery, recasting, repositioning, and/or amplified attention, thus sustaining its constitutive exaggerations (inflation), while at once exposing these exaggerations to those of viable competitors such that exaggerations are mutually disclosed as exaggerations, as neither absolutely responsible nor irresponsible, thus as available to questioning, reframing, and exploration of their implications, and perhaps thereby to transformation (deflation): this is the life-breath of a perspective's dialectical development.

For a perspective to maintain itself as a perspective rather than rigidify into dogmatic assertion and thus falsify itself, it must address itself to the strife-ridden scene of human plurality. Hence the need to re-introduce the various psychoanalytic schools in the context of their disagreements, specifically, their disagreements in perspective. *How* a perspective is articulated matters deeply to its standing as a perspective. In addressing itself to other *subjects*, to other agents/patients who may be compelled by other questions, interests, and other such foci, who may respond otherwise to matters of shared concern, a perspective becomes freighted with the responsibility of compelling self-articulation, thus self-interrupting, a question to itself. Presenting a perspective involves both a gesture of inflation (e.g., bringing the excluded or marginalized to the center or at least to a certain emphatic prominence) and a gesture of deflation (a moment of non-rigidity in which exaggerations are exposed as exaggerations). Presenting a perspective thus means maintaining fidelity, through a both hyperconfident, exaggerated and provisional, qualified mode of presentation, to human plurality and that in virtue of which human concerns and manners of concern are in(de)finitely diverse — call it nature's solicitous sublimity, its in(de)finite granting and exceeding of perspective.

Articulating a perspective is not just announcing an opinion or throwing out an idea.[161] It is a complex ethical-existential, political, cognitive, and rhetorical achievement, the stakes of which are nothing less than — though surely not the whole of — the acknowledgment of nature and humanity. To articulate a perspective is to sustain dialectical solidarity with nature's excessive significance, its elicitation of and irreducibility to in(de)finitely diverse perspectives, its givenness to manifesting — mattering, becoming — otherwise, and with those through whom it so manifests. A well-articulated perspective is an expression and acknowledgment of human dignity: an expression of having created/discovered a range of uncoerced responsiveness to the possibilities for insight and interaction afforded by phenomena through which a life assumes significant shape and on which its exemplary value is staked; an acknowledgement that others, qua subjects (at once agents and patients), may be — indeed are — differently but not irresponsibly oriented, compelled by other currents of concern to create/discover routes of responsiveness — manners of assessment and emphasis, focalization of interest and attention, and corresponding modes of conduct — through which individuation is achieved otherwise; thus an acknowledgement, however dim, of the in(de)finite excess or priority of nature with respect to the human. A perspective, addressing an emphatically human scene, opens humanity onto the in(de)finite priority of, its reflectively irrecuperable traversal by, nature.

NOTES

1. For example, cf. Darian Leader (1997) "Phantasy in Klein and Lacan," esp. pp. 87-88.

2. See also Glover's (1955) discussion of the questionnaire he sent to members of the British Society, the responses to which demonstrated significant diversity in analytic field, indeed much more than was expected.

3. See also her earlier, quite extraordinary statement in (1954) "The Widening Scope of Indications for Psychoanalysis: Discussion," pp. 608-10.

4. Wallerstein, Kernberg, and their ilk notwithstanding. Concerning the consensus problem, cf. Seitz (1966), Sklansky et al. (1966), Weber et al. (1966), Thomä et al. (1976), Fisher and Greenberg (1977/85), Werman (1979), Runyon (1981), Spence (1982), Peterfreund (1983), Rosenbaum and Muroff (1984), Fossage and Loew (1987), Bernardi (1989), and Hunter (1994). For Wallerstein's credo, cf. *The Common Ground of Psychoanalysis* (1992), p. 242. For Kernberg's elaboration of the dream, cf. (2001) "Some Recent Developments in the Technical Approaches of English Language Psychoanalytic Schools." For expression of commitment to unity ("an open unified conception," as against "fragmentation . . . a step toward death") where one might least expect it, cf. Green (2004).

5. To be clear, I mean to repudiate the widely influential view that theories of technique can be derived in a strict sense from theories of pathology (the medical model). This view is so prevalent that it can be found in authors as different as Fenichal and Reich. Quite influentially, Fenichal (1945) claims that "The theory of neurosis has the same relation to psychoanalytic therapeutic practice as pathology has to internal medicine: inductively arrived at through particular practical experience, it furnishes the foundation for further practical work. It represents an attempt to ascertain that which is regular in the etiology, the manifestation, and the clinical course of neuroses, in order to furnish us with a *causally direct method of therapy and prophylaxis*. Nothing could be demanded of such a theory that a medical man would not demand of pathology" (8; emphasis added). Anticipating Fenichal, Reich contends that "It can be said that all questions of technique cluster around one essential question, namely whether and how a clearly defined technique of analytic treatment can be deduced from the psychoanalytic theory of psychic illness" (Reich 1945 [1933], p. 3). I highlight this disagreement in part because I believe that it is largely as a result of the conviction that technique can be deduced from theories of pathology that most psychoanalytic theorizing until the relationalists focused on theories of pathology at the expense of technique, which is unfortunate since neither sophistication in nor proliferation of theories of pathology are known to correlate with therapeutic advances.

6. This is a bit misleading. It is not as if repression is a discrete force to be opposed to the specific force of the return of the repressed. Rather, repression and its breaching are manifestations of the pleasure principle. Though repression may be more or less intense depending, say, on the relation of the repressed to a highly invested self-image, and though repressed wishes may be more or less intense (there is always, for Freud, a question of energetics), libido is the operative force, not repression or the return of the repressed. And though Freud is committed to a *dynamic* unconscious, the dynamic of repression/resistance and return is governed by a single principle, the pleasure principle.

7. "What decides the purpose of life is simply the programme of the pleasure principle" (SE 21: 76).

8. Of course, Freud recognizes the limits of this program: "When one thus sees that the unconscious never overcomes the resistance of the conscious, one must abandon the expectation that in treatment the reverse process will take place to the extent that the conscious will fully dominate the unconscious" (Freud to Fliess, Letter 69).

9. Hyperbolizing a bit, Freud at one point suggests that "in combating these resistances lies the task of therapy" (SE: 225).

10. Also cf. SE 13: 182-3.

11. Though he sets them out as hard and fast rules, Freud knows full well that his criteria for genuine analysis are eminently contestable. In his terms, "I think I am well advised, however, to call these rules 'recommendations' and not to claim any unconditional acceptance for them" (SE 12:123; also cf. the letter to Pfister of 22 October 1927). Or as he says elsewhere, "this technique is the only one suited to my individuality; I do not venture to deny that a physician quite differently constituted might find himself driven to adopt a different attitude" (SE 12:111). As we will see, a psychoanalytic perspective proceeds from judgment – from a particular "constitution," from a certain configuration of sensibility and urgency that compose an "individuality" – and is itself a form of judgment. (To be sure, Freud was not open to unlimited variation in psychoanalysis. Cf., for instance, *New Introductory Lectures on Psychoanalysis*, where, with reference to Rank, Freud says, "This may be a school of wisdom; but it is no longer analysis" (SE 22: 143).

12. To be more precise, for Freud, unconscious memory-traces and wishes are mutually transformative and further subject to transformation according to the logics and imperatives of unconscious metabolism; hence they are, in principle, objectively present but not stably present.

13. As Freud says in "Constructions in Analysis," sometimes the analysand need not find the analyst's interpretations true in her own experience or memory so long as s/he really believes them to be true.

14. For an account of the Lacanian treatment of perversion and psychosis, cf. Bruce Fink (1999) *A Clinical Introduction to Lacanian Psychoanalysis*, chapters 7 and 9; Jacques-Alain Miller (1996) "An Introduction to Lacan's Clinical Perspectives" in *Reading Seminars I and II*; Jean-Claude Schaetzel (1993) "Bronzehelmet, or the Itinerary of the Psychotherapy of a Psychotic" in *How Lacan's Ideas are Used in Clinical Practice*; and Schaetzel (1988) *Clinique différentielle des psychoses*. Also of note is the Lacanian-Winnicottian account of psychosis by Piera Aulagnier (2001) in *Violence and Interpretation*.

15. The Real is a red herring in the Lacanian literature. Though it is surely important to Lacan's theory (especially in the later years) and technique, it is far less so than most commentators assume. Thus no account of the Lacanian clinic would be complete without some commentary on the Real, but I will confine such commentary to a footnote in order to counterbalance the stress placed on it by most commentators.

The Real is the dimension of the ineffable that lines the Symbolic and the Imaginary, causing them to tremble and thereby serving as the impetus for their perpetual reconsolidation or transfiguration. More precisely, it is not the Real *per se* that motivates the reconsolidation or transfiguration of the Symbolic or the Imaginary, for the Real is not an agency – it is rather an excess that overwhelms us and in response to which we are both thrown off balance and motivated to reestablish our bearings. The encounter with the Real is the *spur* of the form-giving impulse: its motivation and limit, irritant and impasse, that which gives rise to the "activation energy" of symbolization and at once the jagged rocks upon which symbolization founders. It is the "hard kernel" that cannot be metabolized by our efforts of schematization or psychic processing, yet that in response to which they are propelled yet again.

Though the Real names a principle of material resistance or excess, speaking at this level of generality misses something crucial: the notional structure of the Real is utterly idiosyncratic; what the Real "is" is a question for each individual. This is to say, the Real is registered in each individual's tendency to *repeatedly return* to certain scenes (behaviors, fantasies, word choices, relationships, etc.) without knowing why and often without even realizing it. The Real is registered precisely in the compulsive quality of certain pursuits particular individuals undertake or attachments they form (again) almost despite themselves, in those actions or activities that are motivated (driven) by principles that seem to forever elude reflective appropriation and often seem contrary to self-interest. The Real is the inexplicable, the limit to rational self-comprehension (*Seminar IV*, p. 67). In terms of subjective experience, the Real names a sense of being here, yet again . . . and yet not knowing what one has gotten oneself into. The Real cannot be decoded into determinate content; it is not subject to analytic deciphering as repressed desires, fundamental fantasies, or even core signifiers may be. It is both under- and over-determined, as under- and over-determined as the core signifiers around which turn and out of which are organized the associational networks structuring each individual psyche. (Because of this, in Lacan's lexicon "the Real" sometimes names certain relatively well-structured impasses – say, those turning around the affects or *jouissance* of parents or previous generations that are unconsciously transmitted – more than a principle of excess that shuts down the possibility of structured experience. In this sense, the Real names a relatively determinate unconscious content or pattern, but only insofar as this content or pattern articulates an impasse and remains ineffable, that is, only insofar as it exceeds our capacities to assimilate it, to make sense of it, negotiate it, and move on.) The Real is endogenous yet inimical to the order of meaning, it is the ex-timate kernel of representation and self-representation, that which must be excluded in order for one's images of self and world to maintain their consistency, and so that which, if confronted, generates therapeutically significant destabilizing effects.

In one sense, then, the Real names our split-ness, our inhabitation by an "other scene" that is constitutively nontransparent. But the Real is not the unconscious. It is a name for our emphatic passivity, a passivity beyond passivity, a passivity that cannot be converted into any form of self-directed activity. Such conversion precisely marks one's distance from the Real, the subsiding of its sublime force. We may learn to avow various unconscious impulses and fantasies, maybe to some extent even our *desire* itself, but the Real cannot be so avowed. There are no ways to accommodate oneself to it or cultivate forms of acknowledgment appropriate to it. "It" is the floodgate that must remain for the most part closed if our cognitive maps, projects, self-representations, and world-orientations are to remain stable enough for us to gain our bearings. Hence it is that which, if partially confronted, produces therapeutically significant effects of dislocation and disorientation, of psycho-symbolic rupture. But again, this encounter must be limited, for fully opening onto the Real would throw us into a limbo from which there would be no foreseeable return. The full accession to the Real, allowing its full force to be felt, would overwhelm us, cause our worlds to crumble. The Real is the limit, the indigestible kernel that cannot be incorporated by the processes of psychic metabolism without unraveling the psyche entirely.

The Real is *the* figure of inadmissibility. Its admission would unravel the structures of admission and exclusion by which experience is structured, overwhelm the principles of selectivity through which the world comes into focus. While various figures of abject life (psychosis, criminality, *homo sacer*, etc.) may serve as cultural placeholders for the Real, their very figurability bespeaks their distance from the Real. The Real is the name of the paradoxical principle (*archē*) of an-archy that is held at bay in order for the ordering operations – the patterning and structuring – of experience to take hold. Admitting what were once abject forms of life into the fold may modify the structures of inclusion/exclusion around which a particular individual or community is organized in incredibly important ways (this is often a matter of life and death), but insofar as the individual or community can reorganize itself, it has not fully admitted the Real.

The Real can be figured as the upsurge of phenomenalization prior to and forever in excess of schematization – it is the constitutive outside, the exception or excess that must be excluded if reality is to maintain a sense of consistency. Again, the configuration of an individual psyche or cultural order may change significantly upon altering its practices of constitutive exclusion, but to admit that against which or those against whom individual or collective identity has been negatively defined is not to utterly shut down the very possibility of experience, which is what the full admission of the Real would entail. The Real is a principle of massive, insurmountable inconsistency, of ravishing chaos. If one insists on framing it as a form of experience, it could be said to be akin to that of *le corps morcelé*, i.e., the experience of each organ or zone, barely defined in itself, striving for its own satisfaction without a sense of the whole person being yet available.

To put one final gloss on it: one's sense of reality may admit of a great degree of latency but the admission of the Real would amount to the utter breakdown of capacities for selective attention through which latencies come into view as the possible horizons of *my* life course: in the face of the Real, one can no longer say "I." And this is why it is so important in the Lacanian clinic. The Real names the radically impossible – that which cannot be extrapolated as the potential fate of the self or world we have come to know. The Real is both "too much" and "not enough"; it is the elemental upsurge of life irreducible to its anthropocentric registration, that which cannot be contained within the bounds of possible experience. A dangerous yet fecund resource indeed.

16. Though it is inevitable that more will be read into the insistence that the client follow the fundamental rule – and though more may be there – the point is to refrain from informing the client what the analyst would like, what her image of happiness or the good life is, what she considers worthwhile ambitions or a more felicitous manner of negotiating with the material with which the client is struggling. The client is considered already too engrossed with the question of the other's desire, considered to believe that if the other's desire could be fully known and fulfilled, an all but forgotten state of peace and plentitude, of unlimited bliss would return.

17. Scare quotes here mean to indicate the anomalous character of Lacan's notion of "cause." Such a "cause" does not initiate or determine a predictable sequence of effects; quite to the contrary, for Lacan, such a "cause" is the wellspring of a certain efficacy that cannot be comprehended as an instance of a pregiven rule or law, as the activation point for the mechanical unfolding of a pregiven sequence. This "cause" is not a principle. On Lacan's account, the sciences are mistaken and insufficient to psychoanalysis insofar as they reduce causality to the starting point of a fully intelligible, mechanical sequence of law-governed effects. Rather than thinking a cause as an origin of an unbroken chain held together by the force of law, Lacan thinks causality as interruption, beginning, that from which the future in its unpredictability will have arisen, or in other words, as the activation of capacities for development that will have interrupted the facile functioning of a normalized, lawful or law-like state of affairs. "Cause" in this sense bespeaks resistance to calculability, to life outside law, or in Reiner Shürmann's terms, "life without why." For an elaboration of Lacan's notion of causality, cf. Bruce Fink (1996) *The Lacanian Subject*, pp. 138-141.

18. Cf. *Seminar X*, session of June 12, 1963.

19. For instance, signifiers such as words, phrases, or images are inscribed early on, before one has any sense of what they might mean, and yet are felt to be profoundly, indeed overwhelmingly significant, so significant, in fact, that they become subject to primal repression an effort to evade their terrifying (in)significance. Such Master Signifiers are subsequently resistant to symbolization – they manifest in deadlocks and impediments to free association – yet in their very resistance to symbolization, they incite efforts of symbolization that turn around them. Thus foreclosed, such Master Signifiers give meaning but are themselves without meaning: they are the kernel of the Real on which we choke (out meaning).

20. Once the transference neurosis is established, "[t]he analyst is considered to want from . . . [the client] the same thing the parents wanted, whether that was blood, solace, pity or whatever. The analysand's notion of what the Other wants is projected and reprojected, but the analyst continually shatters it or shakes it up by not being where the analysand expects him or her to be" (Fink 1999, p. 57).

21. Though it is an ambitiously anti-normalizing enterprise, there is surely a normative, or what Lacan would perhaps call "ethical," orientation of the Lacanian clinic.

22. "[T]he cause of the unconscious . . . must be conceived as, fundamentally, a lost cause" (*Seminar* XI, p. 128).

23. Of course, the risk is that scansion, oracular speech, and other such techniques will reinforce the client's assumption that the analyst knows the truth about her. Cf. Joël Dor 1994, chapters 2 and 3.

24. On oracular interpretation, cf. "D'un discours qui ne serait pas du semblant" (*Seminar XVIII*, session of Jan. 13, 1971).

25. Implicitly here, Lacan suggests that Freudian, and for that matter, any other version of analysis, may routinely support pathology due to its uncritical attitude about routine. The mutual pathologization of interpretation-types will be important for us later, as will a point implicit in the theory of the short session, namely that analysis can be effective only if it transpires outside of the limited time and space of the clinic.

26. Consequently, in addition to acting as a stand-in for the Other, the analyst will often position herself as ever more of a blank screen; for, if Imaginary rivalry leads to resistance to

interpretation through false and placating agreement with an idealized rival or through rebellious attempts to become the true authority vis-à-vis a hated rival (you, the analyst, know nothing, I am the one who Knows), then inhabiting the position of the blank screen both facilitates projection and diminishes rivalry, thus resistance.

27. Intentionally inaccurate interpretations, let us note in passing, are far from viable objects for validation by standard scientific protocols.

28. Notice that Ferenczi, unlike Lacan, does not assume that the one enters analysis only when symptoms fail to yield sufficient satisfaction, for this would imply that adequate tension already obtains.

29. Cf. Ferenczi, "The Principles of Relaxation and NeoCatharsis," "Child Analysis in the Analysis of Adults," and "Confusion of Tongues Between Adults and the Child."

30. "Analysis on its own is intellectual anatomical dissection . . . . Kindness alone would not help much either, but only both together" (Ferenczi 1985, p. 207).

31. Though there are certainly discontinuities between Ferenczi and Alexander, the latter's notion of a "corrective emotional experience" sheds some light on Ferenczi's technique: "The parental intimidation is corrected by the more tolerant and sympathetic attitude of the therapist, who replaces the authoritarian parents in the patient's mind. As the patient realizes that his modes self-assertion will not be punished, he will experiment more boldly. At the same time, he can express himself more freely towards persons in authority in his present life. This increases the ego's capacity to deal with aggressive attitudes which anxiety had previously repressed" (1963, pp. 286-7).

32. Cf. Ferenczi (1955 [1919]) "On the Technique of Psycho-Analysis" and (1955 [1919]) "Technical Difficulties in the Analysis of a Case of Hysteria."

33. By 1925, Ferenczi says that active procedures must be of an "elastic compliancy," meaning that they may or may not be used depending on the case (*Further Contributions*, p. 221).

34. Cf. "The Further Development of the Active Therapy in Psycho-Analysis" in *Further Contributions*, pp. 198ff.

35. The relaxation technique was developed in 1930 consequent upon repeated failures of earlier incarnations of the active technique to help clients relive or otherwise get in touch with early traumatic experiences.

36. Cf. "On the Technique of Psychoanalysis," in *Further Contributions*, pp.177ff.

37. Ferenczi varied the active technique throughout its development. Sometimes the third phase came first.

38. "The fact that infantile sexuality exists obviously remains undisputed, yet much of what appears as passionate in infantile sexuality may be a secondary consequence of the passionate behavior of adults, forcibly imposed on children against their will and, so to speak, artificially implanted in them . . . . Children want no more than to be treated in a friendly, tender, and gentle way" (Ferenczi 1985, p. 79); "the premature forcing of genital sensations has a . . . terrifying effect on children; what they really want, even in their sexual life, is simply play and tenderness, not the violent ebullition of passion" (Ferenczi 1955 [1930], p. 121).

39. Also, let us note in passing, although Ferenczi's later development of mutual analysis would seem to significantly mitigate the risks that Lacan's perspective exposes, because Ferenczi insists that mutual analysis, if it is used, must *follow* the establishment of basic trust, for only this allows for a mutual regression to "tenderness," it would hardly quell Lacan's primary concerns.

40. For Ferenczi's worries about psychoanalytic *theory*, cf. Stanton (1991) p. 86, 135-139. Also cf. Sabourin (1985), pp. 160-82 and Balint (1949), p. 216.

41. Such deadlock, as we will see, is certainly not confined to disagreements between Lacan and Ferenczi. Just to give one further example, in anticipation: what Lacan deems pathogenic engrossment in the desire of the other, Winnicott would consider a manifestation of a false self, implying that what for Lacan is the fundamental matrix is pathology is but epiphenomenal.

42. Cf. Beck (1992) *Risk Society*, (1999) *World Risk Society*, and (2008) *World at Risk*; Beck and Ritter (1995) *Ecological Enlightenment*; Beck and Weisz (1995) *Ecological Politics in an Age of Risk*; Mythen (2004) *Ulrich Beck: An Introduction to Risk Society*; Adam, Beck,

and Loon (2000) *The Risk Society and Beyond*; Beck, Giddens, and Lash (1994) *Reflexive Modernization*; and Giddens (1990) *Consequences of Modernity* and (1991) *Modernity and Self-Identity*.

43. For a detailed sociological description of the world under the imperative of ongoing self-revolution, cf. Zygumnt Bauman (2005) *Liquid Life* and (2006) *Liquid Love* and Jeremy Rifkin (2001) *The Age of Access*.

44. Think of the CEO who speed dates, practices yoga, meditates, and does whatever else promises to keep her "up to date," socially integrated. A voracious consumer of whatever figures social belonging, she is ripe for the latest trend. Or perhaps she accepts (gender, ethic, national, religious, etc.) normalization in her private life and yet remains altogether amenable to the perpetual recasting of her identity, projects, etc. in terms of her work life, e.g., a venture capitalist who regularly attends Catholic mass and is a staunch patriot. Here, social normalization becomes an open secret and seductive transgression in an economic order that mandates perpetual renovation and "thinking outside the box."

45. Incidentally, it is possible that Freud would be particularly unnerved by such language given that, at a vicious moment in the midst of their "breakup," Fliess had called Freud a "thought reader" who projects his ideas into the minds of his patients.

46. "Quite often we do not succeed in bringing the patient to recollect what has been repressed. Instead of that, if the analysis is carried out correctly, we produce in him an assured conviction of the truth of their construction which achieves the same therapeutic results as a recaptured memory" (SE 23: 265-6).

47. A related disagreement between Freud and Ferenczi concerns the terms in which central conflicts are elaborated. In "Confusion of Tongues," Ferenczi even suggests that tenderness vs. passion is to replace impulse vs. ego or superego as the primary terms of conflict.

48. Though this is not the place to explore this point in detail, it is worth recalling that such self-sufficiency pertains to a state prior to clear-cut subject-object differentiation; thus it is not exactly that the infant later turns to the caregiver for the sake of satisfactions that cannot be autoerotically facilitated, for she is always already in relation to her caregivers. Were she not, such a "turn" would be inexplicable. Such a turn is then a qualitative transformation, not a categorically new orientation. Cf. Alan Bass (2002) *Difference and Disavowal: The Trauma of Eros*.

49. Of course, Lacan as much as Freud would be profoundly suspicious of Winnicott's deflation of the tendency to self-evasion, as he would be of Winnicott's claims concerning the drive or tendency to healing and development. For Lacan, the analysand does not have a genuine desire to change or attain heightened self-consciousness (at least not in the ways Lacan would consider fundamental). On the contrary, Lacan suggests that the analysand is passionately self-distorting – ignorance is perhaps her most cultivated passion. The analysand is so committed to her ignorance of, say, the impossibility of total satisfaction, self-mastery, or that which is irreducible to objective presence or absence, that which is not of the order of the simply intelligible (the Real) – generally, to her ignorance of finitude – that the analyst will have to promote the mimetic incorporation of her desire as the analysand's "cause" in order to induce the analysand to break through her resistances to self-knowledge and, to the extent possible, bring the Real into symbolization.

50. Klein's misgivings about the propriety of analytic pedagogy – misgivings manifest in the Controversial Discussions that may have become unduly rigidified as a result of the aggressively polemical character of those "discussions" – prevented her from following Winnicott on this point.

51. Nonsurvival would mean retaliation, withdrawal (attitudinal change in the direction of suspiciousness or diminished receptivity), defensiveness, or, obviously, psychological crumbling.

52. As do his inheritors. Ghent, for instance, speaks of a fundamental striving for growth and development, of the "impulse to psychic healing," and of "a *longing* for the birth, or perhaps rebirth, of true self" (cited in Mitchell and Aron 1999, p. 214). In a similar vein, Bollas (1989) speaks of the "destiny drive."

53. It is never finally clear whether, for Winnicott, suppressed developmental needs are properly unconscious or not.

54. Winnicott's distinctive structure of blindness and insight will be elaborated in greater detail in chapter 4. While the failure to include Klein in this chapter may seem inexcusable, this wrong will be redressed in chapter 4. A fuller account of Kleinian theory is provided in Rosen-Carole (2011) *Lacan and Klein, Creation and Discovery*.

55. Cf. Ernst Kris' famous plagiarism case in "Ego Psychology and Interpretation in Psychoanalytic Therapy." According to Kris, the case shows not only that the traditional id focus (employed in the client's first analysis) does not work as well as the ego psychological focus on all three agencies, it also demonstrates the significance of empirical facts to the conduct and outcome of analysis: Kris discovered that the client who claimed to be a plagiarizer was in fact the victim of plagiarism, and with this, everything changed.

56. For Freud, "the recognition of our therapeutic limitations reinforces our determination to change other social factors so that men and women shall no longer be forced into hopeless situations" (cited in Hale 1970, p. 90-91).

57. Cf. Hartmann and Kris (1945) "The Genetic Approach in Psychoanalysis."

58. On the reading advanced by many ego psychologists, Freud privileges the intrapsychic at the expense of neglecting the porous interface of the psychic and the social; his basic unit of developmental analysis is the infant rather than the infant-caretaker dyad, just as the basic unit of his clinical analysis is the infantile in the adult rather than the infantile-ego-environment complex.

59. "All through childhood a ripening process is at work which, in the service of an increasingly better knowledge of and adaptation to reality, aims at perfecting these functions, at rendering them more and more independent of the emotions until they become as accurate and reliable as any non-human mechanical apparatus" (Anna Freud (1945) "Indications for Child Analysis," p. 86).

60. E.g., for Lowenstein, analysis should correct distortions brought about by defense mechanisms in addition to lifting amnesias (1982, p. 53), and in order to do so, the analyst must serve as a prosthetic ego (1982, 55). Furthermore, for Lowenstein and others ego psychologists, the point of insight and verbalization is to subject what was repressed to reality-testing, whence unconscious ideas and impulses become presumably harmless. Indeed, with great optimism, Lowenstein even contends that once material becomes conscious, it resists future repression even if it is forgotten (1982, pp. 64-5).

61. The aspiration to equidistance and objectivity would no doubt be extremely problematic for Lacan, and at least the latter would be problematic for Klein, since, on her account, phantasy and oscillations between paranoid/schizoid and depressive anxieties are unsurpassable. Concerning Klein's reticence regarding claims to objectivity, cf. John Phillips (1998) "The Fissure of Authority: Violence and the Acquisition of Knowledge" in *Reading Melanie Klein*.

62. Or when not a positive spin, at least a neutral spin. For Anna Freud, there is no obvious benefit to exposing ego-syntonic defenses to analysis: if these defenses are valued aspects of the client's character and are not obviously responsible for her suffering, why call them into question? Why must analysis always make its way to the most primitive strata? Many ego psychologists have followed Anna Freud's lead here, e.g., Kris, who worries more about the rigidity – i.e., contextual inappropriateness – of defenses than about the fact that they are defenses (1982, p.198). Whether or not one agrees with her on this point, her demurral brings out, by way of contrast, something of the aggressiveness of father Freud's Enlightenment spirit.

63. Note that once again psychoanalytic argument proceeds by pathologizing an opponent's views.

64. Even though the notion of neutral energy descends from Freud: "We have reckoned here as though there existed in the mind – whether in the ego or the id – a displaceable energy, which, neutral in itself, can be added to a qualitatively differentiated erotic or destructive impulse, and augment its total cathexes. Without assuming the existence of a displaceable energy of this kind we can make no headway . . . . It seems a plausible view that this displaceable and neutral energy, which is no doubt active both in the ego and in the id, proceeds from the narcissistic store of libido – that is desexualized Eros" (SE 19: 44).

65. Cf. Jünger (1930) "Totale Mobilmachung."

66. In the words of David Rapaport, "We would all agree that liberation from crippling defenses is the aim of our work. In the meantime, however, there is also something we keep in the back of our minds and some of us may even keep it in the foreground: The patient needs to find his place in society and lead a useful, productive life" (1954, p. 587). Also see Hartmann's (1939) discussion of the urgency of "social compliance."

67. Hartmann agrees: "the patient comes to . . . the analyst . . . in the hope of being freed from limitations of his capacity for work and his enjoyment of life" (1964, p. 341).

68. Cf. Anna Freud (1936) *The Ego and Mechanisms of Defense* and (1966) *Normality and Pathology in Childhood* and Wilhelm Reich (1933) *Character Analysis*.

69. Cf. David Shapiro (1965) *Neurotic Styles*.

70. Cf., for example, Spitz (1945) "Hospitalism—An Inquiry Into the Genesis of Psychiatric Conditions in Early Childhood" and (1965) *The First Year of Life: A Psychoanalytic Study of Normal and Deviant Development of Object Relations*.

71. With Mahler and Jacobson, clinical innovations were motivated by a desire to assist those who had been more or less dismissively labeled "psychotics," and especially "childhood psychotics." These were patients of whom it was believed that because their libido is narcissistically absorbed, they are unamenable to transference analysis. Given their flimsy hold on reality, transference regression was considered dangerous; and since they are lacking in object libido, transference likely won't develop in any case. Recall that Freud's study of psychosis is a reconstructive reading of Schreber's memoirs, not an examination of clinical experience.

72. For instance, with Mahler and Jacobson, psychotherapy aims to reinitiate the arrested development of those suffering from early environmental depravations that catastrophically inhibited the development of identity, which is to say, the working out of acceptable forms of connection and separation.

73. "Every analyst had a full caseload, and those with middle-European accents had two-year waiting lists whether they were good or not" (Kramer 1996, p. 44).

74. Cf. Zetzel (1958), Greenson (1965), and Meissner (1981, 1982).

75. Ego psychologists tend to ignore the claims and implications of Freud's (1914) "Mourning and Melancholia" that became important to object relations traditions and various development-oriented theorists including Mahler and Jacobson, who, one can well see by now, do not neatly fall in with the ego psychological perspective as presented here. Regarding the heterogeneity of ego psychology: Eissler too is something of an anomaly; and Brenner, while squarely within the ego psychological tradition, differs significantly with Hartmann over the significance and scope of conflict and compromise. The extravagance of Hartmann's emphasis on the resolvability of conflict is revealed by contrast with Brenner, in whose work the terms "neutralization," "secondary autonomy," and "change in function" do not even appear (cf. Brenner 1982).

76. Cf. Russell Jacoby (1983) *The Repression of Psychoanalysis*, especially chapters 6 and 7.

77. Such insistence on integration and accommodation may be (and its therapeutic expression may promote), from Julia Kristeva's perspective, a hyperbolic counter-investment: an overinvestment in a symbolic order from which one finds oneself, in whole or in part, excluded. Cf. "Women's Time" in *New Maladies of the Soul* (1995). Likewise, from Winnicott's perspective, such an integrationist and accommodating ethos might well be deemed a manifestation of (and its therapeutic elaboration may support) the sycophantic, overly compliant proclivities of a "false self." Winnicott might well wonder whether the issue sidestepped by ego psychology's integrationist ethos is the *quality* of investment, that is, its contribution to a genuinely meaningful, reflectively redeemable life practices. Cf. Hartmann (1964), p. 8

78. Whether subtending and exceeding this ideological investment and its therapeutic elaboration is an identification with the aggressor – a ruthless pursuit of unconditional social integration – is a question that cannot be pursued here.

79. More precisely, where an optimistic ideology of voluntaristic individualism was materially supported by an imperative of socially serviceable self-sacrifice, where promises of unlimited self-improvement (freedom) were predicated on heeding demands for ongoing malleability, ultimately, where one must cope or crumble (plasticity was the rule).

80. Notice in passing that this "American" ideology – optimistic confidence in self-creation and progressive development, the conviction that personal and social flourishing are in principle limitless and mutually supporting, that is, wholly dependent on individual ambition and cunning, etc. – even bracketing the complex transnational history of its implantation and development on American soil, was, within the limited scope of our concern, to a significant extent developed and secured by trans-Atlantic voyagers who were not often prone to stay on American soil, indeed whose subsequent comings-and-goings across the Atlantic, both in person and vicariously through their work, contributed to the development of this "American" ideology. Cf. Paul Gilroy (1993) *The Black Atlantic*, and concerning immigrants' screening, and thereby, revitalization of the "American dream," cf. Anne Anlin Cheng (2001) *The Melancholy of Race*.

81. Cf. Hartmann (1964), p. x.

82. "And now, in the next place, listen to what my feeling is with regard to the city which we have described. I may compare my feeling to something of this kind: suppose, for instance, that on seeing beautiful creatures, whether works of painting or actually alive but in repose, a man should be moved with desire to behold them in motion and vigorously engaged in some such exercise as seemed suitable to their bodies; well, that is the very feeling I have regarding the city we have described. Gladly would I listen to anyone who should describe in words our city contending against others in those struggles which cities wage; in how proper a fashion it enters into war, and how in its warring it exhibits qualities such as befit its education and training in its dealings with each several city whether in respect of military actions or in respect of verbal negotiations" (19b3-c9; translation modified).

83. Cf. Levinas (2008) *Totality and Infinity*, p. 21.

84. To be clear, Hartmann does not categorically neglect conflict – "conflicts are part and parcel of human development, for which they provide the necessary stimulus" (1964, 12); "in applying psychoanalysis to sociological problems, the theory of human conflicts is its most important contribution to this science" (1964, 35) – he deemphasizes and circumscribes it.

85. More broadly, Hartmann's ambition is to study and support the ego insofar as it organizes perception, memory, and motility, serves as a protective barrier against excessive external and internal stimuli, tests reality, and facilitates action as against motor discharge, thus insofar as it promotes synthetic and calculative rationality ("thinking") is related to thinking, inhibition, delay of discharge and gratification, drive and affect regulation , management of object relations, conviction in the reality of self and world, adaptive regression, signal anxiety, and adaptive defenses and character organization – generally, adult competences and autonomy (1964, 115).

86. Ever scientifically scrupulous, Hartmann underscores that primary autonomy is an assumption (1964, xi).

87. Cf. Hartmann (1964), p. 105.

88. Cf. Ernst Kris 1952.

89. "[C]onflicts are part and parcel of human development, for which they provide the necessary stimulus" (1964, 12).

90. Hartmann suggests that irrational forces can be rationally coordinated into a coherent life practice (1964, 56).

91. From a critical Lacanian perspective, although ego psychology's ambitious interest in cultivating self-scrutiny may render it apt for clients negotiating with the liquid modern world, by fostering superego development and promoting adaptive defenses, it risks consolidating rigid character structures, thereby limiting the scope and efficacy of the self-scrutinizing aptitudes it cultivates. From a classical Freudian perspective, ego psychology's emphasis on reality testing may conspire with resistances to transference and regression and against defenses against "irrational" unconscious wishes, thereby fundamentally impeding analysis.

92. "Men make their own history but they do not make it just as they please; they do not make it under circumstances chosen by themselves, but under circumstances directly encountered, given and transmitted from the past. The tradition of all the dead generations weighs like a nightmare on the brain of the living" (Marx 1979, p. 103).

93. Cf. Hartmann (1964), p. 16.

94. "How sound our general statements and our predictions can be depends in the last resort . . . on how far a general theory can be developed" (Hartmann 1964, 104). Although developing a general, scientifically valid psychology was central to ego psychology's research agenda, the focus of the present chapter – various conceptions of what makes analysis essentially analysis – requires forgoing direct discussion of efforts to systematize and scientifically corroborate (e.g., via developmental observation studies) psychoanalytic theory.

95. "The theory of drive primacy and drive taming and the theory of movement from dependency to autonomy and from narcissism to object love are---or have gradually become---part of a supraordinated moral system in scientific disguise" (1984, 208).

96. Here we can already note a limit to Kohut's concern with the socio-historical that is not unrelated to his developmental commitments: a blindness that conditions his insights. Failing to concern himself with the socio-historical conditions and effects of reification, alienation, and individualism, Kohut, one might say, re-psychologizes psychoanalysis – though of course the failure is not unique to him and may not be avoidable. Can the want of meaningful connections to others and to our own life practices be adequately comprehended prior to a sustained analysis of or addressed without major modifications to capitalism, understood as a complex of social practices that motivates the appearance of social life as obdurately opaque, sectorally insulated, and immune from large-scale individual or communal intervention, that is, as reified in Lukacs' sense? How well can the conditions for meaning and value, i.e., successful individuation, be understood in the absence of an analysis of social fragmentation and the alienation of the worker from the means of production (generally, tendential alienation from the institutional media of social reproduction), the specialization of labor (generally, mutual disinterest and the hegemony of instrumental rationality, i.e., the privatization of interest), the transformation (neutralization) of the bourgeois principle of self-determination into the abstract ownership of labor power (generally, ideological individualism), and the transformation (neutralization) of the anti-bourgeois principle of equality into the abstract equality of all before the law (generally, rationalization)? The pertinence of the Marxist framing of these questions will soon become apparent.

97. At times, Kohut even goes so far as to suggest that however ubiquitous the drives may be, they are as such pathological, and in this sense not "normal" (1984, p. 27). At other times, more consistent with critique of Freud and ego psychology, he suggests that only the *experience* of the drives as fragmentary and fragmenting is an indication of pathology, and furthermore that to pathologize the drives "as such" would be to reify the drives, which should be scrupulously avoided. Incidentally, given that the fragmentary and fragmenting experience of the drives is, for Kohut, a signal of pathology, one can see how quickly discussions between self psychologists and Lacanians become gridlocked in mutual accusations of supporting pathology.

98. There are three related points to note with regard to this passage, the significance of which will later become clear. First, it is unclear whether the "nonhuman," and so the "self-destruction" of the human, is a terrible and extreme permutation of the human or marks the transubstantiation of the human. Is the nonhuman or "the human's self-destruction" the outermost limit of the human or does it concern a crossing of the threshold of the human, something ontologically discrete from the human? The figure of the nonhuman and of human self-destruction gesture toward a zone of indistinction, a unique zone in Kohut's thinking, otherwise given – at the levels of both form and content – to resolution, closure, self-regulation, and harmonious self-integration.

Second, Kohut speaks of "the human's *self-destruction*" rather than, say, "self destruction" even though the selfobject milieu is clearly responsible for the breakdown. Although Kohut insists on the constitutive sociality of subjectivity, might the social be thought here, and perhaps elsewhere, as the *mere occasion for or catalyst of* self-centered processes? How complete is Kohut's break from the monadic conception of the subject? To what extent can changes in the intersubjective milieu affect the basic shape of human life? Specifically, are there preordained limits to viable social transformation and consequently individuation?

Third, the claim that "[w]hat leads to the human's self-destruction . . . is . . . indifference . . . the nonempathically responding world" does not simply mean that pathology can be traced back to depressive caregivers, but rather that caretakers' depressive withdrawal as much as their encroaching, smothering intimacy are experienced as nonresponsive, coldly indifferent, and as such are pathogenic; both manners of rearing fail to support the child in the way she needs in order to feel viable as an independent source of agency and value while at once meaningfully connected with others. Kohut's basic question is not, What has become of repressed wishes? What has become of the fate of the drives? Rather, his question is, How do we achieve adequate separation and connection? How do we attain a secure sense of being (and being valued as) an individual as well as (and *by*) being (and being valued as) bound to others? While we must not fail to appreciate Kohut's insistence on the need for caregivers to respect their children's separateness, specifically, to manifest concern for their children as (emergently) distinctive individuals, there is still a question of whether, on Kohut's conception, adequate caregiving means being responsive to a generic set of needs or requires responsivity to children's unique dispositions and distinctive temperaments, broadly, to their singularity. At the core of Kohut's theory of pathology is a theory of universal developmental needs. In light of this, we must ask whether adequate empathy means attention to universal-typical or, at least in part, singular needs. How exactly does Kohut understand the notion of need? Further, because it is tethered to a theory of universal developmental needs, and so to a normative developmental trajectory, we need to ask about the extent to which Kohut's conception of individuality admits of singularity or unanticipated variations. As with the question of the "inhuman," here too it is a question of the relation between the universal and the particular, specifically, a question of whether the universal can be inhabited in a way that fundamentally alters its shape.

99. Think here of the typical teenager who, in response to what seems but the slightest narcissistic affront, explodes in rage and/or retreats to her room and anaesthetizes herself with music or drugs, or seeks solace by immediately recounting the tale of this terrible transgression to friends who she means to recruit into her righteous rage. Or think of the aggressive outbursts that occur, day after day – in bars and clubs, for instance – when following upon a minor trespass on someone's personal space, the "victim" of such trespass lashes out and threatens the "transgressor" with violence or admonishes him with a cold, withering glare. Or think of what regularly happens on the metro and in the streets: a commuter, distracted by the concerns of the day or perhaps annoyed and slightly jostled by the crowd, takes an aggressive step forward and bumps someone who, in turn, repays the favor with a stern, intimidating glare or some manifest expression of exasperation. Most often, this is followed by a shot of the eye to others who are called upon to produce subtle signs of collective disapproval or by a rolling back of the eyes and tilting back of the head, as if the offended party is registering a complaint with the Almighty. In what profound jeopardy the self must feel if the need to secure boundaries is *this* intense. How flimsy must bonds to the community be if, given the slightest injury or disrespect, one immediately appeals to a community of aggressive disapproval. As a final example, consider someone (the author specifies a borderline personality) who

> beneath [a] normal (and sometimes quite sophisticated) exterior . . . suffers from uncontrollable rages, inner emptiness, and lack of self-esteem and . . . is usually unable to form lasting affective relationships. Each attempt he makes to establish an intimate relationship with another person sends back to him an image of himself that he finds unbearable. Thus he seeks in solitude a semblance of authenticity to provide himself with an illusion of an inner life that will not be imperiled by the gaze of the other. The analysis . . . reveals a childhood marked by a lack of gratifying responses and by the scarcity of usable ideals. Their yearning and their needs were ignored by a parental gaze that was indifferent or even cruel. Because of this, they are unable to internalize a self-image stable enough to allow them to get involved in life [even though their normal and sometimes quite sophisticated exterior would lead us to believe otherwise]. (Gurewich 1998, p. 38; bracketed comments added)

100. As there are quite a few points of convergence and agreement between self psychology and ego psychology that are seldom noticed in the literature, let us attend to a few lest my concentration on their divergences give rise to distortions (and because this will reveal the applicability to self psychology of a number of criticisms leveled at ego psychology). Although

the emphasis on conformity is not as pronounced in self psychology as in ego psychology, it is nonetheless insistent. Consider, for instance, the following description of therapeutic progress: "the patient had made progress in the analysis . . . features of his personality that had formerly tended to isolate him (rebelliousness, nonconformity, resistance) were being replaced by attitudes which, while still making him feel special and superior . . . did so in a nonisolating, friendly, and socially acceptable way" (1984, p. 120). Of course, rebelliousness, nonconformity, or resistance may be, as they were in this case, defensively exaggerated, contributing to suffering so extreme and failures so regular and unintelligible that it motivates one to seek therapy. Aggressively pursuing a sense of personal value and distinctiveness, indeed so aggressively as to guarantee the failure of his pursuits, the client to whom Kohut refers in this passage could not but resist whatever was experienced as normative or expected. He was so contrary and contentious (his incessant negativity recalls the narrator of Dostoyevsky's *Notes From Underground*) that the recognitive consolidation without which his desired self-image would remain but a fantasy was hardly forthcoming. But even if, classically, Kohut is interested in facilitating the renegotiation of self-defeating and suffering-inducing forms of life rather than promoting conformity, he is just as reticent as ego psychologists to call into question the value of social acceptance and harmonious and integrated ("friendly") functioning. To be sure, Kohut is more concerned with the client's *compulsive* nonconformity and the fragile narcissism underlying this than with nonconformity *per se*. To the degree that ego psychology is focused on objectivity, i.e. the client's reality-testing aptitude and ability to realistically integrate her pursuits with those of the community, self psychology is focused on subjectivity, on whether the client is vitally – enthusiastically and authentically – engaged in her life practices and secure in her social bonds. But the narcissistic maturation and sense of individual authenticity and social embedding at which Kohut's clinic aims may require substantial modifications to nonconforming or rebellious trends. Self psychology, like ego psychology, though to a lesser extent, does seem to proscribe or pathologize radical resistance. Neither is inclined to read madness as (perhaps necessarily) convoluted social critique, the expression of the unsayable.

Kinship between ego psychology and self psychology is also evident in Kohut's clinical ambition to support the client's realization of basic ideals and ambitions via basic talents. The general thrust of his thinking gives rise to the impression that these basic ideals and talents are at least socially acceptable and likely socially esteemed; at least he never says otherwise. Furthermore, like ego psychology, self psychology promotes enhanced adaptation: the cohesive self at which it aims is said to be more flexible, better able to face rejections, slights, and disappointments, thus better able to achieve her core ideals and ambitions in the face of difficulties. Indeed, Kohut describes the sufficient accretion of self structure accomplished by successful analysis as supplanting "maladaptive" behavior. Although the ability to face rejections and disappointments while remaining committed to one's goals is necessary irrespective of their content and all the more important the more abrasive or unfamiliar, thus difficult to accomplish, their content, the ambitions and talents to which Kohut lends support are, on the whole, perfectly confluent with the dominant social order. One wonders whether profound dissatisfaction with and attempts to radically alter the status quo would seem pathological to Kohut, whether he would read them as failures to achieve an adequate balance of separation and connection, reducible to developmental deprivations, and so in need of therapeutic correction? *So it seems, self psychological therapy, at least on Kohut's conception, promotes steadfast commitments to socially acceptable goals and the adaptive capacity to realize them.* To put it a bit harshly (but just a bit): unlike ego psychology, self psychology does not just insist that we become realistic, adaptive, and socially productive, it demands our enthusiasm, enjoining us not just to do it, but to like it!

101. Freud sounded an early warning against, while at once (arguably) exemplifying, this gesture: "In scientific matters people are very fond of selecting one portion of the truth, putting it in place of the whole and then disputing the rest, which is no less true, in favor of this one portion. In just this way a number of schools of opinion have already split off from the psychoanalytic movement, some of which recognize the egoistic instincts while disavowing the sexual ones, and others attribute importance to the influence of the real tasks of life while overlooking the individual's past" (SE 16: 346). Also see note 160 below.

102. I take it that when Kohut suggests that analysts' "theories . . . must function as suggestions or proposals, not as commands or laws," by "theories" he means metapsychological theories or a certain range of them (1984, p. 153).

103. There is a long history of debasing "need" in psychoanalysis, especially amongst those influenced by Lacan. For example, cf. Laplanche (1976) *Life and Death in Psychoanalysis*. For an attempt to rethink the role of need in psychoanalysis, cf. Alan Bass (2006) *Interpretation and Difference: The Strangeness of Care*.

104. One might wonder whether the cool confidence with which psychoanalytic theory is applied to cinema, literature, politics, history, folklore, mythology, science, and so forth, as if a universal hermeneutic key able to unlock the secrets of all disciplines is also a manifestation of defensive decisiveness.

105. "[T]he old theories of the analytic cure, although correct within their respective frames of reference, were *incomplete*" (1984, p. 75).

106. For a similar account, cf. (1973) Neumann's *Depth Psychology and the New Ethic*.

107. A similar diagnosis is advanced by Putman (2000) *Bowling Alone*.

108. Despite an arguable sociological astuteness, Kohut remains psychologistsic insofar as, ultimately, the social transformations he tracks are explained and evaluated in terms of the psychological needs they satisfy or fail.

109. This is analogous to the process that Winnicott elaborates in much greater detail under the heading of transitional phenomena. This process will be discussed in chapter 4.

110. In Winnicott's idiom, preemptory maternal preoccupation, the madness of early motherhood.

111. "our sharing routes of interest and feeling, modes of response, senses of humor and of significance and of fulfillment, of what is outrageous, of what is similar to what else, what a rebuke, what forgiveness, of when an utterance is an assertion, when an appeal, when an explanation – all the whirl of organism Wittgenstein calls 'form of life.' Human speech and activity, sanity and community, rest upon nothing more, but nothing less, than this. It is a vision as simple as it is (and because it is) terrifying" (Cavell 1962, p. 74).

112. I say "drive or need" because, as opposed to the reigning conception of the drive, here there is no source, the aim is constant (only the object may vary), and there is no limit to reflective recuperation. Since such a "drive" is not subject to sublimation, neutralization, defensive adaptation, or conflict, nor is there independent energy associated with it, it is not quite a drive. But insofar as it is a fundamental source of movement, a guiding force, it is akin to a drive.

113. For indirect contestations of this claim, cf. Agamben (2002) *Remnants of Auschwitz*, Levi (1988) *The Drowned and the Saved*, and Arendt (1998) *The Human Condition*, specifically their respective discussions of the Musselman.

114. Cf. 1984, p. 40.

115. E.g., methods of validating psychoanalytic predictions, however refined, can never put to rest the skeptical worry about consensus-bias: predictions may be validated only because treatments observed are conducted as the validators would conduct them.

116. Thus it is near-inevitable that some will contest whether psychoanalytic judgments convey content, i.e., amount to knowledge at all – in this respect, psychoanalysis finds itself in a situation akin to that of artistic modernism: the potential for aversive responses to its claims and their ongoing unsettledness is internal to the nature of such claims. "[B]eing so committed [i.e., having a belief] must be understood as taking up a stance in an *inferentially* articulated network – that is, one in which the commitment carries with it various others as its *inferential consequences* and *rules out* others that are incompatible [latter emphases added]. Only as occupying a position in such a network can it be understood as *propositionally* (and hence *conceptually*) contentful . . . . For it to be knowledge one is attributing, one must also take the commitment to be one the believer is in some sense *entitled* to" (Brandom 2003, p. 118).

117. For a more nuanced reading of Hegel's notion of *Geist*, cf. Merold Westphal (1979) *History & Truth in Hegel's Phenomenology*, chapters 5 and 6; and Robert Pippin (2008) *Hegel's Practical Philosophy: Rational Agency as Ethical Life*.

118. For a diametrically opposed reading of Hegel, cf. Gillian Rose (1981) *Hegel Contra Sociology*.

119. Cf. Idit Dobbs Weinstein (1995) *Maimonides and St. Thomas on the Limits of Reason* (1995), especially "Introduction" and chapters 5-7. Note that Kohut's affinity to the figure of the Maimonidean prophet is as loose as his affinity to Hegel and Marx adequately understood.

120. To be sure, here as elsewhere Kohut may qualify his claims about the ever-present prospects for developmental completion, express a certain hesitation or scrupulousness (notice the language of "realizable possibility"), but the firmness of his faith in the realizability of that developmental completion, and therewith a harmoniously integrated self, shines forth. Consider the following passage: "It is *certainly imaginable* that, even in adult life, the repeated experience of optimal frustration in an archaic homeostatic selfobject environment brought about in the analytic situation would lead, as in earliest infancy, to the birth of a nuclear self" (1984, p. 8; emphasis added). Though Kohut explicitly qualifies his clinical ambition as no more than imaginable, or more precisely, plausible (not just imaginable but "certainly imaginable"), the locution "certainly imaginable" suggests an undaunted security in his convictions despite their evident want of demonstrative certainty.

121. Presumably, complete frustration of developmental need is what makes a patient unanalyzable.

122. The rhetoric of "need" is extraordinarily pervasive. To name just a few instances, Kohut speaks of the need for narcissistic sustenance, of the need to express anger when frustrated, and of "maturation-directed needs for structure building" (1984, p. 71).

123. Cf. J.M. Bernstein (2009) "Sexuate Being: Foundations for a Feminist Legal Philosophy?" in Heberle and Pryor (eds.) *Imagining Law: On Drucilla Cornell.*

124. A related question is whether Kohut likewise falls prey to this mistake when he extrapolates the basic features of pathology and of the psychoanalytic clinic from his analyses of narcissistic personality and behavioral disorders. He would not be alone here. Regularly in the history of psychoanalysis, theoretical reckoning with experiences afforded by a certain sector of the patient population is presented as an account of the whole of psychopathology or of psychic life altogether and as able to provide therapeutic guidelines for the treatment of all patients, if not more. Such is psychoanalytic "development." Freud noted, while (arguably) at once exemplifying, this tendency many times: "All out apostates always grasped part of the truth and wanted to declare it as the whole truth" (Freud to Jones 1993, p. 635); "It is an almost human characteristic of these 'secessionist movement' that each of them takes hold of one fragment out of the wealth of themes in psychoanalysis and makes itself independent on the basis of this seizure – selecting the drive for mastery, for instance, or ethical conflict, or the mother, or genitality, and so on" (SE 16: 143-4); "There must, of course, be *something* correct about in [Adler's] theory of 'individual psychologists'; a small particle is taken for the whole" (SE 22: 142). As an example among others, consider Anna Freud's massive extrapolations from her work with Dorothy Burlingham's children.

125. Cf. 1984, pp. 56 and 104.

126. It should be noted, however, that the intolerances that fuel Kohut's fervent conviction in the drive to development also give rise to a certain tolerance for what others are prone to stigmatize as pathological. For instance, Kohut welcomes defenses and resistances insofar as they safeguard the self for future development. As with Anna Freud, there is evidence in Kohut's work of a profoundly depathologizing impulse. He may accept affection or hostility as elements of the transference relation rather than interpret them as defenses against underlying unconscious libido or aggression; rather than simply situate them as pathogenic phenomena, Kohut may consider superego demands as occasions for their fulfillment and thus for self esteem; in contradistinction to ego's psychology's emphatic adaptivism ("realism"), he depathologizes the infantile, claiming that a kernel of infantile vitality and excitement must be preserved if later life is to be vibrant and self-esteem adequately established, and further that preserving such a kernel will not, contra ego psychological worries, induce fixation or regression; generally, he depathologizes narcissism, considering it a source of vitality, creativity, meaning, and enthusiasm. But of course, this depathologizing impulse has its limits. For instance, as we have seen, Kohut situates what Freud would consider ordinary psychosexual development as an expression of distorted selfobject relations, a byproduct of developmental deficit to be eradicated.

127. Cf. 1984, pp. 13-14.

128. Though he does not thematize this concern, Kohut like Laplanche is interested in redressing the one-sided focus on fantasy provoked by Freud's revision to his original seduction theory.

129. Kohut makes clear his conviction that selfobject failures are the *ultimate* causes of pathology – "the self psychologically informed . . . identifies *causal sequences*, he shows the patient that his feelings and reactions are *explained by* this experiences in early life" (1984, p. 25; emphases added) – but never claims that they are the *only* causes. Because it is so tempting to read Kohut as reducing all pathology to selfobject failure, let us cite one more passage that seems to follow this protocol, but when carefully considered resists it. When Kohut claims that "the little boy's manifest horror at the sight of the female genitals is not the deepest layer of this experience but . . . behind it and covered by it lies a deeper and even more dreadful experience---the experience of the faceless mother, that is, the mother whose face does not light up at the sight of her child," he seems to be saying that castration anxiety is but a symptom of *the real problem*, namely, a withholding or depressed mother – selfobject failure (1979, p. 19-20). To be sure, Kohut posits want of affirmation as "deeper," "the deepest layer," "behind" horror at the female genitals and "covered by it." But this veil, what manifests on the surface, is not to be taken lightly. Even though this veil can be removed – castration anxiety seen as a cover for the plight of selfobject failure, a fantasy, and in a way a healthy one (insofar as the need for affirmation is sustained and its terrible disappointment concealed, thus its consequences held in check) – it is not to be dismissed: its removal may even require its sustained and serious attending rather than a rush to rip it off (how else than by leading the patient to see his drive to development as preserved even in his anxieties will he be invested with confidence ample enough to support developmental reactivation? Might such confidences, in this context, even amount to an incremental advance in development?). Here and elsewhere, Kohut is cautious not to propose that one go plodding forth to the archaic, ignoring everything epiphenomenal. Rather, he affirms, analysis must slowly make its way from the surface to the depths – at one point he even flags this bit of classical wisdom as something he is willing to accept on face value (on faith) (1984, p. 22). Even if Kohut maintains that "[d]isintegration anxiety . . . . is the deepest anxiety man can experience," that does not mean that other anxieties, say, castration anxieties, are negligible (1984, p. 16). It may even be that understanding disintegration anxiety requires attending to its various manifestations, that disintegration anxiety is nothing but the grammar of its variable expressions – though Kohut never goes this far.

130. Cf. Kohut (1977-8) *The Search for the Self*, Volume 2: 783-92.

131. For an emphatic counterpoint, cf. Jacqueline Rose (1993) "Negativity in the Work of Melanie Klein" in *Why War?*

132. Cf. Walter Benjamin (1969) "The Task of the Translator" in *Illuminations* (ed.) Hannah Arendt.

133. Inappropriate functioning is not simply a matter of overtly sexual or sadistic acts on a caregivers' behalf; rather, it is a matter of styles of care, e.g., smothering a child with kindness (experienced as stifling and cruel insofar as it massively inhibits expressions of anger), treating a child in a prohibitive or rejecting manner, exhibiting tendencies to withdraw, or engaging in subtly competitive hostility: "[i]t is often by focusing our attention not on the content but on the form of parental behavior that we can best answer the decisive question of whether . . . [it] will create a traumatic or a wholesome atmosphere" (1984, p. 15). Notice the subtle displacements of nearly all of Ferenczi's core claims.

134. Such enthusiastic optimism is most prominent in his discussions of psychotic and borderline patients. On the basis of his theory of pathology, Kohut recasts the distinction between psychosis and neurosis, insisting on gradation where many (although certainly neither Freud nor Klein) claim clear-cut, categorical distinctions. Setting the various pathologies along a continuum of narcissistic maturation, Kohut claims that anyone, even borderline or psychotic individuals, can develop self structure, become free from pathological sexuality and aggression, thus come to concern themselves, predominantly, with their "basic program."

This is in stark opposition to Freud, who, especially in his early work, connects psychotic "rejection" (*verwerfen*), hallucination, and projection with defenses against sexuality, claiming that even if the specific psychotic defense is dissolved, the basic irritant, sexuality, persists. Later, Freud emphasizes the reversion of libidinal object cathexes to ego cathexes and the attempts to restore a link with reality (the ego, no longer in touch with reality and under the sway of the id, concocts delusions, a new relationship with reality) as the primary characteristics of psychosis, but even so, for Freud, psychosis like all pathology centrally involves the inherent tumult of sexuality, its irreducible and uncircumventable excessiveness: a psychotic defense may be dismantled, but some form of defense is inevitable given the ambivalent, conflictual nature of sexuality.

For Kohut, the main issue is not sexuality; it is, rather, that psychotic and borderline individuals have not developed the outlines of a nuclear self in early development. Thus, given the right sort of modulations of their selfobject relations (i.e., therapy, but perhaps not only), they can develop more mature self structure. Or in extreme cases, namely, with respect to psychotics who are unable to build nuclear self structure to the point where significant developmental advance, let alone completion, seems realizable – and this, I believe, is Kohut's single concrete concession that complete development may not be realizable for some; though given the general thrust of his thinking, one may suspect that Kohut might be tempted to attribute such psychotics' extremely stultified development to the underdevelopment of his own technique (notice the grammar of sin) – the therapist will seek to build and buttress existing defenses and teach the client how to use her defensive structures to realize what goals he may (1984, p. 9).

One step further along the gradient, Kohut places narcissistic personality and behavioral disturbances. These manifest the rudimentary outlines of a nuclear self, but self structure is incomplete: the self is enfeebled, prone to fragmentation and an intense feeling of disharmony when subject to the narcissistic injuries to which it is particularly sensitive. However, given the right sort of selfobject relations, self structure will be consolidated, at which point those once suffering from narcissistic personality and behavioral disturbances will come to live basically "normal" lives, i.e., will be predominantly focused on realizing their basic ideals and ambitions by calling upon their basic talents and skills in order to overcome what they will come to see as nothing but contingent impediments to their socially productive self-realization.

Finally, conflict neuroses arise when the self is unable to realize its "creative-productive potential" because its "energies [are] absorbed" by the Oedipus complex (1984, p. 10). Here, classical analytic protocols will facilitate disencumberment from Oedipal hang-ups, allowing the client to focus her energy on realizing her basic ambitions.

Given the drive to or need for development, pathology is essentially correctible. Where others see epic conflict or the inherent disharmony of the human, Kohut sees potential.

135. Although it often seems that Kohut's emphasis on empathic immersion is quite at odds with ego psychology's concern for systematization and the validity afforded by external observation, there is much greater confluence between the two than is often noted.

136. The procedure outlined below, Kohut maintains, is primarily suitable for neurotics because its primary component is transference analysis. It will not be fitting for psychotic or borderline individuals, who, he suggests, are in a certain sense (initially) unanalyzable, (preliminarily) in need of another sort of therapy (1984, p. 71). Even though, as we saw earlier, Kohut's theory of pathology projects the possibility of bringing psychotics and borderlines to complete structural development, or if not, at least of helping them use their defenses in a more satisfying and productive manner, his technique is not the means by which to do so.

137. Although, Kohut qualifies, understanding and explanation can sometimes run together from the get-go, for the most part they remain discrete: in the understanding phase, for a long while, the analyst patiently refrains from overhasty interpretation; eventually s/he becomes talkative, verbalizing that s/he understands what the patient feels, or something like it, and thereby establishes an empathic bond (Cf. 1984, p. 177). Too quick or too much interpretation will be experienced by the analysand as anxious and defensive, thus will impede the development of a secure empathic bond.

138. ibid.

139. Interestingly, Mitchell and Black (1996) illustrate alter ego or twinship transference with the example of a client who yearns to feel that "a like-gendered analyst shares a sensibility about being male or female" (161). Of course, there is nothing necessarily wrong with this yearning, but insofar as Kohut would probably never for a moment consider that seeking shared sensibilities about gender, and what's more, the "proper" embodiment of those sensibilities as a

way to shore up a sense of personal integrity and social solidarity *may* be defensive, the limits of his socio-critical acuity, especially as it bears on the limits of his awareness of his normative involvements, may become limits to the efficacy of his therapy. Might yearning to learn that you, like me, experience "our" gender in an essentially similar way be in the service of avoiding, say, (1) anxieties surrounding a dim or disavowed awareness of the indeterminacy and instability of gender or matters for which gender, indeterminacy, or instability (or their various conjunctions) have come to stand or become closely associated in my particular psychic economy, (2) coming to terms with the loss or foreclosure of same-sex object attachments that condition the rigidity of my attachments to heteronormatively configured gender identity [cf. Judith Butler (1997) *The Psychic Life of Power*], or (3) the fact or the worry that I don't experience the link between sex, gender, and sexuality in a heteronormative way, or desire not to, and as the associated anxiety and/or stern superego admonishments.

140. The language of theories as "helpmate not masters" is repeated at 1984, p. 204.

141. Cf. 1984, chapter 2.

142. Implicitly, of course. Kohut seems to not have been familiar with Lacan's work.

143. Or her ultraorthodox claim in "Flight from Womanhood" (1926) that penis envy is often a defense against Oedipal wishes, inadequacy being easier to bear than guilt.

144. Cf. Klein (1977) "Love, Guilt, Reparation."

145. One guess – not about its origins but about its contemporary insistence: the tendency to interpartisan subsumption and pathologization indicative of the impulse to sanctify a perspective as the one true theory may be a response to, indeed the consequence of an internalization of, cultural/scientific skepticism about psychoanalysis (further amplified by an inevitable moment of intra-psychoanalytic skepticism). This is to suggest that, ironically, psychoanalysis tends to seek (idealized) science-like certainty, models itself on (idealized) science, hence tends toward self-mythologization, in consequence of its susceptibility to the skepticism of scientistic culture vis-à-vis its practices; yet its efforts to secure such certainty (via subsumption, pathologization, etc.) promote the picture of chaotic speculation that attracted scientific skepticism in the first place.

146. Later, Mitchell attempts to integrate the insights of these several camps, but his conciliatory efforts beg the question. If each camp accuses the other of pathological collusion, would not an integration of their insights be open to the charge of pathological collusion from all sides – a charge amplified insofar as integration involves what proponents of any single camp would consider distortions of their views, dilutions of their techniques? Why would Mitchell expect those involved in mutual pathologization to accept his arbitration? If acceptance is unlikely, what purpose does such arbitration serve? "On the one hand, an aggressively interpretive approach misses the need of the analysand to establish the narcissistic integration and runs the risk of discouraging the gambit and driving the transference underground. Grandiosity and idealization interpreted as defenses against anxiety, aggression, and separation are not appreciated as efforts to reach the object through familiar patterns, preferred modes of connection and intimacy. Thus, in Kernberg's discussion of these issues, narcissistic configurations are understood as defenses against anxieties generated by oral aggression within early object relationships, rather than as expressions of these object relations as entrenched familial patterns throughout childhood. The danger here is of encouraging resistances to the expression and establishment of these key transferential configurations and compliance with what can only be experienced as the analyst's insistence on less narcissistic, more 'real' perceptions and relations. On the other hand, a receptive, unquestioning approach misses the function of the narcissistic integrations in perpetuating old object ties, and runs the risk of consolidating them . . . . The danger of not appreciating illusions as vehicles for preserving entrenched familial patterns is of encouraging resistances to the resolution of these transferential configurations, and what can only be experienced as the analyst's own investment in and encouragement of compulsive narcissistic illusions" (1999, pp. 171-2).

147. Cf. Bernstein (2001), pp. 75-135.

148. Or, in a Wittgensteinian mood, one might say "a practice."

149. Compare Wittgenstein: "If language is to be a means of communication there must be agreement not only in definition but also . . . in judgments. This seems to abolish logic but does not do so" (PI § 242) While maintaining caution regarding his representational idiom, also

compare Husserl: "However we may change the world in imagination or represent to ourselves the future course of the world, unknown to us, in terms of its possibilities, 'as it might be,' we necessarily represent it according to the style in which we have, and up to now have had, the world" (1970, p. 31).

150. Though ambivalently and inadequately, this is something to which Freud gestures: "at the stage of description it is not possible to avoid applying certain abstract ideas to the materials at hand, ideas derived from somewhere or other but certainly not from the observations alone" (SE 14: 117).

151. This does not mean that the displacements enacted by emerging perspectives are easily recognizable to any party involved. That which has been of central, orienting significance to the tradition(s) from which a perspective departs may become clear, if at all, only upon such departure or in later attempts to come to terms with its consequences (which means, in principle, inconclusively).

152. To his credit, in a number of places Freud seems to recognize the exaggerated character of his constructions, though he isolates this insight, failing to thematize or reflexively incorporate it. For instance, at one point he presents his focus on childhood as if an exaggerated response to an exaggeration: "The emphasis which is laid here upon the importance of the earliest experiences does not imply any underestimation of the influence of later ones. But the later impressions of life speak loudly enough through the mouth of the patient, while it is the physician who has to raise his voice on behalf of the claims of childhood" (SE 17: 183). Of course, many – e.g., Fromm – would disagree with Freud's self-assessment and claim that he *did* in fact underestimate the influence of later experiences. Likewise, Freud sometimes approaches but never fails to subtly or unsubtly repudiate the perspectival character of psychoanalytic knowing, e.g., "I am making use here of a series of similes, all of which have only a very limited resemblance to my theme and which are also mutually incompatible. I know this, and I am not in danger of overestimating their value, but I am led by the objective of illustrating from different sides an extremely complicated topic which has never yet been represented" (SE 2: 291). Other examples of this tendency are evident in the manner in which Freud revises his texts. Though the – frequent – revisions often contradict or substantially modify the claims of earlier editions, Freud does not suppress what is challenged, modified, or abandoned and replaced, allowing different perspectives to remain in view. However, the confident tenor of his revisions suggests that older views are preserved as merely of historical interest or as records of temptations to be avoided.

153. Cf. de Man (1983) *Blindness and Insight: Essays in the Rhetoric of Contemporary Criticism*, esp. p. 106.

154. "There is *only* a perspective seeing, *only* a perspective 'knowing'; and the *more* affects we allow to speak about one thing, the *more* eyes, different eyes, we can use to observe one thing, the more complete will our 'concept' of this thing, our 'objectivity,' be" (Nietzsche (1989) *On the Genealogy of Morals*, p. 119; original emphasis).

155. Of course, there are various ways of suggesting: inviting, encouraging, tutoring, uninsistently making room for, clearing obstacles and undermining impediments to its assumption, etc.

156. Cf. Dieter Henrich (1994) "The Concept of Moral Insight and Kant's Doctrine of the Fact of Reason," in *The Unity of Reason: Essays on Kant's Philosophy*.

157. For elaborations of such a dream in the context of psychoanalysis, cf. Ferrell (1981), pp. 144-5 and the writings of Robert Wallerstein.

158. For a precursor of this strategy, cf. Nietzsche (1989) *Genealogy of Morals*, pp. 74-8.

159. Allow me to suggest in passing that theorizing untheorizability (in the sense of purporting to generally comprehend or demonstrate it), thematizing unthematizability, or otherwise advancing a general (context-absorbing) thesis regarding irreducible remainders as often occurs in discussions of "the event," "the thing," or "the Real," is abstract identity-thinking, therefore self-defeating.

160. Such a turn, however, need not be the final fate of the dialectical development of insight as if, in a vulgar pragmatist vein, politics were revealed as the "truth" of cognition. Indeed, as the medium of normative self-consciousness, the political may undergo transformation via dispersal. Turning back upon and rearticulating itself in, as, and through such a medium, the

dialectical development of insight may unfold by rendering prominent questioning tacit throughout such as what we count as advances in various domains, why they are so counted, how domains are divided, thus who we are and might become – which suffices to say that in becoming practical-political, the dialectical development of insight does not abandon cognitive interests for power projection.

161. I am not claiming that all psychoanalytic schools succeed in presenting themselves as perspectives. Quite to the contrary, my claim is that they would come into their truth were they to do so, thus I am urging such a development and undertaking it in a very preliminary way. Though psychoanalytic schools cannot be thought as anything but perspectives in the sense I have been elaborating (they are surely not the sites of privileged access to universal and univocal truth), most – if not all – fail to understand themselves as such and falsify themselves as a result. Perspective in the sense I am elaborating is the suppressed *structure* of psychoanalytic knowing, a structure deflated in order to inflate, i.e., bring into prominence, the specific insights or therapeutic prospects (contents) of each school.

Chapter Three

Conflict and Controversy

INTRODUCTION: PROMISCUITY IN SCHOOL

Psychoanalytic plurality is truly breathtaking — at once inspiring and bewildering.[1] There are certainly points of overlap where partisans of various persuasions find themselves in agreement even if their respective reasons for their shared positions differ. For instance, most analysts agree that analysis of resistances should precede analysis of repressed content. Even concerning more contentious topics such as how to treat schizophrenics, there is a great deal of agreement between adherents of Sullivinian, Kleinian, and various object relations traditions.[2] Yet efforts to specify what would be essential to psychoanalysis, say, its distinctive object domain, quickly reveal its irreducible equivocity. Even incredibly abstract claims such as "psychoanalysis is an inquiry into the unconscious and its manifestations" fail to comprehend, let alone usefully elaborate, a variety of practices pursued by self-proclaimed and sometimes generally recognized analysts, e.g., those for whom the unconscious is not always at issue or may even be of relatively marginal concern (e.g., Reich, Laing, and to a lesser extent, Winnicott, Kohut, and development-oriented strands of ego psychology).

The most cursory glance at some typical controversies should be enough to make the radical plurality of psychoanalysis amply evident. There are, for instance, severe disagreements over schemas of psychosexual development (compare those of Freud, Abraham, and Klein, or compare Mahler's separation-individuation developmental theory with the developmental theory of Kohut or Erikson), the relevance of empirical research to their formulation, and their role in or bearing on theories of pathology and therapy.[3] Then there is the related question of whether pathogenic phenomena should be traced back to empirical experiences (Ferenczi, Kohut, Winnicott, Guntrip (1961,

1968, 1971), Laplanche, Bollas, Masterson and Rinsley (1975), Epstein (1979), sometimes Kris,[4] to a certain extent Sullivan (1953, 1962), Fromm, and Thompson), or predominantly treated as "psychic reality" (a certain Freud, Lacan, Klein, Schafer).[5] Related as well is the dispute about whether psychic phenomena should be taken as tokens of universal structures or archetypes. On the one side of this dispute would be a certain Freud, Jung, and Lacan, and on the other, the trio of Maria Torok, Nicholas Abraham, and Nicholas Rand, as well as Laplanche, Bersani, and a certain Bion, Bollas, and Kristeva.

Further, there are weighty disagreements about matters of metaphysical stature such as the nature of the human, or more specifically, that of our relations to others and to culture generally. Such disagreements often play out in disputes about seemingly less grandiose topics such as the status of the drives, e.g., in relation to questions such as (1) whether drive life is wholly endogenous or at least semi-autonomous as Freud and Klein contend, or is significantly and extensively shaped by "external" experiences, specifically, those involving early relations to primary caregivers, as Erikson, Kohut, Sullivan, Fromm, Thompson, Kernberg, and others claim; (2) whether there is a death drive, as Ferenczi, Fenichel (1945), and Kleinians insist[6] in disagreement with Fairbairn, Lear, Fenichel (1935),[7] and the Schultz-Henke group[8] — various ego psychologists such as Hartmann and Lowenstein do not exactly accept the "death drive," although they do believe there to be inherently aggressive impulses;[9] Kohut wavers; and (3) whether classical drive theory is still viable, as many classical Freudians maintain, in opposition to Sullivan (1953), Fairbairn (1954), and Guntrip (1969), who more or less wholly relinquish drive theory in favor of a theory of endogenous object-seeking[10] — between these extremes are many working in object relations and British independent traditions who hold that object attachments are both intrinsic and immensely important but do not wholly repudiate classical drive theory.[11]

Then there are disagreements over clinical questions such as (1) whether breaking the rule of neutrality and equidistant or free-floating attention is acceptable and/or inevitable, or more specifically, when, how and to what end are analysts to administer gratifications or engage in various supportive measures (e.g., are supportive measures simply propedeutic to interpretation or a primary medium of therapy?[12]); (2) whether there is ever need for self-disclosure on the part of the analyst, and if so, what would be its appropriate role and manner? Generally, the question is: What is the proper or most efficient structure of address to maintain in the clinical setting? Should the analysand be kept intentionally unsettled so that her desire is mobilized, her defenses thrown off-kilter, and thereby, her unconscious able to resonate with the analyst's speech and express itself in excess of ego-induced restrictions? Or should the analysand be held, secured in a stable space of relative psychic safety in which she is addressed in primarily ego-syntonic terms that allow her to slowly reactivate her suppressed needs and/or repeatedly return to and renegotiate compromises brokered in a relatively immature or overburdened state, perhaps even amplify the adaptive aptitude of her ego, defenses, etc.?

Another sort of clinical dispute concerns the authoritative delineation of specifically psychoanalytic therapy. E.g., are therapies that are recognizably psychoanalytic in orientation but involve psychopharmacological supplements genuinely instances of analysis? Or what of therapies that make use of psychoanalytic concepts, insights, and methods, but not exclusively? Concerning the latter, it is worth noting that there are currently over 400 recognized psychotherapies in the U.S. alone, a great many of which, though professing a certain allegiance to the psychoanalytic tradition, diverge quite noticeably from classical analysis. Examples of quasi-analytic practices include brief analysis (Balint, Malan, Sifneos), the use of analytic insights and structures of attention by doctors, therapists, social workers, and mental health counselors who are not trained as psychoanalysts, and the various therapeutic practices that bear some resemblance to those of the Freudian tradition but are much more in line with Franz Alexander's advocacy of "corrective emotional experiences."

Though one's stance on these disputes may give some indication of one's partisan commitments, this is not necessarily the case. An overall partisan stance, in other words, cannot necessarily be inferred from a survey of specific commitments, hence may not be a deductively integrated totality. This might strike us as curious, and it leads us to the initial topic of this chapter: psychoanalytic plurality in excess of partisan differences. In order to present the plurality of psychoanalytic perspectives, the last chapter reconstructed the core commitments of various schools and staged small-scale debates between them. The price of so doing was marginalizing the many differences between analysts that are irreducible to interpartisan disagreements, along with the often unsettled character — hence content — of partisan commitment itself. Finding that the resources of no single school are sufficient to successfully negotiate with or even account for all that confronts them daily in clinical practice or via engagements with the psychic dynamics of the aesthetic and political phenomena with which they are concerned, with accelerating frequency and mounting intensity, analysts and the analytically inclined are becoming pluralistic. Though partisan sympathies have hardly vanished, many — perhaps most — analysts and analytically inclined individuals do not identify with and draw exclusively from a single analytic school.

Even among analysts who identify with a particular school, much that transpires in clinical practice does not derive from and even may be in tension with official persuasion.[13] Freud, certainly, did not always adhere to what was to become classical Freudian technique: he openly expressed concern for his clients, loaned them money and in certain cases arranged for donations, accepted at least one analysis gratis, instructed analysands in the basic tenets of psychoanalysis, gave them gifts, and lectured to them on the origins of artifacts in his consulting room, the history of archeology, and ancient Egypt.[14] As Glover emphasized already in 1955: "*even in so-called classical analysis of the psychoneuroses, the approach of different analysts varies not only in numerous points of detail but also on many important points of policy*" (165; original italics). Those committed to the classical analysis of psychoneuroses, Glover later underscores, vary in "every imaginable way" (373). Corroborating this point and echoing Glover's slide into hyperbole, Friedman, in his *Anatomy of Psychoanalysis*, contends that "[i]f treatment as written about seems so discursive and intellectual and neat and cool, perhaps treatment as it happens really works on the basis of what every psychotherapist feels daily: personal push and pull; nameless, theory-less, shapeless, swarming interaction" (1988, 12). Exaggerating the excessiveness of analytic practice with respect to doctrinal commitments, Friedman brings such excess clearly into view, while, via his seemingly rhetorical "perhaps," tempering this exaggeration with an allusion to the extent to which analytic interaction and reverie are conditioned by inherited, theory-mediated structures of attention, hermeneutic commitments, conceptions of appropriate end states, and so on. Dialectical tension is sustained, though coarse.

Though it may not yet be at risk of collapsing into eclecticism, psychoanalysis is a hotbed of promiscuity. Not only do different schools theorize and respond to the same clinical and cultural material in very different ways,[15] within a single school there are often significant divergences reflecting the disparate, even incompatible, clinical and extra-clinical aims, hermeneutic protocols, and understandings of basic theoretical and clinical principles of its adherents. But even this does not go far enough. Differences obtain not only between and within schools, but within each analyst. For instance, every interpretation on which an analyst settles emerges from out of but never finally transcends a shadowy realm of interpretive outcasts. Lingering in such shadows are creatures variously developed: some are ill-defined, but barely born; some adolescent, awkward yet powerful; some stiff and brittle, clearly well past their prime; some curiously stunted, containing a kernel of compelling insight but lacking the reach of vision to find its nourishment; some hypertrophied, dauntingly imposing in their general applicability yet too coarse, never quite right; some downright mangled and ghastly or merely mistaken; some fully developed yet idle — intriguing, perhaps even valid, but useless; and some compelling alternatives that for whatever reason didn't make the cut. Contra Friedman, what lurks in such shadows may be the spawn of an overabundant disciplinary inheritance as much as of its lack of traction. Irrespective of their sources, however, the creatures that haunt the shadowy realm of interpretive abjection, supposing exposure to it is sustained, exert a drag on interpretive confidence, draw it back to its conceptually unmasterable impetus, the concrete — conceptually exorbitant and elusive yet, or rather because, eminently, indeed multiply conceptualizable — suffering of the psychic, and thereby sustain the open-ended character of the psychoanalytic experiment, bring psychoanalysis into its truth (yet again, always again) by preserving the interpretive indeterminacy of the objects of which it treats. That is, what persist in the shadows is a reservoir of remainders, the unpursued yet untranscended, that, if heeded, which need not mean directly attended, trouble the easy confidence which the "ah ha" element of insight and the impressive results of psychoanalytic therapy risk letting run wild.[16]

As Bersani puts the point in his typically overstated way, "overdetermination . . . defines the psychoanalytic mind — that is, the mind that has renounced none of its interpretations of the real" (2000, 157). What this overstatement conceals is, first, that analysts regularly refrain from or don't even consider developing certain interpretations as others are pursued, and what is not sufficiently developed *cannot* be renounced for the same reason that it cannot be claimed. Refusing to renounce what cannot be renounced or claimed but merely forgone is not an accomplishment or attitude characteristic of "the psychoanalytic mind" but a category mistake. Second, a vast number of interpretations are renounced as an analysis unfolds, and perhaps for good reasons. Contra Bersani's idealism, their slow shading into oblivion, at least in certain cases, may be a blessing — to assume otherwise is to discount the possibility of seriously misguided or even silly ideas arising, as does happen, and to presume that analysts are perfectly well analyzed, whatever that would mean, and in particular that they do not struggle with countertransference. Nevertheless, what is to be appreciated in Bersani's overstatement is what he is driving at: unavoidably and often without due appreciation, analysts allow various interpretative possibilities to commingle, to confront, question, and qualify each other, and thereby to sustain the difficulty of analytic knowing. Not only because analysts entertain multiple interpretations that are not readily compatible ("overdetermination"), but also because, contra Bersani, each specific interpretation is developed by suppressing, neglecting, or foreclosing multiple alternatives ("the psychoanalytic mind" is not self-transparent), and because the material from which interpretations are forged is both limited[17] and inexhaustible, no interpretation can redeem a claim to exhaustive and incontestable truth, thus only by sustaining exposure to the ill-assured and incomplete character of analytic knowing is analytic truth sustained.

That psychoanalytic interpretations are contestable from a number of directions is not news, but that they are not regularly susceptible to decisive refutation, or why they are not, may be. Conversely, an analytic interpretation, however well supported, cannot wholly exclude alternatives; it is a suggestion, a normative venture however inferentially or deductively assembled,[18] a questing first and foremost for felicitous authority, not validity.[19] As we will see, the associations and other material from which interpretations proceed, thus interpretations themselves, give voice to an unending though not entirely indeterminate past and its aftermath as forever unconsolidated psychic structure; because interpretations are mediations, to an extent constructive but not free-floating, they are both eminently contestable and, likely, bound to get or to do something right (on a certain conception of the analytic process). If interpretations falsify themselves when they overstate their case — claim either demonstrative certainty or self-evidence and thereby disclaim their normative interests, context-mediated significance, hence distinctive object domain — and such distortions are both compounded and concealed by the scientific deflation and/or domestication overstatement invites — psychoanalytic dogma is an open invitation to scientific skepticism and its echo, a moment within an interminable because mutually provoking conflict between aspirants to unimpeachable universality, combatants bound to the site of their conflict (certainty) as to a vanishing memory of authority neither can revive and, in a way, neither wants to see return, but which neither can let go for fear of total collapse — then sustained dialectical tension may be the manner (the *how*) of psychoanalytic truth.

But this is all by way of anticipation. What this, the previous chapter, and the subsequent chapter should make clear is that not only are reasons for commitment to one school rather than another wanting in demonstrative force, so too are reasons for commitment to one interpretation or type of interpretation rather than another — generally, that no appeal to the particular (*this* particular case, or even more locally, this particular manifestation of, say, anxiety) will do to authoritatively resolve the question of what to make of and how to treat clinical, or more broadly, psychic phenomena. Correlatively, what was gestured toward in the previous two chapters and should become increasingly visible in this and subsequent chapters is how deep the rabbit hole goes, that is, the immensity, complexity, and mutual implication of theoretical and clinical issues involved in seemingly local questions. Finally, this and the previous two chapters seek to suggest, albeit obliquely, that the diversity of psychoanalysis reflects something about the nature of its objects — specifically, as will be claimed in chapters 5, 6, and 7 that the objects of psychoanalytic inquiry are ontologically indeterminate, partially pliable to interpretive constitution or inflection, both discovered and created.

INTERPRETATIONS OF INTERPRETATION

To be sure, when it comes to questions of interpretation, there are certain points of across-the-field agreement. For instance, contemporary common sense holds that intervention-heavy analysis tends to be experienced as intrusive, even persecutory, and didactic — likely, it will be either defensively comforting or disorganizing. But then the question is: What is "intervention-heavy" analysis? For Lacan, who compares the analyst to the dummy in bridge,[20] Freud must have seemed a rather intervention-heavy analyst insofar as he was given to pose direct questions, quote Shakespeare and otherwise illustrate analytic concepts, propose interpretations and even genetic reconstructions relatively early in the course of analysis, etc. A Freudian whose basic interpretive demeanor is to grunt inquisitively now and again will likely find Kleinian interpretive practices intervention-heavy, just as s/he may find Lacanian practices of intervening to direct the analysand's attention to words or themes that have been glossed over excessive and untoward. But absent explication of and warrants for the criteria in virtue of which acceptable practices are distinguished from those that are excessively didactic, "deep," or interventionistic, such accusations are but self-aggrandizing assertions.

And although there is broad agreement that in principle *everything* in analysis is subject to interpretation, there is no consensus about how much emphasis to put on different material, how interpretive inferences are to be drawn (e.g., what are the rightful roles of empathy, countertransference, and conscious reasoning, including reasoning informed by developmental theory and other high-order mediators, in formulating interpretations — if indeed interpretations are construed as inferences rather than, say, immediate identifications or acknowledgements of what is manifestly expressed?), how much stock to put in the analysand's and the analyst's interpretations at various points in the analysis, how to organize and address interpretations (should interpretations be more explanatory, clarificatory, confrontational, skeptical/provocative, or reassuring? And when so? This is related to the question of whether analysis should be more expressive or supportive, with whom or in what specific contexts, and to what end(s)?), and what is expressed or implied in the material that unfolds in the clinic: the self striving for development (Winnicott, Kohut), the id in conflict with itself and/or the demands of reality (Freud), or the desire of the Other and manifestations of the transindividual unconscious (Lacan)? Though most analysts agree that dreams, symptoms, inhibitions, slips and parapraxes, affective comportment and especially affective shifts, movement profiles,[21] fantasies, patterns of object relation, transference enactments, word choice, pace of speech, and the styles and themes of and hesitations in free association are eminently interpretable, while some analysts tend to interpret such material in terms of developmental or selfobject needs, others tend see in it resistances to repressed infantile desires.

Even the conventions that tend to constrain and organize interpretation are by no means universal. They alter historically, and even when certain of such conventions predominate, there are always significant exceptions. For instance, although there is an increasingly prevalent focus on "here and now" material,[22] certain analysts — especially Kleinians — gear their attention more to the resonance of transference material with archaic affects, phantasies, and object relations than others. As before, here it is a question of what exactly is "here and now." Related are questions concerning how to interpret the structure(s) of addresses informing the analysand's speech. Is the analysand addressing the analyst as (a) a concrete other in the room, who, as a mental health expert, can offer pragmatic advice, (b) a figure from her past, (c) a fantasy projection of some sort, (d) a needed receptacle or container for inadmissible affects or self-states, (e) a projection of an image of herself as healed or an otherwise idealized figure, (f) a needed selfobject resource, (g) an imago woven from a variety of historical and fantasmatic threads, (h) some combination of the above, or (i) all of the above? In other words, what or who is speaking in the "talking cure," to whom, and to what end(s)? Is it primarily the analysand's ego that is addressing the analyst, or through her speech are the questions, desires, and traumatic disturbances of others (social cohorts or ancestors) conveyed? Related to this quagmire are questions concerning the status of unconscious-to-unconscious communication (can one unconscious communicate with another only through the subtext of direct speech and deeds or might unconscious communication transpire in a manner more akin to telepathy?) and how to understand the unconscious as such if it is such as to be comprehended "as such" (what logics or tendencies govern its metabolism of experience and unconscious content? Is the unconscious to be understood primarily as a seething cauldron of repressed wishes striving for satisfaction or might it harbor far more than wishes, e.g., memory-traces of *all* experiences, both empirical and phantasmatic, or even a certain manner of "experiences" (memory-traces) the individual never directly lived through, as Freud's phylogenetic and esthetic speculations suggest? Might the unconscious or an unconscious be an articulation of transhistorical transmissions of trauma, affect, patterns of object attachment and revulsion, etc.?). What or who are we hearing when we hear voices from "the other scene"?

There is disagreement about at what point in the treatment to interpret and at what point to remain silently attuned,[23] about whether, and if so, how genetic explanation is to factor in, about what the aims of interpretation — or more broadly, of therapy — are, about how to account for and evaluate the efficacy of interpretation and of therapy generally, and about what validates an interpretation. Contenders for the latter include, just to name a few:

1. confluent or confirming evidence from empirical sciences or other forms of external confirmation[24]
2. confluence with an accepted model of mind
3. pattern matching (e.g., the form of the current symptom seems to be configured from behaviors, fantasies, affects, defenses, etc. associated with the suffering of the traumatogenic instance; generally, e.g., if the symptom — or more broadly, the subsequent state — is formally similar to aspects of its attributed antecedent, it is held to be plausible that the antecedent is the cause of the symptom)
4. repetition of an interpretation's theme or some of its terms in newly emergent material[25] or via enactment
5. enhanced fluidity of free associations, e.g., broaching specific topics that previously could not be entertained or tarrying with those that, when broached, were quickly curtailed
6. the (sustained?) dissolution or development of a defensive configuration such as a symptom, inhibition, or impasse; generally, noticeable modifications to the analysand's anxieties and/or defenses, whether this means a weakening of defenses or, in line with the ambition of certain strands of ego psychology, their strengthening and development)
7. heightened creativity or imaginative capacity
8. a "telling" dream[26]
9. the tapping of archaic emotions
10. greater affective intensity, availability/tolerance, complexity, and/or modulation
11. the ability to complete or even just contemplate certain endeavors or negotiate with desires that were otherwise blocked or defensively distorted — generally, avowal
12. strengthened affective bonds with others and/or oneself
13. diminished fixations
14. a greater sapping of the Real through symbolization
15. a more coherent or perhaps less brittle sense of self or greater self-esteem
16. a sense of vitality and authenticity, e.g., an enhanced sense of the meaningfulness of experience
17. reorientation toward the social, whether this means a sense of secure connection to the social world or an "enlightened" acknowledgment of intractable alienation
18. genuine interest in the interpretation
19. a strong affirmation or negation of the interpretation (the interpretation generates resistance)
20. shifts in topic or manner of speech or comportment (e.g., newly significant contrasts, contiguities, analogies, repetitions, moments of

relaxation, shifts in emphasis, idiomatic choice — new or different uses of tropes, clichés, slang — direction or sequencing of associations, or tone — pitch, melody, rhythm, smoothness or difficulty of delivery, etc.)
21. the release of new material (e.g., new thoughts, memories, dreams, moods, impulses, etc.)[27]
22. a more intense engagement with or a new openness to one's analysis
23. an enhanced experience of the significance of and of one's responsibility for one's words and deeds, and with this, diminished alienation in language and action, an expanding acknowledgement of the dialectical intertwining of self and world, of the voluntary and the involuntary [28]
24. enhanced aptitude for tolerating, reflecting, and working through within the space of ambiguity and tension
25. greater facility in verbalization or narrative capability
26. enhanced ego aptitudes including capacities for self-observation and integration of overwhelming affects, fears, desires, anxieties, and sensations
27. changes in level and/or quality of object relations
28. changes in the nature of the analysand's motivations for change
29. enhanced reality-testing
30. the analysand's agreement or conviction, what Harry Stack Sullivan calls "consensual validation" (1940, 163)
31. the appearance of a defense that was neither previously manifest nor suggested by the interpretation (Wisdom 1967)
32. telling accentuations or declines in the analysand's anxiety[29]
33. vitalization — agency-enhancing, self-expanding availability to (rather than closing off or deadening of) experience, to possibilities for going on in heretofore unimagined ways[30]
34. successful mourning of an impossible or unwanted desire or fantasy
35. expert consensus[31]

The proliferation of validation criteria proceeds in tandem with that of conceptions of health/desirable transformation, rendering prospects for consensus dismal. Unfortunately, rather than motivating practical self-consciousness and mutual interest via normative dispute about the relative value of various criteria, hence about the aims of analysis, the wide and proliferating array of validation criteria supports dogmatism as analysts, succumbing to the skeptical temptation arising from their encounters with criterial multiplicity, reactively padlock themselves into the presumptive propriety of their practices, instrumentally appealing to just those criteria that best confirm their interpretive choices. Relativism about what can in principle count as criteria for validity — superficial tolerance — feeds insular dogmatism about the propriety of the criteria to which one appeals, which, because motivated, indeed saturated by the specter of skepticism, can never be assertive enough: prone to self-augmentation and increasing irrationality. Although analysts are now by no means willing to accept Freud's (1917) bold contention that interpretation is self-correcting (whatever in the analyst's conjecture is inaccurate drops out or is withdrawn and replaced by something more correct), they are not for that reason any less self-assured than was Freud.

Even though consensus on the relatively specific question of what validates an interpretation is not readily forthcoming, one might still expect at least some measure of consensus concerning the broader question of the criteria according to which better interpretations can be distinguished from worse. Though it would be contentious to deny the prevailing consensus regarding grossly negligent, counterproductive, or improbable interpretations, or that regarding generally productive, e.g., defense abating, adaptation facilitating, or new material eliciting interpretations, consensus on these matters is hardly uniform (Lacanian, Jungian, and Kleinian interpretations often run afoul of this consensus) and the criteria in virtue of which consensus is achieved are coarse, excessively equivocal; they fail to do the discriminating and norm explicating, thus practice orienting, work expected of them. Overstating the point a bit, one could say that such consensus is merely empirical, of the sort established by opinion polling. When adjudicating between competing interpretations, one may appeal to any of the aforementioned criteria such as production of confirmatory evidence, provision of insight, therapeutic efficacy, or thematic affinity of symptoms and sources, as well as to the following:

1. clinical parsimony (one interpretation gives rise to many effects, speaks to many levels, or resounds with and draws together an abundance of material)[32]
2. logical consistency[33] and/or coherence[34]
3. comprehensiveness
4. confluence of evidence
5. conformity with the findings of other sciences (e.g., developmental research)[35]
6. basic intelligibility[36]
7. patient corroboration

But by what criteria are we to judge these criteria? What makes satisfying a particular criterion or range of criteria an authoritative validation of an interpretation or a viable way to adjudicate between competing interpretations?

Compounding our difficulties, each criterion suffers from internal defects that embolden the case against it pressed by those who assume the authority of another. Normative gridlock seems all but unavoidable.

With regard to the parsimony principle, one could well ask: Isn't the real issue the *quality* of effects, their contribution to the advancement of therapeutic goals, rather than their mere multitude? Is the high ranking of parsimony in the therapeutic context not peculiar, perhaps an indication of quantitative fetishism? And if so, in the service of what? A defensive fantasy of intimacy or interpretive mastery? An identification with scientific totalization? An anxious flight from the temporality of analysis? A freighted concession to economic rationality? Complicity with the client's efforts to circumvent trauma's inertia, its dead weight? Fair enough, perhaps, but what counts as an advance? Isn't the therapeutic efficacy principle either too vague or too partisan to be helpful in adjudicating between better and worse interpretations? And what traction does it have on the question of validity anyway? Of course, most will accept that relative gains in reflective, emotional, and practical freedom, diminished suffering and severity of symptoms, and/or (slightly more controversially) enhanced adaptation are obvious markers of therapeutic advance, and this seems right, especially as concerns those whose impetus to analysis is tremendous suffering and extreme practical impairments and impasses as opposed to, say, general interest in self-exploration or relatively small-scale quality of life issues. However, first, that an interpretation facilitates freedom, diminishes suffering, or promotes adaptation may speak in its favor, but to have factors in its favor does not necessarily support a claim to *validity* (all of Grünbaum's objections to the "tally argument" would be relevant here), let alone resolve (if it even enters the arena of) the debate about the relative value of criteria. Is Brenner's rather mild claim that "symptomatic improvement is a *necessary criterion*, though not in itself a sufficient one, for validation of a line of interpretation and the conjecture(s) on which it is based" (1976, 58) any less hasty or any less disconcerting than Freud's bold assertion that "When it turns out that the assumption of there being an unconscious enables us to construct a successful procedure by which we can exert an effective influence upon the course of conscious processes, this success will have given us an incontrovertible proof of the existence of what we have assumed"? (SE 14: 167) Are criterial claims beyond the bounds of reasonable dispute? Must we say that here the spade turns? Second, appealing to the therapeutic efficacy standard just pushes the problem back a step. One imagines that for just about any interpretation one can make the claim that it somehow generates freedom, diminishes suffering, or the like, or at least that it is part of a process that eventually issues in such ends. Though appeal to the therapeutic efficacy principle may shed critical light on the parsimony principle (or perhaps reveal that the parsimony principle is a technicist elaboration of the therapeutic efficacy principle), so doing hardly suffices to convert the unconverted, especially since continuing appeal to the parsimony principle (or something similar) seems necessary in order to adjudicate between interpretations that all in some way satisfy the (vaguely fashioned) therapeutic efficacy principle. Support for the relative priority of the parsimony principle fares no better. Even were one to win the concession that an interpretation can be parsimonious only if true (though that seems to be at most an empirical generalization, not an a priori truth), basing the case for parsimony on that claim just sidesteps the questions of whether and why concerns with truth ought to outweigh concerns with clinical efficacy. But of course such evasion will not be allowed to stand for long, and we will end up right back where we started.

The logical consistency and coherence principles offer no way to adjudicate between (more or less) equally consistent or coherent interpretations or between interpretations that assume and meet different criteria for consistency or coherence, thus no way to comparatively evaluate different degrees of inconsistency or incoherence. Further, they risk inciting analysts (and vicariously, analysands) to downplay or artificially domesticate inconsistent or incoherent material, to concoct coherence and consistency there where there is real trauma, tension, or contradiction.[37] Of course, any standard may prompt manipulation, but given the conjunctions of (1) analysts' interests in theoretical production and anxiety over scientific credibility, (2) the extravagance of social demands for rationalization, e.g., characterological prescriptability and surveillability (standardization), and the aggressive mass mediation of the consequences of abjection, and (3) the interests of analysands in achieving intelligibility, that is, the pain of analysis and of what encourages its entrance, the risk seems particularly severe. Thus, to be more precise, the risk is not of incitement but of complicity with and aggravation of standing incitements. More straightforwardly, there is no obvious reason to discount interpretations that are attuned to and reflect what may be the incoherence of their subject matter. Hence Freud's cautionary statement regarding the interpretation of dreams: "It is only with the greatest difficulty that the beginner in the business of interpreting dreams can be persuaded that his task is not at an end when he has a complete interpretation in his hands — an interpretation which makes sense, is coherent and throws light upon every element of the dream's content. For the same dream may perhaps have another interpretation as well, an 'overinterpretation,' which has escaped him" (SE 5: 523). And of course, to dismiss incoherent and inconsistent interpretations would be to rule out Lacanian interpretive practices a priori. Generally, if the truth of trauma is inconsistent and incoherent, i.e., manifest in associations irreducible to a hidden code that can be consistently and coherently rendered and in the "wild" variability, and from the perspective of self-preservation or the pleasure principle, irrational character of symptom formation, then would fidelity to these principles not destitute analytic practice? Furthermore, if matters psychic are partially indeterminate, both created and discovered in the course of treatment, all too consistent and coherent interpretations would be self-falsifying and perhaps therapeutically pernicious, would perhaps simultaneously forfeit their therapeutic and cognitive authority (the latter mattering especially if the appeal to such principles is a means of pressing the claim that truth should be valued more highly than therapeutic effectiveness or of adjudicating between competing practices that have achieved or tend to achieve equivalent results). Finally, even if psychic phenomena are fully determinate, might not a consistent and coherent interpretation be consistently *wrong* and/or *unhelpful*?

The same sorts of concerns apply to the comprehensiveness principle, and where it eludes them it runs into objections applicable to the basic intelligibility standard. E.g., might not a comprehensive interpretation be wholly, or at least largely, off the mark, and whether or not accurate, flatly unhelpful? Further, from Freud onward, comprehensive interpretations are often reserved for relatively late stages of analysis, and perhaps with good reason — as noted, "deep" interpretations proposed early may be overwhelming and disorganizing or (along with the analyst who proposes them) subject to defensive idealization. So either the standard is very seldom applicable or its general applicability may be a symptom of analysis having become didactic and counterproductive.

The production of confirmatory evidence criterion seems to beg every pertinent question. The questions of what counts as evidence and why it should be so counted tends to be answered by invoking the authority of tradition or by means of brute self-assertion, which is no answer at all,[38] or by appeal to further criteria. That is, the criterion is either overdetermined or underdetermined. Further, for it to do the work expected of it, it would have to provide a compelling answer not only to the question of why certain phenomena that follow an interpretation are genuinely confirming but also the question of how to assess the relative weight of various confirming phenomena. Part of the difficulty is that the basic features of the analytic context provide ample occasions for skepticism about the confirmatory evidence that emerges within it. E.g., confirmatory memories, associations, etc. may be produced or emphasized on account transference pressures. Insisting that transference is analyzable may to some extent alleviate but will never fully abate such worries.

The confluence of evidence criterion is subject to similar concerns about over- and underdetermination; and with it the problem of relative weighting is magnified. What evidence is relevant? How should various streams of evidence be weighed? What to do when competing interpretations are equally confluent with the available evidence or equally confluent with the different streams of evidence to which they appeal? Presumably, a criterion should block or at least provide critical leverage against the arbitrary intervention of subjectivity. Would a criterion that failed in these respects — that deferred rather than defused skepticism — still count as a criterion?

Likewise, the provision of insight and the therapeutic efficacy criteria are either too vague to do the discriminating work wanted from them or so determined in advance as to support skeptical demurring on the ground of illicit overconstriction. Conjointly, they raise the question of how to comparatively evaluate insight as against effectiveness. Not all insightful interpretations are helpful. If they were, issues of timing, etc. would never arise. Delving into psychoanalytic literature — or really any sophisticated psychological literature — would be just as useful as clinical analysis. And not all helpful interpretations are insightful, at least in any strong sense. Grossly inaccurate interpretations may incidentally perform therapeutically desirable functions (containing, reassurance, etc.) as a result of the relations in which they are embedded. Certainly not all helpful interpretations are true. If they were, genuine plurality in psychoanalytic perspectives would mean that practices with incommensurable commitments couldn't achieve roughly equivalent outcomes. Also, if only true interpretations were helpful, a range of ordinary clinical developments would be unintelligible; e.g., that, as often occurs, a helpful interpretation is revoked or at least substantially modified at later stages of the analysis or subsequent to termination.[39] Indeed perhaps interpretations must be indefinitely revisable, subject to ongoing elaboration, if therapeutic progress is to be possible — though if so, that claim that all helpful interpretations are true would either render analytic practice unintelligible as a whole — self-contradictory — or have to trade on the suppressed equivocity of "helpful" and/or "true," thus would have to contend with a different set of worries. Lacan even claims that Freud's cures were effective precisely because they were erroneous and indoctrinating (2004, 77-9/289-291).[40] It is hard to imagine an analyst pursuing an insightful interpretation expected or discovered to be unhelpful, but clinical conscientiousness does not resolve the question of what validates an interpretation unless mooting the question, i.e., assuming the primacy of the demands incumbent to the clinical context, suffices for its resolution. And the question may not be so easily mooted. First, the clinic is not the only context in which analytic interpretations are issued. Is cultural criticism and the like simply to be left in the lurk? Second, theoretical innovations may proceed in relative autonomy from clinical concerns though they may issue in interpretive prospects the evaluation of which is required for the evaluation of the theoretical innovations they operationalize. Assuming the roughly equivalent therapeutic value of well-timed (etc.) interpretations, inter-theory evaluation may require appeal to something like the criterion of insightfulness if it is not to be cast off as an arbitrary affair. Third, even if the primacy of the clinical context is assumed and it is agreed that efficacy trumps insightfulness, the claims of the latter will likely reemerge when the former is equivalently attained by multiple practices. Put otherwise, it is not so hard to imagine an analyst adjusting her higher-order — metapsychological and suchlike — commitments or realigning her partisan positioning because, even though her practice works well enough, she has become convinced that her conceptual scheme is false or comparatively inadequate. Such transformations have been frequent from Freud onward and attest to the lasting concern for the value of insight.

The criterion of conformity with evidence from other sciences faces difficulties similar to those into which the confluence of evidence criterion runs. If the hunch behind this criterion is that its satisfaction suggests that what an interpretation assumes or proposes is mechanically possible, its satisfaction, because hard to avoid, doesn't amount to much. Indeed, appeal to this criterion may seem a way of sidestepping the question. If its attractiveness trades on the assumptions that veracity trumps all, and that an ascending order of veracity is unproblematically available as a means of discriminating between cases, it is hard to defend, even hard to formulate in want of a compelling, comprehensive theory of science. Again, the basic problem is under- or overdetermination: content, thus discriminating power, is purchased at the price of repudiating interpretations that are not without their virtues, which invites skepticism regarding the criterion; but if too open-ended, it becomes inert. The criterion seems always on the cusp of collapse. Specifically, it leaves unaddressed the questions of which sciences or specific discoveries or evidence-confluent hypotheses should be authoritative when adjudicating between psychoanalytic interpretations and why — is it just a concession to the reigning scientistic ideology, a public relations ploy? What to do if the evidence for incommensurable interpretations is roughly equivalent? Could the criterion assimilate — make intelligent use of — its tendential or systematic crisis? And what to do if an interpretation conforms to evidence from one sector of scientific research but contradicts or is dissonant with evidence from another? A problem all the more vexing if the criterion is appealed to in order to evaluate the relative merit of several such interpretations. Isn't a great deal hanging on the assumptions of the deductive-nomological integrability of science, hence the systematic lawful integrity of nature, and the incomparable cognitive satisfaction of such a science?

The basic intelligibility principle is either too weak or too strong. Its weak/pragmatic version cannot but be satisfied, thus cannot but fail as a criterion: it is meaningless. Such a standard is ill-equipped to handle any level of conflict, amounting to a dismissive shrug if appealed to in order to adjudicate between several interpretations contending that only through them or best through them can sufficient sense be made of certain phenomena. Even when confronted with an ordinary, low-key situation in which there are two competing interpretations, one of which can make sense of certain sectors of the material that another cannot, or makes slightly better sense of this material than its competitor, and vice versa, it has nothing to say but congratulations and condolences to both. Evaluating its strong/transcendental version, if it is not simply a self-absorbed assertion, must await the specific deduction through which the claim to rational necessity would be established. However, even were such a deduction valid, the principle may not generalize, i.e., constrain others to its satisfaction on pain of forfeiting their claims to rationality. Establishing necessary conditions for the possibility (rational intelligibility) of certain phenomena, to wit, the transcendental ambition, itself elaborates a contestable — not rationally necessitated — range of commitments, e.g., a concept of an object (which prescribes the object domain of transcendental reflection, circumscribing its reach, hence its validity; transcendental reflection never simply concerns the conditions of possibility for experience altogether, for there is no "altogether," only phenomena under a certain description) and what may be another facet of the same, the interests of inquiry (which introduces a moment of nonself-sufficiency, hence non-closure, into transcendental reflection; transcendental deductions are indelibly interested, unfolding under the auspices of a — usually silent — hypothetical imperative, e.g., that the necessary conditions of possibility must be established for valid experience in the sense established by empirical science — the understanding of which is itself contestable). More directly, non-necessitated operations within the space of reasons constitute the possibility, while undermining the self-closure, of the transcendental pursuit of rational necessity. Even if valid in its own terms, a transcendental deduction fails to compel in want of a defense of its guiding interests and correlated premises. Its slightly weaker version faces difficulties that turn on its want of probative power — would it not validate any interpretation just so long as there happen to be no competitors, thus running into the "3 Big P's" problem: validating notoriously objectionable theories such as Ptolemyan astronomy, phrenology, and phlogiston?

Appealing to patient corroboration is notoriously problematic. Among the many reasons this criterion comes up wanting are: First, it yields false positives.[41] Explicit confirmation of an interpretation may occur under the pressure of positive transference or currents feeding defensive idealization; may be a reaction-formation promoted by negative transference (say, a means to private abuse of the analyst for proposing an interpretation so absurd or manifestly false, or a supplicating reaction to the terror provoked by negative transference); may be instigated by anxiety pertaining to analysis as such or to what is now being confronted or one expects will be confronted if the interpretation is not acceded to; or it may result from suggestion or operate as a stalling device, diversionary tactic, and/or way of concealing or preparing for reservations. Second, it yields false negatives. Explicit repudiation may function as a freighted denial of the value of the analyst's contribution (in order, say, to avoid or discharge the anxiety of intimacy or to maintain secondary gains from symptoms presumed threatened by the interpretation), as a rejection of and perhaps partial retribution for the frustrations and helplessness of therapeutically sustained regression and dependency, etc. Third, as a practice-guiding principle it risks promoting collusion with the analysand's fantasies.[42] Fourth, patient corroboration is often imprecise, especially during earlier stages of analysis, and may be misleading. As John Forrester puts the point, exaggerating just a bit, "a 'no' may mean a 'yes,' and a 'yes' almost certainly does not mean this particular 'yes'" (2000, 318).[43]

Concerning the thematic affinity standard, even if it too did not suffer from the overdetermination/underdetermination problem, as Grünbaum notes, overstating the case slightly,

> it would be wrong to suppose that there is typically thematic affinity between the ideational or affective content of a repressed desire and the symptoms that provide an outlet for it. As Breuer and Freud emphasized at the outset (S.E. 1893, II:5), 'the typical hysterical symptoms' or outcroppings of repressed ideation do not have any apparent thematic connection at all to their presumed causes. And, as Freud stressed later, the products ('derivatives') of the dynamic unconscious that are thrust back into consciousness usually have a relatively distant topical connection to the repressed motif in which they presumably originated (S.E. 1915, XIV: 149-51, 190-1). (in Clark and Wright 1988, 7)

In sum, when adjudicating between competing interpretations, we face a situation of radical undecidability, that is, a situation in which decision, as opposed to deduction, is unavoidable — supposing that unself-conscious inheritance in a culture such as ours is a certain manner of decision: expositive, relational, and in need of ongoing maintenance and extension; a perpetually precarious accomplishment. Prospects for discovering formulas that would absolve us of responsibility — foreclose our opportunities — for shaping and staking claims about what constitutes better and worse, or valid and invalid interpretations — generally, norms of practice — are fortunately however frustratingly remote. Normative contestation, thus, to some extent, polemic, or their energetic avoidance, i.e., insular conformism, are the only options available; and neither bodes well for residual hopes that a final resolution will be reached. Within a liberal, post-traditional culture, specifically, an ambivalently, i.e., regressively inclined, post-Kantian culture in which substantive reason (religion or metaphysics) is rationalized (dissolved) into three tendentially self-enclosed spheres (science, art, morality),[44] a culture in which moral and aesthetic norms are not just distinguished but, tendentially, categorically and institutionally isolated from one another and from truth-bearing practices (science) and institutionally separated from the center(s) of social production and reproduction (broadly, the economy and its ancillary culture industry), and in consequence of their enforced autonomy (sequestration to privacy), etiolated and distorted,[45] rendered incapable of raising claims to social truth; in a culture that is sustained by manipulated self-interest, a culture in which reason has become private/instrumental rather than disclosive of — a medium for expression and recalibration of — shared normative sensibilities, thus a culture hardly deserving the name, normative dispute tends toward obtuse self-assertion and/or academic acrobatics. Wanting for the minimal subjective and objective conditions for its efficacy, it is bound to remain unresolved — to say the very least; in question, clearly, is the possibility of determinate negation. And even to the extent that normative dispute remains viable, it presupposes, and so can never overcome, the value of evaluative multiplicity,[46] i.e., of individuality; thus resolution, if at all attained, will be forever tentative and revisable, already destabilized by the specter of future skeptical detraction. About such questions, as with questions about ethical propriety or the excellence of a work of art, dispute may be waged — claims advocated and countered, perhaps some degree of agreement achieved — but no citing of facts or norms will automatically carry conviction; there will always be a madness to the decision, such "madness" reflecting the reasons of others, known or unknown, on the basis of which they (would) demur, thus reflecting the unappeasable voice of skepticism within the imperfect consolidation of conviction.

What should be clear at this point is that (1) claiming that psychoanalysis is interpreting with a view to pathology, psychosexuality, and the unconscious — *if* we can say this[47] — hardly suffices to clarify the nature, scope, and status of psychoanalysis, what transpires in the course of any particular analysis, or the nature, scope, and status of psychoanalytic cognition; and (2) psychoanalytic plurality is extrapartisan and insurmountable: consequential disagreements (institutionally internal skepticism) are neither reducible to partisan divergences nor rationally-demonstratively resolvable.

CONFLICT OVER CONFLICT

One of the most persistent psychoanalytic controversies — peculiarly, perhaps, a controversy as seldom thematized as it is intensely charged — concerns the role of conflict in psychopathology. Ultimately, the question is: What is to be considered pathological, hence what pathogenic? Although this larger dispute was treated extensively in the last chapter, briefly returning to it and focusing on a certain prominent sector of it, namely, the place of conflict in accounts of psychopathology, will prove worthwhile if so doing discloses (1) the unity-in-difference of psychoanalysis, i.e., the inter- and intrapartisan alliances and divergences taking shape around the question — or otherwise stated, that psychoanalysis is neither monolithic (ruthlessly dominating differences into a closed conceptual scheme) nor eclectic (unable to configure its component beliefs in any meaningful way); (2) the underivability of partisan identification from where one stands on this topic, or conversely, the underivability of where one stands on this topic from partisan orientation — generally, the underdetermination (more precisely, the asystematicity) of partisan identity; and (3) the nontotalization of each camp, whether due to internal conflicts or other sources — call (2) and (3) aspects of psychoanalytic sublimity.

For Freud, it is always sexuality, specifically, repressed and conflicted desire, that is pathogenic or at least a crucial element in the pathogenic matrix. Sexuality induces conflict and defense (primitively, repression) because various desires are irreconcilable with each other, with our avowable or desired self-images and projected courses of life, and/or with the social norms to which — through socialization and/or public enforcement — we are compelled to accede. Desire in its fervent polyvalence is always potentially pathogenic because potentially conflictual: sexuality makes life (im)possible, takes form primarily as wish. Symptoms, for Freud, are compromise formations, deferred and distorted pursuits of satisfactions that can be had in no other way given the individual's other desires, commitments, and constraints; thus therapeutic action is constituted by the deactivation or diminishment of defense, paradigmatically, the reversal of repression whereby desire is released and may be negotiated afresh.

Conflict is clearly central for Freud, as it is for many contemporary Freudians and others. For the Sandlers, conflict between the past unconscious and the present unconscious is central. For Jacob Arlow (an important figure in the development of ego psychology), "[e]ssentially, psychoanalysis is a psychology of conflict" (in Blum 1980, 193). Such statements are especially noteworthy given that a guiding premise operative in the work of many ego psychologists is that much adaptation, learning, and maturation need not assume or express conflict. Many in the ego psychological tradition presuppose a significant degree of ego autonomy, a conflict-free dimension of ego functioning. For Hartmann, for instance, ego functioning is an independent variable, in principle relatively autonomous from the drives and the environment (1964, 105). As a consequence of their confidence in the relative autonomy of the ego, many ego psychologists restrict the scope and significance of conflict in their accounts of pathology, focusing instead on factors that diminish ego strength, hence inhibit adaptation, that is, on whatever renders the ego susceptible, say, to imperious id and superego demands. Yet as already indicated, disagreements persist among ego psychologists. It is none other than Ernst Kris who characterizes psychoanalysis as the study of "human behavior viewed as conflict" (1975, 6); and Charles Brenner, a staunch ego psychologist, is frequently adamant about the centrality of conflict.

Though in different ways, Anna Freud, Fairbairn, Guntrip, Winnicott, Hartmann (to a degree), Spitz, Jacobson, Mahler, and Kohut contend that pathology results, at least to a great extent, not from conflict but from arrested development. Of course there are disagreements among such figures concerning the sources of arrested development (parental character pathology, failures to consolidate narcissistic structure, a problematic social or selfobject environment, etc.; libidinal fixation, not arrested development *per se* plays a role in Freudian theory), its essential features, and how it can be reactivated, but despite such disagreements they broadly agree on the central significance of arrested development in pathogenesis, or at least that, routinely, too much weight is placed on sexuality and conflict in accounts of pathogenesis and that developmental deficit should be given its due.

Though not inaccurate, to claim the conflict/developmental deficit debate is a major fault line in the psychoanalytic landscape would be overly simplifying. First, some deny a categorical distinction between conflict and developmental deficit. As Wallerstein claims, "We feel this to be a spurious distinction, and each of us (Wallerstein, 1983a; Weinshel, 1990) has counterposed a broadened construction of the concept of conflict in psychoanalysis. Within these constructions, the so-called deficit phenomena described by self psychology can be at least as fruitfully considered as manifestations of conflict. Similar critiques have been advanced by Segel (1981) and Treurniet (1980)" (2004, 246). Second, exemplarily, Freud concedes in *Studies on Hysteria* that "partial traumas" may be involved in pathology and that these are irreducible to conflicted sexuality. Indeed, there seem to be a wide array of pathogenic traumata that fit into neither the conflict-centered nor the arrested development models. Contenders include: abandonment trauma (Germaine Guex), hospitalization trauma (Spitz), early separation trauma (Bowlby), birth trauma (Rank), and cumulative trauma (Masud Khan, 1963, 1964).[48]

WHATEVER HAPPENED TO GENETIC RECONSTRUCTION?

Traversing the psychoanalytic field is a great divergence concerning the role of genetic reconstruction.[49] While some analyses involve no or austerely minimal genetic reconstructions (e.g., preponderant focus is on present adaptive urgencies), others involve fairly frequent and sweeping genetic reconstruction (the reconstructions may be assumed, as in the case of less interpretation inclined practices, or explicitly conveyed). Genetic reconstruction certainly persists, but is slowly being eclipsed by interest in "here and now" material.[50] What can be known of the patient's particular developmental history, whether through reconstructive interpretation or empirical inquiry, increasingly plays a confirmatory or hypothesis-generating rather than therapeutically central role.[51] Yet not so long ago, sweeping reconstruction was a hallmark of psychoanalytic practice.[52] E.g., Freud's interpretations of Dora, the Wolf Man, the Rat Man, da Vinci, Schreber, and Woodrow Wilson — i.e., interpretations irrespective of whether or not they are addressed to a client — all involve grand claims about the relation between present suffering, symptoms, creativity, and practical difficulties, and prior, often Oedipal, conflicts or traumas. For Freud, recall, the "principle constituents of the theoretical structure of psychoanalysis" include "the etiological significance of sexual life and of the importance of infantile experiences." For Freud, at the root of every adolescent and adult neurosis is an infantile or childhood neurosis; hence, given his theory of therapeutic action, the need for sweeping genetic reconstruction. In his words, "analytic work deserves to be recognized as genuine psycho-analysis only when it has succeeded in removing the amnesia which conceals from the adult his knowledge of his childhood from its beginning (that is, from about the second to fifth year)" (SE 17: 183).

This claim, or rather, the orientative conviction it expresses, had a lasting impact on the psychoanalytic community. The penchant for genetic reconstruction was so strong that in 1958 Erik Erikson expressed concern about the prevalence of psychoanalytic "originology . . . a habit of thinking that reduces every human situation to an analogy with an earlier one, and most of all to the earliest, simplest and most infantile precursor which is assumed to be its 'origin'" (18).[53] Clearly Erikson's caution was not heeded as well as he would have liked, for in 1964 Hartmann acknowledged the prevalence of genetic claims in psychoanalysis, including ego psychology (1964, 103ff, 306). Although Hartmann, Kris, Lowenstein, etc. were intensely concerned with present demands on adaptive flexibility, their support for such flexibility included a genetic reconstructive component. Again in 1985 Daniel Stern felt compelled to admonish psychoanalysts for correlating each adult pathological state with one or more infantile events and thereby collapsing the immense differences between infantile and adult-pathological states. Still today, although genetic reconstruction is practiced less extensively than it once was, sweeping reconstructions are prominent features of certain Freudian, Kleinian, ego psychological, British Independent, and Kohutian therapies, and are by no means confined there.[54] And although genetic reconstruction has significantly dwindled of late, the prevalence with which psychoanalysts either directly participate or take a keen interest in developmental research, particularly in the U.S. and even more so in the U.K., testifies to an abiding concern for historical precursors of present suffering and flourishing. Indeed, not infrequently, it is to developmental research that one appeals in order to adjudicate between plausible and implausible genetic reconstructions and prognoses. Further evidence of the abiding if migrating concern for the deep past is provided by the increasing prevalence of efforts to identify and therapeutically utilize a drive for redevelopment, or more generally, to theorize pathology in terms of a stunted development and organize practice in order to facilitate developmental advances that have not been sufficiently fostered by the analysand's early or current caring environment (ego psychology, Kohut, Winnicott, Guntrip, Balint, etc.). Though not necessarily prone to sweeping genetic reconstruction, the large and expanding number of analysts involved in these developments make a great many assumptions, not necessarily shared by their clients, about what their clients suffered in infancy and early childhood and how this bears on their current difficulties, attachment patterns, and so on. Concern with the deep past, however modified the form of this concern, certainly persists.

However, as we have already seen, the tradition of genetic reconstruction is not without its detractors. Already in 1924, Ferenczi and Rank suggested that transference interpretation need not aim at genetic recovery of an infantile neurosis. Late in his career, even Freud increasingly emphasized the need to tarry with the material that emerges in transference *as it emerges* rather than focusing therapy on the analysis of presenting symptoms or rushing headlong into sweeping genetic reconstruction. Kris still employs genetic reconstruction but underlines the constitutive underdetermination, thus inexactitude, of reconstruction: "not only were the events loaded with meaning when they occurred; each later stage of the conflict pattern may endow part of these events or their elaboration with added meaning" (1956, 77). This gesture remains fairly typical in ego psychology. For Seitz, reconstruction is still significant, but only as a means of corroboration. In the Kleinian field, although reconstruction still plays a role, it increasingly takes the backseat to interpretations of here and now object relations. Fonagy (1999) condemns reconstruction and especially the pursuit of recovered memories as therapeutically useless and "damaging to the field" (215).

Often, the reasons for eschewing or downplaying sweeping genetic reconstruction, especially in earlier stages of therapy, are something like the following: (1) Allowing the patient's associations — which ordinarily tend to dwell on present difficulties — rather than the analyst's diagnostic categories, engrained habits of attention, and suspicions about the source(s) of pathology in early life to organize the analysis enhances the efficacy of interpretation because interpretation of here and now material meets the least degree of resistance.[55] (2) Allowing patterns, themes, etc. to come into view gradually, as they reemerge time and again, often when and where least expected, that is, on the basis of scattered though repeated confrontations and tactful, periodic interpretative clarifications, rather than by means of sweeping genetic reconstructions insisted upon by the analyst, better persuades the analysand of both the determining force of the unconscious in general (thereby enhancing susceptibility to/interest in analysis) and the specific force, i.e., the surprising persistence, pervasiveness, and significance, of particular patterns encountered. (3) Focusing analysis on manifest symptoms, difficulties, etc., and all the more so on their genetic determinants, may detract from or even support defenses against more elusive and/or overdetermined material, specifically material that is abrasive to narrative or thematization, thus material not subject to elucidation through sweeping genetic reconstruction. Or more strongly, certain traumas may remain inconspicuous and thus unnegotiated precisely because the analysis remains focused on developmental, e.g., Oedipal or pre-Oedipal, determinants of present suffering. Thematic focus on symptoms or their genetic reconstruction may gear the analysis to units of meaning that are, in a sense, too grand, and thereby obscure what needs to be explored if the therapy is to progress. If trauma is that which cannot or can only very superficially and problematically be integrated into dominant self-images, if it is marked by the faltering of self-narration, then a more patient and protracted labor of listening, attention to psychic material that remains veiled under the cover of more perspicuous symptom structures and elaborations of genetic determinants, may be required. (4) Genetic reconstruction may be therapeutically counterproductive because it detracts focus from the transference, where all the (therapeutic) action is: recollection is unknowing repetition. Bollas, for instance, claims that "any recollection of the past must be viewed as a phantastical reading that reflects present-day internal object relations, so recollecting the past only serves the selective aims of the present. Since a patient thinking of his history does so in the presence of the analyst, such historical considerations must be regarded as unconscious representations of the patient's present experience of the analyst . . . To consider contemporary issues or the past is to collude with the patient's splitting of the transference and to accept the projective identification of the elements of the transference into the narrative objects that refer to persons and events external to the analytic relationship" (1989, 193).[56] Or as Klein more cautiously puts the point, "The patient may at times try to escape from the present into the past rather than realize that his emotions, anxieties, and phantasies are at the time operative in full strength and focused on the analyst" (1952, p56n). (5) Genetic reconstruction, as with deep interpretations generally, may reactivate drives with which the patient is ill-equipped to negotiate, especially if pertinent defenses have not yet been analyzed, which means especially at earlier stages of analysis (Lowenstein 1982, 45).

In sum, even though sweeping genetic reconstruction has been by no means retired from the contemporary clinical repertoire, insight is no longer held to be coextensive with dramatic pronouncements about the genetic determinants of symptoms, inhibitions, or anxieties in the way it once was.[57]

Although the current waning of sweeping genetic reconstruction is particularly pronounced in ego psychology and certain sectors of Kleinian practice, it is hardly confined there. Speculating, the diminished role of genetic reconstruction may have to do with the ascending prominence of countertransference analysis. Perhaps the depth and breadth of insight figured by genetic reconstruction has given way, at least to a significant extent, to the depth and breadth of insight promised by countertransference analysis.[58] Especially but not exclusively for those involved in object relations traditions, countertransference analysis promises refined and comprehensive insight into transference material, thus promises to be of orientational significance for therapeutic intervention therein. The shift from genetic reconstruction to countertransference analysis — a shift in the privileged medium of insight and a shift in what is desired from insight: no longer a dramatic climax but rather wide-ranging relevance — has to do with changing views of the role of the analyst. It is no longer as prevalently assumed as it once was that the analyst's interpretations raise unconscious content to consciousness and thereby cure or set the analysand on the path to the cure, i.e., the path along which she will, if sufficiently devoted to her task and not excessively encumbered by external impediments, create/discover more felicitous ways to negotiate with previously dynamically unconscious material. There are many operations that analysts now consider therapeutically efficient other than disclosing deep insights into the analysand's psychosexually tumultuous past and its bearing on present troubles. Rather than elaborating the Oedipal or pre-Oedipal history of current affects, desires, symptoms, patterns of attachment, and so on as if this on its own (say, because it moots the force of repression) is maximally therapeutically effective, or as if the progressive avowal of sweeping genetic reconstructions entails that the analysand's structures of defense have been modified sufficiently for her to find more mature and gratifying ways of negotiating with the erotic and/or aggressive material previously held defensively at bay, analysts are increasingly prone to focus on their responses to transference in order to (1) determine how they are positioned in the transference, that is, how and with what expectations they are being addressed, and then (2) develop effective responses to the transference material brought into more fine relief by countertransference analysis.[59] Countertransference analysis is *sometimes* the medium of analysts' interests in divesting a residual (and perhaps transferentially amplified) fantasy of sovereignty, to remain aware of the fallibility of their interpretations and other manners of intervention — if the analyst is aware that her impulses to intervention or interpretive constructions are countertransferentially mediated, her practical confidence may trigger a therapeutically beneficial skeptical counterweight — and adjust their therapeutic practices accordingly; for instance, by keeping a more open ear to material that is dissonant with respect to established interpretive convictions or by seeking out signs of defensive compliance.[60]

SELF-ANALYSIS

Whether self-analysis must be a central component of psychoanalytic therapy, whether self-analysis can be as effective as clinical analysis, thus whether psychoanalysis is bound to its institutional formations, are longstanding and significant yet quiet, often implicit questions coursing through the history of psychoanalysis. Although there is heterogeneity within each pole and a spectrum between them, a clear polarity emerges between Freudians and Lacanians, on the one hand, and those that give greater weight to some version of corrective emotional experiences, on the other. Of course, self-analysis is a necessary component of any analysis. Even on the classical model where the analyst is assumed to be a source of objectivity tasked with maintaining an austere detachment, i.e., with sustaining and evidencing neutrality, in order to render conspicuous the contextual inappropriateness of the analysand's responses to her, to utilize her position as an uninvolved bystander to mirror back the analysand's conflicts, and in order to arrogate the necessary authority to her interpretations, working through the material thus illuminated and later interpreted requires self-interpretive work. And even for those who privilege some version of corrective emotional experiences, interpretation, thus self-analysis, is a feature of the therapy. If clinical psychoanalysis is to be at all successful, self-analysis *must* be effective, at least in terms of using insights and aptitudes provisionally acquired in the clinic when contending with life outside the clinic. Specifically, if it is to be at all successful, psychoanalytic treatment requires that the analysand, eventually without prompting (e.g., interpretation) by the analyst, (1) notice herself responding in typical defensive, self-undermining, or undesirable ways to a specifiable range of situations both within and beyond the clinic, (2) reflect on her motivations to defensively recoil from or otherwise evade certain features and latencies of the current situation, e.g., reflect on the future(s) to which her habitual responses will likely commit her, why she is so committed, what desirable alternatives might be available, what about these alternatives is desirable, and what their pursuit would in fact require, and (3) find new, less damaging and/or self-defeating ways to work through these situations. More locally, self-analytic aptitude is a condition for avowing the analyst's interpretations, which is clearly crucial for certain forms of analytic success. Finding the analyst's interpretations true in one's own reflective experiences and meaningful in one's own terms — which may be, indeed, often are (especially at later stages of therapy) quite different from those offered by the analyst — both within and beyond the clinic, substantially supports, and sometimes may be a condition of, the persuasiveness and/or efficacy of these interpretations.[61] Finally, if no analysis, because no life, is complete, if the termination of analysis is by no means coextensive with an all-embracing, fully satisfying cure, ongoing self-analysis will be needed as, inevitably, the analysand is forced to negotiate with, say, conflicts or traumas that will not have been sufficiently analyzed, if at all, in the course of treatment.[62] The success of analysis is both necessarily limited — e.g., complete dissolution of conflict would mean the eradication of passion, thus of formative relationality, condemning the "cured" to mindlessness, i.e., a frictionless, yawning abyss there where subjectivity once struggled to accomplish itself — and to whatever extent attained, contingent upon the inculcation of self-analytic prowess useful for negotiating with difficulties that did not manifest within or were for various reasons neglected by the therapy.[63] However, even if all agree that self-analysis must be a component of clinical psychoanalysis, its therapeutic centrality is disputed. So too is the related but distinct issue of whether self-analysis is equally effective when pursued independently of the clinical setting.

Freud was a great believer in the efficacy of self-analysis. How could he not be? Aside from his cultural inheritances, he only had his self-analysis to go on,[64] and however just it may be to decry the *many* mistakes he made as a clinician, he was clearly competent as an analyst and for the most part happy enough and successful in terms of his work and personal relationships. Nevertheless, Freud introduced doubts about the efficacy of self-analysis that are influential to this day.[65] Famously, Freud said to Fliess, "self-analysis is really impossible, otherwise there would be no illness" (Letter of 14 Nov. 1897). Though this could mean that pre-analytic self-analysis is impossible, which would simply be true by definition, this is probably not what Freud meant — there is no contextual reason for such a claim; if sensical, that claim would have to be, say, a jocular chastisement of an extraordinarily naïve claim about the all but titular practice of psychoanalysis prior to his innovations or otherwise humorously intended, and the context of his letter to Fliess does not support such an interpretation. Likely, he meant that self-analysis deprived of the methodologies and specific insights cultivated by psychoanalysis is condemned to failure, or at least gross inadequacy, which may be a bit hubristic and overstated, but is at least arguable. But even if so, it still may be that self-analysis in the sense we are interested in — the forms of self-analysis practicable in a world where there has been a mass dissemination of psychoanalytic ideas — holds out the prospect of being as effective as clinical analysis. And of course, it was Freud himself who insisted on the impossibility of categorically isolating "neurosis" and "psychosis" from "normalcy," that is, on the inevitability of neurotic and psychotic moments in or features of an otherwise fulfilling and functional life (what Freud would call a life of ordinary misery), thus there is no reason to believe that, for Freud, clinical practice, as opposed to self-analysis, could give rise to a world in which "there would be no illness," thus no reason to believe that, for Freud, self-analysis is categorically and necessarily inferior.

However, there is reason to doubt the efficacy of self-analysis. Keeping with Freud for the moment, one plausible argument against self-analysis is that "in self-analysis the danger of incompleteness is particularly great. One is too soon satisfied with a part explanation, behind which resistance may easily be keeping back something that is more important perhaps" (SE 22: 234). Self-analysis, in other words, seems ill-equipped to negotiate with flights into health and other forms of defensive complacency. Why wouldn't something like natural vanity impede its systematic development? Furthermore, self-analysis may be found wanting on the following counts:

(1) Affective deficit: without the artifice of the analytic setting, its ways of inducing regression and intensifying transference and thereby granting access to the affective intensity of material routinely defended against, one may be unable to adequately work through the affective fullness — which means, also, the emotional content — of the material encountered: insights will be relatively superficial and ineffectual to the extent that they are merely intellectual (dissociated).[66] Or if what a particular client needs is to survive the affective intensity of certain highly defended against material or its phantasmatically anticipated consequences, then the regression induced by the clinical setting, coupled with the analyst's maintenance of an atmosphere of emotional safety sufficient to sustain the regression, may be necessary to tap the relevant material.

(2) Memory deficit: assuming that we are motivated to repress (forget, neglect, downplay, etc.) defensively distort, or otherwise marginalize difficult material, the analyst's retention of insights gathered in the course of analysis and capacity to recall them in a timely way, to remind the analysand of them at precisely the moments s/he is motivated to repress them, may be necessary for a great deal of therapeutic success, especially in early stages of analysis. And especially if successful analysis requires interpretations that develop from comparisons of current associations with previous material, having an analyst to keep in mind a more global context and make these connections seems crucial to the success of the analysis. Indeed, having an analyst to assume the burden of memory and interpretation, at least at early stages of therapy, seems necessary for the analysand to allow herself to become caught up on the reverie of free association, thus to produce a maximum — or perhaps a necessary minimum — of interpretable material. Psychoanalytic concepts aside, assuming natural vanity and a consequent propensity for self-evasion, another's perspective seems, at the very least, extraordinarily useful for purposes of introspection.

(3) Clarity deficit: however ubiquitous transference may be, features of the clinical context such as analytic neutrality allow transference to be revealed as transference much more clearly. The relative recession of the analyst as contradistinguished from the routinely attention-absorbing behavior of others facilitates the analysand's assumption of responsibility for her forms of self- and world-relation. Additionally, the imprecision or incorrectness of an analyst's interpretations may — especially when fueled by transference dynamics — elicit clarifications that may not emerge otherwise.

(4) Resource deficit: as noted, without transference, regression, and an atmosphere amenable to free association, all of which are facilitated by features of the clinical context, less material is likely to emerge. Conversely, without *interpreted* transference, *modulated* regression, and a memory pros-

thesis to support free association, transference, regression, and free association may become too absorbing, i.e., may inhibit the emergence of certain material. Further, certain resources available in the clinic such as the analyst's countertransference are obviously not available in self-analysis. If certain material can only manifest perspicuously in the context of countertransference analysis, self-analysis is comparatively limited. Or if an experience of ongoing care or an insistence on the interpretability of affects, beliefs, etc. is what is needed, self-analysis will be likely less successful.

(5) Futurity deficit: without interpretations of transference, which are certainly much more difficult to produce on one's own — if not cognitively (on an austere understanding of cognition), then at the level of desire — one may miss therapeutically crucial experiences of others' exceeding their transferential positioning, e.g., their nonconformity to pathogenic expectations, and the glimpse of a liberated future that can be had in this way.[67] Such a glimpse may be necessary to induce the hopefulness needed to press on with one's analysis or reinvest in the world.

(6) Usability deficit: if what one needs from analysis is not so much insight in the classical, representational sense as certain types of experiences, then the need of another, specifically, another trained to offer the needed experiences and aware of difficulties salient to their attempted affordance, sets a limit to the efficacy of self-analysis. If what is important in certain analyses is, say, the analyst repeatedly and evidently surviving the analysand's ruthlessness such the latter can disburden herself of pathological expectations that others are vulnerable to destruction by her rage, though one might be able to find a nonclinician to perform this function — one could imagine a certain sort of S&M relationship facilitating the desired outcome — banking on the assumptions that one knows what one needs from an object and that one will find someone willing and able to perform the relevant function is perhaps unwise.

Bruce Fink draws a number of these points together: "One tells oneself lovely stories about the past, one analyzes one's dreams and fantasies to oneself or on paper, but nothing happens, nothing changes. It is all very informative and interesting, and one remembers all kinds of things about one's past, but there is no metamorphosis. Affect is rarely brought into play without the presence of another person to whom one addresses all of these thoughts, dreams, and fantasies" (2004, 142). Or as Freud puts the point in his inimitably aggressive-sympathetic way, "If knowledge about his unconscious were as important for the patient as the inexperienced in psychoanalysis imagines, it would be sufficient to cure him for him to go to lectures or read books. Such measures, however, have as little effect on the symptoms of nervous disease as distributing menu-cards in time of famine has on people's hunger" (SE 11: 225).[68]

On the other hand, there is ample anecdotal evidence of the efficacy of self-analysis. Virginia Woolf, for instance, claims with reference to *To the Lighthouse* that "I suppose I did for myself what psychoanalysts do for their patients. I expressed some very long felt and deeply felt emotion. And in expressing it I explained it and then laid it to rest" (1976, 94).[69] We will return to this issue below.

REFLECTIONS ON THE STATUS OF PSYCHOANALYTIC KNOWLEDGE

At the heart of the question of whether self-analysis and other sorts of experiences and practices are as effective as clinical psychoanalysis is a question about whether psychoanalytic theory and/or practice are medium-bound. Are psychoanalytic knowledge and/or the psychoanalytic cure irrevocably tethered to the clinical context and the various exigencies incumbent thereto?[70] If self-analysis and affiliated experiences/practices yield results comparable to clinical psychoanalysis, if at the very least they yield genuine self-knowledge, then even if such results are not methodologically secured, it is not clear that psychoanalysis is something that transpires only or even primarily in the clinic. Or from a different angle: What are we to make of the various disseminations of psychoanalysis into aesthetics, politics, anthropology, cultural critique, and so on? What is the status of psychoanalytic insights and forms of attention when they are utilized and/or developed in extraclinical settings? Does their validity dissolve upon their detachment from the clinic? Are the various extraclinical employments of psychoanalysis merely provocative, of speculative interest but less than compelling, wanting for authority? First we will ask after the relation of psychoanalytic knowledge to the clinical medium, then turn to the relation of psychoanalytic therapy to the clinical medium.

To say that psychoanalytic knowledge is medium-bound is to say that it is bound to (1) the material recognized as potentially meaning-laden by the psychoanalytic community at a particular time and (2) the interpretive practices, the forms, recognized by that community as methodologically valid. When phrased this way, the claim for the medium-bound nature of psychoanalytic knowledge may sound unpleasantly parochial at best. At worst, it may sound as if the claim advanced reeks of authoritarian-institutionalist voluntarism: an awkward blend of skepticism (the material is cognitively and practically inert, in no way dictates how we conceive it, such conceiving being fully at the discretion of sovereign consciousness, thus as unstable as the whims of such a consciousness and consequently unconvincing — especially to such a consciousness, whereupon instability is amplified and sovereignty belied; form and content are metaphysically hypostatized in their diremption, matter becoming as if a transcendental principle of recalcitrance that cannot but interrupt and thereby provoke the renewed self-assertion of interpretive will, interpretive will finding itself forever wayward, hence tending toward resignation as the emptiness of its infinite freedom is reflected by the frictionless abyss of matter over which it slides, and thus prone to dogmatic reaction) and communitarian idealism (community norms are cognitively constitutive, setting insuperable limits to interpretive innovation, projecting a threshold beyond which only madness lies, thus rendering internal developments — historicality — and cross-communal communication unintelligible, as if magic). To uphold psychoanalytic knowledge as medium-bound is *not* to claim that whatever an empirical psychoanalytic community or its dominant representatives deem potentially meaning-laden and countenance as methodologically valid ways of engaging such material must be so considered. Neither hegemonic opinion nor even unanimous empirical agreement are, for us, adequate to delimit the potentially meaningful from meaning-bereft material or to establish the authority of practices through which potentially meaningful material is to be engaged.[71] We moderns cannot but consider ourselves within our rights to count efforts by the community to naturalize its hermeneutic protocols as violent, regressive, inadmissible denials of creative subjectivity, of our right and responsibility to order and evaluate experience for ourselves. For us moderns, subjectivity is the site through which norms must pass and receive ratification (recognition) if they are to be norms, compelling rather than coercive. The authority of norms is mediated by our free accession to and ongoing avowal/enactment of their terms, by our recognition of such terms as our self-constitutive commitments. While certainly not the self-sufficient origin and proprietor of normative authority, subjectivity is its irreducible mediator, a moment of freedom that cannot be forced but only absorbed: compelled to self-relinquishment whereupon what would be constraints become conditions of self-actualization, of normative self-(re)discovery. The right of subjectivity is infinite, uncircumventable, if right there be. Yet because the right of subjectivity is the right to dissidence and experimentation, including the right to speak in a universal voice irrespective of social particularity and however abrasive to the tradition the content of one's claims may be, under conditions of modernity, which is to say, when exemplarity — innovative inheritance with recalibrating potential — is tendentially deprived of the solidarity — the institutional and intersubjective mediations — it seeks, subjectivity is idiocy: fretful and frequently despairing or exoticized and thereby neutralized anomaly.[72] So to uphold psychoanalytic knowledge as medium-bound is *not* to say that whatever interpretive practices a particular community happens to accept — whether or not these interpretive procedures make a defensible claim to validity or fecundity — are as such legitimate. The notion of acceptance here implies just that the material considered potentially meaning-bearing and the interpretative practices deemed methodologically valid (1) conform to defensible community norms, (2) straightforwardly appear as viable, if modified, continuations of community norms, or (3) appear as warranted or at least warrantable deviations from community norms. All that is blocked are practices whose "warrants" are in principle inscrutable (e.g., interpreting a patient's "aura" in the manner of the worst New Age therapies) and practices which, upon consideration, are found just questionable or problematic but *deeply* implausible or infelicitous when compared with extant alternatives (e.g., newspaper astrology as a way to divine the future or Freud's early employment of hypnotism as a means of uncovering the truth of the past).

Thus the claim that psychoanalytic knowledge is medium-bound does not simply conspire with or reify hegemonic hermeneutic norms, but rather is, or at least can be, a way of insisting that psychoanalytic knowledge is (1) bound to the material recognized as meaningful *within a particular analysis* or related to knowledge that emerges in this way, and (2) bound to hermeneutic protocols that can make a reasonable claim to methodological validity, fecundity, or other such criteria. Within *this* analysis, the material (dreams, pains, behaviors, counter-transference affects and positioning, associations, parapraxes, physical comportment [posture, mannerisms, etc.], emotional tone, etc.) recognized as meaningful by the analyst (or analysand as participating in the analytic function) will serve as the material from which conceptual elaborations of the analysand's psychic life and history are formed and thus from which interpretations (conforming to acceptable hermeneutic protocols) or other therapeutic actions (conforming to acceptable therapeutic norms) proceed. On this conception, the meanings of psychoanalytic concepts and interpretations, as well as the validity of psychoanalytic theories, are circumscribed by — not simply detachable from — the specific analyses in which they are employed. Such concepts and interpretations, however mediated by inherited tradition(s), are singularly inflected — particularized, remediated — by the occasions of their use.[73] They are, to an extent, precipitates of the radically singular experience of therapy — no two analyses are identical — and responsive to the idiolect and therapeutic demands (including specific needs for description and interpretation) operative therein.[74] To insist on clinical primacy is thus to insist that clinical knowledge is that from which other forms of psychoanalytic knowledge (metapsychology, developmental theory, theories of pathology and cure, etc.) arise or to which they indelibly refer; it is to insist that the medium does not disappear behind the message, that psychoanalysis yields knowledge with a practical intent.[75]

To insist on the clinical primacy of psychoanalytic knowledge is to insist that the universal (concept, theory) is irrevocably marked by the particular (singular clinical contexts); indeed that the relation between universal and particular is one of unending dialectical intermediation: clinical context gives rise to the need for, and to some degree the shape of, general claims (concepts, theories) which are tested and specified — expanded, particularized anew, *remediated* — in each new clinical context. In and as the universal, the particular abides. At least within psychoanalysis, the universal is the abode of the particular: the particular emerges in its particularity through its abrasiveness or exceptionality with respect to accepted concepts, theories, and interpretive schemes, inciting their renegotiation or reconfiguration and thus the *appearance* of their *essential provisionality.*[76]

In this light, psychoanalytic concepts are what a Kantian might call "enlarged concepts." Their content cannot be once and for all discursively determined, fractured as they are by their faciliatating exposure to the overabundance and oversaturated character of clinical phenomena, to the inherence of the indeterminate future within the clinical "present." When discussing aesthetic ideas, Kant describes a movement — a dynamic, or one might say in an Aristotelian vein, a nature — of conceptualization apposite for comprehending psychoanalytic knowledge in the following terms: "If we now place under a concept a representation of the imagination belonging to its presentation, but which occasions in itself *more thought than can ever be comprehended in a definite concept and which consequently aesthetically enlarges the concept itself in an unbounded fashion,* the imagination is here creative, and it brings the faculty of intellectual ideas (the reason) into movement;[77] i.e. by a representation more thought (which indeed belongs to the concept of the object) is occasioned than can in it be grasped or made clear" (1987, 158; emphasis added). Analytic contents, and so analytic concepts, are potentially self-exceeding, thus inherently provisional. A Deleuzian might call them virtual.[78]

To its credit, this conception of the medium-bound character of psychoanalytic knowledge acknowledges that psychoanalysis would grind to a halt were its practitioners and theorists to either repudiate or stubbornly adhere to their conceptual and theoretical inheritances. Psychoanalysts must render inherited concepts and theories in their own ways, find their own examples for and applications of them, by seeing how they fit — if they fit — clinical phenomena that, though possessed of all or sufficiently many of the features that warrant the application of a concept, stand out in their singularity and demand a more discerning engagement, a more discriminating elaboration. Working with inherited concepts and theories is unavoidable, but, the medium-bound thesis proposes, these become meaningful only or primarily in the context of the commitments, sensibilities, concerns, experiences, and so forth articulating singular clinical dynamics, and so, perhaps, become meaningful each time anew, each time somewhat differently. On this conception, theory guides but should not, perhaps cannot, rigidly determine practice. *Practice is the creative working through of experience, a matter of both creation and discovery.*

On the analytic stage, concept application is, ideally, a "coherent deformation"[79] of a known rule. But, peculiarly perhaps, such transmuting application may make the rule applied less clear than it once seemed, perhaps even appear less of a rule. As inherited concepts and theories are articulated — applied, illustrated, perhaps also substantiated — they are, on this conception, particularized, allowed to resonate otherwise[80] — but also perhaps to undergo a crisis of intelligibility; in this way, psychoanalysis assimilates it skeptical challenge.

However, even if the insistence on the medium-bound character of psychoanalytic knowledge rightly articulates the potentially interminable intermediation of context and concept along with its crisis-potential, one may yet wonder whether the clinic is the *only* medium that can do so and in so doing mitigate the self-distorting and practically problematic universalizing pretensions and reifying tendencies of psychoanalytic concepts, interpretations, and theories. To be sure, the clinical context can make it emphatically clear that and why inherited concepts, interpretive templates, and theories may be simultaneously and coextensively too abstract and too particular: because formulated via extrapolation — i.e., abstraction — from particular clinical material previously encountered, such concepts, interpretations, and theories are both too abstract and too particular to account for similar yet non-identical material to which they are subsequently applied. Yet is it *only* the clinical context that can make this clear? Is it *only* the singularity of the clinical context that can draw to the fore the provisionality and essential (in)determinacy of psychoanalytic concepts, interpretations, and theories, and so keep psychoanalytic thinking in motion? Why would it not be the case that a concept, interpretation, or theory is particularized through its application to, say, a literary text or film that it illuminates but does not wholly account for? If the thought is that attention to the particular in its simultaneous "rightness of fit" yet incomplete assimilability to the concept is the motor of conceptual development and a source of conceptual precision (self-consciousness), this seems to be so general a statement about conceptual life as to block the appeal to the clinical primacy of psychoanalytic knowledge. Why wouldn't the abrasiveness of the particular vis-à-vis the concept and the ensuing demand to recast the concept in conformity with the permutation revealed by the particular not occur, say, when the application of the concept "projective identification" to political phenomena suggests something new about how projective identification works or what it means? Why should psychoanalytic discoveries only occur in the clinic? Could they? Wouldn't so claiming, at the very least, radically falsify the history of conceptual innovation in psychoanalysis? Thus though a strong case can be made for the need to view psychoanalytic knowledge as medium-bound, this does not entail that the medium to which it is bound is the clinic. Medium means enabling constraint, so the question is: What satisfies that condition?

To say that the *psychoanalytic cure* is medium-bound is to insist that the full force of the psychoanalytic experience, and so its curative or transformative prospects, are available only within the clinic or on its basis. This thesis is even more difficult to establish than the former because it involves the strong claim that self-analysis or other endeavors that have analytic effects (say, artistic production, aesthetic experience, or sustained self-reflection provoked by philosophical texts or conversations) are, therapeutically speaking, second best. For this position to be tenable, the claim that needs to be defended is that the full force of the psychoanalytic experience, the efficacy of the psychoanalytic "cure," requires, minimally, an *other*, and a specifically trained other at that: only when there is another person involved, specifically an analyst, is the therapeutically essential regression, abreaction, and transference (or reactivation of developmental need) provoked, and only with the assistance of a well-trained analyst who is committed to maintaining the clinical setting — say, as a space wherein free association flourishes, where we are supported in our desires for self-knowledge and development, and where we feel vulnerable yet held, safe — can regression and transference, along with the conflicts or unfulfilled expectations or needs subtending transference, be worked through successfully.

The initial plausibility of this thesis comes into view if only we grant that we tend to be our own worst interpreters due to, say, narcissistic, masochistic, or guilt-ridden inclinations to distort our self-images and the interpretations that proceed from them, including the self-interpretations that seek to account for these distortions. On one's own, it is extraordinarily difficult, though surely not impossible, to recognize, say, one's own interpretations of one's suffering or one's routine expectations as utterly implausible if not outright pathogenic. If one accepts the basic tenet of psychoanalysis that subjectivity is to some degree constitutively opaque — i.e., that the unconscious is a principle of self-distortion, that we are highly motivated to defensively distort our self-images, action-interpretations, sources of suffering, and so on — then it seems plausible that one will need *another perspective* to gain access to those aspects of oneself and those experiences that, to various degrees, one prefers to or cannot but conceal or distort. Further, one will need an *authoritative* perspective if the insights granted by another's perspective are to get a grip on tendentially self-occluding or self-distorting subjectivity. For if that to which another's perspective grants access is not to be swept away by the forces that make such a perspective necessary, if that to which another's perspective affords access are precisely aspects of oneself and experiences that one does not know how to, indeed is prone or motivated not to sustainedly avow — negotiate with and explore in anything like their full significance — then not just another's perspective but an authoritative perspective is necessary for self-consciousness and analytic work more broadly. Or even bracketing the standard psychoanalytic premise, if one grants that human beings are *relational and expositive*, that the meaning of our speech and deeds, to a certain extent, can only be disclosed by others affected by them, i.e., if one grants that interpretations of intention are non-exhaustive accounts of the meaning of speech and deeds or even that our interpretations of our intentions are often profoundly limited or even just contestable,[81] then, at the very least, the perspectives of others are requisite for self-understanding and so for the assumption of responsibility. And further, the perspectives of those specifically trained to attend to the unintended or unwanted significance of our speech and deeds may be extremely helpful in this regard.

Even friends are ordinarily of little or at least insufficient help here, for they often express solidarity by tacitly corroborating our self-images and interpretive, especially self-interpretive, convictions even when these seem unlikely or problematic. Unlike analysts, friends tend to either give us the benefit of the doubt or tactfully pass over a great many of our questionable, problematic, or peculiarly freighted self- and world-interpretations. Often we know who our friends are because we sense the trust and affirmation involved in their acceptance of our forms of life and the forms of self- and world-interpretation constitutive of them. Whether out of a sense of solidarity or delicacy or just to avoid coming off as contentious and thereby risking the ruination of the friendship, friends are often willing to let our utterly implausible, problematic, or unexcavated self- and world-interpretations slide. Or, even if there is no true friendship without criticism as a medium of commitment to mutual betterment, even if friendship in a fuller sense involves mutual challenging on sensitive issues and drawing one another's attention to what is routinely ignored or uninterrogated, supposing that a friend will be *as* suspicious of your self- and world-interpretations, *as* inclined to provoke you to probe deeper, and *as* adept at supporting you in this undertaking as an analyst is in most cases not only implausible but places too heavy a burden on friendship. If a friend is doing this for you, you might as well discuss a fee schedule and call her your analyst.

To be sure, we do not always need an analyst to recognize the patterns, conflicts, tensions, and unavowed expectations or need-interpretations structuring our speech, deeds, and other manners and manifestations of self- and object-relation: previous to Freud, humanity was not entirely enshrouded in self-oblivion. Despite the limitations addressed above, friends often perform this critical-interrogative function quite well — sometimes better than one would like. So if an analyst is not *necessary* for insight, or at least not necessary for a broad array of insights, or more strongly, if the relational and expositive character of the self implies that the meanings of our speech and deeds can in some sense *only be revealed by those who are impacted by and implicated in them* (here transference would be a red herring), or somewhat more weakly, by those who are able to judge their impact on others in ways we cannot or are motivated to avoid, then pundits of the medium-bound nature of the cure thesis will have to establish (1) the specific range of insights to which only analysts can grant access and the preeminent therapeutic import of such insights and/or (2) the singular and therapeutically necessary efficacy of analysis with respect to the working through of either a specific range of insights or experiences uniquely facilitated by analysis or of insights and experiences variably attainable. Given the *prima facie* implausibility of the suggestion that clinical psychoanalysis is epistemologically special, i.e., affords access to insights not otherwise attainable (we will return to this), let us turn to experience.

Perhaps there are certain therapeutically essential and not otherwise available *experiences* that clinical analysis fosters. Maxwell Gitelson seems to suggest as much when he proposes that "[i]t is the task of analysis to enable . . . [us] to progress from peripheral to real emotional contact in an *experimentally limited interpersonal situation* — the patient-analyst relationship — so that, *on the basis of this special, controlled experience*, they are able to accomplish in the world at large what the more or less normal do without help. This is not simply a matter of reductive analysis, but also one of concomitant re-education" (1973, 94; emphasis added). On this conception, clinical psychoanalysis facilitates *experiences* of living otherwise — both the undergoing of such experiences and, presumably, a reflective articulation of their compelling character — that, at least for some, cannot be had outside of the experimentally limited clinical context. For instance, by promoting regression to archaic phantasies that, at the level of the unconscious, threaten to annihilate the patient, and by allowing the patient to acknowledge and survive these phantasies and thus experience the prospect of living without a looming and massively encumbering sense of endangerment, the clinician brokers an experience that may be of enormous therapeutic significance.[82] But are such experiences and the emotional reeducation, indeed reorientation, their adequate handling may yield to be had only in the clinic? It is not clear on what ground(s) one could claim exclusivity here. Considering that spontaneous remission and changes in life circumstances have been noted to eventuate in genuine personal transformation from Freud onwards,[83] the exclusivity claim seems rather unlikely. Contingent circumstances such as the ministrations of a superbly sensitive partner, the dynamics of a new work environment, or having a child to care for may respond to the developmental needs of an individual or substantially mitigate, even moot, certain conflicts and/or intense anxieties such that genuine personal transformations on a par with those attainable through analysis ensue. Especially if the individual in question is involved in some form of self-analysis, altered circumstances may impact her sufficiently for many important questions to be productively broached or renewed. Again, although having an analyst might be a more efficient way of getting there, it does not seem to be the only way.[84]

Of course, for some, in fact for many — those who for various reasons (extreme suffering and reflection-debilitating cultural standardization not being the least of them) are not likely to become adept self-analysts — *practically speaking* there may be no alternative to clinical analysis if one is to experience anything like the full force and curative/transformative potential of psychoanalysis. An analyst's periods of silence and evenly suspended attention, for instance, by consistently conveying the message 'go on, there is more to tell,' may afford access to patterns, themes, dissonances, etc. otherwise unavailable. But still there seems to be nothing that an analyst can do that is *in principle* unique. The "limited interpersonal situation" provided by the clinic may have proven *pragmatically necessary* for particular individuals to achieve certain therapeutic goals — for instance, it is extremely difficult to become aware that one is assimilating others to, say, archaic internal objects, unless one undergoes consistent and compelling experiences of another person, e.g., an analyst, in her evident nonconformity to one's internal-object paradigm[85] — but to infer from this that only the clinic facilitates the full force and curative/transformative potential of analysis involves a great deal of questionable counterfactual speculation — claims on the order of: in no conceivable case would changes of life circumstances or spontaneous remission or other sorts of therapies have brought about what clinical analysis was able to.

So even if another's perspective, even another's authoritative perspective, is necessary for expanded self-consciousness and the personal transformations it facilitates, it has yet to be demonstrated that such a perspective need be that of an analyst. Certainly analysts are more adept than most at noticing, conveying, tactfully[86] insisting on, and mediating the exploration of the unintended or disclaimed resonances and implications of speech and unacknowledged presuppositions and consequences of actions, but it is hardly plausible to claim that such aptitudes are unique to them (were they, ethical life would be impossible). And it is equally unlikely that only an analyst can guide us from peripheral to real emotional contact or reactivate and sufficiently provide for developmental need. Sometimes a good relationship will do just fine. But, again, without some support, we are left to our own resources which have proven inadequate to the task insofar as we continue to suffer and/or cause others to suffer in ways we need not. Perhaps, then, the advocate of the medium-bound nature of the cure thesis should claim that what an analyst can do that a friend, partner, self-analytic practice, or altered life circumstances cannot is systematically modify our structures of defense and thereby allow us to retain and work through — broadly, reap the full benefit of — achieved insights and newly available emotional resources,[87] i.e., sustain an affective environment in which we can consistently experience, sustain availability to, and explore new ways of negotiating with defensively repudiated ideations, affects, developmental needs, expectations, and so forth.[88] We all too readily fall back into engrained habits of self- and world-interpretation and old styles of object relation, thus insights achieved and emotional/relational possibilities opened through self-analysis or at the provocation of a friend or partner or altered life circumstances may quickly fade under the pressure to sustain the defenses (and the satisfactions incumbent thereto) that brought about the repressions, disavowals, or old styles of object relation in the first place or have subsequently accrued to them.[89] And compared to the efficacy of insights achieved in and experiences supported by the context of clinically induced regression, abreaction, and transference, insights achieved and experiences facilitated by self-analysis or friendly provocation are often emotionally superficial and all too amenable to defensive compartmentalization or intellectualizing dissociation.[90]

If the analytic setting is properly maintained, it is felt to be a space wherein one is at once safe and emotionally vulnerable. In the clinic, one should feel increasingly safe to feel and say anything, specifically, safe from fears of judgmental opprobrium and from having to contend with the ordinary and ordinarily meaning-constitutive social consequences of one's speech and deeds — consequences that routinely conspire with defenses. The clinical context is an anomalous speech situation: it presupposes the suspension of the implied performative efficacy of speech, specifically, much of its promissory character, its inferential implications, and so the suspension of the routine responsibilities ascribed to and regularly determinative of the meaning of speech acts. In analysis, contra Cavell, we need not mean what we say. In fact, those who insist that they *must* mean what they say give evidence of concretistic and fetishistic thinking that is itself in need of analysis. If you profess love to your analyst, it is not assumed that from thereon you will relate to him or her as one in love would and that you can be held accountable if you don't, indeed must be if words are to mean anything and social life is to attain any semblance of agency-supporting consistency. Ordinarily, speech implies responsibility: it discloses the moral world to and for which one will be responsible, or at least the semantic and pragmatic entailments to which one must be committed on pain of unintelligibility and practical dismissal. But in the clinic, especially in the context of transference, speech is not often received or responded to as implying the practical consequences and semantic commitments it would ordinarily carry. If a client says, "I want to kill my mother," this is not (usually) heard as a statement of genuine intent to kill, as something on the basis of which the analysand can and ought to be judged. Though in one sense analysis is nothing but supported self-interrogation, in another sense, it is a shelter from judgment.[91]

Indeed, on the basis of the holding or containing function of the analyst and the expectation conveyed by the analyst that even the most precarious self states, the most difficult and affectively dangerous experiences, phantasies, wishes, etc. can be (re)encountered, survived, and perhaps renegotiated, one should feel safe to experience and explore material that threatens one's sense of sanity and personal integrity. Rarely if ever is this sense of safety in the face of abject precarity available in self-analysis or in the context of conversations with friends, thus rarely if ever in such contexts does one brush against psychotic dimensions of subjectivity or festering traumas and thereby find oneself in a position to negotiate anew archaic and/or traumatic material or other intensely troubling and troubled self states. Certainly the success of analysis presupposes that ordinarily unbearable material can be undergone and survived or perhaps negotiated anew outside the clinic, but such extra-clinical success would hardly be likely if not for successful clinical experiences. Though friends, literary models, and the like may be impressive, it is not implausible to suggest that their modeling of a well-integrated, mature psyche, say, one that allows for greater permeability of the drives and the ego without suffering breakdown, i.e., their functioning as auxiliary containers or idealized exemplars of negotiating with difficult, perhaps depersonalizing or de-structuring material, will not be as effective as an analyst's. Conversely, conversations with friends, etc. may make us feel *too* safe. Freud may have had a point when he insisted that the frustrations induced by the clinical setting (analytic abstinence, the supine position of the analysand and other impediments to ordinary forms of drive discharge, etc.) are required to generate tension (suffering) sufficient to motivate the client to "do work and make changes" (SE 14: 165, see also SE 17: 179-204). Correspondingly, the analyst's exemplary imaging of more mature psychic integration, of reflective and emotional freedom — generally, the analyst's exemplification of the good life — may be both incomparably effective and crucial to motivate the analysand to give up the securities and satisfactions that, though surely limited, are afforded by his structures of defense. The well-modulated emotional exposure perhaps essential to the full force of analysis is thus, at the very least, difficult to induce and sustain in self-analysis or in conversations with friends.

Likewise, if the experience of empathy and validation, that is, of the acknowledgement and acceptance of one's insuperable narcissism, unremitting vulnerability, diverse and not altogether socialized let alone sociable affects — especially chaotic, conflictual, and negative affects and overpowering erotic sentiments — incomprehensibly sensitive areas, etc., are crucial to the efficacy of analysis,[92] and if these sort of experiences are extremely difficult, perhaps impossible to self-provision and are likely temporally, qualitatively, and perhaps categorically limited when offered by friends or partners, then, again, having an analyst may be practically essential. You can't tickle yourself.

However, let us underscore, there is nothing an analyst might bring to our attention that is in principle barred from independent discovery, and any experience an analyst might facilitate can be, in principle, undergone without such mediation. To suppose otherwise would (1) mystify, idealize, and ultimately falsify the source of the analyst's competence: just as the analyst learned how to be an analyst in her own analysis, we learn how to be analysts in ours; or if this overstates the case, the training contributing to the analyst's formation imparts nothing that cannot be in principle learned independently of certified training institutions, (2) render analytic success incomprehensible: the forms of self-relation fostered by analysis and the possibilities of object relations it opens require elaboration — must be put into practice — beyond the confines of the clinic, and (3) make no sense of how and why therapy can ever come to an end: the termination of an analysis (ideally) requires that the analysand has sufficiently internalized the forms of attention, self- and world-interpretive capabilities, and desire for analysis to continue initially manifest in the figure of the analyst; ideally, the termination of an analysis occurs when the analysand has become a sufficiently competent self-analyst, interested in and able to respond reflectively and effectively (at least more so than before) to difficulties that are bound to occur subsequent to the end of therapy — analysis is *both* terminable and interminable.[93]

Yet there is no reason to deny that with regard to these matters having an analyst can help immensely. If one grants that we are in certain ways committed to our suffering — e.g., that symptoms provide compromise satisfactions (including sometimes relative stability of personality and object relations) to which we are deeply committed for want of subjectively viable alternatives and may accrue narcissistic investment just by dint of being ours; that symptoms, inhibitions, and anxieties ward off expected dangers and so provide genuine comfort; or that pathological self- and world-interpretations proceed from drive conflicts that we have not been able to negotiate more successfully or from ill-provisioned developmental needs that we have not been able to adequately fulfill — then an outside perspective, specifically, a perspective that is not conditioned by commitments to the forms of self- and world-interpretation from which we suffer, and a perspective that, moreover, is cultivated to be suspicious of *precisely* these interpretations, namely, the perspective of an analyst, may be, practically speaking, essential.

But these are no more than pragmatic considerations. They only go to show that an analyst may be an extraordinarily helpful mediator of the full force and curative/transformative potential of the analytic experience, not that an analyst is *necessary* for it. One should not discount the insights acquired, structural changes induced, and therapeutically productive habits encouraged by self-analysis or other sorts of extra-clinical or non-analytic experiences. But neither should one neglect their limits.

A well trained analyst committed to maintaining the clinical setting may be essential to the psychoanalytic process on account of the following. It may be only in a well orchestrated clinical environment that transference will be elicited to the point where a *transference neurosis* is established. For, at least on the standard account, this requires frequent and regular sessions in a demonstrably safe, judgment-free environment, an environment, moreover, where free association is contractually agreed upon, transference is encouraged by and subject to compelling interpretation on the basis of the analyst's partial though emphatic obscurity (unusual unavailability as a concrete person manifesting characteristic habits, beliefs, desires, etc.), regression is encouraged by analytic abstention or sufficiently minimal gratification,[94] and abreaction (perhaps necessary to free libido to invest the analyst and strengthen the transference or to invest other objects, which would perhaps itself be a valuable effect of analysis) is sustained through systematic analysis of defenses. Of course, various persons, figures, and issues — especially but not just those of antecedent emotional significance — can elicit and become the focal point of transference. Indeed, relations with them can become so complex and overdetermined that it can feel as if they mean *everything*. However, there is a difference between an onslaught of transference and a transference neurosis.[95] When nonanalysts come to bear the brunt of transference, understandably, they frequently respond in gratifying or prohibitive ways — one should not underestimate our resourcefulness in eliciting expected responses from our environments — as a result of which the transference may remain relatively superficial, stultified, and due to the fixating, sometimes consuming effect of gratification and prohibition, its analysis, if undertaken, may be impeded. Perhaps only when expectations about how the other will respond and the needs and desires gratified, fantasies and self-images sustained, or more broadly, desire- and anxiety-infused self-and world-interpretations corroborated by such responses are *remarkably frustrated* do we sufficiently regress: our compromise formations no longer work and we are thrown back onto more archaic strategies of pleasure-seeking and object-relating. And perhaps only when such artificially induced regression is sustained under the appropriate care are archaic desires, patterns of attachment and aversion, fears, aggressive urges, fantasies, and so on invoked such that transference is strengthened and deepened to the point where a transference neurosis consolidates, the analysis of which may be crucial for attaining the maximal benefit of psychoanalysis.[96] Or, putting a more developmentalist spin on it, it may be only in the context of the carefully conducted clinical relationship that transference can be elicited to the point where defensively repudiated developmental needs will be sufficiently reactivated and thus able to be avowed and experienced as met if and when they are. For although it may come at the cost of terrible suffering or staleness and rigidity, we may develop "false selves" or in less severe ways superficially adapt to environments that do not respond to our deepest needs, or refuse the affordances of our environments because we dreadfully anticipate our inability to abide, or even survive, inadequate or inconsistent responsiveness. Expanding a bit: it may be only when subtly detected developmental needs — needs the analysand will not allow herself to truly experience no matter how deep her self-analysis goes — are partially gratified by an analyst, that is, tactfully managed on the basis of relative distance from the preemptory urgency of developmental needs and its corollary in/as defense, that the analysand will allow herself to undergo a sustained reactivation of long suppressed needs and contend with the traumatic experiences that led to their suppression, the forms of defense developed to keep these needs and traumas at bay, and the question of whether she is — or under what conditions she would be — ready to allow herself to experience those features of her world that might respond to these needs. Although changes in life circumstances can undoubtedly prove gratifying with respect to suppressed developmental needs, perhaps only under the care of someone trained to tactfully balance gratification and provocation will the analysand be able to contend with regressively released material, e.g., such that a basic sense of cohesive selfhood settles in that allows for the further exploration of the matter at hand or other pressing issues. Or, by metabolizing unbearable affects, wishes, or expectations and returning them in a more palatable form, the analyst may facilitate developmental accomplishments necessary to confront and explore the significance of the material in need of modification/detoxification.

Through abstention, interpretation, and other measures that mitigate superego severity or otherwise modify the analysand's structures of defense, the analyst, perhaps uniquely, may induce regression to patterns of response to frustration (e.g., archaic defenses and habits of object relation) that, upon their return, bear with them long suppressed feelings, fantasies, and beliefs, the reemergence of which may intensify and consolidate the transference and the exploration of which may take the analysis much deeper and make it much more impacting — especially on the Freudian assumption that infantile neuroses subtend adult neuroses. It may be only at the provocation of the *almost* unbearable frustrations systematically generated and tactfully maintained by analysis — given that it is hardly plausible to simply disengage from our routine, that such frustration would be generated by self-analysis is unlikely — that we revert to archaic styles of object relation and undergo the resurgence of repressed or defensively modified wishes or disavowed developmental needs. And it is perhaps only when these are attended at length, which may require the continued provocations of an analyst who refuses to allow us to shy away from them, and when they are interpreted, which may require the presence of mind of someone not directly undergoing them, that therapeutically crucial insights are achieved and structural transformations or inceptive reorientations effectuated. It may be only under conditions of clinically induced frustration and regression that transference becomes sufficiently intense and resilient for frustration to translate into new demands directed toward the analyst or for new feelings, fantasies, or dreams pertaining to her to emerge, i.e., for the development of new material for exploration. What the analyst can offer that self-analysis seemingly cannot is a focal point for and various means for intensifying and sustaining transference projections.

In sum, perhaps it is the specific virtue of analysts that they are some of the least accommodating folk we know; or, more precisely, that they are adept at discerning when accommodation and when refusal of accommodation (e.g., confrontation, provocation, or neutrality and abstinence) is likely to be therapeutically productive and when not. It may be that only by working through the transference neurosis (especially in cases of classical Oedipal neuroses) in the context of regressive abreaction or by facilitating redevelopment through responding in appropriate, tactful ways to transferentially expressed development needs (especially in cases of narcissistic or borderline disorders) that psychoanalysis can achieve its full potential. But is this enough to establish that the psychoanalytic cure is medium-bound? The counterargument would be, roughly, that even if we grant that what is needed for the full force of analysis is a context suited to the development of a transference neurosis, and specifically, tactful handling of the abreaction and regression involved therewith, given (1) the inevitability and ubiquity of transference[97] and (2) the capacity of self-analytic and other therapeutic practices to respond to it in genuinely productive ways, then even if, empirically, clinical psychoanalysis tends to generate outcomes superior to those of other practices,[98] there is no reason to believe that, in principle, the outcomes of various therapeutic practices cannot be equivalent. The foregoing arguments for the medium-bound nature of the psychoanalytic "cure" are at most support for the claim that clinical psychoanalysis is necessary for those incapable of conducting a comparably beneficial self-analysis, especially the severely impaired, but (1) that leaves unaddressed the possibly of the in principle equivalent efficacy of psychoanalytic, nonpsychoanalytic, and psychoanalytically-informed therapies, and (2) that would be a strange place to end up given that the severely impaired are often contraindicated for strictly psychoanalytic treatment. In no way do such arguments establish the general claim that the full force and curative/transformative potential of psychoanalysis is available only by means of the clinic. The pundit of the medium-bound nature of the cure thesis might object that the specific forms of change induced by analysis are not as readily or extensively achieved in alternative therapeutic settings, but this is unconvincing: it establishes the truth of the thesis by defining the full force and curative/transformative potential of analysis in terms that only clinical practice can meet rather than by defending those forms. Such would be an empty victory. The central point is that if it is not shown that working through a transference neurosis rather than ordinary transference distortions and the conflicts, defenses, developmental needs, and traumas with which they are bound up is *the only way* to achieve significant therapeutic progress — a highly dubious claim — then the medium-bound nature of the cure thesis does not stand. Given that all sorts of (self-) therapeutic practices may meet the various criteria for therapeutic efficacy and methodological validity noted in Section II, why would practices that prove to some extent therapeutically effective and methodologically valid not be countenanced as genuine instances of analysis or prove that "analysis" is so emphatically equivocal that claims about the specificity of the clinical context are overwrought? Indeed, how can we speak of "the" clinic?

Though there may be certain functions that in many circumstances an analyst can best perform, it has yet to be established that these functions are *necessary* for the full force and curative/transformative potential of psychoanalysis. Is an analyst necessary to focus the transference to the point where a transference neurosis will consolidate? Likely. But even if so, does analysis of the transference neurosis gives rise to therapeutically necessary or incomparable effects? Likely not. As noted above, even Freud recognized that changes in life circumstances may sometimes be sufficient to undo or moot pathological formations, just as Winnicott and other developmentally inclined analysts expressly deny that — at least in certain cases — sufficient redevelopment cannot be sparked outside the clinic. Having an analyst is extraordinarily helpful in a multitude of ways, and in certain cases self-analysis or other practices will be woefully insufficient in comparison, but all that the foregoing arguments in favor of the medium-bound nature of the cure thesis can establish is the extraordinary usefulness of clinical analysis, not its insuperable necessity or the incomparable worth of its achievements.

I find much convincing in the claims for clinical primacy, especially with respect to those for whom, practically speaking, sophisticated self-analysis is not really an option or with respect to whom banking on analytic effects issuing from changes in life-circumstances, philosophical reflection, aesthetic experience, amicable assistance, and so forth is naïve at best and cruelly dismissive at worst. However, it has yet to be demonstrated that the full force of the analytic experience, its curative/transformative potential, is available *only* in the clinic or that *in principle* the results of clinical analysis are of vastly greater value than, indeed incomparable with, those achieved by other means. And even if one grants analysts the prerogative to define the full force and curative/transformative potential of analysis in terms that only clinical practice can meet, given the massive disparity of analytic aims, that is, given that the aims of analysis as articulated by various practitioners are often conflictual and sometimes radically incommensurable, the medium-bound nature of the cure thesis would suffer under the weight of its own equivocity.[99]

By way of conclusion, let us clarify the motivations for and stakes of the debate about the medium-bound nature of psychoanalysis. It may not be just the legitimacy of self-analysis that is at stake in the insistence on this thesis. Might the insistence on the medium bound-nature of psychoanalytic knowledge answer to a groping desire for a limit? Is its attraction attendant upon the promise of containing and providing a platform for the critique of the unnerving excesses of psychoanalytic speculation? Is the notion of medium a stand-in for the constraint or resistance ordinarily figured by "the facts" in theoretical discourses? Does insistence on the thesis attest to a certain unease about the authority and status of psychoanalytic knowledge? With regard to the medium-bound nature of the "cure," is the insistence on this just a self-interested power ploy, an effort to install an artificial distinction between authentic and inauthentic analysis in the service of securing a sufficient number of clients for practicing clinicians? Is it perhaps an anti-democratic, if beneficently intended, attempt to keep "genuine" analysis confined to the clinic and thus subject to institutional oversight? Or might its attractiveness accrue from the evasion of the significance of psychoanalytic plurality, or more broadly, from the avoidance of clarifying and defending the terms in which psychoanalysis is to be valued, that it enables? That is, does the thesis serve the interests of dogmatism? Psychoanalysis is often used in clinical contexts that are not strictly psychoanalytic and in a variety of extraclinical contexts. Why deny these practices the title of psychoanalysis? Whence the desire to regulate the dissemination of psychoanalysis? Whence the desire to establish the scene of the proper? Must psychoanalysis accede to the impulse to master its domain? And even if it so accedes, can satisfaction be had?[100]

The following will be primarily concerned with the motivations for and stakes of the claim that psychoanalytic knowledge is medium-bound, but as we will see, following this thread will run us into the question of the motivations for and stakes of the claim that the psychoanalytic cure is medium-bound. Further, as we will see with respect to both theses, theoretical and practical issues are mutually implicating.

One plausible reason to insist on the clinical primacy of psychoanalytic knowledge is that so doing allows one to resist what might be considered a false and therapeutically problematic theoreticist framing, i.e., reification, of psychoanalytic knowledge. More precisely, it facilitates a characterization of the *concreteness* of psychoanalytic concepts that seem to do justice to the experience of psychoanalysis and may be independently compelling. Emphasizing the binding of psychoanalytic concepts to singular therapeutic contexts makes visible (or at least suggests) the complex and singular (in)determinacy, i.e., concreteness, of the concepts employed therein and therewith their resistance to systematic codification. For instance, what the Oedipus complex means *for this analysand* may be significantly different from its meaning as typified in the literature, for the literature develops concepts and theories via extrapolations from exemplary cases that may be different in important respects from the case at hand. Indeed, insisting on the singular significance of the Oedipus complex in the present case may retrospectively unlock the differences congealed within the transmitted concept, further contributing to its dynamic (in)determinacy. One might then claim that knowing what the Oedipus complex *is* requires acknowledging the possibility that each manifestation of the Oedipus complex may be a singular, unanticipated permutation of the concept, that the example always threatens to alter the shape of — or, at the limit, call into crisis — the rule or concept of which it is an example.[101] The insistence on the clinical primacy of psychoanalytic knowledge may thus promote clinical sophistication, i.e., fine-grained attentiveness, and work against dogmatic fixation. In short, the thesis asks one to expect to be surprised.

By suggesting that psychoanalytic concepts are open-ended constellations, that they attain to, at most, provisional stability, this insistence may afford insight into the specific nature of psychoanalytic knowledge, and correspondingly, that of its objects. Additionally, by keeping us attuned to the specific developments of each analysis, those that may not be best understood in the terms of one's own or any prevailing theory, it may motivate a critical attitude toward one's own convictions and interest in others', which may in turn be crucial for the efficacy of analysis generally (cf. Kristeva 1995, 35). More emphatically, this insistence may be a means of suggesting that the ossification of psychoanalytic thinking into presumptively stable doctrines is an abdication or violation of the eminently questionable character of psychoanalytic knowing and of the uniqueness of its objects. At the very least, this insistence may keep us attuned to the uniqueness of what unfolds in each analysis and thereby help us resist the temptation — perhaps amplified by the affective "messiness" and frequent confusions of analysis — to mechanically apply concepts and interpretation-templates and provides leverage for criticism of those who do. In sum, this insistence may be in the service of keeping analysis (and therewith analysands) open to its (their) futures, its (their) need for ongoing recasting and adaptation.[102]

Thus, insisting on the medium-bound character of psychoanalytic knowing provides a compelling response to charges against psychoanalytic *methodology* leveled by the likes of Adorno, Deleuze, Foucault, and Irigaray. The gist of the charge against methodology is that psychoanalytic interpretations, concepts, and theories abstract from, indeed violently suppress, silence, or collude with obliviousness to the value of concrete particularity, e.g., sexual difference or socio-historical context, and thereby signal their complicity with later modern commodity culture (reification, interchangeability), bourgeois individualism (abstract, ornamental, and system-syntonic individuality), and/or phallocentrism. Tyrannical subsumption at the formal level signals cryptonormative material implications. More specifically, methodological subsumption is found problematic on account of the following:

(1) It is theoretically insulating, thus dogma supporting, and self-defeating insofar as theory aspires to concrete determinacy.

(2) It is practically self-defeating insofar as variables and nuances that may be crucial for therapeutic success are neglected.

(3) It privileges and further naturalizes instrumental rationality — the assumption is that conceptual subsumption is driven by the imperative of instrumental domination — thus displacing the rationality-potential and challenge of concrete insights into distinctive cases and retrenching the form of rationality from which we suffer, i.e., that in accordance with which objects/others are either resources for our projects or superfluous, waste: a recipe for disaster. Formally, it reproduces and naturalizes the abstraction from use-value (sensuous particularity) to exchange value (context-indifferent concepts, myth), thus promoting the form of rationality that, materially, secures or at least conspires with nihilism, e.g., politics concerned only with system-integration, and its supplementary stabilizing mechanism: commodity culture.

(4) Concepts are never pure: they are formed via extrapolation from exemplary cases, thus stained with a residue of particularity. Consequently, when an analysand is induced to identify with a concept, i.e., induced to employ the concept in her self-interpretation, she assimilates her self-image to an inconspicuous norm. In short, psychoanalysis is normalizing, insufficiently *analytic*.

Additionally, insisting on the clinical primacy of psychoanalytic knowledge allows for two plausible and desirable ways of framing the relationship of psychoanalysis to the exact sciences. *On the one hand*, if psychoanalytic knowledge is bound to or at least substantially mediated by the practical demands incumbent to singular therapeutic relationships, its conceptual and theoretical generalizations will be — or should be — conspicuously artificial and speculative, i.e., eminently questionable. If psychoanalytic concepts and theories are extrapolations from or ultimately related to singular clinical contexts oriented toward the alleviation of suffering and/or pathology rather than the formulation and testing of scope-defined or universal theorems, their difference in character from natural scientific knowledge becomes evident, and therewith their evaluation by the epistemic protocols of the latter becomes evidently inappropriate (or at least external and perhaps unnecessary).[103] Insisting on the clinical primacy of psychoanalytic knowledge may be a way of insisting on the epistemically *unambitious* character of psychoanalytic knowledge. On this conception, psychoanalytic knowledge need not aspire to scientific validity. Indeed, it may not even be representational, thus may not be appropriately evaluated in terms of correspondence. From this deflationary perspective, criticism of psychoanalysis' purported presumptions to causal explanation and scientific standing as fraudulent or inappropriate (Grünbaum, Popper, Habermas, Ricoeur), or of its theories as inconsistent, irreconcilable, or otherwise epistemically objectionable may be dismissed as simply off target. Insisting that psychoanalysis means to be helpful for those seeking its specific forms of care rather than to issue in demonstratively certain and universally valid knowledge, that it does not aim to *explain* in the ways that the exact sciences seek to explain, i.e., through ever more comprehensive laws, supports those so inclined in their decision to calmly walk away from the heated debates about the scientificity of psychoanalysis.[104]

However, if this deflationary acceptance of the speculative character of psychoanalytic knowledge is not to undermine the possibility of criticism, i.e., support dogmatic insularity and polemicism, some means of adjudicating between diverse interpretations, concepts, and theories will be necessary. A "natural" (i.e., prevalent) temptation, then, is to claim that validity is predicated on therapeutic efficacy. To be sure, this gesture is tempting[105] and not without its virtues. Indeed, interest in predicating validity on therapeutic efficacy may be a major motivation of insistence on the claim that psychoanalytic knowledge is medium-bound. In its favor, this measure provides a way of evaluating the respective validity of interpretations issuing from different psychoanalytic schools, differing interpretations issuing from the same school, and even different interpretations entertained by a single analyst: those that yield the best outcomes — in a yet to be defined sense — should be privileged. Further, predicating validity on therapeutic efficacy may moot some of the force behind the suspicion that psychoanalytic interpretations are simply stories among indefinitely many others, no more than logically possible vectors of illumination: not only are they hermeneutically coherent and compelling, *they work.*[106] And so doing allows for an abatement of anxiety over the historical forms of psychoanalytic concept and theory formation (which may to no small extent fuel excessive enamorment with the experimental scientific study of psychoanalytic concepts and theories). What would it matter, say, that in Freud's metapsychological reflections he speculatively generates postulates just for the sake of the argument's advancement or the phenomena's intelligibility (Ptolemism), that in various works he appeals to evidence from speculative history and questionable ethnology, that he keeps on piling constructions upon constructions, that energetics as a whole may be deeply implausible, or that specific runs of argument are extremely problematic, even gender-biased or heteronormative, if what ultimately matters is that the practice works (or how well it works in comparison with others)?

Finally, insisting that validity is predicated on therapeutic efficacy may be a means of insisting on the substantive nature of reason generally, viz. that reason remains rational only insofar as it is keyed to the demand for sensuous happiness, or conversely, that reason tends toward self-destruction (rationalization and reification) when it occludes its functionality and historicity.

Though tempting as a criterion for validity, clinical efficacy is extremely vague and as such fails to function as a means of adjudication. It can almost always be satisfied: aggressivity, silence, a missed appointment, a change in affective tone, various new associations or the consolidation of trends in the material presented, remission of symptoms or diminishment of inhibitions or anxieties, just as the emergence of new symptoms, inhibitions, or anxieties, generally, anything new or significant in an analysis, may count as a therapeutic effect. Given the extent of what may count as effective, given disagreements over desired effects, and given that purported effects may be but contingently related to a specific intervention, mere coincidence,[107] the extraordinary capaciousness of the criterion renders it feeble as a criterion.[108] If, on some conception of efficacy, the criterion validates all interpretations, it hardly counts as a criterion; rather, it just moves the problem back a step (i.e., to the interpretation of "efficacy"). Given the diversity of analytic aims and conceptions of therapeutic progress, and given the diversity and indeterminacy of understandings of the link(s) between them, the satisfaction of the criterion will satisfy no one seriously concerned with evaluating competing practices.[109]

From the purview of clinical analysis, this measure will not do. The identity of validity and therapeutic efficacy does not allow for distinctions between interventions whose effects issue from power imbalance, suggestion, placebo, or other variables and those that result from good clinical practice.[110] If psychoanalytic technique is to progress, it must be able to account for its failures and evaluate competing recommendations for revision, yet this does not seem possible if validity is identified with a diffuse sense of efficacy.[111]

From the epistemological purview, there are numerous problems with predicting validity upon therapeutic efficacy. For instance, proof of the theory would depend on the measuring instruments the theory has created, viz. the various standards of therapeutic efficacy and their criteria for application. Further problems are:

(1) *If possible alternative causes of efficacy are not ruled out, the "validity" claimed is evacuated of any sense.* Symptoms, inhibitions, etc. that are not specifically analyzed sometimes disappear in the course of therapy. This may be due to changes in the analysand's living or work environment; it may be a way of concealing the sources and significance of symptoms and inhibitions and/or preserving the compromise satisfactions to which they give rise; it may be because other symptoms, inhibitions, etc. have taken up their work or because analytic work in a (seemingly) separate domain has had far reaching effects; it may be because the therapeutic agency is some (or several) feature(s) of the relational dynamic rather than a particular (series of) intervention(s); or as Freud (1926) suggests, remission of symptoms, etc. sometimes may just be "spontaneous." Diminished signal anxiety, or more broadly, increased freedom of (re)action — enhanced adaptive facility — may result from living through dangerous feelings, fantasies, desires, and so on in the relatively sheltered safe-haven of analysis — generally, from recondi-

tioning or reprocessing — rather than from a valid interpretation or specific intervention; or it may be the other way around; or the results may issue from specific combinations of ambient factors and interventions. Generally, it may be that any number of factors involved in an appropriately maintained analytic relationship — the ongoing emotional availability of the analyst, the analyst's support for it and consistent non-impingement on the patient's vulnerability, the experience of surviving one's own or the analyst's aggression or desire, empathic emotional support either at a point of severe regression or generally (i.e., "holding"), the analyst's performative exemplarity, e.g., her manifest facility in making connections between past and present or otherwise experientially diverse material, that is, her compelling enactment of integrative reflection and the confidence to follow suit it induces, etc. — rather than specific interpretations or other manners of intervention that give rise to therapeutic effects; or it may be the converse; or it may be some manner of conjunction of specific interventions and ambient factors that is responsible for the results. How would one validly identify and bracket the many and diverse variables to sort this out? Even were it possible to validly identify the variables — that is, assuming, implausibly, some way to guarantee the validity and exhaustiveness of descriptions of context and influencing agencies — it is difficult to imagine that such bracketing would be compatible with conducting an analysis — a double bind seems unavoidable. And even if this aporia is merely apparent, even if it were ethically and practically feasible to systematically suspend validly identified variables (one by one and in all relevant combinations) in the course of *an* (extremely long) analysis, the claim that validity is attendant upon therapeutic efficacy would still be problematic because its sense supposes that the efficacy under consideration pertains at some level of generality, which would not yet be demonstrated. For this, confirmation by multiple analyses will be inadequate given that different combinations of factors — not just factors of therapeutic practice but factors of the context established by the analysand's psychic life — may yield equivalent results. What would still need to be demonstrated is that the object domain is sufficiently homogenous, that what works for one will work for sufficiently many others and for the same reasons. But since different combinations of factors may yield the same results — both *ex hypothesi* and as suggested by the research that shows that diverse psychoanalytic practices yield basically equivalent results — demonstrating the homogeneity of the object domain would be extremely difficult. In short, the mitigation or resolution of pathological formations does not necessarily entail that the interpretations and interventions that immediately precede it or are thematically related to the pathological material — *or* diverse and (partially) diffuse contextual variables — are valid. It is extremely difficult, perhaps impossible, to identify and rule out various possible determinants of therapeutic results in order to establish the causal efficacy of one or a select few.[112] Although sophisticated experimentation no doubt could — and should — make headway into this problem, seemingly insuperable obstacles to meaningfully predicating validity on therapeutic efficacy abound.

(2) *Too few cases are studied and such studies do not involve sufficient methodological precautions to support generalizations about efficacy, wanting which the meaning of "validity" is again emptied out, becoming practically inert and theoretically bankrupt.* This problem may not be insuperable, but at least for the time being it weighs heavily against predicating validity on therapeutic efficacy. Hartmann disagrees, rejoining that

> It is sometimes argued that psychoanalysis has actually studied only a comparatively small number of cases. But this argument misses the point. In every individual case we often gather hundreds of data pertinent to a problem in question, contiguities in free associations or other observed regularities. That is, every clinical 'case' is actually hundreds of cases, scientifically speaking. Or, rather, we can say that for every 'case' there is often a great wealth of instances in which every single hypothesis that comes into play can be tested. (1964, 307)

But such observed regularities should be considered hypotheses, not the testing of hypotheses. A number of commentators such as Marshall Edelson (1985) agree with Hartmann, arguing that large and representative sample groups are not necessary to validate the efficacy of various therapeutic practices since single subject research in the clinical context allows for a wealth of opportunities to assess this. E.g., since "working through" means delivering the same interpretation time and again in diverse contexts, there will be ample opportunity to test the impact of the interpretation in question. But even if the epistemic credentials of single subject research are routinely underappreciated, if the sense of predicating validity on therapeutic efficacy presupposes that such efficacy amounts to law-like regularities (given scenario z for object domain y, x interpretation will produce the desired effects), then methodologically regulated assessment of a large number of cases will be necessary to mitigate the selection-bias problem and the problem of alternative causes of therapeutic results. In order to test claims about therapeutic efficacy, randomized sampling, control groups, and other methodological precautions are needed.[113] Otherwise, claims to generalized efficacy may trade on selection-bias, contingent correlations, and placebo, suggestion, or other alternative causes of therapeutic results. And, interestingly, when these controls are in place to some extent, it ends up that the efficacy of psychoanalysis is not greater than that of expressive or supportive psychotherapies where very different methods are employed. Finally, how to institute sufficient methodological precautions, e.g., establishing relevant and valid differences and similarities between cases and controlling for valid and relevant differences is hard to fathom.

(3) *Clinical events may not be reproducible.* If validity requires confirmation by independent inquirers who replicate an experiment step by step, then, assuming that no two analyses, because no two individuals, let alone relationships, are identical[114] and that potential terms of comparison and criteria of salient sufficient similarity are contestable, that is, assuming that "the given" is a myth and that what needs to be established as sufficiently uniform across cases is not all that clear, the clinical medium seems inimical to supporting validity claims. Agreement in interparty ratings on the basis of which claims to valid description of what transpires in a case are made may only attest to hegemonic interpretive sensibilities, shared conceptual schemes, rather than the truth of the matter.[115]

(4) *Concepts and interpretations are either too abstract or too particular to be validated by therapeutic efficacy.* Lower-level, experience-near claims, e.g., in this case, interpretation x was followed by result y) are too particular to support generalizations about efficacy, thus to meaningfully bear on the question of validity. Higher-level, experience-far claims (e.g., metapsychological claims) are too abstract to be validated by therapeutic efficacy due to the indeterminate link between the higher-level claim and the observations that are said to confirm it: inferences from therapeutic efficacy to the validity of higher-level concepts are massively underdetermined. The equivocity of higher-level concepts contributes to this problem.

(5) *Higher-level concepts are too equivocal to be validated by therapeutically efficacious interpretations or other manners of intervention.* In a NIMH study of ego functioning, "ego functioning" had 12 different meanings, none of which were securely univocal and the relations between which were unclear, as were their criteria for application: reality testing; judgment; a sense of the reality of the world and the self; regulation and control of drives, affects and impulses; regulation and control of object relations; thought processes; adaptive regression in the service of the ego; defensive functioning; functioning of a stimulus barrier; autonomous functioning; synthetic-integrative functioning; and mastery-competence (Bellak and Walkup 1992, 98-101). In Hartmann's (1950) "Comments on the Psychoanalytic Theory of the Ego," the ego is defined by the following functions: organization and control of motility and perception, providing a barrier against external and internal stimuli, conducting action and thinking, inhibiting and delaying gratification (including defensive modes), issuing anticipatory danger signals, establishing character, and synthesis. Given the polysemy of the concept and the indeterminacy of its semantic range, what exactly would be validated by therapeutically effective interpretations in which, at some level, the notion of the ego played a part?

Or to give another example: Ken Lewes argues in *The Psychoanalytic Theory of Male Homosexuality* (1988) that there are at least 12 variations of the Oedipus complex.[116] If this is so, a clinically efficacious interpretation that directly or indirectly concerned "the Oedipus complex" would be too indeterminate to meaningfully validate the concept. Often, psychoanalytic concepts seem to name broad and internally diverse themes, complex assemblages, or as Jung would have it, "tropes"; they do not seem to possess the precision necessary to be validated in the clinic or elsewhere.

Sometimes, of course, specifying what one means when using a higher-level concept will help.[117] Further, this is not to deny that higher-level concepts ordinarily map onto a range of recognizable phenomena that partially specify their meanings. Insisting on equivocity as a challenge to validity does not imply repudiating or disavowing the disclosive, practically and cognitively orientative, authority of our criteria. Though, say, "transference" may be a highly equivocal term, it does possess an ordinary range of referents: professing love to one's analyst or lashing out unprovoked, frequent tardiness or missed sessions, garrulous or taciturn speech, consistent rejection or manifest misunderstanding of interpretations, sleeping in the session, excessive absentmindedness, etc.[118] But this just shows that operationalization is to some extent possible, that our words function in and are facilitated by our practices, not that psychoanalytic concepts are sufficiently semantically stable, mutually differentiated, and determined in their range of applications (as concepts involved in statements of law-like regularities must be) to be validated, let alone validated by therapeutic efficacy. Or perhaps it suggests that the notion that referential validity presupposes impersonal rules of reason that correspond precisely to a self-subsistent and systematically integrated object domain, i.e., the notion that metaphysical and epistemological realism are necessary criteria for genuine cognition, is, as Wittgenstein came to believe, a destructive fantasy, or at least that it is so with respect to the phenomena under consideration here. Do psychoanalytic concepts name natural kinds or do they, as Moss (1985) suggests, gather and organize otherwise evanescent words, affects, and clues in the therapeutic dialogue?

It is surprising that generations of analysts have ignored Freud's insightful comments on this topic.

> The true beginning of scientific activity consists . . . in describing phenomena and then proceeding to group, classify and correlate them. Even at the stage of description it is not possible to avoid applying certain abstract ideas to the materials at hand, ideas derived from various sources and certainly not the fruit of the new experience only. Still more indispensable are such ideas – which later become the fundamental concepts of the science – as the material is further elaborated. They must at first necessarily possess some measure of uncertainty; there can be no question of any clear delimitation of their contents. So long as they remain in this condition, we come to an understanding about their meaning by repeated references to the material of observation, from which we seem to have drawn our abstract ideas, but which is in point of fact subject to them. (SE 14: 117)[119]

(6) *If psychic material is overdetermined, and all the more so if a source of overdetermination is that psychic phenomena are partially pliable to interpretive constitution – not simply a self-standing and autointerpreting object domain but to some extent inchoate, determined and redetermined by evolving frames of reference – its conceptual elaboration(s) and theoretical ordering of such concepts will be underdetermined: partial, selective, never fully exhaustive of the inordinate density and complexity of psychic phenomena. Consequently, claims to validity drawing on such material will be underdetermined, indeed perhaps so underdetermined that they lose their sense.*[120] And even if validity can be understood as distinct from the ideal of unimpeachable and/or exhaustively explanatory objectivity, its dissociation from the latter undermines its function as a criterion for adjudicating between diverse forms of conceptualization and systematization. If validity is not an objective register of absolute reality, if apparently contradictory interpretations reflect different foci or a contradiction in the overdetermined material, then validity cannot do the work it is called upon to perform. Predicating validity (so understood) on therapeutic efficacy will not resolve interanalytic debates or convince the unconvinced that psychoanalysis yields genuine knowledge.

(7) *The therapeutic efficacy standard is prone to yield false positives.* Interpretations that generate positive therapeutic effects and may also be avowed by the analysand are sometimes, actually rather often, later disclaimed or qualified by the analyst, analysand, or both. A recovered memory may be a screen memory. An effective interpretation may be accepted and used because the analysand's structures of defense forbid accepting a more accurate or more affectively impacting interpretation — i.e., the interpretation may be accepted only in intellectualized form. Generally, interpretations may be accepted and used defensively, e.g., to attain a form of "oral" gratification or "tactile" grasp, or on the basis of transferential framing as a gift, a token of affection, an invasive injury over which to brood, evidence of the omnipotence or magical powers of the analyst or whomever the analyst tokens in transference, etc. Various factors that conduce to compliance — a flight into health — may contribute to the efficacy of false or problematic interpretations and interventions. Further, insight in one area may (and often does) operate as defense in another, thus therapeutic success is itself an equivocal standard — e.g., new material brought forth might be a form of resistance to tarrying with a prior topic; newfound or enhanced facility in free associating may conceal covert, defensive narcissism. Or therapeutic progress following an interpretation or other manner of intervention may be contingently related to it.

A subset of this problem concerns the false positives that may result from placebo effect.[121] For instance, the consolidation of transference may, in fact in most cases will, lead to the production of new material. Does this mean that transference or the new material it encourages is *valid*? Likewise, nothing more than the intelligibility that *any* interpretation affords may bring about therapeutic results. Interpretations that feel deep or incisive or otherwise conform to the analysand's expectations about what a good interpretation should sound and/or feel like may also yield therapeutic results. John Forrester considers placebo effect to include "the visit to the doctor, the ambiance of the clinic or the doctor's office, the way in which the doctor negotiates the encounter, the little signs of bodily consolation offered, the confidence and understanding that the doctor can draw upon, especially if the doctor and patient have a long collective history of medical encounters both urgent and mundane" (1997, 62). This list can be extended indefinitely given the paucity of evidence concerning what precisely generates positive therapeutic results: suggestion, seduction, regular opportunities for "venting," and a host of other variables may play a role, perhaps a decisive one. That positive results may be attributed to or involve placebo effect is not the real problem. Rather, the problem is that what makes for good psychoanalytic practice, i.e., what consistently (with reference to a specified object domain) gives rise to therapeutic results better than placebo, is unknown. Thus claims to validity forwarded on the basis of "therapeutic efficacy" are too imprecise to do any meaningful work. If the category of "false positive" cannot be precisely determined and so distinguished from valid results, the notion of validity is undermined.

Another aspect of the problem concerns the determination of "positive results." Can we say, along with Göethe, "*Was fruchtbar ist, allein ist wahr*" if fruitfulness in the short term is followed by stagnation or decompensation in the long term or if by "therapeutic efficacy" we mean, say, the transformation of an affectless smile into manifest anxiety or depression? ("Vermächtnis")[122] Is the attainment of positive results as obvious as Gitelson suggests: "[i]t is recognizable in a glance, a postural change, or a nuance of vocal inflection in the moment at which the therapist has struck the first true note"? (1973, 34) Or is "positive results" an emphatically normative category, thus endlessly contestable?

(8) *The therapeutic efficacy standard is prone to yield false negatives.* Lack of expected positive results may result from a variety of factors.[123] Freud considers the following potential impediments to expected analytic success: constitutional strength of libido, viscosity or mobility of libido, strength of the aggressive drive, strength and history of a pertinent defense mechanism (e.g., to what extent it is bound up with the analysand's basic, practice orienting self- and world-conceptions and ego functioning), quantity and quality of traumatogenic (external) events in "actual" neurosis, the analyst's skill and the skill of the training analyst; and penis-wish/masculine protest (SE 23: 252). False negatives may also result from motivations for entering analysis that lead to a relatively superficial engagement in it: "If the

patient enters analysis only because of the social repercussions of the behavior, engaging in the arduous analytic process may serve only to deceive others [and herself]; the aim is not the reduction of mental pain but the achievement of some social gain — for example, acquiescing to the wishes of a spouse or conforming to the demands of the courts or an employer" (Brody 1990, 27). Or they may result from the guilt-expiating value of illness, from masochistic tendencies, from inadequate environmental support, or from currents of psychic life conducing to envious spoiling of the analytic work. It is difficult to imagine why the vast variety of factors that may undermine therapeutic efficacy should be considered reasons for repudiating the interpretative hypotheses involved. At the very least, predicating validity on therapeutic efficacy *alone* seems an inadequate way of assessing psychoanalytic knowledge and practice. If nothing else, so doing makes it extremely difficult, perhaps in some cases impossible, to specify the conditions for therapeutic failure, thus for disconfirmation of a hypothesis.

Also, if, as seems plausible, correct interpretations may remain ineffective for a long time, e.g., because defenses are not sufficiently abated, appealing to *immediate* effects when considering claims to validity may be misleading. Yet it is difficult to say whether therapeutic success is the longforthcoming result of specific prior interpretations or consequent upon any number of intervening factors.

(9) *If validity is predicated on therapeutic efficacy, then what is in all relevant senses (minus one) a valid interpretation would become invalid if delivered poorly – inaptly timed or phrased — and consequently failed to generate positive therapeutic results.*

(10) Related to the problem of equivocity and false positives, *inexact interpretations yield therapeutic effects*. Important therapeutic transformations — e.g., reduction of anxiety, strengthening of social bonds, enhanced adaptation, etc. — may not validate immediately preceding or thematically linked interpretive hypotheses and/or auxiliary hypotheses but only something in their general neighborhood. Given the complexity of psychic life (overdetermination, multiple functioning, etc.), even mutative interpretations that are specific and concrete in Strachey's sense may be woefully inexact. If psychic phenomena are to some extent indeterminate, or if, generally, interpretation is wholistic and context is partially indeterminate, not self-sutured and objectively present, this problem is insuperable. Again, the question is *what* is validated by therapeutic efficacy? If this question cannot be precisely answered, the therapeutic efficacy standard will not be able to perform the necessary work of adjudication.

(11) *From the point of view of ambitions to achieve objectivity, the data is biased.* From the side of the analysand, there will be selection bias and non-methodologically regulated interpretation in dream reports, recollections, descriptions of present difficulties, responses to the analyst's interpretations,

etc. That is, on standard psychoanalytic premises, defensive and other manners of (more or less) nontransparent motivation are irreducible and pervasive. Verbalization itself — both what is said and how it is said — may be considered a weak form of selection bias to the extent that it is influenced by the analysand's psychosexual history, ideological and otherwise categorical commitments, i.e., social history, and other such factors that may be resistant to transparent discursive recuperation. No matter how closely s/he adheres to the fundamental rule, censorship and other forms of selectivity are inevitable; indeed they must be if the theories of psychic determinism and dynamic defense are defensible. Free association is never entirely free. If it were, it would be useless — completely incoherent. From the side of analyst, desire for intelligibility (especially when the material feels chaotic and overwhelming, which is to say, usually), positive or negative attention, theoretical confirmation, and so on may bias presentations or prior formulations of case material. There is always an agenda. Of course the problems of precipitous schematization, ulterior motives, and so forth are not unique to psychoanalysts, but if formulation of what transpires in the clinic cannot be corroborated by repeated independent experimentation, it is particularly pernicious for them.[124] And here too historical formation, categorical commitments, and the like will to some extent determine what material is given attention, how it is attended, and how it is presented.

At the extreme, a narcissistic collaboration may develop in which each party allows the other to "do their job well," at which point what seems an ideal analysis is anything but: the analysand "free associates" endlessly and seems to make use of the analyst's insights, the analyst impressively draws together diverse material into coherent patterns and sharp interpretations, and yet, at a certain level, the analysis is gridlocked. A great deal of surface change masks vicious adherence to deeply engrained pathological formations.

(12) *What is validated by therapeutic efficacy may fail to measure up to other reasonable standards for validation.* An interpretation that leads to positive therapeutic effects may be internally incoherent, loudly or softly protested by the analysand, incongruous with other sectors of clinical material, contradicted by the findings of the best science available, palpably noncomprehensive, or may otherwise fail to meet what seem to be reasonable standards for validity.

Additionally, some political risks of predicating validity on efficacy are:

(1) Lending to successful practice (on any conception) and thus to any number of normative commitments an ideological veneer of "truth." To embolden normative commitments by attaching to them the emblem of validity and thus with the connotation of truth would likely lead to further self-insulation and mutual provocation.

(2) Contributing to the reign of instrumental rationality. Without an elaborate metaphysics to support it — specifically, to support the claim that therapeutic practice at least, and perhaps practice generally, is effective if and only if the explicit and implied concepts, interpretations, and theories involved, or at least a significant range of them, are accurate — or a concession that the notion of validity invoked has parted ways with aspirations for truth, predicating validity on efficacy would debase and replace questions of truth with those of utility. Though irreducible to them, the standard would collude with hegemonic interests centered on the commercial payoff of knowledge. "Truth" would be colonized by the victorious if not vanquished as a relevant concern.[125]

Finally, predicating validity on therapeutic efficacy unnecessarily and implausibly discounts the contributions of culture-critical employments of psychoanalysis, including their potential contributions to psychoanalytic knowledge. Literature, film, political and historical phenomena, and other such material are obviously not analysands — they do not respond to interpretations, e.g., by producing new associations or dreams, overcoming inhibitions and anxieties, and so on; texts might seem to solicit certain interpretations, but they do not *desire* them[126] — but it is not clear that this is sufficient reason to discount wholesale the possibility that psychoanalytically informed interpretations in these fields may be immanently valid and/or contribute to psychoanalytic knowledge generally.[127]

On the other hand, the insistence on the clinical primacy of psychoanalytic knowledge supports those so inclined to insist on the proto-scientific character of psychoanalytic knowledge. Perhaps psychoanalysis is a "young" science that has yet to develop the resources — clarification of basic concepts and research methodologies, hypothetical-deductive systems, empirical testing procedures, etc. — to take a stand as a full-fledged natural science. So suggests Wallerstein, and quite influentially. On this naturalistic interpretation of psychoanalysis, psychoanalysis is but a low level scientific practice of data gathering and hypothesis construction that does not claim to have established empirically generalizable theories or models from which deductive predictions can be made and subsequently tested that would allow it to present itself as an explanatory natural science. But given the proper clarification of concepts, systematization of hypothesis (experience-near distinguished from experience-distant), generation of models, discovery of laws, creation of valid testing procedures, etc., psychoanalysis may yet attain to natural scientific standing.[128] That clinical phenomena are the source and/or ultimate reference of psychoanalytic knowledge does not mean that the epistemic ordering and evaluation of psychoanalytic knowledge need transpire within the clinic.

NOTES

1. I mean the language here to invoke and repudiate Kurt Eissler's statement that "It is breathtaking to review what Freud extracted during the course of four decades, from the free association of eight subjects who each lay on the couch for 50 minutes per day. The input-output quotient was here truly enormous. The question, however, remains: Did Freud extract from his patients' associations all the knowledge that is to be gained from the psychoanalytic situation? With one qualification, to be dealt with presently, I would say that the answer is yes" (1969, 465).
2. Cf. Kernberg (1976), pp. 127-8.
3. Cf. Sandler et al. (2001) *Clinical and Observational Psychoanalytic Research: Roots of a Controversy.*
4. Interestingly, although Kris' famous plagiarism case convinced many of the import of acknowledging certain features of empirical reality, he was the one of the editors of the Freud-Fliess letters who expunged Freud's various "post-September 1897" (the date conventionally taken to signal Freud's "decisive break" with the seduction hypothesis) comments about the bearing of empirical matters on pathogenesis.
5. An intermediate position – though slanted toward the primacy of psychic reality – is staked out by Kernberg (1992): "I conceive of internalized object relations as not reflecting actual object relations from the past. Rather, they reflect a combination of realistic and fantasied – and often highly distorted – internalizations of such past object relations and defenses against them under the effects of activation and projection of instinctual drive derivatives" (in Hamilton 1992, p. 33). Klein occasionally makes similar gestures, e.g., "The Origins of Transference" (1952).
6. Ferenczi claims to have introduced the notion to Freud; cf. *Final Contributions* (1955), p. 16.
7. In this earlier work, Fenichel proposed that Freud's notion of the death drive signaled a capitulation to capitalism.
8. Cf. Kernberg in Bergmann (2004) *Dissidence and Controversy in the History of Psychoanalysis*, p. 141.
9. Actually, Lowenstein is a little more noncommittal than Hartmann, claiming that only biological research will tell whether or not there is a death drive (1982, 79). And what Hartmann rejected when he repudiated the death drive is rather different from what others mean by the term. On his understanding, the death drive means that "self-destruction is the only alternative to destruction" (1964, p. 87).
10. Bowlby also advocates abandoning classical drive theory but without committing himself to a theory of endogenous object seeking understood as those mentioned would understand it.
11. E.g., Otto Kernberg, who contends that "[u]nconscious intrapsychic conflicts are never simple conflicts between impulse and defense; rather, the drive derivative finds expression through a certain primitive object relation (a certain unit of self- and object representation); and the defense, too, is reflected by a certain internalized object relation" (cited in Blum 1980, p. 210). Kernberg acknowledges the insistence and importance of the drives, but in contrast to classical Freudians, he upholds that drives are always already interpreted through object relations, thus that the intrapsychic is never fully dissociable from the social and historical matrix of individual development. He is, one might say, midway between Freud and Erikson.
12. Bibring suggests that supportive measures ought be propedeutic to interpretation when he asserts that interpretation is the "supreme agent in the hierarchy of therapeutic principles" (1954, p. 763), as does Strachey when he positions interpretation as the "ultimate operative factor in the therapeutic action" (1934, p. 152), and as does Gedo (1979) when he points to instances when the satisfaction of certain basic needs and wishes must precede interpretations and other interventions.
13. "As analysts, we may agree with certain basic tenets: we should maintain our focus on the patient's inner reality . . . . But again and again, we fail to adhere to these precepts. Despite our best intentions, we seem to have a fundamental disinclination to maintaining these positions" (Schwaber 1992, 359-360). See also Parsons (1992) and Fonagy et al. (2001), pp. 3-14.

14. Cf. "'Wild' Psychoanalysis" (SE 11: 219-227); Ruitenbeck (1973) *The First Freudians*; and H.D. (1956) *Tribute to Freud*.

15. An illuminating example of this can be found in Bernheimer and Kahane's *In Dora's Case*, where a great many analysts and theorists return to Freud's infamous Dora case and provide wildly disparate evaluations of Freud's work and reinterpretations of the clinical material. See also Pulver (1987).

16. Bollas gestures in this direction as he writes, "For me . . . any interpretation is always only partly true, as the narrowing of focus essential to the organization of comment about another person inevitably means that all other possible comments are at that moment unspoken" (1989, p. 73).

17. For instance, free association – thankfully – is never entirely free. Selection, focus, and organization, e.g., resulting from unconscious ego compromises and defenses, is always at work. And associations are addressed to another person (or figure) in a particular context, say, transference, which exerts a further organizational influence. Indeed, part of the point of listening to free associations is to pinpoint how and why they are *not* free flowing.

18. The irony that formal logic is insufficiently constraining for psychoanalysis rather than the converse is not to be missed. Another irony worth noting is that though it is often accused of running afoul of the canons of scientificity, the manner in which psychoanalysis inverts and subtly displaces the binary of the context of discovery and the context of justification, which is often central to such accusations, has yet to be appreciated.

19. More strongly, psychoanalytic interpretation is not oblivious to the empirical but premised on a rejection of the equation of the empirical and the self-evident or otherwise statically "given."

20. *Écrits*, p. 598.

21. For the first sustained discussion of this of which I am aware, cf. Ferenczi (1955) "Thinking and Muscle Innervation" in *Further Contributions*, p. 230ff.

22. Cf. Arlow (1987), Gabbard (1997), Gabbard and Westin (2003).

23. And of course there is disagreement about what remaining silently attuned involves. Is it a matter of holding and containing (Bion, Winnicott), empathic resonance (Kohut), keeping open the space of interpretability (Freud, Loewald), or attunement to the dimensions of senselessness and opacity of clinical material and thus to the excessiveness of the subject vis-à-vis the Symbolic (Lacan)?

24. Freud occasionally advocates this standard, for instance in the context of his objection to Rank. There, Freud claims that since "it is not credible that a child should retain any but tactile and general sensations relating to the process of birth," it cannot be the case that "the infant has received certain sensory impressions, in particular of a visual kind, at the time of birth, the renewal of which can recall to its memory the trauma of birth and thus evoke a reaction of anxiety" (SE 20: 135; also cf. Freud 1909). At various moments throughout his career, Freud appealed to a correspondence theory of truth (as in his appeal to family corroboration of his seduction hypothesis in "Aetiology of Hysteria" – but by no means just there, the standard pops up in an on-again, off-again fashion throughout Freud's career), a coherence theory of truth (1923), a production of new material/indirect responses standard (1915-17, 1937), a postdiction standard (1920), a cross-corroboration by converging clinical findings standard (which is related but not identical to the coherence standard), and a standard that would have validity turn on successful prediction of similar findings in other cases (1919, 1922). For logically confused but influential elaborations of the external validation standard, cf. Rubenstein (1983) and Eagle (1985).

25. There are many variations of this standard. Some insist that the development of the interpretation's pattern or theme must manifest in substantially different threads of associations. Some hold that the confluent associations must be especially affect-laden. Others are satisfied with less.

When Freud elaborates this standard, he claims that the repetition of the material in the patient's associations must particularize or recast ("extend") the interpretation: "[t]he 'Yes' has no value unless it is followed by indirect confirmations, unless the patient, immediately after his 'Yes,' produces new memories which complete and extend the construction" (SE 23: 262).

Another variant of this standard would be finding oneself again and again confronted by the same theme or material but none the wiser for it – except perhaps insofar as one has attained some insight into the limits and pathogenic value of knowingness. Lacan's advocacy of this standard is manifest in the following: "And there is only one method of knowing that one is there, namely, to map the network. And how is a network mapped? It is through the fact that one returns, one comes back, one keeps coming across the same path, it always overlaps and cross-checks itself in the same way; and in the seventh chapter of *The Interpretation of Dreams* there is no other confirmation than this – 'Speak of chance, gentlemen, if you like. In my experience I have observed nothing arbitrary in this field, for it always meets up with itself, cross-checks itself in such a way that it escapes chance'" (*Seminar XI*, p. 45; translation modified).

26. SE 19: 115.

27. Cf. Freud 1915-17 and 1937, especially SE 23: 262. One variation on this standard holds that interpretations are validated if they yield new insights on the part of the analysand, but only if the insights obtained involve a new organization of memories or the discovery of new meaning(s) in familiar material. Pundits of this standard often point out that such insights are regularly accompanied by arousal or excitation, which they take to be a compelling indication that the insight, and so the interpretation that sparked it, is valid.

28. As Jonathan Lear puts the point, "interpretations may well be getting the facts of the psychological or historical reality right (correspondence), they may be forming a compelling narrative with which to understand one's own life (coherence), but all of this can be done in a defensive, removed way – as though one were standing outside one's life trying to understand it" (2000, p. 310). The facilitation of significance to which I referred as the "sensibility" of analytic interpretations in Chapter 1 by no means necessarily confers validity in the standard sense, but, I would suggest, is an unavoidable criterion for the evaluation of psychoanalytic practice.

29. Cf. Steiner 1993.

30. Cf. Mitchell 2005; for explicit advocacy of this standard, cf. pp. 196-9 and 213. Note, however, that Mitchell's elaboration of this standard is highly variable – the content shifts in important ways from page to page even though a central emphasis on enlivening is evident throughout.

31. Clearly the overlapping content of some items above would allow for a more austere grouping, but minor variations (which are not readily noticed under general headings) seem as significant as general categories in this context. If the separation of what could be synthesized seems to belabor the point, I trust it does not do so excessively, i.e., so artificially as to undermine the point being made about criterial multiplicity. For taxonomic convenience, 4-34 can be grouped under the heading of "therapeutic efficacy"; 5, 6, 7, 9-17, 20, 21, and 23-29, 33, and 34 can be grouped under the heading of "mental, emotional, and relational freedom."

32. Cf. Boris 1998, p. 119.

33. Appeals to logical consistency (along with appeals to conformity with empirical knowledge) are prevalent among ego psychologists. Cf., for instance, Hartmann 1964, p. 71. Though the popularity of this standard are hardly confined to ego psychological circles. Rand and Torok (1997), for instance, propose that "[r]ather than debate the scientific or nonscientific status of psychoanalysis," they will "apply the standards of internal coherence only, treating Freud's ideas as self-contained entities that stand or fall on the merits of their own consistency" (6).

34. Those who champion the claim that an interpretation's truth is a matter of its fit with narrative patterns generated in analysis such as Spence (1982), Lussier (1991), Schafer (1983, 1990), and Wallerstein (1988) advocate a version of the coherence standard. Davidson (1986) too should be included in their ranks, as should Freud, at least when he explicitly favors coherence over correspondence (1923). Others who are not comfortable with wholly relinquishing a correspondence theory of truth, of which there are many, profess a qualified commitment to the coherence standard, e.g., Marcia Cavell (1993). A different version of the coherence standard is advanced by Hartmann, who claims that "[h]ypotheses on these early stages can be tested as to their agreement or disagreement with the basic concepts of analytic theory" (1964, p. 118; Hartmann claims Glover (1947) as an ally on this point).

35. Perhaps the first glimmer of an appeal to developmental research was Freud's objection to Rank's theory of birth trauma discussed above. The appeal was to a speculative theory of development, not empirical research, but the basic idea is the same: developmental theory adjudicates between the mechanically possible and impossible (later, it would be more frequently appealed to in order to adjudicate between the probable and improbable).
cross-cultural anthropology,[129] neuroscience, etc.[130]

36. This principle stipulates that certain clinical phenomena cannot be made sense of, or sufficient sense of, without certain psychoanalytic concepts; call it a minimal concession to idealism. For instance, as Kernberg (1975) claims, without the concepts of splitting and projective identification, little if any sense can be made of the phenomena central to borderline disorders. Freud makes use of the principle frequently, e.g., to justify the assumption of unconscious mentation (SE 14: 166-167) or to defend his focus on the deep past (SE 10:152). The principle of basic intelligibility may be construed either pragmatically (no other available concepts make any or sufficient sense of the phenomena) or (quasi-)transcendentally (without certain concepts, the phenomena at stake are entirely or largely unintelligible). Though many analysts explicitly advocate the (quasi-)transcendental construal, when pressed, they ordinarily revert to the pragmatic construal. Interestingly, as if they know better but cannot help it, certain analysts suggest a strong, (quasi-)transcendental version of the principle through its explicitly pragmatic elaboration. Witness Bruce Fink as he queries, "Why should we bother to concern ourselves with analytic discourse at all, if it is just one of several or one of many" and then responds, "because *it allows us to understand the functioning of different discourses in a unique way*" (1995, p. 129). Framed by a question that cannot but be rhetorical (were it not, the answer proposed would be question begging in the extreme, no answer at all), Fink's language of uniqueness conceals a claim to the right and proper (barely) beneath a defensive surface that would have us take the unique as the nonsubstitutable but not necessarily superior. Spence (1982) seems more honest, and more supportable, when he discusses the provisioning of basic intelligibility in terms of aberrant life becoming intelligible (thus, though he does not make this point, revealing itself as not so aberrant after all, and perhaps thereby revealing those lives found readily intelligible as more "aberrant" than they once seemed). Bion, as usual, is difficult to read on this question, but he seems to fall on the weak side: "[i]n practice it is possible, and desirable in the interests of beneficial therapy, to observe and interpret the evidence that supports this theory and which this theory explains in a way that no other theory does" (1984, p. 31).

37. It is worth recalling here that throughout the history of psychoanalysis there has always been both a pronounced interest in and equally emphatic worry about the value of coherence. Freud's debate with Adler, for instance, largely revolved around the latter's commitment to theoretical coherence.

38. That is, if the question is what confers intersubjective validity in the sense of methodologically secured objectivity or rationality constitutive cognitive commitment. This is not to deny, however, the expressive value of criterial assertion; its nonself-sufficiency, hence diagnostic value for sociohistorical understanding, or more generally, its practice-probative value; its nonself-subsistence, i.e., involvement in open-ended individual and collective practices of self-creation and -discovery; or its direct claims on cognition. Claims to intersubjective validity need not be based on the methodological neutralization of subjectivity: may be fulfilled other than by the discovery of impersonal laws or rules of reason. Claims to intersubjective validity may be claims to exemplarity, searching claims seeking to speak in a universal voice – seeking to heed, that is, neither reify nor neglect, and convey concept-excessive compulsion, emphatic experience, in the medium of conceptuality – their fulfillment ever-uncertain because lastingly dependent on the effective solicitation of other subjects, on enhancing – expanding the reach of or refining – others' sensible responsiveness, that is, on desirous recognition. Promising to refine or refound others' conviction and orientation in the sensible world, such claims are strictly unredeemable, as precarious as practice. To pursue intersubjective validity via searching assertions of criterial authority would be to internalize the specter of skepticism rather than frantically seek its dissolution (dis-illusion) and thereby avoid the distortions – the empty abstraction and consequent system-idealization – entailed by the endless iteration of disbelief.

39. "The interpretation was accepted, the distress cleared up quite quickly, and the analysis went on. Two years later (the analysis having ended in the meanwhile) . . . it came to him that what had troubled him at the time . . . had been a very simple and obvious thing, sadness that his mother was not there to enjoy his success . . . and the guilt that he had enjoyed it while she was dead had spoilt it for him" (Little 1951, p. 32).

40. One tempting way around this dilemma, predicating validity on therapeutic efficacy, i.e., dropping truth as an independent criterion, will be discussed later in the chapter.

41. For empirical corroboration of this claim, cf. Robbins (1963); regarding false positives in patient corroborations of genetic reconstructions, cf. Breger (2000), esp. p. 274.

42. Cf. Grossman (1996).

43. In response to such concerns, some analysts contend that if a patient-corroborated interpretation gives rise – whether immediately or via associations – to a very precise memory, the corroboration is trustworthy. However, secondary revision may be in play, and as Van der Kolk and Van der Hart (in Caruth (1995) *Trauma: Explorations in Memory*) suggests, extreme precision of memory in the sense of immediate envelopment in the memory, memory with no manifest dimension of construction or modification, may token unnegotiated trauma.

44. Cf. Jürgen Habermas (1987) "Philosophy as Stand-In and Interpreter," in Baynes, Bohman, and McCarthy eds., *After Philosophy: End or Transformation?*; Habermas (1981) "Modern *Versus* Postmodernity"; and J.M. Bernstein (1992) *The Fate of Art*, pp. 225-32.

45. E.g., morality isolated from the aesthetic becomes motivationally inert, say, a merely intellectual deduction or application of the moral law, thus immoral because object-insensitive: if not just a curiosity, a pursuit of purity renewing itself on the occasion of moral uncertainty – others' sufferings. Of course, the conclusions of such moral deductions may pick up motivational force, but only extrinsically, parasitically: (weakly) as a necessary means for pursuing any ends whatsoever in a complex, deracinated social order or (strongly) through its embedding in an extant psychomotivational economy – but in either case, in a way that belies morality's claim to autonomy. If morality survives its categorical and institutional separation from the aesthetic – if the good does not collapse into the desired (nihilism) or the willfully posited (cynicism), if it still carries conviction, it is because this separation is false. Or, conversely, the aesthetic isolated from the moral becomes a mere matter of feeling, cognitively incapacitated, unable to speak – institute, enhance, radiate, or otherwise authoritatively intervene in the basic schema(s) of – social truth. Hounded into psychological privacy and institutional marginality, aesthetic experience, whether as delectation, inspiration, or distress, is seamlessly integrated into the social as a harmless preserve of feeling; such evident social disdain giving rise to distortions in the aesthetic, e.g., the aesthete's fetishization and the philistine's instrumentalization of art.

46. Cf. Rawls (2005) *Political Liberalism*.

47. There are serious disagreements about whether interpretation need be the primary modus operandi of therapy (Kernberg claims that interpretation is "the basic instrument of psychoanalytic technique," a claim with which Brenner, Arlow, and Pine agree; Balint, Kohut, and Winnicott surely doubt this), and if not, when is interpretation expedient and when not? (1992, p. 121) E.g., when might interpretation induce false compliance or provoke a psychotic break? Or when might interpretation contribute to a stalemated analysis because the issue in need of addressing is precisely the analysand's resistance to interpretation as such? In such a case, what is needed may be, as Alan Bass suggests, "phenomenological" description of the resistance rather than interpretation of repressed content. And even if it is conceded that analysis need not always proceed as a primarily interpretive endeavor, if it is agreed that sometimes analysis should be pedagogical in some fashion, still, questions remain concerning with whom (just children and psychotics, or sometimes with neurotic adults) to what extent, and how?

48. Related to the question of the pathogenic primacy of conflict is the controversy over the sufficiency of structural theory, in which conflict plays a central role. The sufficiency of structural theory is advocated by Arlow and Brenner (1964) but contested by those who claim that treating cases of severe psychopathology requires expanding the therapeutic focus well beyond conflict (Balint, Kohut, Kernberg, Searles).

49. The following is an example of genetic reconstruction: "'Up to your *n*th year you regarded yourself as the sole and unlimited possessor of your mother; then came another baby and brought you grave disillusionment. Your mother left you for some time, and even after her reappearance she was never again devoted to you exclusively. Your feelings toward your mother became ambivalent, your father gained a new importance for you' . . . and so on" (SE 23: 261). The "and so on," testifying to the underdetermination of experience, its retrospective revisability consequent upon unforeseen developments in the life of which it is a part, is as significant as the explicit content of the interpretation, the fundamental or at least freighted schema it elaborates.

50. Even in Kleinian circles, i.e., amongst analysts for whom the archaic or primitive is of central significance, there is increasing interest in and engagement with the here and now. Such interest and engagement brings Kleinians into a perhaps surprising – though certainly limited – proximity with intersubjectivists. Cf. Mitchell and Aron (1999), p. 253. However, in light of the metapsychological commitments of a great many Kleinians, generally, their conviction in certain structurally innate and unsurpassable schemas of anxiety management and elaboration, perhaps what should be surprising is not their current focus on the here and now (the endless replay of the archaic in the contemporary) but that it is only lately that such a focus became explicit. A Lacanian would likely caution, though, that immersion in the here and now risks neglecting the dimension of the Symbolic for that of the Imaginary. Specifically, Lacanians often contend that focus on the here and now is just another way of strengthening the ego – i.e., by confronting it with and seeking the integration of its repressed libidinal and aggressive content – thus that as a result of this focus analysis will consign itself to supporting an ego that, they presume, is (1) already strong enough, indeed likely too strong, (2) definitionally or at least largely defensive, and (3) responsible for the repressions, demands for intelligibility, and fantasy of sovereignty from which, in no small part, the analysand suffers. To support the ego is to buttress the structures of defense that analysis claims to undermine and thereby to inhibit the release of desire – e.g., from the constraints of ego-governed, and through the mediation of the ego, socially-governed, psychic life – and forestall the freedom and accommodation to the irrecusably enigmatic dimensions of desirous subjectivity at which analysis should aim. Further, to the extent that tarrying with the here and now makes the analyst's interpretations more palatable, then (1) it is a sly way of maintaining the analyst's posture as the *sujet supposé savoir*, which is counterproductive on the Lacanian conception of treatment (briefly, so long as the analyst is positioned as an expert who Knows and thus can Cure, the analysand will abdicate responsibility to the analyst and fail to fully engage his or her own analysis) and (2) the analyst's ego and the concern for meaning, both of which Lacanians would situate at the level of the Imaginary, will govern the analytic scene, indeed will be mimetically incorporated by the analysand, and this will forestall or even tradeoff with therapeutically necessary attention to the nonsensical – to the enigmatic quality of signifier and to the unconscious as composed of signifiers, that is, to the dimensions of the Symbolic and the Real where, Lacanians suggest, the real analytic work is done. Against a focus on the *meaning* of here and now associations, affects, and object relations, Lacanians tend to urge attention to that which is irreducible to – or more strongly, continually abrasive to and interruptive of – the order of meaning. *If* an analyst is to interpret here and now material, Lacanians often urge, first, a prior protracted encounter with the nonmeaning of clinical material, second, a mapping of the unique network of signifiers and connective structures (particular configurations of metonymy, metaphor, etc.) that articulate the particular analysand's unconscious, and only then, and only in a limited way, attention to the *meaning* of material in the here and now. For it is only once both analyst and analysand have a sense of the relation between various signifiers that emerge in the course of the analyst's speech and have caught a glimpse of the Master Signifiers that never show up directly but silently organize the clinical material, that attention to the here and now will be appropriately contextualized, that is, understood both in its specificity and ultimate unintelligibility.

51. Cf. Cooper (2000), p. 279; Rustin (2000), p. 60; and Kernberg (in Hamilton 1992). Even Roudinesco's (2001) claim that genetic reconstruction has an extremely diminished role, though still an important one, in clinical practice is something of an anomaly. That transference interpretation need not aim at genetic recovery of an infantile neurosis was suggested by

Ferenczi and Rank as early as 1924. And even when genetic determinants are appealed to as confirmation, it is often not in the clinic – as a means to embolden the analyst or analysand's confidence – but in the literature attempting to secure the validity of psychoanalytic knowledge against charges of wild speculation. This is part of a larger trend toward pragmatism: conviction that an interpretation is valid if therapeutically effective (on a wide measure). Frequently, so long as analysts can evade or mitigate charges that psychoanalysis is merely pseudoscience or obscurantist mysticism, i.e., charges that it is evidently *false*, they are comfortable asserting that the validity of psychoanalytic knowledge is secured by its therapeutic efficacy. The prevailing sentiment is: if it works, it is valid enough; or, if it works, it must be valid even if we cannot quite (yet) say why. About this trend toward pragmatism more will be said later.

52. At one point, Freud even apposes psychoanalytic and genetic explanation in such a way as to suggest their identity: "The idea of men's receiving an intimation of their connection with the world around them through an immediate feeling which is from the outset directed to that purpose sounds so strange and fits so badly with the fabric of our psychology that one is justified in attempting to discover a psycho-analytic – that is, genetic – explanation of such a feeling" (SE 21: 65).

53. See also Rado 1956.

54. For a fairly recent defense of reconstruction, cf. Blum (1994a) "The Value of Reconstruction in Adult Psychoanalysis" and (1994b) *Reconstruction in Psychoanalysis: Childhood Revisited and Recreated.*

55. On the other hand, the late Freud also notes in "Constructions in Analysis" that interpretations are often rejected, even if true so far as it goes, until the whole story is told. Patients are prone to reject interpretations on the basis of their partiality – they feel false because they do not yet say all there is to be said, as if they were hiding or balking at something.

56. Despite this objection, Bollas employs genetic reconstruction. Cf. Bollas (1989), pp. 49, 57, and 193ff.

57. On the diminishing import and changing assessment of memory retrieval, cf. Kris (1956), Laplanche (1992), and Caper (1999). That focus on the past is still sufficiently extensive to motivate contemporary rebuke is indicated, for instance, by Frank Summers (2005) *Self Creation: Psychoanalytic Therapy and the Art of the Possible.* It should also be noted in passing that whether one opts for more here and now or more reconstructive interpretation depends in part on the age of one's clientele. Historically, there has been comparatively little genetic reconstruction in child analysis. Or if there is some measure of reconstruction in child analysis, it is often not in the service of returning unconscious material to consciousness such that it can then be avowed, repudiated, or otherwise worked through, but rather for the sake of containing and processing material that, when returned *as meaningful* alleviates some of the anxiety consequent upon its previously unbound, unintelligible character. Also in passing it should be noted that although, in certain cases, Melanie Klein practiced and advocated deep and early constructions in child analyses – it is a common misconception that this is *all* she did – without a prior analysis of resistances, quite often her technique was much less heavy-handed. More often than not, Klein allowed play to develop for quite some time, just as adult analyses allow associations to gradually unfold.

58. Cf. A. Reich (1973), pp. 344-360.

59. As Hoffman makes clear, (1) countertransference analysis need not be insularly introspective because (2) the distinction between countertransference and transference interpretation is not categorical. "Systematic use of the patient's associations as a guide to understanding the patient's resisted ideas about the countertransference" is, for Hoffman, "a critical element of the interpretive process in the social paradigm [without which] . . . . there is a danger that the analyst will rely excessively on his own subjective experience in constructing interpretations" (in Mitchell and Aron 1999, 66). That is, the analysand's identification with, resistance to, assumption in a displaced form, or other manner of response to perceived or fantasized countertransference is itself a topic for transference analysis. Cf. Lipton (1977), Gill (1979, 1982), and Gill and Hoffman (1982a, 1982b).

60. In accord with the guiding concern of this chapter to underscore the vast, extrapartisan plurality of psychoanalytic practices, it is worth noting the numerous ways in which countertransference can be interpreted.

It may be held that (1) the countertransference indirectly reveals how the analyst is transferentially positioned and thereby what shape the analysand's conflicts have taken or how and at the urging of what sort of pressures the analysand is projecting the conditions of her development and/or healing onto her relationship with her analyst. Call this complementary countertransference interpretation: if I, the analyst, feel X, this is likely because the analysand feels Y; this is likely the case because I, the relatively well-analyzed analyst, know that I tend to feel X when others are feeling Y or because it makes sense in this particular instance that I would feel X if the analysand is feeling Y. For instance, because the analyst feels like responding in a way that would be contextually inappropriate or unhelpful; or because s/he feels compelled *not* to respond in a certain way because doing so would be to give in to a temptation, to collude with a seduction; or because s/he feels that s/he has attained insights that the clinical material thus far fails to sufficiently warrant, the countertransference is read as revealing what in or of the analysand must have given rise to the analyst's condition, e.g., the analysand's needs, need-interpretations, or conflicts. In complementary countertransference interpretation, the countertransference is taken as a medium in which is revealed the sorts of responses from the analyst that would facilitate the reactivation or less encumbered progression of the analysand's currently stunted development; or on the contrary, the analyst's transferential positioning as an ideal figure who *can and should* gratify various of the analysand's developmental needs – but in doing so would inhibit the reactivation of developmental needs and/or impede the analysand from organizing her life in such a way that these needs will be provided for more consistently elsewhere, that is, would become compliant with anxiety-infused defenses such as defensive dependency; or that the analyst is positioned as an ideal ego who can bear the analysand's conflicts, etc. and work through them in an exemplary way, thereby concretely demonstrating to the analysand the possibility of another path, an opening to the future of freedom she longs for; or that the analyst is positioned as an ego ideal who images a desired and/or feared self-state of the analysand. In any case, on this model the interpretation of countertransference is an indirect interpretation of transference that proceeds by, first, recognizing that something in the analyst is out of place, thus is worthy of attention, and then, second, reconstructing what in the analysand could have given rise to it. Proponents of this form of countertransference interpretation include Grinberg (1962), Racker (1968), Grostein (1981); Ogden (1982), and Tansey and Burke (1989).

Or it may be held that (2) the countertransference reveals the unavowable affects, impulses, self-states, etc. projected into the analyst rather than onto the transferentially laden analytic relationship. In this model, call it the telepathy model, analysts attend to unconscious-to-unconscious communication by focusing on feelings and inclinations that arise in them as if from nowhere, or at least in a manner that feels strange, out of place, more powerful than the context would lead one to expect, and are inexplicable as an effect of transferential complementarity. A prime example of this understanding of countertransference is the Kleinian notion of *projective identification*. As opposed to projecting *onto* the analytic relationship –figuring the analyst within a schema of conflicts or developmental needs that, because defended against, cannot be readily recognized as the principles organizing the analysand's relations with her analyst – the analysand projects unavowable or dangerous elements of herself – unconscious content – *into* the analyst. Thereby, she seeks to manipulate or destroy her analyst, to lodge within her inadmissible and frightening or good yet vulnerable, perhaps immanently threatened elements of herself. Projective identification is registered, for instance, in the analyst's contextually inappropriate, and when subject to complementary countertransference interpretation, inexplicable, sudden ebullience, redemptive urges, lethargy, frustration, aggression, or anxiety. These are ordinarily taken to reveal the unbearable, terrifying toll of the death drive, e.g., the analysand's sadistic desires to control and destroy and/or her efforts to preserve a perpetually precarious good object. They are taken as crucial clues to the analysand's phantasmatic elaboration of paranoid/schizoid and/or depressive anxiety. On this model, however, the analyst takes a sadistic inclination (or defense against it, e.g., lethargy or somatic pain) or a direct or mediated experience of annihilation anxiety within herself as evidence of either (a) an upsurge of sadism or annihilation anxiety on the part of the analysand or (b) as evidence of the analysand's unconscious effort, thus need, to convey something about herself that is so remote from consciousness yet so insistently clamoring for expression (e.g., transgenerationally transmitted trauma), that it can be conveyed by no other means. For an illustration of this way of handling the countertransference, cf. T. Jacobs (1991). If the difference between this understanding of countertransference and the former is hard to make out, this is in part because the difference is not categorical but rather reflective of metapsychological commitments that practitioners of both forms of countertransference interpretation may share. Kohutian and Winnicottian countertransference analysis, for instance, certainly blend features of both forms. A highly inexact way of stating the difference would be to say that practitioners of the former are more concerned with revealing transference *illusion* than the latter. A better way of stating the difference would be to say that (1) the difference is formal: the former necessarily involves reconstructive inferences while the latter need not, and (2) this formal difference, though real and not insignificant, is the unacknowledged site of a conflict that far exceeds it and cannot be resolved in its terms – a conflict concerning metapsychology and developmental theory, ultimately, concerning the sources of authority of psychoanalytic conceptions of suffering and pathology, therapy, and appropriate end state(s). The contests over this formal difference are symptoms.

And just as there are many ways of interpreting countertransference, there are many manners of response to the insights it yields. (1) Austerity: if the analysand expresses a need, then especially if the analyst is a classical Freudian or Lacanian, it is the task of the analyst not to gratify it but instead to help her explore it, especially with regard to the particular form her need-interpretation takes. Though, of course, facilitated exploration is certainly not confined to orthodox Freudian and Lacanian practices. (2) Gratification: if the countertransference reveals unmet developmental needs, the analyst will to some extent provide for them in order to reinitiate or further the analysand's development. Though, of course, when gratification amounts to debilitating collusion is a judgment call. (3) Impetus to effective transference interpretation: if the countertransference reveals how the analyst is positioned in the transference, the analyst will draw on it when formulating interpretations in order to address the analysand *through* the transference, that is, such that interpretations may be received *as the analyst's interpretations* rather than as demands, insults, or longings expressed by the figure who the analyst is transferentially positioned as (the same words said by your father and by your analyst tend to be received in very different ways). Though, of course, differences will arise concerning the basic frame of transference that such interpretations mean to reveal and disrupt. (4) Symbolic graft: if the countertransference reveals unspeakable dimensions of oneself or the haunting insistence of suffering passed on through the generations yet never directly spoken of, then the analyst may contain and metabolize the projections by naming them, binding them into symbolic form. Though, again, the basic scheme of interpretation will differ amongst analysts, as will the degree of concern with getting the interpretation right. This list is far from comprehensive. The point is simply that even among those who tend to employ countertransference interpretation, analysts are a motley crew. In particular, neither theory of pathology nor theory of development necessarily controls theory of technique; and theory of technique is certainly influenced by metapsychology but does not necessarily derive from partisan commitments.

Finally, it is worth noting that, though ascendant and increasingly so, faith in countertransference is not universal. Lacanians tend to worry that countertransference analysis eclipses the Symbolic and the Real for the Imaginary. Cf. *Seminar I*, pp. 40-43/30-33. The thought is that countertransference, at least when treated as the royal road to the significance of the transference material (conflicts, developmental needs, primitive anxieties and their phantasmatic elaboration, transgenerationally transmitted pathogens, etc.) is yet another way of remaining at the level of the ego – of calculation, schematization, and false certainty – and thereby simultaneously evades the unconscious and the proper analytic aim of releasing the analysand from the orders of meaning that unduly shackle her in(de)finite desire and generate suffering and pathology. The analysis remains at the level of the ego insofar as, on the side of the analysand, the transference material, needs expressed, and perhaps even unclaimed anxieties or self-states projected are largely mediated by the analysand's ego, and on the side of the analyst, the transference material etc. is received by – recognized as such by, and schematized in accordance with the proclivities of – the analyst's ego. The analyst's ego, after calculating what the analysand must feel or need given that she herself feels a particular way or after lending a valence of certainty to a metapsychological assumption informing the disavowed interpretation issues a number of treatment protocols, further calculations, aimed at bringing the unconscious to consciousness, mitigating anxiety, or providing developmental support for mature, adaptive flourishing – i.e., at supporting the ego. So long as analysis involves so much (implicit or explicit) schematization and the aim of countertransference analysis is to support the analysand's ego (or this is its systematic effect, as with anxiety regulation), there will be something amiss as far as Lacanians are concerned.

61. If the analysand is consistently docile, obediently accepting the analyst's interpretations as if revelations from on high, the emotional significance of the material is likely obscured in order to maintain defenses (e.g., dissociation) and/or sustain a counterproductive transference idealization, a fantasy wherein the analyst, as expert possessed of all the answers, is the source of salvation – a fine way of avoiding the real work of analysis.

62. Even Freud acknowledges that a successful analysis will not preclude the recurrence of the difficulties that brought one to analysis in the first place, let alone immunize against outbreaks of other problems (SE 23: 211-53).

63. Lacan's "promotion" of the patient to the status of "the analysand" was motivated by a recognition that, for the most part, or at least in very important ways, it is the client who is doing the analyzing. The "and" in the French "analysand" is equivalent to the (gerund) "ing" in the English "analyzing." Thus to call the client an analysand is to acknowledge that her working through the material is a necessary component, even perhaps the central component, of successful analysis. Of course, Lacan's choice of the term "analysand" also had to do with his aversion to the term previously used to describe patients, "(psych)analysé," which, derived from the past participle, suggests a less active and central participation of the client and that the process of analysis had finished, or could.

64. Although Freud occasionally allowed close friends/colleagues to engage him in something approximating analytic sessions, he never underwent a full analysis.

65. Cf. "Recommendations to Physicians" (SE 12: 116) and "Editor's remarks to The Unconscious" (SE 14: 202).

66. For a contrary view, cf. Mahony (1987) *Freud as Writer*.

67. Others certainly don't always act in accord with our expectations, but, especially if motivated, we are likely to rationalize away our disappointed expectations, thus maintain them, e.g., by attributing such disappointment to unforeseeable contextual factors – "today s/he must have been in a very good mood." Perhaps only or most effectively through in the systematically repeated failure of an analyst to fulfill our expectations, say, for retributive punishment consequent upon an aggressive outburst, do we learn that our anger does not *entail* punishment and that we may be invested in a fantasy of this entailment for various reasons.

68. Freud's skepticism about self-analysis is also found at SE 12: 116 and SE: 14: 202.

69. Cf. Beardsworth (2004) *Julia Kristeva: Psychoanalysis and Modernity*, chapter 4. Lacan, with reference to Joyce, said that through his writing he went as far as one can go in analysis (1971, p. 3). If, as in now commonly accepted, Kohut's (1979) "The Two Cases of Mr. Z" is a report on his successful self-analysis subsequent to an unsuccessful orthodox analysis, this too may be considered anecdotal evidence of the efficacy of self-analysis. See also Sutherland (1990), pp. 392-493.

70. Concerning the potentially medium-bound character of psychoanalytic knowledge, or at least of certain sectors of it, cf. SE 13: 85; SE 10: 233-36; SE 13: 92-94; and SE 12: 59-79. For Lacan's (cagy) statement of the medium-bound nature of therapy thesis, cf. (1958) "*Jeunesse de Gide ou la letter et le désir*": "psychoanalysis is only applied, in the proper sense of the term, as a treatment, and thus to a subject who speaks and listens" (*Écrits*, p. 747; however, see Lacan 1971, esp. p. 3). Lacan also advances a version of the medium-bound thesis, likely pertaining to both psychoanalytic knowledge and psychoanalytic therapy, in *Seminar XIII:* "I affirm that it [the analytic *cogito*] does not exist, however singular this may appear to you, that it only exists, I would say, in a completed form from the agency of the psychoanalytic clinic and therapeutics" (session of 12 Jan. 1966).

71. And even if, impossibly, empirical agreement was deemed adequate as a norm on the basis of which to distinguish between the meaningful and the meaningless and ground the authority of interpretive activity – impossibly because such deeming would give the lie to the

self-evidence of the criterion of empirical agreement, directly contradict it – such a criterion would still be of no avail in psychoanalysis since "the community" has from the beginning, and it seems irrevocably, divided into many camps and relatively autonomous units within such camps. What is disclosed by the collective diversity and internal hegemony struggles and fragmentation in each school is that there is and forever may be no psychoanalysis in general, no genre naming a common, abstract identity that comprehends, and so from which can be derived, the various camps in their *differentia specifica*, thus no medium (*the* clinic) to which psychoanalytic knowledge could be bound.

72. The tendential isolation (de-worlding) and consequent distortions of subjectivity under conditions of modernity helps explain both attractions to and skepticism about psychoanalysis, especially the interimplication of attraction and skepticism, that is, the beleaguered authority of psychoanalysis.

(1) Psychoanalysis concretely demonstrates, though in an isolated setting that renders generalizations problematic, what we sense but cannot find the words to say, thus cannot fully believe and practically elaborate: that our practices are inadequate to the attainment of our ends, thus that we do not know our true ends (the means through which ends are pursued being the medium through which the meaning of those ends are specified). Of course, when addressing the systematic misfire of our ambitions, psychoanalysis tends to focus on the psychosexual history and/or idiosyncratic features of the psychical economy and/or object relations of particular analysands, that is, on client-specific sources of practical debilitation, but, I think, its authority is sourced (in part) in what it dimly acknowledges, indeed acknowledges almost despite itself: that the social world, by making our ends impracticable, makes them unknowable, thus renders us fundamentally unknown to ourselves. Its refusal of a romantic reification of the individual, its oblique acknowledgment of the social incapacitation of robust individuation, i.e., of the want of social resonance with the practices and principles incipiently emerging in analysis through which they would be sustained and developed (psychoanalytic "pessimism"), is, I think, a source of the authority of psychoanalysis. A premise of psychoanalysis is that our practices are systematically distorted: we seek what we officially reject, refuse what we seek (e.g., devise means for the attainment of our aspirations that guarantee their failure or repudiate ends upon their attainment), and generally lurch about attempting to compose some semblance of a coherent life from independently and/or mutually incoherent, perhaps conflictual, impulses. The authority of psychoanalysis, then, emerges in part from its quiet (necessarily quiet, almost mute) acknowledgment, its institutional-practical elaboration, of what we sense but cannot say (especially in the vocabulary of psychoanalysis): that we suffer from our instrumentality, that we cannot recognize ourselves in our privileged form of reason, thus that we need to be saved from ourselves, that what we need is not just augmented instrumental efficacy but a world where what is begun in the clinic (and analogously anomalous sites) will be socially recognized, supported and encouraged – call it solidarity. The authority of psychoanalysis picks up on the residual authority of something yet undead in us – call it the demand for happiness, natural ends, or substantive reason – as measured by which our instrumental practices feel fundamentally inadequate, systematically askew. But because that from which we suffer is, under current social conditions, necessarily inchoate – a different dispensation of truth-practices premised on and elaborating fundamentally transformed conditions of intersubjective and institutional solidarity would be required to concretize such suffering – its acknowledgment of what we sense but cannot say, what we cannot publicly avow, cannot genuinely think or put into practice under current socio-cognitive arrangements, and the authority it arrogates through such acknowledgment, cannot but be weak and wavering. Such authority is not practice legitimating and/or directive. It is the authority of an insupportable and impracticable conviction; the authority of helplessness. (To be sure, that we may be nothing but hodgepodge assemblages of plastic impulses, may not have true ends, is not logically incompatible with psychoanalytic premises. That this logical possibility is not practically-institutionally elaborated – that psychoanalytic practice refuses cynicism – contributes, I think, to its authority.)

(2) Psychoanalytic concepts afford a medium through which sensibility, our affective lives, can be felt capable of achieving collective intelligibility and orientational significance, thus through which a *feeling* of worldliness, of social bonding and material being, can be achieved.

Reactivating a *feeling* of social bonding and material being, the authority of psychoanalysis is that of world-conviction. Yet because contemporary social conditions conduce to the tendential desubstantialization of community and derealization (dematerialization) of subjectivity, that is, enforce contemplative detachment and instrumental self- and world-relations, the promise of psychoanalytic concepts as a medium of material recognition and orientation, of emphatic worldliness, cannot but appear somewhat utopian – it escapes no one that the community of shared sensible significance that psychoanalysis augurs and partially realizes – promises – is as isolated and overburdened as are contemporary communities of taste, i.e., art "communities." Consequently, the authority premised on such a promise becomes the source of defensive demurral – i.e., gives way to skepticism, a moment of identification with the aggressor. Irritated by attraction to a tendentially unrealizable promise – call it the promise of a *sensus communis* – subjectivity preserves a semblance of itself by becoming the "agent" (via reflective reduplication) of its reification. Clinically, this may take the form of an extreme prioritization of adaptation and concurrent localization/limitation of analytic exploration, and may conjoin with various resistances to analysis generally. The authority of psychoanalysis is as weak as our social bonds.

Akin to that of modernist art, the cognitive authority of psychoanalysis is that of the logically liminal modality of the promise; thus it is unsurprising that psychoanalysis is subject to the violent detractions and zealous enthusiasm frequented upon artistic modernism. Psychoanalytic concepts always miss their mark, fall short of – or better, beside – empirical validity. And necessarily so. Like aesthetic judgments, psychoanalytic concepts evoke conceptual synthesis, which they are not, and aspirations to moral universality, which they cannot satisfy. But if they resonate, like aesthetic judgments such concepts incarnate the hope that what they elaborate, however inadequately, can be mutually acknowledged and thereby further realized/concretized: such concepts promise another dispensation of conceptuality and therewith another arrangement of self- and world-relations. To be sure, such concepts cannot but reify and thus betray themselves as they overreach their promissory character and speak in the name of objectivity. But thereby they may generate resistances – a form of skepticism that assumes and may even amplify their authority. When they resonate, and indeed via the resonance of resistances, such concepts register unformulated and tendentially unformulable hopes as well as the indeterminate, excessive or self-transcending character of their objects – human temporality generally. Via resonance, psychoanalytic concepts sounds echoes of a future for our hopes, for ourselves – signal that we are not yet dead, which accounts in part for their attraction. The always complicated, indeed aporetic authority of psychoanalytic concepts, then, hinges on the simultaneity of their promise of a world in which what they dimly and/or distortedly elaborate would *be* more fully, more consistently and/or emphatically, and their registration of the elusiveness of their objects to conceptual capture and so to methods aspiring to empirical validity – their giving (oblique) voice to human freedom. Such authority corresponds to the precision with which singular admixtures of determinacy and indeterminacy can be acknowledged.

(3) Psychoanalytic concepts afford a medium for, thus the promise of the collective recognition of, the experience and expression of resolute individuality; minimally, for the experience and expression of individual excessiveness as a principle of social and political critique, i.e., as an unreconciled demand. While at once they afford a medium in which to acknowledge that nature, though (repeatedly) proclaimed dead by the leading impulses of modernity and the historiographic trends they inform, especially by those discourses beholden to or convergent with the ideology of individualism, yet everywhere rules (pervasiveness but not simply as reified). The authority of such concepts thus depends in part on that of the historical ideals they have come to bear, which is to say, it depends on the capacity of such concepts to sustain antagonism as form: to maintain themselves as the strife-ridden sites, the capaciously mimetic repositories, of both historically transmitted ideals and historical impediments to their realization. In this respect, such authority is experienced as an evanescent moment of relief that one may not be simply delusional.

(4) Psychoanalytic concepts afford a medium for meanings repressed or excluded by prevailing discursive norms and the rationalized practices that underwrite them. Thus psychoanalytic theory gestures toward what it cannot say (saying it would involve conceptualization and so would deny what it is at pains to acknowledge – particularly under contemporary socio-

cognitive arrangements) by pointing back to the clinic – not as a space secured against the depletions of meaning operated by rationalized concepts and practices but as the site of sensuous particularity all but annihilated: incapable of redeeming the abstractness of the concept but signaling that abstractness emphatically as domination.

73. Cf. Schafer (1977), p. 349 and J. Mitchell (2000), p. 55.

74. On this conception, psychoanalytic claims to objectivity cannot be claims to rigorous correspondence with phenomena, at least not in the classical sense. Rather, the specific form of objectivity appropriate to psychoanalytic concepts, interpretations, and theories requires a mimetic moment, a continuing acknowledgement – through both form and use – of the ambiguity of the material from which concepts, interpretations, and theories are constituted; of the ambiguity of what will become of these concepts, interpretations, and theories as they are assimilated and redeployed by the analysand and subject to further transformations in the ongoing clinical dialogue; and of the ambiguous – underdetermined or amethodological – work of interpretation, concept construction, and theorization: what Ferenczi describes as a "constant oscillation between the free play of fantasy and critical scrutiny" (1950, p. 188). Psychoanalytic objectivity is, in part, a matter of attunement to and acknowledgment of the opacity that infuses the concept, and thereby, a matter of attunement to and acknowledgement of human freedom – even, one might say in a Spinozist vein, the unity of freedom and necessity. Like aesthetic judgments, psychoanalytic claims attempt "to grasp the non-conceptual not by means of some allegedly superior non-conceptual methods, but by unlocking the non-conceptual by means of the concept, and the self-criticism of concepts –without reducing what has been comprehended, the non-conceptual, to concepts" (Adorno 2008, p. 74); their objectivity is sourced, in part, in their returning and renewing attention to the discursively excessive source of their discursive operations, the non-identical initiator and impediment to conceptual identification. In brief, psychoanalytic objectivity requires attunement to and acknowledgment of unavoidable errancy (the instability of nature): that resulting from the inherence of the future in the presumptive self-presence of the concept (i.e., from the unanticipatable arrogations of meanings to which concepts are subject in the course of their metabolism by the analysand and their use(s) in the analytic setting and beyond) and that resulting from the demands of analysis (since the material – trends, themes, significant moments, etc. – will have to be conceptualized and concretized for the sake of, and so guided by the needs of, communication with – and within – the particular analysand, the content of psychoanalytic discourse will be keyed to or at least impacted by, thus in some way irreducibly reflective of the demands regulating its expression; and since the content of such expressions is influenced by associations to and assimilation of concepts and interpretations *as expressed*, such content will remain indefinite). Psychoanalytic objectivity will be discussed in more detail in chapter 6. What I would like to briefly suggest here is that, paradoxically, achieving objectivity and constituting itself as a modernist discourse may be (to some extent) one and the same for psychoanalysis.

75. Advocates of this view include analysts of remarkably different persuasions. For instance, Chodorow claims that "[p]sychoanalytic knowledge of the individual and the self is developed in theoretical and in metapsychological writings, but this knowledge is originally derived from the clinical setting, the analytic situation. Thus, an investigation of this setting can give further insight into the differentiated or relational self and help us decide between classical and object-relations models" (in Mitchell and Aron 1999, p. 118). Or as she puts it more emphatically later on: "psychoanalysis can only know the self in the analytic situation; anything else is ungrounded speculation" (120). Harari, who is otherwise not prone to agree with Chodorow about much of anything, claims that "if 'the Lacanian field' has substance and conceptual weight, it cannot be played out or judged outside of the clinical practice of psychoanalysis" (2001, p. lxix). Gitelson's statement of the position makes it clear that the medium-bound thesis implies questions about the propriety of transposing psychoanalytic concepts into other fields of inquiry, and may become a focal point of efforts to delimit and regulate the proper boundaries of psychoanalysis and so elaborate and secure its authority: "We speak of 'applications' of psychoanalysis when often we are engaged in making *extrapolations* based on analogies and assumed continuities. We tend to forget that we have a specific area of competence in individual psychology and that this is based on the discovery of the peculiar psychological phenomena which comes into view in the context of a peculiar dyadic relationship. It

seems necessary to reaffirm that whatever we know with relative certainty about these phenomena, whatever we can predict about them with fair probability, whatever we can verify with reasonable confidence through the supporting observations of our psychoanalytic peers, stems from the peculiar experimental field which has become known as the psychoanalytic situation . . . only in the psychoanalytic situation do psychoanalysts occupy their explicit scientific position for studying their proper material – the unconsciously emerging manifestations of instinct, primary process, affects, conflicts, defense mechanisms, and transferences" (1973, pp. 333-4). Similarly, Rustin (2001) claims that "the equivalent in psychoanalysis of the scientific laboratory is the consulting room. It is inside, and only inside, the consulting room, that the phenomena postulated by psychoanalyst can be clearly observed and distinguished from background 'noise.' It is only there that relevant observations and 'experimental inventions' can be made (these are usually called 'interpretations'), and their effects studied. It is there that most psychoanalytic discoveries have been made, there that the ideas and techniques which constitute the field continue to be developed. It is the consulting room which provides the site to which appeals are made in cases of disputed understanding. It is the role of the consulting room which explains the characteristic form of written presentation of psychoanalytic hypotheses or discoveries. What happens almost invariably in the exposition of new psychoanalytic ideas is reference to clinical cases as the decisive exemplars of the phenomenon in question, or of the techniques used to grapple with it" (36). Shortly after stating this, Rustin (a Kleinian) puts forward a common corollary to the position, namely, that the validation of psychoanalytic claims transpires only (at least the intimation is that it is only, or at least best and primarily) via first-personal clinical experiences: "this sphere of the unconscious can only be investigated in this peculiar setting" (37). Post-Kleinians such as Bion have also professed their allegiance to this principle. Bion often asserts that he is addressing only practicing analysts and that anyone else will not have the experience necessary to understand him. Even Freud, given as he was to building psychoanalytic theory on the basis of reflections involving matters far from the clinical domain, occasionally argued for the priority of the clinical medium, or at least the priority of clinical evidence (SE 16: 255; SE 20: 254; SE 13: 85; SE 10: 233-36; SE 13: 92-94 and SE 12:59-79). Habermas reads Freud as committed to the clinical primacy of psychoanalytic knowledge thesis: "I do not find any basis in Freud for the strict separation between a clinically justified theory of neurosis and a metapsychological superstructure . . . . This separation makes the specific roots of Freudian theory in the experiences of the analytic dialogue unrecognizable" (1984, p. 4, 249). At times, Habermas seems very much committed to the thesis himself, even going so far as to rebuke Freud for imperfect adherence to it: "The derivation of the structural model from the experiences of the analytic situation links the three categories ego, id, and superego to the specific meaning of a form of communication into which physician and patient enter with the aim of setting in motion a process of enlightenment and bringing the patient to self-reflection. In explicating the ego, id, and superego, we must refer back to this context; thus it is not meaningful to describe it in terms of the structural model derived from it. Nevertheless, this is what Freud does. He construes the interpretive work of the physician in the theoretical expressions of the structural model. In this way, the form of communication that was first described from the perspective of analytic technique seems to be theoretically accounted for. In truth, this theoretical exposition does not contain a single element that goes beyond the previous description of technique. The language of the theory is narrower than the language in which the technique was described" (1971, p. 244-5). Later, Habermas repeats, emboldens, and clarifies his earlier insistence on the primacy of the clinic, while at once, perhaps unwittingly, deviating from it, "The basic categories of the new discipline, the conceptual constructions, the assumptions about the functional structures of the psychic apparatus and about mechanisms of both the genesis of symptoms and the dissolution of pathological compulsions – this metapsychological framework was first *derived from experiences of the analytic situation and the interpretation of dreams*. The meaning of this observation bears on the methodology and not only the psychology of research. For these metapsychological categories and connections were not only discovered under determinate conditions of specifically sheltered communication, they cannot even be explicated independently of this context. The conditions of this communication are thus the conditions of the possibility of analytic knowledge for both partners, doctor and patient, likewise. Perhaps Freud was thinking of this implication when he wrote that the claim to fame of analytic work was that 'in its execution research and treatment coincide'" (1971, p. 252; emphasis added; also see pp. 254ff).

Though diverse as the advocates of this thesis are, it is worth noting the comparative prominence and rigidity of this position in the American context compared with the French. Historically, in the U.S. more so than in than France *real* psychoanalysis, thus *real* psychoanalytic knowledge, is claimed to be clinical. Wallerstein's prominence is in this respect exemplary. Although the American pundits of the medium-bound thesis admit interests in the ways in which psychoanalytic concepts and theories are or can be borrowed by other disciplines, these borrowings are much more often construed as questionable – problematically derivative and scientifically suspicious – than is the case in the French context. Part of the reason for this has to do with the fact that, in France, the university has long been a key site of psychoanalytic research. Especially after the heydays of the 50s when the chairs of university-affiliated psychiatry departments in the U.S. tended to be psychoanalytically inclined, the relationship between psychoanalysis and the American universities has been much more tenuous. Additionally, Lacan's philosophical disquisitions and his interest in "mathemes" both required and generated a diversification of alliances; the pursuit of research into "mathemes" in particular required the work of and compelled the interest of those working in philosophy, linguistics, and mathematics. There are, of course, significant exception to this trend, notably concerning those in the American ego psychology tradition. Hartmann, for instance, insists that "psychoanalytic psychology is not limited to what can be gained through the use of the psychoanalytic method" (1964, p. 103; also see pp. 116 and 301).

76. The response to Adorno's and suchlike characterizations of Freudian theory as "tyrannical," then, should be to insist that the *meaning* of a psychoanalytic concept is endlessly inflected or particularized in the singular clinical situation, such restlessness reflecting and in a way acknowledging the non-identical that conditions identifications. Though subsumption is inevitable in psychoanalysis – intuitions without concepts are blind; indeed without concepts as guides, evenly suspended or free floating attention and reverie, thus attention to singular features of the clinical material, would be impossible – the material subsumed need not be taken to be *transitively explained* by a law or law-like process. More pointedly, one could say that Adorno's and suchlike charges mirror the false self-conception of a few prominent analysts, e.g., Hartmann, for whom "the aim of these studies is (besides its therapeutic purpose) to develop lawlike propositions" (1964, p. 324; see also "Understanding and Explanation" pp. 369-403). It is worth noting that Freud frequently acknowledges and foregrounds the provisionality of his claims (SE 4: 281, 536, 568, 598, 610; SE 7: 242; SE 13, 97; SE 23, 159).

77. Though a discussion of this exceeds the scope of this inquiry, let us note in passing that such a faculty, thus nothing less than Kantian reason, may not survive such movement intact. Tracking the dissolution and recuperation and/or reelaboration of reason consequent upon suffering such movement may be a way of understanding Hegel's critical inheritance of Kantian critique and Adorno's reflectively reiterated application of such a manner of critical inheritance (i.e., negative dialectics).

78. That the application of psychoanalytic concepts cannot but risk transforming the concepts applied, that psychoanalytic concepts may be inflected by their uptake (their "performance") in unanticipated ways, nay arrogate connotations and valences that the tradition could not have foreseen as they are employed (and associated to, metabolized, etc.) in singular contexts, is *perhaps* why Freud describes his theoretical inferences and constructions as "intellectual scaffolding" which he "look[s] forward to . . . being modified, corrected, and more precisely determined as further experience is accumulated and sifted" (*Outline*). If Freud is both aware of and to some extent enthusiastic about the dialectical relation between universality and particularity in psychoanalysis, we may do well to review his bolder works and moments in this light. One might notice, for instance, that *The Interpretation of Dreams* moves from didactic generalizations to nuanced particularizations. This is often read as if the former were the truth of the latter; as if the latter portions are only meant to render the former more comprehensible and slightly more specific. But perhaps the movement of the text elaborates a principle of dialectical mediation, a self-critical reflexivity. Of course, the passage from *Outline* may very well express a classically objectivist aspiration. More important than Freud's self-understanding, in any case, is the plausibility of the thought that each use (redeployment) of an

inherited psychoanalytic concept is as much probative as declarative, that through their application, psychoanalytic concepts may be particularized, generating tremors, and at times perchance crises, in their intelligible infrastructure. Such concepts may be more akin to De Manian metaphor wherein the singular is built out of given terms than they are to Kantian determining judgments wherein the universal subsumes – predigests – the particular. At least in the clinical context and perhaps more broadly, the relation between the universal and the particular, the concept and the example, may be one of perpetual negotiation such that each use of an analytic concept conveys a claim to exemplarity. As Adam Phillips suggests, albeit perhaps extravagantly, "The analyst, like a good host, just goes on making introductions" (1995, p. 16).

79. T.J. Clark (2001) *Farewell to Modernism.*

80. To be sure, enthusiasm over the moment or movement of remediation/particularization can be excessive. Witness the problematic collapse of particularization and insight operated by Bollas' "because" in the following: "For an analytic idea to qualify as an insight I think it must undergo a topographic return: from the analyst's comment to a preconscious holding area (an inner mental space) where it evokes instinctual representations, unconscious affects, and unconscious memories, and then returns to consciousness after such inner work has occurred. An analytic idea then, has been transformed into an insight because what was only a theory now bears the patient's instinctual, affective, and memorial print" (1989, p. 96). Particularization may well be, as Bollas initially suggests, a *condition* of insight, but it is unlikely identical with insight – supposing it is would be to conspire with intra-analytic dogmatism and external skepticism.

81. Cf. Cavarero (2000) *Relating Narratives.*

82. "[T]ransference," Hoffman claims, "includes not just a sense of what has happened, or is happening, but also a prediction, a conviction even, about what will happen. The attempt to disprove this prediction is an active, ongoing, mutual effort, which is always accompanied by a real element of uncertainty" (in Mitchell and Aron 1999, p. 64).

83. "As a rule our therapy must be content with bringing about more quickly, more reliably and with less expense of energy than would otherwise be the case, the good result which in favorable circumstances would have occurred of itself" (SE 20: 154; also cf. SE 17: 207). Cf. Eysenck (1952).

84. Pennybacker (1988) has shown that just being afforded the opportunity to talk about and emotionally relive difficult experiences and relationships is a relief; indeed, it is a common finding that even a single analytic session helps somewhat.

85. For Freud's claim that analytic incognito is essential for both transference and its exhibition, cf. "The Dynamics of Transference."

86. Tact, a rather rare disposition, is crucial for determining efficacious moments for and manners of intervention. Efficacious moments for interpretation are often said to be those in which the analysand is significantly disconcerted, evidently troubled but not altogether overwhelmed (e.g., frantically distressed). Such discomfiture is taken as an indication of intense affectivity, a palpating aliveness of, say, conflict, and so of an availability to working through. In the case of severely fractured and precarious patients, those who may well be overwhelmed by interpretation to the point of crisis or collapse – blanket anxiety, rage, depressive withdrawal, etc. – as in the case of analysands who are not so characterizable in general but seem likely to be overwhelmed by an interpretation, unable to use it, at a particular moment of therapy, tact suggests restraint. Cf. Freud (1910) "On 'Wild' Psychoanalysis" and (1926) "The Question of Lay Analysis" and Ferenczi (1928) "The Problem of the Termination of Analysis" in *Final Contributions*, pp. 89 and 100.

87. On Freudian grounds, the efficacy of interpretation requires a number of preparations including, centrally, diminishing the amount of psychic energy used for repression or other defenses. If changes in structures of defense are a condition for the efficacy of interpretations, and it is not likely that such changes will be brought about outside analysis given the secondary gains to which they contribute and the scrutiny-suppressing routinization and interpersonal enabling by which they are supported, then there is some support for the clinical primacy thesis.

88. *If* interpretations produce recall only or primarily because they stimulate primary process connections, i.e., because they activate or generate "conditions more similar to those which existed when the recalled scenes and events occurred," then because the analytic situa-

tion facilitates regression, it best, perhaps uniquely, fosters recall of what was undergone in a primary process-like way (Kris, cited in Lowenstein 1982, p. 134). Or if one finds Kris' interpretive mimesis thesis implausible, one might still accept that the full force of analysis requires sustained regression and that clinical analysis is exceptional in its systematic facilitation of regression. Vastly unlike other sites, in the clinical environment one is induced to regression by following the basic rule of suspending moralized self-criticism as much as possible, having one's range of vision and motility restricted (e.g., by lying on the couch), being confronted with the obscurity of the analyst's personality which puts one in a childlike position of radical ignorance, and so on. On the last point, cf. Kanzer (1961) and Waelder (1960). Additionally, if associations in a state of regression are more fantasy-like or dream-like, that is, more primitive, then perhaps the clinical inducement of frustration is necessary for or at least comparatively much more effective in accessing a wealth of material (cf. Kris 1950, p. 312 and Balter et al. 1980).

89. Freud's recurrently problematic relations with his colleagues, especially those with whom he was initially enamored, may be considered in this light.

90. The perhaps medium-bound or at least medium-facilitated inducement and sustaining of positive transference may also be important to consider in this context. Positive transference, that is, provisionally investing another with the idealizing expectation that she can know and heal, may be a condition for initial willingness to undertake and at certain points for the courage to continue with analysis (how frequently are self-analytic practices, especially of the "journaling" sort, abandoned). Positive transference may also be crucial for a number of analytic successes, especially in the early stages of analysis. For instance, as Freud and others have suggested, sometimes resistances will not be given up except under the sense of obligation to a love object; positive transference may manipulate pathology, induce obedience, in the service of its undoing. And it is difficult to imagine that positive transference is as readily or intensely elicited by self-analytic or less ambitious therapeutic enterprises as by clinical psychoanalysis. Cf. Anna Freud 1980.

Further, advocates of the medium-bound nature of the cure thesis might contend, by consistent nonconformity to expected patterns of response, an analyst may disclose, perhaps render intriguing or compelling, the possibility of a life liberated from the pressures maintaining interpretive inertia and corresponding symptoms and other pathological functions. It is surely not the case that a glimpse of a liberated future can be had in no other way, but it may be the *consistency* or at least *constancy* of the analyst's excess vis-à-vis sedimented expectations, especially when coupled with positive transference, that allows a glimmer of a liberated future to appear as a viable possibility, as something that can be believed in. Analysis injects a spark of hope that may be crucial for therapeutic advancement. Though others may exemplarily figure forth prospects for living otherwise, it may be that the compelling force of exemplarity requires, minimally, both the constancy of the exemplar (thus perhaps the analyst's commitment to maintaining the clinical setting and the particular theories of pathology, therapeutic action, and cure that motivate, sustain, and guide the implementation of this commitment) and sufficient readiness to live otherwise (e.g., enhanced vulnerability, mitigated defenses, liberation of cathexes and imaginative and reflective capacities, etc.; hence the therapeutic apparatus that facilitates this).

91. "A performative utterance will, for example, be *in a peculiar way* hollow or void if said by an actor on the stage, or if introduced in a poem, or spoken in a soliloquy. This applies in a similar manner to any and every utterance – a sea change in special circumstances" (Austin 1975, pp. 21-22).

92. As Jessica Benjamin puts the point, "The experience of a space that allows both creative exploration within omnipotence and acknowledgement of an understanding other is, in part, what is therapeutic about the relationship" (in Mitchell and Aron 1999, p. 198).

93. Though, on the one hand, this implies that analytic success involves a dimension of normalization, on the other hand, it bespeaks the egalitarian ambitions of psychoanalysis – ambitions which, if successfully pursued, generate the resources with which to become aware of and perhaps to some extent to counteract its normalizing effects. The analyst's forms of attention and interpretive capabilities internalized by the analysand may be used against them-

selves, that is, used to call into question the particular forms of attention and interpretative proclivities inculcated by the analysis.

94. Further, through systematic frustration or the right sort of minimal gratification, the analyst can promote the transformation of wishes, expectations, etc. into demands upon the analyst that are *much* easier to detect and explore.

95. Cf. Laplanche and Pontalis (1973), pp. 462-464.

96. Expanding a bit: the analyst's rigorous noncomplicity in our ordinary forms of defense –broadly, our routine ways of getting on in the world – coupled with her relative inconspicuousness as a concrete individual may be requisite to sufficiently strengthen the transference to the point where we revert to typical old ways of securing satisfaction. And when our routine ways of securing pleasure (or whatever it is we seek) are unavailing, especially under the influence of positive transference, we will likely figure the analyst as the one who can satisfy us in the ways we crave, thereby sketching in our relations to the analyst the shape of our desires, fantasies, and/or developmental needs. Then, when frustration is sufficiently abated yet still affectively insistent, we may be in the best possible position to engage the questions of what it is we feel we want (or fear), from whom, and why.

To be sure, some, particularly those committed to some form of relational orientation, may find the discussion of transference neurosis quaint (one prominent relationalist said just that in private correspondence). The point of the present discussion is not to accurately represent clinical psychoanalysis as predominantly practiced or to defend any particular form of analysis but rather to identify what, if anything, supports the claim that the curative/transformative potential of psychoanalysis is medium-bound.

97. On standard psychoanalytic premises, we are systematically prone to repudiate each new dawn in order to reinstall the affective, cognitive, and relational coordinates of a world we (dimly) know ourselves to have lost yet cannot let go of, a failed and consequently frustrating world provisioning only fragile securities and compromised satisfactions yet, paradoxically, a world whose affordance of precarious securities and compromised satisfactions provides the impetus for ongoing attempts at its resurrection. In a standard psychoanalytic idiom, this is called transference.

Analysts pervasively hold that transference is not just inevitable but ubiquitous. In "Five lectures on Psychoanalysis," Freud claims that "transference arises spontaneously in all human relationships just as it does between the patient and the physician" (SE 11: 51). In *An Autobiographical Study*, he amplifies the claim, contending that transference "is a universal phenomenon of the human mind and in fact dominates the whole of each person's relations to his human environment (SE 20: 42; also cf. Freud's *Fragment of an Analysis of a Case of Hysteria* (SE 7: 3-119) and Hyman Muslin and Merton Gill's (1978) commentary in "Transference In The Dora Case"). Ferenczi (1950) quickly corroborated the early Freud's claim regarding the pervasiveness of transference, and by 1913 Jung had extended Freud's claim about the ubiquity of transference to the point where transference was now to be considered the basis for normal human relatedness (cf. Jung (1946) "Psychology of Transference"; also cf. Andrew Samuels (2006) "Transference/Countertransference" for a contemporary Jungian reiteration of the claim). Klein underscored the ubiquity of transference throughout her career (reconfigured in terms of projective identification and the like), especially in her 1952 "The Origins of Transference," and her inheritors have underscored her (and their) adamant adherence to the ubiquity of transference thesis (cf. Elizabeth Bott Spillius (2007) "Melanie Klein Revisited: Her Unpublished Thoughts on Technique"; and Clifford Yorke "Freud or Klein: Conflict or Compromise"). Lacan, who ordinarily went to great lengths to underline his disagreements with Kleinian theory echoes the claim about transference ubiquity in *Seminar I*, esp. p. 109, "The Mirror Stage," and *Seminar XI*, and his inheritors have continued to press the point (cf. Alexandre Leupin (1991) *Lacan and the Human Sciences*). Kohut has advanced this thesis as well in *How Does Analysis Cure?*, as has Loewald (1986) "Transference-countertransference," Kristeva (1987) *Tales of Love*, Gerald Gargiulo (1989) "Authority, the Self, and Psychoanalytic Experience," Stephen Mitchell (1995) *Hope and Dread in Psychoanalysis*, Merton Gill (1984) "Psychoanalysis and Psychotherapy: a Revision"; also cf. Merton M. Gill and Hyman L. Muslin (1976) "Early Interpretation of Transference" and Jane Hall (2004) *Roadblocks on the Journey of Psychotherapy*. The claim is also prominent in attachment theory, as evidenced by

Bowlby (1973) *Separation: Anxiety & Anger. Attachment and Loss Vol. 2*, Bowlby (1979) *The Making and Breaking of Affectional Bonds*; Bowlby (1979) *A Secure Base: Clinical Applications of Attachment Theory*, and later literature in this tradition such as Joseph H. Obegi and Ety Berant (2008) *Attachment Theory and Research in Clinical Work with Adults* and Andersen and Chen (2002) "The Relational Self: An Interpersonal Social-Cognitive Theory." The claim to the ubiquity of transference has even received some corroboration by empirical research: cf. S.M. Andersen and M.S. Berk (1998) "Transference in Everyday Experience: Implications of Experimental Research for Relevant Clinical Phenomena."
Glen Gabbard (2006) "A Neuroscience Perspective on Transference," and Westen and Gabbard (2002) "Developments in Cognitive Neuroscience: II. Implications for Theories of Transference."

By transference, analysts tend to mean the experience of and propensity to respond to events and persons on the basis of interpretive models (psychic templates) that are cognitively and functionally inappropriate to – gross distortions of – the present context, or at least motivated by developmental deficits, defenses, and the like (e.g., experiencing and responding to a person who is not your mother as if s/he were in order to achieve certain satisfactions one does not know how to secure or will not risk securing otherwise). Transference refers to the transferring of expectations, desires, fears, the demands of need, etc. from emotionally important figures or contexts – which may be *ab initio* fantasies or fantasmatic reconfigurations of experience – onto later figures or contexts in order to secure certain satisfactions or meet peremptorily urgent developmental needs. Manifesting as sedimented patterns of object attachment and relation, deep-seated wishes and conflicts that dominate self- and world-relations, character structures, fantasy fixations, defensive tendencies, and the like, transference predigests experience in accordance with standing – often rigid – psychic demands, devastating the fragile incursion of futurity before it can be given a chance to unfold.

That is, transference tends toward totalization. It operates through a passionate insistence into the fore of certain features of phenomena that, because they resonate with unconscious imperatives or developmentally driven needs, take upon amplified, sometimes all-consuming import. Under the long shadow cast by those features of experience that take upon exaggerated prominence at the behest of transference pressures, other features of experience – and so possibilities of self- and world-relation – go ill-attended, suffering neglect and withering from misrecognition. Under the sway of transference pressures we succumb to the most extreme forms of exaggeration and distortion: a motivated focus on certain features of experience that resonate – however obliquely– with longstanding concerns comes at the cost of diminished attention, even obliviousness, to other features of experience that may well warrant consideration and in whose folds another, more desirable future may be harbored. Transference tends toward a stagnant dialectic of blindness and insight: hyperbolic inflations of certain matters coincide with extreme deflations of others. Dominated by the needs and/or desires expressed by transference, we dominate in turn: transference names the overriding urgency to treat others as mere occasions for reelaborating patterns of perception and reaction modeled on perceptions of and responses to, say, one particular, engrossingly important other, developmental impasse, or the like. Locked into the forms of sensitivity (patterns of attention and neglect, value orientations, etc.), beliefs, and expectations that constitute transference, we are caught in a stream of rigidly established cognitive and relational forms and the psychohistorical currents they bear, unable to respond to the specificity of experience, indeed doomed to recapitulate failed forms of experience.

Worked over by the unresolved difficulties that motivate transference, experience bears witness to a past that refuses to pass on, a past whose encumbering presence saps the viability of sustained engagements with the possibilities onto which, indeed as which, the present opens. That is, with greater or lesser intensity, we are bound to experience the present and the futures it anticipates as they resonate with the unfinished business of the past, as an occasion for repeating and trying to somehow master or work though past conflicts, disappointments, etc. [Some version, however weak, of the drive to redevelopment is, I take it, part of just about all psychoanalytic theory – Lacanian theory being a possible exception. For explicit articulations of the drive to redevelopment thesis, cf. Kohut (1984) *How Does Analysis Cure?*; Winnicott (1982 [1971]) *Playing and Reality*; Ghent (1999) "Masochism, Submission, and Surrender:

Masochism as a Perversion of Surrender," esp. p. 214; and Christopher Bollas (1996) *Forces of Destiny: Psychoanalysis and the Human Idiom*. Something like a drive to redevelopment is involved in Sullivan's notion of a drive to mental health and Freud's notion of a drive to recovery (SE 12: 103).] On standard psychoanalytic premises, then, transference is both inevitable and ubiquitous. When it manifests outside the clinic, we tend to call it a symptom, a character structure, a peculiar habit, disposition, or style, or "just the way s/he is." Though Freud's manifest Enlightenment commitments and his conviction in the capacity of the analyst to overcome countertransference to the point of becoming a neutral and objective mirror suggest otherwise, even he occasionally suggests that projection is a normal element of perception, that transference is both inevitable and all-pervasive: "It must not be supposed . . . that transference is created by analysis and does not occur apart from it. Transference is merely uncovered and isolated by analysis. It is a universal phenomenon of the human mind, it decides the success of all medical influence, and in fact dominates *the whole* of each person's relations to his human environment" (SE 20: 79-80; emphasis added).

98. Comparative empirical outcomes will be addressed in chapter 7.

99. For more on the question of the efficacy of self-analysis and its varying historical status, cf. the bibliography in Schott (1985) *Zauberspiegel der Seele: Sigmund Freud und die Geschichte der Selbstanalyse*. The standard works on Freud's self-analysis remain Kanzer and Glenn eds. (1979) *Freud and His Self-Analysis* and Anzieu (1987) *Freud's Self-Analysis*.

100. Laplanche registers his dissent to the restriction of psychoanalysis to clinical practice in the following terms: "there is more to the psychoanalytic experience than clinical psychoanalysis" (1989, 8); "in works on so-called extra-mural psychoanalysis, *psychoanalysis invades the cultural*, not only as a form of thought or doctrine, but as a *mode of being*. Psychoanalysis is a broad cultural movement, and in that sense it is the whole of psychoanalysis which becomes extra-mural" (1989, p. 12); "Theory is often disavowed or denigrated, largely as a result of English empirico-clinicism. The imperialism of so-called clinicism has now reached new heights" (1989, p. 153). However, even Laplanche veers toward a version of the medium-bound thesis: "My thesis as to the role of these neighboring fields is that the domain specific to psychoanalysis emerges because it stands out against them, because it can be contrasted with them" (1989, p. 53).

101. The wide-ranging expression of this view may be surprising, especially in light of the dogmatic polemicism in which those giving voice to it not infrequently engage. That is, the thought is easily admitted but difficult to sustain. "Interpretations deal with the individual experiences of a human being. They aim at widening the conscious knowledge of the individual about himself and should therefore deal with the psychological realities of the individual . . . . interpretations aim at uncovering not . . . the Oedipus complex, but specific individual experiences which constitute the Oedipus complex of the person" (Lowenstein 1982, p. 21). Lowenstein (1957) goes so far as to advocate conducting therapy as if clinical theory did not exist. Likewise, Anton Kris (1983) stresses the need to refrain from theory-governed interpretation (his term for this is "theorectomy"; cf. Klein 1976). "[A]nalysis as a science is always a science of the particular. The realization of an analysis is always a singular case, even though those singular cases lend themselves to some generality" (Lacan, *Seminar I*, p. 29). "But all these terms are rough-and-ready characterizations that have only a very general meaning and value. They do not convey the special note of a particular case and fail to do justice to the nuances and shades of phenomenon" (Reik 1972, p. 174). "[T]he concepts 'obsessional' or 'repressed' could never sum up, to the satisfaction of both analyst and patient, the entire set of sentiments, thoughts, ambivalences and desires that color and add density to everyday experience" (Quiny, "Translator's Introduction" to Pontalis 2003, p. ix). "I say 'table' and I forget *this* table. I say, "He's obsessional,' and I forget the one who is speaking to me. I say, "identification with the father," and I haven't said anything at all" (Pontalis 2003, p. 3). "In the last session I clinked the coins in my pocket while giving myself up to free associations. I casually remarked that playing with money showed anal-erotic tendencies. Freud answered seriously: That is, of course, nonsense. You think of your brothers and are glad that you are now able to send them money" (Reik 1972, p. 258). See also Harari (2001), p. 27.

102. However, overemphasizing particularity may conspire with hysterical structures. On Lacan's account, hysterics tend to question, scrutinize, evaluate, challenge, and insistently

particularize their analysts' interpretations in order to expose the lacuna or gap in the other, i.e., position themselves as an exception, an excess with respect to the analyst's knowledge, and thereby situate themselves as capable of complementing or supplementing the analyst's knowledge, which is a way of adhering to a fantasy of Completion from which they ultimately suffer. "In her position as the one who points out or demonstrates the lack in the Other's knowledge, she becomes a living exception or enigma, always one step ahead of any known theory or technique" (Fink 1999, p. 132). Lacan aside, inherited concepts mediate, and so make possible, clinical attention. Also, there may be reason to refrain from rendering interpretations in an explicitly tentative, provisional, and uncertain manner. For instance, so doing may fail to inspire confidence in the analysand.

Further, it should be noted that this conception of psychoanalytic insight as emphatically singular, resistant – which is not to say simply unamenable – to generalization and extra-therapeutic transposition is perhaps brought into view most clearly by, but does not necessarily presuppose, the medium-bound thesis. There is no reason to believe that the clinic, as against the various settings in which self-analysis is undertaken or psychoanalytic concepts and theories are applied, is the sole context within which such concreteness may manifest.

103. As John Forrester notes, "as is well known, the most significant and telling interpretations are often a well placed and operatically toned analytic grunt." Thus he queries, "How is one to gauge the truth value of grunts, those indispensable media of everyday psychoanalytic communication?" (2000, p. 317). Clinical knowledge need not be formulated with an eye to developing hypotheses that can be integrated into higher order explanatory models or theories from which predictions are made via deduction and then subject to (dis)confirmatory experimentation – though this may be, to an extent, possible and desirable.

104. It also supports those inclined to evaluate the merits of extratherapeutic transpositions of psychoanalytic concepts and theories on a case by case basis, medium-immanent manner.

105. This gesture is so tempting, in fact, that it has served as a rare point of agreement among pundits of remarkably diverse analytic persuasions. Freud, for one, claims that "psycho-analysis is not an impartial scientific investigation, but a therapeutic measure. Its essence is not to prove anything but merely to alter something" (SE 10: 104). The sentiment is echoed in Ricoeur: "[t]he guarantee that the reality of the unconscious is not just a pure figment of psychoanalysts' imagination is provided finally only by therapeutic success" (1974, p. 19). In his earlier work, however, Ricoeur explicitly denied that efficacy is sufficient to demonstrate validity (Ricoeur 1970, pp. 346-7). Soler, a prominent Lacanian, also advocates this thesis: "how do we know that the interpreter is not inventing? How do we know that the meaning that appears between the subject who speaks (in general, or through his or her symptom or the failure of his or her action) and the interpreter is not invented by the latter? There can be only one form of proof, but it's decisive: the fact that symptoms are transformed when they are interpreted. The only proof of the unconscious as speech is the effectiveness of the interpretation on symptoms (1996, p. 44). Other Lacanians have been even more extreme in their (related) prioritization of the value of efficacy. Fink, for instance, claims that "[i]n a certain sense we can say that whether Lacan has a truer reading of Freud than Hartmann does is something of a moot point. What we can say is that, historically speaking, Hartmann's reading was sterile and unproductive. It led to very little in the way of a renewal of research and theorization, whereas Lacan's lead to a huge increase in both (like a good interpretation in the analytic setting, it generated a lot of new material)" (2004, p. 45). The canonical status of this frequent gesture in the Lacanian field is indicated by Dylan Evans's statement in his *Introductory Dictionary of Lacanian Psychoanalysis* that "[t]he value of an interpretation does not lie in its correspondence with reality, but simply in its power to produce certain effects; an interpretation may therefore be inexact, in the sense of not corresponding to 'the facts,' but nevertheless true, in the sense of having powerful symbolic effects" (1996, p. 89). Lacan himself gestures in this direction a number of times, as when he claims that "When all is said and done, it is less a matter of remembering than of rewriting history" (*Seminar I*, p. 14) or that "Analysis is not a matter of discovering in a particular case the differential feature of the theory, and in doing so believe that one is explaining why your daughter is silent – for the point at issue is to *get her to speak*, and this effect proceeds from a type of intervention that has nothing to do with a differential feature" (1988, p. 11). At certain moments, Lacan even identifies "truth" with a

certain analytic efficacy (Seminar of Jan 13, 1971, "D'un discours qui ne serait pas du semblant"). Erik Erikson's (1958) "The Nature of Clinical Evidence" also claims that validity is to be predicated on therapeutic efficacy. In the introduction to *Learning from Experience*, Bion boldly asserts that "[i]n psycho-analytic methodology the criterion cannot be whether a particular usage is right or wrong, meaningful or verifiable, but whether it does, or does not, promote development." Lowenstein too claims that the production of new material signals that an interpretation is correct (1982, p. 27). The therapeutic efficacy standard is also central for Klein, playing a significant role in her debate with Anna Freud over the legitimacy of analyzing children's play. It is equally crucial, on Whitford's account, for Irigaray (1991, p. 35-6). Kohut claims that "The validity of insights obtained will be demonstrated by the fact that the pressure to act out . . . will be diminished in the group" (in Gedo and Pollock 1976, p. 422). Loch, a prominent German object-relationist, insists that what is fruitful is true; more specifically, that if an interpretation generates self-coherence, it's fruitful, thus true (in Smith (ed.) 1977). Jiménez (2006), a relationalist, maintains a qualified commitments to the thesis: "it is essential that psychoanalysis be validated by process and outcome research" (1503). Mitchell, another relationalist, is also committed to a version of the therapeutic efficacy standard (2005, pp. 210-11 and 227). Adam Phillips expresses his commitment to the standard at a metapsychological level when he proposes that "instead of asking, Is there an unconscious, we might ask, In what sense are our lives better if we live as though there is one?" (1995, p. 56). Both the hermeneutically oriented (Woolfolk and Messer in Messer, Sass, and Woolfolk (1988), p. 112; Spence throughout his writings; Ricoeur, cited above) and logical positivists (e.g., Frank) have explicitly advocated versions of this thesis. In Frank's words, "one theory is more practical or convenient than another . . . . . the truth of Freudian or similar theories must not be understood otherwise than pragmatically. It may be convenient or not to accept them" (1959, p. 311; although the phrasing is not unequivocal, exegetical details need not concern us here, for what is at stake is documenting the pervasiveness of a general orientation). Spence puts the point this way: "The more appropriate question concerns what might be called its artistic truth, its significance as a kind of creative endeavor, a putting together of known facts about the patient in a new form that carries a high probability of something happening in the analytic space" (Spence 1982, p. 275). Phillips agrees: "Instead of asking, as one might of a translated text, is it accurate, have we got it right, did these events that we have reconstructed really happen to create the present predicament, we should be asking what kind of life would believing this make possible? What could this translation lead you to do? One would be interested in the possible consequences of the translation; one would be referring forward, not referring back" (2001, p. 146). Jonathan Lear (2003) also advances this claim. Michels' overview, though disquieting, strikes me as an accurate description of a longstanding and still growing trend: "the truth of the theories used by psychoanalysts in guiding their clinical work is not that important. Analysts are concerned with helping patients, not with establishing the validity of psychological theories. They want to know whether a theory is useful in formulating interpretations or other interventions, whether the theory is effective in facilitating the therapeutic process in the consultation room, not whether it meets some philosophic or scientific criterion for truth" (2000, p. 34). Only a few within the analytic community have consistently repudiated this thesis, e.g., Hartmann, who insists that "the problems of validation of psychoanalytic hypotheses ought not to be equated, as has too often been done, with the problem of therapeutic success" (1964, p. 337).

106. We need not corroborate the purported intimacy of instrumental efficacy and empirical accuracy to appreciate that many do, including many of those who challenge the credibility of psychoanalysis.

107. "A determined skeptic to whom we point out that, say, the explanation and analytic treatment of a vehemently repressed impulse has effected a radical change in the patient's inner life, can always retort that there is no guarantee that the change is due just to the said process. Success cannot decide the question" (Reik 1972, p. 375).

108. A related though separate problem is that with regard to analysands who are associatively flighty or cautious and inhibited, as many are in the beginning stages of analysis, association or resistances may not be to *the specific interpretation*; that is, the criterion yields false positives.

109. A separate difficulty, though related to the topic of equivocity, is that it would be strange to say that efficacy entails validity if, as is reported, patients with very similar symptoms and forms of characterological organization react very differently to very similar interpretations. Cf. Anna Freud (1954) "Problems of Technique."

110. Ironically, then, though presumably in the service of warranting the claim to the medium-bound nature of psychoanalytic knowledge and/or therapy, it renders irrelevant distinctions between analytic and non-analytic therapy.

111. In particular, negative therapeutic reaction would be indistinguishable from therapeutic efficacy or rendered incomprehensible.

112. This leads to "gaps between psychoanalytic theory and the success and failure of psychoanalytic therapy, so that the failure of therapeutic techniques is compatible with the truth of this theory [since the technique is not strictly derived from the theory], whilst the success of those techniques may provide little support for it . . . . [since it may be that] success is better explained by an alternative theory of technique" (Keat 1981, p. 159).

113. For a creative handling of the thorny control group issue, cf. Leichsenring, Rabung, and Leibing (2004).

114. "What I say may sound like other comments delivered to other patients, but it is not the same" (Bollas 1989, p. 58). "In transference the analyst risks the dissolution of his own knowledge, that is, of what the patient presumes his knowledge to be and of the knowledge that he has brought to bear in other cases. Each analysis modifies – or should modify – at least some of the beliefs about psychodynamics that I held before hearing what the analysand had to say" (Kristeva 1988, 51). Lacan stresses even more emphatically the need for "ever renewed ignorance that prevents anyone becoming a 'case'" (*Écrits*, p. 322). On standard psychoanalytic premises, "primary process" functioning – individuals metabolizing (condensing, displacing, and representing) what they undergo in singular and unpredictable ways – is a source of irreducible differences between analyses.

115. The incompatibility between (1) the metaphysical and epistemic realism invoked here and (2) the invocation of the myth of the myth of the given above is merely apparent. The latter challenges the notion of metaphysical realism, the former is in the service of subjecting the epistemic and metaphysical assumptions of claims to valid description based on interparty ratings to immanent critique.

116. Bersani identifies 18 (2000, p. 170).

117. For instance, given that terms such as representation, repression, resistance, energy, inhibition, and displacement were already used in Herbart's psychology, and terms such as pleasure principle, tendency towards stability, mental energy, and mental topography were already used in Fechner's experimental psychology, specifying the specifically Freudian or otherwise psychoanalytic meaning(s) of these terms will clear up certain confusions.

118. Cf. Glover (1955).

119. Freud stresses the provisionality of his theoretical formulations on many occasions, e.g., SE 4: 281; SE 5: 536, 568, 598, 610; SE 7: 242; SE 13: 97; SE 23: 159.

120. As Bersani puts the point with characteristic hyperbole, "The logical incoherence that results from the breakdown of conceptual distinctions accurately represents the overdetermined mind described by psychoanalysis" (2009, p. 100). Cf. Atlan's (1992) and Morin's (1981, 1982, 1983, 1985, 1991) discussions of hypercomplexity, which, they suggest, entails indeterminacy and undecidability in many sectors of modern science.

121. What is to be deemed placebo effect as opposed to the efficacy of non-classical technique is a related problem.

122. Kernberg provides a chilling account of a transformation of relatively affectless experience into affectively intense experience that should caution us against immediately deeming such transformations "fruitful": "The effect of my focus on this 'absence' [the emotional unavailability of the analysand and of the analyst as experienced by the analysand] in the transference was striking: the patient began to experience anxiety in the sessions. Over a period of several weeks, his anxiety increased, and his associations changed significantly. He developed an intense fear of me, with an image of me as somebody totally unreal, who presented the facade of a friendly psychoanalyst that covered an underlying frightening empty space. He was alone in the middle of a devastating experience of himself as damaged, disintegrating, inca-

pable of being either a boy or a girl. It was as if only dead objects surrounded him" (in Hamilton 1992, 40). Kernberg's interventions were certainly "effective," but the question of whether such interventions should be deemed therapeutically effective or disastrous cannot be decided locally. And even if Kernberg's practice proved incontestably beneficial in the long term, because the causal links – if there are any – between the initial interventions, the intense anxiety, and the ultimate results are unclear, the question of whether the initial anxiety should be considered a positive therapeutic result of his focus on absence remains undecided. Hartmann (1951) is one of the few psychoanalytic theorists to raise the question of the relation between immediate consequences and therapeutic results, but fails to make any headway into it. Or consider a more straightforwardly equivocal case: "my interpretations of this material stimulated further dreams and associations which appeared to confirm them, but without producing the slightest effect on the patient nor any modification in her symptoms" (Lowenstein 1982, p. 115).

123. Incidentally, because some of these may involve idiosyncratic features of the analysand, analyst, or analytic relationship, they may be sources of ongoing suspicion that one's therapeutic technique was "correct" however ineffective, i.e., sources of dogmatism about technique.

124. Appeals to analysands' avowals of interpretations are of no avail, for these may issue from the force of suggestion, a desire for intelligibility coupled with a lack of alternative compelling stories (which is what often brings clients to analysis in the first place), or their defensive value, as when interpretations are avowed in order to disclaim responsibility and relieve guilt ('if my difficulties and symptoms are determined by infantile traumas, they are not my responsibility'). Or they may result from motivated overcompliance, as when confirmation of an interpretation by an analysand functions as a transference-laden attempt to win praise or secure ingratiation. Or they may be a form of narcissistic or depression-deferring exhibitionism ('Look, its me! You see me!'). Or apparent compliance and conviction may be covertly combative or dissimulate a terrible rage. The hermeneutics of suspicion cannot avoid turning back on itself. Or perhaps what is affirmed when an analysand avows an interpretation is the desirability of the illocutionary and projected perlocutionary effects of the interpretation.
With regard to suggestion, let us note in passing that suggestive recruitment into an interpretive apparatus may be, paradoxically, a condition for whatever objectivity is possible in psychoanalysis. "By explaining things to him, by giving him information about the marvelous world of psychical processes into which we ourselves only gained insight by such analyses, we make him, himself, into a *collaborator*, induce him to regard himself with the objective interest of an investigator, and thus push back resistance, resting as it does on an affective basis" (SE 2: 282; emphasis added).

125. Cf. *Écrits* 595.

126. Cf. Rosen (2007) "On the Fate of Psychoanalysis and Political Theory."

127. Though problematic in a variety of ways, the gesture of predicating validity on therapeutic efficacy is not to be lightly dismissed. One might, for instance, see this gesture as an exaggeration and important as such, for against the backdrop of this exaggeration, the import conventionally placed on established validity in its ordinary sense(s) can be queried as to whether it is itself excessive. If the thesis is an exaggeration, if its development adheres to the logic of perspective, there would be a history – or a variety of histories – to elaborate were we to account more fully for its compelling power. Such accounting might begin with medicine's desperate wanting for therapeutic efficacy in Freud's day and the role this might have played in his attraction to the standard.

128. The prospects for psychoanalysis becoming a natural science will be considered in chapter 7.

129. Hartmann, for instance, claims that "[t]he plasticity of the infantile situation and its limits, the degree to which it can or cannot be influenced by cultural factors, are best delimited by anthropological studies rather than by analyzing individuals of the same culture. In such problems anthropology has a certain experimental value and can, in certain cases, contribute material which will verify or negate psychoanalytic assumptions" (1964, p. 24).

130. Strenger (1991), for instance, holds that psychoanalytic claims must be both theoretically coherent and confluent with the accepted body of knowledge emergent from related sciences.

Chapter Four

Insecurity in Analysis

INTRODUCTION: ONE OR MANY?

Many are convinced that theoretical disagreements in psychoanalysis would be resolved or at least sapped of much of their significance were the relative uniformity that prevails at the level of clinical technique and, correspondingly, with respect to the description of concrete clinical phenomena, appropriately acknowledged. Those so convinced assume that that although experience-far concepts, e.g., metapsychological concepts, may vary considerably, how analysts interpret particular clinical phenomena, at least when such interpreting is phrased in experience-near, low-level terms, cannot be *that different*. Wishing to halt the unseemly rancor of psychoanalytic polemicism, wanting psychoanalysts to acknowledge their common identity and pursue a common good, advocates of this stance suggest putting theoretical disagreements on the backburner in order to focus on the commonality that prevails at the level of "on the ground" clinical work.

One extremely influential exponent of this position is Robert Wallerstein. The two primary claims of Wallerstein's "One Psychoanalysis or Many" (1992) are that a uniform observation language — e.g., "the patient was acutely distressed over the coming cancellation and was reacting unhappily and resentfully to that announcement" (51) — can be consensually established, indeed is to a great extent already in place, and that "[w]hen we reach beyond the interactions of the analytic consulting room, beyond the elucidation of the present unconscious, beyond, that is, the clinical phenomena captured in and explained by our *clinical* theory, to a more encompassing, more generally explanatory, more causally developmental accounting of mental life from its earliest fathomable origins, we are getting into another realm. This other is the realm George Klein called the unnecessary *general* theory that we should sever and cast out by an action dubbed 'theorectomy,' the realm that the Sandlers call the *reconstructed* past unconscious, the realm of our pluralistic theoretical perspectives in psychoanalysis" (51-2).[1] In other words, psychoanalytic knowledge is medium-*bound*.

This strategy at least offers a reasonable explanation of why the outcome rates of psychoanalytic practices whose practitioners understand themselves to differ considerably on theoretical and technical issues are frequently (more or less) equivalent: no one does what they think they are doing, i.e., pursuing a relatively unique range of goals in a relatively unique manner, rather, analysts all do something sufficiently similar under a certain description.[2] That is, theoretical disagreements reflect forms of systematic self-misunderstanding.[3] Though certainly appealing, reduction to clinical common ground presents a number of difficulties. First, it is not clear what the normative force of a consensually established observation language would be, why it should be accepted. Even if, implausibly, equivocity, indeterminacy, diverse criteria of salience and concept application, and so forth were sufficiently reducible for its empirical accomplishment, what would make a consensually established observation language legitimate rather than just empirically hegemonic (e.g., merely reflective of prevalent interpretive dispositions)? In order to accrue consensus, a proposed observation language would have to be extremely vague and admit a tremendous equivocity if psychoanalytic plurality is genuinely robust, which is to say, if the establishment of the observation language has a point, but then it would fail to establish the substantive unity at which it aims; and if it were sufficiently determinate (semantically exclusionary and inferentially articulated) to elaborate substantive unity, again given the empirical premise of robust plurality, it would rule out a variety of interpretive practices, empirically undermining or merely imposing (thus normatively undermining) consensus. If the authority, even the intelligibility, of conceptual practices is bound to their revisability and defeasibility, their being implicitly subject to challenge, thus to their being implicitly addressed to diverse others — if, as Hegel puts it, "Self-consciousness attains its satisfaction only in another self-consciousness" (*PhG* 175) — then an observation language is provisional and contestable or crudely authoritarian, i.e., wanting for normative authority. Consider Wallerstein's claim that what "unites us all as psychoanalysts" is the conviction that clinical theory is a theory "of transference and resistance, of conflict and defense" and is concerned primarily with "the present unconscious" (52). A consensus elaborated in these terms is either extraordinarily superficial and trades on equivocity so extreme as to empty language of meaning, or manifestly a product of authoritarian imposition (could Kohut recognize his practice in its terms?).[4] Second, the inference from a consensually established observation language or its possibility to unity at the level of clinical theory is hardly convincing. The former may be a prerequisite for the latter, but does not entail it. Third, one might think that Wallerstein moves too quickly and treats plurality too lightly when he casts "our pluralism of theoretical perspectives" in terms of "the various scientific *metaphors* that we have created in order to satisfy our variously conditioned needs for closure and coherence and overall theoretical understanding" (52-3). Is his consignment of theoretical languages to such a high altitude not of a piece with his haste to dismiss their bearing on concrete clinical phenomena? One need not be a sophisticated philosopher of science to suspect that observation languages and theoretical languages are co-constitutive or mutually implicating, thus that disagreements over the latter may impact the possibility of consensus with respect to the former. Or from another angle, one need not be Derrida (cf. "White Mythology") to have a reasonable suspicion about the facility with which Wallerstein distinguishes metaphor from literal meaning. Wallerstein claims that "[i]n regard to clinical theory, I view the theory formation, aided though it is in its conceptualization by the symbolisms of our metaphoric constructions, as nonetheless sufficiently experience-near, anchored directly enough in observables, to the data of our consulting rooms, that it is amenable to the self-same process of hypothesis formation, testing, and validation as any other scientific enterprise" (56). This is uncompelling. By fetishizing "observables," Wallerstein displaces the questions he should be addressing. Excising metapsychology in order to identify putatively theory-neutral "observables" would render the hypotheses formulated too few and too vague to be of much value; testing the hypotheses admitted would not do much to adjudicate between competing interpretative practices.[5] Fourth, if descriptions imply conduct, i.e., a range of appropriate responses, the diversity of therapeutic responses to similar phenomena (if genuine) weighs against the possibility and authority of consensus over descriptions. In short, Wallerstein may seriously misunderstand the relation(s) between semantic and pragmatic dimensions of language. Fifth, one might worry that austere restriction of psychoanalytic knowledge claims to low-level, experience-near terms would unnecessarily foreclose questions concerning the cognitive authority of cultural-critical employments of psychoanalytic forms of attention, i.e., would relegate "applied psychoanalysis" to the domain of mere speculation, and would thereby forfeit a significant source of psychoanalysis' claim to cultural interest.

Wallerstein's strategy will not normatively, i.e., authoritatively, resolve the problems pursuant to plurality, e.g., the prevalence of dogmatic insularity, interpartisan polemicism, and the widespread failure of psychoanalysts to learn from one another in a way that conduces to theoretical and/or practical progress understood with reference to shared criteria. And he knows this. Nor will his confidence that observables can anchor scientifically validated clinical theory, thus a common identity, find much resonance among those for whom this matters most. And he knows this too — though perhaps not why (likely, his scientistic condescension stands in the way). "[E]ach of these theoretical explanatory contexts . . . will be persuasive indeed to the adherents of that viewpoint, who in fact will look at it as *the* useful and natural way in which to understand *the phenomenon, the clinical interaction*" (52; emphasis added). Even were they presented with "evidence" of unity, partisans would likely continue to assume their commitments as "articles of faith" (56). Supposing that interpretations of concrete clinical phenomena, if salient, will vary as greatly as metapsychologies, the program Wallerstein advocates would merely conduce to a disavowal of the significance of psychoanalytic plurality. Wallerstein's program for one psychoanalysis at the level of clinical theory and toleration for many metaphors at the level of metapsychology would yield at best superficial, largely irrelevant unity while covertly suppressing the extent and significance of plurality through the norms operative in its understanding of what counts as the basic data of psychoanalysis and the observation language in which this data must be couched: a formula for the return of the repressed if ever there was one.[6]

This chapter seeks to rebuke the claim that adequately attending to concrete clinical phenomena resolves or moots theoretical differences. Differences in the interpretation of particulars will be shown to reflect larger differences in perspective, the reducibility of which is perhaps conceivable, but not without artificially dissolving the question at stake: whether the method of reduction can be translation by the language of a clinical common ground. By working from the inside out, that is, by showing how differences in perspective are implied in the description and treatment of particular clinical phenomena, this chapter seeks to underline the depth and breadth of psychoanalytic plurality.

Some of the ancillary goals of this chapter are:

(1) to show just how much would need to be corroborated by scientific experimentation if it were to pronounce upon the validity of psychoanalytic knowledge claims and/or practice, thereby anticipating the arguments of subsequent chapters regarding the difficulties involved in appealing to experimental science as a means of adjudication between competing psychoanalytic perspectives, interpretations, or practices;

(2) to continue the work of familiarizing the audience with the diversity of analytic perspectives begun in chapter 2, specifically, to partially redress the omission of Klein in that context;

(3) to bring the specificity of psychoanalysis into more fine relief by contrasting it with behaviorism;

(4) continuing a point from chapter 3, to underscore the possibility of significant plurality internal to a psychoanalytic school (multiple possible Freudian interpretations of the same phenomenon will be elaborated);

(5) to specify that even if psychoanalytic perspectives always involve exaggeration and distortion, both of features of the phenomena under consideration and of other traditions that would elaborate and account for these

phenomena otherwise, not all forms of exaggeration and distortion should be treated equally (an example of an unhelpful and flatly incorrect interpretation of what constitutes a Freudian interpretation will be provided);

(6) to suggest that the pursuit of self-knowledge requires knowledge of and dialogue with alternative perspectives, thereby (a) continuing the investigation of the nature of perspectival knowing and (b) providing reason for analysts to quell their mutual hostility or desist from their facile assumption of familiarity (eclecticism) and seek nuanced knowledge of the work of those in other camps (or different sectors of the same camp);[7]

COMPLICATION: ON CONCRETENESS

As Gregory Hamilton notes in the introduction to his object relations anthology, *From Inner Sources*,

> According to this [object relations] model, the patient's expectable feelings of security with the doctor are not repressed at the beginning of therapy because of unconscious erotic or aggressive transference or unconscious association with a previous unfortunate medical event. A secure feeling is absent because, on the one hand, the patient had never been provided a good-enough holding environment to feel secure and, on the other hand, whenever she begins to feel safe, she splits off and projects that affect to protect it from being swallowed up by her overwhelming anxiety (1992, xviii).

Throughout, Hamilton's stresses that even when Freudians, object relationists, and others agree *that* certain clinical phenomena are significant — here, a ubiquitous sense of anxiety or discomfort in early stages of analysis, a peculiar inability on the part of analysands to feel at ease in the presence of a mental health professional —*how* such phenomena are understood will differ significantly. Some, Hamilton suggests, will attribute the unease to negative conditioning: previous "unfortunate" medical events have prejudiced the client against medical practice altogether. I assume Hamilton is either (1) just referring to a commonsense view of the ordinary discomfort attending a visit to a doctor's office or (2) alluding to a more strictly behaviorist view of such discomfort. If the former, the language of repression in the claim that "the patient's expectable feelings of security with the doctor are not repressed at the beginning of therapy because of . . . unconscious association with a previous unfortunate medical event" is out of place or at least extremely contentious. If the latter, the language of repression and unconscious association must be ironically intended (or careless). The irony would be twofold. First, behaviorists do not tend to work with the concept of repression or the concomitant, broader notion of dynamic psychic life. Second, insofar as they assume that current psychic events (e.g., insecurity in the clinic) can be transparently explained by (this would be the force of Hamilton's "because" in this context) previous psychic events ("previous unfortunate medical event[s]"), behaviorists part ways with standard psychoanalytic conceptions of the unconscious, e.g., as (1) a source of (quasi-)transcendental opacity, (2) subject to overdetermination and therefore non-linear causality, and (3) not simply pleasure seeking and pain avoiding.[8]

For behaviorists, if a "previous unfortunate medial event," say, an experience with an inept therapist, generates anxiety over the prospect of being mishandled again, there is no reason to doubt that (1) even if it is unpleasant to consider, the prior experience is fully consciously recuperable, (2) though obviously impacting, it may not be extremely meaningful, i.e., bear on the constitution of a vast variety of wishes, fears, beliefs, self-images, expectations, interpretive dispositions, etc., and (3) once experiences of the present analyst's competence are sufficiently repeated, or at most, once one undergoes the right sort of cognitive-behavioral training, the anxiety will abate. From the comparatively sanguine standpoint of behaviorism, the association between the "unfortunate" medical event and current medical events is entirely eradicable, subject to complete *overwriting* by positive experiences of medical practice. What's more, this overwriting can be accomplished with relative ease because the anxiety inducing association (medical practice = pain) is relatively isolated and superficial (from the point of view of psychoanalysts). It is not, as psychoanalysts tend to suspect, integrated with "deeper" (perhaps ineradicable or at least firmly entrenched, complex, obscure and even self-secluding) psychic structures, needs, or trends, e.g., used as an acceptable expression of or outlet for, and thus as a means of concealing, other inadmissible anxieties that perpetually surge forth. For behaviorists, the association is not subject to unconscious metabolism that would significantly transform the material, e.g., via displacement, condensation, or representation, and render efforts to isolate and recover "it" forever problematic. Rather, given their model of mental malleability, i.e., their technological model of the mind, the prior association can be identified and annulled via overwriting; the possibility that it is indelibly inscribed in an evolving unconscious matrix, thus always potentially in excess of self-appropriative enterprises, is not considered. For behaviorists, pathogenic associations are readily identifiable and eliminable, like an inflamed appendix.

For many psychoanalysts, on the contrary, psychic inscriptions (memory-traces) are both eminently modifiable, their meaning(s) and function(s) subject to ongoing redetermination via primary, secondary, and other processes — on standard psychoanalytic premises, psychic inscriptions are not self-subsistent units of meaning but rather more or less freighted moments of relational configurations, not triggers of law-governed effects but features of complex causal networks — and never wholly eliminable, banished without a trace. Although some analysts emphasize this more than others, all view the unconscious as a principle of distortion, overdetermination, and consequently opacity, thus view psychic life as in principle, partially unavailable to conscious appropriation and modification. Of course, on standard psychoanalytic premises, there are bound to be returns of the repressed and other upsurges of unconscious material — otherwise psychoanalysis would be a form of mysticism. And of course, on standard psychoanalytic premises, psychic life is available to some degree of intentional modification — otherwise psychoanalytic therapy would be a charade. But, again on standard psychoanalytic premises, what returns or surges forth, thus becoming available to alteration, may not be exactly what was once repressed or originally inscribed.[9] Rather, what returns or surges forth is, for instance, a repressed wish or *ab initio* phantasy *as* modified in the course of its unconscious sojourn — as subject to intensification, association with and so coloration by links with other unconscious contents, and integration into a variety of psychic demands, trends, phantasies, and so forth that may seem — and in fact may be — rather remote (thematically distinct) from the original wish or phantasy. What returns or surges forth is, furthermore, what is now admissible to consciousness, thus filtered through currently dominant structures of attention and concomitant concerns. Whether or not defenses play a large role in such filtering — most analysts assume they will — distortion will be ineliminable: the past is constitutively imperiled; it never survives the accomplishment of the present intact.

Most analysts agree that without modifications to the analysand's structures of defense — which may be in principle only partially effective; character structures may be considered defensive sedimentations — unconscious contents will return in a form that placates the prohibitions instituting repression, thus perhaps in a form influenced by the motivating conditions of such prohibitions. And even when defenses are modified and once defensively compromised or repudiated material becomes subject to avowal and integration, the work of avowal and integration cannot but transform (to some extent) the meaning of the material. To discover/create different, more satisfying ways of negotiating with such material (1) changes its meaning if it was once experienced as a vortex of obscurity into which or immobile and unintelligible rock against which one repeatedly stumbled, or in some other way a rigidly insistent, all too stable yet opaque feature of one's psychic landscape; and (2) means releasing it from associational gridlock into more free circulation, into new contexts, new frames of reference and forms of life that will influence its meaning and import: integration and avowal modifies what the material was-to-be, what it will have meant; and if the work of analysis is interminable, or to the extent that it remains unfinished, so will be the meaning of the material.

In short, if what presents itself is the product of (ongoing) unconscious metabolism and becomes available through currently dominant structures of attention and concern, including those cultivated by the therapeutic practice, and especially if inferences from (putative) presentations of distorted material to originating sources (both of the distortions and of the material distorted) are underwarranted, if the here and now is as complexly determined as the there and then, and neither is subject to lawful derivation, then an unqualified return to origins and the possibility of thoroughgoing self-reconstruction such a return promises are ruled out in principle. In contradistinction to behaviorists for whom "unconscious" material is wholly amenable to conscious recovery and manipulation, for psychoanalysts, psychic life remains elusive to strategies of self-excavation and self-determination. Behaviorists tend to view "the unconscious" as a neutral field of inscription in which psychic contents, primarily beliefs and affects, become associated but remain externally related, indeed an assembly plant where associations are contingently forged and may be erased/overwritten in accordance with autonomous construction designs.[10] Psychoanalysts, on the contrary, give credence to the relative autonomy and ongoing activity of the medium with respect to its contents. Proceeding without the axiom of the ultimate excessiveness and elusiveness of unconscious materials and processes vis-à-vis strategies of self-awareness and self-mastery, or at least putting much less emphasis on this, behaviorism brings into relief the limits assumed by psychoanalytic theory with regard to our capacities to break out of patterns of conflicted, self-defeating, undesirable, contradictory, or otherwise "irrational" or "dysfunctional" behavior. Against the backdrop of behaviorism, even Anna Freud looks like a pessimist.

But given that irony is hardly Hamilton's dominant rhetorical modality and given that the subtly vituperative pathos of this irony — if irony it is — in a presentation of the salient differences between object relations theory and other psychological theories would be untoward, indeed counterproductive, perhaps Hamilton does not intend to invoke behaviorism with the phrase "association with a previous unfortunate medical event." Perhaps the terms "repressed" and "unconscious" should be stressed rather than "association" and the phrase "previous unfortunate medical event." Perhaps the latter, strongly invoking behaviorist views, is simply out of place and a red herring. Recall that "association with a previous unfortunate medical event" is framed as a possible cause of the *repression* of "expectable feelings of security with the doctor." It may well be, then, that Hamilton's claim that "the patient's expectable feelings of security with the doctor are not repressed at the beginning of therapy because of unconscious erotic or aggressive transference or unconscious association with a previous unfortunate medical event" is not meant to counterpose object relationist views to those of behaviorists and Freudians but only to the latter. If so, "unconscious erotic or aggressive transference" and "association with a previous unfortunate medical event" would not be intended as the explanations of insecurity at the beginning of therapy given by Freudians and behaviorists respectively, but as two possible explanations given by Freudians. If this exegesis is correct, Hamilton is not ironic, he is just wrong. There are many possible Freudian interpretations of anxiety in early stages of analysis, but "unconscious association with a previous unfortunate medical event" is not one of them.[11]

This is not to deny the obvious — that certain therapists, even some who call themselves or who we might want to call Freudians, frequently draw from disparate traditions. A therapist who deems herself (predominantly) Freudian might also draw on behaviorist concepts, hermeneutic procedures, models of the mind, and therapeutic techniques when, in her judgment, the circumstances call for it. However, if such a therapist is (predominantly) Freudian, some anomaly or difficulty would be required to motivate departure from ordinary forms of interpretive practice, and *ex hypothesi*, there are none. Especially since we are considering not just a ubiquitous phenomenon but a ubiquitous phenomenon within early stages of analysis, it is not clear what the circumstances could be that would motivate a Freudian to depart from her ordinary forms of interpretive practice. *Ex hypothesi*, these have yet to be even tried. Or a heterodox Freudian might interpret insecurity in early stages of analysis as consequent upon association with a "previous unfortunate medical event," but in so doing, s/he would be performatively declaring the limits of classical or prevailing Freudian practice, perhaps attempting to inhabit the category "Freudian" in a way that extends it meaning beyond its classical or prevailing determinations, but would not be, in the relevant sense, offering a Freudian interpretation. And again, if subversive inhabitation of the category is to prove convincing, not just willfully discontinuist, some plausible elaboration of the experience of prevailing or classical Freudianism as restrictive and some reasons for the redetermination of Freudian practice in the manner performatively proposed would have to be implicit in the performance. Yet, given the context, none can be made out.

Now, there are a number of possible Freudian interpretations of the phenomenon. A Freudian may ascribe insecurity or anxiety[12] in early analysis directly to the unbearability of eros or aggression elicited by the transference (assumed to have a quick onset), i.e., to a constitutionally excessive quantity of eros or aggression brought into play by the transference and tending to suffuse the analytic scene or some component of it, or to the disconcerting because (in the context of current psychic structure) overstimulating experience of eros or aggression prompted by the transference. Or a Freudian may attribute it to a reaction formation motivated by the onset of transference and perhaps related to whatever has facilitated its quick onset or unusually immediate intensity. The transferential positioning of and unconscious fantasizing about the analyst as, say, "the subject supposed to know" and/or expert capable of curing (redeeming? purifying? annihilating?) may make the analysand uneasy about confronting this authoritative figure (and that with which or those with whom authority is associated) with her aggressivity and/or desire or about the vulnerability of her fantasized transparency, or about confronting certain affects, beliefs, memories, fantasies, and so on that the analyst, qua fantasized subject who knows, will surely unearth, or about having to undergo and perhaps also wanting to undergo the sorts of transformations that she fantasizes the analyst will insist upon, perhaps about fantasies of self-annihilation associated with her idea of analysis, which may be connected with troubling masochistic impulses and/or a defensively repudiated desire for health and difficult memories and fantasies associated therewith (e.g., hope for success may be linked with intense fear of abandonment and/or the fantasized consequences of failure), or about her passivity in the face of the fantasized omniscience and/or omnipotence of the analyst. A Freudian may consider this massive unease or insecurity as revulsion and/or desire that ciphers revulsion and/or desire connected with warded-off material and manifests as anxiety. And she may interpret this anxiety as the analysand's way of (1) indicating to the analyst that there is material with which she does not want to negotiate or is conflicted about negotiating with, (2) providing herself with a justification to leave or emotionally retreat from while remaining in analysis, i.e., to avoid working through distressing material or undertaking the arduous work of personal transformation, (3) attempting to neutralize in advance the effects of analysis (or what they are fantasized to be) by rendering herself so anxious as to be unanalyzable or by offering her anxiety as a seduction to the analyst's interpretations and thereby setting herself up to believe that whatever transpires in the analysis is the effect of her seduction, that the analyst has been duped and so isn't really all that insightful, that the analysis isn't "real," that she can evade confronting difficult material and disown her efforts, and/or (4) anesthetizing herself (via the consistency and/or intensity of her anxiety) in order to forestall and/or perhaps facilitate the work of analysis. Or a Freudian might consider the insecurity to be provoked by some particular quality of the analyst or therapeutic environment and fantasmatically mediated memories associated therewith or as only contingently associated with the entry into analysis (perhaps the patient has recently started decompensating or has become extraordinarily anxious due to changes or crises in her political environment or in her romantic- or work-life). Or a Freudian might ascribe the insecurity to fantasies about the fate of erotic and/or aggressive impulses evoked or intensified by the entry into analysis, e.g., fantasies wherein eros and/or aggression leads to disastrous consequences, worries about which give rise to anxiety and/or repression, which, due to its permeability, issues in returns of the repressed, thus enhanced anxiety. Or a Freudian might consider whether the insecurity is an elaboration (and/or concealment) of unconscious guilt: what feels like insecurity about therapy, or what *has become* insecurity in therapy, is guilt associated with what one is in therapy to confront or fantasizes one will confront, or is anxiety in the service of concealing the pangs of guilt. Or the insecurity might be ascribed to a fantasy of punishment provoked by unconscious guilt and/or fearful anticipation of, and perhaps desire for, (continued) transgression, a fantasy wherein punishment at the hands of the therapist, and vicariously, whomever or whatever the therapist (or perhaps the therapy) stands for, would settle accounts, reinstitute a desired equilibrium, and thereby provide relief,[13] or if not relief, just restore Order. A Freudian might then elaborate the insecurity as an incipient negative therapeutic reaction: the analysand feels anxious or insecure because unconsciously she has committed, believes she will commit, and/or desires to commit a wrong so grievous that she (would) no longer deserve(s) healing, indeed any respect whatsoever, and is unconsciously seeking therapy as a painful scene of punishment (which would make it anxiety-enhancing). Perhaps she is thereby seeking to restore the balance of the world, to let justice reign, i.e., is in the grip of a narcissistic sacrifice/salvation fantasy; perhaps she is seeking to prevent such a terrible misdeed by subjecting herself to a brutal exposure of her dark deeds or desires; or perhaps she is seeking absolution for her (future) sins via a rigorous confessional practice. Of course, she also may be seeking therapy in order to divest from the framework of retributive, malicious justice — and giving up that framework and the possibilities for expiating self-sacrifice, thus for unqualified Justice and whatever is associated with it, that it affords may be anxiety inducing. Further, perhaps, part of her defense against acknowledging her (fantasmatic, empirical, anticipated, and/or desired) wrongdoing and what it means to her is a pervasive and indefinite sense of anxiety now localized and somewhat relieved in therapy or a newly emergent, diffuse yet severe anxiety in therapy. Perhaps a nebulous cloud of anxiety functions as a defense against specific anxieties and vice versa. Or perhaps anxiety issuing from other sources has become recruited into such a defense.

Or a Freudian might understand the phenomenon as follows: The analysand either generally or perhaps only upon entering analysis is overburdened by powerful erotic and aggressive wishes. These wishes may immediately trigger repression, thus anxiety.[14] In any case, these wishes are overburdening because the analysand's psychic apparatus is relatively immature, consequently intense wishes threaten subjective collapse — depersonalization or destructuration; and/or their intensity, content, associated ideas and/or the intensity thereof, and/or fantasmatic framing rebuff the privileged (highly invested) self- and world-interpretations of the analysand, rendering such wishes unavowable on pain of extreme dissociation, loss of self and world — perhaps such wishes are unmoored from their object-sources and become magnified to frightening dimensions as they are integrated with, say, wishes the gratifications of which are anticipated to be, however pleasurable, massively unpleasurable. Hence, although these wishes, if extant outside of the field of analysis, are ordinarily defused by defenses, the therapeutic framework (including the impulse of the analysand to confront elements of herself that are otherwise staved off, the non-participation of the analyst in typical defenses, the inability to discharge anxiety or distract oneself through physical movement, etc.) renders these defenses unavailable or of limited efficacy, so the wishes and perhaps whatever is associated with them resurge, are experienced as painfully dissonant, dangerous, or overwhelming, and thus give rise to repression and so to anxiety or are deemed inadmissible by the superego (prohibited) and/or ego (unintelligible or dangerous) and thus give rise to (super)ego syntonic signal anxiety[15] or are converted into anxiety consequent upon prohibition of their discharge or induce an anxiety generating struggle with the (super)ego, etc. Perhaps these intense wishes (and their correlates) are transferred onto the analytic field, enacted in relationship to the analyst — repeated rather than remembered — as a last ditch defense; transference at least renders them intelligible/ego-syntonic ("it is the analyst who is causing this distress") and so presumably manageable ("if it is the analyst who is causing this distress, my dealings with her can resolve it"), and/or disguised, thus placating the superego — transferred onto the analytic field, such wishes are defensively distorted (the issue is with the analyst, and not with so and so figure and/or situation from the past), and thereby, perhaps, a highly cathected and unavowable image of their original source(s) and so of oneself is preserved. Or perhaps the wishes etc. are transferred onto the analytic field at the behest of a self-healing propensity — they rush to the fore *so that* they can be dealt with otherwise than in the ways that have been developed heretofore, ways that cannot have been extraordinarily successful given that, presumably, their failure has in part motivated the individual's entry into analysis — yet nonetheless trigger repression, thus anxiety, or conduce to the suffusion of the analytic scene with signal anxieties. Unprepared to acknowledge, let alone renegotiate their relationship with the primary source(s) of these wishes and affects, the relationships with others that have been conditioned by and so in part sustain the defenses to which these wishes and affects contribute, the ideational contents and so forth associated with these wishes and affects and what they imply for the individual's self-image, and so forth, the analysand, when subject to the resurgence of wishes that generate or anticipate significant unpleasure, repress the ideational content of the wishes and transfer the charge elsewhere (divestment of one content corresponds to intensified investment of another, e.g., what appears as an intense erotic wish is dissimulated aggression or vice versa), and/or convert the affects associated with the wishes into a dischargeable form, i.e., anxiety. Further, since repression is highly permeable, signal-anxieties may develop, and since the wishes, etc. are now associated with the analyst and/or the therapeutic context, signal anxiety suffuses the therapeutic scene (in Freud's revised theory of anxiety, anxiety triggers repression). And if repression (also) generates anxiety, the ability of the therapeutic context to release the repressed may, especially in early stages of analysis, lead to repeated efforts of repression, thus to enhanced anxiety.

All of these are possible Freudian interpretations of an analysand awash with anxiety in early stages of analysis.[16] But a Freudian would not say that "unconscious association with a previous unfortunate medical event" explains repression and consequently the massive anxiety or independently explains the anxiety.[17] Such an association may be a component of a much more elaborate scheme, but on its own, such an association is by no means a Freudian explanation. Indeed, Freudianism constitutes itself through excluding what are, from its perspective, local and superficial explanations of this sort.

Further, to impute the claim that "the patient's expectable feelings of security with the doctor are . . . repressed at the beginning of therapy because of . . . [the pain coextensive with] unconscious association with a previous unfortunate medical event" to Freudians is to profoundly misunderstand the Freudian theory of repression. Within the Freudian tradition, repression does not automatically result from pain — if it did, we would be stark raving mad, psychotic one and all.[18] Rather, for Freud, repression is the repression of images, ideas, or memory-traces (ideational representatives) connected with drives the gratifications of which are anticipated to be both pleasurable and extremely, indeed unbearably unpleasurable. Repression ensues when the anticipation of unbearable unpleasure overwhelms the desirability of pursuing the drive's satisfaction. For Freud, repression is never the repression of affect, e.g., pain, thus cannot have as its object the pain coextensive with a "previous unfortunate medical event."[19] Even though many contemporary Freudians admit the repression of affect as well as ideational content, they still would not claim that pain alone triggers repression, much less the presumably mild pain associated with "an unfortunate medical event." In the Freudian tradition, it is always *this* quantity and/or quality of pain that cannot be borne by *this* individual due to her particular constitution and psychic makeup that triggers repression and other defenses — of course, some levels and probably some types of pain cannot be borne by anyone, and so some generalities obtain — thus "unconscious association with a previous unfortunate medical event" *on its own* is no explanation.

Hamilton's framing of the differences between Freudian and object relationist understandings of insecurity in early stages of analysis is either flatly wrong on at least one point or extremely convoluted, as is *very* often the case when pundits of one school present the views of another. Although perspective involves inflation and deflation, exaggeration and distortion, this need not assume the form of simplistic and falsifying depictions of contrary views. It may be difficult to define the difference between (1) revealing the inflations and deflations, exaggerations and distortions of various schools or particular interpretative dispositions by setting them into dialogue and (2) mutual caricaturing, but it is not hard to identify. And on this difference a great deal hinges — call it the opening of the world. Damage to the image of the other may be, simultaneously, damage to one's self-image, perhaps a form of self-loss, *if that image comes into relief, indeed comes into its truth, in dialectical tension with competing views.*

PERSPECTIVE AND DIALECTIC

If one propounds a doctrine, a systematically integrated, comprehensive explanation of the phenomena with which one is concerned, then questions concerning the relation(s) of this doctrine to other possible doctrines dealing with the same phenomena may not be of much interest, indeed may not even arise. If one's doctrine satisfactorily explains every aspect of the phenomena under consideration, seamlessly integrates the phenomena into discrete and systematically integrated formulas, and provides ample illumination, relevant practical orientation, and adequate, continually verified predictions, then even if other doctrinal elaborations of the phenomena with which one is concerned are possible — e.g., due to the perhaps inevitable underdetermination of theory by evidence[20] and/or the reflexive underdetermination of doctrinal content by efforts to achieve doctrinal self-consciousness[21] — the *meaning* of one's doctrine will not be dependent upon them; nothing internal to the doctrine presses for a consideration of alternatives. Doctrines can be challenged by data that exceed their comprehension and disproved by falsifying evidence. They may become immanently unsatisfying or they may simply fall out of service when the questions to which they respond are no longer pressing. But their meanings qua doctrines are not necessarily dependent on their distinctiveness from competing views. (Or at least such is their ideology.) If, however, object relations theory is not a doctrine in this sense, if it is a perspective, or more precisely, a heterogeneous series of partially overlapping perspectives, if it is a novel series of developments, of compelling contestations, within the psychoanalytic tradition rather than a self-sufficient monad, if it is rightly understood as supplementing rather than supplanting standing psychoanalytic theories and practices, i.e., if its rational authority is sourced in the guidance it provides for particular patient populations and/or its compelling capacity to foreground significant features of all patients that would be otherwise neglected or insufficiently appreciated and introduce ways of productively responding to them, then its significance, its meaning and import, will only emerge in dialogical tension with co-contenders to the mantle of psychoanalytic (or more broadly, psychotherapeutic) prominence. Psychoanalysis is and must be pluralistic.

If the distinctiveness, the concrete meaning and compelling character, — of a psychoanalytic perspective is recognizable, thus actual, only against the backdrop of alternatives,[22] if its significance — meaning and meaningfulness — is a function of its implicit and/or explicit citation and negation or emendation of alternative perspectives, if its meaning, its specificity as a perspective, is achieved by and to the extent that it maintains itself — takes a stand — amidst other perspectives, then a psychoanalytic perspective appears in its ownmost specificity, comes into its truth, only when and to the extent that it is maintained in dialectical tension with real competitors rather than false foils, only when "in the mix." The truths delivered by a psychoanalytic perspective are those of a historical discourse of suffering and healing/transformation under conditions of modernity rather than those of a metaphysical discourse of universal truth. The rational authority of psychoanalysis is resolutely historical.

Dialectical tension here names a process through which perspectives disclose themselves through mutual mediation, come into view in relation to one another as exaggerations, as interest-mediated complexions of blindness and insight, as inflated elaborations of various foci, which is to say, as nourished by their rootedness in a finite — embodied and historical — stance, or more precisely, as composed by the history-suffused metabolism of perceptual disposition, desire, imagination, reflection, and phenomena. Perspective is inflation, as inescapable and ordinarily unnoticed as breathing: first — if we can speak of a first moment — a selective, thus "informed" drawing in of phenomena, of what is there to give itself (inhalation), then a testing and refining or (re)processing (metabolism), finally a giving back to phenomena an inflection or cast (exhalation) that is not simply imposed but rather responsive to the experiential/phenomenal specificity, conceptual possibilities, and lasting indeterminacy of that which is there to be given/taken . . . and once more a drawing in . . . Perspective proceeds according to the structures of care — the "prejudices," sensibilities, concerns and interests — that organize and orient attention and reflection and are subject to transformation in the course of this metabolic interaction. Yet while breathing transpires in relative solitude, a perspective necessarily unfolds in the company of others. Thinking is a public affair, always in dialogue with other perspectives.[23]

Akin to the content of speech-acts, the meaning of a perspective is constituted by its (often implicit) repetition or re-citation of an inherited code and invocation of a concomitant set of enabling constraints — i.e., conditions of warranted assertability, broadly understood — that are to some extent negated by means of the novel inflection, contextualization, and development that the perspective (or speech-act) *is*. A perspective is intelligible, has content, only insofar as it is identifiable as a redeployment of a reiterable code, a reactivation of a precedent, thus as a recognizably distinct development of traditionally transmitted orientations vis-à-vis phenomena of collective concern. Whether and to what extent a perspective accrues authority, then, depends in part on whether and to what extent such novel inflections, contextualization, and development can be seen as a regeneration of tradition rather than a spontaneous posit, a willful self-assertion merely cloaked in the language of convention. Like a felicitous speech-act with respect to signs, a perspective develops by releasing and reclaiming phenomena from traditional forms of unintelligibility, by means of their placement in unanticipated yet in certain ways analogous contexts that allow them to resonate and signify otherwise. A perspective, like a speech-act, draws on and releases phenomena from — without simply forgetting or denying — established horizons of meaning; it releases phenomena from their traditional contexts of intelligibility *by* provisioning a new context in which they are re-presented otherwise, re-elaborated. And thereby, a perspective testifies to the irreducibility of phenomena to their sedimented contextual determinations, thus to its own provisionality. A sign must be subject to indefinite recontextualization, thus inherently liable to alterations of meaning, in order to sustain its iterability as a sign, its identifiability as the sign it is taken to be. A perspective must wrest phenomena from established forms of attention and orientation, thus (even if only implicitly) preserve these forms as a lasting backdrop, in order to attain its distinctiveness and sustain its provisional truth. A condition for individuation of both signs and perspectives is a want of sovereignty. The life of signs, like the life of perspectives, is a matter of generativity, not simple intentional production — a matter of generation and regeneration, thus of death and struggles for inheritance.

The dialectical interplay of perspectives *enfolded in the (virtual) presentation of a particular perspective* implies that a perspective unfolds in truth only when manifest as a claimant within a horizon of alternatives, a genuine field of plurality. The presentation of a perspective as a perspective thus achieves precision — truthfulness — by preventing an invariably partial and exaggerated orientation from appearing as the whole — from dominating the scene of inquiry and concealing the alternatives alongside which it takes a stand. Consequently, a perspective in truth depends on *viable* alternatives. The truth of a perspective is maintained, in part, through the explication of its partiality or provisionality and through the mediation of compelling alternatives. A perspective sustains itself as a perspective, maintains its truthfulness, only against the manifest backdrop of other ways in which the phenomena may give themselves, may be gathered, metabolized, cohere and orient otherwise. Thus a perspective in truth is set against itself, dialectically constituted: it must at once compellingly elaborate phenomena from its point of view and acknowledge the perhaps indefinite capacity of the phenomena with which it is concerned to become and appear otherwise. Which means that it must assert itself while acknowledging the compelling yet immanently contested character of other perspectives — must internalize skepticism as an exappropriating principle. Rigor with regard to perspective is a matter of sustained attentiveness to the concrete texture of determinacy and indeterminacy of the phenomena under consideration, thus to the ever-questionable quality of one's presentation.

Perspectives sustain themselves as such, attain to truthfulness, by manifestly remaining in dialectical tension with one another, incorporating this tension in the principle(s) of their development, and thereby allowing this tension to suffuse and mobilize the scene of inquiry, thus freeing phenomena for further elaborations, i.e., acknowledging the inherence of futurity and therewith their morality as best they can, and attesting to their dependence on the freedom of others. The tension with other views embodied by a perspective is its very life-blood, what allows it to maintain its focus, to organize the structures of its concernful attention, and remain responsive to a field of phenomena irreducible to its selective presentation, to this or that perspectival elaboration, thus responsive to the endless demands of freedom. Perspective gathers-in while releasing, letting-be; concretely and compellingly elucidates while allowing the mystery and opacity — the inherent excess — of phenomena to remain. Or more precisely, perspective becomes truthful in so doing *if and insofar as* the phenomena under concern, perhaps phenomena generally, are not simply identical with any determinate conceptualization but rather are a panoply that can be perspectivally unfolded and acknowledged in many ways. That is, if, as Aristotle suggests, being is said in many ways.

Although necessarily exaggerated and tending toward totalization — i.e., pretense — perspective bears, indeed is constituted by, respect for viable alternatives: self-limitation is a condition for authentic self-assertion. And by means of its inherent respect for others, a perspective bears respect for the propensity of phenomena to indefinitely manifest otherwise, for the inexhaustible richness and overfullness of phenomena, their excessiveness with respect to focalized presentation. Perspective embodies respect, is constituted by the space it preserves for others — an inherent negativity; immanent dissensus and dissuasion — thus by its openness to the unforeseen. Dialectically mobilized, perspective at once tends toward totalization and sustains space for otherness, allowing the world to abide in its exquisite and inexhaustible shareablility. Dialectical tension thus names a certain character, comportment, or bearing, an *ethos* of perspective. To think perspective is to think the interimplication of ontology, ethics, and epistemology.

Perspective involves a double bearing, a double imperative, thus an ineradicable tension: the urge to expansiveness or comprehensiveness is met and limited by implicit demands for hesitation and self-constriction; the urge to self-conscious self-restriction is challenged by the impulse to elaboration, by an unavoidable animating enthusiasm. Perspective *indeed* — for perspective, though by no means reducible to a subject, let alone volition, is a certain doing, the activity of metabolism, of mediating alterity — involves a certain ethical bearing: desire and aptitude for abiding in the dialectical tension, always on the verge of collapsing, without which perspective becomes pretense, self-dissimulating, doctrinaire, or haphazard opining — disclaiming its bonds to phenomenality and others, becoming uncommitted.

Dialectically elaborated thought is thought-in-motion, thinking-on-the-way (*meta ta hodon*), thought that maintains fidelity to itself insofar as it sustains and manifests itself as a movement from out of a certain rootedness (embodied stance, tradition, interlocutory scene) on the way to certain ends, both known and unknown, and always in view of alternative perspectives. Dialectical thought is implacably intermediate and interested. In virtue of the dialectical — expositive, relational, and open-ended — character of perspective, what it brings into view exceeds the terms of its disclosure, i.e., emerges as necessarily contorted. What becomes available by means of a perspective is mediated — implicitly measured — by other perspectives *as mediated* by this perspective, thus as constitutively off-kilter, suffering inherent dislocations, subject to an unrelieved errancy. Perspective is endlessly impure; its reflexivity is restless, thus its consolidation indefinitely deferred — and on account of its hyperbolic reflexivity, it is far from simply self-absorbed but rather expresses its bonds to or respect for phenomenality and others.

Dialectically mobilized, perspective strives for distinction yet — or rather precisely on account of this — always finds itself beside itself, in view of and in dialogue with an extimate other (or several). Constitutively unsettled, non-identical with itself, perspective develops questionably, precariously, unable to sovereignly take its own measure, yet compellingly, through the mutually implicated and ongoing creation/discovery of competing views and the creation/discovery of its determinacy. Inceptively emerging from disquieting discontent with received tradition, a perspective is initially formed through (often implicitly) recasting — recontextualizing and thereby recreating/rediscovering the significance of — the questions, concerns, sensibilities, and strategies of those it thereby claims (and if successful, constitutes) as its predecessors and current interlocutors in light of its discontent and in view of an explanation thereof, and therewith begins to create/discover its distinctive questions, concerns, sensibilities, and strategies. Subsequently, its self-specifying self-elaboration proceeds via recurrent, however tacit, reference to the perceived inadequacies of its constitutive others — their impasses, limitations, and untapped latencies — that is, by means of the reworking of other perspectives into the animating principles of this perspective's development. Consequently, its constitutive others, remobilized in the effort to surpass them and bearing an incommensurable point of view that despite (or rather in virtue of) disagreement cannot but be in a certain way reauthorized, trouble the pretense of a perspective to self-sufficiency, become sources of ongoing demands to re-view the perspective into which they are recruited, which means to recreate/rediscover this perspective and therewith themselves. And conversely. Dialectically constituted, perspective is endlessly self-surpassing, overabundant thus inconsistent, a matter of unending generation and destruction, thus mimetically appropriate to the liveliness of phenomena. Attentive to blind spots in its predecessors' and interlocutors' perspectives and seeking to supplement them, a perspective develops by, e.g., illuminating what perhaps only by its lights can be seen as heretofore murky matters and/or pursuing what can only now be seen as unrealized potential, yet cannot stop, indeed its truth requires, its elucidations and/or pursuits to become subject to critical scrutiny by (what it sees as) the perspective in need of supplementation, i.e., requires recreation/rediscovery by what it constitutively excludes. A perspective will hardly accede to such a measure, but by remaining exposed to it, it expresses its blindness to the extent possible, which is to say, imperfectly because always, in a way, from its own point of view — and so sustains its truth as a perspective. When practiced with tact rather than vituperative pathos, mutual pathologization is a dialectical virtue. The dialectic of perspective(s) is as much akin to maieutics as it is to epistemology.

Thus we ought not rest content with simplistic, summarily dismissive and self-aggrandizing depictions of contrary views if the viability of alternatives feeds the dialectical tension, the life-force, of our own perspectives. If the development and presentation of a perspective involves the citation and negation of alternatives, then, although strong misreadings may suffice, there is at least *prima facie* reason to pursue rigorous engagements with competing views. Given that the quality of citation — e.g., the deft discerning of what is said and what is at stake; of what is clarified, what foreclosed, and what faintly resounds; of what is intended and what provokes, unsettles, contorts, eludes, or marginally appears in the course of what is said; of the questions implicitly responded to and contexts assumed; of the constituting elements (sensitivities, sources of enthusiasm, axioms, anxieties, etc.) of the discourse and the constitutively or contingently excluded — may determine what can be said by way of negation, i.e., the quality of one's saying-otherwise; the demand to engage seriously and sensitively with alternatives emerges from the authority of one's own perspective and is not easily overridden. To fail to heed the richness, the compelling insights, the distortions and perplexities, the impasses, and even the madness of what resides in alternative accounts may dull the critical inheritance by means of which one's perspective is constituted. Damage to the image of the other by way of neglect or distortion is simultaneously damage to one's self-image if that image comes into dialectical relief within a field of genuine plurality. Without genuine competitors — which again *may* be (retroactive) fabrications, but if successful, not simply ornamental foils — dialectical tension diminishes, the space of thinking constricts and its animus may wither and fade, the points of contrast against which one's views come into focus becomes hazy, and so one's perspective will inflate into a caricature or atrophy into a doctrine, i.e., falsify itself. Diminishment of the other is at once self-diminishment.

Psychoanalytic "schools" such as the object relations perspective Hamilton is advancing are neither privileged conduits of truth nor elements of a systematic, all-encompassing theory that would deliver the whole truth. "The whole is the untrue." (Adorno 1974, 50; trans. modified). What can be gleaned from each "school" aside from its distinctive insights, hermeneutic strategies, and elucidations of health and suffering is a lesson concerning our strange situation: ineluctably between ignorance and wisdom,[24] blinded by our insight, exaggerating for the sake of truth, marginalizing in the name of justice. Each psychoanalytic perspective suggests, for it can never fully demonstrate, a single piece of wisdom about the human condition: that we are irrevocable intermediate, living at or as the interval, dialectically mobilized.[25] Between ignorance and wisdom, we are learners one and all, striving to catch up with our own best insights and constitutive commitments.[26]

INSIDE OUT

In opposition to Freudian explanation(s), the object relations purview maintains that it is not repression and its vicissitudes that accounts for the insecurity. Repression is a primary feature of psychic life dominated by conflict,[27] and the Freudian focus on conflict — both the axiom of its ineradicability and the weight placed on it in theories of pathology and technique — marks a point of divergence between Freudians and many object relationists.[28] This is emphatically the case for D.W. Winnicott and the British Middle Group, for whom conflict is a developmental achievement and of comparatively limited significance, and to a lesser extent for object relationists influenced by American ego psychology such as Kernberg and Kohut. In Hamilton's presentation of the object relations perspective, insecurity in early stages of analysis hinges on two factors: one developmental/environmental and one quasi-structural. With regard to the former, like behaviorists, object relationists stress the importance of conditioning, but unlike behaviorists, they would be prone to not attribute the insecurity to thematically related events in adolescent or adult life, e.g., "unfortunate" experiences with medical practitioners or the trauma of previous illness (or at least not just to these). Rather, the possibilities of conditioning in adolescent or adult life are considered to be themselves profoundly conditioned by what transpires in emotionally supercharged infantile and early childhood relationships with primary caregivers, or what Winnicott calls the facilitating environment.[29] Patterns of relationality are established and entrenched in early life, as are relationally conditioned stress points, and these significantly influence the course of later development. More specifically, for certain object relationists, early relational forms become paradigms upon which later relations are modeled, preferred relational configurations that are repeatedly sought, or sources of significant and lasting distress that motivate compensatory forms of life.

For instance, to account for a child's pleasure-seeking behavior, an object relationist would emphasize not an innate drive for gratification or tension reduction — these may be conceded but are not stressed — but rather that early infant-caregiver relations were routinely organized as exchanges of pleasure or were insufficiently pleasurable or otherwise so distressing as to motivate monofocal pleasure-seeking as a privileged compensatory strategy, perhaps a medium of minimal subjective consistency.[30] The focus is not on the pleasure — as an intrinsic good, as functionally/evolutionarily significant, or as an indication of the preeminence of the pleasure principle — but on the relational form or on the signal of relational crisis. If the infant-caretaker relationship is not predominantly or consistently pleasure oriented, according to certain object relationists, the child may accept and later reproduce whatever relational patterns prevail rather than abandon the bond[31] or latch onto pleasure-seeking in order to organize a life left in shambles. Some suggest that children will even identify with pathological characteristics of their caregivers in order to secure connection: connection is compulsion, an ineluctable good — even when an opening onto the worst. Early relationships with caretakers are so significant, certain object relationists claim, that parental imagos, privileged forms of relationship to them, and self- and world-conceptions mediated and elaborated by these relationships manifest an extraordinary resiliency. Generally, from the object relations purview, *the need for relation is a prime mover of psychic life and meaningful relation a primary goal.*

Against Freud's emphasis on libido as plastic and primarily discharge-seeking — of course there are exceptions, e.g., his discussion of melancholia,[32] but regularly on Freud's account, those facilitating discharge seem eminently interchangeable, mere occasions for drive discharge rather than significant others with whom one could be in intrinsically meaningful and valuable relationships — object relationists stress the adhesiveness of libido, its attachment to specific objects and relationships from the get-go, and its functioning as a medium of meaning. This pattern of emphasis might be understood as a radicalization of Freud's contention that finding an object is always a refinding:[33] it is not only traces of the object or of the libidinal satisfactions it first facilitates that are rediscovered in an infinite array of substitutes, but (also) form(s) of connection with the object, lasting bonds to the self- and world schematizations they mediate. For Freudians, development occurs as discharge is frustrated and the demands of reality are consequently accommodated (the reality principle is a fate, even a species, of the pleasure principle), while pathology arises from excessive libidinal frustration (which yields compromise formations — symptoms, somaticizations, inhibitions, etc.) or excessive gratification (which yields difficulty with impulse control). For object relationists such as Winnicott and Kohut, (one might also think of Mahler, Masterson, Guntrip, and Jacobson) a *drive for development* will unfold if provided a context of competent handling, holding, and provisioning, including provisioning for relational needs,[34] while pathology results from inadequate environmental/parental provisioning, holding, and handling. Or at least these are the patterns of emphasis characteristic of Freudians and object relationists, respectively. In contrast to Freudians, object relationists stress that objects are not merely soldered onto drives and that the psyche is not primarily governed by the pleasure-unpleasure principle (seeking a certain quantity and/or consistent level of excitation); rather, they maintain, relationships are relatively autonomous goods, compelling irrespective of their impact on tension regulation: continuity and quality of relation are the commanding impulses.[35]

To give the point about development and pathology a more Kleinian accent: via the projection of internal object relations, potentially new experiences are ciphered through old expectations, schematized such that the developmental gains they augur, say, opportunities for individuation and self-actualization, are squandered.

The central point in this context is that if early relationships are not conducted such as to be permeated by a basic sense of security — a sense of trust in the amenability of others/the world to one's needs and desires, to one's developmentally appropriate flourishing — later relationships, whatever their objective qualities, will be suffused with insecurity. Thus, a patient may become profoundly insecure or perhaps depressed in early stages of analysis if, in the context of early rearing, an ordinary, reliable, good-enough caregiver egregiously failed or due to environmental circumstances could not provide adequately, suddenly dissolving the prevailing sense of security and thereby instituting confusion and provoking unbearable aggressivity. From then on, a generalized insecurity may prevail, or perhaps, convinced to her core that if a good person turns up, s/he will soon enough, though at some unexpected point, disappoint radically, reactivate confusion, and be hated, which is unbearable, the infant becomes deeply depressed (Winnicott 1996 [1971], 125-7); or perhaps prior to or oscillating with that depression, profoundly insecure — waiting for the other shoe to drop. The very promise of analysis may be at the root of the insecurity.[36] In Hamilton's concise phrasing, "[a] secure feeling is absent because . . . the patient had never been provided a good-enough holding environment to feel secure" (xviii).

While this account accords with the behaviorist view that the patient suffers from associational fixation, an inability to learn to live otherwise, for object relationists, reconditioning will alter this dire situation only if, contra behaviorists, by "reconditioning" one means facilitated regression to a condition of extreme depression or point of developmental arrest, which is sustained for quite some time and thereby allows the individual to experience unmet needs as unmet — and the complex of affects, ideas, impulses, fantasies, dispositions, etc. associated with these needs and their inadequate provisioning — in the context of their being met reliably, however minimally, by a therapist. Neither behaviorism nor object relations theory assumes a fundamentally conflicted psyche or ineradicable tendencies to self- and world-distortion and -evasion;[37] and both give therapeutic priority to the accomplishment of individuation through creative adaptation to the environment. However, unlike behaviorists, object relationists stress that prospects for reconditioning are severely constrained by the weight of the past, specifically, by the relational/character dispositions arising from the attainment or failure to attain good-enough holding and handling.

While a Freudian analysis might privilege questions of desire and ambivalence and so focus on the (dis)satisfactions resulting from the repetitive, (quasi-)compulsive pursuit of and fantasmatic elaboration of conflicted desires — e.g., an Oedipus complex — and the disavowals, anxieties, and compromises that follow in their wake, object relations analyses tend to focus on (1) the repetitive — and not necessarily pathogenic — pursuit of relational configurations and maintenance of meaningful bonds, which are assumed to be compelling irrespective of, or not primarily on account of, the libidinal satisfactions they yield or their contributions to the maintenance of the pleasure principle, and (2) the pathogenic consequences of relational crisis. Contra Freudians' sexualized suspicion, many object relationists maintain that intimacy, mutual understanding, and various other forms of connectedness are sought after for their own sake. Consider Winnicott's claim that "Id relationships are only meaningful to the infant if they happen in a framework of Ego-relatedness," by which he means meaningful connection without which desire will be experienced as assault (cited in Phillips 1989, 100). The focus is on meaningful bonds, and Oedipal impulses are framed as contingent consequences of their breakdown; the intimation seems to be that Oedipal aggressivity is ultimately a strategy for sustaining bonds under duress.

On the object relations view, relational patterns first established with primary caregivers or in response to their failures cannot be easily abandoned or readily revised in part because, on their revised understanding of libido, libido (or, for Winnicott, the "True Self") not only aims at connection with others (libido as Eros), but tends to adhere to relational patterns first established in a state of radical dependency (libido as conservative, participating in the nature of the death drive).[38] Within an object relations analysis, pathogenic relational patterns are the primary focus and may be understood as reenacting a state of developmental arrest — say, a traumatic experience of the world becoming suddenly unreliable, unamenable to the individual's flourishing, thus awash with anxiety — and so provides clues about what needs would have to be met for the reinitiation of development and, ultimately, the pursuit of creative individuation, i.e., some measure of spontaneity. The basic point about pathology is that when needs are not met due to environmental deprivations or inadequate caregiving, pervasive insecurity may arise. This insecurity may manifest directly or be deflected through hyperbolic narcissism: mutually entwined disavowals of dependency and denials of insecurity that feed a fantasy of isolated and insulated autonomy that yet can never be comfortably inhabited — incessantly attempting to secure an inviolable, quasi-omnipotent autonomy, such narcissism proves unsatisfying, and not just because of the inevitable faltering of its delusional program. In either case, the individual will be prone to feel unreal or inauthentic, not quite alive, fundamentally inhibited, stagnating, unable to tap her creativity or spontaneity. A fear of breakdown or devitalization prevails — a somatic memory of developmental crisis.

From the object relations perspective, both behaviorists and Freudians are asking the wrong questions because they are preoccupied with peripheral effects of relational compulsions and their developmental matrix.[39] They can't see the forest through the trees; the insecurity reelaborates, perhaps is a way of holding onto, a relationship in distress. If a good-enough holding environment does not obtain, insecurity is near inevitable and will likely be amplified in situations such as analysis where typical defenses are, or are expected (fantasized) to be, rendered impracticable. Anxiety is pervasive in early analysis because the analyst is assimilated to anticipations of inadequate holding;[40] contra behaviorists, attempted *disengagement* rather than different forms of relationship will be the consequence of difficulties assimilating the present to the purview of the past. Thus, object relations theory affirms that it is "because . . . the patient had never been [or was not consistently enough] provided a good-enough holding environment to feel secure" that a pervasive mood of insecurity manifests, as elsewhere, in the early stages of therapy. Even if insecurity in early analysis generally or in some particular case cannot be fully explained or is not best explained by reference to the faltering of a holding environment and consequent implantation of a core sense of oneself as unsupported and ill-cared for, perhaps not capable of being well-supported and cared for, in part, what makes object relations theory distinctive is its insistence on this dimension. Even if only as an exacerbating factor, object relations theory would insist that it still requires attention. Certain categorical commitments, thus temptations to pathologize and subsume other perspectives, cannot be dislodged; perspective is constitutively exaggerated even when fair handed.

The object relations account would stress that the insecurity in early stages of analysis is one amongst many manifestations of a basic sense of insecurity issuing from inadequate provisioning of a good-enough holding environment. Making sense of that commitment requires an elaboration of the notion of a good-enough holding environment. A good-enough holding environment means, basically, the modulated provisioning of care and support sufficient (i.e., at the right time and to the appropriate extent) for successful psychosomatic development, meaningful connection, and eventually individuation, e.g., availability to connection without impingement and allowance for separation without abandonment. More precisely, it refers to the felicitous caregiving of those who, first, impart — or for Winnicott, augment and sustain — a sense of wholeness and integrity — a sense of selfhood — to an infant who would otherwise experience herself as either (1) ambiently diffuse, primarily in a state of "going-on-being," which is the minimal substratum out of which or backdrop against which experientially unconnected — or at least relatively unconnected; proto-conceptual — feeling-states (what "for us" are and "*for* one" will be needs, impressions, and desires) emerge and back into which the infant fades if its needs are adequately met (this is Winnicott's picture of the average infant) or (2) fractured by the pulsations of drives, enveloped in a proto-world shrouded in phantasy, inundated by a barrage of unstable and often invasive and persecutory images and sensations, anxiety ridden, sensorially and affectively overwhelmed — overburdened by stimulation from within and without — rent by the upsurge of need, desire, and frustration, and so pulsing and convulsing, unsettled, staggering along, wanting for the securing/stabilizing pace of a primary, integral rhythm — generally, disintegrated or disintegrating rather than unintegrated (this is closer to Klein's and Bion's picture of the average infant). Good-enough holding and handling is initially the relational conduct by means of which self-relation is instilled or the necessary minimum of subjective consistency is established — and originary prosthesis.[41]

Radically exposed, absolutely vulnerable, their access to pleasure and avoidance of pain predominantly mediated by the ministrations of their primary caregivers, entirely dependent on their caregivers' affectionate concern for the consolidation of meaningful bonds (for significant alterity, the emergence of a meaningful world), and subject to overwhelming affective states the far side of which — absent consistent care — cannot even come into view, infants are bound to experience their caregivers as absolutely important — the essential.[42] On the condition of such hyperinvestment, the good-enough primary caretakers' behaviorally evident images of the infant — e.g., as vulnerable but capable of healing, as fragile but enveloped in protective care, as needy but whose needs can be adequately if imperfectly met, as whole if incomplete, as capable of abiding the sensuous peaks of pleasure and pain and of bearing through their sometimes uncertain rhythms, as able to bear and contain tension and anxiety, as capable of self-soothing, as connected rather than abandoned, as a source of pleasure and value; eventually, as able to survive parental dissatisfactions, as someone whose reparative gestures are welcome, and as on her way to a more satisfying and self-actualizing future — will become captivating, privileged and idealized self-images that the infant assumes and aspires to. Such images cannot but be trusted. Although reliably adequate holding, handling, and facilitating contribute to more sophisticated modalities of trust in oneself and others, the consolidation of a world hospitable to self-realization, there is from the beginning an absolute, nonoptional entrustedness: *being-in-trust*. *For want of connection and meaning, the infant assumes, indeed cannot but assume*, images of herself and her relational significance conveyed through the comportment of her caregivers. Meaning and connection can be had here in no other way. Mimesis is a medium of transubstantiation, perhaps prior to the possibility of desire.[43]

On Winnicott's view — also, with qualifications, on the view of other British Middle Group object relationists such as Masud Khan, Charles Rycroft, Peter Lomas, Marion Milner, and John Klauber — holding and handling good-enough to support development (more complex forms of self- and object-relation, i.e., advancing individuation) will involve, next, the ordinary madness of maternal reverie in which a caretaker (or caretakers) immediately and *almost* preemptively responds to the infant's hunger and other needs. This style of caregiving must last as long as the infant requires a sense of omnipotence and omnipresence, i.e., would feel impinged upon and severely distressed if its ongoing "self-"absorption were interrupted. Failures here, Winnicott claims, result in suspended development. If its needs are not tended nearabout immediately and adequately, including its need for a sense of omnipotence and omnipresence, eventually the infant will either (1) withdraw under the weight of primitive agonies, withering and perhaps paradoxically becoming anesthetized by such agonies to the point of near-insentience or (2) become prone to extraordinarily superficial, however convincing, compliance as its primary form of connection with the world; integration and adjustment to the socio-symbolic order there will be, but with only a threadbare minimum of semiotic/affective investment. Such excessive, overcompliant integration bespeaks fundamental detachment and dissociation — what Winnicott calls a "false self." Hypervigilant attention and ongoing compliant adjustment to the emotional states of others — say, a depressed and withdrawn parent — will be the means by which one attempts to secure care for one's basic needs and preserve the possibility of development in a more nurturing environment; but this trades-off with developing a genuine self, which, for Winnicott, emerges from testing out need- and drive-interpretations and strategies for securing their satisfaction. (Winnicott more than most, and perhaps more than is plausible, stresses the genuine self as a discovery, the subject/object of a dawning awareness, but this need not detain us.)

Under optimal (normal[44]) conditions, eventually the primary maternal preoccupation supporting the infant's sense of omnipotence (e.g., creating the breast when hungry) and omnipresence (its "identification" with its world-as-good), and thereby its subjective investment of the world, fades into a responsive but not too responsive style of caregiving that facilitates the infant's learning to tolerate the strain of desire, frustration, and ambivalence, and to respond adaptively to its environment. With the waning of — or weaning from[45] — omnipotence/omnipresence, new, developmentally necessary forms of self- and world-relation become possible. The path to these is paved by caregivers' continual survival of onslaughts of aggression and ruthlessness, their acceptance and undergoing of such assaults without retaliation, collapse, or withdrawal. By not changing in any fundamental way when the infant expresses anger or fantasizes the caregiver's destruction — including such changes as assuming a stance of stoic imperviousness — the caregiver supports the consolidation of object-permanence and object-integrity: the first object is a subject.[46] In other words, the manifest survival of caregivers in the face of infantile fantasies of destructiveness, enactments of frustration, or ruthlessness evince their independence from the ambience of omnipotence/omnipresence, subtly disclosing the irreducibility of the world to the fancy of the infant and thereby introducing the possibility of significant otherness. Their non-destruction, repeatedly experienced, sets a reassuring limit to fantasy. Even when the infant is consumed by rage and fantasizes omnidevouring destruction, the object is still there, satisfying and connected. The dialectic of fate is suspended: destruction of the other (in fantasy) does not entail self-destruction. Creativity, which Winnicott associates with aggressiveness, spontaneity, and complex forms of object relation, can be risked when objects endure. A real object can be loved as well as hated, appreciated as well as bemoaned.

Additionally, according to Winnicott, caregivers' survival, especially when imperfect, functions as a needed form of recognition. Refraining from withdrawal or various forms of retaliation is not always easy. Both inevitably and (if mild) fortuitously, some measure of frustration with the infant will be expressed. Expressing frustration in minor doses acknowledges the unacceptable in the infant, allowing it to feel *real.* If a real object is complex, a source of frustration and incitement to aggression as well as loving and lovable, so too must the infant be if real.

By allowing the infant to undergo moderate frustration, experience tension, ambiguity, and ambivalence, the care-giver facilitates the partial divestment of omnipotence, the grip of which is further loosened as the caretaker indulges the madness of quasi-omnipotent play with a transitional object and otherwise facilitates experiences of transitional phenomena. Transitional phenomena are experientially intermediate between subjective omnipotence or primary creativity — the world as created by the infant — and normative (objective and/or intersubjective) constraint — the world as what would be agreed upon as shared reality, what is "objectively perceived" and can stand up to reality-testing (Winnicott 1996 [1971], 2, 11). Experiences with transitional phenomena support a gradual, thus bearable, transition from primary in-differentiation (processive self-and-world differentiation/articulation with some schematic, conceptual or proto-conceptual consolidation but no Big Difference between self and other or inside and outside) to recognition of emphatic externality and significant otherness. Such phenomena lie "between the thumb and the teddy-bear, between the oral eroticism and the true object relationship, between primary creative activity and projection of what has been introjected, between primary unawareness of indebtedness and the acknowledgment of indebtedness" (1996 [1971], 2).

From the infant's perspective, "both these things are true [of the transitional object]: the infant created it and the world provided it. This is the continuation forward of the initial task which the ordinary mother enables her infant to undertake, when by a most delicate active adaptation she offers herself, perhaps her breast, a thousand times at the moment that the baby is ready to create something like the breast that she offers" (Winnicott 1950, 143-4).[47] Transitional phenomena are in a way pure phenomena because indeterminately hybrid: neither hallucinations nor yet objects (comprehended by scientific laws and preschematized through socially mediated regimes of intelligibility and interest), and sometimes simply things (asymbolic sensory presences). Transitional objects are special objects that, by means of the quiet grace of caregiving, need not abide by "the rules" slowly dawning on the infant. They are marked out as the objective sites of subjective discretion — primary property. They are objects that the infant is allowed to treat as if omnipotently when its sense of omnipotence is fading — anchors for primitive rapprochement and relieving mediators of regression (including regression to asymbolic states of "going-on-being" and its analogues), while at once sponsors of symbolism and facilitators of creativity, experimentation, and adaptation, thus bridges to reality. Transitional objects will be cuddled and loved, invested with warmth and comfort that they in turn provide when the consolations of the world are unavailing. They will also be mutilated, and by surviving, support a wavering recognition of abiding externality and significant alterity *within* the slowly dissolving (and sometimes startlingly challenged) horizon of infantile omnipotence. And they will be "toyed with": tested, squeezed, wondered over, dreamed with — the objective support of physical and fantastical inquiries. But they will also be enjoyed as brute things simply subject to sensory commerce, safe havens from the stress of meaning.

Although sometimes experienced as mere, undemanding things, transitional objects will be more frequently experienced as quasi-independent, alive, glowing with warmth and radiating solace, yet never a challenge to the infant's self-absorption, its receding, thus intensely important, sense of omnipotence. Transitional objects are experienced as "an *almost* inseparable part of the infant": somehow distinct yet hazily so, not altogether other yet not simply a product of the self; somehow alive (warm, glowing, caring, a source of effects in a manner unlike other objects) yet not self-moving; external, sturdy, consistent yet bound up with fantasy play, thus highly malleable (Winnicott 1996 [1971], 7; emphasis added). As such, they symbolize (or are the ground of symbolism — Winnicott is unclear and sometimes ambivalent about this[48]) part-objects such as the breast, and so provide solace by recalling the breast; they are quasi-external repositories of pleasurable memories that the infant can call upon to re-spark feelings of omnipotence, i.e., "recharge" feelings of powerfulness and importance sufficiently to support its various world-explorations (thus its initial discovery of finitude: of who it is both for others and for itself, of various internal and external constraints, and so on). Yet, crucially, transitional objects are not the breast; they are both similar to and different from the breast, i.e., *symbols*. Affording experiences of differentiation, schematizing and schematized by what they are not, e.g., the breast, transitional objects pave the way for acceptance of differentiation (similarities and differences) between and within self and other. Because they are steady sources of solace and encouragement, fostering both rejuvenating calm and wondrous enjoyment, they can facilitate toleration of multiplicity and ambiguity (which they both contain and signal the generality of), and so support early forms of reality-testing. From their initial differentiation reality radiates; their enjoyment transmutes into its acceptance and investment. Or from another angle, becoming more intensely invested than the mother of primary in-differentiation, the mother as breast/part-object that the infant "creates" when hungry, etc., transitional objects allow the infant to explore a proto-world, a space-time beyond caregivers' immediate ministrations, and create/discover what it can be within it. Thereby, transitional objects allow the infant to begin negotiating separateness and connectedness, the concomitant creation and discovery of individuation and worldliness.

The infant, partially abrogating its omnipotence so long as it can do what it will with its transitional object, which sometimes, and importantly, means doing nothing, just being there with it or knowing it is there, begins to play creatively with the world — the world which, like the transitional object, indeed emanating from it, is rich with possibilities, a scaffolding for imaginative play and site of ongoing discoveries. S/he begins to dream with the world and thereby embrace reality. So long as tensions and frustrations are alleviated and/or compensated by consistently adequate care or temporarily abolished by reversion to quasi-omnipotent play or simple sensory commerce with a transitional object, the creative play and interest initially focused on the transitional object remerges elsewhere; ideally, the world becomes a source of pleasure and site of increasingly complex play/discovery.

Transitional objects thus facilitate the transition from object relation to object-use. Object relation is fantasmatic, a projective schematization. As such, it is eventually unsatisfying and unsustainable, both internally limited and giving rise to a sense that one is not really "there," a feeling of being adrift in an ephemeral field of phantoms. The intrinsic dissatisfactions of object relation, perhaps amplified by the decrees of bourgeoning reality-testing, motivate a turn to partially frustrating but enormously pleasurable interactions with concrete objects and others, real beings interaction with whom or with which conveys a sense of mutual presence and whose qualitative complexity far outstrips what can be autonomously projected, thus affording new and exciting prospects for relational development and associated pleasures. Objects *used* are partially resistant to one's desires, but in their resistance they are most certainly *there* and confer a sense that one is *there* along with them. And though resistant to immediate understanding (i.e., fantasy), objects used are not in principle opaque; coming to terms with them will often afford intrinsic satisfactions and unlock further relational possibilities. Object use concomitantly releases — creates/discovers — both self and other. It is "only in being creative," that is, by creating/discovering new forms of object use "that the individual discovers the self" (Winnicott 1996 [1971], 54). Object-use means fantasizing *with* objects/others, fantasizing on *their* as yet indeterminate basis. It is a matter of dreaming well with objects, of play that elaborates the mutually implicated latencies of self and other, of creative adaptation supplanting simplistic subsumption. By putting reality into play, object-use releases possibilities for the mutual development of self and other. Ultimately, for Winnicott, dreaming and living are one (ibid., 31).

The transitional object is gradually divested as transitional phenomena spread out across various regions of existence. The transitional object is neither lost nor internalized but rather fades, dissolves as interest is dispersed elsewhere. It is not repressed or mourned but diffuses into the world at large, transubstantiates. This dispersal supports subjective investment in culture and friendship, developmentally necessary new editions of the holding environment. Conveyed by transitional phenomena to culture and friendship, arenas of intrigue rife with provocations to desire and fantasy, the child is induced to explore the world transmitted to her, the relations in which she finds herself and to which she finds herself attracted, and what these, and so she, can become through her initiative. Culture and friendship are necessary conduits to various forms of individuation; necessary supports for dialectics of creation and discovery, for the work of keeping inner and outer reality separated and connected. Let us note in passing that with regard to culture, Winnicott's focus is not on its value as sublimation or compensation for frustrations and renunciations as Freud's sometimes seems to be. Nor is he focused on its reparative value, as Klein frequently is. Rather, culture is for Winnicott predominantly a relatively stable support for development and individuation, an enabling constraint, and a ready resource for rejuvenation: a home for a developed subject who is also always a *sujet en procès*.

But of course, even if widely hospitable to desire, fantasy, and self-actualization, the constraints correlative to acculturation and friendship may feel abrasive, frustrating, even diminishing, or in any case difficult to abide, thus intermediate experiences, transitional experiences, specifically, the experience of play, will remain continually appealing. In play — whether children's play or play in the mode of art, religion, philosophy, imaginative living, or creative scientific work — a circumscribed sense of subjective omnipotence is indulged. Lost in play, the burden of connecting inner and outer reality slackens, the strain of reality-testing is relieved. When lost in play one is not swept up in delusion, merely projecting, thus simply subservient to internal and/or external nature, i.e., one's impulses and perhaps thereby their cultural mediators, but probing and pursuing latencies ordinarily overlooked, resonances regularly untapped or dampened, constellations normally concealed or unconstructed. Lost in play one does not autonomously overlay reality with the coordinates of fantasy but allows desire to disclose and intrigue; one desires seriously, dreams with the world. Play lights upon the world as com-pliant with desire, folded into its streams, and thereby interprets and concretizes it. Although due to the teleological animus of his writings Winnicott tends to gloss over this despite its developmental importance, play must involve moments of release from meaning and desire, moments of sensuous immanence providing relief (thus not entirely asymbolic) from all forms of normative striving.

Transitional phenomena support vitality, imaginative and creative living, a sense of reality as infused with indeterminacy, with possibilities for co-becoming with objects and others. If experiences with transitional objects and transitional phenomena are inadequately tendered, the consequences may be (1) coarse or artificially intense compliance with social forms from which one remains subjectively dissociated, thus extreme disorientation and insecurity within the social forms one inhabits, (2) lack of investment in even one's own pursuits and forms of life, generally, a propensity to simply go through the motions in a routinized, rigid manner, and/or (3) ensnarement in concretistic fantasy: fantasy that does not play upon experience, unlocking its prospects and exploring its mysteries, but is projected over a world devoid of interest or too distressing to bear — a self-insulating and perhaps painful effacement of significant otherness. Although Winnicott never says as much — this may be a cost of his deflation of dynamism in favor of developmental sequencing and horizontality generally — concretistic fantasy seems to involve the registration and repudiation of symbolic meaning(s), perhaps an attack on specific meanings or on symbolization or meaning as such, i.e., on possibility, indeterminacy or underdetermination, and/or the social supports and/or intrapsychic conditions of meaning (otherwise how would one explain its aggressive self-assertion, its unremitting rejection, thus discrimination, of what would destabilize or interrupt its smothering consolidation?), and so may issue in severe mental dysfunction, miseries of extreme alienation, severe depression, and/or a torrent of anti-depressive manias and paranoid counter-investments that seek to compensate for and conceal severe depression and alienation. And these may involve or generate profound disorientation, insecurity, or anxiety,[49] as may failures to meet developmental needs generally. Significant and lasting insecurities may result from failures of adequate holding and handling at every stage and developmental transition.

"A secure feeling is absent because . . . the patient had never been provided a good-enough holding environment to feel secure" — such a statement is so compressed and formalized as to border on aphorism. It is hardly a local, low-level claim but rather a cipher for complex commitments at the levels of developmental theory, theory of pathology, theory of health, and hermeneutics. Its intelligibility depends on *that much.*

Before we proceed to the second half of the story, namely, to the quasi-structural point that "whenever she [the patient] begins to feel safe, she splits off and projects that affect to protect it from being swallowed up by her overwhelming anxiety," we need to establish, if only in a provisional and schematic way, the confluence and dissonance of Kleinian object relations theory and the broadly Winnicottian object relations perspective that Hamilton is presenting. Only thereby will the distinctiveness and significance of Hamilton's second claim come into view.

Beginning with points of confluence: Klein and other object relationists agree on the primordiality[50] and primacy of object relations, i.e., that certain objects are not merely grafted onto drives and so easily abandoned or exchanged but rather are fused with drives, that these object relations are incomparably or at least extremely significant, that object relations generally are much more significant for the theory and practice of psychoanalysis than the tradition tends to admit, thus that questions pertaining to wishes and defenses (the classical Freudian matrix of symptomatology) may be subordinated to and framed by, or at least are in great need of supplementation by, questions concerning the modes and consequences of object relation. In the words of Otto Kernberg, "Unconscious intrapsychic conflicts are never simple conflicts between impulse and defense; rather, the drive derivative finds expression through a certain primitive object relation (a certain unit of self- and object representation); and the defense, too, is reflected by a certain internalized object relation" (cited in Blum 1980, 210). Drives are always already interpreted through object relations.[51] Object relationists emphasize the endurance and importance of object relations as much as Freudians emphasize their contingency vis-à-vis drive pressures. Correlatively, they agree that tension reduction is not the primary psychic principle — nor do they seek to put a principle of anxiety reduction in its place.[52] Rather, although as we will see presently, anxiety is central to Klein's account of development and pathogenesis, as with other object relationists, her concern for the development of adequate forms of separation and connection tends to displace the primacy of economic principle.

Klein differs from many object relationists in claiming that while individuals vary with respect to the intensity of anxiety to which they are prone and the quantity of anxiety to which they are subject,[53] anxiety is a constant, a universal feature of psychic life. Consequently, for Klein, insecurities in some form or another are inevitable. So rather than interpret insecurity in early analysis as resulting from failures of the holding environment, a Kleinian could interpret it as one amongst indefinitely many expressions of constitutional anxiety. Or a Kleinian could, and likely would, attempt to elaborate the sources of this particular irruption and formation of anxiety rather than rest content with such indefinite pronouncements at the level of metapsychological generality. But even if a Kleinian were to do so, constitutional anxiety and its fates would still play a role in the more nuanced interpretation. From Klein's perspective, as opposed to the object relationist view Hamilton is presenting, although caretaking can influence — partially mollify, channel and perhaps productively organize, reinforce, or exploit and exacerbate — constitutional anxiety, there can never be caregiving good-enough to eliminate or even substantially abate constitutional anxiety, thus some measure of insecurity is inevitable.

The Kleinian infant is from the start and throughout later life wracked by anxiety for at least three reasons. First, the infant is subject to the overwhelming force of need: the infantile body flares up with need, explodes into fits of crying, and even when some degree of psychosomatic integrity is achieved, the upsurge of need may still be suffered as a disintegrative force. Second, infantile desires — distinct from needs — demand immediate, absolute, and impossible satisfaction, thus generate tension and frustration, which for Klein are synonymous with anxiety. Third, the death drive *ab initio* threatens the infant with annihilation. This anxiety-inducing threat is defended against by paranoid-schizoid mechanisms in the service of the infant's self-preservation, and so, by implication, in the service of preserving of the mother/breast who/which, in this state of primary narcissism, the infant does not experience as distinct from itself — or at least the accent is not on distinctness. The infant, presumed to be attached to herself/the breast from the beginning, bound and driven by an embracing *conatus* equiprimordial with Eros and Thanatos, experiences her "self"-directed aggressivity (primary masochism), perhaps amplified by aggression-inducing frustrations, as a threat that cannot be borne. Thus she splits herself into good and bad elements and deflects (projects) the threatening aggressivity outward, discovering/creating an object world which, because suffused with aggressivity and thus threatening, and in conjunction with ongoing "self-"directed aggressivity, motivates the projection of good elements of the self for the sake of their preservation. The object world, like the self, is defensively split into good and bad elements.[54] The death drive, though hardly domesticated, is harnessed in the service of self/object-preservation. The world beyond the breast initially comes into view as, and to a certain extent remains, a repository of projected aggression, a phobic construction. Its early contours, textures, shapes, and consistencies are modulations of or alighted upon in virtue of their resonance with the aggression and frustration which the infant is unable to bear and against which its implacable aggressivity soon turns, fueling the world's aggressive onslaught. Although, for Klein, the world is not simply a phobic construction, self and object attain initial distinction as, and to some extent remain, riven into zones of precarity. Anxiety abounds.

More precisely, (1) splitting the proto-ego into good and bad elements[55] allows for (2) projection of the death drive into, indeed as, an exterior/not me and (3) redirection of the death drive, which cannot be simply projectively expelled, away from the self/breast and onto the aggressivized exterior, which (4) temporarily secures the good ego/breast supporting experiences of the good, e.g., the excitements, satisfactions, and calm, afforded by the good ego/breast, and thereby supporting an availability to alightment upon — creation/discovery of — its analogues, i.e., further experiences of the good, which in turn (5) contribute to the consolidation of the good ego/breast, shoring it up when the infant is frustrated or racked by anxiety, e.g., submerged in terror that the bad will intrude, contaminating, corroding, or simply destroying the good, and (6) allow the external world to be experienced as participating in the nature of the good, as, at least in certain sectors, providing satisfactions, pleasures, comforts, and (or as) defenses against aggressive, persecuting elements. Moreover, (7) projection implies control within the framework of infantile omnipotence — omnipotence is obviously not the exclusive framework of infantile experience, but it is, on Klein's account, resilient despite what she suggests it is up against — thus projection of the death drive yields a sense of control over it, which enhances the infant's confidence in its/the good breast's survival and the ongoing availability of the good. (8) Confidence in the availability of the good is further emboldened by defensive idealization. Splitting and occasional safekeeping of good elements by projection contributes to experiences of the good, which in turn generates confidence in its resiliency. But this confidence can be overwhelmed by the reassertion of the death drive: aggressivity and threats of annihilation seeming to emerge from within and without. Thus the good — both within and without — is intensely exaggerated, defensively idealized. This supports a phantasy of the good as being as omnipotent as the infant sometimes experiences or once experienced itself to be or as omnipotent as the bad elements/objects appear to be from the point of view of the terrified infant sensing itself on the verge of annihilation. All of this supports (9) splitting the object-world into good and bad elements, thus (a) the identification of bad objects as discrete sources of threat, independent and isolable from the good, and so subject to evasion or counterattack, and (b) the identification of good objects as allies and steady sources of solace and joy, eventually subject to introjection, which contributes to the consolidation of a sense of safety and supports self-esteem. (10) However, frustration inevitably sets in, which, enhancing constitutional anxiety, outstrips the solace afforded by interior(ized) or exterior(ized) good objects — splitting, the central defense, cannot keep the good and the bad far enough apart; the bad seeps into and saps the good — threatening the infant with the immanent prospect of utter collapse and unremitting pain. The absence or waning of the good cannot be tolerated, thus is framed as an attack by the bad. (11) Therefore, since splitting gives rise to an object-world populated by persecutory, invasive objects against which the infant's auto-replenishing and frustration fueled aggressivity turn, and so from which it will fear retaliation, its basic defense against annihilation anxiety issues in the multiplication of anxieties: the self-defense is self-defeating insofar as it promotes anxiety, thus the need for defense, which yields further anxiety, and so on.

An initial compromise: better a persecutory world with endangered oases of goodness than abandoning the breast/self. Presumably, were it not for the vicissitudes of projection, the unrelieved peril resulting from an inherent and "self-"directed death drive would motivate construal of the breast as the sole source of destructiveness, and so its abandonment; but given Klein's assumptions about the omnipotent/omnipresent ambience of early infantile experience, to abandon the breast would be self-abandonment,[56] indeed the end of everything, thus such an option proves unviable. Projective identification secures the self and binds it to the world, but at the price of the world's phobic structuration: subjectivity is coextensive with anxiety.

Eventually, *if* the constitutional disposition of the individual (sufficient love) allows for this,[57] a tendency to reparation and depressive integration will arise which helps resolve — albeit temporarily — the internal impasse of the paranoid/schizoid position and renders the unavoidable resurgence of anxiety more manageable, less overwhelming. Felicitous caregiving, in addition to containing, organizing, and assuaging the infant, can activate a constitutional disposition to love, e.g., to repair the object torn asunder under the pressure of innate aggressivity; but — and here Klein's divergence from Winnicott and object relationists in the Fairbairnian tradition generally is most evident; a restriction of scope amounts to a major theoretical disagreement — if a sufficient disposition to love is not inherent, there is nothing that can be done: immured in a phobic, phantasy laden world, development will be stultified. And even given a sufficient disposition to love and felicitous caregiving, *at best* terror over annihilation (paranoid anxiety) partially gives way to anxiety over abandonment (depressive anxiety): the psyche remains rent by psychotic anxieties.

In part, what promotes the transition to depressive integration is envy, the destruction of the good *as such* or at least as idealized. Envy throws into crisis the stable but feeble defenses against anxiety marshaled in the paranoid-schizoid position and eventuates in their reorganization. Utterly exposed, absolutely dependent, and racked by anxiety, the infant experiences — *must* experience, i.e., defensively idealize — the breast as a replete and inexhaustible source of goodness. While anxiety and/or frustration ignite(s) paranoid-schizoid defenses, the idealized goodness of the breast sparks envy: a phantasmatic destruction of the good brought on by the unbearability of its slow, partial, and sometimes inadequate provisioning. Consequent upon inevitable dissatisfactions that disrupt the infant's sense of omnipotence, and/or in consequence of innate, aggression fueled suspicion, the breast is phantasized as hoarding goodness, and so must be destroyed.[58] Envy contaminates the good, spoils it, ravages its purity. In Klein's words, "from the beginning [a "beginning" subsequent to a primordial condition of primary narcissism in which self and other are indistinct] the destructive impulse *is turned* against the object and is first expressed in phantasied oral-sadistic attacks on the mother's breast, which soon develop into onslaughts on her body by all sadistic means. The persecutory fears arising from the infant's oral-sadistic impulses to rob the mother's body of its good contents, and from the anal-sadistic impulses to put his excrements into her (including the desire to enter her body in order to control her from within) are of great importance" (1952, 293; emphasis added). Envy, which is evidently continuous with projection, a development within or immanent crisis of the paranoid/schizoid position that induces its reconfiguration, aids depressive integration — the undoing of splitting and diminishment of associated anxieties — by rendering the schizoid world uninhabitable. Spoiled by envy, the idealized good — the "good breast" — is no longer a source of solace or ally against persecuting objects; and because the phobic/schizoid world is sustained by oases of idealized good, ruining them renders paranoid-schizoid defenses and the phobic world they structure unsustainable and thereby encourages new strategies of object relation and anxiety management, specifically, investment in and negotiations with a *complicated* world — a world in which availability to the good is simultaneously exposure to the bad (abandonment, mistreatment, etc.), a world of ambivalence and ambiguity. Only with less idealized good objects and less demonized bad objects can depressive integration, i.e., acknowledgement of (orientation within) ambiguity and ambivalence, be pursued. And only depressive integration[59] can — albeit imperfectly — sustain the interruption of the self-defeating cycles of paranoid/schizoid defenses brought on by envy and relieve the crisis to which it gives rise.

Hamilton's quasi-structural suggestion that "whenever she [the patient] begins to feel safe, she splits off and projects that affect to protect it from being swallowed up by her overwhelming anxiety" draws heavily on Klein but is certainly not Kleinian *avant la lettre*. Klein would not claim that a patient is prone to split off and project a feeling of safety upon its initial onset but rather when that feeling of safety is imperiled. Of course, given Hamilton's (implicit) suggestion that the patient is on a continuous state of overwhelming anxiety, he and Klein may agree that splitting and projection ensue only when the positive affect is endangered. But Hamilton's claim still seems a departure from Klein given that Klein would be unlikely to countenance his description of the patient as subject to continuous overwhelming anxiety. Such for Klein would imply an unusually extreme crisis-state unlikely to localize in insecurity in early stages of analysis. If overwhelming anxiety is continuous, as Hamilton implies, Klein would expect the patient to be completely nonfunctional; not possessed of psychotic features but embroiled in psychosis of the most extravagant sort. For Klein, if a patient is constantly in the throes of such extreme paranoid anxiety, s/he is not someone whose leading feature is likely to be anxiety in early stages of analysis. This divergence from Klein should not be surprising given that the subtitle of Hamilton's anthology is *New Directions in Object Relations Psychotherapy*. In proximity to Klein, Hamilton implies that the patient wants for depressive integration: continuously consumed by anxiety, when she does experience safety in the midst of such ongoing, overburdening, persecutory anxiety, she projects it in order to phantasmatically protect it, and so preserve herself from the worst. But given Hamilton's intimations regarding the remediability of this propensity to projection (even bracketing his subsequent discussion, confidence that this propensity to projection can be remedied, ultimately that substantial restructuring of the patient's dispositions of object relation is possible, is implied by the framing of the quasi-structural, quasi-Kleinian point by the Winnicottian developmental/environmental point), he likely considers it a signal of developmental arrest, of stagnation in a surpassable *stage* of development, rather than an expression of a recurrent *phase*, as it would be for Klein. In contradistinction to Klein, Hamilton seems to consider this propensity to projection, thus absorption within the phantasmatics of preservation, something that can be fully or at least largely overcome if handled well. Against Klein, Hamilton seems to conceive failure to secure depressive integration as a contingent result of environmental/parental depravation, thus seems to conceive projection and persecutory anxiety as subject to extensive amelioration through analysis. This is what makes his point quasi-structural rather than structural: paranoid projection is not an inexorable feature of psychic life as it is for Klein: paranoid-schizoid mechanisms do not (at best) inevitably oscillate with depressive dynamics as they do for Klein.

Given the Winnicottian tenor of the earlier point, and given that the second point cannot be given a directly Kleinian construal, perhaps Hamilton's second point means to invoke Winnicott's claims that (1) paranoid-schizoid defenses likely result from inattentive holding or waiting too long for parental support and provisioning, (2) envy results from tantalizing care-giving (1996 [1971], 82), and (3) the phantasies of and anxieties pertaining to disintegration considered average and expectable by Kleinians are rather "a sophisticated *defense*, a defense that is an active production of chaos in defense against unintegration in the absence of maternal ego-support, that is, against the unthinkable or archaic anxiety that results from failure of holding in the stage of absolute dependence." (1965, 61). If so, then Hamilton is tacitly pressing Winnicott's general indictment and redescription of Kleinian metapsychology: Klein misunderstands her own discoveries and innovations; she had not described universal features of psychic life, identified pathological invariants, and charted the course of healthy (-enough) development as she thought she has, but has only described development within the parameters of a faulty holding environment. Subsumed within Winnicott's conceptual apparatus, Klein's psychoses become failures of early parental holding and handling. Given the implicit Winnicottian overdetermination of Hamilton's account, *malgré lui*, the subtitle of his anthology (*New Directions . . .*) must be construed ironically. And this in two senses. First, Hamilton is simply rehearsing and applying Winnicottian theory. Second, what is claimed as new is preeminently archaic: appealing to a master in order to confer authority on eminently contestable claims. What is new, if anything, is the surreptitious character of this gesture; the pressure of plurality inducing the appeal to authority to proceed on the sly. What is new, if anything, is the character of Hamilton's anxiety.

Here we witness a clash of universals. Klein's emphasis on "internal" constitution, disposition, and development clashes with other object relationists' accentuation of the holding environment. Klein's casting of object relations in predominantly intrapsychic terms clashes with others' recasting of object relations in more objective/intersubjective terms. Thus here we witness an attempt to resolve conflict by situating one's predecessors or interlocutors as attending to a mere part of a whole to which one has unique access, to mere effects of causes that one has at last discerned (metaleptic catachresis). So here — again — we witness the breakdown of conversation, the evasion of argumentation, the devolution of perspective into doctrine signaled by attempted conceptual engulfment — a strategy modeled on the image of scientific progress but as if designed to be unconvincing, indeed as if solicitous of mimetic rejoinder, seeking mutual embroilment in cycles of revenge. Here we witness the regimentation of conceptuality to barely concealed aggression. The tolerant veneer of manifest eclecticism such as Hamilton's dissimulates, but barely, latent conceptual aggression. Perspective is precisely what eclecticism conceals from view.

While eclecticism that selectively appropriates with smug indifference to the concrete claims, challenges, hermeneutic and historical context(s), and motivating questions and interests of the work pilfered disguises its aggressive disdain in its performance of capacious interest, eclecticism of Hamilton's sort — surreptitiously subsumptive dogmatism — all but lays it bare. It preserves good conscience by avoiding direct, thus undeniable, acts of aggressive appropriation self-assertion — self-absorption, "just working things out for oneself," is its primary form of self-dissimulation — but provides itself ample opportunities for (explicit, i.e., wounded and defensive, thus presumably excusable or retractable, or disavowed, e.g., manifestly self-restrained) aggressive reanimation by so thinly disguising its disdain as to surely provoke — or at least support a fantasy of provoking — its targets' outrage and therewith their subsumptive rejoinder; the open secret of its aggression is the trap it lays for the predator that, if trapped, it will become.

Hamilton seems aligned with object relationists such as Winnicott, Fairbairn, Balint, Bowlby, and Guntrip, all of whom explicitly maintain that anxiety, and all the more so intense anxiety of the sort under discussion here, is conditional rather than constitutional, specifically, the consequence of inadequate caretaking. For those who follow Fairbairn, frustration consequent upon deprivation leads to destructiveness and anxiety over one's destructiveness. Splitting, which for Klein is an intrinsic disposition recurrently triggered throughout life, is for Fairbairn a consequence of inadequate holding, specifically, the result of identifications with aspects of caretakers who are not sufficiently present to the infant.[60] For Klein, anxiety-ridden relations to internal objects are inevitable; for Fairbairn they are compensatory substitutes for more desirable forms of empirical relation. Winnicott echoes this point and the numerous deep disagreements subtending it, claiming that the "internal object depends for its qualities on the existence and aliveness and behavior of the external object. Failure of the latter in some essential function indirectly leads to deadness or to a persecutory quality of the internal object" (1996 [1971], 9-10). Perhaps the earliest precursor of this gesture is Anna Freud's suggestion that projection and introjection are not inherent and inevitable responses to inherent and inevitable anxieties, but rather signals of developmental disturbance.

Or perhaps Hamilton is more influenced by Bion, who claims that infantile affects are experienced as intrinsically overwhelming and threatening annihilation, thus are bound to provoke intense anxiety, but also claims that caretaking and its therapeutic proxy can contain, modulate, and return potentially overwhelming affects in a much more palatable form. Or perhaps he is influenced by Kohut, who, furthest from Klein with regard to these matters — he is almost Rousseauian — denies original aggressiveness. For Kohut, aggressiveness is a symptom of failed parental-environmental efforts to allow the infant to develop in a self-integrating and self-regulating manner. But that his allegiances are unclear and his claims vaguely conciliatory does not relieve Hamilton's account of the specter of subsumptive violence. A sword sheathed or just the cloaked hint thereof may serve to intimidate and provoke no less effectively than one brandished openly. Such subtlety only protects the self-image of its bearer.

So what are we to make of such intense anxiety in early stages of analysis? One option is siding with a non-Kleinian or neo-Kleinian object relations perspective which assumes that those well cared for need not recurrently manage threats of annihilation consequent upon primary (self-)destructiveness and its vicissitudes by means of splitting and projection, thus that adolescent or adult patients embroiled in paranoid/schizoid anxieties and defenses — assuming this, or something like it, to be an adequate interpretation of extreme insecurity in early analysis — suffer from the remediable consequences of depravations or inadequacies in the facilitating environment. In such strands of object relations theory, relatively harmonious or at least non-traumatic relations with others are the norm, while intense anxiety in analysis and other such pathological extremes are the fallout of infelicitous caregiving to be compensated by proxy in the course of analysis. Or one might side with Kleinians, who assume that infants' object relations are pervaded by paranoid, and later, depressive anxieties (desire is even figured as a form of anxiety) which are bound to manifest throughout life and should surely be factored into accounts of, therapeutic expectations regarding, and techniques for treating extreme anxiety in early analysis.[61] Another option is sustaining respect for multiple perspectives and thereby sustaining the questionability of the phenomenon, generally, learning to abide and perchance to profit from the persistent questionability of psychoanalytic interpretation. This is not to suggest that analysts simply shrug in the face of uncertain phenomena. Such skeptical aloofness is obviously impracticable. And it would manifest the residual hold of desires for certainty, for the Absolute, rather than contribute to their mourning. Rather, it is to suggest that in view of the sometimes awe-inspiring results of clinical interventions (or what are presumed to be such), the wide-ranging and sometimes impressive extra-clinical applicability of certain psychoanalytic concepts — all too often clinical or otherwise practical success conduces to the conviction that "if it works, it must be right, or at least pretty close to the mark." — the partisan (or anti-partisan, eclectical) rigidity frequently fostered by transference to teachers, the myriad other manners by which the emphatic questionability of psychoanalytic interpretations and implied commitments may be overwhelmed and occluded, and (self-)distortions thereby instituted, the pursuit of one's own practice, and of psychoanalysis generally, may be well served by an ethos of resolute openness to the emphatic questionability of phenomena mediated by respect for the plurality of perspectives. Such respect is evident in critical scrupulousness rather than the condescension of feigned familiarity. At stake is nothing less than psychoanalytic *thinking* the development of psychoanalysis beyond stalemated partisan polemics (however cleverly concealed) and empty (i.e., uncommitted) eclecticism.

As we have seen, not only are reasons for commitment to one school rather than another wanting in demonstrative force, so too are the reasons for commitment to one interpretation rather than another. Even granted agreement that the analysand's behavior is best characterized as extremely insecure, nothing about this initial agreement entails a Kleinian interpretation that foregrounds or factors in constitutional anxiety or an object relationist interpretations that denies constitutional anxiety or keeps it in the background; a Freudian interpretation that assumes the earlier theory of anxiety or a Freudian interpretation that assumes the revised theory of anxiety; an object relationist interpretation that is more in line with Bion, Winnicott, Spitz, or Fairbairn. Nothing is resolved by appeal to the particular. Further, if conceptual determinacy is mediated by premises and inferential entailments and incompatibilities, then the claim that agreement concerning the description of local, low-level phenomena will obviate higher level disagreements trades on a gesture of reification — is but an obfuscation. Clinical description, indeed conceptuality generally, is inescapably normative — an ongoing dialectic of creation and discovery.[62]

NOTES

1. Other who claim that metapsychology has little if anything to do with psychoanalytic practice and should be expelled include: Gill (1976), Klein (1976), Schafer (1976), and Gedo (1979).
2. Cf. Wallerstein (1992), p. 55.
3. One might consider this argumentative form as generalized Kohutianism.
4. The same can be said of Gabbard's (1995, 2001) claim that concern for countertransference constitutes the contemporary clinical common ground.
5. Or presuming to excise metapsychology while surreptitiously relying on some particular version of it, which seems more likely, would undermine the validation of a unified clinical theory. Although Wallerstein quickly retracts the claim that metapsychology is wholly immune from experimental investigation (57), he still fails to consider the interimplication of metapsychology and clinical theory.
6. In regard to the implicit Hobbesian and Kantian resonances of this program, cf. Garsten (2009) *Saving Persuasion*, chapters 1 and 3.
7. A certain ambiguity in the initial presentation of object relations theory resulting from simultaneously drawing on Fairbairn and Winnicott, an ambiguity all the more palpable when the discussion comes to center on Winnicott, and a tension between the commitments involved in what will be called, respectively, the "developmental/environmental" point (broadly Winnicottian) and the "quasi-structural" point, along with the consequent vagueness, I take to signal the cost of inadequate attention to nuance. What I take such tension and ambiguity as are evident in the following reconstruction Hamilton's presentation of the object relations perspective as it bears on the explanation of insecurity in early stages of analysis to indicate is that the "spontaneous consent" of (and to) eclecticism may conceal theoretical confusions and conspire

with the avoidance of hard questions. However, given the temperament of the psychoanalytic field today, this worry is to be urged cautiously.

8. If Hamilton is alluding to a behaviorist view, what he intends by the term "unconscious" is more closely akin to what psychoanalysts deem "preconscious": material that is contingently non-conscious in the sense that it is just not available to consciousness at the moment rather than (strongly) defensively repudiated (dynamically unconscious) or originally subject to partially or exclusively unconscious registration.

9. Notice that the denial of epistemic realism assumes metaphysical realism. A more consistent position for psychoanalysis may be a denial of (or skepticism about) epistemic realism on the basis of linguistic holism and indeterminacy.

10. As has often been pointed out, behaviorism seems particularly well suited to "American" optimism about and ideological imperatives for radical self-creation and responsibility.

11. With some modicum of charity, one could interpret "the absen[ce]" of "a secure feeling" (from the second sentence) as the core phenomenon in the first sentence, rather than absence of security *consequent upon some manner of repression* of which several possibilities will be considered (as the first sentence strongly implies when read in isolation). Thus one can avoid attributing to Hamilton the belief that "unconscious association with a previous unfortunate medical event" is a possible Freudian explanation of repression, which it clearly is not. But then one would have to attribute to Hamilton the belief that, for a Freudian, "unconscious association with a previous unfortunate medical event" is a possible explanation of the absence of a secure feeling with the doctor at the beginning of therapy, which, though more plausible than the belief that "unconscious association with a previous unfortunate medical event" is a possible Freudian explanation of repression, is still not plausible. What *could* make "unconscious association with a previous unfortunate medical event" a possible Freudian explanation of the absence of a secure feeling with the doctor at the beginning of therapy would have to be (obscurely) packed into the phrases "unconscious association" and "unfortunate medical event" (the latter phrase would have to be construed as an extremely politic circumlocution, a neutralizing reference to profound trauma or to a heavily freighted experience, though there are no contextual indications to support this reading).

12. Though Hamilton never directly says as much, I assume that for him anxiety and insecurity are largely synonymous. Though the demand of brevity precludes this, I think that this assumption could be substantiated through a reading of his introductory essay and other writings.

13. Reich (1949) considers self-induced suffering the price that many pay to assuage feelings of guilt and access sexual pleasure; Rado (1933) considers self-induced suffering a preemptive strike whereby one accepts a lesser evil in order to avoid a more catastrophic one; Waelder (1933) and Fenichel (1945) link it to an effort to actively anticipate what one feels one will be passively subject to, and perhaps thereby (as Eidelberg 1933a, 1933b, and 1934 suggests) control and regulate it. Such would all be the converse of the Richard III-type scenario where existing injury or deformity preemptively exculpates (at least in fantasy), providing a blanket license to do as one will (cf. SE 14: 314-15). On the latter model, a series of injurious and/or immoral actions are construed as righteously justified compensation through which one alleviates one's pain or takes one's due, exempt from the moral evaluation appropriate for those who have not had to bear serious and perhaps irreparable (maybe early and abrupt) injury. On this model, serious and perhaps irreparable injury is considered advance payment exonerating any viciousness, a fantasy that secures identification with a jealously guarded self-image as a victim and may be held in place, in part, by the comfortable stability of the self-image it supports.

14. In Freud's first theory of anxiety, developed in "Anxiety" (1917) and "The Uncanny" (1919), anxiety is the precipitate of repression. Since the object of repression is presumed to be exclusively ideation [later, Freud wavers on this point: "*If* we wanted to differentiate more sharply between the vicissitude of the *idea* as distinct from the *affect*, and reserve the word repression for the affect, then the correct German word for the vicissitude of the idea would be disavowal [*Verleugnung*]" (SE 21:153; emphasis added).], Freud is compelled to speculate about the fate of the affective dimension of the repressed impulse. Repression, Freud claims in

this earlier work (and let us note, by means of a *conditional* statement: the line begins, "If in the first place psycho-analytic theory is correct in maintaining that . . ."), converts "every affect belonging to an emotional impulse, whatever its kind" into anxiety (SE 17: 241). Anxiety is affect transformed and discharged; it brings the psychic apparatus back to a bearable level of tension or acceptable rhythm of pleasure and unpleasure. The early theory of anxiety assumes the relatively smooth, unchallenged functioning of the pleasure principle.

15. In Freud's later theory of anxiety, motivated by his revised drive theory (the dualism of ego or narcissistic libido and object libido is replaced by that of Eros and Thanatos) and introduction of the second topography (1923), anxiety is conceived as a component of the mechanism of defense, *a trigger rather than a consequence of repression.* In "Inhibitions, Symptoms, and Anxiety" (1926) and "Anxiety and Instinctual Life" (1933), anxiety is elaborated as *fundamentally* signal anxiety; that which brings the paralyzed pleasure-unpleasure principle back into operation. Anxiety in these later essays is a defense against excessive (traumatic) quantities of excitation that have escaped or are anticipated to escape governance by the pleasure-unpleasure principle. However, if we read the later developments as supplementing rather than supplanting the earlier work, we can say that either (1) in early stages of life repression works according to the first model (anxiety early on is a "direct consequence of a traumatic moment," i.e., repression [1933, p. 95]) while later, repression ordinarily operates according to the second model; or (2) anxiety is in one respect a trigger of repression and in another respect – which may only be connected to the first through the equivocity of the term "anxiety" – *also* a consequence of repression. For the later Freud, there may be *at least* three distinct sources of severe discomfort relevant to our discussion: trauma itself (unbound excitation), the management of/defense against trauma, i.e., signal anxiety, and repression.

In the earlier article "Anxiety" (1917), Freud already began to theorize the signal value of anxiety: realistic anxiety [*Realangst*] signals or anticipates an external danger (but if *Realangst* "anticipates" an external danger, this may be because the current situation recalls a previous danger situation, in which case the early Freud is not *so* far from the behaviorist theory of association after all) and trips off a flight mechanism (though seemingly in the service of self-preservation, *Realangst* triggers a flight mechanism but also paralyzes action – in Freud's words, it is "a mere abortive beginning" – and so is of limited self-preservative value), while neurotic anxiety follows from the repression of an idea connected to an impulse that signals danger (significant unpleasure if pursued). Neurotic anxiety is governed by the economic considerations of the pleasure-unpleasure principle; it is specified as the discharge of libido that has become unmoored from its ideational content in the course of the latter's repression. Libido, in conflict with a prohibition or intolerance, undergoes the repression of its ideational component while its libidinal energy is transformed into and discharged as anxiety: when libido cannot be discharged as libido, it is discharged as anxiety; no matter what, the pleasure principle reigns. However, with the change from the first to second topography (unconscious-preconscious-conscious to id-ego-superego), dynamic considerations in general and the dynamic operations of the ego in particular are given more attention, and under these conditions the signal value of anxiety, which is a matter of the ego managing its weakness vis-à-vis id impulses, takes center stage. Furthermore, Freud soon begins to reflect on what exceeds or is "beyond" the pleasure principle (this topic is already broached in "The Uncanny" [1919] before it is famously elaborated in *Beyond the Pleasure Principle* [1920]), which is the crucial framework for his revised theory of anxiety. Anxiety, especially in "Anxiety and Instinctual Life," is construed in relation to (1) an unbearable, unbound, traumatic quantity of excitation and (2) danger signals of the reemergence of traumatic excitation that are produced or detected by the ego and call the pleasure principle back into action. In the revised theory of anxiety, anxiety is thought in terms of the dynamic operation of the ego, or more precisely, *as the limited discomfort that the ego allows or induces in order to provoke the binding operation of the pleasure-principle* that has been circumvented by an excessive quantity of excitation or its anticipation: "it is only the magnitude of the sum of excitation that turns an impression into a traumatic moment, paralyses the function of the pleasure principle, and gives the situation of danger its significance" (SE 22: 94). On this account, the ego solicits the pleasure-principle, manufactures the conditions under which the pleasure principle will resume its dominance; here the ego is first and foremost in the service of the pleasure principle. The differences between the first and second theories, then, greatly turn on Freud's attention to what lies "beyond" the pleasure principle and under what conditions the pleasure principle can prevail. Ultimately, for the later Freud, signal anxiety is the recollection and release of unpleasure by the ego in just the right dose to incite repression of the relevant impulses and so maintain governance by the pleasure principle.

In addition to elaborating anxiety as a technique of the ego, in the later theory the differences between *Realangst* and neurotic anxiety are much less emphasized. In the later theory, anxiety is equated with danger signals produced and marked as such by the ego that alert one to threatened repetitions of unbearable, unbindable, traumatic quantities of excitation. The task of the ego is to evade *psychically real* dangers (whether or not they are *realistic*) evoked by drive impulses. These dangers are, we might say, following Freud's distinction in *Moses and Monotheism*, "historically" but perhaps not "materially" real. These dangers are anticipated or imagined to result from following through on various impulses, or more precisely, *were once* anticipated, imagined, or experienced to follow from pursuing drive impulses when the individual was in a state of relative immaturity: "The ego notices that the satisfaction of an instinctual demand *would conjure up* one of the well-remembered situations of danger . . . the ego anticipates the satisfaction of the impulse and permits it to bring about the reproduction of the unpleasurable feelings at the beginning of the feared situation of danger. With this the automatism of the pleasure-unpleasure principle goes into operation and now carries out the repression of the dangerous impulse" (1933, pp. 89-90; emphasis added). [Interestingly, as a side note, notice that the ego is conceived not as the seat of reality testing but of imagination, as speculative, perhaps even fanciful. It is not the empirical consequences of the pursuit of an impulse but the ego's imaginative anticipation of its satisfaction that brings about the reproduction of the (beginnings of) unpleasurable feelings. And not only is the ego imaginative, its efforts to avoid the full force of recollected experiences of unpleasure compel it to peremptorily induce the unpleasure it fears even if its immediate context differs radically from relevant prior contexts: the self-preservative efforts of the ego are irrational and self-injurious. The ego is bathed in dread.] In sum, the ego, under the weight of its own anticipatory imagination of trauma, notices that (1) what can now be seen as a potentially dangerous impulse was experienced previously, and (2) the gratification of the impulse was once (actually or imaginatively: even though Freud says that the situations of danger the ego attempts to avoid are "well-remembered," on Freudian grounds there is no reason to believe that these memories are necessarily of empirical events) associated with certain dangers. The ego then (prudently?) allows these dangers, or more precisely, the uncomfortable feelings suffered at their beginnings, to saturate the psychic scene just enough to provoke the pleasure principle, and so repression, into operation. Anxiety (signal anxiety) is thus a technique of defense, a stratagem of the ego.

Here we will open a brief parenthesis. Although the basic contours of and motivation for Freud's later theory of anxiety are well known, as far as I am aware, certain subterranean currents of the later theory have yet to be noticed, let alone explored. Indeed the logic of the passage cited above is hardly as clear as it initially seems, and quite fortuitously, the questions that it provokes bear on a number of issues pursued throughout this text, perhaps even gesture toward a Freudian theory of perspective, or even if not, bear on the topic of Freud and science that will be broached in the final chapter. In the interest of drawing out what has yet escaped attention, I will cite the passage again and intersperse commentary in brackets. "The ego notices that the satisfaction of an instinctual demand [On the one hand, it seems that the ego just *notices*, i.e., observes from an external, neutral position, that "the satisfaction of an instinctual demand would conjure up one of the well-remembered situations of danger." Indeed it seems as if what the ego notices is that the satisfaction of an instinctual demand would conjure up a well-remembered danger situation *because* such satisfaction would actually entail such danger – i.e., observes an empirical regularity and sufficiently similar contexts. It is as if the connection between the demand and the danger situation is firmly established, grounded in a realistic assessment of the empirical implications of the demand. But on the other hand, if we stress that "the ego notices that the satisfaction . . . *would* conjure up one of the well-remembered danger situations," then perhaps the conjuring has not already happened, the ego does not notice an extant danger, and we may begin to suspect that the ego plays a role in this conjuring, perhaps in some way inflicts the danger it claims to notice upon itself. Might it be that the satisfaction *would* conjure up one of the well-remembered dangers only if the ego conjures one of them? That the demand may perhaps yield uncompromised satisfaction – only empirical investigation could tell – but for the ego's fretful (anxious) impediment? When the ego "anticipates the satisfaction of the impulse and permits it to bring about the reproduction of the unpleasurable feelings at the beginning of the feared situation of danger," might this permitting of reproduction be in fact a construction? Might the ego be claiming to anticipate what it will itself do, namely *project* a situation in which the impulse is too dangerous to be pursued. Might this implicate the ego in a ruse of reason, a self-fulfilling prophecy? Might the ego, quite irrationally (i.e., unconstrained by context) or at least highly imaginatively project the situation that it claims (and Freud claims) compels it to develop signal anxiety? Might the ego generate its own nightmares? If so, why is Freud reticent to acknowledge the self-inflicted terror and more broadly, the imaginative work of the ego? When Freud claims that the ego anticipates danger in pursuing a impulse, is he taken in by the ruse of the ego, presenting the product of its activity as inevitable, thus complicit in the ego's rationalization of its preemptive strikes? Might Freud be identified with the ego? And why would the ego claim this inevitability, claim to anticipate as an empirical fact transparently recorded what it will itself do? What are we to make of an ego, presumably the seat of reality testing, that participates in such obfuscations, rationalizations, disavowals, etc.? Indeed, what are we to make of an ego, presumably the bearer of the gentle voice of enlightenment, that gives rise to its own nightmares?] would conjure up [The rhetoric of conjuring evokes primitive religion, superstition, magic, perhaps alchemy – might the specter of Jung be looming? – as if what is at work in the ego's ostensibly rational anticipation is the invocation of a specter, a somehow fictional as opposed to strictly realistic danger. In light of this rhetoric, one begins to wonder if what the ego conjures is a danger that *would likely follow* from the reemergence of the impulse in the here and now or whether the ego conjures a danger scenario that *was once* associated with the impulse due to different developmental conditions, e.g., due to the relative weakness or immaturity of the ego, but hardly likely to follow in the current context? Is the ego unable to distinguish or unconcerned with distinguishing differences between past and the present? The ego, Freud makes plain, is not fully autonomous from the unconscious. Might this inability to or lack of concern with distinguishing between the here and now and there and then be an expression of the timelessness of the unconscious? What implications would this have for the separation and connection of the ego and the unconscious, the claims of reality and of psychic reality? To put the point somewhat exorbitantly: if a want of distinction between the past from the present is the hallmark of neurosis and a central feature of transference, what does this suggest about the ego? Might the ego be itself quite mad? Or if the ego does not directly conjure the danger but notices what is otherwise conjured and attempts to avoid it, what are we to make of the ego's gullibility? If the danger it "notices" presupposes the suppression of the difference between dangers to an individual in a prior state (e.g., of relative immaturity) and the individual in her current state, then in the service of what is the ego's susceptibility to danger convocations? Winnicottian and Kohutian considerations of suppressed injuries, need, and self-states wait in the wings.] one of the well-remembered situations of danger [which presumably *were once* empirically or at least experientially coeval with the pursuit of the impulse. Freud makes it seem as if what will be conjured up is precisely what was previously empirically encountered or experienced: it is not just conjured but well-remembered. Impacting, perhaps. But well-remembered? Are not memory-traces subject to transformation in the course of their unconscious sojourn? Subject to displacement and condensation, variable investment and phantasmatic framing and reframing? Could Freud be suggesting intrapsychic transparency and internal realism? However well-remembered these situations of danger may be, the danger *as* remembered/conjured may not be exactly what was originally experienced. And likely would not be given that psychic, bodily, and social development significantly transform what will count as danger. Freud again seems pressured to disclaim or all too available to complicity in the disclaiming of the imaginative, speculative, constructive operations of the ego. Indeed, of the insuperability of imagination generally. Why so? The danger remembered/conjured up/imaginatively elaborated by the ego (or which the ego corroborates or at least does not reject), may not be reasonable from the point of view of the present, let alone realistic from the point of view of an external observer or the individual's "observing ego." Upon reflection, it may seem completely absurd. Perhaps in some cases what is noticed or conjured up is a screen memory or otherwise defensively distorted. Perhaps "well-remembered" is a euphemism for "traumatically inscribed." If so, the ego may be irredeemably prone to or complicit with flights of fancy, insuperably ensnared by defensive pressures, by no means the source of clear thinking and guarantor of objectivity. And if this is so, it may be difficult, indeed exceedingly difficult, to secure the conviction that reason will eventually gain a hearing – a Freudian credo. Might Freud's Enlightenment convictions be at stake and under pressure here? If the ego is supposed to be the seat of reality testing and rationality but we have reason to doubt its neutrality, sovereign immunity, and clear-sightedness, then might the distinction between reality and fantasy or psychic reality, between historical and material truth, come under pressure? How might one distinguish between the unconscious and observing ego? Or from the other side, central to Freud's revised theory of anxiety is the *psychic reality* of danger, but if the interface of psychic and material reality is as porous as is here suggested, and is furthermore epistemically insecure, then might material reality bear on the development of signal anxiety more than Freud wants to admit? Might material reality be more significant than Freud is willing to admit throughout his late work And might Freud's inflation of psychic reality and deflation of material reality be related to, perhaps in certain ways conditioned by, his complicated relationship with Ferenczi? We will return to this question shortly. For now, let us notice that if material reality plays a greater part in the development of signal anxiety than Freud wants to admit, i.e., if we bracket the speculations above and stress that "[t]he ego [as a medium of reality testing] notices that the satisfaction of an instinctual demand would conjure up [because its satisfaction would actually reproduce the basic coordinates of] one of the well-remembered situations of danger, that is, if we suppose that such drive satisfaction would actually be dangerous in the current context (this correspondence being what makes the danger situation "well-remembered"), then the preeminence of the pleasure principle may come into question. The revised theory of anxiety means to acknowledge the preeminence of the pleasure principle and specify the mechanisms through which the crises it undergoes are quickly, indeed automatically abated. But if material reality plays a larger role in the development of signal anxiety than Freud acknowledges, perhaps the pleasure principle is not as sovereign as it seems – its crises may not automatically initiate reparative mechanisms, or even if they do, these may be feeble, even irrational. Perhaps there is life (material reality) and psychic life "beyond the pleasure principle" to an extent that even Freud's reflections in *Beyond the Pleasure Principle* fail to acknowledge, or actively avoid. Might we consider Freud's prioritization of the intrapsychic and specifically of the pleasure principle a repression of the claims of *life*? Or of the functional demands of organismal life and/or historical complexity and contingency? To speculate, if Freud is averse to considering material and psychic life radically beyond the pleasure principle, this might have something to do with an inability to think, or perhaps resistance to thinking, "life without law," life beyond the equilibrating law of the pleasure principle and the automatism of the ego and/or the psyche, life outside the conditions of (decently) homeostatic self-composure that the dominance of the pleasure principle presumably facilitates and that may be, for Freud, the energetic and psycho-affective conditions for rationality. Again, it may be Freud's Enlightenment convictions that are under pressure here. Further, if material reality plays a greater part in anxiety, and perhaps more broadly, psychic life, than Freud is ready to admit, then his methodological insistence on psychic reality in general and his privileging and elaborate development of what he once called neurotic anxiety (as opposed to real anxiety) in particular may have something to do with the turmoil surrounding his freighted debate with Ferenczi, who around the time of Freud's revisions to the theory of anxiety was emphasizing the import of empirical-material history to psychic life in general and pathogenesis in particular, and who died in 1933, the year that Freud published "Anxiety and Instinctual Life." If/when Freud makes it seem as if what will be conjured by the ego is precisely what was previously experienced – this would not be a concession of the significance of material reality but an absorption of the "realistic" (transparent, factual, etc.) notion of reality involved therewith into the concept of psychic reality – and thereby falls behind his own insight that memory-traces are subject to ongoing transformation and distortion in the unconscious – an insight that in part motivates the imperative to focus on psychic reality – might there be a melancholic – denied and distorted – identification with or concession to Ferenczi at work? An identification then denied and degraded (melancholic self-laceration?) through Freud's recurrent and energetic – all too recurrent and energetic? – insistence on the primacy and inevitable transformations and distortions of psychic reality in his late work?] . . . the ego anticipates [imagines? more or less accurately recalls an imagination of? gullibly, interestedly, or neglectfully conspires with an imagination coming from elsewhere of?] the satisfaction of the impulse and permits it to bring about the reproduction of the unpleasurable feelings at the beginning of the feared danger situation. [The ego "permits" (produces?) an upsurge of unpleasure that was once, perhaps *in a different stage of development* or at least amidst very different circumstances, connected with the impulse. Recall in this context Freud's linking of ego development with transformations of fundamental structures of concern. The infantile ego detects danger situations bearing on its utter helplessness; the young ego, painfully aware of its relative insufficiency, is prone to detect specific danger situations concerning object loss, loss of love, and helplessness; the phallic phase ego (at least in boys) focuses on detecting danger situations of "threat" (Freud flags castration threats, but whether he considers them real or imaginary is an open question) and will also be alert to the two previous paradigms of danger; finally, the latency stage ego attends to all former danger situations as well as dangers from the superego. Anxiety is "awakened as a signal of earlier situations of danger" which may no longer prevail. Such "awakening" thus may be an auto-induced, wholly fantastical nightmare; not grounded in a perception of identity but the instituting of analogy. Is this not a description of paranoid tyranny? (SE 22: 94) Also, whence Freud's confidence in the ego's capacity to judiciously dole out just the right amount of unpleasure to provoke the repressive operation of the pleasure principle whereby it reinstates its sovereignty? Whence his rationalistic imagination of the ego's automatism? His confidence in its tact? His presumption that it will inflict only sublatable (economical) wounds? Whence such idealization?] With this the automatism of the pleasure-unpleasure principle goes into operation and now carries out the repression of the dangerous impulse" [Dangerous from what point of view? And what of the fate of the affects connected with the resurgent impulse and the beginning of the well-remembered danger situation?] (SE 22: 88).

There are three points I would like to underline. First, the ego, on Freud's terms, even if the seat of reality testing may not be entirely well-qualified for the task (classically understood). Its mediation of the "demands of reality" may involve exaggeration and deflation, the interarticulation of blindness and insight and of creation and discovery, at least inflection and perhaps gross distortion. The ego may not afford simple, unmediated contact with "reality." More particularly, second, the ego may exaggerate, even fantasmatically concoct dangers that aren't "really" there and may fail to notice realistic dangers to which its structure of attention blinds it; consequently, it may not be a locus or guarantor of reason. Third, if true, the above would warrant Freud's insistence on *psychic reality*, but since he is prone to disclaim or deflate these points, accounting for his insistence on psychic reality requires us to look elsewhere. Finally, let us note by way of anticipation that in view of Freud's developmental account of the ego's forms of danger-registration, a *contrast between an object relations focus on developmental history and a Freudian focus on conflict and repression may be misconceived.*

16. In all such accounts, expectable feelings of security with a doctor are not *themselves* repressed, as Hamilton suggests a Freudian would consider them to be – they are not significant enough to be repressed – though their absence could be considered in some way related to repression: the anxiety may be an aid to faltering repression, a component of a complex repressive mechanism, a consequence of repression, and so on. And in all such accounts, Freud's focus on psychic dynamics, especially defensive dynamics, is preserved, as is his disposition to attend closely to overdetermination. (To be fair to Hamilton, Freud sometimes uses the terms "repression" and "defense" interchangeably, or almost so. Cf. Laplanche and Pontalis (1974), pp. 390-94).

17. The insistence on the various and varied Freudian interpretations is meant to give some sense of what Bersani describes (see chapter 4) as the overdetermination of the psychoanalytic mind.

18. In fact, for Freud and within the Freudian tradition, abiding certain degrees of pain (frustrations) is the motor of many productive developments, e.g., reality testing and character formation. Also for Freud and certain of his inheritors, pain (tension-raising) is coextensive with the inscription of memory-traces and eros, thus is an ineliminable feature of psychic life,

encountered both before and after primary repression, before and after each secondary repression. Cf. Bass (2002) *Difference and Disavowal: The Trauma of Eros.*

19. SE 22: 59-67.

20. Cf. Feyerabend (1975) *Against Method*, Hesse (1980) *Revolutions and Reconstructions in the Philosophy of Science*, Putnam (2004) *The Collapse of the Fact/Value Dichotomy and Other essays*, and Standford (2006) *Exceeding Our Grasp: Science, History, and the Problem of Unconceived Alternatives.*

21. Cf. Gabriel (2009) *Mythology, Madness and Laughter: Subjectivity in German Idealism.*

22. Thus to a certain extent indefinitely deferred – "virtual" – because the mutual specification of perspectives is ongoing.

23. In her *Lectures on Kant's Political Philosophy*, Arendt insists that thinking is a communal affair, necessarily involving other perspectives: "'enlargement of the mind' . . . . is accomplished by comparing our judgment with the possible rather than actual judgments of others, and by putting ourselves in the place of any other man" (1989, p. 43). To think (judge) in Arendt's sense is to attempt to make out that to which we have blinded ourselves, to foreground that which we have foreclosed, or at least to provisionally amplify that which we have minimized in order to secure the insights and stabilize the practices to which we are committed. Thus, to think is to courageously undertake to sustain passivity, to sturdy attention in the face of that which we tend to shy away from or block out, to suspend or provisionally modify our privileged habits of attention, perhaps indeed to alter our very forms of life, our structuring sensibilities, risking self-loss for the sake of self-enhancement. Imaginatively putting oneself in the place of another is to assume the perspective that an other emblematizes. Though it may seem (and in some sense may be) hubristic to identify and successively inhabit others' perspectives, that the perspectives provisionally assumed are imaginary (emblems) rather than empirically attributed is a signal of respect for the internal relation of concrete others to their perspectives, an acknowledgment that their perspectives are *theirs*, bound to their life practices. In part, what binds a perspective to a concrete other, makes it *her* perspective, is the singular manner in which it is inhabited and thereby elaborated. Because this cannot be foreseen, it can only be imagined.

Coming at this from another angle, consider what Arendt means by "possible rather than actual judgments of others." Likely, Arendt does not mean an indefinite array of opinions that – who knows? – an other may randomly put forward. Haphazardly posited opinions are not judgments in Arendt's sense; they are not attributable in the relevant sense to an other, are not judgments "*of others*" (the details of Arendt's version of Kant's apperception thesis need not detain us here). When she speaks of possible judgments of others, likely, the emphasis is distributed equally between "of others" and "possible." To imagine the possible judgments of others is not to skeptically shrug and concoct wild possibilities. Rather, "possible rather than actual judgments of others" are judgments that this or that particular other could conceivably put forward or be committed to, thus judgments imaginable on the basis of concrete, actual experiences, judgments *made possible* by the actuality of the other. Without experiences of concrete others and their often surprising and spontaneous but not completely *ex nihilo* judgments, imagination would suffer from its lack of constraint, would have nothing to work with; what could be gleaned from "another's perspective" would be only what one puts into it. Thinking lives off the dialectical interplay of sedimentation and the shudder of surprise. Without actual experiences of concrete alterity, we may extend but not enlarge the mind, supposing that enlargement, as a figure of growth, requires rupture and regeneration. [Compare "The Crisis in Culture": "The power of judgment rests on a potential agreement with others, and the thinking process which is active in judging something is not, like the thought process of pure reasoning, a dialogue between me and myself, but finds itself always and primarily, even if I am quite alone in making up my mind, in anticipated communion with others with whom I know I must finally come to some agreement. And this enlarged way of thinking, which as judgment knows how to transcend its individual limitations, cannot function in strict isolation or solitude, it needs the presence of others 'in whose place' it must think, whose perspective it must take into consideration, and without whom it never has the opportunity to operate at all" (220-1).]

The exegetically crucial question is: what sense would it make to *compare* "our judgment with the possible *rather than actual* judgments of others" if by "possible" we mean randomly posited, merely logically possible? What would be the point of this (self-)comparison? By "possible rather than actual judgments of others," Arendt likely means a range of judgments that *become possible* for others on the basis of their conditioned but not fully determined metabolism of experience, and so become imaginable by us on the basis of encounters with them. What we deem possible is retrospectively determined (imagined, projected), thus conditioned and enriched by experience. "Let's face it. We're undone by each other. And if we're not, we're missing something" (Butler 2004, p. 19). The embryonic kernel of what may-yet-be is given in and through experience. Possibility (becoming-otherwise) is itself a dimension of reality (qua becoming); it is epistemically belated.

The insistence on the internal relation between thought and imaginative plurality is echoed in Arendt's essay "Socrates," where she affirms that "the escape of the philosopher from the realm of plurality always remains an illusion: even if I were to live entirely by myself I would, as long as I am alive, live in the condition of plurality" (20). Nothing, Arendt seems to suggest, not even abject isolation, can destroy plurality (an echo of this sentiment can be found in Arendt's final charge against Eichmann in *Eichmann in Jerusalem*). On Arendtian grounds, one might well ask: did not the camps aim at and might not totalitarianism have succeeded at destroying human plurality? Is not plurality, thus humanity, a *condition*, as the title and substance of *The Human Condition* and much of the content of her other work suggests? And is not a "condition" precarious, subject to destruction and thus in need of perpetual securing (whether in the mode of maintaining or renewing and reworking)? Even if Arendt's emphasis on the ineradicability of plurality is overwrought, her point is well taken. (Also, that Arendt supports her claim that plurality is ineradicable with a thought experiment involving total isolation, thus by invoking a context in which the significance of plurality is artificially put out of play, further indicates that this overwrought insistence on the ineradicability of plurality is not her considered view. To be sure, Arendt is prone to anxiety over the eradicability of plurality, and therewith the destitution of action (the replacement of *acting* in common –"power" – by "action" coordination: ideological subsumption and/or the regulation of the pursuit of private interests), but even in passages where such anxiety is evident seems to understand plurality as a contingent condition. For instance, in the following passage Arendt explicitly (anxiously) identifies "the concept of man" with plurality and further characterizes plurality as the "nature" of the human (yet as an *alienable* "nature"), as if determining the *essence* of the human in a classical metaphysical gesture, while at once alluding to the possibility of an ontological transmutation of the human, thus presenting the concept of the human, and so plurality, as a precarious condition, indeed one capable of multiple manners of realization: "if it does not belong to the concept of man that he inhabits the earth together with others of his kind [this seems to be a criticism of Heidegger's ontologization of plurality as *Mitsein*, i.e., of his overlooking the institutional and intersubjective conditions necessary for the realization of "the concept of man"], then all that remains for him is a mechanical reconciliation by which the atomized selves are provided with a common ground that is essentially alien to their nature. All that can result from that is the organization of these selves intent only on themselves into an Over-self in order somehow to affect a transition from resolutely accepted guilt to action" (1994, 181-2).

24. Cf. *Symposium* 201d-212d.

25. In Heideggerian terms, a thrown projection [*geworfener Entwurf*].

26. As Oscar Wilde once said, "anything worth doing is worth doing badly."

27. In addition to furthering the claim about the inevitably perspectival character of knowing, part of the point of the previous (long) footnote is to underscore that (1) repression need not be involved in the Freudian account of anxiety (recall that Freud's early article "Anxiety" (1917) explicitly relates the signal value of anxiety to *Realangst*); (2) if the ego is as mad as it sometimes seems, or at least if the ego cannot be said to yield unqualified access to reality, that is, if the ability to distinguish between psychic and material reality is epistemically insecure, then, (a) as much a Freud would resist it, a Freudian account can at least allow for questions about the impact of what may well be material reality on anxiety and (b) the object relationists' attempt to account for insecurity in early stages of analysis by appealing to the effects of

external reality, specifically the effects of early care, may be problematic (which proves our point that limited understanding of one's opponents leads to limited self-understanding); and (3) if the ego projects, imagines, or activates the danger situations whose realization it attempts to thwart, then *conflict* (classically understood as conflict between the id and the ego or the id and the superego) may not play as significant a role in the account as it seems. Even in the revised theory of anxiety, signal anxiety can be understood as a strategy by which the ego manages its weakness vis-à-vis id impulses *that may or may not be repressed*, and even, perhaps, vis-à-vis what may well be *external events* or *its own projections of danger*. In any case, conflict may not play the role it seems to.

28. One exception would be Fairbairn, whose departure from Freud turns not on a de-emphasis of repression but a redetermination of the model of repression. For Fairbairn, memory-traces and desires are repressed not because they violate the pleasure-unpleasure principle but because they threaten to release unavowable object ties with which they are associated; primarily, relational patterns that cannot be integrated are repressed.

29. The facilitating environment is the adaptive context of good-enough caregiving in which the caregiver provides for the particular and evolving biological and psychological needs of the infant (and later, the child) by means of his or her emotional and behavioral responses, and does so in a way that allows that infant's maturational process to unfold without undue interference or interruption such that, eventually, a "true self" can emerge.

30. Fairbairn and Guntrip would be at one end of the object relations spectrum where drive theory is largely if not altogether repudiated and development posited as turning on the need for meaningful relationships and connections, while Klein would be at the other end where drive theory is sustained.

31. For certain object relationists, the need to conserve relational forms established in early life – irrespective of their quality – is central. For others, early relational depravations set into motion compensatory strategies that are not readily abandoned for fear of utter catastrophe. To give an example close to Winnicott's heart (he was appointed Psychiatric Consulate to the Government Evacuation Scheme in the County of Oxford in 1940): of the children evacuated from London during the Second World War, those who had extreme and seemingly inexplicable difficulties adapting to their new homes – the caretakers were affectionate, supportive, understanding – were often those coming from homes in which they had not, in Winnicott's assessment, received adequate care.

32. As many object relationists note, Freud's "Mourning and Melancholia" departs from his usual characterization of object ties as contingent, merely soldered onto the drives, and from his claim that tension reduction is the primary governing force of psychic life. There, Freud begins to entertain the consequences of seemingly ineradicable commitments to particular objects/others.

33. However, the claim that finding an object is always a refinding may come under pressure, or at least look rather different, in light of the suggestion of the ego's imaginative operations discussed above. Failure to attend closely to the texts and not just the stated positions of one's interlocutors may blind one to difficulties in – and possibilities of – one's own perspective.

34. Bion is difficult to situate in this context. He denies an inherent *desire* for development, but whether or not he assumes a *drive* for development is an open question. Klein will be discussed later.

35. From a certain object relations perspective, we are both prone to conserve relational configurations latched onto in early life and gluttons for meaning. Lacanians would surely worry that such an object relations perspective is a reification of pathology at the level of metapsychology. For advocacy of the relatively autonomous good of attachment from a slightly different perspective (relational rather than object relations), cf. Mitchell (1988), esp. pp. 26 and 33.

36. If this is what Hamilton has in mind, it might help explain why he speaks of repression of "expectable feelings of security" when (presumably) characterizing the Freudian position. On this sort of object relations account, a feeling of security (or some positive feelings) is what sparks the insecurity, and Hamilton might think that, for a Freudian, when an idea and/or feeling vanishes or converts into its opposite, it must be due to repression.

37. Or at least neither stresses these to the degree the Freudians do. Within the manifestly diverse object relations tradition, emphasis on conflict and tendencies to self- and world-distortion and -evasion varies considerably. But however diverse, object relationists tend to place less weight on these then do Freudians, and unlike Freudians, tend to frame them as developmental accomplishments rather than pathogenic primitives.

38. For Fairbairn, who was the first to suggest that libido is "object seeking," i.e., seeks connections with others as its fundamental aim, the viscosity of libido accounts for the prevalence of repetition compulsions much more persuasively than the typical Freudian account.

39. Cf. Winnicott (1996 [1971]), p. 104.

40. One way to think about the aim of analysis generally is as seeking to interrupt the subsumptive mechanicity of (false, reifying) determinate judgments and facilitate reflective judgment (interpretive and thereby practical freedom) by recalling or otherwise reactivating the motivating conditions under which reflective judgments consolidated and dissimulated themselves as (false and pathogenic) determinative judgments and supporting the working through of affiliated experiences, fantasies, etc. (i.e., the practice of reflective judgment).

41. Although agreement that relational dynamics condition self-integration prevails amongst object relationists, significant disagreements persist concerning how such conditioning is to be understood. On Winnicott's (1945) view, a potential for self-integration is activated and sustained, and an innate tendency to self-integration is enhanced, by parental ministrations. When the infant is "kept warm, handled, and bathed and rocked and named," a feeling of integrity ensues, and coupled with "acute instinctual experiences which tend to gather the personality together from within," sediments an initial sense of self ("Primitive Emotional Development," p. 150). The consequent provisioning of comfortable warmth, regular patterning of cleanliness and dirtiness (e.g., changing, bathing, wiping), rhythmicity of rocking and of speech directed to the infant, treating the infant as distinctive, individuated ("naming"), e.g., as a seat of desires, a subject of experiences, a source of various effects, and in another sense of "naming," *interpreting the infant's needs and desires through one's responses to them*, e.g., interpreting a cry as hunger, a grimace as overheatedness, a smirk as coyness and inducement to play, all contribute to the coalescence of a sense of integrity, even, to a degree, of subjective specificity, that complements and corroborates the infant's sense of cohesiveness induced by the rhythmicity of drive surges, the cyclicality of need, and "instinctual experiences which tend to gather the personality together from within." Objective patterns become (or support) the schemas of subjectivity. Holding and handling allow the infant to be experimental, even chaotic, wild, mad, and yet contained; to be all over the place, in bits and pieces, without succumbing to a sense of crisis or disintegration. In the context of good-enough holding and handling, this mediated self-containment, the infant can experience its variable states and impressions as variations on a theme (itself). Gradually, the infant comes to experience differentiation only from out of a milieu of integration. In want of a primary rhythmicity and patterning, there will be psychosis. E.g., in conjunction with adequate feeding – nurturance (often the breast) arriving, a thousand times over, exactly when needed or not terribly far therefrom – good-enough holding and handling will facilitate the infant's experience of itself as omnipotent, as creating the bountiful world orchestrated by entrusted caregivers; and its emergence from omnipotence, its transition from an overly capacious, unsustainable model of self-integration, to the sort of self-integration that depends on negotiating with the world, is possible only in virtue of the self-confidence mimetically incorporated from the facilitating environment its caretakers provide (including their indulgence of omnipotence fantasies).

For Bion, on the contrary, there is no such innate tendency to self-integration. On his view, infants are initially racked by raw anxiety and aggressivity that conduce to a looming sense of annihilation, of being on the cusp of a perilous falling away or disintegration into bits and pieces. Accordingly, a good-enough caregiver must (1) accept this anxiety and aggressivity, e.g., allow herself to become uncomfortable, and (2) respond with relative calm rather than franticness or unconcerned imperviousness, e.g., by putting the infant's anxiety and aggressivity into words and/or interpreting them through her responses in a manner that mitigates their severity. Only if caregivers contain "beta elements" (confused thoughts and feelings associated with intense aggression and anxiety) by accepting, transforming, and returning them as "alpha elements" (the thoughts and feeling minus the torrential anxiety that made them unbearable, indeed so unbearable that "logical connections" – inferences and schematized relations – between them could not be established), will the psychoaffective conditions obtain for the infant to develop a sense of safety in its skin and on this basis eventually come to experience itself as a relatively robust and resilient subject – at least able to survive the anxiety and aggression on whose inevitability and consequentiality Bion to a much greater extent than Winnicott insists. For Bion, containing means permuting the infant's anxiety- and aggression-burdened thoughts and feelings into more palatable forms. Through a sort of alchemy or magic of suggestion, caregivers transubstantiate their inordinately aggressive and anxiety-racked little monsters into children: a second birth. If attention and containing are sufficiently provisioned, the infant gradually absorbs, along with the transformed thoughts and feelings, the caregiver's organizational, anxiety-alleviating and aggression-modulating capabilities. It becomes able to self-sooth, to transform persistent beta elements into alpha elements. Because he does not share Winnicott's conviction in an innate tendency to self-integration, Bion more than Winnicott stresses the need for caregivers' *exemplarity* and the mimetic media through which this exemplarity works its magic.

Like Bion, Spitz does not share Winnicott's conviction in an innate tendency toward self-integration. Further setting him apart from Winnicott, Spitz doubts that the rhythmicity of drive surges provides even a minimal sense of subjective consistency. And in contradistinction to Bion, Spitz claims that the infant is not so much racked by aggressivity and anxiety as s/he is bombarded by a maelstrom of unmetabolizable stimuli from within and without. Further, contrary to Bion, Spitz does not emphasize caregivers' exemplarity as what gives rise to an incipient sense of selfhood. Rather, closer to Winnicott, he claims that this is an effect of a "dialogue" between the stimuli to which the infant is subject and the facilitating environment. First, through touch, posture, bodily tension, vocal rhythm and tone, and other such features of her somatic comportment toward her child, the caregiver generates an affective climate that becomes the infant's initial sense of cohesiveness. Then the good-enough caregiver will spontaneously undergo regression to her earliest experiences and thereby reopen channels of communication through which the relatively inchoate experiences of her infant can be understood. On this basis, the caregiver will be able to appropriately sooth her infant, preventing overstimulation – which is for Spitz, along with extreme understimulation, the main impediment to early development. Subsequently, Spitz stresses, the good-enough caregiver as auxiliary-ego will slowly induce greater consistency and determinacy in her infant's experiences by behaviorally and linguistically interpreting its inchoate affects and the stimuli in which it is awash. By means of the words and deeds through which caregivers repeatedly mark and metabolize stimuli to which infants are subject – determining them as, say, "food," "frightful/bad," or "pleasurable/explorable" – they introduce a basic (proto)conceptual framework that will be slowly soaked up by the infant so long as her level of stimulation is well-regulated. Once merely subject *to* stimuli, the infant becomes a subject *of* experience, *for* whom stimuli bear discernible significance, or more precisely (because what is at stake is the co-constitutive binding of significance to experience, the dissolution – or extreme curtailment – of the possibility of encountering mere stimuli), one for whom phenomena are – for the most part – intrinsically if unevenly and unstably significant. Through this "dialogue" between the stimuli to which the infant is subject and the caregiver's conceptual apparati, once intrinsically overwhelming stimuli become bound and bearable, meaningful, the basic elements of a nascent world-orientation, a subjectivity. Further development is envisioned as the result of increasingly sophisticated variants on this mimetic model. E.g., the good-enough caretaker will begin to introduce proto-narrative sequences (first upset, now better), eventually inspiring complex forms of self- and world-relation that elaborate a meaningful and hospitable world.

42. It should be noted that for Winnicott, caregivers are initially experienced as dimensions or aspects of the omnipotent infantile self and only later experienced as discrete, independent beings. The following assumes some acknowledgment of their ontological independence.

43. This is not to say, however, that an infant simply incorporates the conscious and unconscious images of and assumptions about her manifest in the manner of her caretakers' relations to her. For it is not as if these images and assumptions are transparent and self-interpreting. Such images may be fragmentary and elusive, both to the infant and to the caregivers (the mysteries of the ancient Egyptians were mysteries to the ancient Egyptians . . .). They

may be highly complex and overdetermined, contradictory, repressed, too charged for the infant (and sometimes the adult) to bear. They may be connected with caretakers' experiences, desires, and so forth of which there are yet no experiential corollaries and for which there are yet no interpretive schemas in the infant. Conveyed by mood, gesture, patterns of vocal inflection, play, specific manners of response and non-response, distributions of attention, complicated routines, and so on, the meanings of these images are hardly self-evident – only through repetition and holistic interweaving are they instilled. Connected to caregivers' experiences, feelings (including feelings about matters of which the infant is largely or entirely unaware), regimes of categorical salience and proclivities of concept application, and structures of unconscious or more broadly intrapsychic meaning, such images may be opaque if not wholly unintelligible to the infant. Indeed, such images may be for the most part enigmatic signifiers, far from simply appropriable. Perhaps only as mediated by phantasy (enigmatic images may even be a primordial spur of phantasy) or prior to phantasy, some other manner of unconscious or proto-psychic metabolism, will these images be assumed. Yet however various and uncertain are the modes of incorporation, object relationists assume that what needs to be transmitted will be. Their attention gravitates not toward the subtle perturbations or other consequences of lasting enigma but toward the consolidation of the minimum necessary conditions for selfhood.

44. On the one hand, Winnicott continually affirms that most parenting is good-enough. But on the other hand, he claims that "there will never be enough psychotherapists to treat all those who are in need of treatment," which implies the contrary (1982, p. 19).

45. The "internal" impasse of omnipotence is resolved only by "external" mediation.

46. Cf. the work of Jessica Benjamin, especially *Bonds of Love* (1988) and *Like Subjects, Love Objects* (1998).

47. "Mothering," for Winnicott, "includes fathers, but fathers must allow me to use the term maternal to describe the total attitude to babies and their care" (1982, p. 141).

48. Cf. Winnicott (1982), p. 6.

49. Insecurity may ensue because the analyst is too interested in meaning or concrete defenses against its possibility. "An opportunity for rest has been missed because of the therapist's need to find sense where nonsense is. The patient has been unable to rest because of a failure of the environmental provision, which undid the sense of trust. The therapist has, without knowing it, abandoned the professional role, and has done so by bending over backwards to be a clever analyst, and to see order in chaos" (1982, p. 56). Incidentally, although this is obviously directed against Kleinians and Lacan is nowhere on Winnicott's radar, one might extrapolate from this a critique of Lacanian technique, an indictment of the therapeutic deployment of the category of the Real and of certain features of the Symbolic. An extreme divergence from Lacan might be noticed at this point of profound intimacy of interests.

50. "I have often expressed my view that object relations exist from the beginning of life, the first object being the mother's breast which to the child becomes split into a good (gratifying) and bad (frustrating) breast" (Klein, *Developments in Psycho-Analysis*, p. 293).

51. Although object relationists agree that drives are always already interpreted through object relations, this does not imply agreement that the intrapsychic is indissociable from the social-historical conditions under which object relations develop; Kleinians more than others grant credence to the relative autonomy of the intrapsychic.

52. Fairbairn (1952) more than other object relationists emphasizes the impulse to object seeking whether or not this results in a reduction of tension.

53. For more on the Kleinian theory of anxiety, cf. Rosen-Carole (2011) *Lacan and Klein, Creation and Discovery*.

54. Klein is never quite clear about this. Sometimes she seems to suggest that the creation/discovery of the world as (partially) a repository of aggression follows upon experiences of frustration. Perhaps this pertains more to the consolidation of the phobic world sourced in the interplay of an originary death drive and equally originary conatus.

55. Klein sometimes suggests that this splitting occurs under the pressure of proto- or early superego imperatives that seek to institute distinctions between the admissible and the inadmissible.

56. Cf. Klein et al. (2002 [1952]) *Developments of Psycho-analysis*, p. 275.

57. Cf. *Envy and Gratitude*, pp. 187-8.

58. Klein sometimes stresses that envy is not a result of frustration, but is simply an attack on the good qua good. Whether this is convincing or not need not concern us here.

59. Cf. Susan Isaacs (1948) "The nature and function of phantasy."

60. Cf. *Freud and Beyond* (1996), p. 120.

61. E.g., for Kleinians, interpretations aim to bring together split off parts of the self, i.e., facilitate integration and thereby restructuration of anxiety.

62. At this point I would like to direct the reader to *Lacan and Klein, Creation and Discovery*, which was written as the next chapter of this text but proved too lengthy to include.

Chapter Five

Subjectivity: A Dialectic of Creation and Discovery

> [A]nalysis is always more and something other than analysis. It transforms; it translates a transformation already in progress.
>
> —Derrida, "Eating Well"

ONTOLOGICAL INDETERMINACY

If psychoanalytic plurality is irreducible, psychic life or at least certain features thereof must be epistemically and perhaps ontologically indeterminate — and vice versa. To say that psychic life is epistemically but not ontologically indeterminate is to advance a transcendental realist thesis: psychic life subsists in itself — is stably self-present, fully determinate — although our epistemic access to it is insuperably limited or insecure; either something about it inexorably resists comprehension or it is fully comprehensible but we can never be certain that we have hit the mark. To say that psychic life is ontologically indeterminate is not necessarily to advance a strong empirical idealist thesis, i.e., to claim that psychic life is but a raw resource for sovereign interpretive construction, nothing in itself. Nor is it necessarily to advance a classical transcendental idealist thesis, i.e., to claim that certain forms — cognitive mediations — are unavoidable (constitutive of experience) and/or necessary for the scientificity of inquiry. Thus to say that psychic life is ontologically indeterminate is not necessarily to commit oneself to the classical corollary of transcendental idealism, namely, empirical realism, i.e., to claim that although such forms are themselves contingent — they are not necessarily exhibited by all forms of life or even all forms of inquiry undertaken by rational beings — within their compass knowledge is as certain as can be; once we acknowledge our finitude (necessary mediations), and forgo the fantasy of attaining subject-independent knowledge and measuring our knowledge against this cognitive ideal (the "really real," what is altogether independent of experience), skepticism loses its bite: is either no longer corrosive, becoming immanent to the empirical realist pursuit, or no longer coherent, evidently asking for the impossible; finitude turns out to be not a limit in the sense of an impediment but a condition of possibility, indeed the framework for the pursuit of the infinite.[1] In the following, the claim that psychic life is ontologically indeterminate involves both a weak empirical idealist thesis (psychic life is partially — and unevenly — pliable to interpretive constitution) and a weak transcendental idealist thesis (certain categorical coordinates are historically uncircumventable and in that sense necessary conditions for intelligibility as a person; they are not subject to transcendental deduction, thus do not claim transhistorical validity as constitutive conditions for experience and/or valid knowledge, but rather are elements of a reigning epistemē — material aprioris.) Thus it means to delimit a new dispensation of idealism: dialectical idealism.

DIALECTICAL IDEALISM

Oriented toward ontologically indeterminate subjectivity, dialectical idealism may be of more limited applicability than Kant's transcendental idealism, Schelling's objective idealism, and Hegel's absolute idealism, though its elaboration of transcendental-historical necessity (the material apriori) and its underscoring of the multiple manners of satisfying such transcendental conditions, thus their underdetermination, i.e., its insistence on the dialectic of creation/discovery, if compelling, may have consequences bearing on all other forms of idealism. If accounting for even a limited domain (subjectivity) demands a formulation of transcendental and empirical idealism as dialectically interarticulated, the ambition of idealism to deliver a definitive statement of the conditions of (im)possibility for rational satisfaction may find itself unsettled from within.

Hegel's absolute idealism (arguably) absolutizes the purview and self-appropriative power of reflection by rendering the object domains over which reflection ranges precipitates of its generative/synthetic activity, i.e., not natural givens but normative delimitations. Schelling's objective idealism skeptically insists on the reflective irrecuperability of the possibility of reflection itself — thus of reflection's generative activity — by demonstrating that the genesis of an object domain over which reflection may range, i.e., the assemblage of a system of categories or determination of a symbolic field, cannot itself be unproblematically accounted for within the field of reflection. Any such accounting would be constituted, therefore incomplete.

It would involve a new layer of description, a regime of reflection itself in need of accounting, thus would indefinitely defer the self-totalization sought. Schelling's skeptical idealism is bound to aspirations to totalization no less than Hegel's absolute idealism. As the preeminent contemporary commentator on Schelling, Markus Gabriel, puts the point, "Hegel does not achieve any absolute closure of form. There is no logical 'absolute form,' as Hegel believes, precisely because reflection in its all-embracing claim to positivity cannot sufficiently reflect its being conditioned by a process which is not always already reflective" (2009, 41). Reflection is necessarily constituted, therefore cannot provide a neutral account of its constituting activity; it finds its insuperable internal limit in what Schelling calls mythology. The autopoiesis of reflection remains its blind spot. The conditions for determinacy are indeterminate, and such indeterminacy is the groundless ground of Notional freedom, thus the Notion cannot close upon itself; it remains fractured and propelled by the ineffable.

Schelling's skepticism, however, is unconvincing because it suppresses the distinction between a context of discovery or genesis and a context of justification, and thereby glosses over the question of salience. Excess is not ontologically or logically guaranteed unless reflection *must* pursue seamless self-integration, unconditionally satisfying self-transparency; a self-justifying, fully — albeit perhaps provisionally — satisfying dispensation of reflection is *conceivable* if the demands of and on reflection are historically variable. There is no *a priori* reason that the necessity of a regime of reflection could not be deduced from within its own terms. Of course, the necessity of that regime of reflection may not be binding on all, and its conditions of emergence may be obscure, but these conditions are not necessarily salient to its satisfactions. Why *must* preconditions always be accounted for? In what sense is *the possibility of determinacy* a *presupposition* of determinacy? Why would (or when would) the impossibility of accounting for the possibility of determinacy be salient to the determination (or evaluation) of determinacy?[2] Schelling's claim that reflection is conditioned by and actualizes itself as an indeterminate process — an animus — for which it cannot account is a theoreticist displacement of history that either addresses a very strange question of justification — why would the sort of self-closure Schelling demonstrates to be impossible be necessary, valuable, significant, rationally obligatory, etc.? — or illicitly makes an interesting question of discovery/genesis into a misleading question of justification while denying the available responses to this question (e.g., Fichte's account of the summons[3]).

Schelling radicalizes Hegel's ambition to render the purview of reason absolute, bringing brute existence and mere meaningfulness into the equation in order to interrupt it; but existence and meaningfulness *per se* need not demand explanation (this is one possible lesson of Hegel's *Logic*) — they could just be recursive posits or phenomenologically granted axioms of inquiry. Or empty categories. Schelling (and perhaps following him, Heidegger) reifies the absolute as withdrawing with each determination of a fundamental object domain or arrangement of categories (metaphysical order; epoch of Being), objective idealism now shading into transcendental realism. Refusing to relinquish the idea of the absolute, desperately introjecting and thereby preserving the salience of immediacy (as always already lost and distorted), Schelling's skepticism twins the systematic ambitions by which he has clearly been seduced.[4] Perhaps such ambitions are better mourned and divested (or in Hegel's idiom, forgiven) than so negated. Schellingian mythology is melancholy reified.

If Hegel's purported satisfaction with his achievement of reflective self-closure is what Schellingian skepticism means to corrode with demonstrations that self-understanding necessarily involves reiterated recursive abstraction, thus self-loss, then Schelling may be fighting against a false foil. Arguably, Hegel's dialectical mobilization of categories means to absolutely expand the reach of idealism (normative self-consciousness) by releasing it from its orientation toward and promise of consummate categorical stability (an orientation and promise of Kantian provenance). Various empirical realisms geared to diverse categories and variably motivated (yet always "historically informed") manners of their interarticulation may be what, on Hegel's conception, the absolute autonomy of reflection amounts to. The genuine disagreement between Hegel and Schelling, then, may concern Hegel's *methodological* presupposition that the rational is the actual and the interests it bears.[5] An "ethical" disagreement. Putting this possibility aside, as its defense would demand a lengthy exegesis unsuited to this context, and one burdened with the fact that even if Hegel gestures in the abovementioned direction at crucial moments, there are many passages supporting Schelling's reading, let us say that at least from Schelling's perspective, Hegel's interest in underwriting the unlimited ideality of reflection inherits Kant's claim that rational satisfaction (the satisfaction of the demands of reason) means absolute determination.[6] But of course the same can be said of Schelling's denial that reflection can close on itself. Schelling certainly, and Hegel perhaps, remains within the orbit of the absolute, bound to the promise of unqualified rational satisfaction even when reflecting on its irredeemability. "Mythology" is just the creative-poetic expression of the thought that though ever-beckoning, such satisfaction cannot be had. It is the mania of despair; such skepticism a short step to *ennui*.

What Schelling reifies as the moment of mythology generated by reason's attempt to coil around itself is from the perspective of dialectical idealism a hypostatization and thus distortion of perspectival self-consciousness issuing from contingent dialogical interaction. Unlike Hegel's absolute idealism and Schelling's objective idealism, dialectical idealism is not oriented toward the completion or interruption of reflective self-closure (totalization). Rather, it assumes along with the ontological indeterminacy of its subject matter, the displacement of the Kantian horizon in which rational satisfaction means absolute determination. It seeks more diverse and insecure satisfactions issuing from dialectically driven inquiry and its immanent dissonance. Where Schelling would insist on the immanent exterior of mythic ineffability, dialectical idealism would underscore the historically ineluctable conditions for self-consciousness and their realization in dialectics of creation/discovery, universalization/particularization, blindness/insight, inflation/deflation — generally, the variable but not arbitrary interface of the transcendental and the material. Unable to chart a course through steady streams of deduction, dialectical idealism hiccups its way along, drawing attention to obscurity in the concrete contexts of perspectival development — where it might matter.

INDETERMINACY AND IDENTITY

As understood herein, to claim that psychic life is ontologically indeterminate is not to suggest that psychic phenomena can just be crafted any which way by the mystical force of interpretation or that the success of diverse castings must be equivocal because relative to diverse interpretive schemes. That would be both obscurantist and highly implausible. Although the significance of the past can be modified via investments in new or reconfigured narrative or symbolic frameworks that allow the sedimented significance of past events to loosen and subside as latent meaning-potentials of these events are realized, as Lady Macbeth discovered to her great dismay, "What's done cannot be undone" (Act V, Scene 1). Psychic life is historical: irreversible and incessantly intermediate. Though trauma may be remediable, its incendiary force is inextinguishable; remediation, i.e., (re)symbolization or (re)integration, is conditioned by, and however obliquely and unwittingly, disclosive of the fact and perhaps the nature of the trauma. The range of realizable meaning-potentials of past events are conditioned by individual and collective developmental histories.

Although one's self-image can change considerably via new interpretations of formative events, of what events have been formative, and of individual and collective latencies, ongoing social recognition of a reformulated self-image is a condition for its coherence and endurance, its very practicability. Interpreting it so can only make it so, when it can, if the interpretation's precipitate, the newly formed or reformed self-image, achieves sufficient social corroboration: intersubjective recognition and institutional support.

To be sure, interpretive revisions may render us available to futures — experiences, forms of individual and collective self-realization — that our current psychic structures and dispositions inhibit. By means of interpretive reorientation we may alight upon and become attuned to prospects for realizing that which has been buried under the weight and suffering of our psychosocial status quo, become more available to or at least capable of lending consideration to, that which has been tendentially muted or distorted by the entrenched forms of selective attention to which our psychic histories, conflicts, and the like have given rise — and so to what keeps such forms of selective attention in place, what keeps us committed to our suffering and ignorance. Interpretation may yield more expansive, attuned, and fulfilling forms of perception and response; freedom of imagination, feeling, and thought; freedom of initiation and for responsibility (the dialectic of agency). One might even say that the point of inducing and interpreting transference is to remobilize drives for the sake of new beginnings. But we cannot interpretively will our way into our dreams.

If the claim were that psychic life is unlimitedly available to interpretive will, akin to prime matter for certain strands of Medieval theological nominalism, it would rightly fall prey to suspicions of spuriously divinizing either the self or the social, depending on where one locates the source of interpretive authority.

But to contest strong empirical idealism is not necessarily to accede to transcendental or any other form of realism. In fact, to venture the claim that psychic life is ontologically indeterminate is to suspend the assumption on which any realism regarding the psychic must be based: that the psyche is a fully positive substance, that there is a paradoxically mind-independent nature of the mind or subject-independent reality of the subject to which beliefs may correspond, and in corresponding with which, become knowledge, and with respect to which therapeutic interventions can decisively hit or miss their mark.[7] It is thus to propose that investigations of psychic life that are primarily oriented toward representational accuracy, i.e., aspire to deliver third-personal, intersubjectively verifiable knowledge of psychic structures, contents, and processes, or presume a privileged position from which the third-personal truth of psychosexuality can be dogmatically proclaimed, are categorically misleading. This is not to deny that representational ambitions are often appropriate and informative. It is to suggest, however, that psychic phenomena may confound efforts to construe them as consistent, enduring, and systematically integrated substances fully present to the classical representational regard. If and to the extent that certain aspects of psychic life are distorted when construed from, or occluded by, a third-personal, contemplative vantage-point, e.g., if the spectatorial stance must miss subjectivity's excessiveness vis-à-vis particular subjective determinations, representational programs will have to acknowledge their limits. If and to the extent that certain aspects of psychic life are intrinsically elusive — self-effacing or self-distorting, e.g., evident only in the difficulties, perturbations, inconsistencies, or breakdowns of symbolization or self-narration, or manifest only as that which the vividness of memory conceals — the clarity and coherence of representational depiction, its confident capture of the matter at hand, may signal its infelicity, hence require representation to bend toward witnessing, testimony, or otherwise oblique indication. Or, less pertinent to our immediate concerns but still to the point of clarifying the limits of representation vis-à-vis psychic life, if certain psychic phenomena arise and/or develop spontaneously, in ways that cannot be accounted for by any psychic mechanism, if certain psychic phenomena are in this sense singular rather than particular, then the systematic aspirations of the representational program will have to acknowledge a fundamental limitation.

Two distinct sets of claims may be involved in the claim that psychic life is ontologically indeterminate:

(1) Psychic life is partially (and unevenly) pliable to interpretive constitution; and interpretive self-constitution is a necessary and ongoing feature of human subjectivity — its (constitutively provisional) achievement *is* the achievement of (constitutively provisional) subjectivity.

(2) There are evident moments of spontaneity in psychic life; and such spontaneity may signal not just contingent epistemic incompletion but ontological indeterminacy.

Commitment to psychoanalysis as an irreducibly pluralistic enterprise only entails commitment to the former conception of psychic indeterminacy. And fortunately so, for the latter conception may amount to a misplaced concretion of spontaneity: what seem to be empirically spontaneous developments "in the mind" may only *seem* that way because knowledge of the mental is not yet systematically complete, or worse, because we have confused the syntactic and semantic indeterminacy of intentional contents — that there is no definitive description of an intentional content; that the meaning of a belief, desire, hope, or fear may be successively redetermined with alterations to its bearer's fundamental forms of self- and world-comprehension, or more generally, with its differential place in variable contexts of significance — with the empirical operations of the mind itself. Indeterminacy figured as spontaneity may be but a reified image of our ek-static temporality, our self-transfigurative capacity, indeed our freedom. Worse still, the ontologization of indeterminacy as empirical spontaneity may, paradoxically, displace our freedom through its reified rendering as but blind nature. In the ontologization of spontaneity one may detect extreme anxiety, a dogged and doomed attempt to preserve freedom we fear we are on the cusp of loosing or have already lost. The ontologization of spontaneity may be a metaphysical displacement of melancholy.

To say that psychic life is ontologically indeterminate in the first sense is to claim that in the context of human beings, who are necessarily and constitutively self-interpreting and socially mediated, the significance of psychic phenomena, thus to a degree, developments and dispositions of psychic structure, remain underdetermined; the significance of psychic material is, as such beings are, inexorably expositive, relational, and reconfigurable. From a slightly different angle, one could press the claim by focusing on the phenomena rather than the context: a great many psychic phenomena, including aversions, anxieties, beliefs, desires, moods, fantasies, feelings, and self-images are relatively, though variably, inchoate; they are not self-subsistent, decisively definable contents, and this not just because they are context dependent, thus open-ended constellations of meaning, but because "in themselves" they are not fully individuated or discursive — they are as fuzzy and fluctuating as experience, perhaps partaking of its weak concept-transcendence. For the present purposes it matters little whether one emphasizes indeterminacy as sourced in socially mediated self-interpretations through which the symbolic and affective significance of experience is shaped and reshaped or in the inchoateness, the inherent and insuperable negativity or excess of possibility, of certain psychic phenomena. Either way, the inevitable excess of psychic life vis-à-vis interpretive concretion comes into view. So the basic point might be phrased as follows: a wide array of psychic phenomena attain their evolving, ever-indeterminate significance in a matrix of socially mediated yet irreducibly individuated interpretive self-constitution.

To say that we are *necessarily* self-interpreting and socially mediated is to say that (1) the content of experience, like the subject of experience, does not come fully forged. The content of experience cannot be derived from the objects of experience or their circumstantial arrangements, i.e., involves our activity; and correlatively, the coherence of the subject of experience, thus the possibility of meaning, of having experiences rather than merely being at a causal nexus, is not guaranteed by the sequentiality of undergoings — it too involves our activity. The content of experience does not come ready made, or to the extent that it does, like ready made paint, remains stranded in mere possibility, is no more than suggestive, until involved in a practice; nor is the unity of the subject of experience, thus the horizon of meaning, implied by merely being the locus of various undergoings identifiable from a point of spectatorial abstraction. Consciousness implies self-consciousness, and self-consciousness is an activity: the underdetermined, ongoing assumption of a stance on our experiences, thus on ourselves, whereby we become selves (provided sufficient social recognition; subjectivity implies intersubjectivity). The content of experience depends on our interpretively innovating or assuming (i.e., ratifying or recasting) a socially suggested or naturally prompted interpretation of experience, integrating the experience as interpreted into our operative forms of self- and world-understanding, perhaps revising or recalibrating them accordingly, *and in doing so making it ours*. Self-consciousness is necessary activity.

As should be clear, to say that we are necessarily self-interpreting is not to subscribe to a triumphalist metaphysics of self-determination and thereby discount the extent to which socialization prescribes the significance of various experiences. From infancy onwards we are exposed to, indeed relentlessly bombarded by, socially normative interpretations of our experiences. Social integration and reproduction require a minimum symbolic hegemony, though of course symbolic hegemony ordinarily extends far beyond such functional requirements. Subjectivity is constituted, in part, by unremitting susceptibility to socio-symbolic suggestion. Indeed, the very "activity" of self-interpretation is so deeply conditioned by formative socio-symbolic influences that attempting to distinguish the contribution of the self from the contribution of the social, to demarcate the authentic from the inauthentic, is often a fool's game, an open invitation to befuddled consternation and dogmatic reaction. Especially when efforts to distinguish what comes from the self as opposed to the social treat the self as a positive entity — a fact — rather than a normative status, the results are regularly confounded paralysis and flight into a fantasy of privileged self-access and self-interpretive sovereignty.

As should be equally clear, however, the claim that socio-symbolic influence is unavoidable must be strictly distinguished from the presumption of its sovereign efficacy.[8] The coding of experience through socio-symbolic suggestion, however strong, consistent, and pervasive, and however well supported by normalizing institutions and punitive apparati, ordinarily operates in a contested field. Symbolic hegemony is usually unstable and incomplete, requiring reconsolidation through the continual integration or marginalization of competing symbolic options (including those to which it may unwittingly give rise).[9] Not infrequently, the reconsolidation of symbolic hegemony relies on abusive displays of alternatives — specters of madness, depravity, immorality, precarity, abject unintelligibility, crisis and catastrophe of every sort rendered as the consequences or content of such alternatives — that aim to incite revulsion, and so anxious reattachment, but may prove attractive supports for subversive appropriation and contestation or circumvention, and even if not, keep hegemony unstable by binding it to alternatives. Because symbolic hegemony often sustains itself through the managed spectacle of crisis at its collapse (what it excludes is immanent to its strategies of survival); because it is ordinarily unable to overwhelm — assimilate or marginalize — or even identify and target the array of alternatives; because its assimilations and marginalizations may misfire, triggering unanticipated consequences including tensions, resistances, redeployments, and reconfigurations; because its interpretive networks cannot easily efface the heterogeneous, thus potentially reconfigurable, elements of which it is constituted; and because it relies on resistance, or at least the possibility thereof (which is the promise of every newcomer), symbolic hegemony is tendentially unstable and incomplete. And because socio-symbolic codes must be assumed and elaborated in a unique context of significance, that is, a unique life — a life composed by a unique history, associative patterning, metabolizing tendencies, relational configurations, etc. — their assimilation may be the occasion for individualizing inflection and redirection. The reproduction of symbolic hegemonies necessarily opens them onto the chance of reformulation or differential accentuation; each occasion of interpretive assumption is a possible occasion for resisting, rejecting, or idiosyncratically elaborating (working through) socially suggested meanings. Helping out in the kitchen may be repeatedly coded as "being a good girl," but as chance may have it, resistance to parental desire, authority, and expectations (and all that is bound up therewith) may constellate around just this scene of interpolation, turning it into a privileged site of resistance and individuation. Contrary to the interpellative intention, "being a good girl" may become what one least wants to do. And because idiosyncratic elaboration, if sustainable, requires social recognition, it may become exemplary, subject to broader uptake and therewith a multiplication of differential inflections.

Likewise, even if certain interpretations of our experiences are naturally prompted, we are not thereby relieved of responsibility for assuming them: ratifying or elaborating and integrating them. Assuming such responsibility is assuming subjectivity (or attempting to). To say that certain interpretations may be naturally prompted is to say that young children may be predisposed to construe, and older children, adolescents, and adults predisposed to consider construing, a certain range of phenomena through particular concepts, schemata, and interpretive orientations. The most likely contenders for this sort of natural authority are concepts, schemata, and interpretive orientations whose scope of employment and specificity cannot be adequately accounted for by inductive explanation (because the properties of the objects are so heterogeneous that induction cannot explain the consistency with which particular forms of categorization and interpretation are employed) or social-mimetic explanation (because the concepts and interpretive orientations appear, if at all, only marginally in social environment; if they do show up, their apparent social significance pales in comparison with the weight they have for the child).[10] This cognitive endowment may include, for instance, categorical distinctions between the living and the non-living,[11] distinctions of kind among the living (i.e., folk species differentiation), the idea that human beings are divisible into enduring kinds with innate characteristics (what Lawrence Hirschfeld calls "the idea of race"),[12] and interpretive-evaluative orientations such as in-group bias.[13] But that we may be naturally *prompted* to employ or reckon with such categories, concepts, interpretive orientations by no means entails that we are preordained to assume them. Even if insuperable, the authority of nature is certainly not overwhelming. These classificatory and interpretive impulses may be queried, rejected, or elaborated by older children, and perhaps even younger children can be taught to override their insistence. Even if certain categorical inclinations cannot but be contended with, they are not on their own normatively binding.

Next, to say that we are *necessarily* self-interpreting is to say (2) that assuming a relatively stable interpretive stance on a range of issues considered fundamental to one's identity — e.g., the meaning of one's attachments and frustrations, the ranking of one's values, the significance of one's sexuateness, etc. — is necessary for intelligibility as a person, which in turn is necessary for viable social and psychological existence. Viable claims to personhood involve practices of performative self-figuration (expressive self-interpretation) though which one takes a stand on — assumes and elaborates — certain features of subjectivity that have come to be considered — or in certain cases, that one performatively presses a novel claim for consideration as — constitutive of the human condition. Exactly what one must take a stand on may be socially and historically variable, but even if there are no universally necessary, minimal conditions for (recognition of) personhood, those that are socially and historically in force are near-uncircumventable terms through which personhood must be figured; circumventing these terms would require compellingly instituting others, nothing less than an act of Kantian genius, i.e., performing personhood in such a way that though the performance fails to satisfy the prevailing terms of intelligibility, its claim is still, and on its own terms, which have through its efficacy become our terms, persuasive; to successfully circumvent prevailing terms of intelligibility, a performance must condition its own reception, render its internal criteria for evaluation socially exemplary, institute a new rule, and even then, perhaps, the terms it institutes must compensate for and so remain in dialogue with the terms ostensibly circumvented — as is more evidently the case with supplementation or reconfiguration. For instance, if being sexuate is considered coextensive with being human, then performatively articulating one's sexuate being (e.g., desire, identifications, and kinship commitments) will be necessary to achieve intelligibility and social standing as a person.

Certainly the sort of self-interpretation under consideration is no merely mental or private affair, no intimate dialogue of the soul with itself. Rather, it is a preeminently public activity of expressive self-elaboration (= interpretive self-realization). Introspective reflection on what it means to bear such-and-such characteristics, desires, attachments and aversions, historical inheritances, identifications, moral and political commitments, relational predilections, etc. may be involved, but these reflections are as if nothing if they are not enacted through individuating practices of self-figuration, publicly legible performances in which identity stakes a claim to expressive realization. Nothing harbored in the innermost recesses of the heart certifies the truth of identity. *Identity is performative or not at all.*

In this context, the distinction between public and private is as troubled as that between (self-)description and performance, passivity and activity, or individuation and inheritance. If the epitome of privacy, namely, introspective reflection by means of which one seeks to discover who one truly is, must draw on inherited terms and through words, gestures, and deeds manifest in, must *be*, publicly staged acts of self-expression through which one creates and recreates a public persona, if such self-creation or — personification is not voluntaristic self-fashioning but proceeds for the most part as the assumption and elaboration of socially prescribed terms of intelligible subjectivity, and if performative self-realization is a medium of collective self-discovery, a way a social body discovers its limits and possibilities, then with regard to identity the private can be cleanly distinguished from the public as little as self-description can be held apart from performative self-realization.[14] Subjectivity is an intersubjective dialectic of creation and discovery.

Finally, to say that we are *necessarily* self-interpreting[15] is to say that (3) we must continually schematize, or in narrative terms, emplot our actions and experiences if they are to count as ours, register as the actions and experiences of a single, abiding subject, the protagonist of her own life story.[16] The intelligibility of action and experience generated by the ongoing, recursive, retrospective, and anticipatory gestures of narrative emplotment is a condition for subjective integrity, the experience of oneself as the subject of meaningfully connected actions and experiences rather than subject to, a merely episodic point of convergence of, blind causal forces. It is a condition for assuming a first-person perspective, for the experience of oneself as a singular, unsubstitutable doer of deeds and bearer of consequences rather than an object of unintelligible necessity — or only third-personally intelligible. Thus it is a condition for the experience, indeed the very possibility, of agency, for intelligibility as a doer of meaning-bearing deeds that, together with one's formative experiences, condition one's future development, and for which one can be held and hold oneself responsible. Through narrative we turn temporal succession, the happenstance of going-through, into significant sequence and thus into a course of life that can be acknowledged as ours. Narrative transforms what would otherwise be merely juxtaposed or abstractly (e.g., lawfully) coordinated events into the formative experiences and expressive initiatives of a developing subject. Through narrative self-elaboration, we project a future and thereby stake a claim as to what would count as a continuation of *this* life by regathering the past as our past. By recounting and reckoning with what we have done and what we have suffered, we come to have a past that can be acknowledged and a future that can be lived as ours. By transfiguring a succession of events into significant sequences, narrative self-elaboration gives birth, concurrently and coextensively, to a subject and a world. Through narrative, we claim ourselves by claiming a world in which, stretched between past and future, we feature as fundamental points of reference: a world comes to gravitate around us, a world whose coherence or lack thereof reflects our own. To self-narrate is to construe oneself as the subject of experiences and doer of deeds that collectively compose — or at least lay claim to composing — the dramatic developments of one's life course and that set the terms for one's future development. What would otherwise be a mobile locus of causal interactions or spectator of impersonal sensations (as in certain moments of Flaubert and Proust), becomes a subject of experience.

Or to put the point the other way around, those events that resist integration into our fundamental forms of self- and world-comprehension, that cannot be woven into narrative self-elaboration even as incitements to its reconfiguration, affix us to a space-time of dead repetition, impact a moment of unassumable immediacy, an insuperable inertia, into subjectivity that intermittently dislocates the first-person perspective, swamping it in a mass of objectivity. Such events encrust another place, another time into the narrative fabric; they are not just dissonant but radically external to experience, alienating us at once from ourselves and our constitutive others as they absorb us into their dead weight. Such events exert a traumatic efficacy by disrupting the narrative metabolism through which experience, selfhood, and worldliness are concurrently and coextensively unified and by means of which the future comes into view as a continuation of the past, there where what lies latent can be worked out.[17]

That we are necessarily self-narrating, though, does not mean that we can or must organize our experiences into a unified trajectory of unbroken linear progress. That would be to conflate narrative with (idealized) conceptual synthesis, to reduce the thrown projection of a life, the dialectical creation/discovery of a self, to the step-wise unfolding of a determinate principle: to map the deductive order of logic onto the material order of life. If successful, self-narration strikes a balance, each time unique, of consonance and dissonance. Far from rendering all actions and experiences immediately intelligible, fully self-present, narrative self-envelopment implies endless exposure to indeterminacy and plurivocity. If the significance of our actions is not immediately given but rather determined by the consequences they will have initiated, including the prospects for anticipatory and retrospective self-narration they will have opened, narrative self-recuperation will always be a moment too late and too soon, self-presence indefinitely deferred. Narrative self-elaboration, if constitutively belated and self-supplementary, will be the unresolved story of a subject-in-process. And if the consequences our actions will have initiated, including the prospects for retrospective and prospective narratability they will have opened, concern not simply ourselves but an undeterminable multitude of others, our life stories are never simply our own. Action's reverberations in excess of intention and unconfinability to first-person assessment mimetically correspond to narrative's essential retrospectivity and expositivity[18] — the dialectical interplay of which gives rise, in literary terms, to the demand for sequels, spinoffs, and backstories (demands constitutively suspended — issued but unfulfilled — by modernist, i.e., autonomy inclined, literature). The fulfillment of our stories requires, and is indefinitely deferred by, their telling by others. Indeed, our stories cannot but become a collective concern if they are to have any sort of conclusion.[19]

The narrated self is a complexion of determinacy and indeterminacy, a chiasmus of past and future, the subject of in principle indeterminate, because redeterminable, multiply relatable actions and experiences, a nodal point in a web of power relations. If at all adequate, narrative form will have to accommodate this by elaborating its subject as a problematic individual rather than an epic hero playing out an allotted fate, i.e., find some way to express the excess of ek-static temporality and relationality vis-à-vis represented content.

Far from securing replete self- and world-intelligibility, the consistency afforded by narrative form is precisely the context within which various actions and experiences can stand out as problematic — and not just as anomalies to known laws of development but as potentially formative events freighted with as yet undecided significance, as enigmatic openings onto futures whose realizations depend on whether and how their provocation is assumed. Only against the backdrop of narrative consistency can events manifest as opaque developments in the dramas of our lives and thereby challenge our privileged forms of self- and world-comprehension. The consistency afforded by narrative form is the context within which we can become problems for ourselves, spurred to work out (create/discover) the significance of our actions and experiences through further action and interpretive work. The world-orientation afforded by narrative self-elaboration is the context in which events can exert their estranging and disruptive force, what makes for the difference between inert or merely causally effective externality and the challenge of an event. As a condition of possibility for subjective integrity, narrative cohesion is a condition for a certain range of traumas (if traumatic impingements are always impingements upon structures of expectation).

Much of what it means to say that we are *constitutively* self-interpreting is implied above. In one sense, it is to propose that we become who we are by assuming sufficiently consistent,[20] coherent, and socially corroborated interpretive stances on our actions, inclinations, experiences and memories.[21] Below the threshold of achieving subjectivity and simplifying for the sake of heuristic convenience, one might say that, for instance, when children are beset by troubling affects associated with dependency and attachment and find themselves in need of a framework to make sense of and perhaps bind and thereby modify or temper, or in some way get a handle on their experiences of loss, threat, frustration, excitement, desire, and dependence, they may commit themselves to an Oedipal narrative/fantasy:[22] tending to interpret the relatively hazy state of primordial attachment and aversion to or frustration by one's caregivers in terms of Oedipal ambivalence is just what it means to be Oedipally ambivalent; likewise, tending to interpret frustration as abandonment or withholding, abandonment or withholding as an expression of aggression, the suffering of aggression as a standing motive for revenge, the standing possibility of vengefulness as reason to fear punitive repercussions, and so on, is just what it is to be in the paranoid-schizoid position; or tending to interpret others' weaknesses, faults, failures, and suffering as opportunities to be of assistance and elaborating these interpretations in social interaction is just what it is to be a kind person.[23] On the assumptions that (1) experience is not fully formulated upon impact but conceptually (under)determined, constituted by conceptual mediation yet more dense than its conceptual elaboration, thus indefinitely subject to reinscription, i.e., conceptualized if coherent yet conceptually inexhaustible or weakly concept transcendent — this is perhaps most evident with regard to affect; and (2) memory is pliable because meaning is pliable,[24] the claim is that experience and memory achieve determination, and we along with them, as they are interpretively cast: semantically and syntactically organized

What we undergo is for the most part, and especially initially, rather vague, not exactly confused but ill-defined.[25] How we remember the past and locate ourselves in its legacy may be constrained by the incontestable impact of certain events but is not simply determined by them.[26] The contents and structures of experience are not immediately given in full-fledged form; they are relatively amorphous and (in part because) mutually conditioning, of lastingly indeterminacy insignificance. Even after the initial imprecision of experience fades under the weight of settled interpretative commitment, its indeterminacy does not simply evaporate but ordinarily transmutes into the hazy lining of memory. Psychic phenomena are ontologically indeterminate: relatively though variably inchoate, neither transparently given to conscious immediacy nor fully positive contents registered by and warehoused in the unconscious, lying in wait for decoding and retrieval. Their — thus our — semantic and syntactic organization involves, in a certain sense, the ontological generativity of self-interpretation.

With respect to psychic phenomena, then, the question of what it is (and so the question of who I am) undergoes an enduring crisis. If and to the extent that "it" is not a stable, enduring substance, some bit of absolute reality the comprehensive understanding of which would explain both the entity itself and the history of its variously distorted conceptualizations; if and to the extent that "it" is not a mind-independent reality, thus a truthmaker for statements asserted of it, then what the classical question "What is it?" (*ti esti*) is driving at is better obtained obliquely, perhaps through a conjunction of questions and inquiries that register the singular complexion of determinacy and indeterminacy of the subject matter, its constitution by a dialectic of creation and discovery.

Lest this be heard as a metaphysical hypostatization of the distinction between mere, indeterminate sensation and conceptual formulation, that is, as positing sense data as the raw material of socially mediated interpretive self-formation, let us underscore that even rare experiences of what can be called pure sensory impressions acquire their putative purity only by manifesting *as* abrasively unassimilable to reigning conceptual mediations, and thereby preserve an essential reference to them. The apparent concrete givenness of pure sensory impression is anything but; such experiences are *abstract* precisely in virtue of their abstraction from, i.e., suppressed mediation by, our ordinary conceptual orientations. What can figure *as* purely sensuous, in other words, depends on our conceptual dispositions; "the purely sensuous" can only be *posited* as such.

Were sense impressions as immediate as they are sometimes claimed to be, we could not build concepts from them since the work of the reproductive imagination through which sense impressions are associated on the basis of their resemblances requires concepts or proto-conceptual schemas in virtue of which resemblances can be discerned as resemblances. Hume's mistake, in other words, was to deny the necessity of (proto-)concepts for the discernment of resemblances and thereby leave the question of how concepts are formed an empirical question — supplemented by some evolutionary speculations and gerrymandering of the scope of the concept — in order to avoid making the matter wholly mysterious.[27] But treating concept formation as an empirical question will never explain the intra- and inter-personal consistency of conceptual composition from extremely heterogeneous sensations. Though appeal to Platonic archetypes would leave the matter just as mysterious — this would be just another way of stating the problem, not solving it — perhaps Plato's *forms* can be understood as our natural and cultural conceptual endowment, our inherited and engrained habits of gathering appearances, in light of which attention is cued to various similarities and differences. Sense impression is not the raw stuff of the world but a moment of indeterminacy abstracted from a dialectic of determination.

Likewise, much of what it means to say that we are necessarily and constitutively *socially mediated* is implied above. Broadly, it is to propose that subjectivity, indeed experience, unfolds for the most part as an assumption — ratification or recasting — of socially inherited terms or interpretive dispositions; that subjectivity implies subjection. It is to suggest that we are inexorably relational and expositive, thus never in full control of the significance of our words, deeds, experiences, and self-images; that relationality and expositivity are internal to subjectivity. Although by wording the world we come to have a world, those words are, thus that world is, never simply our own. Inherited terms are the largely insuperable coordinates for interpretive self-constitution. However much given to idiomatic innovation, the necessary and constitutive self-interpretation of (what may thereby become) our actions and experiences requires reference to social regimes of intelligibility and ongoing corroboration (acknowledgment, desirative investment) if it is to prove practicable — a medium of expressive self-realization rather than a fantasy consigned to incoherence and/or rigid repetition. The innermost recesses of psychic life are necessarily permeable to social influence, although not a neutral medium for social inscription. Psychic life transpires not "in the head" but in intersubjective space, indeed as an intersubjective dialectic of creation and discovery. The exquisite permeability of experience, affect, meaning, and self-image to social mediation is most clear in the case of young children: through their physical, vocal, and emotional comportment, generally, their responsive dispositions, caregivers shape the meaning and affective structure of their children's relatively inchoate experiences.[28] And to the extent to which we remain childlike throughout our lives, vulnerable and dependent, the mutuality of meaning — hence indeterminacy — is irreducible.

The discussion of the second set of claims will be brief since they do not directly follow from the plurality premise and require consideration in a more fitting context (chapter 7). To venture the thought that psychic life is, to some as yet unspecified extent, spontaneous is to deny that psychic life is of a piece with deterministic natural processes, i.e., stable mechanisms that reliably respond to stimuli in programmatically predictable and systematically reconstructable ways. It is to entertain the prospect of *de novo* mutation at the level of psychic processing and so to urge consideration of psychic life as, in part, epistemically indeterminate because ontologically indeterminate. If certain features of psychic life are genuinely spontaneous, unpredictably cropping up here and there in the midst of established regularities or what had seemed to be deterministic mechanisms, the possibility of a systematically complete metapsychology or theory of the mind comes under pressure. To risk the thought of psychic spontaneity is to call for a rethinking of the human as insuperably heterogeneous, categorically underdetermined. All the more so if certain spontaneous psychic developments are neither immediately meaningful nor ultimately recruitable into the order of meanings, the thought of psychic spontaneity presses for an ethos of humility with respect to what is presumably most proximate as it sends a tremor through the anthropo*logical* horizon.

To say that psychic life is ontologically indeterminate in the senses sketched above is not to advance a comprehensive "theory of the mind." If certain psychic phenomena are either strictly other to the order of significance or tenuously poised between the orders of sense and nonsense, there will be exceptions to the first model of indeterminacy. There may be strictly meaningless organic aspects of psychic life, as in Hobson's well known anti-psychoanalytic theory of dreams as meaningless and bizarre mental discharges, and there may be certain psychic tendencies that either altogether evade or partially resist incorporation into the order of significance, as in Jonathan Lear's theory of spontaneous mental self-interruption, certain Lacanian conceptions of the death drive and the Real, Santner's notion of "significant stress," Laplanche's "enigmatic signifiers," a number of crucial Kristevan concepts, etc. And of course, the intelligibility of the second model presupposes that the scope of spontaneity, thus indeterminacy, is limited. The claim that psychic life is ontologically indeterminate is certainly exaggerated.

Rather than implausibly denying that psychic life is ontologically determinate and epistemically determinable, this chapter seeks to sponsor a dialectical engagement of determinacy and indeterminacy. The suggestion is that psychic phenomena may be best conceived as complex admixtures of sense and nonsense (content and enigma), historical weight and future eventuality (being and nothingness), generally, determinacy and indeterminacy. By no means do I want to deny that we can make genuine discoveries about psychic phenomena,[29] but I do want to suggest that discovery may be no mere unveiling but rather partially — though depending on the specific phenomena at stake, variably — constitutive of what is found.

Objections from within psychoanalysis to the suggestion that psychic life is ontologically indeterminate, especially when the suggestion is strongly urged, are not difficult to imagine. Is not insisting on the indeterminacy of affect or the vagueness of inner life a typical evasive tactic?[30] Might not the suggestion of the ontological indeterminacy of psychic life risk collusion with resistances? A Winnicottian might worry that the claim is a generalization of the self-perception of a false self. A Culturalist — e.g., Karen Horney — might worry that it opaquely reflects, indeed reifies or ontologizes, the pathological impact of a cultural/historical symbolic collapse. A Jungian might worry that acceptance of the ontological indeterminacy of the psychic, specifically, acceptance of the necessity of retrospective self-elaboration/constitution (*Zuruckfantasieren*), may result in blindness to the current difficulties and disturbances concealed or avoided through certain manners of recreating one's past — generally, blindness to the symptomatic value of self-narration.[31] Potential for abuse certainly does not warrant wholesale repudiation — that would token an impracticable fetishism of purity — but the defense-value of the suggestion is reason to be wary.

NOTES

1. Although (a certain version of) empirical realism may be independently compelling and desirable — there have been many intimations of this throughout — (1) it is not implied by the

claim that psychic life is ontologically indeterminate; and (2) to the extent that the dialectical conversion or defusing of skepticism by empirical realism binds it to the quests for certainty or claims to the absolute against which and sometimes in league with which skepticism often historically took (and still frequently takes) a stand, i.e., if the conversion or defusing of skepticism conveys into empirical realism a constitutive contrast with passions for the absolute which become a condition for its intelligibility, an undischargeable, unmetabolizable inheritance is introduced — as, inversely, (on Lukacs' reading) Kierkegaard's leap of faith bears with it the doubt it presumably overleaps and which becomes central to the experience of faith, enjoining the (impossible) experience of immediacy in reflective mediation, thus aporia (cf. Lukacs 1980 [1962] *The Destruction of Reason*). Or from another angle, if transcendental idealism involves a Table of Categories, a secularized Table of Laws, then stabilizing empirical realism by binding it to transcendental idealism may expose its domesticated skepticism to unwelcome and unruly guests: apparitions of the absolute at, indeed as, its margins. Empirical realism's failure to achieve absolute immanence may be reason to resist or remain ambivalent about commitment to it.

2. Why must the "paradoxical 'existence'" of a "domain of all domains" be "presuppose[d] in order to make sense of the existence of a multitude of mutually determining object domains"? (Gabriel 2009, p. 90) Is it "only 'natural' that we attempt to make sense of the senseless facticity we confront by naming it"? (ibid) If by such naming we achieve "the distance necessary for contingency to have a liberating effect," then what specific forms of bondage or suffering, and so what horizon(s) of satisfaction, are presupposed? (Gabriel 2009, p. 93).

3. Cf. Bernstein (2007) "Recognition and Embodiment."

4. "Contra Hegel, the very existence of intelligibility owes itself to a process it cannot account for. This is the point of introducing the indeterminate conditions of determinacy into logical space. If there are experiences of elusiveness which cannot be overcome, then logical space must have properties which point to a dimension which is not logical" (Gabriel 2009, p. 60). How are the demands of reason imagined such that this impasse would amount to their nonsatisfaction? To what extent might Schellingian mythology bear traces of Christian theology?

5. Indeed, one valence of Hegel's claim that the rational is the actual may be a swipe at Schelling: the rational character and rational potential of the actual is all the reason there is and need be; the non-actual is the non-rational, i.e., the mythological, and so what?

6. It is "subjectively necessary," Kant claims in the *Critique of Judgment*, to presuppose "that nature does not have this disturbing boundless heterogeneity of empirical laws and heterogeneity of natural forms, but that, rather, through the affinity of its particular laws under more general ones it takes on the quality of experience as an empirical system" ("First Introduction" pp. 397-8/209; also cf. *CPR* A556/B584 and B599ff.). Compare Hegel: "The 'I' is as it were the crucible and fire which consumes the loose plurality of sense and reduces it to unity . . . The tendency of all man's endeavors is to understand the world, to appropriate and subdue it to himself; and to this end the positive reality of the world must be as it were crushed and pounded, in other words, idealized." (*Encyclopedia Logic*, p. 69). A more typical passage in which Hegel seems to commit himself to the thesis that rational satisfaction is attained only upon complete determination is: "However, to knowledge, the goal is as necessarily fixed as the series of the progression. The goal lies at that point where knowledge no longer has the need to go beyond itself, that is, where knowledge works itself out, and where the concept corresponds to the object and the object to the concept. Progress toward this goal is thus also unrelenting, and satisfaction is not to be found at any prior station on the way" (*PhG* ¶ 80; translation modified following Pinkard). Also cf. Hegel's *Philosophie der Religion*, pp. 393 and 429ff.

7. To be sure, empirical realism in the Kantian tradition is concerned with consolidating realism with regard to the "outer" (e.g., underwriting scientific knowledge of nature) rather than the "inner." When concern turns to the "inner," it intentionally overshoots it, as evident in Kant's transcendental psychology. So to restrict the scope of the central realist assumption (thoroughgoing determinacy) is not to directly contest empirical realism as pursued within the Kantian tradition, for that tradition already implements such a scope restriction. It is in psycho-

analytic and empirical psychological traditions that one finds various implicit or explicit transcendental and empirical realist claims regarding psychological phenomena in the mundane sense. However, the Kantian intuition that psychic life resists realist construals, once explicated, may have far reaching reverberations that amount to a serious challenge to the Kantian tradition.

8. Cf. Judith Butler (1997) *Excitable Speech*, especially "Sovereign Performatives."

9. Cf. Foucault (1990) *The History of Sexuality, Vol I: An Introduction*, pp. 92-102.

10. Cf. Bernstein (2002) "Re-enchanting Nature," pp. 223-5 and 237-9. Also see Bernstein (2001) *Adorno: Disenchantment and Ethics*.

11. Cf. Michael Thompson (2008) *Life and Action*.

12. Cf. *Race in the Making* (1996).

13. Cf. Max Weber (1978) *Economy and Society*, p. 43ff and 932ff.

14. To say that intelligible personhood requires the assumption of a relatively stable interpretative stance on a range of issues considered fundamental to identity is not to deny that identity is performed sometimes with greater consistency, sometimes with less, or that personal and/or political exigencies may make it crucial to express one's inconsistency in diachronic or synchronic terms, or even to maintain or manifest a certain unintelligibility. Regimes of social intelligibility are not infinitely lenient, *relatively* consistent and recognizable forms of self-interpretation/figuration are necessary for social legibility, and it is all too easy to imagine inconsistent interpretations/realizations of one's desire, sexuate being, or value-priorities, and all the more so obstinately opaque forms of self-expression, being socially coded to mark their bearers as something less than or other than persons. The specters psychosis and abjection haunt the thresholds and police the borders of social intelligibility. But social intelligibility is not an all or nothing affair.

15. The necessity at stake here and throughout is obviously normative. Though it would be misleading to say that such necessity is merely hypothetical — i.e., something that must be accommodated *if* one is interested in viable social identity, as if one could be simply unconcerned with one's social standing, totally aloof from the social regimes of recognition through which one becomes intelligible to oneself and others and acknowledged as a participant in and salient bearer of the consequences of collective practices — perhaps one can say that this form of necessity is *conditional* in the sense of being a fundamental condition for the form of life in which one values one's capacity to value and realize one's values through self-actualizing social performances, a condition for leading a life. And if one does not value oneself in this sense, nothing else *can* matter. Such is the necessity of a material apriori.

16. Whether and to what extent social reification and fragmentation impede successful self-narration is a question that will have to be left for another occasion. On this, cf. J.M. Bernstein (1984) *Philosophy of the Novel: Lukacs, Marxism, and the Dialectics of Form* (1984).

17. In part, the (depleted, overburdened, insecure, yet sometimes compelling and felicitous) authority of psychoanalysis in fragmented and reified conditions of modernity is sourced in its capacity to keep narrative practice, thus subjectivity, alive — partially, precariously. That its authority is conditioned by modernity's destitution of narrative practice is one reason to consider psychoanalysis a historical discourse of suffering and healing *under conditions of modernity* rather than a metaphysical discourse of universal truth.

18. Gertrude Stein, whose flair for autobiography is well known, perhaps knew this best of all. Cf. Stein (1933) *Autobiography of Alice B. Toklas*.

19. When it comes to explicit narrative self-elaboration, who or what prompts us to tell out stories and the when and where — broadly, the power dynamics — of invitations to confessional intimacy or self-revelatory confiding surely condition the accounts that ensue. Emphatically but not exclusively, explicit narrative self-elaboration, however much an occasion for narcissistic jubilance, is always guilty and estranging: one never quite fits the terms and schemas in which one gives an account of oneself. Cf. Denise Riley (2000) *Words of Selves*. Self-narration implicates us in a persistent disquietude, is endemically inconclusive.

20. Cf. Heidegger (1962 [1927]) *Being and Time*, p. 369.

21. For a compelling demonstration of how wide-ranging inconsistency can be compensated by strict coherence and consistency with regard to a select few matters, and how paired

down the context of social corroboration can become, see Edward Albee, *Who's Afraid of Virginia Woolf.*

22. Klein might deny this and insist that there are innate ideas such as "the breast" — the point is not uncontroversial. However, even Klein from time to time refers to the status of her statements as "hypothetical inferences" (cf. Klein 1944, p. 775 and Rosen-Carole (2011) *Lacan and Klein, Creation and Discovery*).

23. Cf. Ian Hacking (1995) *Rewriting the Soul: Multiple Personality and the Sciences of Memory* for intriguing examples regarding multiples. Hacking argues that "[t]he disorder becomes a way of seeing childhood and its terrors. It is not that one split early in life in order to cope. Rather, in therapy, one begins to see oneself as having split at that time in order to cope . . . . We should not think of multiplicity as being strictly caused by child abuse. It is rather that the multiple finds or sees the cause of her condition in what she comes to remember about her childhood, and is helped thereby. This is passed off as a specific etiology, but what is happening is more extraordinary than that. It is a way of explaining oneself, not by recovering the past, but by redescribing it, rethinking it, refeeling it . . . . The soul that we are constantly constructing we construct according to an explanatory model of how we came to be the way we are" (93-4).

24. As Freud puts the point, "Our childhood memories show us our earliest years not as they were but as they appeared at the later periods when the memories were aroused. In these periods of arousal, the childhood memories did not, as people are accustomed to say, emerge; they were formed at that time. And a number of motives, with no concern for historical accuracy, had a part in forming them, as well as in the selection of the memories themselves" (SE 3: 322). Or as he says in a letter to Fliess, "the material present in the form of memory traces [is] subjected . . . to a rearrangement in accordance with fresh circumstances to a reinscription . . . the memory is present not once but several times over . . . laid down in various kinds of indications" (6 Dec 1896). Or from another angle, "Truthfully returning to a reverie does not involve a faithful correspondence to a past state of affairs, but rather a sort of re-creation, allowing again the freedom of movement. Recalling the reverie is calling it forth, regenerating meaning." (Friedlander, 2004, p. 27). Also cf. Sartre (1961) *Psychology of Imagination*, esp. p. 198.

25. Bracketing cases of ideological saturation.

26. Cf. Judith Herman (1992) *Trauma and Recovery.*

27. Plato initiates this type of criticism, e.g., in the *Meno* where Socrates queries whether we can find or even make sense of searching for a unity or pattern in particulars without (in some sense) prior experience of the unity or pattern. Kant continues this form of critique and gives it a modern cast when he claims that the "unity of synthesis according to empirical concepts would be altogether accidental, if these latter were not based on a transcendental ground of unity. Otherwise, it would be possible for appearances to crowd in upon the soul, and yet to be such as would never allow of experience. Since connection in accordance with universal and necessary laws would be lacking, all relation of knowledge to objects would fall away" (CPR A 111).

28. Cf. Bion (1962). On Gitelson's account, "Just as the mother is the target for the child's drives and, in her capacity as auxiliary ego, guides their form and function — thus introducing the operation of the reality principle — so does the analyst draw the focus of the unconscious tendencies with which a patient enters analysis and, in his diatrophic function, provides the irrupting instincts and revived developmental drive with direction and purpose" (1973, 324).

29. "One of the things psychoanalysis means in calling itself a science is that analyst and patient may make genuine discoveries about how the patient sees things, what she wants, phantasizes, believes, remembers, and so on, consciously *and* unconsciously" (M. Cavell 1993, p. 74).

30. Cf. SE 10: 186.

31. As is well known, narcissistic patients in particular may employ narrative as a privileged form of defense against transference and free association.

Chapter Six

Objectivity: A Dialectic of Universalization and Particularization

It is equally deadly for the spirit to have a system and not to have one. It must therefore, perhaps, decide to combine both.

- Friedrich Schlegel, *Athenaeum-Fragments*

THE IMPOSSIBLE IDEALITY OF PSYCHOANALYSIS

Beholden to a double demand, psychoanalysis is irrevocably aporetic. Composed of two antagonistic impulses, one toward universalization and another toward particularization, the discourse and practice of psychoanalysis are fraught with tension. Psychoanalysis cannot but employ and strive to refine widely applicable, inferentially articulated, and explanatory concepts. The efficacy of analytic listening and its cultural appeal require that analysts attend to clinical and cultural phenomena as familiar or potential tokens of types bound together in relations of inference and exclusion. Yet for the very same reasons, psychoanalysis cannot but seek to sustain its exposure to the abrasive particularity or shrouded significance of the clinical or cultural events to which it attends. Indeed, in order to reactivate its constitutive conceptual inheritance, psychoanalysis must tarry with that which cannot be readily encapsulated by received theory and may prove refractory to any conceptual determination, thus systematization.[1]

Precariously poised between inflationary currents and deflationary countercurrents, psychoanalytic discourse and practice are ever off-kilter, unable to repose in themselves, untotalizable. They cannot but propose bold generalities, and fidelity to the discourse and practice of psychoanalysis implies seriously undertaking such conceptual adventures, sustaining their claims to truth. But in the name of the recalcitrance of the material they treat, in solidarity with the unassimilated, the inchoate, and the fugitive, out of adherence to the ekstatic temporality of their subjects, i.e., in the names of freedom and the future, and as a signal of respect for others, they must also express critical hesitations regarding these ambitious proposals, interrupt their tendency to totalization, strive to keep in view and work against the tragic blindness of knowingness. At once, psychoanalysis strives for a mythical totality that cannot but remain opaque and promises a discretion that cannot be fulfilled. Equally modest and immodest, "[t]he un-naïve thinker knows how far he remains from the object of his thinking, and yet he must always talk as if he had it entirely" (Adorno 1973, 26).

On the one hand, the work of conceptual determination in psychoanalytic discourse and practice is both necessary and desirable (e.g., as a medium of freedom from pathological, and perhaps socially enforced, self-obscurity or fragmentation), but as it asserts itself over or comes into conflict with the singularity, opacity, and pliability of the material it treats, its awkward violence is revealed (if only in its steely countenance). Although conceptuality is internal to experience, conceptual determination or explication effaces the first-person perspective, disenfranchising that which it seeks to contain and comprehend. Of course, for certain analysands, an analyst's universalizing pronouncements (or intimations) may be quite salutary, especially in early stages of analysis, e.g., may position the analyst as a containing, empathic, calming presence, perhaps reminiscent of parental figures through whose quasi-omnipotence the world became hospitable, and so may allow the analysand to relax, feel safe, and engage in her analysis more fully. But as insistently particular and allusive psychic phenomena are occluded or become condensed in a concept, the concept accrues a power to make its addressee feel neglected, misrecognized, even obliterated. We all have experiences with or can easily imagine employments of psychoanalytic concepts that intend annihilation: "You're being neurotic," "That's perverse!" etc. Though unusually conspicuous in such abusive deployments, the power to efface is intrinsic to and always to some degree manifest in even the most well-intentioned and highly adept uses of psychoanalytic concepts. An interpretation, especially a diagnosis, can feel like a form of social death. Setting aside for a moment the stigma attached to their particular contents, the appositeness of general terms may feel like an erasure of individuality, captivation by the cold grip of the concept — emphatic substantiality — the affective corollary of its compelling employment; while the inappositeness of general terms, the feeling that one fails to fit neatly within interpretive or diagnostic concepts — which is to say, the discomfiture that may bespeak their efficacy, e.g., in mobilizing affect, investment, and self-articulation — may exacerbate feelings of unintelligibility, uncontainability or unmanageability, feelings of social misrecognition, indeed ostracism or persecution, thus feelings of guilt.

Recruitment into conceptual generality, as much as resistance to it, is permeated by guilt. If an interpretation is compelling, the one to whom it is addressed may feel comforted by the recognition — relieved that her suffering is meaningful, that the life that bears this suffering is still woven into the fabric of social intelligibility, that her difficulties are understandable and thus perhaps manageable, that someone is trying to help, that her suffering is not punished by social expulsion, etc. — and at once mutilated and mortified. Mutilated by the interpretation's conceptual cuts and, suppression — which may feel like denial, debasement, or rejection — of singular sufferings, longings, anxieties, etc. within the field of its conceptual operations ('Not even those whose profession demands the utmost attention to human variation — i.e., analysts — can see who I am. Am I human? Am I here?' Interpretation always verges on caricature.). Mortified by its insinuation that one is but an interchangeable instance of a general rule, scripted there where one feels opaque or frantically innovating, mechanical there where one feels most unique (and not only due to the narcissization of defenses); or that the meaning of one's words and deeds is contained in a stratum transcendent to experience, that what one took to be life is but allegory. Psychoanalytic concepts are death-bearing even as they revive the affective and reflective life of the suffering.

Attempts to evade the guilt and distress of conceptual enframing immediately imperil prospects for recognition, thus for freedom or even survival. Yet the unavoidability of conceptual mediation need not imply its uncritical acceptation. Undergoing displacement and distortion by conceptual generality may occasion a certain contestation, a reassertion of singularity, a dynamization of subject and concept. As Julia Kristeva suggests, "this interpretive construction, which can be as portentous as my own desires will allow, is nevertheless my only way — *the* only way? — to guide the analysand's speech from being completely eclipsed toward a state of relative autonomy" (1995, 123). Varying this thought: the disconcerting heteronomy of conceptual captivation may solicit analysands' resistances, which may in turn spark, or already take the form of, a certain affective and symbolic autonomy, a measure of independence from or radiating reanimation within the cold grip of the concept. That is, resistances may spark or take shape as felicitously idiosyncratic self-expression, a transcendence of the concept through the concept, a challenging of conceptual closure through conceptual constellation, an elaboration of the non-identical through an uneasy avowal and specification of the identical.

Even then, conceptual (re)determination involves suppressing and distorting aspects of the phenomena under consideration that do not immediately or exhaustively lend themselves to its terms, corralling relatively inchoate phenomena into firm conceptual casts, and intervening there where one presumes to lay bare — thus at once falsifying the phenomena and the conceptual claim. Psychoanalytic concepts are exaggerated, dominating, bound to miss their mark, always bordering on caricature. The singular is coarsened as it is marshaled under the universal, becoming the particular; muted in and through a profusion of discourse; misrecognized in the medium of its recognition, thus rendered impossible by the conditions of its actualization. And if, say, due to their resonance with archaic sufferings, interpretations are experienced as voracious, objectifying or obliterating, authoritarian or otherwise aggressive impositions, etc. — risks amplified by transference — then irritation, repudiation, rigid hyperinvestment in a contrary symbolic order, blind obedience, or withdrawal rather than self-specification may ensue.

But the coarsening entailed by the concept, the massifying effect of its too broad brushstrokes, may become a condition for (qualified) liberation and specification as the abrasive particularity of the material stands out against or overflows its conceptual figuration. Perhaps in and through the silence enforced by the onslaught of discourse, singularity mutely insists, inscribing tremors in the concepts, interpretations, and theories that seek to enclose it, exposing them to a dim yet insistent perturbation that refuses them their desired stability. Perhaps this will only provoke their reassertion, i.e., anxious efforts to vanquish such instability by means of monotony or saturating expansion, but perhaps (too) it will have become the animating impulse of self-specification exceeding the reigning conceptual compass. Perhaps, paradoxically, bold conceptual claims give muted voice to the singularity of the material and self-transcending character of the subject they disavow and come into their truth by virtue of what is unanticipatedly spoken through and against them.

On the other hand, if refraining from a mechanical application of received concepts, interpretive templates, or theories in order to tarry with the novelty, infinite intricacy, mobility, obscurity, and indefinite interpretive pliability of *this* client's clinical productions becomes a wholesale refusal to name what is there to be seen or heard, an egregious abdication of analytic responsibility, a freighted disavowal of tradition-mediated insight, perhaps an assault on thinking is underway. In a psychoanalytic idiom, attempts to evade the discomfort, guilt, and resistances induced by psychoanalytic concepts may symptomatize a hysterical solicitation of Law,[2] a paranoid penchant for unimpeachable systematicity,[3] a mutually deforming dissociation of affect from intellect characteristic of certain obsessional-neurotic discourses,[4] masochistic self-mortification, or what may at first look the same, melancholic aggressivity. Enveloping clinical material in a fantasy of unmediated positivity (or absolutely internal mediation) or succumbing to a fetishism of the ineffable or "the event" is no less violent than conceptual subsumption, and no more sustainable. Repudiating conceptual mediation, were this even possible, would signal an insupportably naïve, romantic faith in immediacy, a surreptitious demand for self-presence, perhaps a presumption of the possibility of immediate fusion harboring its own dangers and disavowals. The structural deceit of the concept — concealment effected through disclosure, necessary and necessarily false identification of the non-identical — distressing as it may be, is of a piece with its powers to channel, filter, and productively shape the relatively inchoate affective life of those who suffer from a want of meaning and reshape and reactivate the ossified, self-destructive, or otherwise damaging psycho-significative structures of those who suffer from regimes of rigid meaning.[5]

Psychoanalysis dreams of conceptual capture so efficient, so pure that it would leave nothing festering in the dark, dank corridors of the unconscious wherein, presumably, so much havoc is wreaked[6] — only to have its dreams disturbed by that which scoffs at the violent imbecility of its sanguine program. Equally, psychoanalysis dreams of a pure heterology, of unremitting and undiminished sensitivity to the traces of the other that differ from and defer representational knowledge — only to find itself in a nightmare of collusion with social and psychic forces that, often to devastating effect, organize and enforce the unintelligibility and incoherence of certain feelings, fantasies, longings, self-images, and the like.

Hedged in by violence and stupidity on both sides, tending toward one exaggeration or another, psychoanalysis wavers between impulses to which it cannot fully accede. As discourse and practice, psychoanalysis is given to a fundamental disquietude, constitutively troubled.

UNIVERSALIZATION AND PARTICULARIZATION

At best, psychoanalytic discourse and practice respond to this double injunction by attempting the impossible, that is, by organizing themselves as dialectics of inflation and deflation. Within the terms of such a dialectic, ideally, the universalizing thrust of extravagantly encompassing and explanatory concepts, concepts that claim to be completely coherent, transparent, transmissible, and systematizable, meets with and is partially offset by acknowledgements of the singularity, opacity, and indefinite futurity of material that resists generalization, i.e., that demands the continual qualification, recasting, reconstellation, or rejection of the concepts through which it is elaborated. Thereby, the claims of the first-person against representational abstraction are acknowledged within the medium of conceptuality, becoming its principle of dynamization.

How this might occur in psychoanalytic discourse has been discussed earlier in terms of a dialectical development of perspective — an issue that will be revisited below. In the clinical context, the norms of intelligibility implicit in the analyst's practice and the necessity of the analysand's self-interpretation, coupled with conceptual and interpretive underdetermination, positive transference, commitment to and encouragement of free association, internalization of the analytic function, working through, and/or effective interpretation may suffice to sustain a dialectic of universalization and particularization. But what we will be concerned with is a limit case — the prospect that strategic employments of the violence of universality may conduce to the development of such a dialectic. The violence of conceptual positing, if handled with tact, and especially if the transference is well established, may elicit a desire for recognition on the part of the analysand precisely because the universals to which s/he is submitted induce various discomforts of misrecognition; and the desire for recognition may take shape as or lead to the development of a more concrete discourse, one that resonates more fully with *this* analysand. The mutilations and mortifications of judgment which humble interrogative rhetoric can conceal but not circumvent may, if deftly handled, spark symbolic-affective reanimation.

Dialectically organized, psychoanalytic discourse and practice may awaken insights that transcend the propositions out of which they are constituted. This would be a form of dialectic akin to that described (and practiced) by Socrates in *The Republic*, specifically at 533c8 where, through dialectic, propositions or hypotheses are said (and shown) to open onto what transcends and thus, in a way, destroys them, or more precisely, onto what infuses them with restless negativity.

To be sure, attempting to leverage the violence of universality against itself is a risky endeavor. Propelled by misrecognition, and especially when caught up in the transference, the desire for recognition may take shape, for instance, as a sadistically satisfying rebuff by means of which one seeks partial compensation for the narcissistic wound of misrecognition, or as a fantasy of merger with the object of transferential desire, or as a means to secure the attention and affection of that object and perhaps thereby to dissipate anxieties pertaining to one's sense of invisibility or entombment elsewhere. Or the strategy may misfire in a host of other ways. For instance, parts of an interpretation or senses of a concept that fail to resonate with the analysand, just don't make sense in terms of her experiences, may be latched onto, hyperinvested, in virtue of their failure of fit, construed as necessarily opaque signs of her ineffable identity, the privileged, private idiom of her ownmost selfhood (rather than perfectly intelligible but off the mark descriptions), and so support a fantasy of immediate self-presence and necessary social invisibility/unintelligibility.[7] Rather than provoking resistances and felicitously idiosyncratic, conceptually dynamizing forms of self-expression, misrecognition may induce rigid identification with the experience of being elsewhere, ineffable, unrecognizable. The strategy takes great risks with those susceptible to defensive, insulating attachments to ineffability as a means of securing a sense of unique identity[8] demanded and undermined by the prevailing ideological/institutional complex. Thus it is extremely risky in a world such as our own where individuation is aggressively demanded, idealized, and capitalized on, yet in which the socio-symbolic resources necessary for robust individuation are underdeveloped, and so susceptibility to resolute identification with the ineffable is pervasive. But as risky as this operation is, its advantages if successful are clear. The violence of interpretation may provoke resistances that lead to, or already take the form of, the querying, recasting, reconstellation, or rejection of the offending interpretation. By motivating or taking shape as critical questioning, repudiation, or transformational reiteration of the interpretation, such resistances may yield forms of self-expression much more redolent with the concrete (in)determinacy of the analysand. Or even if misrecognition does not impel the analysand to articulate her difference from the terms through which she has been interpellated, her resistances may function as a guide directing the analyst to that which has been overlooked, marginalized, one-sidedly developed, or contorted through the particular interpretation.[9]

Through the resistances it may inspire, the violence of the concept can guide conceptual insight to the urgency of its reworking and to the limits of its medium, that is, to more refined conceptual insight, and at the limit, to "the consistent sense of nonidentity" that emerges in and through the succession of resistances to conceptual enclosure (Adorno 1973, 5). On the analytic scene, the coercion of thought may be the medium of its deliverance (Adorno 1973, 48). The all too rigid meaning, the exaggerated and one-sided truth posited or implied by the analyst, may motivate, directly or indirectly, the imaginative elaboration of alternative concepts, conceptual constellations, or other forms of description and expression that are more felicitously disclosive and perhaps therapeutically significant. By provoking resistances, the constraint of the concept may keep the phenomena *in question and in motion*, supporting an interminable dialectic of universalization and particularization.

Psychoanalysis cannot avoid the violent stupidity of universality; it can only seek to turn it against itself. The violent exaggerations and effacements inherent to conceptual description, i.e., interpretation, if they spark a succession of resistances that incite or take the form of refinements to the proposed interpretation[10] or transconceptual expressions of that which the interpretation contingently or conceptuality constitutively occludes, may be crucial for therapeutic efficacy. Perhaps only a challenging interpretation will be challenged: scrutinized, idiosyncratically inflected, qualified, supplemented, supplanted, or exposed to psychic currents that refuse, perhaps are intrinsically inimical to, conceptual formulation, i.e., sufficiently invested to be productively worked through. Perhaps only a challenging-challenged interpretation will harness drive energies, attract relatively amorphous psychic phenomena, and/or become affectively freighted sufficiently to become subject to avowal, or at least something with which to contend.[11]

Recall the scene in Hitchcock's *Rear Window* where Jeff's (James Stewart) insurance nurse Stella (Thelma Ritter) slaps a bit of cold massage ointment onto his back, and in response to his consterned "Do ya ever heat that stuff?" insists a bit caustically, but caringly, that "It gives your circulation something to fight." The very coldness of the concept may set ablaze resistances to it, and in and through these resistances, a critical engagement with, perhaps a discursive reworking and/or affective and associative engorgement of the concept may be kindled, perhaps to the point where the concept conflagrates and comes into view in its essential provisionality. That is, if the misrecognitions — deformations, occlusions, avoidances, and obliterations — effected by the concept induce resistances, the failure of the concept to capture its material (or its success in *only capturing* its material) may open onto fine-tuned conceptual redescriptions and/or transverbal and perhaps transconceptual elaborations of that which the concept elides, obscures, or aggressively recruits into its regime of intelligibility.

When tactfully handled, unavoidable interpretive violence becomes manifest as immanent failure, indeed manifest failure becomes part of the meaning of the interpretation — in a way, a measure of its success. To acknowledge the necessity of failure would be to set conceptuality off on a course from which there is no return, a course of incessant striving to thetically recuperate the abrasive particularity to which it has, perhaps despite itself, yet again given rise, thus with respect to which it is constitutively belated. If provoked by the particularizations it inspires, universalization finds itself motivated by its impossibility;[12] its very form demanding and forbidding its final success. If the actuality of a concept is, in part, the reiterations and transconceptual reworkings onto which its failures may incessantly open, then the primacy of possibility is immanent to, though non-identical with, its actuality: the concept is aporetic. There is difference *in* and *through* the concept.

Tactfully handled, concepts assume dialectically mobilized meanings, meanings that are at once discursively determinable and "multifaceted, indefinable, set ablaze" (Kristeva 1995, 125). As the eminently tactful Julia Kristeva puts it, "[b]y giving a name to that which cannot be formulated, I put it into question. I make an affect into a question" (1995, 89).[13]

But only if the interpretation resonates; only if it hits on or speaks to something that it does not quite comprehend, or if it conspicuously avoids or mischaracterizes something it thereby renders potentially pertinent. Only if the interpretation is sufficiently impacting to regather and mobilize affect and symbolization, which means only if defenses are well-analyzed or otherwise mitigated, may its resonance transmute into the desirous pursuit of self-elaboration. Only if the cold grip of the concept does not leave its addressee cold, withered, may its violence prove reanimating. The interpretation must be doing more than it can know.

To be sure, the abrasive particularity or indefiniteness onto which the concept may open are as little pure or self-subsistent as the concept. Generally, that which eludes or confounds conceptual capture, disclose(s) itself not in empathic, wordless communion but only in the fold of conceptuality — at a moment of infelicity or dialectical impasse which may also be a moment of remobilization, the initiation of unforeseen lines of development. Only because it is not wholly sealed off from *logos* but rather its appropriated-inappropriable, "inner" perturbation can what exceeds conceptualization become at all evident or effective. Specifically, that which insists in its irreducibility to conceptual enframing can do so only vis-à-vis this or that particular concept or line of conceptual development. The course of particularization, even as it interrupts the closure of universality, and however indefinite, is itself necessarily dominated by universality, conditioned — though perhaps not altogether predigested, perhaps impacting the very terms by which it is conditioned — by the specific terms (universals) with which it refuses to reconcile.

Psychoanalysis cannot but strive for universality: the resistances through which emerge that which is unthought or unthinkable by the prevailing conceptual order "appear divergent, dissonant, negative for just so long as the structure of our consciousness obliges it to strive for unity," for just so long as the "demand for totality will be the measure for whatever is nonidentical with it" (Adorno 1973, 5-6). Conceptual determination is an enabling condition for what is thus a necessarily qualified independence from it. Equally, psychoanalysis cannot but strive to remain true to singularity if it is to avoid the most egregious abuses.

Ideally, psychoanalytic discourse and practice will both *capture* the phenomena with which they are concerned within the privileged terms of a particular perspective and *release* them from (within) these terms into a field of redeterminability maintained discursively by other perspectives and clinically by the singular psychic life of the analysand.[14] Dialectically mobilized, the strife-ridden scene of analytic thinking keeps in view its material's *problematic* character and thereby, that of the psychoanalytic enterprise itself. Striving at once to deliver determinate insights and to be continually self-surpassing with respect to particular interpretations, general partisan orientations, and at the limit, the assumption of the total intelligibility of the psychic, psychoanalysis reveals that *self-negation, the permanent prospect of limited or unlimited overhaul, is inscribed in its impossible essence.* As an emphatically modernist, i.e., self-revolutionizing, discourse and practice, psychoanalysis is as well characterized by theoretical tenets, interpretation programs, therapeutic protocols, and the like, as it is by its self-surpassing momentum, its intrinsic difficulties and imbalances, generally, its fundamental disquietude.

At its best, psychoanalysis remains in irresolvable tension with itself, foregoing neither the risks of extrapolating from its source materials, integrating its newly won insights with its conceptual endowment and making the necessary revisions to maintain coherence, even formulating its insights in audaciously apophantic or declarative terms,[15] nor that of recalling and attending to the singularity and enigmaticity of this material in order to restrain its tendencies toward reification, partially counteract or make amends for the violent subsumptiveness and accusatory aspects of its universalizing thrust, and support the independence of its clients. Poised between the accusative and the vocative, between assertion and evocation, actually always having slid toward one side or the other, at best, psychoanalysis restlessly strives and fails to get on an even footing with itself. An impossible profession indeed.

THE DIALECTICAL ADVENTURES OF LACANIAN DOGMATICS

Let us take the risk of learning from Lacan, for the dialectical drama of universalization and particularization (virtually) *internalized in and conducted through the moment of universality* is most pronounced in and so best illustrated with reference to Lacan's teachings. In Lacan's writings and seminars, the strategic involution of universality means to inscribe a call for a return to things themselves, to phenomenality in excess of its conceptual determinations, a return to or reactivation of creative self-articulation and intersubjective dialogue, within the level of universality itself. It means to keep universality exposed to its discursively irrecuperable source material and structurally unachievable aim, to unseal phenomenality and its innovative uptake, thus to solicit subjectivity, through — thus mediated by — the concept that is not itself fully conceptual.[16] In the undischargeable demands for remediation or particularization inscribed in the hyperbolic assertion of universality, an essential mobility is maintained. Lacan's ambition is to effect an axial turn toward mimetic-material expression within the medium of the universal.[17]

So what exactly is the conceptual operation of interest? By *not* providing demonstrations or, often, even examples[18] of his most important and novel claims, Lacan at once demands disciples to simply accept his assertions as dogma *and* urges interlocutors to think through the matters under concern in their own way, with originality and concern for contexts he could not have foreseen, by developing arguments for and examples of his claims. Lacan's gamble is that as his addressees devise examples and arguments to elaborate and support his convictions, these supplemental efforts will lend valences to his claims that he never intended, could never have intended, setting them off on an unpredictable but perhaps not arbitrary course and thereby exposing their essential iterability or underdetermination, the imbrication of creation and discovery. For a moment, Lacan's universalistic assertions would be pure means.

Venturing decisively bold yet decidedly vague truths, Lacan gambles on the chance that as much as these seductively confident certitudes risk arresting reflection — a risk that, on his account, must be taken if the force of the insight is to be effectively conveyed; recall Adorno's claim that "[t]he unnaïve thinker knows how far he remains from the object of his thinking, and yet he must always talk as if he had it entirely") — and thus risk self-falsification, i.e., reification, their imprecision, when conjoined with their seductive character, may motivate efforts to concretize them, to substantiate them, and that such efforts will expose the provisionality and partiality of his claims, and by implication, those with which they are supplemented. By conspicuously avoiding argument and exemplification, Lacan at once makes manifest his convictions, attempts to extend their claim, and allows his bold assertions to come into proximity to their truth by encouraging their reiterative assimilation by others. By not identifying the intuitions that would fulfill his significative intentions, because the referents of his discourse are never clear — one never knows exactly *what* he is talking about — Lacan encourages prolific probative applications of his concepts and claims, experimentation and speculation — which, because these concepts and claims regularly find a point of purchase (or several), risk becoming falsified as a universal hermeneutic key, an ultimate metaphysical code — and therewith their recurrent displacement and transfiguration. Through this eminently risky operation, the resiliently underdetermined, manifestly determinable character of Lacan's concepts and clams, and the phenomena they bear (metaphorize), may be released into the space of thinking and allowed to unfold along multiple trajectories. By such means the intransigent difficulty of psychoanalytic thinking would be foregrounded, its turbulent dialectical mobility (re)activated, the risk of petrification held off for yet another moment. Lacan seeks to dynamize universality, to cause it to implode as a dialectical stutter of expansion and contraction, assertion and self-critical hesitation, retraction, or revision. He seeks to elaborate compelling insights with which to work, and which, from time to time, we must unwork, *in the form of* revealed truths with which to rest content.

Lacan also gambles on the prospect that his strident assertions, precisely in virtue of their manifest violence and seductively masterful demeanor, will provoke resistances that will cause them to be queried, reconfigured, supplemented, or supplanted. By engaging in conceptual violence so extreme that it cannot be ignored or readily swallowed — the smug, doctrinaire quality of his discourse is repulsive,[19] motivating concern for saving the phenomena from the sovereign violence of his conceptual decrees . . . to attempt to debunk his commentaries on, say, psychoanalytic, literary, or philosophical texts is to take the bait — he seeks to turn the violence of the concept against itself. By maintaining a posture of masterly aloofness, a self-absorption and inaccessibility that is sometimes not so far from coquetry,[20] he unnerves and repulses there where he attracts. Conjointly, the manifest violence and seductively masterful demeanor of his strident assertions mean to incite Oedipal revolt: revolt against the Law's arbitrariness, its violent neutralization of differences, its usurpation by charismatic authority, its stultifying stability and gross inadequacies, and its undischargeable demandingness (what it demands is hardly clear, in its grip one is always guilty). In short, Lacan's discursive display of sovereign violence means to hystericize. If the provocation proves successful, Lacan will always have been the first and best anti-Lacanian: the ab-solute master.

Through the involution of universality, phenomena are recalled; not presented in their purported positivity but re-presented, remembered, called upon from a certain distance within the universal. Phenomena are recalled in their obscurity and indefinite futurity, their particularizability; if successful, the involution of universality will recall and thereby reactivate phenomena, thus recall and reactivate the perspectival character and immanent dialogical dimension of psychoanalytic discourse and practice. By means of the involution of universality, the particular is announced as an aporetic phenomenon — gestured at as the trace of the concepts it will have solicited and outstripped.[21] In this way, Lacan allows the exorbitance of phenomena to manifest in the closest proximity to and just out of reach of conceptualization — to resonate and provoke.

Lacan certainly does not refrain from definitive pronouncements on the truths of suffering and subjectivity, but by speaking and writing in a manner that is conspicuously opaque and condensed, that is difficult,[22] sometimes barely intelligible or contradictory, in need of unpacking at every turn, and always in need of review, his discourse strives to mimetically accommodate its objects. Acceding to that in its objects which both solicits and rebuffs or reverberates beyond conceptual articulation, Lacan's discourse seeks to win what objectivity it may by remaining *true to* its objects. In virtue of its perspicuous inadequacy, its obvious failure to rigorously determine its objects, its powerlessness, Lacan's discourse seeks to attest to its claimedness by its objects — to *their* claim. By homing in on and infusing itself with that in its objects which both provokes and resists conceptual determination — their opacity, condensation, contradictory elements, allusiveness, insecure intelligibility, etc. — Lacan's discourse recalls and seeks to reactivate the phenomena, and therewith, dialogical interactivity. With Lacan, the interminability of the dialectics of universalization and particularization, creation and discovery, i.e., the dilemma of psychoanalytic knowing, is delivered to self-consciousness. Measured by the demand for totality, his concepts and theories are always less than concepts and theories, and thus more: overflowing with a content that cannot be captured by any discrete formulation, they demand dialogical engagement.

By means of a superbly subtle — perhaps too subtle — conceptual operation, Lacan urges his addressees to ruminate over what he says, to create/discover what this discourse might mean — what the phenomena it addresses might (yet) be — within the space of their experiences, conceptual and imaginative operations, etc. His audacity is the medium of his undoing. For Lacan and those who follow him, psychoanalysis will always involve "an element of exaggeration, of over-shooting the object, of self-detachment from the factual, so that instead of merely reproducing being it can, at once rigorous and free, determine it. Thus every thought resembles play, with which Hegel no less than Nietzsche compared the work of the mind" (Adorno 1974, 126-7).

Although he clearly prefers to intrigue, sometimes Lacan makes his intentions clear: "You don't understand dis writing [*stécriture*]. So much the better — it'll give you a reason to explain it" (*Seminar XI*, 253; Bruce Fink's translation in *Lacan to the Letter*, 176-77); "I strive to ensure that access to the meaning [of what I say] not be too easy, such that you must contribute some elbow grease of your own (or work hard at it) [*mettre du vôtre*]" (*Seminar XIX*, Jan. 6, 1972; Bruce Fink's translation, *ibid.*, 178).

Lacan's wager is on dogmatic self-assertion provoking his addressees to associate to his claims in ways that will permit their development in multiple, unanticipated directions, thus to become co-authors — who, were they to acknowledge themselves as such, would acknowledge the essentially (in)determinate character of the claims they take over. He means for his addressees to revoke his title to the letter by claiming it themselves and thereby revealing all such claims as false. Projecting a scene of obedient discipleship, he seeks for his concepts and theories to become objects of free-floating attention, of innovative variation and manipulation. At the limit, what he seeks to show is that, enamored and engorged with their impossible objects, psychoanalytic concepts are not exactly concepts, i.e., rules establishing necessary and sufficient criteria for instantiation, but rather, perhaps are more akin to promises and remembrances.[23]

But despite all this, Lacan is no doubt compelled by his conceptual insights and innovations, and interested in transmitting this compulsion. He seeks to sustain psychoanalysis as a problematic field within which conflict and creativity are encouraged, to keep psychoanalytic thinking vital, enmeshed in a scene of mutual problematization the loss of which may entail the loss of the specific character of psychoanalytic objectivity; but he also means what he says.

TRAVERSING THE END OF METAPHYSICS

As reserved, self-critical, or eclectic as it may be, psychoanalysis cannot but drift toward a metaphysical discourse of universal truth. As modest as one must be in view of that which may exceed and complicate one's theoretical and therapeutic apparati, one's perspective must be coherently and compellingly rendered, therapeutic protocols brought to bear on what would otherwise persist in painful, pathogenic unintelligibility or rigidity. Interruptions may ensue, but the urgency of consolidation and application is irreducible. Seeking to sustain itself as a perspectival discourse, to acknowledge its constitutive incompletion, by sustaining the dialectics of universalization and particularization, creation and discovery, psychoanalysis strives to maintain its vitality and remain true to its objects, to ward off the risk, which it cannot but court, indeed to which it has always already to some extent succumbed, of stabilizing into definitive doctrines. Psychoanalysis is never fully itself; its ideality remains forever compromised.

Unavoidably, one impulse or the other dominates. The dialectic of universalization and particularization is no homeostatic counterbalancing. Within the work of a particular theorist, the course of a particular therapy, and across the field, psychoanalysis vacillates between bold assertions (or intimations) of the truths of suffering and subjectivity, what Adorno would call "metaphysics running amuck" (1973, 155), and critical scrupulousness: retraction, revision, or hesitation. Even when the former means to become the incitement to and medium of the latter. Audacious theoretical proposals and routine therapeutic protocols oscillate with excessive emphases on the radical heterogeneity or singularity of the clinical or cultural event.[24] There is no balance to be won: psychoanalytic discourse and practice are ever-exaggerated. Unable to repose in itself, constitutively aporetic, psychoanalytic thinking keeps its practitioners off-balance, inflating and deflating, permanently conflicted, anticipatory and on edge.[25] As Adorno concisely puts it, "nothing is true in psychoanalysis except its exaggerations" (1974 §29).

OBJECTIVITY IN PSYCHOANALYSIS

Perhaps it is precisely insofar as it is multilayered and contra-dictory, surprising and difficult, elusive, opaque, even sometimes bordering on unintelligibility that psychoanalytic discourse mirrors (mimetically accompanies) its objects — the unconscious in particular and psychic phenomena in general — attaining a form of objectivity appropriate to the enterprise. By giving itself over to both an impulse to universalization and an impulse to particularization, an impulse to discovery and to (re)creation, to consolidation and to speculation, i.e., by giving itself over to the forever uneasy, nonprogrammatic work of dialectical elaboration, perhaps, almost despite itself, psychoanalytic thinking is able to attain a certain objectivity, to acknowledge its objects as complex, evolving admixtures of determinacy and indeterminacy, and to recognize itself in their reflection. Its tempestuous lability, its vexing difficulty and para-doxicality, may be the way (*ton hodon*) in which psychoanalytic thinking registers — adheres to and performatively acknowledges — the specific objectivity of its objects, what it is to be such an object: an aporetic methodology. If so, it may be the sense of difficulty, danger, and frustration beleaguering psychoanalytic discourse and practice, the feeling of being fated to failure, that signals the achievement of a certain manner of objective attunement.

Might a certain manner of mimetic performance — rather than or in addition to adequation and systematic integration — be a way in which objectivity is attained? If so, what would be the value of such objectivity?

The strain on countenancing this conception of objectivity is not slight: paradoxically, its attainment involves a failure to fulfill the traditional criteria for objectivity. Objectivity in this anomalous sense is attained insofar as discourse never quite corresponds to its objects but rather remains continually co-responsive with them: a medium of bidirectional transformation. For psychoanalytic discourse to strive for objectivity in this sense is for it to both attempt to draw out its objects' conceptual contours and draw attention to its impassioning prepossession, its inhabitation and animation by the insistence of that which indefinitely resists and demands the recalibration of conceptualization. Or from the other side, such objectivity would be a matter of allowing objects to respond to discourse by both manifesting in its terms and manifestly resisting total assimilation to them, hence driving discourse into speculation. Objectivity in this sense names not unassailable knowledge but a certain urgency and unsettling motility of insight: commitment to phenomena manifesting as dialectics of universalization and particularization, creation and discovery — thoughtful self-dispossession.[26]

NOTES

1. "I happen to think however, as do all analysts, I imagine — and that is very unpleasant for me — that I only go forward on paths already mapped out. If I have never heard of infantile sexuality theories or of the primal scene, the death instinct or castration anxiety, no doubt I would have only been able to drift along on the flow of words and images. Yes, but what if what I have learned prevents me from hearing? What if I get hooked on the already-named-identified out of fear of losing myself? . . . A deafness, a blindness, brought about by knowledge . . . . There is no initial beginning . . . . In whatever matter, we always come after and yet we are perpetually starting something. Each analysis, however many years we have been in practice, is the first time" (Pontalis 2003, pp. 95-6).
2. Cf. Kristeva (1995) *New Maladies of the Soul*, p. 68.
3. Cf. Freud (1911) "Psychoanalytic Notes Upon an Autobiographical Account of a Case of Paranoia (Dementia Paranoides)."

4. Cf. Kristeva 1995, 45ff.

5. Compare Toqueville's (1990) discussions of "intermediary powers" and "new secondary powers" forestalling the collapse of democratic equality (especially the moment of horizontality, i.e., solidarity) into equal susceptibility to domination by the bureaucratized state (verticality) and thus the destruction (via the regressive massification) of individuality (esp. pp. 298, 304, 318). Toqueville's conception of "intermediary powers" and "new secondary powers," thus Montesquieu's (1989 [1748]) treatment of "pouvoirs intermédiaires," might be fruitfully compared with the notion of "theoretical intermediaries" developed herein.

6. Cf. SE 14: 149.

7. Cf. Adorno 1973, p. 39.

8. Cf. Kristeva 1992, esp. pp. 33-94.

9. A premise of the claim that conceptual overkill can provoke resistances and thereby sustained questioning, rejection, or substantial reworking is that the analysand lacks a more affectively resonant, experientially accommodating, practically felicitous, or otherwise more suitable discourse to set against the interpretations proposed. Often, part of the impetus to engage in clinical analysis is a disconcerting want of meaning, or at least workable meaning, a want of expressive resources adequate to and of interpretive resources adequate for negotiating with experiences that are intensely significant yet unintelligible or rigidly confined within an order of meaning from which one suffers, e.g., a want of symbolic resources to effectively bind distressing affects or ideations or to support adaptive success in various social dynamics. More conventionally expressed, one tends to enter analysis when symptoms no longer suffice. This, along with the earlier point about transference, is why, at the risk of a certain distortion, the clinical context rather than the practice of psychoanalysis more broadly is the framework for this discussion. The incitement of particularization, dynamization, etc. by universality is certainly conceivable outside the clinical frame (we will return to this in the following section), but there is no denying that certain features of that frame strongly contribute to its efficacy.

10. To be sure, resistances are not the only route to refinements and recalibrations. Associational broadening and deepening of an interpretation, for instance, need not be considered an expression of resistances. Particularization, in short, does not necessarily hinge on transference-laden or otherwise freighted reactions to misrecognition. This is not an apologia for early, deep, and frequent interpretations or self-assertive audacity but an account of the self-surpassing potential of tactfully employed conceptual/interpretive boldness. Interpretively overburdening the analysand, crowding out her room for reaction, will be counterproductive, i.e., will likely result in seduction or withdrawal.

11. Again, the challenging character of the interpretation need not issue from the misrecognition effected by conceptual captivation, mortification and mutilation. Quite to the contrary, the challenge may issue from the difficulty of integrating and working through an interpretation that has hit the mark. Or it may issue from the provocative character of the interpretation's content.

12. "To define identity as the correspondence of the thing-in-itself to its concept is hubris; but the ideal of identity must not be simply discarded. Living in the rebuke that the thing is not identical with its concept is the concept's longing to become identical with the thing. This is how the sense of non-identity contains identity. The supposition of identity is indeed the ideological element of pure thought . . . but hidden in it is also the truth moment of ideology, the pledge that there should be no contradiction, no antagonism . . . . The untruth of any identity that has been attained is the obverse of truth. The ideas live in the cavities between what things claim to be and what they are" (Adorno and Horkheimer 2002, p. 149).

13. Or from another direction, and a bit extravagantly: "A good interpretation, by contrast, is something we cannot help remaking (in psychoanalysis the orders the patient is being given are turned into questions). In this sense, psychoanalysis, as Laplanche suggests, 'de-translates' the patient's material; it undoes the patient's habitual, defensive associations in the service of spontaneous recombinations. Loose ends become newer beginnings" (Phillips 1998, p. 33).

14. As we will shortly see, this distinction may not hold.

15. Part of the inherent risk of psychoanalysis, then, is that by asserting such bold and generalized insights, it gives scientific inquiry, especially that of skeptical, disconfirmation-bent sort, points of traction.

16. Cf. Adorno 1973, p. 10

17. Compare Adorno: "A true priority of the particular would only be achievable by virtue of a transformation of the universal. Simply bringing it into existence is a complementary ideology" (1973, p. 313; translation modified).

18. Cf. *Seminar XIX*, Jan. 6, 1972 and *Le Séminaire, Livre XI: Les quatre concepts fondamentaux de la psychanalyse*, p. 253.

19. Although, as the history of Lacan's reception well shows, repulsion can be converted into attraction or even be itself attractive.

20. Cf. SE 3: 55-6.

21. "[T]he truth of such disintegration is achieved by way of nothing less than the triumph and guilt of integration" (Adorno 1997, p. 45).

22. Cf. *Écrits*, p. 412/493.

23. Lacanian conceptuality may thus be conceived as an inheritance of the Hegelian speculative proposition. Cf. Hegel (1986) *Werke in zwanzig Bänden* 3: 37, 57, 59-61 and 6: 243.

24. E.g., "the language of psychoanalysis offers clues not solutions, calls to action for the interpreter but not interpretations" (Bowie 1993, p. 16).

25. Although acknowledging the indelible exaggerations of psychoanalytic discourse and practice may temper the acerbic tone of interpartisan conflict, it may also be its motivation.

26. Compare Derrida (1994): "One can desire, name, think in the proper sense of these words, if there is one, only to the immeasuring extent that one desires, names, thinks still or already, that one still lets announce itself what nevertheless cannot present itself as such to experience, to knowing" (p. 30).

Chapter Seven

Science and Satisfaction

> Mediocre spirits demand of science a kind of certainty which it cannot give, a sort of religious satisfaction.
>
> —E. Jones

THE SCIENCE QUESTION, *VIA NEGATIVA*

If questions such as what distinguishes better from worse psychoanalytic practice, more from less legitimate insight, and authentic psychoanalysis from frauds and derivatives are unlikely to be resolved by partisan self-assertion and pathologization of competing claims, might polemical paralysis and sweeping skepticism be avoided by submitting these questions to the tribunal of science? Might not process studies effectively distinguish valid from invalid psychoanalytic practices? Might not outcome studies effectively adjudicate between better and worse clinical practices? Might not infant observation studies be brought to bear on questions of the relative plausibility of competing psychoanalytic reconstructions, developmental theories, and theories of pathology and cure that rely on developmental theories? Might not the consonance or dissonance of the findings of contemporary neuroscience with various psychoanalytic claims be pertinent to their epistemic evaluation and mutual comparison? Is not scientifically certified empirical knowledge the epistemic gold standard, thus the methodological protocols of modern experimental science the ideal criteria for evaluating controversial and competing psychoanalytic claims?

Even if appeals to the methodological criteria and results of the modern natural sciences cannot resolve the normative questions of what makes for better and what for worse psychoanalytic practice and what constitutes genuine psychoanalysis, and even if psychoanalytic claims are in various respects, e.g., with regard to their metaphysical or ontological presuppositions, incommensurable with the types of claims that the paradigmatic modern sciences are designed to assess, thus appeals to the methodological criteria and results of such sciences question begging, submitting psychoanalytic claims to the tribunal of science may yield pertinent if not decisive results and may, precisely there where psychoanalytic claims prove refractory to the evaluative procedures, because incommensurable with the metaphysical assumptions, of the modern natural sciences, disclose in greater detail what it means to be committed to psychoanalysis.

Formulating psychoanalytic claims such that they would be amenable to experimental scientific investigation would mean operationalizing them, i.e., submitting them to something akin to eidetic variation, and determining their inferential implications, and this may be a way of learning about them: in terms of both their possibilities and their limits. Even if casting psychoanalytic claims in the language appropriate to experimental scientific inquiry, i.e., the language(s) of causality, and hierarchically organizing them for the purposes of deduction, prediction, and experimental (dis)confirmation significantly distorts these claims, might not reflection on what precisely is distorted or occluded bring these claims, and what it means to be committed to such claims, into more fine relief? Even if drawing inferences from psychoanalytic claims is not the same as making causal or probabilistic predictions, the demand for the latter might at least raise questions of why we balk at it, what sorts of inferences we are willing to countenance, and why. In short, although scientific authority is insufficient to dissolve intrapsychoanalytic conflict, its deliverances may be well worth considering, even rationally obligatory to take into account; and although modern experimental science may not be the rightful measure of claims concerning psychic life in view of the deterministic presuppositions of the former and the ontological indeterminacy of the latter, there may be a cognitive yield from addressing the question of the scientific credibility of psychoanalytic claims *via negativa.* Numerous psychoanalytic claims do not measure up well against the demands of modern science, but that does not entail their dismissal as mystifying pseudo-science. Rather, reflectively engaging the nonsatisfaction of the demands of modern science may prove illuminating with regard to the claims and commitments of both psychoanalysis and science.

To be sure, the turn to science is not irresistible. Commitments to psychoanalysis can be staked on the value of the praxis, as vulnerable as that terrain may be. Concern with the specter of skepticism evoked by transcendental realist[1] presuppositions or objectivist aspirations, as much as attempts to exorcize such a specter, may no doubt strike us as tiresome and bizarre — evidence of residual commitment to a starting point long since shown to be unviable. Further, the temptation to conflate cognitive authority with experimental scientific validation *should* be resisted: hastily corroborating experimental modern science as the sole source of knowledge-certification bespeaks an idolatry of science that feeds its anonymous authority, distorts our understanding of its results and its promise, and contributes to the destitution of *thinking* in a more expansive sense. But if those committed to psychoanalysis are to enter into dialogue with those who are not persuaded by first-personal elaborations or social scientific "demonstrations" of the value or cognitively compelling character of psychoanalytic insights and forms of attention, especially those for whom modern science is *the* method of obtaining valid empirical knowledge and *the* royal road to reliable instrumental efficacy, then engaging their interlocutors by submitting psychoanalytic claims to the tribunal of science may be an unavoidable starting point.

Or, skeptical interlocutors aside, in order to temper tendencies to chauvinistic, stultifying and falsifying presumptiveness about our particular psychoanalytic commitments, would we not do well to submit these commitments to the tribunal of science? Might not the failure of these commitments, or of psychoanalysis generally, to measure up against the demands of science provide a productively skeptical rejoinder to the passionate intensity with which we tend to invest forms of attention and insights that have made significant contributions to our flourishing, consolidated as our orienting perspective, and perhaps have been hard won? Might scientific skepticism not temper the expansionist urge of commitment, an urge that threatens to devolve into hegemonic imposition or at least a fantasy thereof? Perhaps the irreducible plurality and perspectival character of psychoanalysis or the now well-entrenched ethos of eclecticism will suffice in this regard. But given the fervency and frequency of polemical self-assertion and mutual pathologization, tactfully dosing scientific skepticism, though no doubt risky as it may fuel the polemical fires it means to diminish, is not a strategy one can easily dismiss.

There is as little reason to idolize science as there is to shy away from it. If psychoanalytic claims are to be submitted to the tribunal of science, the first question must be: What is "science?" Might it be as heterogeneous as psychoanalysis? If so, how can "it" adjudicate psychoanalytic claims? Those who disparage psychoanalysis on the grounds of its failure to meet scientific standards rarely agree about the specific standards to which psychoanalysis should be held accountable. Such critics tend to agree — as, increasingly, does the psychoanalytic community at large — that psychoanalysis should be measured by the standards of "empirical science" (Edelson 1984, 1985; Fisher and Greenberg 1985; Grünbaum 1984, 1993; Kline 1981; Masling and Schwartz 1979; Nagel 1959; Wallerstein 1986). But while Grünbaum (1993) and Popper (2003 [1963]) advocate holding psychoanalysis accountable to the standards of (their conceptions of) modern physics, Sulloway (1979) and Webster (1995) advocate holding it to the standards of (their conceptions of) evolutionary biology. Even were there agreement about which specific science(s) provide(s) the right model, it would still have to be shown that the model science(s) (1) provide(s) useful criteria for assessing psychoanalytic claims in particular and/or (2) warrant(s) the claim to exclusive rights over knowledge-certification.

Let us consider these two requirements in turn.

(1) A good standard for assessing psychoanalytic claims would be one that allows insights or practices that are empirically more successful to win out over those that are less successful. Hence, just finding a science whose epistemic standards psychoanalysis can meet, like geology (arguably), or one that it cannot meet, like mathematical physics, simply sidesteps the question. But as we saw in chapter 2, one school's standards for success often match another school's depiction of pathology. Such standards are always contentious. And as we saw in chapter 3, there are numerous criteria for interpretive success, which we can now characterize as criteria for empirical success, some of which any insight or practice will surely satisfy and the ordering of which is an irresolvably contentious affair. The problem, then, is how to adjudicate between insights and practices that meet different standards for success and/or (more or less) equally well satisfy shared standards. Further, if we accept the claim advanced in chapter 1 that the success of psychoanalytic praxis is to be gauged by its felicity in attuning us to various features of experience *as* significant and orienting our responses to them in a way that contributes to our flourishing, by its capacity to keep us in touch with others and with ourselves, to yield a world within which our forms of perception, reflection, and response are *sensible* (meaningful, experientially weighty, and propitious for achieving our ends), then we have a standard for empirical success that fails to do the work we expect a standard to do, namely, objectively and unproblematically discriminate between more and less successful practices. In view of this standard we can make *judgments* about the worth of various insights and practices, but it is no algorithm or decision rule.

We might then look to cases in which individuals successively undergo multiple analyses with practitioners of different persuasions and attempt to measure the flourishing and foundering to which each analysis contributes. But methodological difficulties abound. Are the positive or negative results of later analyses influenced by the client having been through analysis, or a particular form of analysis, or analysis with a particular analyst previously? What results from deferred or cumulative efficacy and what from the specific character of the later analysis? Might not the commitment to undergo or the need to undergo multiple analyses indicate a bias in the sample? Are those who consent to participate in studies representative of analysands as a whole? How might one establish a representative sample? Are suffering and healing subject to statistically significant sampling? What secures the objectivity of their common measure? How variable is the human in terms of psychological makeup and responsiveness to various therapeutic practices? Might the presumption of the relative homogeneity of the human be a residue of uninterrogated metaphysics? (Maimonides, for one, denied the presupposition.) Also bearing on the question of sample bias is the question of whether the client having previous experience with analysis, or more specifically, having experience with (a) different style(s) of analysis, or perhaps (a) specific style(s), influences how subsequent analyses are conducted, either generally or with respect to particular (sorts of) therapists. Even if we started from scratch and introduced randomized therapy assignment, a variety of studies have shown that even a single interview conducted for assessment and diagnostic purposes can have a positive therapeutic influence (Fisher and Greenberg 1996) and that just being in analysis, or in any sort of formal or informal therapy, correlates with positive outcomes.[2] Randomized assignment would go very little way toward alleviating the difficulty of attributing positive or negative change to specific practices — and the problem of characterizing change as positive or negative would remain untouched. Further questions include: How representative of the school is the particular analyst? And to what extent is this an empirical question? Given that analysts are becoming increasingly eclectic and even those who believe themselves to be committed to a particular school often deviate from its norms (which are themselves contested), how can the relationship between praxis and outcome be determined? Beutler (1991) suggests that in order to adequately differentiate between therapeutic practices, we would need to generate a list of the variables relevant to the specificity of the treatment (i.e., variables related to the particular therapy, therapist, phase of treatment, and patient type), and even a short list would range from about 1,000 to 1.5 million combinations. Luborsky (1993) concurs, adding that although differences in symptom severity, capacity to form treatment alliances, therapeutic competence, treatment model, adherence to the treatment model, and other such variables are extremely important to consider when undertaking comparative outcome studies, these variables are regularly ignored.

There are two basic problems with appealing to ideal cases in which a single individual undergoes multiple analyses with analysts of different persuasions, and her involvement in a later analysis is concurrent with the dissipation of a symptom, inhibition, etc. that a previous analysis left in place or only partially or temporarily alleviated. First is the generalization problem. The evidence to date does not suggest that the sort of therapy that is more successful in a particular case *tends to be* more successful than competitors, either with respect to particular issues or generally.[3] The preponderance of evidence suggests that the outcome rates of various forms of psychoanalysis are equivalent; therapeutic results do not seem to be very sensitive to the practices employed, let alone to the theories that guide these practices or in terms of which they are elaborated. One of the only factors that regularly seems to matter for outcome rates is the "match" between analyst and client.[4]

Second is the framing problem. Eliminating symptoms and other such striking results are not the only relevant or even the most important measures of success (though they are surely high on the list). In a situation where symptoms persist and yet one feels that life is more livable, even fuller and more engaging, that one has gained some measure of freedom from self-undermining or otherwise undesirable patterns of behavior, that one is more capable of responding productively and context-sensitively to emotionally complex situations, or that one is more sensitive to dimensions of experience that had been heretofore unnoticed, the persistence of symptoms that another sort of practice, *ex hypothesi*, could alleviate would certainly be significant but it would not necessarily be damning evidence of therapeutic failure or sufficient warrant to prefer the alternative. Generally, the problem is that evaluative criteria are subjects of normative dispute. Precise determinations of the efficacy of specific forms of psychoanalytic practice with regard to specific ailments, especially insofar as this involves contrasting the efficacy of a specific form of psychoanalytic practice with alternative psychoanalytic and non-psychoanalytic therapies used to treat the same ailment(s), would be highly significant to insurance companies. These findings might also be useful for the wise consumer and for purposes of therapeutic referral. For instance, psychoanalysis seems to be particularly effective at relieving peptic ulcers (Orgel 1958).[5] But does "the analytic experiment" not involve reflectively engaging and exploring the question of one's ends: working to project and pursue a singular vision of the good by exploring and clarifying those involvements or ends that claim one as if irresistibly, e.g., in the form of persistent wishes, conflicts, fantasies, patterns of attachment and avoidance, etc.? Are not the interests that tend to bring one to analysis (a better chance at love, resolving a vocational difficulty, breaking out of a longstanding malaise or depression, etc.) often very different from those eventually pursued — at least different in terms of how their pursuit is understood, what such pursuits are taken to involve and to mean? Is not part of the value of psychoanalysis, especially today, that it provides an institutional space in which reflection on ends is encouraged?[6] If, at least in part, the success of psychoanalysis is to be measured by the sense that one's life would be wanting in integrity, orientation, fullness, and significance without the forms of attention, insights, questions, and capacities it enables or encourages, and if success in these terms does not correlate strongly with more measurable successes, then appealing to more measurable criteria like symptom alleviation just cheats: it trades away a good standard *for assessing psychoanalysis* for a good standard *qua standard*.

Perhaps, then, a good standard would be one that allows a theory to win out over its competitors if it can replace its competitors' refuted theories with a more general theory that explains the refuting instances, i.e., explains why a disconfirmed theory was successful and why it failed, and can also make new, observationally confirmed predictions. But are there refuted theories in psychoanalysis? Can there be? There are certainly theories whose relevance has diminished, say, because they fail to take account of social transformations that influence contemporary shapes of suffering and pathology, such as the generalized slackening and surreptitious resurgence of social/moral prohibition, corporate exploitation of narcissism and repressive desublimation, etc. There are theories that respond to questions that, for the most part, we no longer find worth pursuing (the questions have effectively evaporated) or no longer care to pursue, say, for ethical-political reasons, e.g., Freud's theory of penis envy. There are theories now found to be extremely limited, much less informative and useful than competitors, e.g., Freud's theory of psychosis focused on homosexual conflict. There are theories that do not achieve what they seek to achieve, e.g., fail to explain what they (purportedly) seek to explain, such as Freud's theory of Oedipal gender formation. There are theories of technique that contemporary consensus holds to be therapeutically limited or counterproductive, e.g., those that assume as ideal an absolutely neutral, objective analyst who has "overcome" countertransference. Clearly, there are *reasons to prefer* certain theories as opposed to others. But are there *refuted* theories?

For the exact sciences, ideally, refutation results from empirical findings that do not conform to, or more strongly, decisively deny predictions derived from the hypothesis in question. Thus, establishing that a theory or hypotheses is internally contradictory constitutes refutation, though of a less determinate (informative) form, because internal contradiction implies prediction of contradictory states of affairs. One source of worry that this ideal of refutation is impracticable is that, for all known scientific research programs and all but the most local and limited of hypotheses, there is non-conforming, non-confirming, and disconfirming evidence (although not necessarily decisively disconfirming evidence). Hold this thought to the side for the moment. Even were it practicable, this ideal of refutation would only be appropriate for psychoanalysis only if and to the extent that psychoanalysis aims to (or can be fairly characterized as aiming to) establish the laws and causal mechanisms of a well-defined, deterministic object domain (say, the unconscious), or at least develop hypotheses that explain validly classified and observed features of human subjectivity or trends in psychic life and rule out alternative explanations. Does it so aim? And if so, to what extent?

One way to get at why, or to what extent, this ideal of refutation is inappropriate for psychoanalysis is to note that it assumes interarticulated ideals of scientific method, progress, and objectivity, which in turn assume an image of the natural world, which psychoanalysis must hesitate and in certain respects refuse to corroborate. Classically, the ideal of scientific objectivity rests on the assumption that the natural world is empirically and logically determinate: composed of discrete substances and properties in thoroughgoing causal interaction such that, in principle, knowledge of the whole can be deduced from the highest laws of the system, or conversely, inductively established via systematic empirical investigation. The ideal of science to which this image corresponds is one in which a relationship holds "between a body of propositions such that no one of them can be false if the rest are true, and no one of them is independent of the others," thus in which, in epistemically ideal conditions, all propositions can be assigned a truth-value (no indeterminacy), and any true proposition can be deduced from the rest (Woozley, 152). But if psychic phenomena (wishes, fantasies, pains) are neither wholly pliable to interpretive construction nor wholly determinate (substances or properties secured in causal chains that express systematically integrated laws), why should psychoanalysis maintain faith in the epistemic ideal of science and continue to countenance its assumptions? Might the conceptions of natural objects and systems — of nature generally — assumed by the classical ideals of objectivity and refutation be of limited applicability? Is psychic life a substance? Can science rightfully measure something that is, to some degree, inconsistent, incoherent, and indeterminate — say, necessarily and constitutively self-interpreting and socially mediated, perhaps also empirically spontaneous, prone to develop and manifest in ways that cannot be predicted? Can there be a science of subjectivity? If scientific inquiry is powerful but limited; if, as Husserl never tired of demonstrating, science can never ground its claim to provide a totally exhaustive or fully rationally satisfying account of the world;[7] then self-conscious self-restriction when confronted by practices that proceed from different premises rather than imperious imposition is how science can remain true to its promise, i.e., avoid devolution into scientism.

Ideally, science strives to formulate, in simple and elegant equations, the small set of first principles from which all lower-level laws, causal mechanisms, and empirical observations can be derived. That is, it strives to discover the systematic (deductively-nomologically integrated) order of laws that are, at the highest level, unconditional and unrestricted in scope, and at lower levels make up for their lack of scope with enhanced precision. This ideal assumes an image of nature as not just regular and orderly, but wholly deterministic and specifically law-governed. More precisely, it assumes that nature is composed of discrete substances and properties governed by rules (lawfully integrated causal complexes) that precisely ordain their behavior and that these natural substances and properties have exact boundaries. Only on these assumptions can science claim that its epistemic ideal (exact deductive relations obtaining between precise concepts and laws) mirrors nature as such. The classical ambition of science, then, is objectivity understood as deductively closed knowledge of the systematically interrelated whole[8] that is perfectly confluent with all empirical observations: complete empirical and logical determination.

Of course there are certain aspects of nature, say, genetic mutation and other aspects of evolutionary biology; habitat transformation and other aspects of ecology; perhaps the development of wishes, fantasies, neuroses, and other psychical processes, that do not seem to be deterministic/derivable. Regularities in these domains obtain, thus probabilistic causal claims can be ventured and confirmed, but thoroughgoing empirical and logical determination seems an *idealization* in light of available evidence. Perhaps with regard to these areas we lack the necessary data and/or equations. Maybe what seems to bespeak spontaneity or irregularity will reveal itself to be a law-governed operation within a closed system after all. If so, interpretive indeterminacy (taxonomic plurality) may still be a source of skepticism, but skepticism would have lost much of its bite — revealed itself to be seeking for certainty there where certainty is unavailable; contentious or evasive; no longer cognitively useful. To the extent that objectivity in the abovementioned sense is desirable, holding onto the assumptions of empirical and logical determinism and the like, seeing how far one can go with them, remains worthwhile. Desires are not subject to refutation (but rather to collapse, catastrophe, or transformation).

The crucial point with regard to psychoanalysis is that the function of the abovementioned ideal of refutation is to keep the classical pursuit of objectivity efficient and on track; it functions under the auspices of the *hypothetical imperative* of objective knowledge. However, psychoanalysis has reasons to hesitate over corroborating, let alone monofocally pursuing, this ideal of objectivity. These reasons are precisely its experiences of subjectivity: of the ontological indeterminacy of psychic phenomena, their indefinite pliability to interpretive constitution and social mediation. These experiences are *emphatic experiences*, orientational experiences, experiences from which psychoanalysis' hesitations vis-à-vis or denials of thoroughgoing determinism cannot be derived but in which they are sourced. Assuming the premise of subjectivity is as if a matter of conscience.[9]

If the ideal of refutation guiding the classical ideal of science is not entirely appropriate for psychoanalysis, to what kinds of informative failures are psychoanalytic claims prone? What sorts of failures could be appropriately invoked when evaluating a psychoanalytic claim, whether independently or comparatively? Failures of conformity with empirical observations? These certainly matter, though they are not decisive. Such failures would be decisive only if the claims in question aim to explain, in a strong sense, the objects with which they are concerned, i.e., integrate them in a deductive-nomological system all the propositions of which are subject to observational confirmation in ideal epistemic conditions. It may seem suspicious that psychoanalytic theories tend to be sufficiently semantically flexible to account for a great many apparently disconfirming observations in their own terms and sufficiently syntactically flexible to restrict their scope or readjust the status of their claims when they cannot absorb the anomalous findings (e.g., if infant observation studies or neuroscientific experiments yield disconfirming or nonconforming evidence bearing on a certain developmental theory or a theory of pathology or cure that relies on it, rather than conclude that the theory is false or implausible, proponents of the theory can claim that it concerns "the infantile" rather than empirical infants, or more generally, that it is a feature of a theory of therapy that does not aim to explain but to effect various changes).[10] But absent commitment to the classical ideal of objectivity, it is unclear why this amounts to a cardinal sin. Although manipulating semantic and syntactic flexibility to make *ad hoc* changes to hypotheses under pressure is disconcerting, bearing the suspicions it raises rather than rejecting the move for the sake of cognitive calm may be "the price of doing business." Not all vices are cardinal sins, and some vices have their virtues.[11]

What about internal inconsistency? This too matters, but a rigoristic application of the standard would be question begging — tantamount to an immediate repudiation of the psychoanalytic enterprise. Psychoanalysis cannot but entertain the idea that the phenomena with which it is concerned are inconsistent: e.g., I both desire and dread my mother; or Eros and the death drive are for the most part intertwined; or attraction partially converts into revulsion; or I act on the basis of having both registered and repudiated a certain state of affairs; or guided by transferential pressures, I treat an object as an imago in some respects and according to her specific individuality in others. Further, psychoanalytic claims tend not to be sufficiently concrete (if x, then y and only y; and if x, then not z) for a theory that encompasses them to be found internally inconsistent.

The difficulty with determining what could count as informative failure (or something akin to refutation) for a psychoanalytic theory results, in part, from the loose relation between theory, practice, and observation in psychoanalysis. Theory may orient or inform practice, but it does not dictate practice; thus difficulties at the level of practice may bear upon but they do not necessarily invalidate the theory in whose name or under the guidance of which the practice is pursued. Likewise, theory and practice cannot but express some sensitivity to observations, indeed may be reworked in light of new observations, but whatever sensitivity is expressed, the uptake of observations is underdetermined.[12] Conversely, another part of the problem is the overproximous relation between psychoanalytic theory and observation. To the great consternation of its critics, psychoanalytic theories are regularly used to interpret the observations that could serve as evidence for or against them, but, on the classical conception, only observations that do not already reflect the terms of the theory in question can confirm or (decisively) disconfirm that theory.

Would we fare any better with a standard that allows a theory or practice to win out over competitors if it solves the problems of a competing theory or practice more successfully or elegantly; or better, does this while pointing to problems that a competing theory or practice cannot identify; or more minimally, explains and avoids the failures of a competing theory or practice; or even more minimally, reproduces the successful consequences of a competing theory or practice and denounces its mistakes even if it cannot explain or avoid them? Some such standard would be both useful and appropriate for psychoanalysis, but this is because these standards codify criteria for immanent critique. Even though such standards elaborate an ideal of scientific progress keyed to the classical conception of objectivity, their value and pertinence is not confined to that enterprise. Their application does not amount to an appeal to the tribunal of science. Further, appeals to such standards are not without their difficulties. First, what precisely are "the problems" to which a psychoanalytic theory or practice is addressed, and what is involved in solving them more successfully, are often difficult to determine. Second, if their identification is to have any critical purchase, the problems of a competing theory or practice pointed to must be shown to be problems *for* that theory or practice, which brings us back to the first difficulty. Third, in the vast majority of cases it is extremely difficult to show that the failures that a replacement theory or practice solves or problems that it avoids cannot be solved or avoided by better application or adjustment to the prevailing theory or practice; part of the difficulty results from the indefinite boundaries/terms of psychoanalytic theories and practices.

So far we have been concerned with the difficulties involved in assessing psychoanalytic claims with criteria (arguably) appropriate for the modern natural sciences generally. Attempting to establish that psychoanalysis should be measured against the standards of a particular science, say, mathematical physics or evolutionary biology, involves further difficulties.

On the one hand, it is *prima facie* implausible that psychoanalysis should be held accountable to the range of epistemic standards and methodological virtues unique to or uniquely privileged by a particular science — that just sounds like cognitive imperialism. On the contrary, just as it seems *prima facie* inappropriate to measure evolutionary biology by the criteria of mathematical physics or vice versa, it seems inappropriate to measure psychoanalysis by the standards of any particular science unless the science (ultimately) has the same object domain as psychoanalysis (which for the moment we can assume is false; this claim will be substantiated in the discussion of reductionism below) or can vindicate a claim to exclusive title to the methodological and epistemic criteria that yield genuine knowledge (which too for the moment we can assume is false; we will dispute this in the discussion of the second requirement below). But on the other hand, the epistemic standards and methodological criteria shared by the various modern sciences are diverse, so diverse that a psychoanalytic claim meeting for failing to meet any particular one will hardly constitute endorsement or repudiation by the tribunal of science; and since the ordering of these diverse epistemic standards and methodological virtues is a matter of judgment, absent commitment to the classical conception of objectivity, meeting or failing to meet some number of them does not amount to vindication or condemnation by the tribunal of science (indeed what such criterial diversity suggests is that the adjudicatory system of science is as pluralistic and contested — procedurally and teleologically underdetermined — as the juridical system). Yet not so diverse that they appropriately bear on all theoretical and practical claims.

Some of the epistemic and methodological criteria to which most sciences hold themselves or can be held accountable are:

1. increases truth content: predicts new or novel phenomena or discovers new aspects of the world, e.g., new respects in which models resemble the world or ways in which the resemblance between a model and the world are different than heretofore thought
2. reliabilism: practice or belief A is generated by reliable process X, and there is no equally reliable process Y that would lead to not-A
3. consilience of inductions: e.g., the Whewellian criteria of convergence of different lines of evidence for a theoretical view (revamped Scholasticism)
4. consistency: hypotheses agree among themselves, new hypotheses agree with accepted theories
5. empirical adequacy of models: models yield true hypotheses regarding observables
6. simplicity of equations or equations that are easier to solve than competitors
7. precision: terminological clarity and/or transparency of data
8. operationalizability
9. indubitability of inference: strong material entailment or logical necessity
10. descriptive and/or deductive completeness
11. discriminatory power
12. predictive power[13]
13. explanatory power
14. efficiency in identifying and/or solving problems and/or generating interesting questions: Laudan (1977, 1984), for instance, claims that the acceptability of a scientific tradition and its associated theories should be measured by their rate of problem-solving effectiveness, that is, by the number and import of problems solved by the tradition in a particular span of time, or by their effectiveness in otherwise guiding practice successfully

15. sensitivity to data or falsifiability
16. high degree of logical probability or empirical verification
17. unity of and/or greater degree of scope
18. adequacy to preferred set of observations
19. robustness
20. contribution to consistently successful interaction with some aspect of the world (manipulation, control, planning success) or technological developments
21. standardizability and/or quantifiability of findings
22. measurement of something not yet measured
23. provisioning of a legitimate paradigm: an exemplary solution that provides the model for other solutions and further research (or some other version of wide applicability)
24. avoidance of *ad hoc* hypotheses
25. saves the phenomena[14]
26. production of new or better or more useful information
27. increased capacity to refer to natural kinds and/or specify referents (of natural kind terms) descriptively
28. establishment of objective dependencies
29. contribution to the unity of science
30. full literal truth

Critical rationalists tend to prefer theories that increase content, take falsification seriously, and avoid *ad hoc* hypotheses. Logical empiricists tend to prefer theories that are precise, based only on measurable data, and avoid vague and untestable ideas; for the sake of precision and certainty, they risk shutting out the world, losing truth, effectiveness, and interest. Constructive empiricists prioritize empirical accuracy. The question is: by what right does one claim that one's privileged satisfactions are absolutely satisfying, enjoined upon all?

Given that the epistemic and methodological criteria appropriate to scientific inquiry and theorization are diverse (the above list is quite partial; and absent commitment to the aspirations of and metaphysics subtending the classical conception of objectivity, there is no reason to believe that these criteria entail one another or are subject to simultaneous satisfaction) competition or at least heterogeneity *within and between the sciences* may remain irresolvable. One equation or treatment may give only a rough estimate of the relevant features of the phenomenon or process under consideration, but is comparatively easier to solve or work with than another. A theory may be better than competitors, but seemingly absurd and suspected false.[15] Predictive power is impressive, but predictive closure encounters challenges in chaos theory and the various life sciences, indeed only obtains in highly restricted circumstances, and by no means implies descriptive completeness.

Neither is descriptive completeness guaranteed by empirical success, for empirical success by no means implies that all or even all the relevant properties or variables are known. Simplicity seems like a hoax, a relatively haphazard way of cutting down the range of alternatives, or else an ontotheological-economical axiom.[16]

Scientific contents, aims, and objects are perhaps irreducibly diverse. It is far from certain that any set of epistemic and methodological criteria will be unproblematically privileged, established as a scientific absolute, *absent a hypothetical imperative that dictates the end of scientific inquiry.*[17]

(2) If the first requirement abounds in difficulties, fulfilling the second is downright implausible. The neo-Kantian project of establishing a tribunal to which all subsidiary sciences must appeal is and will likely remain in utter disarray.[18] At present, there is no compelling reason to believe that there is some special surveying science that can properly order and assess the various special sciences and thereby yield a systematically complete knowledge of everything. Rather, the question of what makes for better or worse scientific practice seems to be a question best posed *for* — to and by — local scientific communities or research programs, and is amenable to diverse answers depending on their objects and objectives. The reign (or dream) of scientific monotheism has been effectively contested by the resurgence (or acknowledgment) of vibrant scientific polytheism; there seems to be no master science that can organize the findings of the special sciences into a deductively complete or otherwise systematically secure account of the whole; epistemic and methodological virtues seem irreducibly diverse, practice- and interest-sensitive.[19] Absent at least a reasonable suspicion that this or that science may be the master or model science, whether or not psychoanalysis measures up well against the standards and/or findings of some particular science no longer seems an urgent question.

The sources and consequences of the crises to which the neo-Kantian ambition has succumbed are diverse. Here we will focus only on why a project crucial to its success is now in such shabby shape, namely, theory reductionism. Roughly, theory reductionism is the dream of unifactorial or suchlike explanation, that is, explanation of the whole of nature via the restricted vocabulary of a single special science that concerns itself with the most simple natural elements, structures, and processes from which all others can be derived. Theory reductionism, to the extent that it is relevant to the neo-Kantian project, implies ontological reductionism. On the premises that (1) the basic elements of the reducing theory and the structures of reduced theory are identical, (2) nature is divvied up into natural kinds, and (3) scientific theories can be hierarchically organized and deductively complete because nature is a closed system of laws that fully determine the behavior of all natural substances and properties, the ambition of reductionism is to demonstrate that every theory but one (ecological theories, geological theories, biological theories, chemical theories, various physical theories, etc.) can be derived from a theory of simpler entities.

Given the proliferation of subdisciplines with specialized vocabularies and the unpersuasiveness of efforts to date to reduce them — at present, even basic physics seems irreducibly divided into the world of the very large (general relativity theory), the world of mid-ranged objects (quantum theory), and the world of the very, very small (e.g., superstring theory, but theories about this realm come and go relatively rapidly) — the first premise finds itself in troubled waters. But perhaps the ideal is still worth pursuing.

Concerning the second premise, in *The Disorder of Things* (1995) and elsewhere, John Dupré argues convincingly against taxonomic realism: the idea of one unambiguously correct taxonomic theory. As Dupré has shown, there are countless legitimate ways of classifying nature, none of which can prove itself superior to others absent agreement about the goals of inquiry. If different goals require different taxonomies, and no goal can prove itself to be *the goal* of science, the assumption of determinate natural kinds is highly questionable.[20]

One way of reformulating the worries about the first two premises would be to say that the formulation and corroboration of theories and hypotheses are underdetermined by evidence. As the history of science shows, there are multiple, mutually inconsistent accounts of any body of evidence that are either empirically equivalent[21] or equally satisfying (though perhaps in different registers, that is, in view of different aims); and there is no compelling reason to believe that it will ever be otherwise. As Mary Hesse would put it, empirical data cannot constrain theories or hypotheses to one.[22] Or as Descartes would have it, the sensations that yield and/or vindicate the hypothesis "there is fire" can also be explained by accounts of evil demons or life-long dreaming.

But perhaps the Cartesian-skeptical route to the strong conclusion that theories and hypotheses are *inevitably* underdetermined by data is hasty — itself underdetermined by evidence. Perhaps what Hesse should have said is that science has *not yet* developed to the point where empirical data can constrain theories or hypotheses to one and *may never*. Perhaps the most that one is entitled to say is that, so far, the history of science provides reason to suspect that there will always be an equally satisfying or at least competitive alternative for any description or explanation of data. The history of underdetermination does not entail a discrediting or dissolution of faith in the ambition of developing a rigorously complete deductive-nomological theory of the natural world wherein firm and final theories and hypotheses rule out competitors, but it can make this faith evident as such, i.e., demonstrate that this ambition lives on credit of faith. Indeed, this "unsettling" history may be the ground of such faith. Even if deductive-nomological integration were achieved, interpretive indeterminacy would not be surpassed. At most, it would become of less concern: exiled.

The third premise is likewise problematic. If it is not simply a stipulation, the most compelling basis for belief that nature is organized by laws through and through is an argument from enumerative induction, and this is not terribly plausible. As Nancy Cartwright has repeatedly shown, often what happens at one instance (some causal process) is not a reliable guide to what happens at others (is not universalizable into law) absent shielding conditions. That is, (1) the extent to which nature is law-governed and (2) the extent to which the establishment of law-governance is sufficiently explanatory have been overestimated as a result of tendencies to gloss over the *ceteris paribus* and *ceteris absentibus* clauses that allow complex, often unique causal processes to be shielded off in the formulation and verification of regularity laws and covering laws. Only by means of these clauses can science abstract from the specific parameters and complexes of causal interactions sufficiently to formulate general laws; but what the resultant law gains in scope, it loses in precision and (mechanical-reconstructive) explanatory force (what one might call "truth"). The mathematical precision of equations through which laws are expressed masks their inaccuracy. Often, to the extent that a law succeeds in its own terms (wide scope), it loses the world.

If, at most, nature partakes of a patchwork of laws — in restricted conditions laws dictate behavior, but ordinarily these conditions do not obtain; causal interactions do not perfectly conform to models of abstract laws absent shielding conditions — then deductive closure is off the table. Classical mechanics, electromagnetic theory, and special relativity theory exhibit appreciable success in reducing diverse phenomena to their vocabularies *so long as* the phenomena reduced reliably occur in situations where all their causes and the arrangements of these causes are known, and these too can be described in the reducing vocabulary. But this is rare, usually limited to artificial constructs (experiments, devices, etc.). Reducible phenomena are only those generated by causes that produce these and only these effects, and these seem to be few and far between. Causes tend to produce a wide array of effects depending on the arrangement of other causes; often the only way to formulate laws comprehending complex causal interactions is to try to forget — i.e., bracket — the specificity of their objects. Thus, discoveries pointing in the direction of irreducible natural complexity — there seem to be many means to the same end rather than strict lawful dependencies of particular ends on particular sets of means[23] — call the third premise into question.

Further, deductive closure might obtain and scientific theories might be subject to indubitable hierarchization only if Cartwright and others are wrong — merely trading in appearances — when they suggest that even where nature is law-governed, it is governed in different domains by different systems of laws that are not related to one another in a systematic, let alone uniform, way.

With regard to theory reductionism directly, certainly theoretical vocabularies can supplement or supplant one another, but it is unclear how, say, biology or ecology could be reduced to the (or a) vocabulary of physics without loss. Of course, the registration of loss assumes the concerns of biologists or ecologists, but it is unclear why the concerns of physics are overriding even if the latter's concerns are maximally adapted to the ideal of deductive-nomological integration. Without begging the question by simply asserting that the satisfaction of its cognitive criteria constitutes replete explanation, it is unclear why the categorical composition of physics should be assumed adequate to the diverse pursuits of diverse sciences (or that if it is not, the "sciences" to which it is inadequate are less than entitled to the name), especially since the categorical composition(s) of physics exclude(s) — or hastily reduce(s) — categories central to other scientific pursuits, e.g., the category of life understood in biology as involving self-movement, self-healing and self-preservative propensities, holistic arrangements and interactions of parts that support functions other arrangements would satisfy, teleological directedness, etc. Physics may describe the mechanisms of biological processes and interactions, but without begging the question regarding adequacy of explanation, it cannot vindicate a claim to reduction. Part of the problem with theory reductionism, then, is the residual ambiguity consequent upon unavoidable interpretive parasitism: reduction is possible only if the vocabulary of the *reduced* theory is preserved as a guide to the phenomena reduced.

If strong reductionism is problematic, are weaker versions any less so? Perhaps, but giving up even an inch on the claim that all theories can be reduced to and derived from one special theory of simple entities, structures, and processes means giving up on the claim that the reducing theory is the rightful measure of all theories. Mitigating the problems pertaining to strong reductionism implies abandoning the pursuit of the absolute satisfaction it promises (and the attendant metaphysical presuppositions), thus leaving open the question of the motivation for (weak) reduction. For instance, in one weaker incarnation, reductionism is pursued as a program of describing everything that matters to the motion of bodies in the restricted vocabulary of physics. Assuming this to be possible, it would still have to be shown that knowing about the motion of bodies is all there is to know about nature, or else why successful subsumption in such terms is cognitively compelling — it does not necessarily imply maximal empirical adequacy, arrogating successful consequences may mean taking on board associated insufficiencies and failures, etc. If the aim is just to redescribe rather than reduce *and derive* all other theories, why would descriptive hegemony warrant replacement, let alone cognitive satisfaction?

A stronger version of reductionism, mechanical reductionism, aims to explain wholes (the whole of nature or a specific natural system) in terms of the functional (mechanical) interaction of its parts. The problem is that even if the relevant parts and their properties can be unproblematically identified (so bracketing Dupré's worries about taxonomic realism), and the functioning of these parts and their properties are simple and uniform (so bracketing Cartwright's worries about causal complexity and irregularity), it would still have to be shown that nature is a deductively closed mechanical system if replacement and cognitive satisfaction are to be warranted. And this is an assumption unavoidably underwarranted by whatever success mechanical reductionism achieves.

A FREUDIAN SCIENCE?

We will now turn to Freud's comments on the scientific standing of psychoanalysis, not out of reverence for Freud but because Freud's oscillating inflation and deflation of psychoanalysis as a natural science is instructive in three respects. First, it registers an anxiety concerning the authority of psychoanalysis still faced today. Second, it suggests something significant about the objects of psychoanalytic knowledge: that they are neither altogether amenable to lawful determination, prediction, or transparent explanation nor altogether resistant to generalization, predication, or explication; neither so abrasively singular that their conceptualization can only be viewed as a violation or abdication nor determinate entities whose law-governed manifestations could be, in principle, deduced from a systematically complete knowledge of the psyche. Third, it shows why appeals to Freud will be of no avail in sorting out the question of whether psychoanalysis should be treated as a natural science. Although Freud's pronouncements on the question hardly constitute good reasons for treating psychoanalysis as a natural science or not, since so much of the literature — especially the literature attempting to debunk psychoanalysis as pseudoscience — has concerned itself with establishing Freud's opinion on the topic in order to criticize or endorse it, if we are to alter the terms of the question of the relation of psychoanalysis to science, we would do well to begin by engaging it on its own terms.

1. Inflation: Psychoanalysis is a Natural Science Among Others

Freud characterizes psychoanalysis as "a natural science like any other" (SE 23: 158; see also SE 20: 47) and laments the "gross injustice that people have refused to treat psycho-analysis like any other science" (SE 20: 58).[24] In unambiguous terms he upholds that "the intellect and mind are objects for scientific research in *exactly the same way* as *any* non-human things. Psychoanalysis has a special right to speak for the scientific *Weltanschauung*"(SE

22: 159; *emphasis added*[25]). Further, Freud proclaims, "Spirit and soul [*Geist und Seele*] are objects for scientific research like any non-human things," "[t]he contribution [of psychoanalysis] consists precisely in the extension of [scientific] research to the area of the soul" (SE 22: 159). In a similar vein, he contends that "[t]he hypothesis we have adopted of a psychical apparatus extended in space, expediently put together, developed by the exigencies of life, which gives rise to the phenomena of consciousness only at one particular point and under certain conditions — this hypothesis has put us in a position to establish psychology on foundations similar to those of any other science, such, for instance, as physics" (SE 23: 196). Even when Freud succumbs to Kantian-type skepticism about things-in-themselves, he maintains that however ultimately unknowable reality may be, the scientist, e.g., the psychoanalyst, can and does attain valid insight into dependency relationships ("On the History of the Psycho-analytic Movement").[26] Freud continually claims that the motives into which psychoanalysis inquires are a species of cause (SE 4: 81-2; SE 5: 541-542, 560-1; SE 10: 199). So committed was Freud to establishing the conformity of psychoanalysis to the epistemic standards of classical science that on a number of occasions he insists that psychoanalytic theory validation proceeds by hypothetico-deductive inductivism (SE 14: 77, 117; SE 20: 32).[27]

Freud describes the intention of *The Project* as furnishing "us with a psychology which shall be a natural science: its aim, that is, is to represent psychical processes as quantitatively determined states of specifiable material particles and so to make them plain and void of contradictions" (SE 1: 355). His conviction in the confluence of psychoanalytic and natural scientific pursuits was so profound that it was easy for him to imagine psychopharmacology supplanting psychoanalytic technique: "The future may teach us to exercise a direct influence, by means of particular chemical substances, on the amounts of energy and their distribution in the mental apparatus . . . . But for the moment we have nothing better at our disposal than the technique of psycho-analysis" (SE 23: 182). When Freud claims that "[t]his line of approach is *derived directly* from pathological clinical observations," he even seems to embrace, or at least veer toward, a positivist conception of science according to which concepts (in the weak form of observation-statements) are to be directly inferred from theory-neutral observations, thus eliminating dubious inferences beyond the observable (SE 1: 356; emphasis added).[28]

There is no denying that Freud's influence by Helmholtz, which led him to uphold, from time to time, that fundamental laws of nature must be obeyed in the psyche and that, specifically, the pleasure principle and nirvana principle obey the law of the conservation of energy. Even when Freud insists that, for instance, "the laws of unconscious activity differ widely from those of the conscious," the gist of the claim seems to be that unconscious laws differ in content, not in form, from the laws of consciousness (SE 12: 255-6). At one point, Freud even calls for a unity of science approach to the special sciences, signing a manifesto in favor of such a project. Presumably, he had faith that psychoanalysis would discover the laws of the unconscious and would thereby contribute to the systematic integration of knowledge of the natural world (Kertz 1986). Freud could not be more clear in his contention that, psychology, once it recognized unconscious mentation, became "a natural science like any other" (SE 23: 159; also see SE 14: 59).

How can we understand Freud's propensity to extravagant generalization if we do not assume that he was — anxiously, desirously — attempting to develop psychoanalysis as a science among others? To give just a few examples: for Freud, the case of Anna O. shows that the cathartic method works; the case of Lucy R. shows the purposefulness of repression; the case of Elizabeth Von R. demonstrates hysterical conversion (pleasure becomes pain) and shows that conflict leads to symptoms as compromise-formations and that the cure comes through the ability to bear the conflict; the dream of Irma's injection provides evidence for the theory of dreams as wish-fulfillments (SE 4: 121); and Dora's case demonstrates the theory of transference (admittedly, not successfully accommodated to, but rather wrongly neglected and retrospectively inferred). *The Interpretation of Dreams* means to show that dreams are a witness to and model for regression; and the Schreber case, as Freud indicates in a letter to Jung, illustrates and means to partially explain the dynamics of paranoia he observed in Fliess during their disagreements (cited in Gedo and Pollock 1976, 418). Freud's notes on the Rat Man show that he was accumulating material for a theoretical demonstration of obsessional neurosis on the basis of that case, and even the published material advances bold generalizations: obsessive neurotics are concerned with conflicts about aggression and submissiveness, cruelty and gentleness, dirtiness and cleanliness, disorder and order; these conflicts lead to cruelty or a reaction-formation against it; and conflicts between hating one's parents and fear of giving free rein to this hatred generate a severe conscience and guilt. Although the unpublished notes include a number of observations and reflections pertinent to the case that do not strictly fall in line with the exhibition of Freud's theory of obsessional neurosis, their excision from the published case report is telling. If not in the course of the therapy, then in the report on it, Freud is monofocally attentive to the aspects of the Rat Man's case that support his elaboration of the etiology and structure of obsessional neurosis. By exaggerating the prominence and significance of certain variables and deflating others, Freud's presentation of the case material sacrifices nuance and complexity, even arguably distorts the material, in order to render certain sectors of material *paradigmatic*.

Perhaps, Freud's pronounced propensity to generalize and willingness to put forward ambitious theoretical statements on the basis of rather shanty evidence[29] is attributable not (just) to speculative daring or self-promotional interests but (also) to a desire to craft a scientific image for psychoanalysis by dint of the universality of its claims. Even if he knew full well that his generalizations and theoretical constructions were speculative in the extreme, he may have been attempting to utilize his authority to determine the appropriate *shape* of psychoanalytic claiming.[30]

Freud was prone to deliver striking generalizations: "the original helplessness of human beings is thus the *primal source of all moral motives*" (SE 1: 379); "[u]npleasure remains the sole means of education" (1954, 428); "nothing but a wish can set our mental apparatus at work" (SE 5: 528). His desire, even haste to universalize and thereby establish the scientific character of psychoanalysis may be related to why Freud, e.g., in *The Interpretation of Dreams*, claims to prove a great deal on the basis of self-scrutiny. Freud often gives greater weight to introspective data than to intersubjectively corroborable observations — "I have found love of the mother and jealousy of the father in my own case too, and now believe it to be a general phenomenon of early childhood" (Freud to Fliess Oct 15th 1897, Letter 71, 223) — but perhaps this is not because he was unconcerned with scientific credibility, but just the reverse.

As the development of his own work attests (his assessments of other psychoanalysts' work is a separate matter) for Freud, theoretical development should proceed in accordance with the scientific ideal: through the elaboration of ever more encompassing generalizations. At times, it even seems that generating a comprehensive theory of the mind is his highest priority. For instance, the hypnoid hypothesis is less generalizable than the conflict/defense hypothesis, and was abandoned in favor of the latter; the seduction hypothesis is less generalizable than the Oedipus complex, and the latter won out; the theory of actual neuroses is less generalizable than the revised theory of anxiety, and subsequent to its development, Freud concerned himself predominantly with the latter. Freud's claims to conceptual development often take the following form: the old is found to be a special, limited case of the new; more precisely, older theories are found to be part of a whole which was not yet seen. For instance, with the revised theory of anxiety, the anxieties pertaining to actual neuroses, infantile phobias, and psychoneuroses are gathered under a new, unifying explanation. The relative advancement in coherence and universality afforded by the revised theory of anxiety makes it, on Freud's account, obviously superior to the less integrated array of previous theories. Even if to do so meant (quietly) violating its evidentiary protocols, it seems that, throughout his career, Freud was highly interested in casting psychoanalysis on the model of explanatory natural science.

When the prospect of developing an explanatory, natural scientific account of the neuroses within his lifetime seemed dismal, the difficulty Freud faced in accommodating himself to this suggests that he both desired to develop psychoanalysis as a natural science among others and despite it all maintained faith that psychoanalysis would eventually yield a more than "merely clinical" explanation: "Perhaps in the end I may have to learn to content myself with the clinical explanation of the neuroses" (1954, 137). Even as his aspiration to certify psychoanalysis as a natural science comes to appear unrealizable, all Freud can say is that he *may* have to content himself with "clinical explanation" — it is as if nothing can dissuade him from pursuing the dream of a systematically complete and universally explanatory theory of the mind.

It is as if nothing could shake Freud's confidence that psychoanalysis is, and so will someday assume the title of,[31] a natural science.

> Whereas the psychology of consciousness never went beyond the broken sequences which were obviously dependent on something else, the other view, which held that the psychical is unconscious in itself, enabled psychology to take its place as a natural science like any other. The processes with which it is concerned are in themselves just as unknowable as those dealt with by other sciences, by chemistry or physics, for example; but it is possible to establish the laws which they obey and to follow their mutual relations and interdependencies over long stretches. (SE 23: 158)

In contrast to the psychology of consciousness that never went beyond broken sequences, failed to discover the forces (laws) of which these sequences are *obviously* expressions, Freud suggests, psychoanalysis pursues so far as possible a systematic account of the law-governed whole, thus earning its title as a natural science. A master tactician, Freud even preempts the objection to the entitlement of psychoanalysis to natural scientific standing on the basis of its limited deliverances and partial unverifiability by pointing to the equal failure of the accepted sciences to deliver deductively and descriptively complete, mutually integrated systems that rule out alternative interpretations of the data, decisively putting skepticism to rest. The incompleteness of psychoanalytic knowledge and its susceptibility to skeptical suspicion is no different from that of the accepted sciences, Freud protests. Also note that, on the one hand, Freud's thing-in-itself skepticism and his distinction between establishing laws and following "mutual relations and interdependencies over long stretches" puts subtle pressure on the self-image (the concomitant epistemological and metaphysical commitments) of natural science. The intimation of Freud's thing-in-itself skepticism is that realism, because it assumes as fundamental a distinction between subject and object, makes skepticism unavoidable. Though perhaps for different reasons, neither Freud nor natural science can appeal to transcendental idealist strategies to suture knower to known, make the known *known necessarily*, thus neither can claim with absolute certainty that the "in itself" is accurately captured by any categorical construction. And if following mutual relations and interdependencies is not exactly the same as "establish[ing] . . . laws," then, presumably some degree of taxonomic pluralism with regard to establishing laws and their interconnections, or more broadly, some degree of underdetermination of theory by evidence, thus some limit to positive verification, is unavoidable. Theories cannot be reduced to one, and if so, nature may not be as thoroughly nomological or systematically integrated as natural science stipulates. If there is a valid distinction between establishing laws and following mutual relations and interdependencies , phenomena cannot be entirely law-governed. If accounting for phenomena in terms of causal powers realized under various initial conditions and accounting for phenomena in terms of the universal laws under which they fall are at least sometimes distinct, if there are relationships and dependencies that can be empirically verified and yet are not instances of general law, or at least are not best accounted for in terms of the latter, then the restricted rationalism of the natural scientific image of the world, and obliquely, the metaphysical commitments constraining scientific rationality, become evident. But on the other hand, despite Freud's reservations about the notion of the thing-in-itself, he speaks of the "unconscious in itself," the truth behind appearances. Even if rigorous scientific rationality yields reason to be wary of the self-image of natural science, criticisms of this self-image must be quiet, Freud implies, for the sake of pressing the claim of psychoanalysis to natural scientific standing: "the other view, which held that the psychical is unconscious in itself, enabled psychology to take its place as a natural science like any other." Whether or not natural science is what it is taken to be, psychoanalysis deserves recognition as a natural science. If natural science pursues the thing-in-itself (the lawfully integrated whole), so does psychoanalysis. If natural science eventually recognizes the implausibility of this pursuit, so much the better for psychoanalysis' claim to recognition. Generally, the strategy is to keep criticism of natural science hypersubtle, thus the prospect of narcissistic injury and consequent vindictiveness minimized, while loudly broadcasting any reason to uphold psychoanalysis as a natural science.

Why such inflation? To speculate, perhaps Freud was profoundly worried that psychoanalysis would not be considered proper science in a culture that officially assumes — or fantasizes — a hard and fast distinction between scientific knowledge and artistic fancy and tends to immediately assimilate new discourses to one or the other, allowing little opportunity for recategorization, and believed that permitting psychoanalysis to be relegated to the side of art would impede it from being taken sufficiently *seriously*.[32] Perhaps as a hyperbolic rejoinder to both extant and anticipated consignments of psychoanalysis to artistic whimsy — or even to pathological fantasy; the racialized discrimination faced by "the Jewish science" may certainly be pertinent here[33] — Freud presents psychoanalysis as *perfectly* in line with science (perfectly assimilated).[34] "Despite what some people say, I am not an artist," Freud protests in a letter to Lou Andreas-Salomé (in Pfeiffer 1966, 196).

As early as 1919, Havelock Ellis wrote an essay in which Freud's pursuits are positioned as artistic creations, not science. Ellis' claim was all but inevitable given the prevalent belief that concern with the soul, especially with the madness to which the soul may succumb, plunges inquiry into the inscrutable depths of interiority and the irrational about which no scientifically valid claims can be made. Replying to Ellis, Freud contends that "we cannot but regard this view as a fresh turn taken by resistance and as a repudiation of analysis" (SE 18: 263). This could be a *fresh turn* taken by resistance only if resistance has previously assumed other guises. Presumably, one of the prior forms of resistance Freud has in mind is the widespread neglect of psychoanalytic developments (and their anticipations in poetic and philosophical discourses), which was but barely giving way to serious cultural interest. Once psychoanalysis begins to secure serious cultural interest, Freud suggests, its significance is registered and repudiated as it is cordoned off to the marginal realm of artistic innovation, deemed but a speculative — however ingenious — flight of fancy. Meeting excess with excess, perhaps, by insisting emphatically on their scientific credentials, Freud attempts to do what those who had previously developed analogous insights failed to do, namely, secure a serious and lasting reception for his insights.[35]

Perhaps this also provides a clue to why Freud was so keen to acknowledge similarities between his insights and those of past poets and philosophers, yet never did much more than acknowledge such similarities in passing. A consummate strategist — his identifications with famous military strategists are well known — perhaps, Freud' gestures toward poetic and philosophical ancestors may be in the service of advancing the cause of psychoanalysis simultaneously on two fronts. Perhaps Freud *both* wants to assimilate the authority of poetry and philosophy so as to secure the authority of psychoanalysis amongst those for whom poetry and philosophy are authoritative, and wants to assimilate the authority of science to secure the authority of psychoanalysis amongst those for whom science is authoritative. If so, recalling analogies with the poetic and philosophical predecessors without tarrying too far with these analogies and thereby giving the scientifically-rigid motive to dismiss psychoanalysis would be an appropriate strategy.[36]

2. Deflation: Psychoanalysis Is Not a Natural Science

Quite boldly, Freud announces that "psychoanalysis is not an impartial scientific investigation, but a therapeutic measure. Its essence is not to prove anything, but merely to alter something" (SE 10: 104). He knew full well that psychoanalysis is not exactly science, or at least not an exact science. Thus he describes it as occupying a "middle position between medicine and philosophy" (SE 19: 217). From very early on, Freud recognized his propensity for theoretical daring in contrast to Breuer's methodological asceticism (cited in Gedo and Pollock 1976, 169). Underscoring to the point of wildly exaggerating its uniqueness, Freud characterizes psychoanalysis as "*sui generis*, something new and singular that can be understood only with the help of new insights — or, if you will, new assumptions" (SE 20: 189-190). Later in the same essay, Freud provocatively characterizes the analyst as "a secular minister of souls [*ein weltlicher Seelsorger*]" — far from a neutral scientific observer (SE 20: 225). Well aware that his investigations concern psychic developments that are not rule-governed, thus cannot be perfectly predicted or verified with certainty, and so presumably aware that unlike the exact sciences, psychoanalysis cannot aspire to deductive-nomological closure, Freud contends: "the allegedly traumatic experience, though it *does* have a relation to the symptom, proves to be an impression which is normally innocuous and incapable *as a rule* of producing any effect" (cited in Gedo and Pollock, 1976, 219; latter emphasis added). Psychoanalysis, Freud suggests, is a (singular) science of the singular, emphatically attentive to precisely what one would suspect *would not* occur.[37] Paradoxically, psychoanalysts must expect to be surprised; theirs is an anomalous science of anomaly.[38] Note how careful Freud is to qualify the experience under investigation as an *alleged* trauma, keeping in view the speculative or at least epistemically insecure character of the inquiry and certainly doing nothing to suppress the allegation that the observations involved are theory-mediated. Although Freud claims that some manner of dependency relations are involved in the development of symptoms, and presumably these can be identified ("the allegedly traumatic experience . . . *does* have a relation to the symptom"), it is not incidental that he describes the conditioning event, the alleged trauma, as an "impression," an "experience." Whether the impression or experience at stake is something the analysand recalls or an analytic reconstruction, it is nonverifiable in the ordinary scientific manner, i.e., via predictive confirmation and deductive integration. Is it incidental that throughout his writings Freud uses the term "guess" 218 times and terms akin to "speculation" 108 times (Guttman, Jones, and Parrish 1980) or that he repeatedly describes his claims as "theoretical fictions"? (SE 5: 598 and 603; SE 12: 220; SE 14: 231; SE 20:194; SE 23: 235 and 239)

If science strives to articulate clear connections (laws) between undeniable facts, and if, as Freud's rhetoric continually makes clear, both "the facts" and their relations are (ontologically) anomalous and (epistemically) highly contestable in psychoanalysis, then psychoanalysis is surely no science. Even if Freud's penchant to generalize is interpreted as an attempt to articulate psychic laws, these "laws" are quite unlike those of physics in that they have very little explanatory power and specificity. In physics, ideally, increasing degrees of universality entail increasing degrees of specificity; but as Freud repeatedly intimates and sometimes boldly proclaims, it is just the reverse with psychoanalysis.

At least a certain degree of ambivalence, perhaps a rather nonchalant attitude or even a critical reticence about the scientific standing of psychoanalysis can be discerned in Freud's use of the language of causality. If by "cause" Freud means the necessary and sufficient antecedents of observed and predictable effects, or more strongly, the necessary and sufficient antecedents of observed and predictable effects *and only these effects*, that is, if Freud's use of the language of causality intends to align psychoanalysis with the ideal image of exact science, then, first of all, the warrant for speaking in this way is *conspicuously* absent.[39] Second, that Freud feels compelled to qualify the language of causality by apposing it to the language of motivation, as when he speaks of an anticipation of incapacitation by illness as "the cause [*Ursache*] or motive [*Motiv*] of falling ill," suggests that his notion of cause does not precisely conform to the ideal scientific notion (SE 10: 199). The apposition to *Motiv* both independently introduces a hint of ambivalence and quietly draws attention to the language of causality such that one can hear in "*Ursache*" itself [the origin or source of the thing or the original-thing or source-thing] a certain ambivalence about whether psychic "causes" are to be understood as necessary and sufficient antecedents or, more loosely, as speculatively reconstructed historical backdrops or otherwise useful origin-stories, even myths. If anticipation of incapacitation by illness is "the cause" of falling ill, "cause" cannot be understood as either necessary or sufficient for the effect *in general or in this particular case*. We often anticipate illness without succumbing to psychopathology; and Freud would never claim that *just* this anticipation causes the illness: it is the revival of infantile neurosis and arrogation to itself of a number of conflicting drive-investments, etc., not the anticipation *per se* that contributes to the illness, and even an account of such contributions is not fully explanatory.[40]

Might we understand Freud's use of "cause" here (and not just here) as *both* an (overhasty?) ornamentation of psychoanalytic claims with scientific signifiers *and* an expression of unconcern with, or even a self-conscious transgression of, the "proper" use of scientific terminology (perhaps even a subversive rearticulation of the language of causality and so a covert critique of the discourse and ideality of "the proper")? Considering the mismatch between what Freud describes as "causes" and causes in the (ideal) sense the exact sciences give the term, *on the one hand*, Freud's language of causality seems to evince an anxious identification of psychoanalysis with science. But even if so, such anxiety might not be an expression of Freud's need to see psychoanalysis as a science, but rather of his need to display it in such a light for others. That is, the anxious invocation of the language of causality may be an anxiously pursued strategy designed to induce those who would otherwise fail to take psychoanalysis seriously to do so. If this is Freud's game, he cannot expect the ruse to last for long. At most, then, this language must function as the expression of a promise that future work will bear out the scientific character of psychoanalysis in general and its anticipatory use of the language of causality in particular. But given that Freud provides no reason to believe that this promise will be fulfilled, its function seems to be largely instrumental, holding open a place for psychoanalysis in a scientistically inclined culture until that culture's rigid identification of science with certified or authoritative knowing slackens. In short, the anxiety evinced may be social anxiety both motivating and resulting from reigning scientistic commitments, and Freud's rhetorical complicity may be, in his estimation, a delaying strategy made necessary by the social circumstances of the promulgation of psychoanalysis (perhaps also a means of immanent critique). *On the other hand*, it may be that Freud is simply unconcerned with making causal claims in the manner of the exact sciences of his day. It may be that, when speaking of causes in the way that he does, he is shrugging off the admonitions he knows full well will follow. Freud regularly speaks of causation as genesis, likely motivation, or plausibly determining influence (SE 4: 81-2; SE 5: 541-2, 560-1; and SE 10: 199). It may even be that, when speaking of causes, Freud is performatively protesting the hegemonic appropriation of the language of causality, even the language and criteria of authoritative cognition generally, by the exact sciences and suggesting that such language and criteria are, at least to some extent, irreducibly subject to social contestation. Is it just the "science" of psychoanalysis he had in mind when he speaks of "scientific terms, that is to say . . . figurative language [*Bildersprache*]"? (SE 18: 60) It may also be that Freud's invocation of the language of causality exploits the disturbance of the ideal self-image of science issuing from empirical inquiry: "the tubercle bacillus is not disqualified from being the cause of tuberculosis just because many carriers of the bacillus do not develop the disease — just as many who experienced childhood seductions do not become hysterics" (SE 3: 209). Perhaps Freud, like many in the medical field at the time, construes cause as capacity, specifically as a capacity that, excepting restricted cases, will be realized or not depending on the arrangement of parameters and other causes.

Consider in this context Freud's notion of overdetermination. Although overdetermination might be understood to imply the ontological claim that multiple interacting causal factors constellate to produce the phenomenon under concern, and these causal influences cannot be reduced to expressions of covering or regularity laws, thus that the phenomenon under concern contests the image of nature as nomologically totalized, but is not for that reason cognitively opaque, the way Freud uses it, overdetermination regularly implies the epistemological claim that the causal complex responsible for the phenomenon at issue is ultimately inscrutable. Admonishing the hubris he senses in the classical conception of nature as wholly transparent to scientific inquiry, perhaps seeking to justify speculative daring against positivist asceticism, and contending that obscurity and perplexity lie there where matters seem most clear, thus, perhaps, that common sense, even scientific common sense, may function as a force of concealment in virtue of its obtrusive obviousness (and further that destabilizing sedimented doxa may require critique to enact the overdetermination and opacity it seeks to foreground, i.e., involve itself in literary maneuvers; the multiply mediated character of Freud's allusive claim itself recalls Plato's dialogues as much as its content directly evokes Heraclius and Aristotle), Freud maintains that "We still show too little respect for Nature which (in the obscure words of Leonardo which recall Hamlet's lines) 'is full of countless causes that never enter experience'" (SE 11: 137).[41] Even when pressing a claim for the superior precision of psychoanalytic over against natural scientific knowledge, Freud insists that "[i]nternal objects are *less unknowable* than the external world" (SE 14: 171; emphasis added). So when Freud describes overdetermination as "*the principle of the complication of causes*," the ambiguity of the expression is not to be taken lightly (SE 6: 60-1). This "overdetermined" expression may suggest that (1) overdetermination means fully explicable, even in particular nomologically explicable determination by multiple causal agencies; (2) the ideal of causal determination and principled explication is unsettled by the notion of overdetermination (the etymology of "principle [German] allows us to hear this expression as: the cause of the complication of causes — a consummate expression of negative dialectics); (3) thus that Freud is at least ambiguous, perhaps ambivalent,[42] or even critically wary about the scientific standing of psychoanalysis. Overdetermination might just mean that causal analysis is in principle complicated (which is uninformative). Or it might mean that the causes at issue interact in ways that produce singular, unpredictable effects. And if science assumes that nature is regular, orderly, and to be explained through laws of increasing scope, then the assumption of overdetermination precludes psychoanalysis from attaining scientific standing.

On a number of occasions, even when Freud discusses psychoanalysis as a science, he is careful to keep its differences from the exact sciences in view, if not always in the fore. For instance, Freud maintains that, in the spirit of science, psychoanalysis strives to be sensitive to observational data, but unlike in the exact sciences, advances in psychoanalysis are not determined by strict logical inference from observational data or decisive disconfirmation of predictions: "Psychoanalysis as an empirical science . . . keeps close to the facts in the field of its study, seeks to solve the immediate problems of observation, gropes its way forward by the help of experience, is always incomplete and always ready to correct or modify its theories" (SE 18: 253). Here Freud suggests that psychoanalysis is an empirical science insofar as it attempts to coordinate and account for its observations rather than just thrash about in the ether of speculation; but even so, striving to *keep close* to the facts would certainly not satisfy those who identify scientific inquiry with positivist methodology. Striving to keep close to the facts implies speculative abstraction in need of tempering or concretization by responsible returns to what is observationally evident; thus such striving already intimates a difference between psychoanalysis and (positivistically conceived) science. Likewise, although Freud suggests that psychoanalysis is an empirical science insofar as it seeks to solve the immediate problems of observation, this implies that there are less immediate problems (whether of observation or other sorts, e.g., of theory construction) that it is quite aware it does not solve, perhaps cannot solve. And if solving the immediate problems of observation means generating a comprehensive classificatory scheme, obvious questions about the validity of its taxonomic procedures wait in the wings. Further, even if *as* an empirical science psychoanalysis strives to keep close to the facts in its field of study and so on, the modal *as*, especially when read in light of the above considerations, intimates that this is not the only way that psychoanalytic investigation proceeds, i.e., that at other times psychoanalysis proceeds *as* a much more speculative enterprise. And even when psychoanalysis proceeds as an empirical science, it "gropes its way forward by the help of experience" rather than progressing on the basis of logically necessary inferences and experimentally reliable results. If in this context "experience" is Freud's code word for "tradition" (in addition to signifying clinical and suchlike data), then as guided by "experience," psychoanalysis at once claims scientific credibility and marks its distance from the systematic skeptical debunking of all things "traditional" through which the traditional self-image of science and certain features of scientific methodology were forged. What's more, *as* an empirical science, psychoanalysis "is always incomplete," which is to say, presumably, that unlike the exact sciences, it cannot aspire to the deductive-nomological closure or to contributing to such closure. Perhaps it is also to say that psychoanalysis' sensitivity to data, specifically to the unpredictable, unruly, inordinately complex, and perhaps self-secluding developments and manifestations of psychic phenomena, forbids it from claiming descriptive completeness (some measure of taxonomic pluralism and underdetermination of theory by evidence is inevitable) and from overestimating the extent to which it can develop laws of regularity, let alone necessity. Even *as* an empirical science, psychoanalysis is very different from other such sciences. Perhaps, the determination of the empirical itself is subtly called into question through the identification of psychoanalysis as an empirical science. Finally, it is important to note that we are discussing a line from one of Freud's popular publications. Perhaps especially in such a context, Freud both wants to give an impression of the scientificity of psychoanalysis in order to contribute to its popular credibility *and* wants to acknowledge the differences between psychoanalysis and the exact sciences for his more rigorous readers.[43]

As much as psychoanalysis may be inspired by the spirit of science, it remains available to other spirits, other muses. "If the theory of sexuality comes," Freud proclaims, "I will listen to it" — as if the dawning of the theory of sexuality would be neither a *revelation* immediately affirmed — it would be listened to, sounded out, perhaps interpreted in light of the deliverances of the empirical sciences — nor strictly a result of rigorous scientific inquiry and logical analysis (cited in Gedo and Pollock 1976, 184). One can only speculate here, but it may not be too farfetched to hear Freud suggesting along Maimonidean lines that rigorous empirical inquiry (generally, the perfection, which would involve the self-limiting, of demonstrative knowledge) is the precondition for revelation and so for the development of knowledge that cannot be had without revealed premises.

Why would we ever think that Freud, the author of *Moses and Monotheism*, *Totem and Taboo*, *Civilization and its Discontents*, and *Beyond the Pleasure Principle* (with its professedly speculative elaboration of the death drive) would ever presume that psychoanalysis is simply a natural science among others? Even in view of his late claims that one can do nothing for patients and should be content with psychoanalysis as a research method, it is not as if Freud conducted controlled experiments, dedicated himself to determining the possibilities transforming the clinic into a viable experimental field, or was concerned with systematic theory building. Quite to the contrary, his late writings are among his most speculative and cultural-critical.

In virtue of the concern with meaning, specifically, practically felicitous or pathogenic meaning, constitutive of the Freudian enterprise, Freud perhaps *could* not consider psychoanalysis an exact science, or exactly a natural science in the reigning sense of the term. Consider the following. "In this materialist or, better, mechanistic period medicine made tremendous advances, but it also misunderstood in a shortsighted way the chief and most difficult among the problems of life" (SE 19: 216). Blinded by its insight into mechanism and perhaps all the more by its desire for deductive certainty and predictive confirmation which the study of mechanism promises, the intensity of which desire was perhaps significantly enhanced by the palpable limits of its competence and the regular therapeutic failures to which it was prone, medicine became myopic with respect to "the chief and most difficult among the problems of life": presumably, the problem of meaning, and perhaps more specifically, psychosexual meaning. Clearly, what mechanistic medicine glosses over are irregular or idiosyncratic developments; and although reflectively acknowledging these would be "most difficult" in the context of the dominant self-image of science, it is unlikely that Freud would consider them "the chief . . . problems of life." Besides, in the contemporary medical community the diversity and irregularity of bodily functioning was much more readily acknowledged than in other scientific domains, so simply underscoring bodily anomaly would be redundant with respect to medicine and ineffective with respect to those committed to mechanistic reductionism.

"[T]he chief and most difficult among the problems of life" occluded, or perhaps constitutively excluded, by mechanistic medicine, then, perhaps concerns the notion of life itself — life as normatively articulated, meaning-saturated, thus requiring hermeneutic engagement and not just mechanistic decoding. The chief and most difficult problem, perhaps, is reflectively incorporating a robust notion of life into the horizon of scientific inquiry, or what may amount to the same, reformulating the notion of science, and correspondingly, of nature, consequent upon the inclusion of psychoanalytic inquiry as an empirical (or materialist) practice. That is, "the chief and most difficult among the problems of life" is perhaps the *problematic* — categorically troubling — character of life itself. I suspect that Freud has something like the following in mind: thinking "life" involves thinking part/whole relations, thus normative configurations, thus involves categories excluded or occluded by the reigning image of scientific method (teleology, coherence, etc.) and forms of judgment (specifically reflective judgment) it tends to suppress or epistemically marginalize, and involves considerations of drive underdetermination (broadly, underspecialization), thus the imbrication of orientations toward survival and meaning, thus of natural responsivity to noninstrumentalized nature, thus of the fate of this responsivity, and so the social-historical mediation of nature and natural mediation of socio-historical developments, thus involves the category of historicity, and ultimately involves divestment from an image of science as categorically separate from hermeneutic inquiry, matter from meaning, mechanism from history. Thinking life is a reflexively hermeneutical affair, and as such a more adequate materialism.[44]

CONFLUENCE AND DISSONANCE

1. Confluence

Among analysts and the analytically inclined, interest in establishing or promoting the conformity of psychoanalysis to science, especially to neuroscience (Watt 1986, 1990; Levin 1991, 2002; Schore 1994; Solms 1997; 2000, 2001; Kandel 1998, 1999; Panskepp 1998, 1999; Siegel 1999; Solms and Kaplan-Solms 2000; Semenza 2001;Yu 2001a, 2001b; Roeckerath 2002; Cozolino 2002; Solms and Turnbull 2002; V. Green 2003; Modell 2003; Schore 1994, 1997, 2001, 2002, 2003, 2005; Mayes 2003; Kernberg 2004; Browning 2006[45]), is wide-ranging and rapidly proliferating. Too often such interest is silently premised on, or its results are assimilated by, the desirous conviction that demonstrating the conformity of psychoanalysis to scientific discoveries and epistemic norms translates into instant credibility, or if not, at least entitles psychoanalysis to rational interest. Even more boldly, Mayes (2003), Kernberg (2004), and others claim that modern neuroscience can *(in)validate* psychoanalytic theories. If establishing or promoting the confluence of psychoanalytic methods and claims with scientific discourses and methodological norms advances psychoanalytic practice or research, or mitigates the tendential disenfranchisement of psychoanalytic practices and insights from rational interest, and so, perhaps, the irrational idealization and instrumentalization of science, the enterprise is to be appreciated and encouraged. But too emphatically underscoring or seeking to establish confluence is self-defeating — a reckless pursuit of conformity that abdicates the rational potential of both psychoanalysis and science. Often, the pursuit of confluence effectively amounts to idolizing science and then preying on its projected authority: an anxious ruse of parvenus by means of which no one but they are deceived. To immediately, indeed preemptively accede to the identity of science and rational authority is to obviate the need to articulate and defend the specific objectivity and value of psychoanalysis. And under the spell of scientism, psychoanalysis will no doubt be once again suspected of irrational regression — a suspicion bolstered by its aggressive assimilation by those within the psychoanalytic community who, forsaken by science, reactively repudiate its claim, attempting to inoculate themselves from disparagement by holding steadfast to and loudly proclaiming (perhaps only within insular circles of the likeminded) their abstract difference and self-authorization, i.e., by enforcing their abjection.

Awestruck by Gerald Edelman's neural Darwinism, many give him pride of place in their "science of psychoanalysis" pantheon. Very roughly, the central claim of Edelman's neural Darwinism (1986, 1993) is that a wide range of neural patterns are laid down as adaptive responses to experience. This claim has a great deal of experimental neuroscientific support. Many see in Edelman's work an organic basis for individual psychic differences,[46] specifically for pathological functioning (the claim is that pathological behavior or ideation was once an adaptive response to experience that has since become ossified; this certainly *sounds like* transference). Others have latched onto Edelman's work because it provides an experimentally credible theory of the structure and function of the brain that at least does not rule out a wide variety of psychoanalytic claims. But Edelman's theory is both too capacious and too restrictive. Given a weak reading of "adaptive responses," just about any psychoanalytic or psychological claim will find an organic precondition in Edelman's theory. Indeed, the theory sounds like behaviorism minus the optimism about recoding. More precisely, on a weak reading of "adaptive response" (e.g., "seemed to have some instrumental value at the time"), the theory either begs a host of questions about why and to what degree certain responses became ossified (i.e., begs the question with regard to metapsychology) or assumes that all "adaptive responses" are equally prone to ossification and so *denies* metapsychology (especially metapsychologies that involve claims about primordial and lasting maladjustment). Consequently, the theory is unhelpful for debates within psychoanalysis and between psychoanalytic and non-psychoanalytic psychology. On the other hand, a stronger reading of "adaptive response" would rule out far too many psychoanalytic claims, especially metapsychological claims, without compelling warrant. Why believe that all pathological phenomena were once adaptive responses? Or if Edelman's claim is not bidirectional (ossified adaptive responses are pathological but not all pathological phenomena are ossified adaptive responses), what work can this claim do? The most that can be concluded from Edelman's neural Darwinism is that a number of psychoanalytic claims are not impossible, i.e., their organic substratum can be imagined in the context of contemporary neuroscientific discoveries.[47] But this is (very) little more than saying that psychoanalytic claims are logically possible, which is not saying much.

Another theorist often given pride of place in the "science of psychoanalysis" pantheon is Antonio Damasio.[48] Like Edelman, Damasio (1994, 1999) develops a model of the brain well supported by neuroscientific experimentation that does not rule out a number of key psychoanalytic claims. Specifically, Damasio's stratified model of the brain allows for unconscious phantasies and predispositions to be laid down in the earliest years and most primitive regions of the brain. Damasio further claims that these phantasies and predispositions may not be capable of processing through more "advanced," later-developing mental functioning. This model has recently received significant experimental support from a number of studies showing that certain sorts of brain injuries result in severe deficiencies in relational capabilities while leaving (traditionally understood) cognitive capacities untouched (Schore 1994, Shuttlesworth 1998, and Solms and Kaplan-Solms 2000). Like Edelman's, Damasio's model of the brain renders a number of psychoanalytic claims conceivable in the context of contemporary neuroscience, but little more. To be sure, Damasio's work is more confluent with Kleinian theory than ego psychology and various cognitive-behavioral oriented non-psychoanalytic theories (but not with Kleinian therapy, especially in comparison to supportive psychoanalytic or non-psychoanalytic therapy), and it accords more with relation-oriented practices than predominantly interpretation-oriented practices (or perhaps only with evaluative focus on the relational effects of interpretation); and in any case only concerns pathological phenomena sourced in phantasies and predispositions rooted in primitive regions of the brain — a reference class exceedingly difficult to determine and perhaps nonexistent given what was discussed earlier with regard to outcome and process studies. But it provides nothing remotely decisive for debates within psychoanalysis or between psychoanalytic and non-psychoanalytic theory and therapy. No doubt part of the allure of Damasio's work for psychoanalysts is that it seems to provide a scientific basis for the claim to the superiority of psychoanalytic theory and therapy to rationalist strands of cognitive-behavioral therapy (CBT). With regard to therapy, if unconscious phantasies and predispositions are largely unimpacted by later-developing mental functioning, then the holding and containing or otherwise emotionally impacting operations of analysis (perhaps including abreaction and transference analysis) seem much more promising than CBT-like attempts to confront and correct irrational ideas or condition away irrational behavior. But, two empirical claims would have to be established before any confidence in the therapeutic superiority of psychoanalysis is warranted. First, it would have to be shown that and how unconscious phantasies and predispositions largely unimpacted by later-developing mental functioning bear on various forms of pathology. Second, outcome and process studies would need to confirm the superior efficacy of the emotionally impacting operations of psychoanalysis with regard to the pathological phenomena established by the first set of studies. The depth at which phantasies and predispositions are buried in Damasio's model might limit the efficacy of emotionally oriented or other such practices as much as those that aim as rational reconditioning or edification. If Damasio is right, conditioning and CBT have organically imposed limits, but this does not entail that other practices will fare better.

A more promising and highly prominent strategy to establish the confluence of science and psychoanalysis is to construe psychoanalytic claims in a manner that yields predictions subject to experimental confirmation or disconfirmation. Bellak recounts an experiment in prediction that has been performed many times over in the psychoanalytic community: "Along with some colleagues, I arranged for the tape recording and transcription of analyses. A group of analysts was assembled to evaluate and judge the clinical material. One group was responsible for making predictions, while others judged the session material itself. Transcripts were distributed weekly and predictions made regarding the upcoming time frame (next session, next week, next month). Forms were prepared and ratings made. Regular meetings were conducted and, overall, strong correlations were held for the ratings performed" (1993, 12). The hunch behind this sort of research seems to be that if what unfolds in the course of an analysis can be reliably predicted (in terms validated by inter-rater reliability), the phenomena unfolding (under a valid description) must obey regularity laws. If this is to be demonstrated, better controls are needed. First, as it stands, this sort of experiment might simply show that clinical phenomena are *regularly influenced* by the analyst in predictable ways, perhaps precisely those readily identifiable by those participating in the experiment as judges and predictors because they tend to influence clinical material in ways similar to the analyst conducting the experimental sample. What might be demonstrated, then, is that analysts can identify and predict their artifacts.[49] The research supports the ontological indeterminacy of the psychic thesis as well as it supports the claim that the phenomena predicted obey regularity laws.[50] Second, even if we grant the assumption that clinical phenomena obey regularity laws, the experiment does not determine the *extent* to which they do, thus does not close the door on claims that, to an extent, psychic phenomena are spontaneous, unruly, and/or ontologically indeterminate. But failing to do so (bracketing adjustments to the image and claims of science attendant upon quantum mechanics and chaos theory) impedes the characterization of psychoanalysis as fully confluent with science. Third, predictions rendered are often so obvious and vague that there is nothing especially psychoanalytic about them. E.g., predicting that a nymphomaniac will develop an eroticized transference or that a paranoiac will develop a negative transference is insufficiently informative for their confirmation to validate the terms in which they are phrased (as against reasonable non-psychoanalytic alternatives) or the assumption that clinical phenomena obey regularity laws *in the robust sense* (broadly, this is an issue of distinguishing correlation from causation of the sort appropriate for nomological integration). Fourth, when predictions rendered are sufficiently contentful and specific, they are often disconfirmed. One class of predictions ordinarily disconfirmed are clinical collateral inferences: e.g., if x (infantile overstimulation), then y (specific sexual problems).[51] A separate but pertinent point is that no matter how well such predictions are confirmed, their confirmation fails to demonstrate that all that is relevant to, or that what is of utmost relevance to, psychoanalytic theory and/or practice are the rule-bound or probabilistically determinable unfoldings of psychic phenomena.[52]

A brief glance over a select few moments in the history of empirical investigations of psychoanalysis should give us pause before the recent resurgence of science-idolatry within psychoanalysis. From at least the 1920s onward, pundits and detractors of psychoanalysis alike have undertaken and commented on thousands of experiments in order to confirm the credibility of their convictions.[53] Some of these experiments and commentaries are informative and valuable, but when advocates or critics of psychoanalysis allow themselves to become too enamored with science, things turn ludicrous (both comic and tragic-cruel) quite quickly.

Bellak, who believes that "most of Freud's hypotheses can be stated operationally and, in principle, can be experimentally verified, modified, or rejected" — but never says why he holds this to be the case — once attempted to "demonstrate" the notion of projection by using the Thematic Apperception Test (1993, xi). Bellak's hypothesis was that criticism leads to rage, and if subjects are impeded from reacting with outward-directed anger, they will project their rage by ascribing angry events to pictures they are shown. To support this hypothesis, the following experiment was devised.

Harvard undergraduates were shown five pictures and asked to tell a story about what led up to, is going on in, and would follow (narratively) from the five pictures. After the fifth picture, their performances were severely criticized. Then, after each subsequent picture-and-story (five more), the criticisms were repeated (Bellak, 1950). The results: criticism leads to increased ascription of anger to the pictures as determined by an "angry word" count. Setting aside the host of methodological questions one would want to pose, let us simply note that even if "projection" is a statistically significant outcome, the experiment fails to demonstrate projection in any relevant *psychoanalytic* sense of the term. A notion of a dynamic unconscious is hardly necessary to explain the results; cognitive-behavioral theory would explain the results just as well in a very different vocabulary (or a nominally equivalent but inferentially incommensurable vocabulary). The data suggests that what (some) psychoanalysts call projection, or something like it, *might* be operative, i.e., the results admit of (various) psychoanalytic construal(s), but a psychoanalytic notion of projection — assuming there is *one* — let alone the inferences implicated in the content of such a notion, are not *demonstrated*. No alternative explanation of the data is ruled out;[54] the data supports the claim that a psychoanalytic notion of projection is not impossible.

Bellak reports on an equally absurd — and downright cruel — experiment performed by Mower and Ullman (1993, 21), who tried to "prove" defensive regression via ethological experimentation.[55] Rats were trained to turn off a painful electric stimulus by pushing a lever with their noses. Then the lever was rendered inoperative. Later, the situation was rigged such that the painful stimulus would be turned off only if the rats stood on their hind legs. Finally, the situation was rigged such that the rats standing on their hind legs would not turn off the painful stimulus, at which point Mower and Ullman discovered that, lo and behold, the rats tended to return to pushing the lever with their noses. *This* was taken as "proof" for a psychoanalytic notion of defensive regression.

2. Dissonance

At least as instructive as determining the confluence of psychoanalysis and science, and perhaps much more so, is identifying their moments of dissonance. For thereby, we can clarify the nature and promise of the practice and of our commitments to it, further elaborate the specificity of psychoanalytic knowing and of its objects, which together yield its specific objectivity, and thus advance toward determining the criteria by which psychoanalytic claims are appropriately assessed.

To begin with the obvious, the clinic is not a laboratory — Freud's protests to the contrary notwithstanding.[56] Even were the objects under investigation well defined and operationalized, conditions cannot be controlled such that these objects could be isolated from all but influences whose effects are regular and known.[57] Psychoanalysis is as little a laboratory science as astrophysics, geography, ecology, paleontology, geology, oceanography, or sectors of biology.[58] The clinic cannot shield-off influences such as sympathy, guidance, and other sorts of help (or hindrance) from friends and relatives or therapeutically relevant changes in life circumstances; nor can it subtract such influences, as if their efficacy were regular and known, in order to determine counterfactually what would have resulted from the precise conjunction of psychic phenomena and clinical context. As I argued in chapter 3, if the clinic were sufficiently sealed off from such influences, psychoanalytic practice could not possibly be effective. The reigning scientific consensus is that single case studies yield valid generalizations if and only if all the relevant sources of variation are taken into account, that is, if and only if an experimental context is established wherein natures (determinate substances) either (1) act without impediment or (2) are impeded only by processes that are known to give rise to stable and predictable effects. If this is accepted, there is no basis for drawing strong conclusions about dependency relations between phenomena emerging in the course of a single analysis (or several) or between what transpires in the course of a clinical analysis (or several) and what occurs beyond the corridors of the clinic with respect to the individual(s) involved. Generalizations cannot be made on the basis of one or several case studies and nontrivial causal hypotheses cannot be confirmed by uncontrolled case studies.[59] If the psychoanalytic clinic is not a laboratory, this is because the phenomena developing therein may not be determinate substances systematically connected with all other substances; the horizon of nature, and emphatically that of human nature, thus historicity, may exceed the horizon of nomologically or causally integrated substance. If the clinic is not a laboratory, this may be because, unavoidably, *life intervenes*. If it is as unendingly complex, surprising, irreducible to rule and objectification as it seems, life is not a "proper object" of scientific inquiry, or scientific inquiry is itself improper, non-identical with its reigning image. Precisely in its elusive mobility and indefinite complexity, life is perhaps both condition and object of psychoanalytic investigation, or more precisely, an axis thereof.

(But the image of life as unendingly complex, surprising, and irreducible to rule and objectification may be its *memento mori*. If such is life, this may signal its tendential reification rather than its inherently emancipatory exuberance. Neither rationally scrutable nor stable, indeed prone to erratic, abstract differentiation — planned incoherence and superfluity in the service of the consolidation of profit and power — the excess of life may image its withering and despair. Standardized and commodified, life is as overdetermined, opaque, cobbled together, and abstractly other to itself as the system that liquidates it. The romance of life is the flip side of fascism, the inner tendencies of which vestigially-liberal capitalism feels free to express and exploit, having found in the total mobilization of desire an acceptable means by which to sublate what was once its ostensible enemy. Immediately extolling life conspires with its indiscriminate annihilation, indeed all but enjoins it. Thus here we must be extremely cautious. Yet to concede the identity of life with planned obsolescence, unregulated power-grabbing, extorted and fully functionalized uniqueness, the self-occluding, continuously self-"revolutionizing" socialization of desire, and so psychological disarray and social meltdown, to identify life with the coerced arbitrariness of divining the next party dictate or "the next big thing," is to renounce the rational potential of the category, and therewith, solidarity with those who suffer(ed) from its nonrealization: the memory of the future. Along with concern for needless suffering, the future is abandoned to the ever-same. To concede the identity of life and its debasement is to inflict upon the energies of thought, which are the legacies of unredeemable suffering, the petrification of which one despairs; it is to reduce to rubble what remains of resistance: the memory of the damned. In a paroxysm of necrophilia, one absorbs oneself into the image power projects of its victims: nothingness.)

To be committed to psychoanalysis is to strive to give oneself over in self-abandon to, and at once to strive to reflectively integrate, that which in its indefinite dynamism and perhaps unlimited associative complexity, at once reflectively irrecuperable overdetermination and resilient underdetermination, may exceed the determinacy of conceptual formulation, pressuring the concepts through which it is peremptorily yet always belatedly cast into new and unexpected formations. It is to find oneself mimetically negotiating the aporia that which seems to simultaneously demand and resist objectification and systemization. Psychoanalytic knowledge is twilight knowledge: constellations — theoretical intermediaries — dawning with the diminishment of ideal illumination, just prior to the darkness in which they stand out in too fine relief.

To be committed to psychoanalysis is to acknowledge in the medium of speculation, the freedom of thought from mere reproduction of ideologically encrusted and suffering suffused positivity, the vitality of its object, at least the nonexhaustion of its possibility. Speculative excess is solidarity with suffering subjectivity. Psychoanalysis is a labor of love: the condition of its insights is the mimetic madness of its pursuit.

Although comparison with control groups supports stronger claims about dependency relations, the term in which such claims are formulated are eminently contestable, and even assuming the availability of a validated vocabulary, clinical work does not regularly lend itself to comparisons between, say, the effects of a given interpretation with the consequences of withholding that interpretation or responding in a different way to either a single client in significantly similar situations or different clients in significantly similar situations. And the determination of "significantly similar" context is itself perhaps unavoidably contentious. Of course, one can study what follows from different responses to typical or repetitive clinical phenomena (e.g., an enactment trend or recurrent associative motif) both with respect to a single client (the client in "significantly similar" situations) and with respect to different clients in "significantly similar" situations. But if psychic life is as permeable to "internal" and "external" influences and as unpredictable — labile and idiosyncratic — in its metabolism of these influences as most psychoanalytic theories assume and as critical cultural theory suggests it must be under conditions of late capitalism (even B.F. Skinner's efforts to fully condition his responses — basically, to transform himself into a machine — were of limited success), then well supported, strong causal claims about the relationship between, say, specific therapeutic measures and results or etiological history and presenting psychopathology will be few and far between. Strong statistical trends can be established (following x intervention under conditions a, b, and c — but it is never this simple — there is statistically significant probability of y), and these would be highly significant for therapeutic practice (codes of standard practice and best practice are no doubt desirable). But there seem to be too many potentially intervening contextual variables, including those that may stem from innate psychic idiosyncrasy (the object under investigation, say, a particular matricidal fantasy, may differ in its form and significance even if the situations in which it is found are "significantly similar"; context cannot but be a clue to, but perhaps does not control, significance), for strong causal claims to be grounded. Process and outcome studies yield a limited truth.

The core commitment evident in the dissonance of psychoanalytic claims and experimental science aiming to establish exact dependency relations is that psychic life is both radically over- and underdetermined: both conditioned by more factors than can be determinately specified, let alone specified in their mutual influence, and which perhaps include factors prone to self-occlusion or self-distortion and that admit of indefinitely variable, in part because mutually influencing, expression; and to an extent singular and unpredictable, perhaps partially self-constituting, perhaps sometimes simply spontaneous, in its responsivity to conditioning influences. Trends of influence and response can be determined both with respect to specific individuals and transindividually, but it may be that psychic objects are not deterministic natural entities or events about which strong causal claims (x leads to y and only y; and x never leads to z) can be made.[60] On this assumption, the most that one can claim to discern are regularly realized capacities and connections, not determinate causal processes. Consequently, predictions cannot be strictly deduced from hypotheses whose validity would be confirmed by experiments establishing that x psychic state or event leads to y and only y psychic state or event (or to a definite range of states or events) given the influence of z and only z pathogenic influence or therapeutic procedure.

To be committed to psychoanalysis is to give a chance to a world of chance[61] without forsaking the patterns and regularities presenting themselves to rigorous empirical inquiry. It is to affirm the possibility of the relative spontaneity of the psychic, of the unending irregularity of the human, onto which investigations into psychic determination recurrently open. And so it is to mourn the ever-enticing dream of cognitive completion, and therewith, unlimited instrumental efficacy, i.e., the ideal of replete satisfaction. Though variably determinable, the significance and consequences of *experience* are perhaps never fully determinate. A client who manifestly responds to interpretations in a consistent and predictable way may concurrently — subterraneously, pre- or unconsciously — or sequentially experience them, or some of them, as gratifications, repetitions of typical and as such in a certain way consoling depravations, intrusions, humiliations, or condemnations, supports for rationalizing evasion of the work of self-determination, reference points for resentment and transgression, self- and world-disclosing/emotionally clarifying, promises or harbingers of more mature psychic integration or more satisfactory self-elaboration, tokens of genuine interest or concern, affectively overwhelming and chaotic, signals of love, hate, special selection and attention, seduction, and so on. To be committed to psychoanalysis is to be given to aporia.

Next, there are limits to quantification in psychoanalytic research. Even Hartmann — who advocates establishing psychoanalysis as a deductive-nomothetic science, claiming that "how sound our general statements and our predictions can be depends in the last resort . . . on how far a general theory can be developed" (1964, 104); "the concern with developmental problems refers primarily to the history of individuals. But this should not obfuscate the fact that the aim of these studies is (besides its therapeutic purpose) to develop lawlike propositions" (1964, 324); and "the goal of psychoanalysis is not the understanding of the mental, but rather the explanation of its causal relationships" (1964, 377; see also 397 and 401) — recognizes that "[w]e compare the strength of impulses, the tenacity of resistances, the impact of rational tendencies, etc., we infer from the strength of a resistance the force of repression; but one cannot measure these factors (1964, 314; also see 327).[62] To be sure, there have been tremendous advances in the quantification of clinical phenomena and of various components of psychoanalytic theory.[63] The research that undertaken, collaborated upon, and inspired by Wallerstein and Kernberg has greatly contributed to this development. For instance, the Menninger Foundation Psychotherapy Research Project's development of clinically anchored ratings scales has advanced the sophistication and relevance of psychotherapy measurements appreciably. Luborsky and Crits-Christoph's (1990) CCRT and Fonagy and Target's (1997) Reflective Self-Functioning Interview are particularly impressive developments. But the pursuit of quantification is plagued by the semantic and syntactic indeterminacy problem. And it regularly faces a double bind: the yield of quantification is often not obviously relevant to or in accordance with non-quantified conceptions of psychoanalytic theory, except by fiat;[64] and when relevant, quantified data are rarely all that informative, let alone decisive with regard to competing claims, except by fiat.[65] Further, if quantification (and ultimately the classical concept of causality[66]) is inseparably bound to spatiality, i.e., if quantification means isolating and determining (measuring) the position of an entity within a set of spatial coordinates (or determining successive positions of an entity within spatial coordinates in order to quantify cause and effect relations), then to the extent that psychic phenomena are not simply *res extensa*, the yield of quantification will be limited. The ideal of quantification implies a metaphysics that cuts against psychoanalytic commitments. However innovative efforts at quantifying psychic phenomena become, the Galilean-Keplerian impulse to quantification, thus the sharing and comparison of data and precision yielded by quantification, may be profoundly limited by the perhaps partially indeterminate, unruly character of psychic phenomena.

To be committed to psychoanalysis is to be committed to calculating with the incalculable, to expose oneself to and attempt to reflectively accommodate what may be the freedom of phenomena to develop and manifest in ways that cannot be foreseen, that which may in principle outstrip intention. Psychoanalysis implies ab-solute responsibility.[67]

Related to the problem of quantification is that of operationalization. Psychoanalytic concepts are not operationalizable in the strong sense of having determinate rules for application. *Malgré lui*, Ferrell puts the point nicely: "when we use analytic theory to assert that the Ego, or repression, or an unconscious mental event, or some other theoretical concept applies here or there, there is no set of accepted and objectively determinate observations we can make to confirm or to upset our assertion. The theoretical concepts of psychoanalytic theory do seem, therefore, to be *empirically indeterminate*" (1981, 32; emphasis added).[68] If psychic life is semantically and syntactically indeterminate to any degree, operationalization is unavoidably problematic, thus psychoanalytic concepts and theories are underdetermined by evidence. Observable predictions cannot be strictly deduced.

"Words," Freud suggests, "since they are the nodal points of numerous ideas, may be regarded as predestined to ambiguity" (SE 5: 340). If self-obscuring or -distorting, semantically unstable and dynamically relational, and/or ontologically spontaneous, i.e., intentionally and extensionally indeterminate, the material constellated in psychoanalytic concepts, thus operationalizations of such concepts, are constitutively ambiguous. If only because each analysis tends toward a singular idiolect — metaphors and other manners of figurative speech, which, arguably, predominate, are relatively idiosyncratic artifacts of context — what is said and done, and so conceptualized, in a singular analysis is not simply translatable into testable form. In analysis, words and deeds assume a unique weight and webbing. Should they become raw materials for the formulation of concepts sufficiently abstract for unproblematic operationalization, i.e., converted into rules for replicatable identification, their specific weight would be not so much relieved as disavowed. Their sublated significance would become the medium of their evisceration; their reidentification a melancholic obsession with a lost object put ever further out of reach. And swept up in a such a disavowal would be the ontologically indeterminate and socially mediated character of such words and deeds.

Given sufficient shielding conditions, one can of course infer a number of observational correlates of psychoanalytic concepts.[69] But even if the institution of specific shielding conditions were not controversial, as the discussion of psychoanalytic plurality should make clear, such inferences would still be unavoidably controversial. The irreducible plurality of psychoanalytic perspectives precludes the final stabilization of psychoanalytic concepts: if the phenomena are partially indeterminate, and if such indeterminacy is not just due to yet unspecified but in principle determinable arrangements of causal conditions or yet incomplete but in principle completable eidetic variation, the formulation, application, and extension of concepts of such phenomena will remain indeterminate, a matter of judgment calibrated — at most — by the choreography of critique.[70] As Fisher and Greenberg note, "the diversity of the secondary elaborations of Freud's ideas [not to mention the range of analytic innovations that are not strictly encompassed under the Freudian umbrella] is so Babel-like as to defy the derivation of sensible deductions that can be put to empirical test" (1985, 1x).

If psychoanalytic concepts cannot be operationalized in the strict sense, then we must concede to Popper that within psychoanalytic research, negative findings (e.g., x does not regress when frustrated) do not of themselves necessarily invalidate hypotheses (e.g., frustration leads to regression). The burden is then on those committed to psychoanalysis to contest either or both of Popper's inferences: (1) if a theory cannot be decisively disconfirmed by negative findings it is nonscientific; (2) if a theory is nonscientific, it is cognitively discredited.[71] To be sure, non-falsifiability is disconcerting: if disconfirmations of predictions do not invalidate the claims from which they are derived (so assuming for the sake of argument that strict derivations of predictions are possible), then determining when to abandon or reformulate such claims and rethink the problem, the approach to it, or the means of testing conjectures becomes problematic. If its claims are not falsifiable, psychoanalytic theory is an ever-expanding archive of eminently contestable claims rather than a progressively developing science in principle capable of complete determination.[72] But is the capacity to deliver deterministic knowledge of fully law-governed natural entities and their interrelations an absolute methodological criterion? If relatively few (if any) scientific disciplines can plausibly promise to fulfill such a criterion, and if theory reduction and taxonomic reduction are as implausible as has been suggested, then raising such a criterion to the status of a methodological absolute expels far too much from the domain of the cognitively significant to warrant assent. The criterion presupposes *and excludes* the systematic integration of the sciences: it is self-undermining.

Psychoanalysis pursues the admittedly *speculative* and self-interrupting project of tracking and reflectively articulating both trends and anomalies. Even its concern for patterns and regularities is a concern for what is perhaps analogous but irreducible. Psychoanalysis develops not, or not only, by progressively refining its understanding of its objects but (also) by accumulating diverse opinions about matters opinable. Thus insofar as it promotes ruling out claims not fully favored by empirical evidence and prioritizes ruling out impossibilities entailed by universal claims, falsification-driven science assumes an ideal image of nature, a metaphysical-libidinal support, that is neither self-justifying, scientifically credible, nor entirely appropriate for the psychoanalytic enterprise. In comparison with the unlimited — though cautious — psychoanalytic ethos of affirmation, its yes, yes to the tradition-mediated experiences, the conventions and pathos, through which clinical details may become intelligible and perspicuous in their failure of fit with traditional conceptions, which then become subject to scope restrictions and/or reformulation, its affirmation of both particular theory-mediated concepts and irreducible interpretive pluralism, its accession to the indeterminacy yet wide-ranging determinability of psychic phenomena, its concern for generality and singularity, falsification-driven science appears emphatically and unnecessarily negativistic — a hasty rush to eradicate the uncertain. In a psychoanalytic idiom, falsification driven science would be a pure culture of the death drive. Would anything be left subsequent to the subtraction of the uncertain? The Popperian ideal of science is not rigorous but rigoristic, as if a sublimation of raging superego severity.[73]

Crucial to contesting Popper's inferences is defending a notion of causal *powers* with partially indeterminate conditions of activation. While this notion is by no means new to the scientific community — it is as ancient as Aristotle — it tends to be eclipsed, especially in the aftermath of enthusiasm over Newton's integration of celestial and terrestrial mechanics and Einstein's integrative advances, by the assumption of determinism. Framed by this assumption, causal powers are usually considered as activated or not depending on the determinate, if not fully nomological, arrangement of antecedent conditions (whether strictly physical or physical and environmental, as in evolutionary biology and theories of soft inheritance;[74] even chaos theory regularly involves the assumption that phenomena are organized by deterministic systems, the only difference being that what develops in those systems is infinitely sensitive to initial conditions): though x does not always lead to y, if set of conditions z holds and set of interfering conditions v does not hold, the power of x to effect y is necessarily activated. Insofar as it ventures to suspend the assumption of determinism for the sake of a more adequate acknowledgment of the nature (freedom) of its objects, psychoanalysis provisionally denies that the conditions under which the causal powers with which it is concerned are activated can be in principle prospectively or retrospectively specified in full. What is denied is the principle of sufficient reason as all-pervasive, and with it, the image of nature as totalizable. Epistemic opacity is entailed by the assumption of psychic self-occlusion and -distortion, and by the elusiveness of individual histories to first- or third-personal verification. Ontological indeterminacy is entailed by the over- and underdetermination thesis, thus by the creation/discovery thesis, by the allowance of spontaneity, and by the assumption that each unconscious is a unique, evolving, metabolically indefinite associational aggregate.[75] As Lacan compresses the thought, "The human object is distinguished by its neutrality and its indefinite proliferation" (1981, 49)

Impressed by experiences of the emphatically or residually non-identical, psychoanalysis cannot but confront the thought that causal powers *may not be entirely a matter of principle*. Psychoanalysis gambles on the singular: a state of affairs that does not conform to expectations is taken not only as reason to reconsider the expectations but also, at least sometimes (and when cannot be fully specified in advance), as grounds for the suspicion or occasion for the speculation that the phenomena under consideration may be to some extent singular, resistant to explanation via generalization yet not for that unintelligible. In this respect, psychoanalysis takes up the work of the novel in a culture suffused by coldness, unsure about what to call a crisis, thus extremely remote from a language of happiness, and too inundated by transparently manipulative claims to novelty to believe in its possibility. And not only does psychoanalysis speculate on the singular; internally riven, it also risks an impossible avowal of the spontaneous and thereby risks suspending the assumption of all-encompassing intelligibility: an axiom of inquiry descending from Aristotle and as little interrupted by romantic reveries of transport to the ineffable as by the most sophisticated and fallibilist modern science. Not only might the unfolding of psychic life sometimes be as unpredictable as a throw of the dice [*un coup de dés*], in which case it would still be subject to statistical plotting, explanatory recourse to conditioning environmental-historical factors — as in "soft inheritance" theories that seek to account for the activation or failure of activation of a genetic possibility by referring to the experiences of a progenitor — because it still assumes a consistent causal interface, is provisionally put out of play. If, following Kant, unified experience presupposes the "thoroughgoing mutual interaction of phenomena," psychoanalysis risks the destitution of "experience" for the sake of fidelity to experience.[76] Coming into its truth by sustaining the aporias of its objects, psychoanalysis acknowledges that between determinism and its contrary, the evidence is equivocal.

As much as it is committed to establishing the common and regular, *psychoanalysis treads the shifting ground of the empirically and logically indeterminate.* Its manifest dissonance with the at once ascetic and excessive demands of science is the condition of its claim to consonance with nature. This is to contest Popper's inferences not by directly disputing them but by challenging their presuppositions and raising a question about the *onus probandi* and its conditions of adjudication.

The next step in contesting Popper's inferences is to engage them directly by showing that falsifiability is too strong to work as a standard for scientific research, and even if it could, cannot justify its claim to hegemony. What was gestured toward above and now will be clarified is that falsifiability as a methodological absolute would eliminate from the realm of the scientifically, thus cognitively credible so many reasonable and useful scientific theories that acceding to it would render science empty and impracticable, a vacuous ideal. Popper's standard seems but the expression of hyperactive skepticism conditioned by an equally hyperactive desire for certainty rather than something useful for the scientific community, not to mention parascientific inquiry.

Falsification is meant to delineate science from non-science. But even modern physics, due to the central place of probability in it, would not meet the Popperian standard: because probabilistic hypotheses do not exclude anything as strictly impossible, they cannot be conclusively falsified. And as Popper acknowledges, Darwinian theory does not measure up either. The standard runs too far afoul of various reasonable and useful parsings of theories into science and nonscience to be of interest to the scientific community. Arguably, no science meets Popper's standard. If, as Kuhn claims, there are always anomalies, on Popper's terms all theories should be regarded as falsified (1970, 135).

Despite itself, what the measure of falsification discloses is that even the natural sciences are so diverse (perhaps as diverse as their discrete yet overlapping object domains and functions) that efforts to establish a single test for scientificity are bound to be based on the illicit (either arbitrary or interested) promotion of an single science (or more likely, a concocted ideal science) to the status of an ideal model. Identity is asserted, not rationally established; this is ideology parading as the rule of reason.

What Popper wants from the falsification standard is *certainty* about and within the domain of science, but its price is empirical emptiness and irrelevance. "Scientific theories, [Popper] has always claimed, have the logical form of universal generalizations: 'All *A*s are *B*.' The falsity of any such claim follows *deductively* from an evidence statement of the form 'This *A* is not *B*.' All that science requires, claimed Popper, is that observational evidence can thus logically falsify a scientific theory. The most that can be said in favor of so austere a view is that, by refusing to make any inductive inferences at all, it does avoid Hume's problem" (Giere 1990, 27). Falsification is all-important only if nature is empirically and logically determinate and the science of nature is exclusively concerned with universal generalizations — why either claim should be countenanced Popper does not say.

Finally, falsification runs into logical problems. First, if one cannot show that the predictions of a theory are false until they are described in the language of that theory, then if the models of the theory do not fit the observations (if the observations falsify the theory), then perhaps all one has shown is that the theory is inapplicable, not necessarily that it is disconfirmed. Second, "inferring empirical conclusions from a theory . . . . will typically require vastly more by way of premises than merely the theory that is supposedly being exposed to possible falsification," thus it is unclear what is to be concluded from the negative result of an experiment (Dupré 1995, 230). It may be that a crucial component of the theory is false or it may be that an auxiliary premise is problematic. Sometimes the question can be resolved (temporarily) by determining that a problematic auxiliary premise is the source of the negative result, but the possibility of false negatives remains.

Even if falsification worked for science, on what basis could it claim hegemony over cognitive credibility? Why restrict compelling cognition to identity thinking? To elaborate psychoanalytic claims in falsifiable form, i.e., as universal generalizations, may be to falsify these claims by attributing to their objects more empirical and logical determinacy then they admit. If out of fidelity to its formative experiences and in proleptic solidarity with the freedom of its "objects," psychoanalysis does not simply trade in universal generalizations, what warrants the application of Popper's standard? Why is establishing a compendium of still-plausible universal generalizations a categorical imperative for cognition? Why should Popper's desire for certainty crowd out all others? What is beginning to become clear, is that theoretical presuppositions are sourced in experience — phenomenology, desire, metaphysical inheritance, etc. — thus exceed the manners of rational deliberation they condition. Such presuppositions and the claims they condition can be disputed, but not in any simple way rationally overridden. To attempt the latter would be to beg the question. Falsification is certainly unhelpful as a standard *for* psychoanalysis. The sorts of discriminations it facilitates would not help adjudicate between more and less credible, adequate, etc. psychoanalytic theories, better and worse techniques, proper and improper instantiations of psychoanalysis, and so on. The *only* thing it could do is generate skepticism about the scientific standing of psychoanalysis.

Then there are a host of data problems. Some of these can and should be minimized. For instance, as many commentators have noted (most vociferously, Donald Spence), compiling a library of audiovisual records of analytic treatments would facilitate the scientific investigation of analytic practice. Since case studies infrequently and insufficiently explicate the observations and inferences on the basis of which interpretations are formed and other manners of intervention are pursued, the fit of observations to interpretations and the propositions implied other manners of intervention cannot be validated by independent researchers. The worries that analysts construe the data to fit their interpretations (especially when emboldened by therapeutic successes), conflate observation with inference,[77] or selectively present case material to support theoretical claims (i.e., propagandize) would be lessened, though surely not eliminated, if detailed treatment records (and clinical notes) were available for public inspection. All too often, case reports allude to the clinical "facts" in a way that courts charges of self-protective or self-serving case presentation, e.g., charges of retrospectively altering the case material due to a variety of professional pressures. The disparity between the notes for and write-up of the Rat Man case shows clearly that in the write-up Freud only presents "paradigmatic" evidence for his theory of obsessional neurosis. Only because we have the notes is Freud's selectivity conspicuous.[78] If audiovisual records and process notes were much more detailed and publicly available, psychoanalytic practice would be much more scientifically scrutable. Further, were these to be publicly available, the inevitable exaggerations and contortions, inflations and deflations, concomitant trends of blindness and insight — generally, the perspectival character — of psychoanalytic interpretation would be much more evident and perhaps the penchant to bold, authoritative assertion on the part of publishing analysts would be to some extent preemptively diminished. (Of course, peripheral awareness of public scrutiny might transform analytic practice, perhaps destructively.)

Certain data problems, however, are insuperable. First, there is the selection bias problem. As Grünbaum puts it,

> Presumably if the intelligent and imaginative patient is permitted to free associate . . .long enough, his unfettered rumination will in due course yield almost any kind of thematic content of which he had (at least recently) not been conscious: thoughts about death, God, and indeed cabbages and kings. But, if so, how does the analyst avoid a selection bias in the face of the thematic variety [and variable thematizability, i.e., semantic grammatical indeterminacy] of the associations, particularly since imposing some limit on duration is unavoidable. (in Clark and Wright 1988)

Process studies have identified common thematic units and consistent thematic patterns (e.g., the CCRT), but only in a way that begs the question against Grünbaum: why privilege the common and recurrent rather than the anomalous and marginal? Associative trends are not to be overlooked, and repeated returns to various themes are often worth exploring, but so too are "telling" associations that stand out from the thematic thrust of the material. Besides, interpretive processing, whether of central or peripheral material, is unavoidable, and though unevenly, unavoidably contentious. The data are not self-evident.

Though selection bias is insuperable, the force of the charge wrongly attributes to psychoanalysis a strong representational aspiration grounded in the assumption that psychic life in general and free association in particular are taxonomically self-subsistent and fully deterministic. Selection bias is a serious problem for research that aims to deliver discursively transparent, indubitable knowledge of the law-governed development of determinate substances, but much less serious for an enterprise that avows the partially speculative character of its research as a theoretical (material-mimetic) expression of its subject matter: speculation is mimesis of indeterminate subjects, a cipher of singularity. With respect to such an enterprise, the possibility of selection bias — i.e., the possibility of perspective — is but a reason to maintain critical vigilance, not to discard its deliverances.

Further, Grünbaum's advocacy of controlled epidemiological research as a means of verifying psychoanalytic etiological hypotheses should commit him to the claim that observational research of infant and child development can address the selection bias problem as it pertains to the construction of developmental schemes and the articulation of specific developmental claims. In light of data compiled on normal and pathological developmental trends — e.g., data concerning what empirical features of development are associated in a statistically significant way with what later psychic developments — psychoanalytic developmental schemes can be refined and the relative plausibility of psychoanalytic developmental claims pertaining to specific analysands can be evaluated. By Grünbaum's lights, the force of the charge of selection bias should be mitigated if the developmental claim in question maps onto empirically established developmental regularities.

But developmental observational research involves a new data problem: contamination. When experimentally investigating the sort of phenomena pertinent to psychoanalysis, the presence of an observer can be a source of anxiety, reassurance, etc., and so bias the data. If, for instance, the perceived status of the observer as an expert or authority figure renders her an object of dependency, attachment, fear, aggression, etc., the data will be biased. This problem is particularly pernicious for developmental observation studies dealing with isolated children or parents. Naturalized experimental design may help, but this limits the type of data that can be obtained.[79]

Next, there is the problem that psychoanalysis posits objects and processes that are to some extent publicly inaccessible, e.g., self-obscuring or -distorting, and thereby limits the intersubjective corroboration of its methods of data gathering, concept formation and inference licensing, handling of case material, and so on.[80] As opposed to — potentially distorted or partial — manifestations of the unconscious in symptoms, parapraxes, word choice, bodily bearing, and the like, on standard psychoanalytic premises, strictly speaking, unconscious contents and processes are to some extent barred from public (and equally, private) discernment. Unlike dream reports, associations to dreams, and so on, strictly speaking, dream thoughts are not part of the public record. By affirming the opacity unrelieved by the most astute conceptual comprehension, allowing it to resonate in the dialectical engagement of perspectives, psychoanalysis sustains solidarity with the non-identical under conditions of its tendential eclipse, and thereby the promise of happiness in a world in which even the terms of its fulfillment have become unimaginable. Withdrawal from intelligibility obliquely images intelligibility altogether otherwise, just as the assumption of self-sheltering and -disguise preserves the demand for such an otherwise itself otherwise unrecognizable and withering from neglect under the dominant dispensation of intelligibility. To be sure, psychoanalysis does not consider the unconscious to be simply a social artifact, but what it means to be committed to psychoanalytic concepts and theories cannot be separated from the conditions in which such commitments are undertaken: the theories as much as the phenomena theorized are dynamically relational and expositive.

Further examples of material that is assumed to elude public discernment, at least to some extent, include the analyst's processing of clinical material (unconscious listening, or as Reik formulates it, "listening with the 'third ear,'" the work of the analysand's preconscious,[81] etc.) and the analysand's processing of interpretations and other manners of intervention. To be sure, the partial inscrutability of such data pertains as much to the analyst or analysand as to the public, thus about claims of privileged competence with respect to such data one must remain wary even if they contain a kernel of truth, i.e., bear witness to the untruth of transparency. The archive of psychoanalytic data is also a crypt of the *arcanum*. Psychoanalytic knowing is thus subtended by the experience of mourning, speculation the medium of sustaining loss.

Another set of publicly inscrutable data are the indeterminate ideas and associations that inevitably emerge in the course of analysis. These are perhaps best described in a Kantian idiom as (1) that which has the form of a concept yet is not a determinate concept (akin to the beautiful) or (2) that which cannot be gathered into a single representation yet provokes the demand of reason for representation (akin to the sublime). Although not simply inimical to the order of language, such ideas and associations refuse to reconcile with it, are misrecognized as they are recognized. Although insuperable in psychoanalysis, indeterminate ideas and associations are not unique to it; it may even be that indeterminate ideas and associations are insuperable elsewhere as well, indeed generally. If, following Kant austerely, cognition proper (determinative judgment) presupposes the harmonization of the imagination and the understanding, that is, if conceptual articulation is the recasting in the form of a deductively-nomologically integrable concept (or ratification as such a concept) of material (atomistic impressions) gathered by the imagination into a unity amenable to conceptual determination (a single representation) — but, perhaps *pace* Kant, not exhausted thereby; if it were, concept development would be inexplicable, i.e., reason would be opaque — and presented to the understanding as so amenable, then conceptuality presupposes a logically and perhaps psychologically prior organization of impressions into a proto-cognitive unity (representation); indeed this may be identical with a concept but for the understanding's stamp of approval. On Kant's account, then, it is not just in the course of analysis that indeterminate ideas and associations will emerge, rather, this will have always been the case in the course of cognition. Only by reinscribing representation as conceptual determination can the material history of the concept, thus indeterminacy, be effaced sufficiently to satisfy the demands of reason mediated by the understanding. But even Kant cannot deny that in the "experience" of the sublime, thought finds itself agitated and mobilized by the failure of the imagination to gather a series of impressions into a single representation; this failure of the imagination to gather impressions into a unity amenable to proper cognition discloses, through the frustration provoked thereby, the demand of reason for totality that has been operative all along *as well as the possibility of its nonfulfillment* (or fulfillment otherwise). Against the inner current of his thought, Kant admits that sensuous nature is not predestined to determinative judgment, indeed is intelligible otherwise. By granting the possibility of "experience" abrasive with respect to *experience* (transcendental apperception), Kant quietly amplifies his notion of nature and therewith opens the authority of determinative judgment to challenge by its preconditions (reflective judgment and representation — extra- and proto-conceptual schematization). That is, the sublation of indeterminate ideas into independently closed and deductively integrated concepts may not be immune from reasonable challenge. Thus reason may be divided "in itself." The reworking or certification by the understanding of what the imagination presents to it as amenable to conceptual determination, it seems, can only assert its claim on what is amenable but irreducible to its authoritative impress. Indeterminate ideas and associations are the proletariat of faculty psychology.

Another data problem is built into the standard objection that on pain of circularity, the theories and hypotheses that influence the observation and description of data cannot be the theories or hypotheses for which the data serve as evidence (Rubenstein 1976, 1980; Fonagy 1999, 2002). Otherwise, worries about biased, i.e., confirmation-bent, observation and description cannot be avoided. Even if expressing a hyperactive skepticism, the worry is legitimate and indeed in its own way productive, for it shows that psychoanalysis cannot be rightfully considered to pursue unimpeachably valid laws of psychic life. And against its intention, the objection implies that any theory or hypothesis will be underdetermined by evidence and thereby undercuts the measure (absolute certainty) against which psychoanalysis would be found wanting, paradoxically putting psychoanalysis and science on a more even footing. If the theories and hypotheses that influence the observation and description of data cannot be the theories or hypotheses for which the data serve as evidence, then there will be a "semantic gap between statements describing data and hypotheses [that] must be bridged by substantive background assumptions establishing the evidential relation of the data to hypotheses" (Longino 2002, 50). For example, "[b]ubble tracks in a compressed gas are different from the particles whose passage is postulated as producing them, and can serve as evidence for claims about the particles only in light of causal or statistical assumptions about the relation of tracks to particles" (ibid.). Since there are no formal rules for establishing the evidential relations between data and hypotheses or theories, that is, since hypotheses and theories do not specify the data that will confirm them, underdetermination is inevitable and the worry that various interests have permeated the articulation of evidential relations cannot be allayed.[82]

Further data problems are related to the following sets of questions: (1) How can the most intimate experiences of, say, love and loss, be discussed publicly without effacing their specificity, even defacing their value as speech swerves toward cliché — if only, or also, to guard such experiences in the silent reserve that *manifestly* depletes stereotypical speech of significance; standardized expressions anxiously watch over the incomparable, preserving and negating its integrity at the price of its all but ineffability? Do contemporary conditions of socialization afford linguistic resources even remotely adequate to describe the intensity and complexity of much of what is experienced in the course of analysis? Does not the articulation of what is experienced in analysis require that language become "poetic," which is to say, generative, mobilized, even frenetically so, infused with forces it cannot fully regulate or stabilize, prone to grope awkwardly for words and syntax with which to express the qualitative specificity of complex affective experience?[83] (2) Is censorship — more broadly, perspective — not inevitable to some extent on both sides of the couch? Does the articulation of psychic material at a particular juncture of analysis not involve its partial recasting or contextual inflection? Is the articulation of such material not coextensive with some measure of form-giving or re-creation? Do not contextual factors such as the particular vicissitudes of transference obtaining and other features of the interpersonal analytic dynamic condition the elaboration of unconscious and/or historical material? In analysis, are repetition and continuation not at once, to some extent, transformation (or perchance, deformation)? In short, is there pure data to be had? Is not analytic data necessarily context-laden and theory-mediated? (3) To what extent can the analyst's memory and process notes be trusted as public record? Are not certain sectors of analytic data — e.g., the affective atmosphere, transference and countertransference dynamics, and other aspects of the analytic scene that are not easily if at all detectable in audiovisual recordings — unavoidably anecdotal? Might not certain aspects of the significance of the material unfolding only available to the those experientially involved in the scene(s) of its unfolding? Is it possible to strictly differentiate the analyst's observations and interpretations from the presentation of the analysand's self-interpretation, from either party's fantasies, and so forth? Can the entirety of analytic material be translated into propositional form without reduction and distortion? Is a purely descriptive language possible for psychoanalysis?

Then there are a number of methodological problems with testing psychoanalytic claims. For one, no test decisively confirms etiological claims because no test can rule out alternatives. Take, for instance, Freud's hypothesis about the etiological significance of homosexual conflict in paranoid schizophrenia. Experiments attempting to test the hypothesis have proceeded on the assumption that if paranoid schizophrenics display special sensitivity (measured by relative quantity of attention, papillary diameter, judgments of spatial position, and thresholds for tachistoscopic recognition) to stimuli with homosexual connotations (pictures, tachistoscopic exposures, paired stereoscopic presentations, slides, photographs in unstructured spatial contexts), then the hypothesis receives support. And in fact, the studies surveyed in Fisher and Greenberg (1985) show that male paranoid schizophrenics, in contrast to male nonparanoid schizophrenics, do display special sensitivity to stimuli with homosexual connotations (268). But contra Fisher and Greenberg's assessment, this demonstrates a *link* between sensitivity to homosexual content and paranoid schizophrenia, not the etiological significance of homosexual conflict for paranoid schizophrenia. What could possibly demonstrate that? Especially if we follow Freud in assuming that, to some degree, unconscious homosexual conflicts are universal, how could the unique intensity of homosexual conflict in the development of paranoid schizophrenia be isolated and measured? How could one rule out alternative causes sufficiently to decisively confirm the hypothesis? Of course, large-scale, longitudinal developmental-observational studies with experimental components would contribute to the (dis)confirmation of the hypothesis, but decisive confirmation, because this would mean ruling out alternative etiological hypotheses, seems not just infeasible but impossible. Fallibilism is not just an external epistemic virtue but an intrinsic element of psychoanalytic cognition.

Second, there is the vagueness problem. Often, psychoanalytic theories are too vague to test if testing means to yield decisive results. Of course, tests can be devised. For instance, *if* the ego is defined by a set of functions (and so begging the question of operationalization), one can test how well it performs these functions: one can measure aptitudes for reality testing; frustration, anxiety, and ambiguity tolerance; motor function, etc. But these sorts of tests are of limited relevance, especially to the extent that we are committed to the claim that psychoanalytic concepts are indefinitely subject to remediation (medium-bound). A better example would be Fisher and Greenberg's suggestion that we test the validity of Freud's theory of melancholia by "observing a series of individuals as they encounter serious losses and ascertaining whether certain phenomena (e.g., introjection of the lost object, focusing hostility inwards, increased self-criticism)" follow and whether these phenomena are "predictive of the likelihood of developing depressive symptomatology.[84] In addition, the researcher would determine whether certain presumably predisposing variables (e.g., early childhood losses, oral character traits, narcissistic or ambivalent style of object choice) predicted the probability of depression." This, in their estimation, "would be the optimal design for checking out Freud's statements concerning the etiology of depression (melancholia)" (1996, 25). Operationalization would still be problematic, and etiology would not be definitively demonstrated, but the Freudian theory of melancholia could find support through such a procedure, at least enough to warrant analysts acting on the assumption that if an analysand experiences certain types of loss, especially if the predisposing factors for melancholia obtain, a number of therapeutically relevant consequences are likely to follow, i.e., warrant modifying their conduct accordingly.

But even if a psychoanalytic theory does receive support from this sort of experimental procedure, it is still too vague to be deemed valid straightaway. Logical empiricists, holding that all meaningful theoretical statements must be translated into self-evident observation statements, would deny the claim to validity on the grounds of the data problems and problems with operationalization discussed above. Such problems would also preclude psychoanalytic concepts from meeting the criteria of those positivists for whom descriptive terms must be defined through a standardized vocabulary such that the meaning of a sentence can be determined by the conditions under which it can be verified. Nor could psychoanalytic claims be deemed valid according to the standards of someone like Donald Davidson, for whom "our utterances are true or false, *given what they mean*. Who decides this? Until we know what an utterance or inscription means, or know the propositional content of a belief or other thought, we do not know what is needed even to raise the question of truth" (2000, 302). Although a variety of experimental procedures such as questionnaire studies, projective tests (Rorschach Inkblot Test, Thematic Apperception Test [TAT], the Blacky Test[85]), tachistoscopic exposure, and so forth can be used to corroborate (or disconfirm) psychoanalytic claims, the evidence will at most support *judgments* of (or against) the plausibility or usefulness of these claims, not decisively demonstrate (or disconfirm) them.

A related problem of vagueness concerns the remarkable efficacy of inexact interpretations. The archive of this problem is substantial. As early as 1957, Gordon showed that relief from hypnotically induced conflicts may occur when subjects hit on plausible but inaccurate explanations of their feelings. Later, in 1964, Mendell demonstrated that intentionally inaccurate interpretations, that is, interpretations that by design do not follow from the unfolding material, lead to positive changes.[86] Many studies have shown that bogus interpretations are often enthusiastically accepted by the analysand as specifically accurate for them (Forer 1949; Sundberg 1955; Meehl 1956; O'Dell 1972; Dmitruk, Collins, and Clinger 1973; Snyder, Shenkel, and Lowery 1977; Fisher and Greenberg 1985; Farrell 1981, 1992). Farrell, summarizing Forer's findings, states that "The general finding has been that a subject accepts the statements of the bogus account as containing good and revealing insights about himself. He accepts them as being just as accurate as, or even more accurate than, the statements of the genuine account: he accepts these whether they are offered by prestigious or non-prestigious investigators, and whether they are personally complimentary or uncomplimentary" (Farrell 1981, 92). Freud's notorious "tally" argument is thus shown to be wildly overconfident: "After all, his conflicts will only be successfully solved and his resistances overcome if the anticipatory ideas he is given tally with what is real in him. Whatever in the doctor's conjectures is inaccurate drops out in the course of analysis; it has to be withdrawn and replaced by something more correct" (SE 16: 452).[87]

Next, a clinical interpretation is not a hypothesis in the sense of being strictly deducible from a more general theory that thus would be supported by confirmations of the predictions to which the hypothesis gives rise. Though strict logical deduction of a hypothesis (in the sense that this and only this hypothesis among a range of alternatives can be deduced from some theory) may be an unrealizable ideal, this is emphatically so with psychoanalytic clinical "hypotheses."

Finally, if testing psychoanalytic claims requires testing predictions derived from hypotheses, then the assumption of the logical and empirical indeterminacy of psychic phenomena presents a number of problems. First, the assumption of overdetermination (indefinitely multiple complex causal arrangements conducing to similar effects) implies a limit to the derivation of predictions from hypotheses. Second, the assumption of the empirical indeterminacy (the singular, to some extent unpredictable development and concatenation) of psychic phenomena limits predictive prowess.[88] For instance, if one attempts to confirm a given hypothesis by examining the impact of intensified aggression, one will have to contend with the prospect that intensified aggression can be expressed in aggressive behavior, inhibition, affect-laden aggressive thought, dissociated aggressive ideation, semantically ambiguous sublimations, enhanced superego severity, conversion (e.g., into excessive kindness or love), inversion (self-directed aggression), displacement (e.g., onto extraneous people, things, or situations), projection (and so either anxiety or manic denial of anxiety), defensive neutralization and thus blank affect, and so on. Or from another angle, the distinction between independent and intervening variables, if or to whatever extent apposite, is never clear. Third, attempts to predict the *significance* of a certain experience or psychic occurrence run into a difficulty best expressed in analogy with the logic of action: just as intention bears on but does not exhaust the meaning of action or decisively circumscribe its limits, for the meaning of action, the shape of an action, is in part (under)determined by the perhaps unpredictable and unending effects to which it may have given rise, the significance of a psychic event, its meaning or "psychic reality," is (under)determined by the perhaps unpredictable effects to which it will have given rise in the complex, interpersonally permeable and socially mediated circuitry of psychic life. If psychic life is relational and expositive, endlessly subject to retroactive reconstitution or reinflection, its conceptualization is inherently untimely, incommensurable with its content.

EXPERIMENTAL EVIDENCE

1. Evidence that Impacts Psychoanalytic Theory

Psychoanalytic claims are neither altogether amenable nor wholly abrasive to experimental scientific investigation. For the sake of refining and defending commitments to psychoanalysis, it is incumbent upon us to determine more precisely how various psychoanalytic claims fare under experimental scrutiny. We will start by canvassing the experimental evidence underwriting the general plausibility of psychoanalysis, i.e., experimental evidence that suggests that psychoanalysis is at least onto something, is not just whimsical or perverse speculation. Slowly, we will make our way toward experimental confirmations of more specific claims. For the sake of brevity, in this section I will merely cite a number of experiments and reviews, leaving it to the reader to inquire into their methodological validity.[89] The dialectical strategy of the following two sections is to provisionally shift the burden of defense onto those who dismiss psychoanalysis as uncorroborated, even uncorroborable nonsense — an exaggerated correction to be sure, but one that seems necessary if the burden of defense is to be more equitably distributed in the long term, that is, if assessments of psychoanalytic claims by both defenders and detractors, thus debates between and amongst them, are to have any hope of rational advancement — while simultaneously showing, against those who overestimate the significance of empirical studies, that they are at most touchstones for the determination of the cognitive and practical authority of psychoanalysis, not surefire mechanisms for certifying validity and efficacy, and thereby rationalizing authority. Assumptions of judgment and commitment, a burden constitutive of subjectivity, cannot be relieved or redeemed by scientific study.

(1) There is ethological and neurological evidence that what transpires during initial, highly sensitive periods of formation bears on later functioning (Hofer 1980; Damasio 1994, 1999, 2003, 2005; Edelman 1987, 1993). Longitudinal attachment research corroborates this claim (Bretherton and Waters 1985; Belsky and Nezworski 1987; Main et al. 1985; Kobak and Sceery 1988; also see pt. 7a below).

(2) There is support for the postulation of emotional meaning and emotional association from chemoarchitectural and distributed network animal studies (Panksepp 1998, Watt 1999).

(3) Luborsky and Crits-Christoph (1990) have empirically established that the relationship to the analyst is much more akin to relationships with other people than is ordinarily supposed, which perhaps supports the claim that transference is a general rather than strictly clinical phenomenon. More direct empirical support for claim that transference is ubiquitous is provided by Andersen and Berk (1998). Gabbard (2006), and Westen and Gabbard (2002).

(4) There is empirical evidence of "unconscious" perception, memory, and processing ("thinking") (Zajonc 1968; Fowler, Wolford, Slade, and Tassinary 1981; Silverman 1983; Bowers 1984; *American Psychologist* 47(6), 1992, 761-809; LeDoux 1996; Brakel, Kleinsorge, Snodgrass, and Shevrin 2000; Morris and Dolan 2002). "A great deal of research has sought to demonstrate that it is indeed possible for people to be 'unconsciously influenced' (see Dixon, 1971, 1981, for scholarly reviews). The earliest empirical work in this area was probably conducted by Poetzl (1917/1960 who found that those part of a stimulus array that his subjects were unable to report seeing (and were therefore apparently unaware of), emerges in subsequent dreams. Many other studies have since reported similar findings under a variety of presentation speeds (from brief to prolonged) and recovery conditions including dreams, free drawings, imaging, word associations, and Rorschach responses (Allers & Teler, 1960; Fisher, 1954, 1957, 1960; Fisher & Paul, 1959; Fiss, Goldberg, & Klein, 1963; Giddan 1967; Haber & Erdelyi, 1967; L. Luborsky & Shevrin, 1956; Malamud, 1934; Malamud & Linder, 1931; Paul & Fisher, 1959; Shevrin and Fisher, 1967; Shevrin and Fritzler, 1968; Shevrin & L. Luborsky, 1958; L.H. Silverman & D.K. Silverman, 1964)" (Weinberger and Silverman 1990, 304). Somewhat more specifically, empirical studies "support Freud's hypothesis that the perceptual object dimension of a word ["thing presentation"], being functionally distinct from its meaning, can give rise to novel sequential processing, an effect that is more

likely to occur unconsciously (i.e., d’ < 0) and under conditions of anxiety” (Klein Villa, Shevrin, Snodgrass, Bazan, and Brakel 2006).

(5) There is evidence of “unconscious” attitudes and motives (Shevrin and Dickman 1980; Silverman, Lachman, and Milich 1982; Bowers and Meichenbaum 1984; Kihlstrom 1987; Kline 1987; and Bornstein and Pittman 1992). Dixon’s (1981) and Kihlstrom’s (1984) research also supports the contention that thinking, feeling, and acting may be influenced by non-conscious determinants. Empirical confirmation of hypnotic suggestion is further evidence for the possibility of non-conscious motivation. It would not be difficult to devise experiments to support, or to extrapolate empirical support from the archive of psychological experiments for, a wide variety of convictions that inform psychoanalytic theory, e.g., that the patterning of associations is not always immediately transparent; that there are links between physiology and psychic life and to some extent reciprocal influence; that the non-conscious affects consciousness; that there is a constant interplay of non-conscious and conscious processing; that earlier states, perceptions, and capacities are in some way preserved and/or exert influence on later states, perceptions, and capacities, and/or may be reinhabited or reactivated under certain conditions; or slightly more specifically, that infantile experiences influence subsequent development and perhaps psychopathology (as in the Spitz “hospitalism” studies), etc. However, such support would certainly not render psychoanalytic formulations of these vague ideas more compelling than alternative renditions.

(6) There is evidence for repression in Wolitzky, Klein, and Dworkin 1975; Erdelyi and Goldberg 1979; Kline 1981, 196, 208, 436; Fisher 1982, 680; Geisler 1986; Davis and Schwartz 1987; Singer 1990; Newton and Contrada 1992.[90] Levinger and Clark (1961) have demonstrated that associations to words regarded by an experimental subject as “emotional” are more frequently forgotten than associations to words judged by the same individual as “neutral.” Also relevant is Luborsky’s (1996) empirical confirmation of “motivated forgetting.”

(7) O’Neill et al. (1987) provide evidence that the probability of depression is high for those who have experienced both a significant early loss and a recent loss. And there is ample evidence that distinct styles of childrearing differentially impact children’s character structures, specifically that inclinations to exacting self-criticism and orientation toward dependency correlate with particular parenting styles (Fisher and Greenberg 1996, 57). Conjointly, these studies suggest that history matters for pathology and character development but does not strictly entail specific pathological or characterological developments. In virtue of its weakness, the evidence provides some empirical support for the thesis that psychic life is to some extent singular, i.e., anomalous and unpredictable. Further empirical evidence for the thesis that psychic life is not a deductive-nomological machine is provided by Eysenck,

Wakefield, and Friedman (1983); Kirk and Kutchins (1992); and Fisher and Fisher (1993). These studies show that diagnostic categories cannot be reliably distinguished and that a large proportion of individuals who fit one diagnosis fit multiple diagnoses (taxonomic pluralism). This suggests that it is highly unlikely that there are unique causal agents responsible for specific forms of psychopathology and/or classes of symptomatology, thus that in the realm of the psyche, "causes" lead to multiple effects (over- and underdetermination).

(7a) Further — and stronger — evidence that history, and in particular, rearing, influences character structure and psychopathology is provided by the Adult Attachment Interview (developed by Mary Main) and the Strange Situation Test (developed by Mary Ainsworth).[91] These tests, performed thousands of times over world-wide, have proven reliable and valid measures of the relationships between parental personality, patterns of infant behavior, and significant reflective capacity on the part of the infant as s/he matures. The evidence is so strong that on the basis of these tests a plausible case can be made for a strong statistical relationship obtaining between parental personality and infant behavior and development. The Adult Attachment Interview (AAI) tests the ability of parents to register and represent emotionally significant experiences. Specifically, it tests for repression or dissociation as indicated by parental difficulty with holding in mind distressing or emotionally significant experiences. Parental reporting on difficult or emotionally significant experiences that manifests low coherence, just as parental expression of attitudes and opinions in the biographical narrative that are at variance with or seem unsupported by the facts recounted, correlate strongly with emotional difficulties in both the parent and child (the latter as measured by the Strange Situation Test (SST)). More specifically, AAI assessments of the parent indicating that s/he has difficulty reflecting on emotionally significant experiences is strongly correlated with an increased probability that his/her infant will show anxious-ambivalent behavior in SST assessments and that the infant will develop into an adult who will have pronounced difficulty reflecting on emotionally significant and/or difficult experiences. Reflective capacity of the parent is predictive of the infant's attachment patterns, and later, psychological well-being. Even if it is performed before the infant is born or well afterwards, the AAI still predicts and retrodicts accurately (Parkes, Stevenson-Hinde, and Marris 1991).[92]

(8) Some evidence for the ontological indeterminacy thesis is provided by Forer 1949; Marmor 1970; Ross and Conway 1986; Loftus 1979 and 1993; and Brewin, Andrews, and Gotlib 1993. These studies show that memory can be molded by suggestion[93] and by a desire to perceive consistency and continuity between current and past behaviors and attitudes.[94] The thesis is also supported by Eisenstein, Levy, and Marmor's (1994) finding that persuasion and suggestion play a significant role in healing and by the finding of Murray

(1956), Truax (1966), and Masling and Cohen (1987) that therapists unwittingly influence the content of their clients' speech, specifically in such a way that clients reproduce therapists' psychological theories.[95] Ethological-neurological evidence supporting this point (specifically, finding that long-term memories are not permanently inscribed but rather retranscribed and reconsolidated with each instance of activation) is provided by Nader, Schafe, and LeDoux (2000). Indirect support for the ontological indeterminacy thesis, i.e., evidence of suggestibility, is provided by Fisher's (1953) study: "patients under analysis accepted suggestions to dream in 68% of 95 experiments . . . the content of the suggestion influenced the content of the dream produced" (406).

(9) Evidence of defense mechanisms is provided by Vaillant 1977 and 1986; Suls and Fletcher 1985; Ihilevich and Gleser 1986; Cramer 1987 and 1988; and Fisher and Fisher 1993.

(10) More specifically, evidence that projection is used as a defense against anxiety is provided by Suls and Fletcher 1985; Vaillant 1986; Ihilevich and Gleser 1986; Kline 1987; and Cramer 1988.

(11) There is empirical evidence (from subliminal psychodynamic activation experiments) supporting the claim that behavior, and in particular behavior deemed psychopathological, may be to some extent motivated by conflict over libidinal and/or aggressive wishes (for review of the studies, cf. Silverman 1983; Weinberger and Silverman 1987).

(12) Friedman (1952) provides support for claims about the prevalence of Oedipal hostility (although alternative interpretations of the data are not ruled out) through the following experiment. An investigator asks children ages 5-16 to complete two fables having to do with engaging in a pleasurable activity alone with one parent and then meeting the other parent. The children are also asked to compose stories about two pictures, one showing a child and a father figure and the other a child and a mother figure. The children provided negative endings for the fables in which they were initially alone with the opposite sex parent and then met with the same sex parent. Schill's (1966) experiment using the Blacky Test also supports claims about the prevalence of Oedipal hostility. College students were shown a picture of a dog with a knife over its tail as if about to cut it off. Asked who was responsible for the threats, males tended to say "father," while females tended to say "mother."

(13) Decent evidence of transference is provided by studies that show that characteristic and consistent patterns of relating to others are consonant with descriptions of relations to parents and are reflected in relations to therapists (Luborsky, Barber, and Crits-Christoph 1990; Luborsky and Crits-Christoph 1990).

(14) There is evidence that self-directed aggression increases the likelihood of depression, which supports a Freudian understanding of melancholia (Rustein and Goldberger 1973; Abramson et al. 1978; Abramson et al. 1980).

(15) Fisher and Greenberg's (1978) review indicates that Oedipal conflict and the theory of oral and anal personality types are well supported by empirical evidence. Further empirical support for the theory of the Oedipus complex is provided by Silverman, Ross, Adler, and Lustig (1978); Hayden and Silverstein (1983); and Palumbo and Gillman (1984).

(16) Specifically, Fisher and Greenberg report that "[t]he orality index was . . . determined from the frequency with which inkblot responses contained oral references (e.g., food, nurturant figures). Previous studies have demonstrated that this orality index is elevated in persons who are alcoholic (Weiss & Masling, 1970), who are quick to yield (Masling, Weiss, & Rothschild, 1968), and who are likely to be upset by being alone (Masling, Price, Goldband, & Katkin, 1981). The data indicated that the orality scores were positively and significantly correlated with self-reported amount of depression in both samples" (1996, 34). In other words, the orality index corroborates claims about the relation between oral fixation and various dispositions such as dependency, submissiveness, and depression.[96]

2. Evidence that Impacts Psychoanalytic Practice

Next, there is experimental evidence bearing on psychoanalytic practice and its possible refinement. Some of these studies speak to the question of what makes for more and less successful clinical practice, thus may bear on the question of how to adjudicate between options when seeking psychoanalysis. Further, if process and outcome studies can reliably identify those most likely to benefit from specific forms of psychoanalysis as against others, referral may be incrementally rationalized. Again, for sake of brevity, studies will be merely cited rather than explored in terms of their methodological validity.[97]

(1) Fisher and Greenberg's (1996) positive review of the orality index suggests that it would be useful for determining whether or not there is actually an oral issue to work on. Thus it would be useful for adjudicating between better and worse practices *if* what makes for better clinical practice is "hitting the mark," comprehensiveness, and/or explanatory fullness, and especially *if* one supposes that only direct acknowledgement and interpretation of oral issues is a condition for successfully working through them (which means denying the inexact interpretation thesis).

(2) If and to the extent that accuracy of reconstruction or orientation by accurate reconstruction is necessary for or conducive to positive clinical results, a study of 278 university women concluding that level of dissociation discriminates between abused and nonabused participants would be relevant to refining therapeutic practice (Briere and Runtz 1988). Likewise, if "getting it right" matters therapeutically, then Jones' experimental finding "that the increase in phallic imagery following exposure to the subliminal pregnancy

message was not a reflection of a generalized increase in achievement/power fantasies but rather seemed to be anchored in body (phallic) feelings" is relevant insofar as it indicates "that the observed increase in phallic imagery could be better explained within the 'Freudian traditionalist' than the 'culturalist' paradigm. That is, Freud's notion was affirmed that pregnancy induced fantasies relevant to gaining a new phallic body part" (Fisher and Greenberg 1996, 164).

(3) Fisher and Greenberg (1996, 36, 48) report that non-questionnaire studies indicate that high levels of dependency and self-hostility (independently) predict depression. This suggests that analysts of those identified as high on self-hostility or dependency indices might do well to watch out for depressive developments, calibrate their practices accordingly, and perhaps expect and explore amplified self-hostility or dependency (or their vicissitudes) upon the onset of depression. Blatt et al. (1976) and Beck's (1983) studies are pertinent to this point. They show that among those who manifest unusually elevated dependency tendencies, in contrast to those prone to self-criticism and taking responsibility on themselves, events that trigger dependence also trigger depression, while among those prone to self-criticism and introjection, events that trigger self-criticism tend to incite depression. Another piece of pertinent experimental evidence is provided by King and Emmons (1990) and Raulin (1984), who have shown that abnormally high levels of ambivalence are often correlated with depressive inclinations.

(4) Also, if getting it right matters therapeutically, or even if (or to the extent) not, if knowing what to look out for positively bears on clinical results, the following studies would be significant to the refinement of analytic practice: Fisher and Greenberg (1996) report correlations between maternal dominance and sons' sexual difficulties (133); the children of harsh, dominating parents tend to be unusually prone to dependency and self-criticism (Bornstein 1993 and Koestner, Zuroff, and Powers 1991); numerous studies have established a strong correlation between childhood traumas and dissociation; anal trends in mothers are correlated with anal trends in children (Fisher and Greenberg 1996, 102); there is some evidence that obsessive compulsive parents tend to raise obsessive compulsive children (Pollak 1979, 238). Cf. points 7 and 7a above.

(5) There is empirical evidence that certain phenomena tend to cluster, which might be useful for directing clinical attention, i.e., rationalizing clinical inferences and expectations. For instance, "oral qualities" such as an intense need to affiliate with others, pessimism, and passivity often track together (Fisher and Greenberg 1977). Orderliness, obstinacy, parsimony, and investments in control, regularity, and rigidity tend to hang together (Fisher and Greenberg 1977; Masling and Schwartz 1979; Kline 1981; and Fisher and Greenberg 1996, 103, 112).[98]

(6) There is empirical evidence that could be profitably brought to bear on expectations concerning the development of transference and on the manner in which it is engaged. For instance, "oral types" tend to be abnormally sensitive to whether or not they receive approval by those they deem significant; they tend to seek experiences of being in the good graces of those they perceive to have power; they exhibit a noticeable desire for feedback from authority figures; they place high priority on and become deeply invested in relationships that provide nurturance; they are highly sensitive to the (perceived) motives and intentions of others and want to be with others when under stress (Fisher and Greenberg 1985, 133; Fisher and Greenberg 1996, 86).

(7) Although many analysts have stressed that transference interpretations should focus predominantly on the relation with the analyst (Freud; Strachey 1969; Stone 1967; Gill 1982; orientation toward the "here and now" is a contemporary commonplace), some empirical research suggests that it is often more effective to focus on distorted beliefs about all of the significant people in the patient's life (Silberschatz, Fretter, and Curtis 1986; Fretter, Bucci, Broitman, Silberschatz, and Curtis, 1994).

(8) Although many (albeit many fewer in the post-relational moment) analysts claim that the very heart of analysis is transference interpretation, Piper, Azim, Joyce, and McCallum (1991) provide evidence of an inverse relationship between the proportion of transference interpretations and both outcome and therapeutic alliance measures. Others have corroborated the claim that too much emphasis on transference may be therapeutically detrimental (Henry, Schacht, Strupp, Butler, and Binder 1993; Henry, Strupp, Butler, Schacht, and Binder 1993; and Henry, Strupp, Schacht, and Gaston 1994). Høglend's (2004) review (mostly of short term therapies) concludes that "a high dosage level of transference interpretations does not seem to overcome patient resistance and defensiveness and may in fact contribute to a negative therapeutic process" (294). Some have found that resolving the transference neurosis bears much less than expected on other outcome measures, e.g., improved quality of object relations (Kantrowitz, Katz et al 1987) and affect management (Kantrowitz, Paolitto et al. 1986; Wallerstein 1986). Kantrowitz and Paolitto (1986) found, furthermore, that improvements in affect management occur whether or not a transference neurosis is established, let alone resolved. However, there are studies that indicate that therapies primarily oriented toward transference analysis lead to the best results (Malan 1976; Earle 1979; Earle and Goldberg 1984; Marziali 1984; Weber, Bachrach et al. 1985; Luborsky, Cristoph, Mintz, and Auerbach 1988).

(9) Neuroscientific studies identifying visceral indications of psychic processes might facilitate enhanced therapeutic attunement and optimal working alliances (Schore 2005).

(10) Neuroscientific evidence favors suspending the traditional practice of interpreting at moments of affective intensity when the client is known to suffer from PTSD (Yovell 2000; see also Tutte 2004 and Cimino and Correale 2005). Also, there is a growing body of evidence that suggests that even if interpretation-heavy, conflict-centered analyses are best for classical neurotics, more disturbed patients (i.e., borderlines) tend to do better with less interpretation. Fonagy and Target (1996) provide evidence of this with respect to child analyses in particular.

(11) A review of 765 child analyses at the Anna Freud Centre indicates that "disruptive disordered" children were not significantly helped by psychoanalysis, while the more severe and complex cases of "emotionally disordered" children profited from psychoanalysis — all of which bears on the issue of analyzability and rational referral (cf. Fonagy and Target (1994, 1996) and Target and Fonagy (1994, 1996).

(12) Luborsky et al. (1988) find that congruence of CCRT patterns and the content of interpretations correlates significantly with positive therapeutic outcome.

(13) A finding that may bear on rationalizing therapeutic referral is that "more dependent, interpersonally oriented (anaclitic) patients . . . were more constructively responsive to a therapeutic context with greater interpersonal interaction in face-to-face psychotherapy [supportive-expressive therapy], while the more ideational patients, who emphasize separation, autonomy, control, and independence (introjective patients), found the context of psychoanalysis more conducive to therapeutic progress" (Blatt and Shahar 2004, 427).

•

3. From the Mouths of Babes: Developmental Observation

Developmental observation studies may be useful for generating and may bear on the assessment, including the comparative evaluation, of developmental claims. If and to the extent that getting it right matters, these studies may be especially useful for evaluating and refining the conduct of child analyses and adolescent or adult analyses in which genetic reconstruction plays a significant role. For instance, data from developmental observational studies indicates that Oedipal behavior peaks at 4 years and declines starting at 5 years (Fisher and Greenberg 1996, 123). Developmental observational studies also suggest that there cannot be representation of absent objects before about 18 months (M. Cavell 1993, 46). However, although developmental observation studies can be used to differentiate between plausible and merely possible developmental sequences, although they can provide (non-decisive) evidence *against* various developmental claims or modify the status of such claims (i.e., as pertaining to the infantile rather than empirical infants), although they can be marshaled as evidence *confluent* with certain developmental claims, and although perhaps they can be used to "elaborate and augment understanding and strategy," they do little to *corroborate*, let alone *validate* any particular developmental claim or establish the preferability of one developmental claim over another (Knoblauch 2005, 887). At most, developmental observation shows that a particular developmental claim (genetic reconstruction or prognostication) is either not impossible or more confluent with empirical knowledge of development than competing claims. Developmental observation can motivate the specification or refinement of reconstructive hypotheses, clinical prognoses, and metapsychological theories, and it can be generative of new developmental hypotheses and stimulate further research, but it cannot rule out or, conversely, lend much credibility to, any particular developmental claim. And since clinical results do not seem to be keyed to practitioners' developmental theories, it seems unlikely that "getting it right" matters much for therapeutic practice.[99]

Freud opened the door to the now widespread interest in developmental observational research long ago when he announced that "What we inferred from these [adult] analyses was later confirmed point by point by direct observation of children" (SE 16: 310).[100] Since then, researchers have been beating on the door of the nursery, hoping to confirm or disconfirm developmental and related psychoanalytic hypotheses on the basis of what can be observed therein. For instance, contra Mahler, Stern has persuasively shown on the basis of experimental research that infants can differentiate themselves from others within the first several months of life (1985). More recent research indicates that infants can distinguish their mothers within the first few hours of life. To some extent, this evidence countervails theories of primary nondifferentiation. However, as noted earlier, those committed to developmental theories that assume primary nondifferentiation could respond to these findings by claiming that a register of nondifferentiated experience subsists alongside early differentiating capacities, i.e., by restricting the scope of their claims and insisting on compatibility, or by modifying the status of their claims such that nondifferentiation pertains to an "infantile" dimension or experiential register of the child, adolescent, or adult rather than to the empirical infant. A Kleinian confronted with evidence that infants do not possess the powers Kleinians attribute to them could well say much the same. Since interpretive extrapolations from developmental observation are inevitably (though unevenly) underwarranted — "The baby burrowing into its mother's lap may be described equally well as 'wanting to get back to the womb', 'to scoop out the mother's "good" insides', 'to feel safe', 'to take the place of its sibling', and so on" (M. Cavell 1993, 52) — such research cannot rule out hypotheses dissonant with its findings.

Too often, interpretive indeterminacy is anxiously effaced in the literalizing zeal of those who maintain that in developmental observation (or child analysis) they have finally found an authoritative empirical resource confirming or repudiating various psychoanalytic hypotheses. Hartmann, for instance, claims that observations of psychotic patients confirm Freud's theories of primary process operations (1964, 315). But do they confirm or just (arguably) instantiate these theories? Would Hartmann accept, as many have claimed, that modernist painting, poetry, and literature confirm these theories? Likely not, but on what basis is observation of psychotic patients invested with confirmatory power as against the merely illustrative character of modernist painting, poetry, and literature? Brenner (1957) claims that more than ample evidence for Freud's theory of component drives can be gleaned from observations of adult sexuality. After asking "how are we to identify the derivatives or manifestations of the sexual drive at a still earlier age," he suggests that "[w]e can do so by observing: (1) that in the course of . . . development they become a part of adult sexual behavior which is subordinated under and contributes to genital excitement and gratification [in certain cases, or they may maintain a relative autonomy that is not pathological perversion], as ordinarily happens in the case of kissing, looking, fondling, exhibiting, and the like [But can the integration of component drives into adult sexuality be directly observed? Again, wouldn't "observations" of this sort illustrate the theory rather than empirically support it?]; and (2) that in certain cases of . . . sexual development (sexual perversions) one or another of these infantile interests or actions becomes the chief source of adult sexual gratification [But how would this establish that such modalities of adult sexual gratification are sourced in component instincts, that what is observed is a return to origins? The desire to align origin and eventuality tends to obscure numerous possible intermediary moments.]" (25). So, Brenner continues, the evidence for the primacy of orality in early infancy is "to a large extent reconstructive . . . based on the analyses of older children and of adults, but it is also possible to observe quite directly the importance to children of this age, and even older, of sucking, mouthing and biting as sources of pleasure" (25). One could no doubt empirically establish the prevalence of sucking, mouthing, biting etc., but this would hardly be evidence for any particular theory of development or psychopathology, as Brenner implies. Neither observation of adults nor child analysis, as Brenner earlier claims, allows one to "see directly" what in adult analysis is retrospectively inferred, namely, "the great significance of infantile sexual desires as well as their nature" (24).

Is not the fetishism of observation merely the symmetrical inverse of rigid adherence to whatever tradition bequeaths; yet another myth of the given? Does it not support insularity and overconfidence — thus perhaps therapeutic infelicity — matching the fervor of those committed to following Freud come hell or high water? Observation may rightfully induce suspicions about, say, an undifferentiated phase, infantile narcissism, the classical conception of the stimulus barrier, omnipotence fantasies, or hallucinatory wish-fulfillment, but it is no magical mechanism for cognitive authentication, and putting too much faith in its deliverances may promote a hasty suppression of a variety of potentially productive clinical and theoretical hypotheses (Peterfreund 1978).[101]

THE POWERS AND LIMITS OF NATURAL SCIENCE

If the claims of psychoanalysis to cognitive credibility are to be rationally appraised, the presumption that the protocols of natural science are *the* mechanisms of empirical knowledge-certification, i.e., the conflation of scientific validity with cognitive value and authority, must be contested. Thus the final phase of this dialectical strategy is to advance an account of natural science that, however skeletal, is both plausible — a real competitor — and sufficiently deflationary to put pressure on the claim that because natural science yields objective knowledge of universal laws that, when systematically integrated, exhaustively explain and reliably predict the developments and interactions of all natural phenomena, it is the rightful measure of knowledge as such. Though, ultimately, what should be contested is the presumption that the sort of knowledge yielded by natural scientific research is unconditionally satisfying, which would involve not just a deflationary account of natural scientific knowledge but explicit normative defense of the perspectives yielded by, thus the forms of life promoted by, psychoanalysis, in this section I can only prepare the ground for such an undertaking.

THEORIES

A highly influential view, arguably the standard view, of scientific theory is the syntactic view, which holds that a theory is a set of axioms plus its deductive consequences. More precisely, the syntactic view holds that a theory is composed of sets of propositions organized as axiomatic systems that give comprehensive or sufficiently broad accounts of a domain. If "axiomatic systems" are sets of deductively complete and empirically verified systems themselves systematically integrated into a deductively complete, empirically verified totality, and if the axioms of each system, set of systems, and the total system by which such sets are comprehended are true or false statements (including but not limited to universal generalizations), then science has yet to produce a theory. And perhaps never will. This view seems, at most, a regulative ideal. Though not without strategic value, in light of the discussion of reductionism and related matters above and the arguments below, as a description of current or possible scientific theory, this view is untenable.

If, on the contrary, "axiomatic systems" are understood as systems that inferentially coordinate provisionally accepted propositions, that is, propositions (thus, necessarily, propositional arrangements) accepted *instead of* competitor propositions (and propositional arrangements) that have their virtues and can also explain the data, by means of contestable axioms that stipulate and/or interpretive-inferential practices that instantiate norms of theory construction, norms of domain determination and scientific development (e.g., aims and interests), basic observations and experiences (including but not limited to basic statements of fact and universal generalizations), and other such norms and premises taken for granted for the sake of scientific research in general or for the sake of a particular pursuit, then this view aptly describes the actual practice and perhaps the promise of scientific theory development . . . but not only scientific theory development. Indeed, this amounts to saying that scientific theories are composed of (1) shared sets of equations, concepts, experiences, interpretive protocols, and paradigms, dispositions, metaphysical commitments, aims and interests that drive or are employed in the production of models, or more precisely, families of models, that are used to predict, explain, and/or manipulate the world, and (2) claims about the sort of things to which models apply, both individually and generally.[102]

MODELS, HYPOTHESES, EXPLANATIONS

Models are required because the basic concepts and fundamental principles (laws, equations, etc.) of scientific theories are too abstract to describe the concrete phenomena, i.e., specific causal networks and capacities. Nature is non-identical with its most elementary principles. The generality afforded by basic concepts, fundamental principles, and theories is purchased at the price of phenomenological imprecision. Fundamental principles, for instance, describe abstract relations between abstract concepts. At most, they describe capacities of systems that fall under these concepts. On their own, they cannot represent the concrete causal nexuses of which the natural world is composed. Indeed, they cannot even indicate by what systems they are instantiated or if the systems in which they are instantiated are best described in their terms. Likewise, absent modeling, all theories can do is classify and summarize complex events and processes.[103]

Modeling is necessary to show if and to what extent fundamental principles and theories describe the world. But in order to describe the world to which fundamental principles and theories might apply, a model will have to *supplement* the abstract description of the natural world they afford, and this will mean construing the world as much more complex than fundamental principles and theories stipulate, thus forgoing the simplified understanding of nature they promise. The modeling through which fundamental principles and theories are elaborated gives the lie to their pretensions to unveil the formulaic truths of nature. Fundamental principles, theories, and the like are not false *per se* but self-falsifying when they claim self-sufficiency, i.e., claim to compress into basic rules what, once unraveled, is the world in its entirety. As we will see, modeling is the condition of (im)possibility for totalizing truth and all-satisfying explanation.

A model is an object or set of objects that satisfy a set of axioms and allow for the description of phenomena, most often dependency relations, through an equation or set of equations. A model is exactly described by an equation or set of equations not because the totality of concrete situations and capacities of which nature is composed is rigorously and comprehensively described by, or best described by, one or more equations — not because mathematics is the language of nature — but because a model *abstracts and idealizes* (mathematizes) natural events and processes sufficiently for the work of science to proceed: a model is *defined* as something that exactly satisfies certain axioms and equations.[104] This is to say, a model is an idealization, an approximate description of inordinately complex events and processes required to ensure that the conditions of equations are sustained and thus that the work of science can proceed.[105] Models mediate interests. Since even the phenomena regularly held up as paradigm instantiations of equations *always* fail to exactly match the equations by which they are described — to cite a well known example, no actual harmonic oscillator can be reduced to the equation $F = -kx$ — without idealization and approximation, that is, without modeling, scientific research would be paralyzed. Science requires exaggeration, concomitant inflation and deflation, perspective.

To be sure, although models elaborate attenuated truths of the natural world, they are certainly knowledge-bearing. Yet to the extent that they fail to foreground their status as models, to the extent that they succumb to reification, their innermost danger, and presume to provide a fully adequate description of the phenomena modeled, suppressing the excessiveness of phenomena, their availability to other manners of modeling, modeling is a form of (self-) falsification.

The formulation of a model partakes of the perspectival dialectic of inflation/deflation, exaggeration/distortion, creation/discovery, blindness/insight. Models, and so the theories, principles, and equations modeled, never agree with all the known facts in their domain.[106] Formulating a model involves selecting and so screening-off certain aspects of nature, e.g., via the enactment of shielding conditions. Hence enhancement of a model's scope usually trades off with diminishment of its descriptive precision. And modeling often involves asserting aspects of the model for the sake of the model's coherence and usefulness, *not* because these aspects are believed to map onto known aspects of nature. Often, equations are developed from descriptions chosen in large part for their mathematical features, though they may not be the best descriptions on many other counts. Models are not exactly mirrors of nature. They mediate — coordinate, articulate — theories and concrete situations, respecting their differences. Models are principles or processes of interpretive construction, of concept application and elaboration — theoretical intermediaries. Though not mere constructions, they are hermeneutic tools necessary for the development of science. But also that which indefinitely forestalls the realization of the classical ideal of science.[107]

Though there is no algorithm for adjudicating between competing models, some models will clearly be of greater interest than others, e.g., those that allow for more or more precise predictions or more law-like generalizations relative to competitors or that facilitate various desired interventions that others do not. However, no model has yet been developed that maximally satisfies all relevant normative criteria.

Hypotheses, then, can be understood as claiming a similarity between models and real causal manifolds. More specifically, hypotheses can be understood as claiming that an indicated type and degree of homology exists between a model and a real system. On this conception, scientific progress can be understood, in part, as a reflexive specification of the form and empirical adequacy of its claims, i.e., as a movement toward self-consciousness (including acknowledgment of speculative excess) rather than simply toward deductive-nomological totalization.

As noted above, so much are models not exact descriptions of nature that, often, they will have features that are not presumed to have an empirical counterpart. The phase factor in the wave functions of quantum theory, the imaginary part of complex numbers used in electromagnetic theory, and perhaps negative square roots (used in a variety of models) do not correspond to anything in the world. These supplements support the efficacy of the model on the condition of revoking its promise to perfectly reproduce or reveal nature, whether in the language of mathematics or otherwise. Some but not all aspects of a model must be similar to, must simulate, some real system. And a "real system" need mean no more than a pervasive pattern of regularities (specifically, dependency relations) observable given sufficient shielding conditions, that is, given the bracketing of certain observations or the bracketing performed by an experimental setup. Thus a model's claim to realism is highly qualified.

Claims to realism or exactitude of description are further problematized by the impossibility of directly testing a model against observations. If we accept Duhem's (1914) claims that (1) a model must be embedded in an experimental context that is partially defined by other models, and (2) data are significant only relative to the total experimental context, then two conclusions follow. First, since a model must contextualize and thereby concretize a concept or another model, if, as seems plausible, contextualization fails to fully absorb the phenomena (concept or other model and the experiences they bear), that is, if the phenomena can be indefinitely redescribed by new contextualizations, new models, then the meaning of data is *constitutively indeterminate*. Second, the role of negative evidence is systematically ambiguous. Negative evidence does not necessarily indicate that the model tested is mistaken; observations might not match predictions because some other model defining the experimental context does not fit the situation, thus in the face of negative evidence the model tested may be retained given suitable modifications to other models employed in the experimental setup.[108]

That said, it should be unsurprising that both across the sciences and within each science, phenomena are regularly modeled differently for different purposes. Models bring out certain aspects of phenomena, and so far, no model has shown itself to be the all-around best. Indeed, what would make a model the all-around best is systematically ambiguous (see the earlier discussions of diverse epistemic and methodological criteria and of normative dispute among perspectives). Neither has it been shown that accepted models can be coordinated into a deductive-nomological system. At least ideally, the success of a model depends on how precisely it replicates what happens in the world and how much of the world it comprehends, but since enhanced precision and expanded scope usually do not track together (quite the contrary), conflict between models seems inevitable. What will satisfy is as much as question for science as it is for psychoanalysis.

From this perspective, the development of science can be figured as the development of families of models that have demonstrated their worth through exemplary applications to the behavior of kinds of events or systems of interest. But if this is accepted, the development of science, as much that of psychoanalysis, seems an unending, normatively underdetermined enterprise rather than a linear progression toward, or at least in view of, a known terminus.

What view of scientific explanation would be consonant with this account of the role and function of models? If explanation is not to succumb to false generalizations, i.e., render the sacrifice of precision for scope a methodological absolute, it must proceed as detailed analyses of specific compositions of causes and by reflexively articulated approximations of models to phenomena (specific compositions of causes). Since modeling must exceed what fundamental principles (laws, equations, etc.) stipulate, explanation cannot be the same as deduction from fundamental principles. The explanatory power of the fundamental laws and principles of high-level theories is not to be denied, but it does not imply their truth. Rather, truth is obtained through the articulation of low-level causal principles and concrete phenomenological laws. Decreasing explanatory scope increases precision. If this is accepted, explanation should proceed by stating concrete causes and phenomenological laws (specific, context-bound dependency relations) and then fitting them into a theoretical framework, a unifying set of fundamental equations. Fundamental laws are true of objects in models; phenomenological laws are true of reality, or at least more true to reality than fundamental laws.[109] Hence explanation is aporetic, internally riven, ever unsatisfying.

An acceptable, if not fully satisfying, explanation, then, would be one in which the behavior to be explained by a model is derived from facts about the model plus the principles of the theory modeled. What models explain are quantitative or qualitative capacities, capacities for phenomena in restricted circumstances to bring about either qualitative (imprecise) or quantitatively exact, predictable results (Cartwright 1999, 53 and 66-7). Thus a truthful explanation would be a self-consciously qualified explanation, e.g., would involve the statement of the (or at least some) *ceteris paribus* clauses it assumes. If "[t]o explain a phenomenon is to find a model that fits it into the basic framework of the theory and that thus allows us to derive analogues for the messy and complicated phenomenological laws which are true of it," then scientific explanation is an irreducibly analogical endeavor, not a systematic demonstration of deductive closure (Cartwright 1983, 152). The need for models points toward the need to mourn the metaphysical ideal of classical science.

Connectors

Modeling involves the development of connectors. Theories are connected to phenomena by chains of reasoning that connect high-level theoretical principles, mid- and low-level phenomenological laws, and observation statements. Further, if a hypothesis is to be tested, other connectors, namely auxiliary premises, will be needed for the derivation of testable predictions. Connectors are interpretations, thus bears with them an ineffaceable moment of uncertainty and contestability. The necessity of connectors guarantees that, in principle, the conversation of science is interminable.

One important type of connector is a bridge principle. Theoretical terms are abstract, thus require bridge principles to be applied to concrete causal manifolds (real systems). If *ad hoc* applications are to be avoided, bridge principles must be developed to license the application of theoretical terms to a situation described by a model. They tell us what kinds of situations fall within the domain of a theory, i.e., characterize the scope of a theory. Although bridge principles are surely *principles*, they are far from exceptionless, hence non-necessary. As even Hempel admits, bridge principles do not have the character of universal laws; they hold only when circumstances are sufficiently ideal (Cartwright 1983, 132). Or as Cartwright puts it, "the 'right kind of description' for assigning an equation is seldom, if ever, a 'true description' of the phenomenon studied; and there are few formal principles for getting from 'true descriptions' to the kind of descriptions that entail an equation. There are just rules of thumb, good sense, and, ultimately, the requirement that the equation we end up with must do the job" (1983, 133). Because context is not self-specifying, interpretive indeterminacy, hence mediation by interest and tradition, is irreducible.

Connectors are not objective rules that determine how one ought to reason in a given situation. Rather, they are interest-governed elaborations, reflective judgments, that involve science in an unending dialectic of creation and discovery. "To get from a detailed factual knowledge of a situation to an equation, we must prepare the description of the situation to meet the mathematical needs of the theory" (Cartwright 1983, 15). That is, in a certain way, one must create the (concepts of the) objects about which discoveries will be made. Phenomena must be construed, worked up and worked over, in a way that may forfeit absolute precision — "Generally, the result will no longer be a true description" (ibid.) — yet is necessary to yield knowledge. Knowledge is only ever gleaned in the light radiating from a specific perspective. Refusing imaginative mediation, even falsification, or repudiating the uncertainty of perspectival inquiry, would mean forfeiting what truth can be had.

The treatment of phenomena required for, say, the elaboration of an equation, involves the suppression of phenomenological complexity and the deflation of those dimensions of the phenomena that do not conform to the demands of mathematically-inclined inquiry. Hence elaboration involves some measure of falsification or distortion. But this does not mean that genuine discoveries about phenomena so treated are unavailable. Though phenomena are not identical with their mathematized elaborations, discoveries made about the mathematizable dimensions of phenomena are genuine discoveries. It is just that such discoveries, though genuine, are partial and perspectival, hence non-objective in the classical sense.

Laws

With this characterization of theories, models, hypotheses, and connectors in the backdrop, we are now in a position to evaluate the claim that nature is thoroughly law-governed, thus best explained by expositions of laws and their interconnections, ideally by a deductively-nomologically integrated presentation of the totality of natural laws.

If this claim is to be evaluated, we must first address the question: What is a law? One prevalent view of law, the covering law model, holds that laws are universal generalizations. If laws are universal generalizations, then a systematically complete exposition of the lawful operations of nature would be fully satisfying if laws state the governing rules of nature and these governing rules are elements of the deductive-nomological system of nature in which one factor (e.g., a higher-level law) explains another (e.g., a lower-level law) if the occurrence of the second can be deduced from the occurrence of the first.[110] Assuming that all natural phenomena fall under covering laws, the systematically complete exposition of such laws would yield empirically and logically determinate knowledge of nature. Demands for more would be unintelligible, satisfaction would be replete. Some of the most significant difficulties faced by this conception of law and lawful explanation will now be considered.

When applied to specific circumstances, covering laws do not give a correct account of the events and processes they comprehend. They do not precisely represent any situation; they are idealizations, not rigorous statements of fact. Only of a model may statements of law be literally and precisely true, and this for two reasons. First, in order to attain precision, covering laws must flatten out, i.e., homogenize, the complex textures of natural phenomena (objects, events, processes) and thereby lose precision. If they are to be precisely true, they must be true of homogenous classes of objects, of which there are none, thus which must be produced by abstraction and idealization. Second, on its own, a covering law describes, at best, what happens when only a single law obtains, which is never. Covering laws must have the same form when they act together as they would were they to act singly, but then what a single covering law states on its own cannot be exactly true because the effects said to issue from the law on its own would not arise when multiple covering laws act together. The supplementation necessary for truthfulness undermines the formal self-subsistence in virtue of which covering laws lay claim to be basic elements or governing rules of nature.

Like models, covering laws are interest-governed and semantically sensitive to use-context: they make salient features common to certain situations in which the law's users are interested and underdetermine the rendering of that which they make salient. Thus, like models, covering laws are truth-bearing, yet prone to reification and therewith falsification. Their integrity and explanatory power trades off with phenomenological precision, thus the truths and satisfactions they afford are either self-consciously qualified or falsified.

Another way to state the problem would be to say that the covering law model is too selective, lets in too little, to succeed as a satisfying description of nature. First, there are few if any isolated systems, and only of an isolated system could a finite set of covering laws be fully descriptive.[111] Second, there are always more variables of a real system than a covering law or finite set of covering laws accounts for. Covering laws, if there are any, are few and far between.

Although generalizations play a role in all sciences, universal generalizations don't (Giere 1990, 103). In physics, for instance, theoretical laws may be considered abstract formulae that describe no particular circumstances. As is well known, the quantum Hamiltonian, classical force functions, and electromagnetic field vectors do not correspond precisely to anything in the world. There has yet to be found an exceptionless quantitative law or theory in any branch of science. That there might be one day is a *metaphysical* speculation. Even in high theoretical physics it is widely accepted that laws do not apply to a wide range of circumstances, i.e., are not universals. With regard to the life sciences, since species are internally heterogeneous and subject to transformation over time (through mutation, natural selection, etc.), generalizations about species members will have exceptions. If, as Davidson (1967) claims, laws of nature must be exceptionless, we must admit that perhaps there are none.

So far as science can say for now, only given *ceteris paribus* and *ceteris absentibus* clauses, that is, only in ideal or experimental conditions, do covering laws hold. Even ideal cases, e.g., the laws of motion of classical mechanics, are not well-confirmed empirical generalizations. Laws such as $F = ma$ are not empirical claims, let alone empirically verified universal generalizations, but rather general schemas that need to be filled in with specific force functions. Additions to the equation might make it a better approximation to the phenomena it seeks to explain, in light of what seems to be interminable natural complexity, it may be impossible to complete the process of supplementation. Could an equation exactly represent all existing gravitational forces? Since determining the precise laws of motion of even the most simple physical phenomena would involve equations incredibly more complex than any yet written down, and perhaps more complex than *could* be humanly surveyed, the most one can say is that somehow, in principle, it may be possible to determine the true laws of motion. But it seems that these laws would not be universal generalizations. And since science has proven more than capable of doing without them, it is unclear why striving to establish the true laws of motion, or any true laws for that matter, would be a high priority for science, let alone the basis for its cognitive authority and/or social standing (Giere 1990, 66-7). Paradoxically, the impressive success of science calls into question the imperative of absolute truth.

In order to make even paradigm cases of covering laws true, e.g., Snell's law or Boyle's law, an indefinite number of *ceteris paribus* clauses need to be added to the expression of the law, as do clauses restricting the class of phenomena of which the laws are true, but adding these clauses (1) means that the law cannot stand as a universal generalization, and (2) qualifies the explanatory value of the laws because they only explain ideal phenomena. The cost of explanatory power is descriptive power and vice versa. Thus, the other side of the problem is that as laws are suitably adjusted to conform to phenomena, their utility is diminished since this lies in covering a range of related phenomena in which a similar principle is operating. Even if a law could be stated that perfectly covers a specific case, the law would likely be so specific that it only describes that case, surrendering everything we wanted from explanation via law.

There is an aporia at the heart of the covering law model: laws are either too abstract or too concrete. "If . . . 'laws' are to be regarded as universal generalizations, they hover between falsity and vacuity. If stated with sufficient precision to be informative, they are always subject to some exceptions . . . If stated with sufficient generality or qualification to avoid exceptions, they cease to be usefully informative. At best, such 'laws' express only rough statistical generalizations" (Giere 1990, 17). Covering laws are literally false yet false laws are more useful than ultra-qualified true laws would be. Perhaps, like psychoanalysis, science works in the medium of inexact interpretations.[112]

If the ideal situations to which covering laws apply are either experimental situations or natural events and processes qualified by *ceteris paribus* and *ceteris absentibus* clauses, then laws may not be best conceived as expressing the fundamental truths, governing rules, or basic elements or structures of nature, the exposition of which promises to be fully satisfying when systematically integrated in a deductively complete totality. Perhaps it would be better, or at least it would be plausible, to characterize laws as *pragmatic formulas* that exhibit impressive organizing power and facilitate successful interventions in and discoveries about the natural world. On this conception, laws are at once, and indissociably, truth- and interest-bearing. If covering laws are representations, approximations, or idealizations of phenomena much more complex than they can express, then their authority is sourced in their success in guiding our interactions with phenomena of interest. Laws "need only conform enough to the material interacted with to [say] enable the engineer to succeed in getting the gene into the plasmid" or facilitate the specification of new content of a theory; they need not express strict truth, nor need they be deductively integrable components of a nomothetic totality (Longino 2002, 110).

If it is in virtue of their strong claims to objectivity that covering laws succumb to aporia, one might consider withdrawing such claims, or at least keeping them explicit as regulative ideals in the service of a classical metaphysical condition. Perhaps by disclaiming pretensions to rigorous truth or unconditional objectivity, indeed by denying the age old equation of truth, objectivity, and the unconditioned, a pragmatic vocabulary would express the truths of covering laws more truthfully.

The next set of difficulties besetting explanation via statements of covering law concern the metaphysical presuppositions of this form of explanation. If systematically integrated statements of universal law are maximally satisfying, (1) nature must be law-governed through and through such that there is a law or set of laws to cover every case, and (2) every law must be an irreplaceable element of a deductively complete whole.[113] Said otherwise, nature must be most knowable when known most universally: all lower-level laws must be deducible from, and so implied in, higher level laws.

One problem with describing nature as fully law-governed is that laws imply particular concepts of objects that limit their applicability. The law of universal gravitation holds only for non-charged bodies. Coulomb's law does not hold for massive objects. Classical mechanics assumes "small compact masses, rigid rods and point charges; but it is not very successful with things that are floppy, elastic or fluid" (Cartwright 1999, 12). As Kelvin pointed out, Newtonian models apply to things like "point masses, rigid rods, and springs, in general . . . inextendable, unbendable, stiff things" and so "can never simulate very much of the soft, continuous, elastic, and friction-full world around us" (Cartwright 1999, 48). Likewise, "quantum theory extends to all and only those situations that can be represented as composed of central potentials, scattering events, Coulomb interactions and harmonic oscillators," which, though expansive, is not an all-expansive range (Cartwright 1999, 196). No laws, not even paradigm-case laws, are universal generalizations. No laws govern in all domains. Laws are complicated, diverse, and limited in scope.

Given this, and given what was said above about *ceteris paribus* qualifications and the like, though there may be laws to describe every case, the laws that best describe specific cases are not of a form that can be integrated into a deductively complete whole. Laws could be integrated into a deductively complete whole only if nature is composed of homogenous classes of objects whose developments are systematically interrelated and regulated by universal principles, which it is not.[114]

If nature is law-governed through and through, at least in the way required for explanations through laws to be completely satisfactory, given causes would need to necessarily bring about given effects or at least increase the incidence of given effects in a statistically significant way, which they do not (always). A given cause need not bring about or increase the likelihood of an expected effect if the presence of the cause is associated with factors that impede or decrease the likelihood of the expected effect. This is known as Simpson's paradox: regular associations between any two variables in a given population can be reversed in subpopulations if there is a third variable correlated with both variables.[115] Stated otherwise, statements of law-governance assume *ceteris paribus* clauses — clauses stipulating that nothing interferes with a regular association between cause and effect. Causal laws are to some extent ephemeral and epiphenomenal; they arise from and obtain only with respect to a nomological machine (an ideal or experimental situation) in which fixed components with known capacities are arranged in an isolated and stable configuration such that the fixed relation of parts guarantees causal relations. Causes assume initial conditions, and initial conditions, though pervasively patterned, are perhaps irreducibly diverse. The most that can be said with confidence is that natural phenomena are constrained by laws but not determined in every detail, not even statistically

(Cartwright 1983, 49). It is far from certain that the particular is contained in the universal.

Though there may be a law or set of laws to describe every case, such a law or set of laws will not "cover" or "govern" every case: in virtue of their abstractness, laws are not principles that *determine* exactly what happens in a given case; and they do not accurately predict exactly what will happen in cases similar to those in which they are realized. Like laws, theories, and models, causes are abstractions, idealizations. There is always a more concrete description of the event or process for which a causal story seeks to account than that causal story, especially if that causal story takes the form of a causal law. First, causal laws assume, but do not account for, the intermediate factors that, *ex hypothesi*, ensure temporal continuity for individual causes. Assuming for the moment that nature is fully empirically determinate, there must always be something between a cause and an effect that carries the influence of the cause, and since this interval remains opaque in a causal law, causal laws are inadequate descriptions of nature, at least when measured by an ideal of total disclosure. Second, causal stories assume background narratives or prequels, i.e., accounts of initial conditions. Causal stories center on the sparking of a process waiting in the wings or the removal of an impediment such that something happens that would not happen otherwise or would be less likely to happen otherwise *given initial conditions assumed rather than recounted*. If a cause is understood as that which *always* brings about a given effect, there are no causes. If a cause in understood as increasing the probability of each of its effects in the right circumstances, then causal talk is of limited explanatory power and does not imply deductive-nomological integration. Causal laws, then, represent relations between kinds, not events; they are type-type, not token-token relations. Thus causal laws are either too abstract to precisely describe a given case or too concrete to be usefully informative, especially with respect to ambitions to establish natural principles. In contemporary statistical physics as much as in the life sciences, causally relevant antecedents are regularly understood as neither necessary nor sufficient.

Finally, given the well-known difficulties involved in differentiating causes from co-symptoms, and given the extent to which multiple, irreducible treatments of the same causal phenomena are possible (the causal laws that describe the phenomena are not reducible to one), the assumption that every law must be an irreplaceable element of a deductively complete whole is extremely difficult to sustain.[116] Is the image of nature as a deductively-nomologically integrated totality but ideology?

Another prevalent view of law, the conventional view, holds that laws are regularities that obtain among occurent or measurable properties. The instrumentalist theory of law holds that laws are regularities that cover the widest range of circumstances in the most efficient way. Any such view of law that centers on regularity of association rather than strict causal determination and concedes as implausible a view of nature as a systematically integrated totality of determinate substances and properties in thoroughgoing, lawfully regulated interaction, effectively releases science from the mandate to yield cognitive closure — full satisfaction consequent upon absolute determination. Or, if the disclosure of regularities, whether necessary or probabilistic, is claimed as the "truth-maker" of laws, the following objections ensue. First, regularity laws admit of accidental regularities — observed relative frequencies are not even true probabilities — and so even if such laws are, in a variety of contexts, better models than others, their explanatory power is limited. Second, regularity laws occlude singular or relatively rare events. They let in too little to be fully satisfactory and are insufficient for the practice of science, which is not exclusively concerned with regularities but also with what confounds expectations, stands apart as anomalous. Especially when it comes to forecasting and planning, exclusive focus on regularity is not adequate for the practice of science. Third, like covering laws, regularity laws require *ceteris paribus* and *ceteris absentibus* clauses which qualify their explanatory power. Deterministic regularity laws, necessary (necessary regular association between properties), just like probabilistic regularity laws, e.g., those of quantum mechanics, assume given antecedent conditions and non-intervention of confounding factors. Generally, reliable regularity at the level of details is rare; it takes ideal or experimental conditions, what Cartwright calls nomological machines, to get such reliable regularity. That is, reliable regularity requires conditions to be just right for a system to exercise it capacities in repeatable ways. More strongly, we can say, following Cartwright (1999), that there are no regularities in nature absent shielding conditions. $F = ma$ only if, counterfactually, force operates unimpeded. Deterministic regularity laws are falsifying, while probabilistic regularity laws fails to satisfy the grand ambitions of lawful explanation.[117]

That science is best understood as pursuing, let alone must be understood as pursuing, the progressive disclosure of the systematically interconnected lawful operations (rules) of nature, i.e., as aspiring to complete — and completely formalized — determinacy, is less than convincing. Establishing laws and their interconnections is important, but not necessarily because "[s]cientific progress consists mainly in decreasing gradually the number of separate and independent laws through an unceasing extension of their connections" (Compte 6: 600). Cartwright, for instance, has defended the strategy of characterizing the natural world through causal laws because causal laws pick out the right properties on which to condition, thus contributes substantially to the development of science.

Experiments

Given what has been said of the ideality of scientific knowledge, we are now in a position to account for the powers and limits of scientific experimentation. Experiments are nomological machines. They are built to fit or elaborate models. They control initial conditions and intervening variables such that dependency relations can be established, but because they must shield off the inordinate complexity and diversity of the natural world, they cannot perfectly predict or retrodict causal claims about the world outside the experimental setup. Even in an ideal case where the law to be established by an experiment is deductively implied by data together with the description of experimental setup and background assumptions, the law so established is true of a model, not of the world.

The data yielded by experimentation support *extrapolations* from controlled situations (laboratories or technical devices) to less regulated settings, but if there is no perfect parallelism between the controlled and the uncontrolled, the micro and the macro, the cognitive yield of experimental findings is qualified. Experiments cannot establish universal laws of nature. At best, they can establish that laws hold for conditions similar enough to those of the experiment, i.e., suggest an analogy (thus raise difficult questions concerning analogies with and within nature). Since the point of an experiment is to take into account all and only those circumstances that the laws in question govern, the scope of its findings will be limited. Even paradigmatic laws, e.g., the laws of physics, may be literally true only of what we make (Cartwright 1999, 47). And to the extent that circumstances remain which no experimental model precisely fits, the reach of science is limited, its deliverances qualified.

Further, since there are always contingencies in the design, execution, and interpretation of experiments, they may strongly suggest but cannot compel choices among competing theories or hypotheses.[118] What makes for proper experimental execution and what to make of the yield of experiments are subjects of unending, but not unconstrained, negotiation. As ethnomethodologists and sociologists have long argued, establishing what the observational data are, what the results of an experiment are (i.e., distinguishing between a genuine result and an artifact of the experimental situation), what a genuine anomaly is, and so forth, are highly controversial affairs. Though experimental science may yield highly precise and/or informative results, it does not yield unambiguous knowledge, e.g., absolutely clear criteria to determine when x is the case and when not. This is most clear in situations where what it is for an experiment to "work" in the context of a new and controversial area has not yet been operationalized. In such situations, what will count as replication of an experiment is manifestly problematic. Ideally, the conversation of science will be as unending as that of psychoanalysis.[119]

CONCLUDING REMARKS ON IDEALITY, METHODOLOGY, AND OBJECTIVITY

For science to yield unconditionally satisfying knowledge, thoroughly objective and exhaustively explanatory knowledge, nature must exhibit not the least recalcitrance to reason. Nature, fully unshrouded, would have to reveal itself as both thoroughly deterministic and unconditionally available to the methodologically regulated human regard. Nature, then, would be indistinguishable from the projection of reason as the order and structure of all there is, thoroughly ideal.[120] For scientific knowledge to satisfy absolutely, the order and operations of nature must manifest unreserved compliance with human interests in nature's intelligibility and manipulability, and reciprocally, such interests must be aligned with, or rationally regulated by, the deliverances of science — fully in accord with its decisive determination of rational possibility. Possession of nature's formulae would mean implicit possession of empirically certifiable predictions bearing on the unfolding of all natural phenomena. Our predictive prowess and prospects for control would be advanced to their greatest heights — and presumably in harmony. For science to satisfy absolutely, the deep architectonics of nature and the imperatives of human interest must be disclosed as utterly harmonious, essentially identical. Nature and humanity would be as one, fully reconciled, united in the ideality of total self-transparency.

This beautiful, terrifying dream is surely tempting; indeed its powerful allure may have played no small part in the impressive developments of modern science. But it is a dream nevertheless. Far from empirically or metaphysically grounded, it is at most a regulative ideal — perhaps in some ways a dream-image consolidating unfocused desire and unnegotiated, near-imponderable suffering, a romantic reaction to the world's uninterrupted barbarity. The axiom of nature's empirical and logical determinacy has not yet been, and given what we know of the diversity and complexity of nature, likely will not be established as a valid empirical induction. Indeed, this axiom, as an axiom, is strictly indemonstrable. No matter the extent to which nature is found to be empirically and logically determinate, the inference that nature as such is empirically and logically determinate cannot but be a leap of faith, a speculative surplus indemonstrable within the domain it delimits. Likewise, the axiom that the logically and empirically determinate order of nature is unreservedly available to methodologically regulated human inquiry, the assumption that nature and reason are one, can only be taken on credit of faith.

And like all beautiful images, its aggressive integration of the non-identical makes of its beauty something ugly.

Ideally, science would like to bequeath humanity a complete system of mathematical formulas from which the developments of all concrete phenomena can be derived, fully explained and exactly predicted. But deductive closure obtains only to the extent that the only relevant factors at work are those that can be appropriately, indeed uncontentiously, modeled by a theory, which, as we have seen, is never. Unless science can develop a deductively complete system of theories that, both individually and severally, model objects without losing in scope what they gain in precision, its grand promises remain unredeemed, its satisfactions limited. This is not to say that what science offers in the meantime, e.g., powerful organizational schemes, robust predictive power, and genuine knowledge of dependency relations and law-like generalizations within particular systems, is by any means negligible. Science offers a great deal, but not everything promised.

Ideally, science would like to provide secure, repeatable means to obtain reliable results. But to the extent that it is interested in extending knowledge and the means of obtaining it, not just endlessly justifying extant cognitive tools and reverifying hypotheses, science cannot refrain from innovating, speculating, essaying endlessly.

Ideally, science would like to be a linear progression of knowledge accumulation, or better, a progressive integration of the totality of empirical knowledge into a deductively complete system. But, so it seems, diverse interests, sensitivities, and urgencies (perspectives) motivate and organize scientific investigative pursuits, thus science proceeds simultaneously along a number of paths that may not meet in the end. So it seems, the integration science might achieve will involve reflective judgment and so will be, to some extent, irremediably uncertain, fragile, and prone to elaboration otherwise. Scientific content reflects, and if self-conscious, respects, the diversity of knowers.

What a less ideal science of a less ideal nature offers, and can be expected to offer, is enhanced instrumental felicity in and genuine knowledge of the natural world that reveals by concealing, discloses by distorting, approximates, improvises, and idealizes. Science can be expected to yield highly precise knowledge of systems that we make, e.g., technological devises or controlled experimental situations, but less precise knowledge of nature's inordinately complex givenness and becoming beyond the field of volition. Nature is uncircumscribable. Science can be expected to provide powerful organizational and classificatory schemes, but not the one true schema of nature. It can be expected to continue to press on into uncharted realms and to refine, even revolutionize, our understanding of what has become obstinately familiar, adding greatly to the wealth of human knowledge and contributing enormously to our predictive acumen and instrumental efficacy, but not to reach completion, coming to rest in a paroxysm of cognitive satisfaction. Science presses on into new landscapes of ignorance,[121] which often means treading over well-worn ground, mapping the terrain only by striding over or turning a blind eye to some of its empirical features, by exaggerating and inflating, and so invariably deflating and distorting — by idealizing. What science can offer are discoveries not about nature's universal rules but about relatively stable capacities in particular domains and about how phenomena possessed of these capacities behave in more complex settings. Science develops through analogical extrapolations from what is established with a great deal of certainty and precision in artificial systems to what is expected to occur in the less controlled, much more complex order(s) of nature. Shuttling back and forth between the controlled and the uncontrolled, scientific progress may be conceived as an endless specification of the degree to which artificial systems appropriately model nature, as advancing knowledge of nature both in its determinable specificity and its irreducible opacity.

A paramount danger to be avoided in the development of science, then, is devolution into methodologism: the illicit promotion of a particular method that, given particular aims and interests, is arguably appropriate for the investigation of particular sorts of objects, to *the* valid method of inquiry — a surreptitious design on hegemony, a sweeping repudiation of natural complexity and of the scientific significance of human plurality.[122] Methodologism names the penchant to level illusory claims to objectivity by suppressing the ways in which the objects about which one inquires are, indeed must be, schematized or interpretively constituted by the particular method of inquiry, thus bear traces of contingency. It is an effort to efface science's perspectival character that is cognitively stultifying, thus self-defeating, insofar as it enforces an unnecessarily ascetic restriction on scientific development, which it then maroons in the stagnant swamps of positivism as it urges the conflation of knowledge of the objectifications of a particular method, its ob-jects, with knowledge of objects in their pure givenness. Methodologism depletes science of the potential for rational self-consciousness by denying the exorbitance of its object and enterprise.

The ruse of methodologism preys on the desire for and prevalent misunderstanding of objective knowledge. By remaining methodologically *external* to the object of inquiry, it generates an illusory sense that the knowledge it yields is subject-independent, interest-free: knowledge of the thing in itself. This is abstraction and homogenization — voracious idealization, subjective imposition — parading as the royal road to objectivity. In its promise that the properly regulated application of the appropriate cognitive processes — empirical rules or *a priori* principles of understanding — will yield objective (subject-neutral) knowledge of any possible object, methodologism conceals its efforts to enthrone some particular method and its associated interests, orientations, and corresponding concept of an object as absolutely valid, universal. Such a ruse, to be sure, is rarely if ever intentional. Enormously impressed by the prior success of the method promoted to absolute validity, its advocates are most often under its spell.

The concept of an object implied in the method advocated *can* model objects in general, or at least a diverse array of objects. Thus methodologism banks on interest in methodological security and the belief that the proper application of reason will eventually unlock all of nature's secrets being sufficiently strong to generate large-scale readiness to (1) relegate to unintelligibility or irrelevance those objects or aspects of objects that cannot be perfectly or (given various aims and interests) best modeled by the method proposed, hence too the corresponding interests, and (2) convert the limitations dictated by the particular method and its freighted concept of an object into a reason to pursue research into objects so constituted ever further. Structural limitation is denied by its framing as incomplete application; cognitive dissatisfaction is converted into the zealous pursuit of an ever elusive goal (exhaustive objectivity). Methodologism is method in bad faith.

Methodologism forfeits the refined responsiveness to particular sorts of interest-mediated objects that various methods afford, and so their perspectivally inflected cognitive and practical yield, for the sake of sponsoring the illusion of subject-purified knowledge. It trades the varieties of insights and opportunities afforded by diverse modes of inquiry for the particular satisfaction of an impossible quest for certainty and complete control. Methodologism is mythology.

Attempting to immunize inquiry from the recalcitrance or resistance of phenomena vis-à-vis the particular method pursued and its implied concept of an object, and so to the transformations of investigative strategy and object-modeling such recalcitrance or resistance may incite, methodologism sacrifices science's aspiration to objectivity. Or better, objectivities: rigorous expositions of objects as they are, which is to say, as they are possessed of certain capacities, constrained to develop in particular ways in particular conditions and exert specific effects in those conditions, but also as they are given to and indefinitely elaborable through an irreducible plurality of perspectives. By preemptively insulating inquiry from competing forms of disclosure afforded by other methods and their models, and so from the dialectical contestation or interplay of competing perspectives, methodologism lends itself to intemperately bold claims to cognitive exhaustion, risks stultifying the development of science, and sacrificing objectivity understood as a mutually disclosing co-responsiveness of method and object by means of which implicit interests and the like are made reflectively available and objects are recurrently revealed as both informatively determinable by and withdrawing from a particular methodological regard, as complex admixtures of determinacy and indeterminacy, clarity and opacity.

Methodologism is just another reductionism. It attempts to bring "the sensible surrounding world to univocal determination," to efface the multiplicity of perspectives through which nature can be disclosed, and so to sweepingly deny the constitutive interest-mediation of science, by insisting that the proper pursuit of knowledge proceeds through the elaboration of shared foci embedded in a privileged methodology (Husserl 1970, 29). It promises deliverance of a truth "of which everyone who can understand and use this method can convince himself" (ibid 29) — much like what Freud says of psychoanalysis in "Constructions in Analysis." Seemingly possessed of great democratic virtues, methodologism exploiting the value of and extorts desires for sharing, belonging, and connectedness (solidarity) in order to force a reconciliation, a unity achieved through the expulsion of those who do not and that which does not conform. It asks for a common focus, a shared structure of attention, which is not in the least objectionable until it becomes hypostasized, i.e., at the point where method becomes methodologism. Its conniving assault on human plurality, its exorbitant drive to regulate disagreement, is at one with its violence to truth.

Methodologism would repudiate prospects for advancing scientific (self-)understanding for the fantasmatic assurance of community. It is an ethico-political fantasy of stable, harmonious community (both amongst humanity and between humanity and nature) the allure of which is in no small part predicated on the promise of coextensive self-possession (assured investigative propriety) and self-annihilation (a mystical dissolution of subjectivity through which objects become available in their unencumbered self-presence). Might the temptation of methodologism register the unmetabolized anxieties of modern social life? Fixated on and terrified by human and natural plurality, thus indeterminacy, methodologism repudiates them as the abyss of the infinite; but it is from this abyss that it draws its anxious momentum. It cannot fully efface what it seeks to deny.[123]

NOTES

1. Cf. Kant *CPR* A366-80.

2. Pennybacker (1988) reports experimental confirmation that talking about and reliving traumatic experiences generates a sense of relief. Smith and Glass' (1977) review of 375 studies concludes that undergoing any therapy (behavioral, psychodynamic, etc; the studies did not include "proper" psychoanalysis) will lead to one being better off than 75% of the no-therapy population and that the differences in outcome rates between different psychotherapies are negligible. Smith, Glass, and Miller's (1980) review of 475 studies confirms that treatment with psychotherapy (relatively short psychotherapy, averaging 16 sessions each) is better than no treatment. They found that patients undergoing psychotherapy improved at an outcome rate of .85 of a standard deviation; later metaanalyses suggest results up to a full standard deviation (Shapiro and Shapiro 1982). The findings of Prioleau, Murdock, and Brody (1983), as well as reviews by Rachman and Wilson (1980), Kline (1981), and Erwin (1988) suggest that outcomes from psychotherapy (not specifically psychoanalysis) are no better than outcome rates for placebo-treated groups. Slightly more specific evidence is provided by Brill et al. (1964): placebo groups showed as much improvement as the psychoanalytically-oriented treatment group. Sloane et al. (1975) found that just making periodic contact (no placebo) leads to some measure of improvement; and Frank (1983) shows distress dropping after initial interviews, before placebo treatment. These studies suggest that the following factors may impact outcome: spontaneous remission, belief that one is receiving effective treatment, expectation that one will

soon receive treatment, decision to enter therapy, connection with the therapist, and initial discussion of difficulties. More recent studies, such as those of Orlinsky (1994), Wampold (2002), and Hovarth (2005) confirm that the establishment of a therapeutic relationship is consistently associated with positive outcomes.

However, Lambert and Bergin (1994) found that psychotherapy generates results superior to nonspecific treatment, placebo, and no-treatment. Fisher and Greenberg's (1996) review indicates that six studies confirm that the positive changes brought about by specifically psychoanalytic processes are greater than those evident in no-treatment control groups (though there are problems with these studies; also cf. Heinzel et al.'s (1998) review. Leichsenring, Rabung, and Leibing's (2004) review also found that of untreated waiting-list patients and patients treated by family doctors who were in need of psychotherapy, very few experienced any relevant change (d = .12; SD = .19). Leichsenring (2005) found that "controlled quasi-experimental effectiveness studies provided evidence that psychoanalytic therapy is . . . more effective than no treatment or treatment as usual [= by a primary care physician]" (858). Bachrach et al.'s (1991) review is also relevant, as it indicates that (again, though there are problems with the studies — there was no comparison with placebo or wait-list groups, there was a possibility of bias in assessing outcome, and there was no standardization of terms such as "improvement" or "analytic process"), improvement rates for suitable psychoanalytic patients ranged from 60-90%. This figure has been prevalent since the early days of empirical research. The methodologically shabby but still pertinent studies of Coriat (1917) and Fenichel (1930) found, respectively, that out of 93 cases of psychoanalysis, 73% improved, and out of 721 cases, 60% improved. Shortly thereafter, Kessel and Hyman (1933) report a striking success ratio: of 29 neurotic patients treated, 27 clearly benefited from psychoanalysis. A few years later, Jones (1936) reports on an improvement rate a bit below Bachrach's range: only 47% of 59 neurotics treated with psychoanalysis substantially improved. The number jumps back up to the low end of Bachrach's range when, the following year, Alexander reports that of 157 cases, 63% of the neurotics improve significantly from psychoanalysis. Knight's (1941) review of the previous studies plus 100 new cases found a 60% improvement rate for neurotics —just at the low end of Bachrach's range. For more on these "first-generation" studies, cf. Wallerstein 2004, pp. 119-123. Later studies confirm that improvement rates approximate Bachrach's range. According to Goldberger, Reuben, and Silberschatz's review (1976), "[s]even of the 31 studies report improvement rates below 50% and 24 studies report improvement rates above 50%. Eleven studies report improvement rates above 75% . . . . three of six studies of phobias report improvement of rates of less than 50%, whereas three of six anxiety neurosis studies report improvement rates above 75% . . . . eight of the nine studies of compulsions report better than 50% improvement rates, and . . . six of the hysteria studies report improvement rates over 50%" (516). They conclude that "[a]n average of 64.4% of total cases were symptom free following psychotherapy . . . . The rate of improvement in terms of personality adjustment was 58%" (532). Earle (1979) reports significant improvement for neurotic patients in 55-60% of cases. "Third-generation" studies report slightly lower outcome rates. Kantrowitz, Paolitto et al. (1986) and Katz et al. (1987) report that of 22 supervised psychoanalyses in Boston in the 70s, 41% had successful results. For more on the "third-generation" studies, cf. Wallerstein 2004, pp. 133-145. However, a follow-up study of psychoanalyses and psychoanalytic psychotherapies conducted by the German Psychoanalytic Association found that 70-80% of clients experienced positive and stable results, as assessed by themselves, their analysts, independent psychoanalytic and non-analytic experts, studies of sick leave taken subsequent to treatment termination, and questionnaires (Leuzinger-Bohleber et al., 2003). Rudolf et al.'s (1994) study similarly finds that of those treated with psychoanalytic therapy, 76% improved. Leuzinger-Bohleber, Stuhrast, Rüger, and Beutel's (2003) study finds positive, stable change at 6.5 years after the treatment in 70-80% of patients. And de Maat, de Jonghe, Schoevers, and Dekker's (2008) review, which surveys 1,431 analyses, reports similar findings for cases of moderate/mixed pathology.

3. In the face of the available evidence, it is no longer possible to accept Freud's claims that there is no need for statistical comparison with results from untreated control groups or from patients treated by rival therapies (SE 16: 461-2; regarding Freud's aversion to statistics, cf. SE 22: 152) . Already in 1954 Glover noted that, in his experience, psychoanalysis is not

more successful than other forms of therapy. And even when looking to the "rough figures as can be obtained," it does not seem, in his estimation, that "psychoanalysis is notably more successful than other forms of therapy" (1954, 393). On the basis of his experiences, Rangell (1981) concurs: "I have been able to reach convincing elements of patient's infantile neuroses in consistent analytic psychotherapy, with results comparable to what I have come to expect in [strict] psychoanalysis" (680). Fisher and Greenberg's (1985) review concludes that outcome rates for psychoanalysis are comparable to outcome rates for other treatments — Smith, Glass, and Miller's (1980) study agrees; as do the studies of Luborsky, Singer, and Luborsky (1975), Frank (1982), DeLeon, VandenBos, and Cummings (1983), Kiesler (1985), Lambert, Shapiro, and Bergin (1986), Stiles, Shapiro, and Eliott (1986), and von Rad, Senf, and Bräutigam (1998) — and that strict adherence to the psychoanalytic model does not significantly impact outcome. France's National Institute for Health and Medical Research recently published a report on the comparative efficacy of treatment options, finding that out of 1000 studies of therapies that sufficiently respected an evidence-based medicine protocol, the most effective were cognitive-behavioral therapies and the least effective were psychodynamic therapies (INSERM, 2004). However, Earle (1979), Earle and Goldberg (1984), Weber, Bachrach et al. (1985), Rudolf (1991), and Heuft, Seibuechler-Engec, Taschke, and Senf (1996) found that psychoanalysis leads to the highest levels of therapeutic benefit. The claim that outcome rates for psychoanalysis and other psychotherapies are equivalent is reconfirmed by Luborsky and Spence's 1978 study (338), Wallerstein's Menninger Foundation Studies (1986), and Fisher and Greenberg's (1996) review. In the latter, Fisher and Greenberg report evidence that psychoanalysis does not lead to a greater magnitude of effects than psychodynamic psychotherapy (260) and that "[t]he chance to vent thought and feelings in a caring relationship with a strong therapist figure who serves a mediating role between the patient and society is a potent factor common to most psychotherapies as well as influence processes in general (e.g. Frank & Frank, 1991; Strupp & Hadley, 1979)" (212). Later, they add that "[i]t now appears that providing a coherent rational framework for conceptualizing problems may be of more importance than what the particular framework happens to be. Consistent with this idea Luborsky (1984) found that the degree of adherence to a treatment manual (the degree of treatment 'purity') predicted outcome with different treatments regardless of which treatment model was used" (212). Contra the 1985 findings, strict adherence to a particular model does seem to matter for outcome, but it doesn't seem to matter what that model is.

In fact, most of the evidence suggests that what we would expect to impact outcome rates generally doesn't. For instance, Heilbrunn (1963, 1966) undertook two surveys of his practice, finding each time that varying treatment duration and intensity does not impact outcome. A more systematic study was organized by Wallerstein (The Psychotherapy Research Project of the Menninger Foundation, described in *42 Lives in Treatment*) in which, through random assignment, 21 people were treated with psychoanalysis and 21 with psychoanalytically-oriented psychotherapy. Evaluations of these therapies concluded that the "active ingredients" and results of the two types of therapies were basically indistinguishable. More specifically, it was found that there are no unique benefits to psychoanalysis, that longer-term treatment does not positively correlate with better results (contrary to popular belief, longer-term treatment does not yield more lasting effects), and that insight inclined psychoanalysis do not generate deeper structural changes, more stable and enduring changes, or more useful changes than therapeutic practices that are more "supportive" (insight and change are not appreciably correlated) (Wallerstein 1986, 720-730; Wallerstein 2004, 140-141; compare with SE 7: 252ff). What's more, Wallerstein found both that psychoanalysis is routinely conducted in a more supportive manner than expected, and that, arguably, supportive rather than expressive elements accounted for more positive changes than anticipated (2004, p. 144). Eisenstein, Levy, and Marmor's (1994) study agrees with Wallerstein's on the point that insight does not significantly correlate with positive outcome. And Sandell (1999) and Sandell et al. (2000) corroborate the claim that supportive as against "classical" technique is more effective. Also of interest is Andrade's (2005) finding that "[a]s a primary factor in psychic change, interpretation is limited in effectiveness in pathologies arising from the verbal phase, related to explicit memories, with no effect in the pre-verbal phase where implicit memories are found" (697). Support for the claim that interpretations contribute less to insight than expected can be found in Gassner et al. (1982)

and Elliott (1991). However, cf. Friedman, Garrison, Bucci, and Gorman (2005). Heinzel et al.'s (1998) study found no difference in outcome between Freudian, Adlerian, and Jungian therapies. Leuzinger-Bohleber, Stuhrast, Rüger, and Beutel's (2003) study found that the analyst's partisan orientation (whether ego psychologist, Kleinian, self-psychologist, or intersubjectivist) did not significantly bear on therapeutic results for those with "good-enough" outcomes.

The factors that do impact outcome are, generally, rather surprising. One unsurprising factor is length of treatment. Bachrach (1959), Erle (1979), Freedman, Hoffenberg, Vorus, and Frosch (1999), Rudolf et al. (2004), Leichsenring (2004, 2005), and Friedman, Garrison, Bucci, and Gorman (2005) find that those who stay in treatment longer tend to have better outcomes. Kachele (1999) corroborates this claim with respect to clients with eating disorders. That brief therapies are not as effective as they are often touted to be is supported by Westen and Morrison (2001). (However, cf. de Maat et al. (2008) for contrary findings.) On a more surprising note, Eisenstein, Levy, and Marmor (1994) find that factors such as the therapist's personality, values, and style are much more significant than has been acknowledged. Similarly, Strupp, Wallach, Wogan, and Jenkins (1963) find that the analyst's liking the analysand and having shared values and interests are good prognostic factors. Kantrowitz et al. (1989), Kantrowitz et al. (1990), and Freedman, Hoffenberg, Vorus, and Frosch (1999), have established that therapist-patient "match" bears significantly on outcome. More specifically, studies have shown that having an analyst who is experienced as empathetic, warm, and genuine positively effects outcome (Patterson 1984; this gives some support to preferring Kohutian or Winnicottian procedures over others, and reason to expect poor outcomes for Lacanian psychoanalysis) and that having an analyst who is "flexible," e.g., prone to tailor interpersonal style to the patient rather than rigidly adhere to her preferred method, leads to better outcomes (Beutler and Clarkin 1990; Blatt and Felson 1993; contra Fisher/Greenberg and Luborsky). Høglend's (2004) recent review (mostly of short-term therapies) suggests that "[n]on-specific factors, such as understanding, attention, and a good relationship between the therapist and patient account for all, or almost all change (Baskin, Tierney, Minamy, & Wampold, 2003; Frank 1971; Rosenzweig, 1936)" (282). Generally, studies have shown that the analytic relationship (therapeutic alliance) significantly impacts outcome (Horvath and Symonds 1991, Rudolf and Manz 1993, Beutler, Machado and Allsetetter Neufeldt 1994, Lambert and Bergin 1994). Eisenstein, Levy, and Marmor (1994) also find that suggestion and persuasion play a significant role in healing. As noted above, Fisher and Greenberg's (1996) metareview suggests that having a consistent framework within which to conceptualize one's difficulties positively impacts outcome. And if we put together (1) the findings of Ross and Conway (1986), Loftus (1993), and Brewin, Andrews, and Gotlib (1993) that memory can be molded by suggestion and by a desire to perceive consistency and continuity between current and past behaviors and attitudes, with (2) the findings of Eisenstein, Levy, and Marmor's (1994) that persuasion and suggestion play a major role in healing, then it seems that valid insight matters much less for therapeutic outcome than does the therapist's persuasive efficacy in provisioning a coherent framework for self-interpretation. That is, the evidence is much more on the side of the "creation/discovery" thesis than the classical "freedom through self-knowledge" thesis.

Another factor that significantly impacts outcome is the client's character structure. Fisher and Greenberg's (1996) review suggests that "analytically oriented therapists were significantly more effective when working with patients whose coping styles were internal/intropunitive rather than external/impulsive. In contrast, behavioral clinicians obtained their best results with patients relying on externalizing, acting-out coping mechanisms" (250). Summarizing the findings of Blatt and Felson (1993), Fisher and Greenberg (1996) suggest that "patients who were cognitively oriented, self-critical, and concerned with issues of autonomy and self-worth proved more likely than interpersonally oriented, dependent patients to benefit from psychoanalysis" (251).

4. Kantrowitz, Katz, et al. (1989), p. 899; Kantrowitz, Katz, and Paolitto (1990); Kantrowitz (1993), p. 327.

5. However, cf. Suerbaum and Michetti (2002).

6. That psychoanalysis sponsors reflection on ends, and not just in the sense of prudential reasoning in view of accomplishing publicly intelligible aims or deliberation regarding the

ordering of commitments and values, is a crucial feature of its claim to modernism-materialism. Maintaining the clinical relationship rather than immediately acceding to dispositions of emotional and/or ethical response to what unfolds therein — the supervenience of psychoanalytic functionality on "ethical life" — does not deny, but rather suspends, seeking to preserve for another future, the claims of the material registered by such responsive inclinations; makes them (barely, as if an intermittent burst through a field of distortion) audible *as* claims. The *demanding* character of such material, the claim it presses against standing regimes of intelligibility and response (socially sanctified and interpersonally entrenched need-interpretations), thus its significance as *unrecognized injury*, is registered in the self-restraint of the analyst (and eventually, assuming the efficacy of analytic exemplarity, in the reflective capacity of the analysand wherein it becomes a formally productive derangement, an unassimilated residue of nameless need interrupting, and perhaps thereupon reanimating, the projection and pursuit of one's conception of the good). Analytic neutrality — more broadly, commitment to maintaining the clinical environment — is the exilic afterlife of injury having become nearly-mute plaintiveness upon its overcoding by standing regimes of intelligibility and response. Bearing such material with the aims of therapy intact rather than immediately acceding to impulses to alleviate, if only by rendering intelligible, the suffering it expresses, makes of analytic "neutrality" a medium for sustaining suffering and thereby a form of commitment to the freedom of the analysand. Psychoanalysis acknowledges the not yet vanquished insistence of need under conditions of its instrumentalized disparaging and expulsion, preserves an institutional space for undischargeable plaint (a counter-institution *par excellence* — thus an impossible endeavor), by attending to need's at once muted and overdetermined significance. The refusal to defuse and dismiss the significance of need by prompt gratification or interpretation is the echoing silence on the condition of which need might yet become eloquent. Abiding the frustration of nonresponsiveness is a condition for the experience of objective alienation, and thus for freedom.

7. Let's suppose that there is nothing that exceeds science's predictive powers and that it has been able to formulate all of nature, even all social occurrences, in neat equations. Even then the claim to exhaustiveness would be unintelligible. Science's claim to exhaustiveness would have to be measured against some other description of the world that is shown to be both limited and itself explained by science. Even if science could explain why the competing description arose, could solve all of the problems that are solved by the competing description as well as all the problems the competing description left open, and could point to and solve problems that do not even come into view under the competing description, *even then* though we would have every reason in the world to be highly satisfied with science, its claim to exhaustiveness would be unintelligible. The very idea of a competing description negates the claim to exhaustiveness. All that is shown is that it is rationally desirable for a more successful description to subsume a less successful one, not that the more successful description is exhaustive. There may even be reasons to stick with the subsumed description. And skepticism would not be fully blocked. Now, to be more realistic, let's assume that there are features of the world, call them intentionality, spontaneity (human autonomy and unpredictable natural events), meaning, experience, and value, that do not fit into the scientific image of the world. And let's say that that these things matter. If we do, science's claim to exhaustiveness is foiled.

8. Cf. Oppenheim and Putnam (1958); Kant *CPR* A556/B584, A832, B599ff., B679, B682, and *CJ* 397-8/209; Hegel *W* 17: 393 and 429ff.

9. To the extent that psychoanalysts can organize their endeavors in a way that contributes to the pursuit of objective knowledge without faltering in their responsibilities to their clients, there is certainly no objection to their doing so. One could even make the case that therapeutic responsibility obligates psychoanalysts to learn what they can about features of psychic life that are lawfully or probabilistically determinate. But by the same token, they are obliged to suspend the assumption of thoroughgoing lawful or probabilistic determinism and its corollaries, and inquire into therapeutically relevant features of psychic life on the assumption of their ontological indeterminacy. Antinomy is unavoidable. Psychoanalysis may betray itself and its clients by conducting itself in a manner that contributes to the pursuit of objective knowledge inasmuch as this requires the abdication of (1) interpretive resources and practices that science deems unreliable or invalid (countertransference, "listening with the third ear," routine psycho-

analytic inferences, etc.), (2) strategies of interpretation that do not employ conceptually precise hypotheses capable of ruling out alternatives and experimental verification, (3) assumptions that guarantee a limit to its claims to objectivity (the insuperable distortion of unconscious material, psychic singularity and indeterminacy, etc.), and (4) speculations pursued for therapeutically and/or theoretically exploratory purposes. Equally, psychoanalysis may betray itself and its clients if it fails to discern causal mechanisms that bear on suffering and healing, establish valid classificatory schemes, and so on. Emphasizing experiences of singularity and indeterminacy too vehemently results in unnecessary blindness and cognitive vacuity. Psychoanalysis cannot refrain from developing theoretical intermediaries (neither universal generalizations nor a- or quasi-conceptual traces of singular events) without practical self-defeat and cognitive wistlessness. *Pro tem*, psychoanalysis must accede to the demands of science *and* must not fail to see what can be seen, to do what can be done, by suspending those demands and following through on its assumptions of psychic indeterminacy, singularity, insuperable obscurity, and the like. If it turns out that psychoanalytic therapy is so immensely improved by the contributions of objectivity-aspiring science that retaining the manifest image of psychic life becomes irrational, so much the better. Wagering that it will be is neither rational nor irrational.

10. E.g., ethnographic and anthropological evidence of children's sex play may decisively disconfirm Freud's latency hypothesis only if it is construed as a universal claim. For an example of a prominent author who completely misses the boat on this point, cf. Westen (1990) "Toward a Revised Theory of Borderline Relations: Contributions of Empirical Research."

11. Cf. Aristotle, *Nicomachean Ethics* and Hirschman (1997) *The Passions and the Interests.*

12. No doubt we are moving a bit fast and loose here. A more adequate response to the question of what could count as failure within psychoanalysis would first distinguish between various types of psychoanalytic theory (metapsychology, theory of technique, theory of pathology, developmental theory, applied psychoanalytic theory, etc.) and between the various types of claims involved in them (interpretive claims, axioms and principles, practical suggestions, observations, diagnoses, etc.) and then ask what sorts of informative failure(s) each can run into. The basic principles of a more fine-grained analysis, I hope, are evident in this fairly cursory treatment of the question.

13. Interest in predictive power is especially prevalent in contemporary high energy physics, where theories are ordinarily construed as instruments of prediction and devices employed in experimental research are often explicitly designed to yield data that will be highly amenable to simple and elegant formulation in predictive calculations.

14. Cf. Van Fraassen (1980) *The Scientific Image.*

15. As Laudan and others have extensively shown, there are numerous cases in the history of science where it is known that the "best explanation" is false. E.g., although the theory of electromagnetic aether has independent sources of support collected for over a century and a half, it was widely believed to be false (1981, pp. 19-49).

16. I am inclined to agree with Giere that "there is no abstract property called 'simplicity' that some scientific models exhibit to a greater degree than others. It is just not the case that some models in nuclear physics are intrinsically simpler than others in the same abstract way that some models of evolutionary biology are simpler than others. It is useless to seek a general analysis of simplicity in the abstract . . . Of course, adherents of a rival approach are not compelled to agree with the judgment that the excluded models are less simple, or that the features designated as indicative of greater simplicity are desirable" (1990, p. 225). Cf. Eldridge 1997, p. 161.

17. Cf. Kuhn 1970a, pp. 199-200, Kuhn 1970b, p. 262, and Richard Bernstein's discussion of these and related passages in *Beyond Objectivism and Relativism* (1983), Part II.

18. For Kant's statement on philosophy as the arbiter of reason and tribunal of secondary sciences, see (1992) *The Conflict of the Faculties.* On the difficulties involved in elaborating this position, especially the performative difficulties, see Hent de Vries (2001) *Religion and Violence*, pp. 18-122 and (1999) *Philosophy and the Turn to Religion*, pp. 359-430.

19. Further, the various sciences are internally heterogeneous. With reference to the disunity biology, cf. Dupré (1995) and Rosenberg (1994). With reference to the disunity of

physics, cf. Giere (2006), e.g., "the two most fundamental sets of principles, those of quantum mechanics and general relativity, are incompatible. The principles of quantum mechanics presume a flat space-time that is denied by general relativity. But even if someone succeeds in producing unified principles of quantum gravity, it is doubtful that the resulting models could provide an exact fit to any significant portion of reality" (66).

20. Also see Kitcher (1984) "Species." For a treatment of chemistry similar to Dupré's treatment of biology, cf. LaPorte (2004, chapter 4). Also see Scerri (1991, 1994).

21. E.g., Hertz argues in *Electric Waves* that there are three models of Maxwell's electromagnetic theory, all of which imply equivalent predictions and can be expressed by the same equations. Or consider competing interpretations of quantum mechanics: the Copenhagen interpretation was and remains privileged over the Bohm interpretation even though "there is general agreement that the two theories agree on all implications that are empirically detectable. Thus, no experiment could provide decisive evidence in favor of one over the other. But they are conceptually very different. So it is difficult to argue that they are mere notational variants. On the standard [Copenhagen] interpretation, quantum phenomena are inherently probabilistic. The Bohm theory is deterministic. Standard quantum mechanics is incomplete in the sense that it provides no dynamic account of measurement processes. The Bohm theory eliminates this 'measurement problem.' It is fully dynamic. But it is drastically nonlocal, which is to say, it invokes action at a distance. So does the standard theory, though in more subtle ways" (Giere 2006, p. 119n9). For examples of empirical equivalents of aspects of Newtonian mechanics and of Einstein's general theory of relativity, cf. Earman (1993). However, empirically equivalent theories need not remain so. Cf. Laudan and Lepin (1991).

22. Cf. Hesse (1966) *Models and Analogies in Science*, (1974) *The Structure of Scientific Inference*, and (1980) *Revolutions and Reconstructions in the Philosophy of Science*. Also cf. Goodman (1983) *Fact, Fiction, and Forecast.*

23. Cf. Mayr (1975), p. 133. Also see Rosenberg (1994) *Instrumental Biology; or, the Disunity of Science*, in which it is compellingly argued that there may be multiple molecular structures that issue in a single phenotype and many phenotypes that issue from the same molecular structure.

24. Freud's claim that psychoanalysis is a natural science among others has echoed throughout the history of psychoanalysis: "It is only when we consider the social phenomena of adaptation in their biological aspect that we can really start 'getting psychology rightfully placed in the hierarchy of science, namely as one of the biological sciences' (Jones 1936)" (Hartmann 1964, p. 16); "The history of analysis shows in a particularly conclusive way a mutual promotion of observation and theoretical formulation" (Hartmann 1964, 71); psychoanalysis establishes "how thousands of emotional varieties follow the same laws, laws as valid as those of physics and chemistry" (Reik 1972, p. 9); "Like every scientific investigator, he has learned to discern the variety and wealth of organic processes and recognizes how, in spite of great freedom, they obey unchangeable laws" (Reik 1972, p. 246); "[w]ith regard to symptoms, constructions take the form of explanatory hypotheses . . . . they thus become theoretical statements from which singular prognoses can be derived. Generally speaking, these prognoses identify the conditions causally responsible for the neurotic state and claim that the therapeutic success must dissolve these conditions in order to induce change" (Thomä and Kächele 1975, p. 86). For contemporary assertions of this view, cf. Roudinesco (2001) *Why Psychoanalysis?*, Brenner (2002), and Rangell (2004), esp. p. 218. For a contemporary defense of the claim that psychoanalysis *should* be developed as a natural science, cf. Westin (2000) "The Search for Objectivity in the Study of Subjectivity: Reply to Commentary."

25. See also his characterization of psychic events as fully determined, in no way arbitrary, at SE 5: 514.

26. For another instance of Freud's thing-in-itself skepticism, cf. SE 23: 158.

27. He also occasionally suggests that psychoanalytic theory advances by decisive empirical refutation of prior hypotheses, e.g., the seduction hypothesis "broke down under its own improbability, and under contradiction in definitely ascertainable circumstances" (SE 14:17).

28. Concerning Freud's positivism, cf. Milner (2000) "The Doctrine of Science," p. 59n8 and "Constructions in Analysis," esp. p. 260.

29. Cf. the opening of "Mourning and Melancholia."

30. Concerning a possible subterranean influence on Freud's drive to universalization, cf. Gilman (1994), esp. p. 221.

31. "The voice of the intellect is a soft one, but it does not rest until it has gained a hearing. Ultimately, after endlessly repeated rebuffs, it succeeds" (SE 21: 53).

32. Hence his lament to Fliess that *The Interpretation of Dreams* "is not yet sufficiently appreciated *by scientists*" (in Masson 1985, p. 358; emphasis added).

33. Cf. Sander Gilman (1994) *The Case of Sigmund Freud: Medicine and Identity at the Fin de Siècle.*

34. Consider in this context a statement attributed to Freud by one of his analysand's: "But when you write, the public demands that you make things definite, else they think that you do not know what you are saying" (Blanton, 1971, pp. 47-8).

35. If only to mark the partial character of this account of Freud's emphatic and repeated insistence that psychoanalysis is a natural science among others, let us note that more fully addressing the question of why Freud was so prone to underscore and perhaps exaggerate the scientific character of psychoanalysis would require considering if and how so doing responds to question of — and anxieties pertaining to — the relation(s) of science, psychoanalysis, religion, and "race." I suspect that Freud's notion of the scientificity of psychoanalysis is both counter-religious (especially set against the malicious conflation of "race" and religion that would impugn the credibility, certainly deny the universal claims, or indeed support the direct pathologization of psychoanalysis) *and* to an extent anti-Enlightenment, thus incredibly over-determined with regard to racializing discourses; just as I suspect that the illusion whose future Freud considers in *The Future of an Illusion* is as much the reigning self-interpretation of science as it is popular and theological interpretations of religion.

36. "Is it the truth if we describe things as they are without troubling to consider how our hearer will understand what we say? Or is it only jesuitical truth, and does not genuine truth consist in taking the hearer into account and giving him a faithful picture of our own knowledge (SE 8: 115).

37. Cf. SE 4: 182.

38. In Adam Phillips' apt phrase, psychoanalysts are "connoisseur[s] of anomalies" (1995, p. 12). Or as Lacan puts it in his characteristically condensed and dialectically unstable way, "[t]he most particular cases are those whose value is the most universal" (*Seminar VI*, Feb 11, p. 1959). Making plain the ethico-political charge of the claim, Kristeva suggests that psychoanalysis is concerned with "the demassification of the problematic of *difference*" ("Women's Time"). Let us note in passing that very early in his career, Freud thought that it would be possible to establish a constant aetiological relation between a particular causal class and a particular pathological class for all of the major neuroses, e.g., neurasthenia is caused by excessive masturbation or spontaneous emission, anxiety neuroses are caused by coitus interruptus and suchlike frustrations, hysteria in women and obsession in men are caused by sexual, specifically genital-centric traumas in early childhood (SE 3:163).

39. That Freud was at least acquainted with and may to some extent have ascribed to a deflationary sentiment about science is indicated by his notes in his copy of Pearson's *Grammar of Science*. Cf. Gilman (1994), p. 52.

40. At least a note of ambivalence can also be detected in Freud's comment that "our science involves a number of hypotheses — it is hard to say whether they should be regarded as postulates or as products of our researches" (SE 23: 282).

41. Likewise underscoring the nature's moments of irreducible opacity, in "Notes Upon a Case of Obsessional Neurosis" Freud stresses that "the leap from a mental process to a somatic innervation — hysterical conversion — . . . can never be fully comprehensible to us" (SE 10: 157).

42. With regard to Freud's ambiguity or ambivalence about the scientific standing of psychoanalysis, consider the following. "Strictly speaking," Freud proclaims, "there are only two sciences: psychology, pure and applied, and natural science," after which he contends that psychoanalysis is a branch of psychology and thus a science, though not a natural science (SE 22: 179). But after this ambiguous gesture, Freud presents psychoanalysis in as scientific a light as possible: "psycho-analysis . . . . is certainly not the whole of psychology, but its substructure

and perhaps even its entire foundation" (SE 20: 252). If psychoanalysis is not a natural science, at least it is the very basis of science that proceeds otherwise.

43. Correspondingly, it is not incidental that *The Project*, which, as we have seen, intends to develop "a psychology which shall be a natural science" and aims "to represent psychical processes as quantitatively determined states of specifiable material particles and so to make them plain and void of contradictions," was written principally for an audience of neurologists. So too, it is not incidental that the "quantitatively determined states of specifiable material particles" that Freud intends to discuss are neither measured nor (presumably) measurable.

44. For another indication from a different angle that Freud believed that mechanistic science was insufficient *as science*, consider his protests against the reduction of scientific knowing to concern with physical laws at SE 20: 32-3 and SE 14: 77. Also cf. SE 15: 87.

45. See *Neuropsychoanalysis: An Interdisciplinary Journal for Psychoanalysis and the Neurosciences* generally.

46. Also cf. Ansermet and Magistretti (2007) and Harth (1982).

47. There is an enormous amount of research, especially in the field of neuropsychoanalysis, attempting to show that psychoanalytic theories have organic substrata. Cf., for instance, Schore's (2002, 2003) attempts to locate a biological substratum for projective identification and Shuren and Grafman (2002) and Kimura et al.'s (2004) work on the biological basis of transference.

48. To get a sense for the enthusiasm about Damasio among psychoanalysts, cf. Blass and Carmeli's (2007) account of his exuberant reception at the opening session of the 2004 IPA Congress.

49. Even this claim would be underwarranted. One could subject to rigorous experimental scrutiny the claim that analytic neutrality leads to frustration, tension, and conflict enhancement. But positive confirmation does not exclude the hypothesis that, at least sometimes (say, if the analysand is testing unconscious pathogenic beliefs), or always at some level, analytic neutrality (also) provides comfort and relief.

50. More generally, the worry about inter-rater reliability is that it may simply confirm collective immersion in a hegemonic vocabulary.

51. Also, as many commentators have noted, when predictions of later psychic developments based on infantile observation hold up, they do so only in a very general way. Cf. Diem-Wille (1997) in Sue Read (ed.) *Developments in Infant Observation: The Tavistock Model.*

52. If the hunch behind this sort of research is that it can establish that clinical phenomena obey regularity laws, part of its appeal, perhaps, resides in its potential contribution to establishing authoritative criteria for the validation of interpretations capable of adjudicating between competitors. The thought is that if clinical phenomena obey regularity laws and so can be predicted, a *prima facie* plausible criterion for interpretive validation would be: X interpretation is valid if it explains phenomena a, b, and c (observable now) and phenomena d and e (not evident now, but discovered later); Z implies Z1, Z2, Z3 which can occur or fail to occur under specified conditions. Enamored with the prospect of scientific credibility this criterion seems to afford, Hartmann emphatically asserts that successful prediction is *the* standard of validation (1964, 310ff). Cf. Kline in Clark and Wright (1988), p. 226. Criticism of this gesture is implied in chapters 3-5 of the present text. The frenzy over prediction as a route to scientific credibility may also play a role in the enthusiasm for process and outcome studies. That such studies are frequently in methodological disarray, and when not, prone to the extrapolation of inferences they do not support, is, though well known, not as disturbing as one might expect to those "in the know."

53. Depending on what one counts as an experiment and how one dates the origination of psychoanalysis, one might say that experimentation and commentary on experimentation began quite a bit earlier. In the letter to Fliess of 12 December 1896, Freud speaks of his emboldened confidence in the paternal-seduction hypothesis resulting from "Eckstein deliberately treating her patient in such a manner as not to give her the slightest hint of what would emerge from the unconscious and in the process obtained from her, among other things, the identical scenes with the father."

54. Equally, the experimental data from which Dollard and Miller (1950) extrapolate the claim that ideas and affects associated with punishment are excluded from consciousness

through conditioned avoidance are insufficient to support this claim against the Freudian alternative.

55. Appeals to ethological evidence to support psychoanalytic claims are surprisingly recurrent. In 1933 and then again in 1936, Imre Hermann appealed to ethological evidence to support his concept of a "clinging drive." In 1935, Ian Suttie appealed to such evidence in order to establish the scientific credibility of the concept of non-appetitive love (3). Bowlby (1969) marshals Harlow's famous rhesus monkey experiments against Freudian drive theory, specifically against its claims about the libidinal contingency of the source of satisfaction. In 1984, Modell appeals to ethological evidence to support object relations theory against alternative psychoanalytic theories (pp. 199-200).

56. When Freud claims that the analyst uses the clinic "just as a physicist makes use of experiment," he is clearly exploiting a loose analogy: naturally occurring psychic phenomena (defenses, desires, etc.) are replicated and studied in an artificial setting, thus the clinic is a laboratory of sorts (SE 23: 197). Behind this rather implausible analogy, I suspect, are two plausible thoughts. First, in physics as much as in psychoanalysis, experiments are often probative, yielding source material for reflection rather than demonstrations or verifications, and this is not to be maligned. Second, if sufficiently many patients enact the same scenarios, stage the same desires, fears, fantasies, and so forth in the clinic, the claim that what appears in the clinic are exaggerations of typical forms of psychic life (dreams, slips, parapraxes, etc.) becomes somewhat more plausible and the claim that clinical experience can support generalizations about psychic life find some empirical warrant. Of course, such claims are problematic: a general theory of psychic life explains clinical phenomena which in turn warrant the theory in which they are described, and what is meant by "control" and "experiment" in the case of physics is, as we will soon see, not what is provided by the artificiality of the clinic.

57. Wallerstein (2004) disagrees, but equivocates. For him, control means as little as selecting "groups of patients . . . who are alike in certain variables while dissimilar in others" (94). If the variables selected for are not known to lead to regular and predictable effects in known circumstances, is this not classifying rather than controlling in the relevant sense, equivocal between myth and science?

58. Cf. SE 22: 27

59. For an alternative assessment of single case studies, cf. Chassan (1979), Edelson (1985), Jones (1993), and Fonagy and Moran (1993). For a somewhat dated review of the single case design literature as it pertains to psychoanalysis, cf. Waldron (1997). Also cf. the discussion in the "Special Section: Single-Case Research in Psychotherapy" in *Journal of Consulting and Clinical Psychology*, Vol. 61(3), Jun 1993, pp. 371-420.

60. Strong causal claims (dependency relations) assume the precise establishment of initial conditions, determinate contexts. Informative causal claims assume the establishment of uniform contexts. Psychoanalysis, clinical or otherwise, seems unable to deliver either, at least not with the desired degree of determinacy. Both those who seek to establish psychoanalysis as an exact science and those who accuse psychoanalysis of making fallacious causal statements (cf. Grünbaum on the "thematic affinity fallacy") may do well to recall Aristotle's claim that "it is the mark of an educated man to seek as much precision in things of a given genus as their nature allows, for to accept persuasive arguments from a mathematician appears to be [as improper as] to demand demonstration from a rhetorician" (*NE* 1094b24-28). Or its echoes in Freud: "The lack of precision in what I have written in the text above, its abbreviation of the time factor and its compression of the whole subject-matter, may be attributed to the reserve necessitated by the nature of the topic. It would be as foolish to aim at exactitude in such questions as it would be unfair to insist upon certainty" (SE 13: 142n); "Science has only a few apodictic propositions in its catechism: the rest are assertions promoted by it to some particular degree of probability. It is actually a sign of a scientific mode of thought to find satisfaction in these approximations to certainty and to be able to pursue constructive work further in spite of the absence of final confirmation" (SE 15: 51; see also SE 7: 201, where Freud claims that the long detours of clinical reconstruction, coupled with somewhat opaque direct observations, yield "a satisfactory degree of certainty in their findings.").

61. Cf. SE 6: 239.

62. Characteristically, Hartmann then goes on to qualify this concession, stating that "it *may be* that 'more, less, greater than, fewer of, increase or decrease, etc., *may be used more profitably*' than numeration," which implies that although numeration *may* be less useful in a variety of contexts, it is nonetheless possible (Hartmann p. 314, citing Brower (1949); emphases added).

63. Freidman's and Schill's experiments support the claim that the prevalence of fantasies can be quantified, which would bear on the scope of a number of metapsychological theses. Also see Jones (1993), Koenigsberg et al. (1993), Fonagy et al. (2001), pp. 44-60, 313-328, and Waldron et al. (2004).

64. Overemphasizing quantification rigs the game of comparative process and outcome studies against psychoanalysis. As Haynal notes, "behavior therapies have the advantage that they address only *a single* symptom, and any change is, therefore, easier to see [and to quantify]. Psychoanalysis, aiming at different modifications in the representational world, in affectivity and the attitude of life, naturally offers a wider variety of aims, which are difficult both to define and to control" (1993, p. 131).

65. In their review of research on the effectiveness of psychoanalysis, Bachrach et al. (1991) conclude that "[t]he quantitative studies, in particular, have not contributed fresh insights into psychoanalysis, nor have they demonstrated findings with substantially greater rigor than previous clinical investigations" (911).

66. "[T]he scientific concept of causality is inseparably bound up with spatiality: in space, entities are isolable; by reference to its coordinates they can be measured and positionally identified; by means of this reference, velocity and acceleration can be determined, and in this way 'effect' can be *quantitatively* correlated with cause" (Jonas 1982, p. 132). Cf. Kant's (1786) claim that a discipline is scientific only if and to the extent that its concepts are capable of mathematical construction in space (*Metaphysiche Anfrangsgründe der Naturwissenschaften*, p. 470).

67. Correspondingly, if, as Weber claims, the largely successful expulsion and occlusion of "mysterious, incalculable forces" in the effort to "master all things by calculation . . . . means that the world is disenchanted," then to be committed to psychoanalysis, if this means commitment to reckoning with the incalculable, is to pursue a program of reenchantment, albeit indirectly (1958, p. 139).

68. Cf. Nagel 1959.

69. Inferences of observables from metapsychological claims may thus be subject to experimental scrutiny, as in Bruner and Postman's experiments (1947a, 1947b, 1949) showing that emotionally disturbing words are subject to repression (forgetting) with greater frequency than neutral words. This provides some credibility for both the specific hypothesis that emotional disturbance is a cause of repression, and indirectly, to the (or some) higher-level theory of repression. However, these experiments do not satisfactorily operationalize the concept of repression, especially if one assumes, along with Freud and many others, that repression implies counter-cathexis. How would one show that *as a result* of repressing emotionally charged words, other words or ideas take on increased importance? How would causation be distinguished from correlation?

70. A distinct operationalization problem concerns analytic interventions. How can interpretations that begin "I wonder," "Do you think that," "Have you considered," etc. or that amount to no more than a suggestive "really?" "hmmm," "huh," or "say more" be unproblematically translated into propositional content with observable corollaries?

71. Some have attempted to show that psychoanalytic claims are in principle falsifiable and that it was none other than Freud himself who falsified some its claims, e.g., Hospers (1959); Salmon (1959); Glymour (1974, 1980); and Grünbaum (1977a, 1977b, 1978, 1979, 1984). But so doing, they wildly exaggerate the deterministic dimensions of psychoanalytic claims, transforming rhetorical excess, speculative overreach, and wishful thinking into statements of universal generalization. Grünbaum, for instance, repeatedly argues that since psychoanalysts makes claims of the sort "if x infantile conditions, then y correlated clusters of character traits," their claims are falsifiable. Both sides of the falsification debate assume an idealized image of nature as empirically and logically determinate and deductively-nomologically integrated, if only as a presupposition of the epistemic and methodological norms they advocate. An ade-

quate assessment of the epistemic authority of psychoanalysis presupposes acknowledging the contingency of this metaphysical ideal and taking the toll of such contingency in the development of epistemic and methodological criteria.

72. Cf. Sandler (1983).

73. To be sure, the analytic community does not take negative findings as seriously as it should. Psychoanalytic periodicals should be much more willing to publish, or solicitous of accounts of, routine clinical failures, and analysts should be much more inclined to submit articles detailing routine clinical failures rather than just those that confirm received theory, offer bold new insights, or propose therapeutic innovations. But the affirmative ethos of psychoanalytic research is admirable in its own right. Psychoanalytic research "begins" with a double affirmation: a "yes" to tradition-mediated forms of attention and inference and to the experiential density and opacity, the abrasive singularity of the clinical material, its standing out as non-identical though analogous to previous cases and the concepts through which they have been understood. To the extent that this double, "impossible" affirmation is sustained, concept and experience are ceaselessly remediated.

74. Cf. Richards (2006); Mayr (1980, 1982).

75. If that which becomes subject to unconscious association is as variable and singular as a life; if associational structuration is elaborated by principles as diverse and obscure as assonance, consonance, various forms of experiential or linguistic contiguity, puns, jokes, simultaneity, intensity, iconic coherence, homophony, counterpoint, antipathy, cause and effect, thematic or imagistic similarity, and so on, if fully or to whatever extent by principles; and if the same "unit" can participate simultaneously in many associational webs and so develop via singular concurrences of principles, if by principle, then exhaustively detailing unconscious contents and developments, let alone establishing explanatory principles of associational development, is but a pipe dream. When considering the idiosyncratic character of unconscious association, most commentators are quick to focus on the principles by which such idiosyncrasy is regulated, sacrificing particularity to generality and reasserting the common — as if unnerved by a fated fragment of freedom. Perhaps out of pity (and melancholic self-pity) and in the interest of its endurance, such idiosyncrasy is schooled in the neglect that will be socially enforced. Witness, for instance, Grosz's (1990) elaboration of the connection between (what seems to be) the contingency of the "object" of primal repression and the historically variable through ideationally regulated constitution of the unconscious: "Primal repression lays down a primary infantile nucleus or kernel for the unconscious, a series of key memory traces which, from this time on, attract other perceptual traces or experiences associated with them towards the unconscious. These are also repressed, 'pulled' into the unconscious by ideas already contained there. These later repressions — 'repression proper' — constitute the bulk of unconscious contents. They are selected according to their proximity to the primally repressed. The unconscious is largely composed of infantile, oedipal memories and wishes. The unconscious remains infantile in its aims and wishes, governed by impulses that are laid down in our individual (pre-)histories, permanently preserved, unchanged by the passage of time. The criteria for 'selection' of unconscious contents remains within the order of representation; the proximity of terms to the primally repressed nucleus of the unconscious is determined not by any real relation between one idea and the repressed term, but on the basis of usually verbal or signifying relations" (83). Also see Burgoyne (1999) "Interpretation," p. 56.

76. Kant claims that it is "subjectively necessary" to presuppose "that nature does not have this disturbing boundless heterogeneity of empirical laws and heterogeneity of natural forms, but that, rather, through the affinity of its particular laws under more general ones it takes on the quality of experience as an empirical system" (op. cit.). In a similar vein, Husserl contends that "in the phenomenological sphere, there are no contingencies, no mere matter-of-fact connections; all is essentially and definitely motivated" (*Ideas* 2012 [1913], p. 290). An echo of Kant's claim can perhaps be heard in Wittgenstein's proposal in the *Tractatus* that "to understand a sentence means to know what is the case if it is true" (4.024; translation modified following Wellmer).

77. Cf. Hartmann (1958), pp. 305ff.

78. For more on this issue, cf. "The Conceptualization and Communication of Clinical Facts in Psychoanalysis" *IJP*, 75 (5/6), Dec. 1994.

79. Further, general worries along these lines are elaborated by Rosenthal (1966) and Rosenthal and Rosnow (1968).

80. This is not to be confused with positing unobservables, e.g., positing atomic vibration in solids (a relatively uncontroversial and scientifically productive claim).

81. Cf. Victoria Hamilton (1996) *The Analyst's Preconscious*.

82. Cf. Haraway (1974). The worry, though legitimate, can be taken too far, as when Frederick Crews argues that "[t]he most fundamental rule of the game is that a given theory or hypothesis cannot be validated by invoking 'evidence' manufactured by the same supposition" (2000, p. 21); "[i]f you want to establish the truth of a hypothesis or a theory, you need to relate your postulates to data that can be regarded independently as facts by people who are not already members of your group" (2000, p. 52-53). Just looking at the first line cited, one might suppose that Crews is aligning himself with Popper's conviction that for a hypothesis to be falsifiable it must be able to give rise to a counterintuitive prediction. If so, Crews would have to explain why the capacity to yield counterintuitive predictions is necessary for falsification. Though confirming a counterintuitive prediction yields persuasive support for a hypothesis, it is unclear why falsification hinges on the capacity to yield such predictions. But since Crews speaks of validation rather than falsification, perhaps it is not Popper who is in the backdrop. Taking both lines into account, it may be that, as far as Crews is concerned, the rules of the game are established by logical positivists, specifically Hempel. Is Crews not advancing a version of Hempel's (1970) claim that observations interpreted in terms of a new theory cannot be used to refute that theory? (Cf. Hempel 1970, pp. 236ff.) If so, Crews is saddled with the early positivist assumption that there can be a theory-neutral observation language ("data that can be regarded independently as facts by people who are not already members of your group"). And given that this assumption was widely abandoned in the face of its unworkability, Crews would have his work cut out.

83. Cf. Julia Kristeva (1984) *Revolution in Poetic Language*.

84. Supposing that they are distinct from depressive symptomatology. Fisher and Greenberg seriously misunderstand Freud's reflections on melancholy, especially insofar as they attribute to Freud a *theory* of melancholia. But we can push this misgiving aside for the purposes of the present context.

85. Cf. Blum (1980 [1949]).

86. For further criticism of Freud's "tally argument," cf. Grünbaum (1984) and Spence (1982), p. 289. There is, however, a substantial literature denying the meaningfulness of placebo effect in psychotherapy research. Cf. Critelli and Neumann (1984), Dush (1986), Horvath (1988), Lambert and Bergin (1994), Senger (1987), and Wilkins (1984).

87. The well-known efficacy of inexact and incorrect interpretations has done less to inhibit the identification of psychoanalysis as that specific form of therapy in which veridical insight is necessary for therapeutic success than one might expect. Witness, for example, Marshall Edelson: "The claim of psychoanalysis to distinctiveness as a treatment in my view depends upon the claim that the acquisition of veridical insight by the analysand is a necessary condition, although probably not a sufficient condition, for the efficacy of this treatment" (1984, p. 139). Also cf. Peter Lowenstein (2007), "Cultural History and Psychoanalysis" for a strikingly fidelitous reassertion of Freud's "tally argument." There are, however, contrary currents; cf., *inter alia*, Grossman (1999) "What the Analyst Does Not Hear," esp. p. 91.

88. Freud seems aware of this — though his attitude toward it is ambivalent; it is as if Freud cannot sustain the insight, cannot but undercut or even contradict it through the language in which it is advanced — when he claims that "It is very easy to account for this disturbing state of affairs. Even supposing that we have a complete knowledge of the etiological factors that decide a given result, nevertheless what we know about them is only their quality and not their relative strength. Some of them are suppressed by others because they are too weak, and they therefore do not affect the final result. But we never know beforehand which of the determining factors will prove the weaker or the stronger. We may say at the end that those which have succeeded must have been the stronger" (SE 18: 167-168).

89. Concerning the tendency to oversimplification in psychotherapy research, cf. Elliott and Anderson (1994). See also Beck, Ward, Mendelson, Mock, and Erbaugh (1961), Spielberger, Gorsuch, and Lushene (1970), and Derogatis (1983).

90. For a contrary view, cf. Holmes (1990).

91. Cf. Ainsworth et al. (1978), Sroufe (1988), Fonagy (1993).

92. Of course, there are forms of psychological difficulty not indexed to tendencies to disavow a troubled past or diminished reflective capacity. For misgivings about the pertinence of the AAI/SST to predictions of psychopathology, cf. Stern (1985), especially chapter 9.

93. Testimonial evidence (corroborated and uncorroborated) that memories are pliable to suggestion is abundant. E.g., "I myself have a very clear visual memory, detailed and vivid, of having been the object of an attempted abduction while still a baby in a pram. I can still see a series of precise details of where it took place, the struggle between my nurse and the abductor, the arrival of the passersby and the police etc. However, when I was 15, the nurse wrote to my parents that the whole story had been made up by her and that the scratches on her forehead were her own doing etc. In other words, for five or six years, I must have heard the story of that abduction which my parents believed, and drawing on it, I fabricated a visual memory which still remains today. It is a reconstruction, however false, and if the event had been real and the memory consequently true, it is very likely that I would have reconstructed it in the same manner because a recall memory does not yet exist (only a recognition memory), in a baby in its pram" (Piaget 1971; translation by Haynal 1993). Robbins (1963) has provided an empirical demonstration of the susceptibility of memory to popular theory.

94. Also relevant to this, though indirectly, is the evidence against the accuracy of eyewitness reports. Cf. Levine and Wallach (2002), chapter 6.

95. Related evidence of suggestibility is provided by Bornstein's (1990) review.

96. Certain psychoanalytic ideas have not held up under experimental scrutiny. For the sake of not following unlikely leads, it is important to draw attention to these.
(1) Holt (1976) reports evidence that disconfirms the hypothesis that all stimulation is inherently noxious. This speaks against a strong (and misleading, though prevalent) formulation of the tension-reduction principle and certain renderings of the death drive.
(2) There is decent evidence that not fear but affection leads to identification with moral principles, which casts doubt on the link Freud draws between castration threats, superego formation, and moral development (Fisher and Greenberg 1996, chapter 6).
(3) Though the issue is contentious, there is evidence that speaks against Freud's theories of dream functioning (Hobson, Hoffman, Helfand, and Kostner 1987; Hobson 1988, 1997, 1999; Fisher and Greenberg 1996; however, cf. Solms 1997, 1999, 2000, 2001, and Yu 2001a, 2001b, 2003. Braun 1999, like Hobson, denies aspects of Freud's particular theory of dream functioning, but not the claim that dreams are meaningful).
(4) Again, though the issue is contentious, there is neuroscientific evidence supporting the claim that not all memories can be recovered. Traumatic memories that are not explicitly coded may be unrecoverable, thus there may be a limit to the reach of psychoanalytic reconstruction (Pulver 2003). Mancia (2006) contests this view, arguing that implicit memory is subject to influence by modified technique involving concentrated attention "on the modalities of . . . communication such as intonation, rhythms, and tempo of speech, in particular the musicality of the voice, and on the most obviously reconstructive dimensions of dreams. All this will allow the emergence, besides recollection, of emotions [and phantasies] that concern the most archaic and meaningful relational experiences, and that belong to unrepressed unconscious material" (88).
(5) If hippocampal maturity is necessary for explicit memory, and if explicit memory is a condition of repression, then the immaturity of the hippocampus in early infancy suggests that theories of primal repression or early ego-guided repression may be incorrect (Joseph 1996; Siegel 1999; Mancia 2006).

97. Although process and outcome studies are graining in sophistication, an enormous number of them (particularly those undertaken prior to the mid 1980s) are in methodological shambles. Some of the most serious problems include: reliance on a single practitioner, failure to establish what psychoanalysis is and so if it is taking place, lack of no-treatment or alternative-treatment control groups, little to no attention to the question of whether the treating analyst is experienced or inexperienced, no random assignment, reliance on therapist's outcome ratings or ratings of case notes, too narrow focus in outcome assessment on symptom alleviation, the tendency of analysts and analysands to overrate effectiveness, insufficient con-

trols to establish whether results issue from the idiosyncratic style of the particular analyst rather than the method, and failure of comparison of outcome rates with a controlled placebo group. A perhaps irresolvable difficulty is that if what counts as a desired outcome is renegotiated, both formally and informally, throughout the course of analysis, i.e., is to some degree specific to the analytic pair, then ratings of standardized outcome measures will miss something essential.

98. However, the risks of putting too much stock in knowledge of patterns yielded by empirical experimentation include the rigid slotting of clinical material into pre-established frameworks and thus a failure of engaged clinical listening and coming off as all too knowing, which brings it own set of problems.

99. For further criticism of appeals to infant observation in the context of psychoanalytic disputes, cf. Wolff (1996).

100. Also cf. "Formulations on the Two Principles of Mental Functioning."

101. For an attempt to supplement the insecure authority of observation with that of majoritarian inference dispositions, cf. Briggs (1987). To be sure, interest in developmental observation does not entail a slide into reification. For instance, Stern's developmental research, he insists in a debate with André Green, is not so much geared toward hypothesis testing as hypothesis generating (Sandler et al. 2000; for an earlier anticipation of this view, cf. Spitz 1950). The clinical value of observational studies, Stern insists, lies in their contribution to search strategies that facilitate therapeutically useful constructions (Stern 1985, p. 273). Having *not* found evidence that psychological insults or traumas at specific ages or phases result in specific, predictable types of clinical difficulties in later life, Stern insists that the theoretical value of infant observation lies in its contribution to distinguishing between possible and likely developmental claims (Stern 1985, pp. 23, 186). However, with regard to such matters Stern is inconsistent, for he claims that evidence from infant and child observational studies is sufficient to sort out metapsychological disputes. For instance, he claims that data from observational studies requires us to jettison the notion of the stimulus barrier and the erotogenicity of the mouth, side with theories of very early ego functioning as opposed to those that posit the reality principle and the ego emerging subsequently to the pleasure principle and id functioning, and prefer theories that center on experiential wholeness and its loss rather than omnipotence and its traumatic dissolution. Cf. Stern (1985), chapters 10 and 11. An earlier, relatively sober view of the promise of infant observational data is put forward by Kris (1950), who suggests that such data may provide "confirmation or supplementation of insight gained by reconstruction."

102. Some of the language here follows that of Giere (1990), p. 20.

103. Cf. Duhem (1962) *The Aim and Structure of Physical Theory*, p. 7ff.

104. Even this is something of an idealization. That a model may *or may not* exactly satisfy an equation or set of equations (i.e., epistemic indeterminacy) is internal to its nature: "suppose we have a model that is not complete. That means that there are some things in the world not represented by the model. Those unrepresented things may be expected to have some (perhaps remote) causal connections with things that *are* represented" (Giere 2006, p. 66) The point is sharper if we assume, as do those committed to the deductive-nomological vision of science, the thoroughgoing causal interaction of all substances and properties.

105. On idealization and approximation, cf. Scriven (1961), Suppe (1972), Shapere (1974, 1982), Moulines (1976), Laymon (1980), Cartwright (1983, 1999), Feyerabend (1990, 1999), Giere (1990), Longino (2002), and Teller (2001, 2004a, 2004b). For a speculative genealogy of the claim of ideality, specifically mathematical ideality, on science, cf. Husserl (1970), p. 27ff.

106. Cf. Feyerabend (1965), 224ff and (1990), p. 39ff.

107. CF. Heisenberg (1952) *Philosophic Problems of Nuclear Science*.

108. This statement of the problem is a condensed elaboration of Duhem's underdetermination thesis. "A Duhemian predicament is a situation in which (1) a scientist or community of scientists S accepts a hypotheses H and accepts auxiliary assumption A; (2) H and A together imply observation O; but (3) following normal observational procedures, S would accept ~O (not O) on presentation of the relevant stimulus (e.g., performance of the relevant experiment). The predicament consists in not knowing (logically) which of the three possible producers of the contradiction to modify: H, A, or the procedures underwriting acceptance of ~O. Analysts, such as David Bloor, have exploited underdetermination to argue that it leaves scientists at-

tached to H, free to replace A or to blame the observational procedures for the untoward result. Thus any H can, in principle, escape falsification" (Longino 2002, 62). "[T]he constraints of data are not sufficient to compel judgment" (ibid). Put otherwise, science ineluctably involves judgment, i.e., a moment of subjectivity or freedom, thus in principle cannot fulfill its skeptical anti-anthropocentric promise to deliver objective (fully-independent) knowledge of the natural world, reality "in itself."

109. Cf. Cartwright (1983), p. 18ff.

110. For a defense of the deductive-nomological characterization of scientific explanation, cf. Hempel (1965) "Scientific Explanation"

111. The assumption that every bit of nature directly or indirectly interacts with every other bit — one version of the thesis of the unity of nature — may be incompatible with the precise truth of any finite set of covering laws.

112. And even if these problems with the covering law model could be somehow resolved, the claim that statements of law are fully satisfying because they can be integrated into a deductive-nomological system of nature in which one factor (e.g., a higher level law) explains another (e.g., a lower-level law) if the occurrence of the second can be deduced from the occurrence of the first would fail because derivations from fundamental laws involve long series of approximations and corrections.

113. Notice the proximity between scientific and literary idealism, the shared conviction that each single element must be unsubstitutable if the whole is to be absolutely integrated.

114. Cf. Dupré (1995), p. 110.

115. Cf. Simpson (1951) "The Interpretation of Interaction in Contingency Tables."

116. To underline one aspect of what is at stake here, let us recall Kant's contention that systematicity is a condition for scientific knowledge (A 832): if there is no guarantee of systematicity, there can be "no coherent employment of the understanding . . . no sufficient criterion for empirical truth" (B 679), and no empirical concepts or experience (B 682).

117. For a treatment of laws as capacities, cf. Cartwright (1999). In its favor, this view keeps in the fore questions of the conditions under which certain natures or potentials are facilitated or impeded and so mitigates the risk of falsification.

118. Scientists do not follow algorithms when replicating experiments. Rather, they regularly alter the experiment in various ways, e.g., by using slightly different detection instruments.

119. "[T]he hypothesis, in spite of its verification, continues to be and is always a hypothesis; its verification . . . is an endless course of verifications. It is the peculiar essence of natural science, it is a priori its way of being, to be unendingly hypothetical and unendingly verified" (Husserl 1970, 42). On the need to test the validity, usefulness, and adequacy of prevailing standards and theories by research that violates them, cf. Feyerabend (1990).

120. "We form images or symbols of the external objects; the manner in which we form them is such that the *logically* necessary consequences of the images are invariably the images of the *materially* necessary consequences of the corresponding objects" (Hertz 1984, 1).

121. The phrase descends from Helen Longino (2002, p. 188).

122. As Wittgenstein would have it, "There is not *a* method, though there are indeed methods, like different therapies" (*PI* §133).

123. I would like to express my heartfelt gratitude to my research assistant, Patrick Bova, for his intelligent and assiduous contributions to both this work and my previous book, *Lacan and Klein, Creation and Discovery*. I would also like to thank Amy Ring, our daycare provider, for the peace of mind.

References

Abrams, S. (1987) "The Psychoanalytic Process: A Schematic Model," *IJP* 68:441-452.
Adorno, T. (1968 [1950]) "Charakteristik Walter Benjamin" in *Über Walter Benjamin* (Frankfurt am Main: Suhrkamp).
Adorno, T. (1973) *Negative Dialectics*, trans. Ashton (New York: The Seabury Press).
Adorno, T. (1974) *Minima Moralia*, trans. Jephcott (London: Verso).
Adorno, T. (1997) *Aesthetic Theory*, trans. Hullot-Kentor (Minneapolis: U of Minnesota Press).
Adorno, T. (2008) *Lectures on Negative Dialectics*, ed. Tiedemann, trans. Livingstone (Cambridge: Polity Press).
Adorno and Horkheimer (2002) *Dialectic of Enlightenment: Philosophical Fragments*, trans. Jephcott (Stanford: Stanford UP).
Agamben, G. (2002) *Remnants of Auschwitz*, trans. Heller-Roazen (New York: Zone).
Ainsworth et al. (1978) *Patterns of Attachment: A Psychological Study of the Strange Situation* (Hillsdale: Lawrence Erlbaum).
Alexander, F. (1937) *Five Year Report of The Chicago Institute for Psychoanalysis: 1932-1937* (Chicago: Chicago Institute for Psychoanalysis).
Alexander, F. (1963) *Fundamentals of psychoanalysis* (London: Allen & Unwin).
Andersen and Chen (2002) "The Relational Self: An Interpersonal Social-Cognitive Theory," *Psychological Review* 109(4):619-645.
Andersen and Berk (1998) "Transference in Everyday Experience: Implications of Experimental Research for Relevant Clinical Phenomena," *Review of General Psychology* 2:81–120.
Andrade, V. (2005) "Affect and the Therapeutic Action in Psychoanalysis," *IJP* 86:677-697.
Ansermet and Magistretti (2007) *Biology of Freedom*, trans. Fairfield (New York: Other Press).
Anzieu, D. (1987) *Freud's Self-Analysis* (New York: IUP).
Appelbaum, S. (1977) *The Anatomy of Change: A Menninger Foundation Report in Testing the Effects of Psychotherapy* (New York: Plenum).
Arendt, H. (1961) "Crisis in Culture," in *Between Past and Future: Six Exercises in Political Thought* (New York: Meridian).
Ardent, H. (1989) *Lectures on Kant's Political Philosophy* (Chicago: University of Chicago Press).
Arendt, H. (1994) *Essays in Understanding*, (ed.) Kohn, trans. Kimber and Kimber (New York: Harcourt Brace & Company).
Arendt, H. (1998) *The Human Condition* (Chicago: University of Chicago Press).
Aristotle (1984) *Nicomachean Ethics*, trans. with commentaries and glossary by Hippocrates G. Apostle (Grinell: The Peripatetic Press).
Arlow, J. (1987) "The Dynamics of Interpretation," *PSQ* 56:68-87.
Aron and Harris (eds.) (1993) *The Legacy of Sandor Ferenczi* (Hillsdale: Analytic Press).

Atlan, H. (1992) "Self-organizing Networks: Weak, Strong and Intentional. The Role of Their Underdetermination," *La Nuova Critica* N.S., 19–20(1/2):51–70.
Aulagnier, Piera (2001) *Violence and Interpretation*, trans. Sheridan (Philadelphia: Taylor & Francis).
Austin, J. L. (1975) *How to Do Things With Words*, eds. Urmson and Sbisa (Cambridge, Mass.: Harvard UP).
Bachrach, Galatzer-Levy, Skolnikoff, and Waldron (1991) "On the Efficacy of Psychoanalysis," *JAPA* 39: 871-916.
Balint, M. (1949) "Love for the Mother and Mother-Love," *IJP* 30:251-259.
Balint, M. (1965 [1933]) "Character Analysis and New Beginning," in *Primary Love and Psychoanalytic Technique* (London: Tavistock).
Balint, M. (1968) *The Basic Fault: Therapeutic Aspects of Regression* (London: Tavistock).
Balter et al. (1980) "On the Analyzing Instrument," *PSQ* 49:474-504.
Barlow, D. (1981) "On the Relation of Clinical Research to Clinical Practice: Current Issues, New Directions," *J. Consult. Clin. Psychol.*, 49:147-155.
Bass, A. (2000) *Difference and Disavowal: The Trauma of Eros* (Stanford: Stanford University Press).
Bass, A. (2006) *Interpretation and Difference: The Strangeness of Care* (Stanford: Stanford University Press).
Beardsworth, S. (2004) *Julia Kristeva: Psychoanalysis and Modernity* (Albany: SUNY UP).
Beck, Ward, Mendelson, Mock, and Erbaugh (1961) "An Inventory for Measuring Depression," *Archives of General Psychiatry*, 4:561-571.
Bellak, Leopold, and Walkup (1993) *Psychoanalysis as a Science* (Boston: Allyn and Bacon).
Belsky and Nezworski (eds.) (1987) *Clinical Implications of Attachment* (New York: Routledge).
Benjamin, J. (1988) *Bonds of Love* (New York: Pantheon).
Benjamin, J. (1998) *Like Subjects, Love Objects* (New Haven: Yale UP).
Benjamin, W. (1969) *Illuminations*, (ed.) Hannah Arendt, trans. Zohn (Great Britain: Collins/ Fontana).
Bergler and Eidelberg (1933) "Der Mammakomplex des Mannes" *Int. Z. Psa*: 19:547-583.
Bergmann, M. (ed.) (2004) *Understanding Dissidence and Controversy in the History of Psychoanalysis* (New York: Other Press).
Bernardi, R. (1989) "The Role of Paradigmatic Determinants in Psychoanalytic Understanding," *IJP* 70: 341–57.
Bernstein, J.M. (1984) *Philosophy of the Novel: Lukács, Marxism, and the Dialectics of Form*. (Minneapolis: U of Minnesota Press).
Bernstein, J.M. (1992) *The Fate of Art* (University Park: Penn State University Press).
Bernstein, J. M. (2001) *Adorno: Disenchantment and Ethics* (Cambridge: Cambridge UP).
Bernstein, J. M. (2002) "Re-enchanting Nature" in *Reading McDowell: On Mind and World* (ed.) Smith (London: Routledge).
Bernstein, J. M. (2007) "Recognition and Embodiment" in *German Idealism: Contemporary Perspectives* (ed.) Hammer (New York: Routledge):183-205.
Bernstein, J.M. (2009) "Sexuate Being: Foundations for a Feminist Legal Philosophy?" in Heberle and Pryor (eds.) *Imagining Law: On Drucilla Cornell*.
Bernstein, R.J. (1983) *Beyond Objectivism and Relativism* (Philadelphia: U Penn Press).
Bernstein, R.J. (1988) "Interpretation and Its Discontents: The Choreography of Critique," in Messer, Sass, and Woolfolk's (eds.) *Hermeneutics and Psychological Theory*.
Bersani, L. (2000) "Speaking Psychoanalysis," in *Whose Freud?* (eds.) Brooks and Woloch (New Haven: Yale UP).
Bersani, L. (2009) *Is the Rectum a Grave?* (Chicago: U of Chicago Press).
Beutler, L. (1991) "Have All Won and Must All Have Prizes? Revisiting Luborsky et al.'s Verdict," *Journal of Consulting and Clinical Psychology* 59:226-232.
Beutler and Clarkin (1990) *Systematic Treatment Selection: Toward Targeted Therapeutic Interventions* (New York: Brunner/Mazel, Inc.).

Beutler, Machado, and Neufeldt. (1994) "Therapist Variables," in Bergin and Garfield (eds.), *Handbook of Psychotherapy and Behavior change* (New York: John Wiley and Sons, Inc):229-269.

Bibring, G. (1954) "Psychoanalysis and Dynamic Psychotherapies," *JAPA* 2:745-770.

Bion, W. ([1962]) *Learning From Experience* (London: William Heinemann Medical Books) [reprinted by Karnac (London: 1984)].

Blanton, S. (1971) *Diary of My Analysis With Sigmund Freud* (New York: Hawthorn).

Blass and Carmeli (2007) "The Case Against Neuropsychoanalysis: On Fallacies Underlying Psychoanalysis' Latest Scientific Trend and Its Negative Impact on Psychoanalytic Discourse," *IJP* 88:19-41.

Blatt and Felson (1993) "Different Kinds of Folks May Need Different Kinds of Strokes: The Effects of Patients' Characteristic on Therapeutic Process and Outcome," *Psychotherapy Research* 3:245-259.

Blatt and Shahar (2004) "Psychoanalysis — with whom, for what, and how? Comparisons with Psychotherapy," *JAPA* 52:393-477.

Blight, J (1981) "Must Psychoanalysis Retreat to Hermeneutics? Psychoanalytic Theory in Light of Popper's Evolutionary Epistemology," *Psychoanalysis and Contemp. Thought* 4:147-205.

Blum, H. (ed.). (1980). *Psychoanalytic Explorations of Technique: Discourse on the Theory of Therapy* (New York: IUP).

Blum H. (1994a) "The Value of Reconstruction in Adult Psychoanalysis," *IJP* 61:39-64.

Blum, H. (1994b) *Reconstruction in Psychoanalysis: Childhood Revisited and Recreated* (Madison: International Universities Press).

Bollas, C. (1989) *The Shadow of the Object* (New York: Columbia).

Bollas, C. (1996) *Forces of Destiny: Psychoanalysis and the Human Idiom* (London: Free Association Books).

Borch-Jacobson, M. (1991) *Lacan: The Absolute Master* (Stanford: Stanford UP).

Boris, H. (1998) "Tolerating Nothing," in Phillips and Stonebridge (eds.) *Reading Melanie Klein* (London: Routledge).

Bornstein, R. (1990) "Critical Importance of Stimuli Unawareness for the Production of Subliminal Psychodynamic Activation Effects: A Meta-Analytic Review," *Journal of Clinical Psychology* 46:201-210.

Bowie, M. (1993) *Psychoanalysis and the Future of Theory* (London: Blackwell).

Bowlby, J. (1973) *Separation: Anxiety & Anger. Attachment and Loss Vol. 2.* (London: Hogarth Press).

Bowlby, J. (1979) *The Making and Breaking of Affectional Bonds* (London: Tavistock).

Bowlby, J. (1979) *A Secure Base: Clinical Applications of Attachment Theory* (London: Routledge, 1988).

Bowlby, J. (1979) "Psychoanalysis as Art and Science," *International Review of Psychoanalysis* 6:3-14.

Bowlby, J. (1981) "Psychoanalysis as a Natural Science," *International Review of Psychoanalysis* 8:243-255.

Bowlby, J. (1982 [1969]) *Attachment* (London: Hogarth).

Bowman, M. (2002) *The Last Resistance: The Concept of Science as a Defense Against Psychoanalysis* (New York: SUNY Press).

Brakel, Kleinsorge, Snodgrass, and Shevrin (2000) "The Primary Process and the Unconscious," *IJP* 81:553-569.

Bandom, R. (2003) *Articulating Reasons: An Introduction to Inferentialism* (Cambridge, Mass.: Harvard UP).

Braun, A. "The New Neuropsychology of Sleep Commentary by Allen Braun," *Neuropsychoanalysis* 1:196-201.

Breger, L. (2000) *Freud: Darkness in the Midst of Vision* (New York: Wiley).

Brenner, C. (1976) *Psychoanalytic Technique and Psychic Conflict* (New York: IUP).

Brenner, C. (1982) *Mind in Conflict* (New York: International Universities Press).

Brenner, C. (2002) "Reflections on Psychoanalysis," *Journal of Clinical Psychoanalysis*, 11:7-37.

Bretherton and Waters (1985). "Growing Points of Attachment Theory and Research," *Monographs of the Society for Research in Child Development 50 (1-2,* Serial No, 209).
Brewin, Andrews, and Gotlib (1993) "Psychopathology and Early Experience: A Reappraisal of Retrospective Reports," *Psychological Bulletin* 113(1):82-98.
Briggs, S. (1987) *Growth and Risk in Infancy* (London: Jessica Kingsley).
Brill et al. (1964) "Controlled Study of Psychiatric Outpatient Treatment," *Archives of General Psychiatry* 10:581-595.
Brody, E. (1990) *Psychoanalytic Knowledge* (Madison, CT: IUP).
Browning, Margaret (2006) "Neuroscience and Imagination: The Relevance of Susanne Langer's Work to Psychoanalytic Theory," *PSQ* LXXV:1131-1159.
Bruner and Postman (1947a) "Tension and Tension-Release as Organizing Factors in Perception," *Journal of Personality* 15:300-308.
Bruner and Postman (1947b) "Emotional Selectivity in Perception and Reaction," *Journal of Personality* 16: 69-77.
Bruner and Postman (1949) "Perception, Cognition, and Behavior," *Journal of Personality* 18: 14-31.
Burgoyne, B. (1999) "Interpretation" in *The Klein-Lacan Dialogues* (eds.) Burgoyne and Sullivan (New York: Other Press):45-58.
Butler, J. (1997a) *Excitable Speech* (New York: Routledge).
Butler, J. (1997b) *The Psychic Life of Power* (Stanford: Stanford UP).
Butler, J. (2004) *Undoing Gender* (New York: Routledge).
Camino and Correale. (2005) "Projective Identification and Consciousness Alteration: A Bridge Between Psychoanalysis and Neuroscience?" *IJP* 86:51-60.
Caper, R. (1999) *A Mind of One's Own: A Kleinian View of Self and Object* (London: Routledge).
Cappon, D. (1964) "Results of Psychotherapy," *British J. of Psychiatry* 110: 35-45.
Carey, S. (1985) *Conceptual Development in Childhood* (Cambridge, Mass: MIT Press).
Caruth, C. (ed.) (1995) *Trauma: Explorations in Memory* (Baltimore: The Johns Hopkins University Press) .
Cavarero, A. (2000) *Relating Narratives*, trans. Kottman (New York: Routledge).
Cavell, M. (1993) *The Psychoanalytic Mind: from Freud to Philosophy* (Cambridge, Massachusetts and London: Harvard University Press).
Cavell, S. (1962) "The Availability of Wittgenstein's Later Philosophy," *The Philosophical Review* 71(1).
Cavell, S. (1979) *The Claim of Reason* (New York: Oxford UP).
Cavell, S. (1987) *Disowning Knowledge* (Cambridge: Cambridge UP).
Cavell, S. (1988) *In Quest of the Ordinary* (Chicago: Chicago University Press).
Cartwright, Nancy (1983) *How the Laws of Physics Lie* (Oxford, New York: Clarendon Press).
Cartwright, N. (1999) *The Dappled World. A Study of the Boundaries of Science* (Cambridge: Cambridge University Press).
Chassan, J. (1979) *Research Design in Clinical Psychology and Psychiatry*, 2nd edition (New York: Wiley).
Cheng, A. A. (2001) *The Melancholy of Race* (Oxford: Oxford UP).
Clark, T. J. (2001) *Farewell to an Idea* (New Haven: Yale UP).
Clark and Wright (1988) *Mind, Psychoanalysis, and Science* (Oxford: Blackwell).
Clinique différentielle des psychoses: rapports de la Rencontre internationale 1988 du Champ freudien à Buenos Aires (1988) (Buenos Aires: Navarin).
Coiffi, F. (1998) *Freud and the Question of Pseudoscience* (Chicago: Open Court).
Compte, A. (1864) *Cours de Philosophie Positive*, 2nd ed. Paris: Baillière.
Cooper, A. (1986) "Some Limitations on Therapeutic Effectiveness," *PSQ* 55:576-598.
Cooper, A. (2000) "The Changing Psychoanalytic Model of Mind," in *Whose Freud* (eds.) Brooks and Woloch (New Haven: Yale UP):275-280.
Coriat, I. (1917) "Some Statistical Results of the Psychoanalytic Treatment of the Psychoneuroses," *Psychoanalytic Review* 4:209-216.
Cozolino, L. (2002) *The Neuroscience of Psychotherapy: Building and Rebuilding the Human Brain* (New York: Norton).

Crews, F. (1986) *Skeptical Engagements* (New York: Oxford UP).
Crews, Fredrick (2000) "Unconscious Deeps and Empirical Shadows," in *Whose Freud?* (eds.) Brooks and Woloch (New Haven: Yale UP):19-32.
Critelli and Neumann (1984) "The Placebo: Conceptual Analysis of a Construct in Transition," *American Psychologist* 39:32-39.
Crutchfield, Farmer, Packard, and Shaw (1986) "Choas," *Scientific American* 255:46-57.
de Forest, I. (1954) *Leaven of Love. A Development of the Psychoanalytic Theory. Sandor Ferenczi* (New York: Harper).
de Man, P. (1983) *Blindness and Insight: Essays in the Rhetoric of Contemporary Criticism*, 2nd Revised Edition (Minneapolis: U of Minnesota Press).
de Matt, Philipszoon, Dekker, and De Jonghe (2007) "Costs and Benefits of Long-Term Psychoanalytic Therapy: Changes in Health Care Use and Work Impairment," *Harv. Rev. Psychiatry* November/December 2007:289-300.
de Maat, de Jonghe, Schoevers, and Dekker's (2008) "The Effectiveness of Long-Term Psychoanalytic Therapy: A Systematic Review of Empirical Studies," *Harv. Rev. Psychiatry* 17(1): 1-23.
de Toqueville, A. (1990) *Democracy in America*, Vol. 2, ed. Bradley and trans. Reeve (New York: Vintage).
de Vries, H. (1999) *Philosophy and the Turn to Religion* (Baltimore: The Johns Hopkins UP).
de Vries, H. (2002) *Religion and Violence* (Baltimore: The Johns Hopkins UP).
Dahl, Kächele, and Thomä (1988) *Psychoanalytic Process Research Strategies* (New York: Springer-Verlag).
Damasio, A. (1994) *Descartes' Error: Emotion, Reason, and the Human Brain* (New York: Putnam and Sons).
Damasio, A. (1999) *The Feeling of What Happens: Body and Emotion in the Making of Consciousness* (New York: Harcourt Brace & Co.).
Damasio, A, (2003) *Looking for Spinoza: Joy, Sorrow, and the Feeling Brain* (New York, Harcourt Brace & Co.).
Davidson, D. (1967) "Causal Relations," *Journal of Philosophy*, 64: 691-703.
Davidson, D. (1986) "A Coherence Theory of Truth and Knowledge," in *Truth and Interpretation: Perspectives on the Philosophy of Donald Davidson* (ed.) LePore (Oxford: Basil Blackwell).
Davidson, D. (2000) "On Truth," In *Whose Freud?* (eds.) Brooks and Woloch (New Haven: Yale UP).
Debray-Ritzen, P. (1972) *La Scholastique Freudienne* (Paris: Fayard).
DeLeon, VandenBos, and Cummings (1983) "Psychotherapy — Is it Safe, Effective, and Appropriate? The Beginning of an Evolutionary Dialogue," *American Psychologist* 38: 907-911.
Derrida, J. (1985) "White Mythology: Metaphor in the Text of Philosophy," in *Margins of Philosophy*, trans. Alan Bass (Chicago: University of Chicago Press): 207-272.
Derrida, J. (1994) *Given Time*, trans. Kaumf (Chicago: U of Chicago Press).
Derogatis, L. (1983). *SCL-90-R: Administration, Scoring and Procedures - Manual II* (Baltimore: Clinical Psychometrics Research Inc.).
Diem-Wille, G. (1997) "Observed Families Revisited — Two Years On: A Follow-Up Study" in Reid (ed.). *Developments in Infant Observations* (London: Routledge).
Dmitruk, Collins, and Clinger (1973) "The Barnum Effect and Acceptance of Negative Personal Evaluation," *J. Consult. and Clin. Psychol.* 41:192-4.
Dobbs Weinstein, I. (1995) *Maimonides and St. Thomas on the Limits of Reason* (Albany: SUNY UP).
Dor, J. (1994) *Clinique Psychanalytique* (Paris: Ed. Denoel).
Dollard and Miller (1950) *Personality and Psychotherapy: An Analysis in Terms of Learning, Thinking and Culture* (New York: McGraw-Hill).
Dossman, Kutter, Heinzel, and Wurmser (1997) "The Long-Term Benefits of Intensive Psychotherapy: A View from Germany," *Psychoanalytic Inquiry* 17S:74-86.
Douglas, Hull, and Goodman (1993) *How Classification Works: Nelson Goodman Among the Social Sciences* (Edinburgh: Edinburgh UP).

Dreher and Sandler (1993) *What do Psychoanalysts Want?* (New York: Routledge).
Duhem, P. (1962) *The Aim and Structure of Physical Theory*, trans. Weiner (New York: Athenaeum).
Dupré, J. (1995) *The Disorder of Things* (Cambridge: Harvard UP).
Dush, D. (1986) "The Placebo in Psychosocial Outcome Evaluations" *Evaluation and the Health Professions,* 9:421-438.
Eagle, M. (1984) *Recent Developments in Psychoanalysis* (New York: McGraw-Hill).
Earle, J. (1979) "An Approach to the Study of Analyzability and the Analysis: The Course of Forty Consecutive Cases Selected for Supervised Analysis," *PSQ* 48: 198-228.
Earle and Goldberg (1984) "Observations on Assessment of Analyzability by Experienced Analysts," *JAPA* 32:715-737.
Earman, J. (1993) "Underdetermination, Reason, and Realism," *Midwest Studies in Philosophy* 18:19-38.
Edelman, G. (1987) *Neural Darwinism* (New York: Basic Books).
Edelman, G. (1992) *Bright Air, Brilliant Fire: On the Matter of the Mind* (New York: Basic Books).
Edelman and Tononi (2000) *A Universe of Consciousness: How Matter Becomes Imagination* (New York: Basic Books).
Edelson, M. (1983) "Is Testing Psychoanalytic Hypotheses in the Psychoanalytic Situation Really Impossible?" *The Psychoanalytic Study of the Child* 38: 61-109.
Edelson, M. (1984) *Hypothesis and Evidence in Psychoanalysis* (Chicago: U of Chicago Press).
Edelson, M. (1985) "The Hermeneutic Turn and the Single Case Study in Psychoanalysis," *Psychoanal. Contemp. Thought* 8:567-614.
Eidelberg, L. (1933a) "Zur Metapsychologie des Masochismus," *Int Z. Psa*: 19:615-616.
Eidelberg, L. (1933b) "Zur Theorie und Klinik der Perversion," *Int Z. Psa.* 19:620-621.
Eidelberg, L. (1948 [1934]) "Contributions to the Study of Masochism," in *Studies in Psychoanalysis* (New York: Nervous and Mental Disease Monographs): 31-40 [originally published as "Beiträge zum Studium des Masochimus," in *Int. Z. Psa* 20:336-353.
Eissler, K. (1963) "Freud and the Psychoanalysis of History," *JAPA* 11: 675-703.
Eisenstein, Levy, and Marmor (1994) *The Dyadic Transaction: An Investigation Into The Nature Of The Psychotherapeutic Process* (New Brunswick, NJ: Transaction Publishers).
Eldridge, R. (1997) *Leading a Human Life: Wittgenstein, Intentionality, and Romanticism* (Chicago: U of Chicago Press).
Elliott, R. (1991) "Five Dimensions of Therapy Process," *Psychotherapy Research* 1:92-103.
Elliott and Anderson (1994) "Simplicity and Complexity in Psychotherapy Research," in Russell (ed.) *Psychotherapy research: Assessing and redirecting the tradition* (New York: Guilford): 65-113.
Ellis, A. "An Operational Reformulation of Some of the Basic Principles of Psychoanalysis," *Minnesota Studies* 1:131-54.
Epstein, A. (1979) "Effect of certain cerebral hemispheric diseases on dreaming," *Biol.* 14(1):77-93.
Epstein, L. (1979) "The Therapeutic Use of Countertransference Data with Borderline Patients," *Contemp. Psychoanal.* 15:248-275.
Epstein, S. (1979) "The Ecological Study of Emotions in Humans," in Pleiner (ed.) *Advances in the Study of Communication and Affect* (New York: Plenum).
Erdelyi and Goldberg (1979) "Let's Not Sweep Repression Under the Rug: Toward a Cognitive Psychology of Repression," in Kihlstrom and Evans (eds.), *Functional Disorders of Memory* (Hillsdale, N.J.: Erlbaum).
Erikson, E. (1959) *Identity and the Life Cycle: Selected Papers. Psychological Issues 1* (New York: International Universities Press).
Erikson, Erik. (1972 [1958]) "The Nature of Clinical Evidence" in *Insight and Responsibility* (New York: Norton).
Erle, J. (1979) "An Approach to the Study of Analyzability and the Analysis: The Course of Forty Consecutive Cases Selected for Supervised Analysis," *PSQ* 48:198-228.
Erle and Goldberg (1979) "Problems in the Assessment of Analyzability," *PSQ* 48:48-84.

Erle and Goldberg (1984) "Observations on Assessment of Analyzability by Experienced Analysts," *JAPA* 32:715-737.
Erwin, E. (1988) "Psychoanalysis: Clinical vs. Experimental Evidence," in *Mind, Psychoanalysis and Science* (eds.) P. Clark and Wright (Oxford: Basil Blackwell).
Evans, D. (1996) *Introductory Dictionary of Lacanian Psychoanalysis* (London: Routledge).
Eysenck, H. (1952) "The Effects of Psychotherapy: An Evaluation," *Journal of Consulting Psychology* 16:319-324.
Eysenck and Wilson (eds.) (1973) *The Experimental Study of Freudian Theories* (London: Methuen).
Fairbairn, W. (1952) *Psychological Studies of the Personality* (London: Routledge).
Fairbairn, W. (1954) *Object Relations Theory of the Personality* (New York: Harper Collins).
Fairbairn, W. (1958) "On the Nature and Aims of Psychoanalytic Treatment," *IJP* 39:374-385.
Ferenczi, S. (1950 [1909]) "Introjection and Transference," in *Contributions to Psychoanalysis*, trans. Ernest Jones (Boston: Richard G. Badger).
Ferenczi, S. (1950) "Stages in the Development of the Sense of Reality," in *Sex in Psychoanalysis* (New York: Basic Books): 216-239.
Ferenczi, S. (1955 [1926]) *Further Contributions to the Theory and Technique of Psychoanalysis* (London: Hogarth Press).
Ferenczi, S. (1955) *Final Contributions* (London: Hogarth).
Ferenczi, S. (1985 [1932]) *The Clinical Diary of Sandor Ferenczi*, ed. Dupont and trans. Balint and Zarday Jackson (Cambridge, Mass.: Harvard UP).
Farrell, B. (1961) "Can Psychoanalysis be Refuted?" *Inquiry* 4:16-36.
Farrell, B. (1964) "The Status of Psychoanalytic Theory," *Inquiry* 7:104-123.
Farrell, B. (1981) *The Standing of Psychoanalysis* (Oxford UP).
Fenichel, O. (1930) "Statistischer Bericht über die Therapeutische Tätigkeit, 1920-1930," in *Zehn Jare Berliner Psychoanalytisches Institut* (Berlin: Internationale Psychoanalytisches Verlag):13-19.
Fenichel, O. (1945) *The Psychoanalytic Theory of Neurosis* (New York: Norton).
Fenichel, O. (1953 [1935]) "A Critique of the Death Instinct," in *Collected Papers of Otto Fenichel* (New York: Norton).
Feyerabend, P. (1965) "Reply to Criticism," in *Boston Studies in the Philosophy of Science*, Vol. 2 (eds.) Cohen and Wartofsy: 223-61.
Feyerabend, P. (1990) *Farewell to Reason* (New York: Verso).
Feyerabend, P. (1999) Conquest of Abundance: A Tale of Abstraction Versus the Richness of Being, (ed.) Terpstra (Chicago: University of Chicago Press).
Feyerabend, P. (2010 [1975]) *Against Method*, 4th ed. (New York: Verso).
Fine and Fine (1990) "Four Psychoanalytic Perspectives: A Study of Differences in Interpretive Interventions," *JAPA* 38:1017-1047.
Fink, B. (1996) *The Lacanian Subject* (Princeton: Princeton UP).
Fink, B. (1999) *A Clinical Introduction to Lacanian Psychoanalysis* (Cambridge: Harvard).
Fink, B. (2004) *Lacan to the Letter* (Minneapolis: U of Minnesota Press).
Fisher, C. (1953) "Studies on the Nature of Suggestion — *Part II* the Transference Meaning of Giving Suggestions," *JAPA* 1:406-437.
Fisher and Greenberg (1977/1985) *The Scientific Credibility of Freud's Theories and Therapy* (New York: Basic Books).
Fisher and Greenberg (1996) *Freud Scientifically Reappraised* (New York: Wiley).
Flew, A. (1949) "Psychoanalytic Explanation," *Analysis* 10(1):8-15.
Flew, A. (1956) "Motives and the Unconscious," *Minnesota Studies* 1:155-73.
Fonagy, P. (1993) "Measuring the Ghost In the Nursery: An Empirical Study of the Relation between Parents' Mental Representations of Childhood Experiences And Their Infants' Security of Attachment," *JAPA* 41(4):957-989.
Fonagy, P. (1999) "Memory and Therapeutic Action," *IJP* 80:215-223.
Fonagy, P. (1999b) "Research in the IPA," *International Psychoanalysis* 8(1):9-11.
Fonagy, P. (2002) *An Open Door Review of Outcome Studies in Psychoanalysis, Second Revised Edition* (London: IPA).

Fonagy and Moran (1993) "Selecting Single Case Research Designs for Clinicians," in Miller, Luborsky, Barber, and Docherty (eds.) *Psychodynamic Treatment Research: A Handbook for Clinical Practice* (New York: Basic Books):62-95.
Fonagy and Target (1994) "The Efficacy of Psychoanalysis for Children with Disruptive Disorders," *Journal of the American Academy of Child and Adolescent Psychiatry*, 33: 45-55.
Fonagy and Target (1996) "Predictors of Outcome in Child Psychoanalysis: A Retrospective Study of 763 Cases at the Anna Freud Centre," *JAPA* 44:27-77.
Fonagy and Target (1997) "Attachment and Reflective Function: Their Role in Self-Organization," *Development & Psychopathology* 9:679-700.
Forer, B. (1949) "The Fallacy of Personal Validation: A Classroom Demonstration of Gullibility," *J. Abn. Soc. Psychol.* 44:118-123.
Forrester, J. (1997) *Truth Games: Lies, Money, and Psychoanalysis* (Cambridge: Harvard).
Forrester, J. (2000) "What Kind of Truth," in *Whose Freud?* (eds.) Brooks and Woloch (New Haven: Yale UP).
Fossage and Loew (eds.) (1987) *Dream Interpretation: A Comparative Study* (New York: PMA Publishing Corp).
Foucault, M. (1990) *The History of Sexuality, Vol I: An Introduction*, trans. Hurley (NY: Vintage).
Fowler, Wolford, Slade, and Tassinary (1981) "Lexical Access With and Without Awareness" *J. of Exper. Psychol.: Gen.* 110:341-362.
Frank, P. (1959) "Psychoanalysis and Logical Positivism," in S. Hook (ed.) *Psychoanalysis, Scientific Method, and Philosophy* (New York: NYU Press).
Frank, J.D. (1982) "Therapeutic Components Shared by All Psychotherapies," in Harvey and Parks (eds.) *The Master Lecture Series: Vol 1. Psychotherapy, Research, and Behavior Change* (Washington D.C.: American Psychological Association):5-37.
Frank, J.D (1983) "The Placebo Is Psychotherapy," *Behav. Brain Sci.* 6:291-2.
Freedman, Hoffenberg, Vorus, and Frosch (1999) "The Effectiveness of Psychoanalytic Psychotherapy: The Role of Treatment Duration, Frequency of Sessions, and the Therapeutic Relationship," *JAPA* 47:741-772.
Freud, A. (1936) *The Ego and the Mechanisms of Defense* (New York: IUP).
Freud, A. (1945) "Indications for Child Analysis," in *The Psycho-Analytic Treatment of Children* (London: Imago).
Freud, A. (1954) "The Widening Scope of Indications for Psychoanalysis: Discussion" *JAPA* 2:607-620.
Freud, A. (1966 [1954]) "Problems of Technique in Adult Analysis," *Bulletin of the Philadelphia Association for Psychoanalysis*" 4:44-69.
Freud, A. (1966) *Normality and Pathology in Childhood* (London: Hogarth).
Freud, A. (1969) "Difficulties in the Path of Psychoanalysis," *The Writings of Anna Freud*, Vol. 7 (New York: IUP).
Freud, A. (1972) "Child Analysis as a Sub-speciality of Psychoanalysis," *IJP* 53:151-156.
Freud, S. (1953-1974) *The Standard Edition of the Complete Psychological Works*, ed. and trans. Strachey (London: Hogarth Press).
Freud, S. (1954) *The Origins of Psychoanalysis: Sigmund Freud's Letters to Wilhelm Fliess, Drafts and Notes, 1887-1902* (New York: Basic Books).
Freud and Jones (1993) *The Complete Correspondence of Sigmund Freud and Ernest Jones, 1908-1939*, ed. Paskauskas (Cambridge, Mass.: Belknap).
Freidman, L (1976) "Problems of an Action Theory of the Mind," *IRP* 3:259-275.
Friedman, L. (1978) "Trends in the Psychoanalytic Theory of Treatment," *PSQ* 47:524-567.
Friedman, L. (1988) Anatomy of Psychoanalysis (Hillsdale, NJ: Analytic Press).
Friedman, L. (1995) "Psychic Reality in Psychoanalytic Theory," *IJP* 76:25-28.
Friedman, L (1999) "Why is Reality a Troubling Concept," *JAPA* 47:401-425.
Friedman, L. (2000) "Modern Hermeneutics and Psychoanalysis," *PSQ* LXIX:225-264.
Friedman, Garrison, Bucci, and Gorman (2005) "Factors Affecting Change in Private.
Psychotherapy Patients of Senior Psychoanalysts: An Effectiveness Study," *J. Amer. Acad. Psychoanal.* 33:583-610.

Frenkel-Brunswik, E. (1954a) "Meaning of Psychoanalytic Concepts and Confirmation of Psychoanalytic Theories," *Scientific Monthly* 79:293-300.

Frenkel-Brunswik, E. (1954b) "Psychoanalysis and the Unity of Science," *Proceedings of the American Academy of Arts and Sciences* 80:271-347.

Gabbard, G. (1995) "Countertransference: The Emerging Common Ground," *IJP* 76:475-485.

Gabbard, G. (1997) "Challenges in the Analysis of Adult Patients with Histories of Childhood Sexual Abuse," *Canadian Journal of Psychoanalysis* 5:1-25.

Gabbard, G. (2001) "A Contemporary Psychoanalytic Model of Countertransference," *Journal of Clinical Psychology* 57(8):983-991.

Gabbard, G. (2006) "A Neuroscience Perspective on Transference," *IJP* 1286:189-196.

Gabbard and Westin (2003) "Rethinking Therapeutic Action," *IJP* 84:823-41.

Gabriel and Zizek (2009) *Mythology, Madness and Laughter: Subjectivity in German Idealism* (New York: Continuum).

Gadamer, H-G. (1975) "Hermeneutics and Social Science," *Philosophy and Social Criticism* 2(4):307-316.

Gadamer, H-G. (2003) *Truth and Method* (New York: Continuum).

Galatzer-Levy, Bachrach, Skolnikoff, and Waldon (1997) *Does Psychoanalysis Work?* (New Haven: Yale UP).

Gargiulo, G. (1989) "Authority, the Self, and Psychoanalytic Experience," *Psychoanalytic Review* 76:149-161.

Garsten, B. (2009) *Saving Persuasion* (Cambridge, Mass.: Harvard UP).

Gassner et al. (1982) "The Emergence of Warded-Off Content," *Psychoanalysis and Contemporary Thought* 5:55-76.

Gedo, J. (1979) *Beyond Interpretation: Toward a Revised Theory for Psychoanalysis* (New York: International Universities Press).

Gedo and Pollock (eds.) (1976) *Freud: The Fusion of Science and Humanism: The Intellectual History of Psychoanalysis* (New York: IUP).

Gedo and Schaffer (1989) "An Empirical Approach to Studying Psychoanalytic Process," *Psychoanalytic Psychology* 6:227-291.

Gellner, E (1985) *The Coming of Unreason* (London: Paladin).

Gelman, S. (1988) "The Development of Induction within Natural Kind and Artifact Categories," *Cognitive Psychology* 20:65-96.

Gelman, S. (1989) "Children's Use of Categories to Guide Biological Inference," *Human Development* 32:65-71.

Gelman and Wellman (1991) "Insides and Essences: Early Understandings of the Non-Obvious," *Cognition* 38:213-244.

Ghent, E. (1999) "Masochism, Submission, and Surrender: Masochism as a Perversion of Surrender" in Mitchell and Aron (eds.) *Relational Psychoanalysis: The Emergence of a Tradition*: 211-242.

Giere, R. (1990) *Explaining Science* (Chicago: U of Chicago Press).

Giere, R. (2006) *Scientific Perspectivism* (Chicago: U of Chicago Press).

Gill, M. (1976) "Metapsychology is not Psychology" in *Psychology versus Metapsychology, Psychological Issues*, Monograph 26 (eds.) Gill and Holzman (New York: International Universities Press): 71-105.

Gill, M. (1984) "Psychoanalysis and Psychotherapy: a Revision," *International Review of Psychoanalysis* 11:161-179.

Gill, M. (1994) *Psychoanalysis in Transition: A Personal View* (Hillsdale, NJ: Analytic Press).

Gill and Hoffman (1982a) *Analysis of Transference II: Studies of Nine Audio Recorded Psychoanalytic Sessions* (New York: IUP).

Gill and Hoffman (1982b) "A Method for Studying the Analysis of Aspects of the Patient's Experience of the Relationship in Psychoanalysis and Psychotherapy," *JAPA* 30:137-167.

Gill and Holzman (eds.) (1976) *Psychology Versus Metapsychology: Psychoanalytic Essays in Memory of George S. Klein* (New York: IUP).

Gill and Muslin (1976) "Early Interpretation of Transference," *Journal of the American Psychoanalytic Association* 24(4):779-794.

Gilman, S. (1994) *The Case of Sigmund Freud: Medicine and Identity at the Fin de Siècle* (Baltimore: The Johns Hopkins UP).

Gilroy, P. (1993) *The Black Atlantic* (Cambridge, Mass.: Harvard UP).

Gitelson, M. (1973). *Psychoanalysis: Science and Profession* (New York: International Universities Press).

Glover, E. (1952) "Research Methods in Psycho-Analysis," *IJP* 33:403-409.

Glover, E. (1954) "The Indications for Psychoanalysis," *Journal of Medical Science* 100:393-401.

Glover, E. (1955) *The Technique of Psychoanalysis* (New York: International Universities Press).

Glymour, C. (1980) *Theory and Evidence* (Princeton: Princeton UP).

Glymour, C. (1982 [1974]) "Freud, Kepler, and the Clinical Evidence," in *Philosophical Essays on Freud* (eds.) Wollheim and Hopkins (Cambrodge: Cambridge UP):12-31.

Göethe, J. W. (1829) "Vermächtnis" in *103 Great Poems: A Dual Language Book*, ed. and trans. Appelbaum (New York: Dover).

Goldberger, Reuben, and Silberschatz (1976) "Symptom Removal in Psychotherapy," *Psychoanal. Contemp. Sci.* 5:513-536.

Goodman, N. (1983) *Fact, Fiction, and Forecast*, 4th Edition (Cambridge, Mass.: Harvard UP).

Gray, P. (1990) "The Nature of Therapeutic Action in Psychoanalysis," *JAPA* 38:1083-1097.

Green, A. (2001) "Science and Science Fiction in Infant Research," in Sandler et al. *Clinical and Observational Psychoanalytic Research: Roots of a Controversy* (London: Karnac).

Green, A. (2001) "What Kind of Research for Psychoanalysis," in Sandler et al. *Clinical and Observational Psychoanalytic Research: Roots of a Controversy* (London: Karnac).

Green, A. (2004) "Dissidence — Disagreement and Alternate Hypotheses for the Foundation of Psychoanalysis: On the Importance of Examining the Underlying Meanings of Freud's Hypotheses" in *Understanding Dissidence and Controversy in the History of Psychoanalysis* (ed.) Bergmann (New York: Other Press): 113-127.

Green, V. (ed) (2003) *Emotional Development in Psychoanalysis, Attachment Theory, and Neuroscience: Creating Connections* (Hove: Brunner-Routledge).

Greenson, R. (1965) "The Working Alliance and the Transference Neurosis," *PSQ* 34:155-181.

Gressot, M. (1956) "Psychanalyse et Connaissance," *La Psychanalyse*, 2:9-150.

Grinberg, L. (1962) "On a Specific Aspect of Counter-transference Due to the Patient's Projective Identification," *IJP* 43:436-440.

Grossman, L. (1996) "'Psychic Reality' and Psychic Testing," *IJP* 77:508-517.

Grossman, L. (1999) "What the Analyst Does Not Hear," *PSQ* 68:84-98.

Grostein, J. (1981) "The Significance of Kleinian Contributions to Psychoanalysis I. Kleinian Instinct Theory," *International Journal of Psychoanalytic Psychotherapy* 8:375-392.

Grostein, J. (1981) "The Significance of Kleinian Contributions to Psychoanalysis II. Freudian and Kleinian Concepts of Early Mental Development," 8:393-429.

Grostein, J. (1981) "Wilfred Bion: The Man, The Psychoanalyst, The Mystic," *Contemporary Psychoanalysis* 17(4):501-536.

Grostein, J. (1994) "Panel presentation. 'Projective Identification and Countertransference:' A brief commentary on their relationship," *Contemporary Psychoanalysis* 30: 578-592.

Grostein, J. (1994) "Projective Identification Reappraised: Part I: Projective Identification, Introjective Identification, the Transference/Countertransference Neurosis/Psychosis, and their Consummate Expression in the Crucifixion, the Pieta, and "Therapeutic Exorcism," *Contemporary Psychoanalysis* 30:708-746.

Grostein, J. (1995) "Projective Identification Reappraised: Part II," *Contemporary Psychoanalysis* 31:479-511.

Grosz, E. (1990) *Jacques Lacan: A Feminist Introduction* (London: Routledge).

Grünbaum, A. (1977a) "How Scientific is Psychoanalysis?" in *Science and Psychotherapy* (ed.) Stern, Horowitz, and Lynes (New York: Haven Press): 219-254.

Grünbaum, A. (1977b) "Is Psychoanalysis a Pseudo-Science? Karl Popper Versus Sigmund Freud (Part I)," *Zeitschrift für Philosophische Forschung* 31(3):333–353.

Grünbaum, A. (1978a) "Is Psychoanalysis a Pseudo-Science? (Part 2)," *Zeitschrift für Philosophische Forschung* 32(1):49–69.

Grünbaum, A. (1978b) "Popper versus Inductivism," in Radnitzky and Andersson (eds.), *Progress and Rationality in Science*. Boston Studies in the Philosophy of Science, Vol. LVIII. (Dordrecht: D. Reidel Publishing Co.): 117–142.

Grünbaum, A. (1979) "Epistemological Liabilities of the Clinical Appraisal of Psychoanalytic Theory," *Psychoanalysis and Contemporary Thought* 2: 451-526 .

Grünbaum, A. (1982) "Can Psychoanalytic Theory be Cogently Tested 'On the Couch," *Psychoanalysis and Contemporary Thought*, 5(2):155-255;(3):311-436.

Grünbaum, A. (1984) *The Foundations of Psychoanalysis* (Berkeley: U of California Press).

Grünbaum, A. (1988) "The Role of the Case Study Method in the Foundations of Psychoanalysis," *Canadian Journal of Philosophy* 18:654-657.

Grünbaum, A. (1990) "'Meaning' Connections and Causal Connections in the Human Sciences: The Poverty of Hermeneutic Philosophy," *JAPA* 38:559-577.

Grünbaum, A. (1993) *Validation in the Clinical Theory of Psychoanalysis: A Study in the Philosophy of Psychoanalysis* (Madison: IUP).

Guntrip, H. (1969) *Personality Structure and Human Interaction* (New York: IUP).

Gurewich, J.F. (1998) *Lacan and the New Wave in American Psychoanalysis: The Subject and the Self* (New York: Other Press).

Guttman, Jones, and Parrish (1980) *The Concordance to The Standard Edition of the Complete Psychological Works of Sigmund Freud* (Boston: Hall).

Habermas, J. (1971) *Knowledge and Human Interests*, trans. Shapiro (Boston: Beacon).

Habermas, J. (1973) *Theory and Practice*, trans. Viertel (Boston: Beacon).

Habermas, J. (1981) "Modern *Versus* Postmodernity," *New German Critique* 22:3-14.

Habermas, J. (1984) "Questions and Counter Questions," *Praxis International* 4(3):229-249 [reprinted in Bernstein (ed.) *Habermas and Modernity* (Cambridge, Mass: MIT Press) .

Habermas, J. (1987) "Philosophy as Stand-In and Interpreter," in Baynes, Bohman, and McCarthy (eds.) *After Philosophy: End or Transformation?* (Cambridge, MA: MIT Press).

Hacking, I. (1995) *Rewriting the Soul: Multiple Personality and the Sciences of Memory* (Princeton: Princeton UP).

Hägglund, Martin (2008) *Radical Atheism: Derrida and the Time of Life* (Stanford: Stanford UP).

Hale, N. (ed.) (1970) *James Jackson Putnam and Psychoanalysis* (Cambridge: Harvard UP).

Hall, J. (2004) *Roadblocks on the Journey of Psychotherapy* (New Jersey: Jason Aaronson).

Hamilton, G. (1992) *From Inner Sources: New Directions in Object Relations Psychoanalysis* (New York: Jason Aronson).

Hamilton, V. (1996) *The Analyst's Preconscious* (London: Routledge).

Hansel, J. (2000) "Modern Defense Analysis: Three Perspectives on the Same Hours," *JAPA* 48:929-940.

Harari, R. (1991) *Lacan's Seminar on Anxiety* (New York: Other Press).

Harth, E. (1982) *Reflections on the Physical Basis of Consciousness* (New York: Morrow).

Hartmann, H. (1950). "Comments on the Psychoanalytic Theory of the Ego," *Psychoanal. St. Child* 5:74-96.

Hartmann, H. (1951a) "Technical Implications of Ego-Psychology," *PSQ* 20:31-43.

Hartmann, H. (1951b) "Some Psychoanalytic Comments on 'Culture and Personality,'" in Wilbur and Muensterberger (eds.) *Psychoanalysis and Culture*. (New York: IUP).

Hartmann, H. (1958 [1939]) *Ego Psychology and the Problem of Adaptation*, trans. Rapaport (New York: International Universities Press).

Hartmann, H. (1964) *Essays on Ego Psychology. Selected Problems in Psychoanalytic Technique* (New York: IUP).

Hartmann and Kris (1945) "The Genetic Approach in Psychoanalysis," *The Psychoanalytic Study of the Child* 1:11-30.

Haynal, A. (1993) *Psychoanalysis and the Sciences: Epistemology—History*, trans. Holder (Berkeley: U of California Press).

Hayden and Silverstein (1983) "The Effects of Tachistoscopic Oedipal Stimulation on Competitive Dart Throwing," *Psychological Research Bulletin* 23:1-12.

H.D. (1956) *Tribute to Freud* (New York: McGraw-Hill).

Hegel, G.W. (1969) *Philosophie der Religion*, in *Werke* Vol. 17 (Frankfurt: Suhrkamp).

Hegel, G.W. (1979) *Phenomenology of Spirit*, trans. Miller (Oxford: Oxford UP).
Hegel, G.W. (1982) *Hegel's Logic, Being Part One of the Encyclopedia of the Philosophical Sciences*, trans. W. Wallace (Oxford: Clarendon Press).
Hegel, (1986) *Werke in zwanzig Bänden* (Frankfurt am Main: Suhrkamp).
Hegel, G.W. (1991) *Elements of the Philosophy of Right*, ed. Wood, trans. Nisbet (Cambridge: Cambridge UP).
Heidegger, M. (1962 [1927]) *Being and Time*, trans. Macquarrie and Robinson (New York: Harper and Row).
Heilbrunn, G. (1963) "Results with Psychoanalytic Therapy. Report of 241 Cases," *Am. J. Psychother.* 17:427-35.
Heilbrunn, G. (1966) "Results With Psychoanalytic Therapy and Professional Commitment," *Am. J. Psychother.* 20:89-99.
Heinzel, Breyer, Klein (1998) "Ambulante analytische Einzel- und Gruppenpsychotherapie in einer bundesweiten katamnestischen Evaluationsstudie," *Gruppenpsychoth Gruppendynamik* 34:135–52.
Heisenberg, W. (1952) *Philosophic Problems of Nuclear Science*, trans. Hayes (New York: Pantheon).
Hempel, C. (1965/1970) *Aspects of Scientific Explanation* (New York: Free Press).
Hempel, C. (1970) "On the 'Standard Conception' of Scientific Theories," in Radner and Winokur (eds). *Minnesota Studies in the Philosophy of Science* Vol. 4 (Minneapolis: U of Minnesota Press).
Henrich, D. (1994) *The Unity of Reason: Essays on Kant's Philosophy* (London: Harvard University Press).
Herman, B. (1996) *The Practice of Moral Judgment* (Cambridge, Mass.: Harvard UP).
Herman, J. (1992) *Trauma and Recovery* (New York: Basic Books).
Hermann, I. (1933) "Zum Triebleben der Primaten," *Imago* 19:113-25.
Hermann, I. (1975 [1936]) "Clinging — Going-in-Search," *PSQ* 45:5-36.
Hertz, H. (1893). *Electric Waves: Being Researches on the Propagation of Electric Action with Finite Velocity Through Space*, trans. David Evans Jones (Ithaca: Cornell UP).
Hertz, H. (1984) *Die Prinzipien der Mechanik in neuen Zusammenhange dargestellt: Drei Beiträge* (Leipzig: Barth).
Hertz, N. (1983) "Dora's Secrets, Freud's Techniques," *Diacritics* Spring:65-83.
Hesse, M. (1966) *Models and Analogies in Science*, Revised Edition. (Notre Dame, Indiana: Notre Dame University Press).
Hesse, M. (1974) *The Structure of Scientific Inference* (London: Macmillan).
Hesse, M. (1980) *Revolutions and Reconstructions in the Philosophy of Science* (Brighton: The Harvester Press).
Heuft, Seibuechler-Engec, Taschke, and Senf (1996) "Langzeitoutcome ambulanter psychoanalytischer Psychotherapien und Psychoanalysen: eine textinhaltsanalytische Untersuchung von 53 Katamneseinterviews," *Forum der Psychoanalyse: Zeitschrift fuer Klinische Theorie und Praxis* 12:342-355.
Hilgard, E. (1952) "Experimental Approaches to Psychoanalysis," in Pumpian-Mindlin (ed.) *Psychoanalysis as Science* (Palo Alto: Stanford UP).
Hirschfeld, Lawrence (1996) *Race in the Making.* (Cambridge: The MIT Press).
Hirschman, A. (1997) *The Passions and the Interests* (NJ: Princeton).
Hobson, J. (1988) *The Dreaming Brain* (New York: Basic Books).
Hobson, J. (1997) "Dreaming as Delirium: A Mental Status Exam of Our Nightly Madness," *Sem. in Neurol.*, 17:121-128.
Hobson, J. (1999) "The New Neuropsychology of Sleep," *Neuropsychoanalysis*, 1:157-183.
Hobson, Hoffman, Helfand, and Kostner (1987) "Dream Bizarreness and the Activation-Synthesis Hypothesis," *Hum. Nuerobiol.*, 6:157-164.
Hofer, M. (1980) *The Roots of Human Behavior* (San Francisco: Freedman).
Høglend, Per (2004) "Analysis of Transference in Psychodynamic Psychotherapy: A Review of Empirical Research," *Canadian Journal of Psychoanalysis* 12:279-300 .

Holmes, D. (1990). "The Evidence for Repression: An Examination of Sixty Years of Research," in *Repression and Dissociation: Implications for Personality, Theory, Psychopathology and Health* (ed.) Singer (University of Chicago Press: Chicago): 85-102.

Holt, R. (1976) "Freud's Theory of the Primary Process: Present Status," *Psychoanalysis & Contemporary Science* 5:61-99..

Holt, R. (1976) "Drive or Wish? A Reconsideration of the Psychoanalytic Theory of Motivation," in Gill and Holzman (eds.) *Psychology versus Metapsychology: Psychoanalytic Essays in Memory of George S. Klein. Psychological Issues* 9(4) Monograph 36:158-197.

Holzman, P. (1985) "Psychoanalysis: Is the Therapy Destroying the Science?" *JAPA* 33: 725-770.

Hook, Sidney (1959) *Psychoanalysis: Scientific Method and Philosophy* (New York: NYU Press).

Home, H. (1966) "The Concept of Mind," *IJP* 47:42-49.

Horney, K. (1926) "The Flight from Womanhood," *IJP* 7:324-339.

Hornstein, G. (1992) "The Return of the Repressed: Psychology's Problematic Relations with Psychoanalysis, 1909-1960," *Amer. Psychol.* 47:254-263.

Hospers, J. (1959) "Philosophy and Psychoanalysis," in Hook (ed.) *Psychoanalysis, Scientific Method, and Philosophy* (New York: NYU Press).

Hovarth, A. (2005) "The Therapeutic Relationship: Research and Theory [Introduction to Special Issue]," *Psychotherapy Research* 15:3-17.

Horvath and Symonds (1991) "Relation Between Working Alliance and Outcome in Psychotherapy: A Meta-analysis," *Journal of Counseling Psychology* 38(2):139-149.

Horvath, P. (1988) "Placebos and Common Factors in Two Decades of Psychotherapy Research," *Psycho Bull* 104(2):214-225.

Hunter, V. (1994) *Psychoanalysts Talk* (New York: Guilford Press).

Husserl, E. (2012 [1931]) *Ideas: General Introduction to Pure Phenomenology* (New York: Routledge).

Husserl, E. (1970) *The Crisis of the European Sciences and Transcendental Phenomenology*, trans. Carr (Evanston: Northwestern UP).

Muslin and Gill (1978) "Transference In The Dora Case," *Journal of the American Psychoanalytic Association* 26(2):311-329.

Isaacs, S. (1948) "The Nature and Function of Phantasy," *International Journal of Psycho-Analysis* 29:73-97.

INSERM. (2004) *Psychothérapie — Trois Approches Évaluées* (Paris: INSERM).

Jacobs, T. (1991) *The Use of the Self: Countertransference and Communication in the Analytic Situation* (Madison, CT: IUP).

Jacoby, R. (1983) *The Repression of Psychoanalysis* (Chicago: U of Chicago Press).

Jaménez, J. P. (2006) "After Pluralism: Towards a New, Integrated Psychoanalytic Paradigm," *IJP* 87(6):1487-1508.

Jonas, H. (1982) *The Phenomenon of Life* (Chicago: The University of Chicago Press).

Jones, E. (1936) *Decennial Report of the London Clinic of Psychoanalysis, 1926-1936.*

Jones, E. (1957) *The Life and Work of Sigmund Freud, III* (London: Hogarth Press).

Jones, Enrico. (1993) "How Will Psychoanalysis Study itself?" *JAPA* 41S:91-108.

Jones, Enrico (ed.) (1993) "Special Section: Single-Case Research in Psychotherapy" in *Journal of Consulting and Clinical Psychology* 61(3), Jun 1993:371-420.

Jones, Cumming, and Horowitz (1988) "Another Look at the Non-specific Hypothesis of Therapeutic Effectiveness," *J. Consult. Clin. Psychol.* 56:48-55.

Jones and Windholz (1990) "The Psychoanalytic Case Study: Toward A Method for Systematic Inquiry," *JAPA* 38:65-73.

Joseph, B. (1989) *Psychic Equilibrium and Psychic Change* (London: Routledge).

Joseph, R. (1996) *Neuropsychiatry, Neuropsychology, and Clinical Neuroscience: Emotion, Evolution, Cognition, Language, Memory, Brain Damage, and Abnormal Behavior*, 2nd Edition (Baltimore: Lippincott Williams & Wilkins).

Jung, C. (1946) "Psychology of Transference" in *The Collected Works of C. G. Jung*, ed. Read, Herbert, Fordham, Michael, and Adler, trans. R.F. C. Hull, Vol. 16, pars. 353-539 (New York: Pantheon, 1954).

Jünger, E. (1930) "Totale Mobilmachung" in Kriegund Krieger, ed. by E. Jünger (Berlin: Junker und Dünnhaupt); in The Heidegger Controversy, pp. 119-39 as "Total Mobilization," trans. Joel Golb and Richard Wolin.

Kachele, H. (1999) A Multicenter Study of Expenditure and Success in Psychodynamic Therapy of Eating Disorders: Study Design and Initial Results," *Psychother Psychosom Med Psychol,* 49(3-4):100-108.

Kandel, E. (1998) "A New Intellectual Framework for Psychiatry," *Am J Psychiatry* 155:457-69.

Kandel, E. (1999) "Biology and the Future of Psychoanalysis: A New Intellectual Framework for Psychiatry Revisited," *Am J Psychiatry* 156:505-24.

Kant, I. (1975 [1786]) *Metaphysiche Anfrangsgründe der Naturwissenschaften,* in*Kant-Werke,* 10 Vols., (ed.) Weischedel (Darmstadt: Wissen-schaftliche Buchgesellschaft) 8:7-136.

Kant, I. (1987 [1790]) *Critique of the Power of Judgment,* trans. W. Pluhar (Indianapolis: Hackett).

Kant, I. (1992) *The Conflict of the Faculties,* trans. Gregor (U of Nebraska Press).

Kant, I. (1999 [1781]) *Critique of Pure Reason,* ed. and trans. Guyer and Wood (Cambridge: Cambridge University Press).

Kantrowitz, J. (1993) "Outcome Research in Psychoanalysis: Review and Reconsideration," *JAPA* 41S:313-328.

Kantrowitz, Katz, and Paolitto (1990) "Follow-up of Psychoanalysis Five to Ten Years After Termination: III. The Relation Between Resolution of the Transference and the Patient-Analyst Match," *JAPA* 38:665-678.

Kantrowitz, Paolitto et al. 1986. "Affect Availability, Tolerance, Complexity, and Modulation in Psychoanalysis: Follow-up of Longitudinal, Prospective Study," *JAPA* 34:529-559.

Kantrowitz et al. (1989) "The Patient-Analyst Match and the Outcome of Psychoanalysis: A Pilot Study," *JAPA* 37:893-919.

Kaplan, A. (1981) "From Discovery to Validation," *JAPA* 29:3-26.

Kandel, E. (1998) "A New Intellectual Framework for Psychiatry," *Am J Psychiatry* 155:457-69.

Kandel, E. (1999) "Biology and the Future of Psychoanalysis: A New Intellectual Framework for Psychiatry Revisited," *Am J Psychiatry* 156:505-24.

Kanzer, M. (1961) "Verbal and Nonverbal Aspects of Free Association," *PSQ* 30:327-50.

Kanzer, M. (1961/1979) "Freud and the Demon," in Kanzer & Glenn (eds.) *Freud and his Self-Analysis* (New York: Jason Aronson).

Kanzer and Glenn (eds.) (1979) *Freud and His Self-Analysis* (New York: Jason Aronson).

Katz et al. (1987a) "The Role of Reality in Psychoanalysis: Follow-Up of 22 Cases," *JAPA* 35:367-385.

Katz et al. (1987b) "Changes in the Level and Quality of Object Relations in Psychoanalysis: Follow-up of a Longitudinal Prospective Study," *JAPA* 35:23-46.

Keat, R. (1981) *The Politics of Social Theory: Habermas, Freud and the Critique of Positivism* (Oxford: Basil Blackwell).

Kernberg, O. (1975) *Borderline Conditions and Pathological Narcissism* (New York: Jason Aronson) .

Kernberg, O. (1976) *Object Relations Theory and Clinical Psychoanalysis* (New York: Jason Aronson).

Kernberg, O. (2001) "Some Recent Developments in the Technical Approaches of English Language Psychoanalytic Schools," *PSQ* 70:519-547.

Kernberg, O. (2004) "Psychoanalytic Affect Theory in the Light of Contemporary Neurobiology," Paper delivered at 6th International Psychoanalytic Symposium, Delphi, October 2004.

Kessel and Hyman (1933) "The Value of Psychoanalysis as a Therapeutic Procedure," *JAMA* 101:1612-1615.

Khan, M. (1963) 'The Concept of Cumulative Trauma', *Psychoanal. Stud. Child* 18:286-306.

Khan, M. (1964) "Ego-Distortion, Cumulative Trauma, and the Role of Reconstruction in the Analytic Situation," in *The Privacy of the Self* (London: Hogarth): 59-68.

Kiesler, C. (1985) "Meta-analysis, Clinical Psychology, and Social Policy" *Clinical Psychology Review* 5: 3-12.

Kimura et al. (2004) "Interhemispheric Difference in Emotional Response Without Awareness," *Physiology & Behavior* 82:727-731.
Kirsner, D. (1982) "Self-Psychology and the Psychoanalytic Movement: An Interview with Dr. Heinz Kohut," *Psychoanalysis and Contemporary Thought* 5(3):483-95.
Kitcher, P. "Species," *Philosophy of Science* 51:308-33.
Klauber, J. (1968) "On the Dual Use of Historical and Scientific Method in Psychoanalysis," *IJP* 49:80-88.
Kline, P. (1972/1981) *Fact and Fantasy in Fantasy in Freudian Theory* (London: Methuen).
Klein, G. (1973). "Two Theories or One? Perspectives to Change in Psychoanalytic Theory," *Bulletin of Menninger Clinic* 37:101-136.
Klein, G. (1976) *Psychoanalytic Theory: An Exploration of the Essentials* (New York: IUP).
Klein, M. (1952) "The Origins of Transference," in *Envy and Gratitude and Other Works*, Vol. 3 of *The Writings of Melanie Klein* (London: Hogarth Press and the Institute of Psycho-Analysis, 1975): 45-56.
Klein, M. (1988) *Envy and Gratitude & Other Works, 1946-1963* (London: Virago).
Klein, M. et al. (1952) *Developments in Psychoanalysis* (London: Hogarth).
Klein Villa, Shevrin, Snodgrass, Bazan, and Brakel (2006) "Testing Freud's Hypothesis that Word Forms and Word Meanings are Functionally Distinct: Subliminal Primary-Process Cognition and its Link to Personality" *Neuropsychoanalysis*, 8:117-138.
Knight, R. (1941) "Evaluation of the Results of Psychoanalytic Therapy," *Am. J. Psychiatry* 98:434-446.
Knoblauch, S. (2005) "What Are We Trying to Do When We Write About the Psychoanalytic Interaction? The Relevance of Theory and Research to Clinical Responsiveness" *Psychoanalytic Dialogues*, 15(6):883-896.
Koenigsberg et al. (1993) "A Method for Analyzing Therapist Interventions in the Psychotherapy of Boderline Patients," *J. Psychother. Pract. Res.* 2:119-134.
Kohut, H. (1959) "Introspection, Empathy, and Psychoanalysis," *JAPA* 7:459-483.
Kohut, H. (1978) *The Search for the Self: Selected Writings of Heinz Kohut: 1950-1978*, Vol. 2 (ed.) Ornstein (New York: IUP).
Kohut, H. (1979), "The Two Analyses of Mr. Z," *IJP* 60:3-27.
Kohut, H. (1984) *How Does Analysis Cure?* (Chicago: University of Chicago Press).
Kohut and Wolf (1978) "The Disorders of the Self and their Treatment: An Outline," *IJP* 59:413-425.
Kobak and Sceery (1988). Attachment in Late Adolescence: Working Models, Affect Regulation, and Representations of Self and Others," *Child Development* 59:135–146.
Korsgaard, C. (1996) *The Sources of Normativity* (Cambridge: Cambridge UP).
Korsgaard, C. (2009) *Self-Constitution: Agency, Identity, and Integrity* (Oxford: Oxford UP).
Kramer, Y. (1996) "Freud and the Culture Wars," *Public Interest* 124:37-51.
Kris, A. (1982) *Free Association: Method and Process* (New Haven: Yale UP).
Kris, A. (1983) "Determinants of Free Association in Narcissistic Phenomena," *Psychoanal. Study Child.* 38:439-58.
Kris, E. (1950a) "On Preconscious Mental Processes," *PSQ* 19:540-560.
Kris, E. (1950b) "Notes on the Development and on Some Current Problems of Psychoanalytic Child Psychology," *Psychoanalytic Study of the Child* 15:378-394.
Kris, E. (1951) "Ego Psychology and Interpretation in Psychoanalytic Therapy," *PSQ* 20:15-30.
Kris, E. (1952) *Psychoanalytic Explorations in Art* (New York: IUP).
Kris, E. (1956) "The Recovery of Childhood Memories in Psychoanalysis," *Psychoanalytic Study of the Child* 11:54-88.
Kris, E. (1975 [1947]) "The Nature of Psychoanalytic Propositions and Their Validity," in *Selected Papers of Ernst Kris* (New Haven: Yale).
Kristeva, J. (1984) *Revolution in Poetic Language*, trans. Roudiez (New York: Columbia University Press).
Kristeva, J. (1987) *Tales of Love*, trans. Leon Roudiez (New York: Columbia University Press).
Kristeva, J. (1988) *In the Beginning Was Love*, trans. A. Goldhammer (New York: Columbia UP).

Kristeva, J. (1992) *Black Sun*, trans. L. Roudiez. New York: Columbia UP.
Kristeva, J. (1995) *New Maladies of the Soul*, trans. Ross Guberman (New York: Columbia UP).
Kuhn, T. (1970a) *The Structure of Scientific Revolutions* (Chicago: U of Chicago Press).
Kuhn, T. (1970b) "Reflections on My Critics," in Lakatos and Musgrave (eds.) *Criticism and the Growth of Knowledge* (Cambridge: Cambridge UP).
Lacan, J. (1961-2) *The Seminar of Jacques Lacan, Book X: Anxiety, 1962-1963*, trans. Cormac Gallagher (unpublished typescript) .
Lacan, J. (1965-6) *The Seminar of Jacques Lacan, Book XIII: The Object of Psychoanalysis, 1965-1966*, trans. Cormac Gallagher (unpublished typescript).
Lacan, J. (1971) "Lituraterre," *Littérature (Larousse)* 3; republished in Ornicar? 41, April-June 1987:5-13.
Lacan, J. (1971) *Le Séminaire de Jacques Lacan, Livre XVIII: D'un discours qui ne serait pas du semblant* (unpublished typescript).
Lacan, J. (1972) *Le Séminaire de Jacques Lacan, Livre XIX: Le savoir de psychoanalyste, 1971-2* (unpublished typescript).
Lacan, J. (1973) *Le Séminaire, Livre XI: Les quatre concepts fondamentaux de la psychanalyse*, ed. Jacques-Alain Miller (Paris: Seuil).
Lacan, J. (1981) *Le Séminaire III: Les Psychoses* (Paris: Seuil).
Lacan, J. (1982) *Écrits: A Selection*, trans. Sheridan (W. W. Norton & Company).
Lacan, J. (1988/1991) *The Seminar of Jacques Lacan: Book I*, trans. Forrester (New York: W.W. Norton).
Lacan, J. (1994) *Le Séminaire de Jacques Lacan, Livre IV: La relation d'objet, 1956-1957* (ed.) J-A Miller (Paris: Ed. Seuil).
Lacan, J. (1997) *The Seminar of Jacques Lacan: Book III: The Psychoses 1955-1956*, trans. J-A Miller and R. Grigg (New York: Norton).
Lacan, J. (1998) *The Four Fundamental Concepts of Psychoanalysis*, trans. J-A. Miller and A. Sheridan (London: Norton).
Lacan, J. (2004) *Écrits: A Selection*, trans. Fink (New York: Norton).
Lacan, J. (2007) *Écrits*, trans. Fink (New York: Norton).
Lagache, D. (1949) *L'Unité de la psychologie* (Paris: P.U.F) .
Lagache, D. (1950) "Définition et Aspects de la Psychoanalyse," *Rev. Fr. De Psychoan.* 14(3): 384-423.
Lagache, D. (1950) "Fascination de la Conscience par le moi," *La Psychoanalyse*, 3:33-47.
Lambert, Shapiro, and Bergin (1986) "Evaluation of Therapeutic Outcomes" in Garfield and Bergin (eds.) *Handbook of Psychotherapy and Behavior Change*, 3rd edition (New York: Wiley).
Lambert and Bergin (1994) "The Effectiveness of Psychotherapy," in Bergin and Garfield (eds.), *Handbook of Psychotherapy and Behavior Change*, 4th ed. (New York: Wiley): 143-189.
Laplanche, J. (1976) *Life and Death in Psychoanalysis*, trans. Mehlman (Baltimore: The Johns Hopkins University Press).
Laplanche, J. (1989) *New Foundations for Psychoanalysis*, trans. Macey (Oxford: Basil Blackwell).
Laplanche, J. (1992) "Interpretation Between Determinism and Hermeneutics: A Restatement of the Problem," *IJP* 73:429-445.
Laplanche and Pontalis (1973) *The Language of Psychoanalysis*, trans. Nicholson-Smith (New York: Norton).
LaPorte, J. (2004) *Natural Kinds and Conceptual Change* (Cambridge: Cambridge UP).
Laudan, L. (1977) *Progress and Its Problems: Toward a Theory of Scientific Growth* (Berkeley: University of California Press).
Laudan, L. (1981a) *Science and Hypothesis: Historical Essays on Scientific Methodology*. (Kluwer Academic Pub.).
Laudan, L. (1981b) "A Confutation of Convergent Realism," *Philosophy of Science* 48:19-49.
Laudan, L. (1981c) "The Pseudo-Science of Science?" *Philosophy of the Social Sciences* 11:173-198.

Laudan, L. (1984) *Science and Values: The Aims of Science and Their Role in Scientific Debate* (Berkeley: U of California Press).
Laudan, L. (1984) "Explaining the Success of Science: Beyond Epistemic Realism and Relativism," in *Science and Reality* (eds.) Cushing, Dealaney, and Gutting (Notre Dame: U of Notre Dame Press):83-105 .
Laudan and Lepin (1991) "Empirical Equivalence and Underdetermination," *Journal of Philosophy* 88:449-472.
Laymon, R. (1980) "Idealization, Explanation, and Confirmation," *PSA* 1980:336-350.
Leader, D. (1997) "Phantasy in Klein and Lacan," in *The Klein-Lacan Dialogues* (eds.) Burgoyne and Sullivan (London, Rebus Press): 83-95.
Lear, J. (2000) "Truth in Psychoanalysis," in *Whose Freud?* (eds.) Brooks and Woloch (New Haven: Yale UP).
Lear, J. (2004) *Therapeutic Action: An Earnest Plea for Irony* (New York: Other Press).
LeDoux, J. (1996) *The Emotional Brain* (New York: Simon and Schuster).
Leichsenring, F. (2004) "Randomized Controlled versus Naturalistic Studies: A New Research Agenda," *Bull. Menninger Clin.* 68:137-51.
Leichsenring, F. (2005) "Are Psychodynamic and Psychoanalytic Therapies Effective? A Review of Empirical Data," *IJP* 86:841-868.
Leichsenring, Rabung, and Leibing E. (2004) "The Efficacy of Short-Term Psychodynamic Psychotherapy in Specific Psychiatric Disorders: a Meta-Analysis," *Archives of General Psychiatry* 61(12):1208-16.
Leupin, A. (1991) *Lacan and the Human Sciences* (Lincoln: U of Nebraska Press).
Leuzinger-Bohleber et al. (2003) "How To Study the 'Quality of Psychoanalytic Treatments' and their Long-Term Effect on Patients' Well-Being: A Representative, Multi-Perspective Follow-Up Study," *IJP* 84:263-90.
Levin, F. (1991) *Mapping the Mind: The Intersection of Psychoanalysis and Neurosciences* (Hillsdale: Analytic Press).
Levin, F. (2002) *Psyche and Brain: The Biology of Talking Cures* (Madison: IUP).
Levinas, E. (2008) *Totality and Infinity*, trans. Lingis (Pittsburgh: Duquesne UP).
Levine and Wallach (2002) *Psychological Problems, Social Issues, and the Law* (Boston: Allyn & Bacon).
Levinger and Clark (1961) "Emotional Factors in the Forgetting of Word Associations," *J. Abn. Soc. Psychol.* 62:99-105.
Levi, P. (1988) *The Drowned and the Saved* (New York: Vintage).
Lewes, K. (1989) *The Psychoanalytic Theory of Male Homosexuality* (New York: Plume).
Limenatani, A. (1986) "Variations on some Freudian Themes," *IJP* 67:235-43.
Lipton, S. (1977a) "The Advantages of Freud's Technique as Shown in his Analysis of the Rat Man," *IJP* 58:255-273.
Lipton, S. (1977b) "Clinical Observations on Resistance to the Transference," *IJP* 58:463-472.
Little, M. (1951) "Countertransference and the Patient's Response to It," *IJP* 32:32-40.
Loch, W. (1997) "Some Comments on the Subject of Psychoanalysis and Truth," in Smith (ed.) *Thought, Consciousness, and Reality* (New Haven: Yale): 219-31.
Loewald, H. (1986) "Transference-countertransference," *Journal of the American Psychoanalytic Association* 34:275-288.
Longino, H. (2002) *The Fate of Knowledge* (Princeton: Princeton UP).
Loftus, E. (1993) *Memory* (Reading, MA: Addison-Wesley).
Lorenzer, A. (1970) *Kritik des psychoanalytischen Symbolbegriffs and Sprachzerstörung und —Rekonstruktion* (Frankfurt am Main: Suhrkamp Verlag).
Lowenberg, P. (2007) "Cultural History and Psychoanalysis,"*Psychoanal. Hist.*9(1):17-37.
Lowenstein, R. (1982) *Practice and Precept in Psychoanalytic Technique: Selected Papers of Rudolph M. Lowenstein* (New Haven: Yale UP).
Lowenstein et al. (1966) *Psychoanalysis: A General Psychology: Essays in Honor of Heinz Hartmann* (New York: IUP).
Luborsky, L. (1984) *Principles of Psychoanalytic Psychotherapy* (New York: Basic).
Luborsky, L. (1996) *The Symptom-Context Method: Symptoms as Opportunities in Psychotherapy* (Washington, D.C.: American Psychological Association).

Luborsky, Chandler, Auerbach, Cohen, Bachrach (1971) "Factors Influencing the Outcome of Psychotherapy: A Review of Quantitative Research," *Psychol. Bull.* 75:145-85.

Luborsky, Crits-Cristoph, Mintz, and Auerbach (1988) *Who Will Benefit from Psychotherapy* (New York: Basic Books).

Luborsky, Crits-Christoph, et. al (1990) *Understanding Transference: The CCRT Method* (New York: Basic Books).

Luborsky, Singer, and Luborsky (1975) "Comparative Studies of Psychotherapies: Is it true that 'Everyone has won and all must have prizes"? *Arch. Gen. Psychiat.* 32: 995-1008.

Luborsky and Spence (1978) "Quantitative Research on Psychoanalytic Therapy," in Garfield and Bergin (eds.) *Handbook of Psychotherapy and Behavior Change.* (New York, Wiley): 331-368.

Luhmann, N. (1998) *Love as Passion: The Codification of Intimacy*, trans. Gaines and Jones (Stanford: Stanford UP).

Lukács, G. (1980 [1962]) *The Destruction of Reason*, trans. Palmer (London: The Merlin Press).

Lussier, A. (1991) "The Search for A Common Ground: A Critique," *IJP* 72:57-62.

MacIntyre, A. (1958) *The Unconscious* (London: Routledge).

Macmillan, M. (1991) *Freud Evaluated* (Cambridge: MIT Press).

Mahony, P. (1987) *Freud as Writer* (New Haven: Yale UP).

Main, Kaplan, and Cassidy (1985) "Security in Infancy, Childhood and Adulthood: A Move to the Level of Representation," in Bretherton and Waters (eds.), *Growing Points of Attachment Theory and Research,* Monographs of the Society for Research in Child Development, 50(1-2, Serial No. 209):66-104.

Mancia, M. (2006) "Implicit Memory and Early Unrepressed Unconscious: Their Role in the Therapeutic Process (How the Neurosciences Can Contribute to Psychoanalysis," *IJP* 87:83-104.

Mandler, J. (1992) "How to Build a Baby: II. Conceptual Primitives," *Psychological Review* 99:587-604.

Marx and Engels (1979) *The Eighteenth Brumaire of Louis Bonaparte* in *Collected Works*, Vol. 11 (New York: International Publishers).

Masling, J. (ed.) (1983) *Empirical Studies of Psychoanalytic Theories*, Vol. 1 (New Jersey: Erlbaum).

Masling, J. (ed.) (1986) *Empirical Studies of Psychoanalytic Theories*, Vol. 2 (New Jersey: Erlbaum).

Masling, J. (ed.) (1990) *Empirical Studies of Psychoanalytic Theories*. Vol. 3. New Jersey: Erlbaum).

Masling and Cohen (1987) "Psychotherapy, Clinical Evidence, and the Self-Fulfilling Prophecy," *Psychoanal. Psychol.* 4:65-79.

Masling and Schwartz (1979) "A Critique of Research in Psychoanalytic Theory," *General Psychology Monographs* 100:257-307.

Masterson and Rinsley (1975) "Borderline Syndrome: The Role of the Mother in the Genesis and Psychic Structure of the Borderline Personality," *IJP* 56:163-177.

Mayes, L. (2003) "Partnering with the Neurosciences," *JAPA* 51:745-753.

Mayr, E. (1975) *Populations, Species, and Evolution* (Cambridge, Mass.: Harvard UP).

Mayr E. (1980) "How I became a Darwinian," in *The Evolutionary Synthesis* (eds.) Mayr and Provine. (Cambridge: Harvard).

Mayr, E. (1982) *The Growth of Biological Thought* (Cambridge: Harvard).

McIntosh, D. (1979) "The Empirical Bearing of Psychoanalytic Theory," *IJP* 60: 405-432.

Meehl, P. (1956) "Wanted — A Good Cookbook," *American Psychologist* 11:263-272.

Meissner, W. (1981) *Internalization in Psychoanalysis* (New York: IUP).

Meissner, W. (1982) "The History of the Psychoanalytic Movement," in *Psychoanalysis: Critical Explorations in Contemporary Theory and Practice* (eds.) Jacobson and Parmelee (New York: Brunner/Mazel): 3-28.

Meltzer, D. (1978) *The Kleinian Development* (Pertshire: Clunie Press).

Mendell, W. (1964) "The Phenomenon of Interpretation," *Am. J. Psychoanalysis* 24:184-9.

Messer, Sass, and Woolfolk (eds.) (1988). *Hermeneutics and Psychological Theory: Interpretive Perspectives on Personality, Psychotherapy, and Psychopathology.* (NJ: Rutgers).
Michels, R. (2000) "Psychoanalysis and its Discontents," in *Whose Freud?* (eds.) Brooks and Woloch (New Haven: Yale UP).
Miller, J-A. (1996) "An Introduction to Lacan's Clinical Perspectives," in *Reading Seminars I and II* (eds.) Fink, Jaanus, Feldstein (New York: SUNY).
Milner, J.C. (2000) "The Doctrine of Science," *Umbra,* "Science and Truth":33-64.
Mitchell, J. (2000) "The Vortex Beneath the Story," in *Whose Freud?* (eds.) Brooks and Woloch (New Haven: Yale UP).
Mitchell, S. (1988) *Relational Concepts in Psychoanalysis: An Integration* (Cambridge, Mass.: Harvard UP).
Mitchell, S. (1995) *Hope and Dread in Psychoanalysis* (New York: Basic Books).
Mitchell, S. (2000) "Response to Silverman" *Psychoanalytic Psychology* 17(1):153-159.
Mitchell and Black (1996) *Freud and Beyond: A History of Modern Psychoanalytic Thought* (New York: Basic).
Mitchell and Aron. (1999) *Relational Psychoanalysis: The Emergence of a Tradition.* (Hillsdale, NJ: Analytic Press).
Modell, A. (1984) *Psychoanalysis in a New Context* (New York: IUP).
Modell, A. (1986) "The Missing Element in Kohut's Cure," *Psychoanalytic Inquiry* 6: 367-385.
Modell, A. (2003) *Imagination and the Meaningful Brain* (Cambridge: MIT Press).
Montesquieu, C-L. (1989 [1748]) *Spirit of the Laws* (eds.) Cohler, Miller, and Stone (Cambridge: Cambridge UP).
Morin, E. (1981) *La Méthode. Tome 1. La Nature de la Nature* (Paris: Seuil).
Morin, E. (1982 [1969]) *Le Vif du Sujet* (Paris: Seuil).
Morin, E. (1983) "Beyond Determinism: The Dialogue of Order and Disorder. *SubStance* (40): 22-35.
Morin, E. (1985) *La Méthode, Tome 2. La Vie de la Vie* (Paris: Seuil).
Morin, E. (1991). Le Idee: Habitat, Vita, Organizzazione, Usi e Costumi (Milano: Feltrinelli).
Morris and Dolan (2001) "Emotion: The Amygdala and Unconscious Fear Processing," in *Out of Mind: Varieties of Unconscious Processes* (eds.) de Gelder, de Haan, and Heywood (New York: Oxford UP).
Moulines, O. (1976) "Approximate Application of Empirical Theories: A General Explication," *Erkenntnis* 10(2):201-227.
Murray, E. (1956) "A Content-Analysis Method for Studying Psychotherapy," *Psychological Monographs* 70(13).
Nacht, S. (1950) *De la Pratique à la Théorie Psychoanalytique* (Paris: P.U.F.).
Nader, Schafe, and LeDoux (2000) "Fear Memories Require Protein Synthesis in the Amygdala for Reconsolidation After Retrieval," *Nature* 406:722-726.
Nagel, E. (1959) "Methodological Issues in Psychoanalytic Theory," in *Psychoanalysis, Scientific Method and Philosophy* (ed.) S. Hook (New York: NYU):38-56.
Neumann, E. (1973) *Depth Psychology and the New Ethic,* trans. Rolfe (Boston: Shambhala).
Nietzsche, F. (1989) *On the Genealogy of Morals,* ed. and trans. Kaufmann (New York: Vintage).
Obegi and Berant (2008) *Attachment Theory and Research in Clinical Work with Adults* (New York: Guilford Press).
O'Dell, J. (1972) "P.T. Barnum Explores the Computer," *J. Consult. and Clin. Psychol.* 38: 270-273.
Ogden, T. (1982) *Projective Identification and Psycho-Therapeutic Technique* (New York: Aronson).
Oppenheim and Putnam (1958) "Unity of Science as a Working Hypothesis," *Minnesota Studies in the Philosophy of Science* 2:3-36.
Orgel, S. (1958) "Effect of Psychoanalysis on the Course of Peptic Ulcer," *Psychosomatic Medicine* 20:117-123.

Orlinsky, D. (1994) "Research-Based Knowledge as the Emergent Foundation for Clinical Practice in Psychotherapy," in Tally, Strupp, and Butler (eds.) *Psychotherapy Research and Practice: Bridging the Gap* (New York: Basic Books).

Palumbo and Gillman (1984) "Effects of Subliminal Activation of Oedipal Fantasies on Competitive Performance: A Replication and Extension," *Journal of Nerv. Ment. Dis.* 172:737-741.

Panskeep, J. (1998) *Affective Neuroscience: The Foundation of Human and Animal Emotions.* (New York: Oxford UP).

Panskeep, J. (1999) "Emotions as Viewed by Psychoanalysis and Neuroscience: An Exercise in Consilience," *Neuropsychoanal.* 1:15-38.

Parkes, Stevenson-Hinde, and Marris (1991) *The Place of Attachment in Human Behaviour* (New York: Routledge).

Parsons, M. (1992a) "The Refinding of Theory in Clinical Practice," *IJP* 73:103-115.

Parsons, M. (1992b) "Cognition as Interpretation in Art Education," in Reimer and Smith (eds.) *The Arts, Education, and Aesthetic Knowing (Chicago: University of Chicago Press): 71-91.*

Patterson, C. (1984) "Empathy, Warmth, and Genuineness in Psychotherapy: A Review of Reviews," *Psychotherapy* 21:421-438.

Pennybacker, J. (1988) "Disclosure of Traumas and Immune Function: Health Implications for Psychotherapy," *Journal of Consulting Psychology* 56(2):239-245.

Peterfreund, E. (1971) *Information Systems and Psychoanalysis* (New York: IUP).

Peterfreund, E. (1983) *The Process of Psychoanalytic Psychotherapy: Models and Strategies* (Hillsdale: Analytic Press).

Peters, R. (1950) "Cure, Cause, Motive," *Analysis* 10(5):103-9.

Pfeiffer, E. (1966) *Sigmund Freud-Lou Andreas-Salomé. Briefwechsel* (Frankfurt: Fischer).

Phillips, A. (1989) *Winnicott* (Cambridge, Mass.: Harvard UP).

Phillips, A. (1995) *Terror and Experts* (Cambridge, Mass.: Harvard UP).

Phillips, A (1998) *The Beast in the Nursery* (New York: Pantheon).

Phillips, A. (2001) *Promises, Promises: Essays on Psychoanalysis and Literature* (New York: Basic Books).

Phillips, J. (1998) "The Fissure of Authority: Violence and the Acquisition of Knowledge," in *Reading Melanie Klein* (eds.) Phillips and Stonebridge (London: Routledge).

Piaget, J. (1971) "The Affective Unconscious and the Cognitive Unconscious," *JAPA* 21:249-246.

Pippin, R. (2008) *Hegel's Practical Philosophy: Rational Agency as Ethical Life* (Cambridge: Cambridge UP).

Pontalis, J.B. (2003) *Windows*, trans. Quinney (Lincoln: University of Nebraska Press).

Popper, K. (2003 [1963]) *Conjectures and Refutations: The Growth of Scientific Knowledge* (London: Routledge).

Prioleau, Murdock, and Brody (1983) "An Analysis of Psychotherapy Versus Placebo Studies," *Behavioral and Brain Sciences* 6:275-310.

Pulver, S. (1987) "How Theory Shapes Technique: Perspectives on a Clinical Study," *Psychoanalytic Inquiry* 7:141-299.

Pulver, S. (2003) "On the Astonishing Clinical Irrelevance of Neuroscience," *JAPA* 51:755-772.

Putnam, H. (2004) *The Collapse of the Fact/Value Dichotomy and Other Essays* (Cambridge, Mass.: Harvard UP).

Putnam, R. (2001) *Bowling Alone* (New York: Touchstone).

Rachman and Wilson (1980) *The Effects of Psychological Therapy*, 2nd enlarged edition. (New York: Pergamon Press).

Racker, H. (1968) *Transference and Counter-transference* (New York: IUP).

Rado, S. (1933) "Fear and Castration in Women," *PSQ* 2:425-475.

Rado, S. (1956) *Collected Papers, Vol 1. Psychoanalysis of Behavior* (New York: Grune and Stratton).

Rand and Torok (1997) *Questions for Freud: The Secret History of Psychoanalysis* (Cambridge: Harvard UP).

Rangell, L. (1981) "Psychoanalysis and Dynamic Psychotherapy: Similarities and Differences Twenty-Five Years Later," *PSQ* 50:665-693.
Rangell, L. (2004) *My Life in Theory* (New York: Other Press).
Rapaport, D. (1958) "The Structire of Psychoanakytic Theory: A Systematizing Attempt," in Koch (ed.) *Psychology: A Study of a Science* 3 (New York: McGraw-Hill): 55-183.
Rapaport, D. (1960) "The Structure of Psychoanalytic Theory," *Psychological Issues*, Monograph No. 6(2)2 (New York: IUP).
Rapaport, D. (1967 [1954]) "Clinical Implications of Ego Psychology," in *The Collected Papers of David Rapaport* (ed.) Gill (New York: Basic Books).
Rapaport and Gill (1959) "The Point of View and Assumptions of Metapsychology," *IJP* 40:153-162.
Rawls, J. (2005) *Political Liberalism* (New York: Columbia UP).
Sue Read (ed.) (1997) *Developments in Infant Observation: The Tavistock Model* (New York: Routledge).
Reich, W. (1974 [1933]). *Character Analysis* (New York: Touchtone Books).
Reich, A. (1949) "The Structure of the Grotesque-Comic Sublimation," *Bull. Menninger Clin.* 13:160-171.
Reich, A. (1973) "Empathy and Countertransference" in *Psychoanalytic Contributions* (New York: IUP) .
Reik, T. (1972 [1948]) *Listening with the Third Ear* (New York: Arena Books).
Richards, E. (2006) "Inherited Epigenetic Variation — Revisiting Soft Inheritance," *Nature Reviews Genetics* 7:395-401.
Riley, D. (2000) *The Words of Selves: Identification, Solidarity, Irony* (Stanford: Stanford University Press).
Roeckerath, K. (2002) "Projective Identification: A Neuro-Psychoanalytic Perspective," *Neuropsychoanalysis* 4:177-185.
Ricoeur, P. (1970) *Freud and Philosophy: An Essay on Interpretation* (New Haven: Yale UP).
Ricoeur, P. (1974) *The Conflict of Interpretations* (Illinois: Northwestern UP).
Ricoeur, P. (1981 [1977]) "The Question of Proof in Freud's Psychoanalytic Writing," in Thompson (ed.), *Paul Ricoeur: Hermeneutics and Social Science* (Cambridge: Cambridge UP).
Robbins, L. (1963) "The Accuracy of Parental Recall of Aspects of Child Development and Child-rearing Practices," *Journal of Abnormal and Social Psychology* 66:261-270.
Rosen, G. (1981) *Hegel Contra Sociology* (London: Athalone).
Rose, J. (1993) *Why War?* (Oxford: Wiley-Blackwell).
Rosen (2007) "On the Fate of Psychoanalysis and Political Theory," *PSQ* 76:943-80.
Rosenbaum and Muroff (eds.) (1984) *Anna O: Fourteen Contemporary Reinterpretations* (New York: Free Press).
Rosenberg, A. (1994) *Instrumental Biology; or, the Disunity of Science* (Chicago: U of Chicago Press).
Rosenblatt and Thickstun (1977) "Energy, Information, and Motivation. A Revision of Psychoanalytic Theory," *JAPA* 25:537-558.
Rosenblatt and Thickstun (1984) "The Psychoanalytic Process: A Systems and Information Processing Model," *Psychoanalytic Inquiry* 4:59-86.
Rosen-Carole, A. (2010) "Menu Cards in Time of Famine: On Psychoanalysis and Politics," *PSQ* 79:203-233.
Rosen-Carole, A. (2011) *Lacan and Klein, Creation and Discovery* (Lanham: Lexington).
Rosenthal, R. (1966) *Experimenter Effect in Behavioral Research* (New York: Appleton-Century-Crofts).
Rosenthal and Rosnow (eds.) (1968) *Artifact in Behavioral Research* (New York: Academic Press).
Ross and Conway (1986) "Remembering One's Own Past: The Construction of Personal History," in Sorrentino and Higgins (eds.) *Handbook of Motivation and Cognition* (New York: Guilford Press):122-144.
Roudineso, E. (2003) *Why Psychoanalysis?*, trans. R. Bowlby (New York: Columbia).
Rycroft (1966) *Psychoanalysis Observed* (London: Constable).

Rubenstein, B. (1967) "Explanation and Mere Description: A Metascientific Examination of Certain Aspects of The Psychoanalytic Theory of Motivation," in *Motives and Thought* (ed.) Holt (New York: IUP).

Rubenstein, B. (1980) "The Problem of Confirmation in Clinical Psychoanlaysis," *JAPA* 28:397-417.

Rubenstein, B. (1983) "Freud's Early Theories of Hysteria," in *Physics, Philosophy and Psychoanalysis* (eds.) Cohen and Laudan (Boston: Reidel): 169-190.

Rudolf, G. (1991) "Free University of Berlin: Berlin Psychotherapy Study," in Beutler and Crago (eds.) *Psychotherapy Research. An International Review of Programmatic Studies.* (Washington: American Psychological Association.).

Rudolf and Manz (1993) "Zur prognostischen Bedeutung der therapeutischen Arbeitsbeziehung aus der Perspektive von Patienten und Therapeuten," *Psychother. Psychosom. med. Psychol.*, 43:193-199.

Rudolf et al. (1994) "Ergebnisse psychoanalytischer Therapie," *Z. Psychosom. Med. Psychoanal.* 40:25-40.

Ruitenbeck, H. (1973) *Freud as We Knew Him* (Detroit: Wayne UP).

Ruitenbeck, H (ed.) (1973) *The First Freudians* (New York: Aronson).

Runyan, W. (1981) "Why did Van Gogh Cut Off His Ear? The Problem of Alternative Explanations in Psychobiography," *J. Personal. & Social Psychol.* 40:1070–1077.

Russell, R. (ed.) (1994) *Reassessing Psychotherapy Research* (New York: Guilford).

Rustein and Goldberger (1973) "The Effects of Aggressive Stimulation on Suicidal Patients: An Experimental Study of the Psychoanalytic Theory of Suicide," *Psychoanalysis and Contemporary Science* 2:157-174.

Rustin, M. (2001) *Reason and Unreason: Psychoanalysis, Science and Politics* (Middletown: Wesleyan UP).

Salmon, W. (1959) "Psychoanalytic Theory and Evidence," in S. Hook (ed.) *Psychoanalysis, Scientific Method, and Philosophy* (New York: NYU Press): 252-267.

Samuels, A. (2006) "Transference/Countertransference," in *The Handbook of Jungian Psychology: Theory, Practice and Applications* (ed.) Papadopoulos (London: Routledge).

Sandell, R. (1999) "Long-Term Findings of the Stockholm Outcome of Psychotherapy and Psychoanalysis Project (STOPPP)," Paper presented at the Psychoanalytic Long-Term Treatments: A Challenge for Clinical and Empirical Research in Psychoanalysis, Hamburg, Germany.

Sandell et al. (2000) "Varieties of Longterm Outcome Among Patients in Psychoanalysis and Long-Term Psychotherapy: a Review of Findings in the Stockholm Outcome of Psychoanalysis and Psychotherapy Project (STOPP)." *International Journal of Psychoanalysis*, 81(5):921-943.

Sandler, J. (1983) "Reflections on Some Relations Between Psychoanalytic Concepts and Psychoanalytic Practice," *IJP* 64:35-45.

Sandler et al. (2001) *Clinical and Observational Psychoanalytic Research: Roots of a Controversy* (London: Karnac).

Sartre, J-P. (1961) *Psychology of Imagination* (New York: Citadel).

Scerri, E. (1991) "Chemistry, Spectroscopy, and the Question of Reduction," *Journal of Chemical Education* 68:122-6.

Scerri, E. (1994) "Has Chemistry Been at least Approximately Reduced to Quantum Mechanics?" *PSA* 1:160-70.

Schaetzel, Jean-Claude (1994) "Bronzehelmet, or the Itinerary of the Psychotherapy of a Psychotic," in *How Lacan's Ideas are Used in Clinical Practice* (ed.) Schneiderman (New York: Jason Aronson).

Schafer, R. (1975) "Psychoanalysis without Psychodynamics," *IJP* 56:41-55.

Schafer, R. (1977) "The Interpretation of Transference and the Conditions for Loving," *JAPA* 25:335-362.

Schafer, R. (1976) *A New Language for Psychoanalysis* (New Haven: Yale UP).

Schafer, R. (1983) *The Analytic Attitude* (New York: Basic Books).

Schafer, R. (1990) "The Search for the Common Ground," *IJP* 71:49-52.

Scharff, J. (2001) "Case Presentation: Object Relations Approach," *Psychoanal. Inquiry*, 21:469-482.
Schill, T. (1966) "Sex Differences in Identification of the Castrating Agent on the Blacky Test," *J. of Clinical Psychology* 22:324-325.
Schore, A. (1994) *Affect Regulation and the Origin of the Self* (Hove: Erlbaum).
Schore, A. (1997) "A Century After Freud's Project for a Scientific Psychology — Is a Rapprochement Between Psychoanalysis and Neurobiology at Hand?" *JAPA* 45:807-839.
Schore, A. (2001a) "Neurobiology and Psychoanalysis: Convergent Findings on the Subject of Projective Identification," in *Being Alive: Building on the Work of Anne Alvarez* (ed.) Edwards (London: Brunner-Routledge): 57-74.
Schore, A. (2001b) "The Right Brain as the Neurobiological Substratum of Freud's Dynamic Unconscious," in *The Psychoanalytic Century: Freud's Legacy for the Future*, (ed.) Scharff (New York: Other Press): 61-88.
Schore, A. (2002) "Clinical Implications of a Psychoneurobiological Model of Projective Identification," in *Primitive Mental States Volume II: Psychobiological and Psychoanalytic Perspectives on Early Trauma and Personality Development* (ed.) Alhanati (London: Karnac): 1-65.
Schore, A. (2003a) "The Seventh Annual John Bowlby Memorial Lecture," in *Revolutionary Connections: Psychotherapy and Neuroscience* (eds.) Corrigall and Wilkinson (London: Karnac): 7-51.
Schore, A. (2003b) *Affect Dysregulation and Disorders of the Self* (New York: Norton).
Schore, A. (2003c) *Affect Regulation and the Repair of the Self* (New York: Norton).
Schore, A. (2003d) "Special Section: Psychoanalytic Research: Progress and Process Notes from Allan Schore's Groups in Developmental Affective Neuroscience and Clinical Practice," *Psychol Psychoanalyst* XXIII, No. 4:9-16.
Schore, A. (2005) "A Neuropsychoanalytic Viewpoint: Commentary on Paper by Steven H. Knoblauch," *Psychoanalytic Dialogues* 15(6):829-854 .
Scriven, M. (1959) "The Experimental Investigation of Psychoanalysis," in S. Hook (ed.) *Psychoanalysis, Scientific Method, and Philosophy* (New York: NYU Press): 226-251.
Scriven, M. (1961) "The Key Property of Physical Laws: Inaccuracy," in Feigl and Maxwell (eds.), *Current Issues in the Philosophy of Science* (New York: Holt, Rinehart and Winston).
Schott, H. (1985) *Zauberspigel der Seele: Sigmund Freud und die Geschichte der Selbstanalyse* (Göttingen: Vandenhock und Ruprecht).
Schroeder and Dush (1987) "Relinquishing the Placebo: Alternatives for Psychotherapy Outcome Research. *American Psychologist* 42:1129-1130.
Schwaber, E. (1992) "Countertransference: The Analyst's Retreat from the Patient's Vantage Point," *IJP* 73(pt. 2):349-61.
Sears, R. (1943) *Survey of Objective Studies of Psychoanalytic Concepts* (New York: Social Science Research Council).
Seitz, P. (1966) "The Consensus Problem in Psychoanalytic Research," in *Methods of Research in Psychotherapy* (eds.) Gottschalk and Auerbach (New York: Appleton-Century-Crofts).
Semenza, C. (2001) "Psychoanalysis and Cognitive Neuropsychology: Theoretical and Methodological Affinities," *Neuropsychoanalysis* 3:3-10.
Senger, H. (1987) "The 'Placebo' Effect of Psychotherapy: A Moose in the Rabbit Stew," *American Journal of Psychotherapy* 41(1):68–81.
Shapere, D. (1974) "Scientific Theories and their Domains," *The Structure of Scientific Theories* (ed.) Suppe (Urbana: University of Illinois Press).
Shapere, D. (1982) "The Concept of Observation in Science and Philosophy," *Philosophy of Science* Dec. 1982:485-525.
Shapere, D. (1984) *Reason and the Search for Knowledge: Investigations in the Philosophy of Science* (Boston: Reidel).
Shapiro, D. (1965) *Neurotic Styles* (New York: Basic Books).
Shapiro, T. (ed.) *Psychoanalysis and Contemporary Science*, 5 Vols. (New York: IUP).
Shapiro and Shapiro (1982) "Meta-analysis of Comprative Therapy Outcome Studies: A Replication and Refinement," *Psychological Bulletin* 92:581-604.

Shepherdson, C. (2003) "Lacan and philosophy," in *The Cambridge Companion to Lacan* (ed.) Rabaté (Cambridge: Cambridge University Press).
Shuren and Grafman (2002) "The Neurology of Reasoning," *Archives of Neurology* 59: 916-9.
Shuttlesworth, J. (1989) *Psychoanalytical Theory and Infant Development*," in Miller (ed.) *Closely Observed Infants* (London: Ducksworth).
Shuttlesworth, J. (1998) "Theories of Mental Development," *Infant Observation* (1)2: 29-50.
Siegel, D. (1999) *Developing the Mind: How Relationships and the Brain Interact to Shape Who We Are* (New York: Guilford).
Silverman, L. (1983) "The Subliminal Psychodynamic Activation Method" in Masling (ed.) *Empirical Studies of Psychoanalytic Theories*, Vol. 1 (Hillsdale: Erlbaum): 69-100.
Silverman, Ross, Adler, and Lustig (1978) "A Simple Research Paradigm for Demonstrating Subliminal Psychodynamic Activation," *Journal of Abnormal Psychology* 69:158-172.
Simpson, E. (1951) "The Interpretation of Interaction in Contingency Tables," *Journal of the Royal Statistical Society*, Ser. B. 13:238-41.
Sloane et al. (1975) "Short-Term Analytically Oriented Psychotherapy Versus Behavior Therapy," *Am. J. Psychiatry* 132:373-377.
Sklansky et al. (1966) "Verbal Interaction and Levels of Meaning in Psychotherapy," *Archives of General Psychiatry* 14:158-170.
Skinner, B.F. (1956) "Critique of Psychoanalytic Concepts and Theories," in *The Foundations of Science and the Concepts of Psychology and Psychoanalysis*" (ed.) Feigl and Scriven (Minnesota: U of Minnesota Press): 77-87 .
Skinner, B.F. (1965) *Science and Human Behavior* (New York: Free Press).
Smith, J. (ed.). (1977) *Thought, Consciousness, and Reality* (New Haven: Yale).
Smith and Glass (1977) "Meta-Analysis of Psychotherapy Outcome Studies," *American Psychologist* 32:752-760.
Smith, Glass, and Miller (1980) *The Benefits of Psychotherapy* (Baltimore: JHU Press).
Snyder, Shenkel, and Lowery (1977) "Acceptance of Personality Interpretations: The 'Barnum Effect' and Beyond," *J. of Consulting and Clinical Psychology* 45:104-114.
Soler, C. (1996) "The Symbolic Order (1)," in *Reading Seminars I and II* 1996 *Reading Seminars I and II* (eds.) Fink, Jaanus, Feldstein (New York: SUNY UP).
Solms, M. (1997) *The Neuropsychology of Dreams: A Clinico-Anatomical Study* (Mahwah: Lawrence Erlbaum).
Solms, M. (1999) "The New Neuropsychology of Sleep Commentary by Mark Solms," *Neuropsychoanalysis* 1:183-195.
Solms, M. (2000) "Dreaming and REM Sleep Are Controlled by Different Brain Mechanisms," *Behavioral Brain Science* 23(6):843-50.
Solms, M. (2001) "The Interpretation of Dreams and the Neurosciences," *Psychoanalysis and History* 3:79-91.
Solms and Kaplan-Solms (2000) *Clinical Studies in Neuro-Psychoanalysis: Introduction to a Depth Neuropsychology* (London: Karnac).
Solms and Turnbull (2002) *The Brain and the Inner World: An Introduction to the Neuroscience of Subjective Experience* (New York: Other Press).
Sabourin, P. (1985). *Ferenczi, Paladin et Gran Visir Secret* (Paris: Ed. Universitaires).
Spence, D. (1982) *Narrative Truth and Historical Truth: Meaning and Interpretation in Psychoanalysis* (New York: Norton).
Spence, D. (ed.) (1984) *Psychoanalysis and Contemporary Science* Vol. 4 (New York: IUP).
Spielberger, Gorsuch, and Lushene (1970) *The State-Trait Anxiety Inventory (Self-Evaluation Questionnaire)* (Palo Alto, CA: Consulting Psychologists Press).
Spillius, E.B. (2007) "Melanie Klein Revisited: Her Unpublished Thoughts on Technique," in *Encounters with Melanie Klein: Selected Papers of Elizabeth Spillius* (eds.) Roth and Rusbridger (London: Routledge).
Spitz, R. (1945) "Hospitalism—An Inquiry Into the Genesis of Psychiatric Conditions in Early Childhood," *Psychoanalytic Study of the Child* 1:53-74.
Spitz, R. (1950) "Relevancy of Direct Infant Observation," *Psychoanalytic Study of the Child* 5:66-73.

Spitz and Cobliner (1965) *The First Year of Life: A Psychoanalytic Study of Normal and Deviant Development of Object Relations* (New York: IUP).
Springer, K. (1992) "Children's Awareness of the Biological Implications of Kinship," *Child Development* 63: 950-959.
Sroufe, L. (1988) "The Role of Infant-Caregiver Attachment in Development," in Belsky and Nezworski (eds.) *Clinical Implications of Attachment* (Hillsdale: Erlbaum): 18-38.
Stanford, P. (2006) *Exceeding Our Grasp: Science, History, and the Problem of Unconceived Alternatives* (New York: Oxford UP).
Stanton, M. (1991) *Sandor Ferenczi: Reconsidering Active Intervention* (Northvale: Aronson).
Stein, G. (1990 [1933]) *Autobiography of Alice B. Toklas* (New York: Vintage).
Steiner, J. (1993) Psychic Retreats: Pathological Organizations in Psychotic, Neurotic and Borderline Patients (London: Routledge).
Stern, Daniel (1985) *The Interpersonal World of the Infant: A View From Psychoanalysis and Developmental Psychology* (New York: Basic Books).
Stern, Donnel (1997) *Unformulated Experience: From Dissociation to Imagination in Psychoanalysis* (Hillsdale: Analytic Press).
Stiles, Shapiro, and Eliott (1986) "Are All Psychotherapies Equivalent?" *American Psychologist* 41:165-180.
Stiles, Shapiro, and Harper (1994) "Finding the Way from Process to Outcome: Blind Alleys and Unmarked Trails," in *Reassessing Psychotherapy Research* (New York: Guilford).
Strachey, J. (1934) "The Nature of the Therapeutic Action of Psychoanalysis," *IJP* XV:127-59.
Strenger, C. (1991) *Between Hermeneutic and Sciences: An Essay on the Epistemology if Psychoanalysis* (Madison: IUP).
Strupp, Wallach, Wogan, and Jenkins (1963) "Psychotherapists' Assessments of Former Patients," *Journal of Nervous and Mental Disease* 137:222-230.
Suerbaum and Michetti (2002) "Helicobacter Pylori Infection," *New England Journal of Medicine* 347:1175-1186.
Sullivan, H. S. (1940) *Conceptions of Modern Psychiatry* (Washington, DC: William A. White Foundation).
Sullivan, H.S. (1953) *The Interpersonal Theory of Psychiatry* (New York: Norton).
Sullivan, H.S. (1962) *Schizophrenia as a Human Process* (New York: Norton).
Sulloway, F. (1979) *Freud: Biologist of the Mind* (New York: Basic Books).
Summers, F. (2005) *Self Creation: Psychotherapy and the Art of the Possible* (Hillsdale: Analytic Press).
Sundberg, N. (1955) "The Acceptability of 'Fake' versus *Bona Fide* Personality Test Interpretations," *J. Abn. Soc. Psychol.* 50:145-147.
Suppe, F. (1972) "What's Wrong with the Received View on the Structure of Scientific Theories?" *Philosophy of Science* (39):1-19.
Sutherland, J. (1990) *The Autonomous Self: The Work of John D. Sutherland* (ed.) J. Scharff (Northvale: Jason Aronson).
Suttie, I. (1935) *The Origins of Love and Hate* (London: Free Association Books).
Tansey and Burke (1989) *Understanding Countertransference: From Projective Identification to Empathy* (Hillsdale, NJ: Analytic Press).
Target and Fonagy (1994a) "The Efficacy of Psychoanalysis for Children: Prediction of Outcome in a Developmental Context," *Journal of the American Academy of Child and Adolescent Psychiatry* 33:1134-1144.
Target and Fonagy (1994b) "The Efficacy of Psychoanalysis for Children with Emotional Disorders," *Journal of the American Academy of Child and Adolescent Psychiatry* 33:361-371.
Taylor, Charles (1992) *Sources of Self* (Cambridge: Harvard UP).
Teller, P. (2001) "Twilight of the Perfect Model," *Erkenntnis* 55:393-415.
Teller, P. (2004a) "How we Dapple the World," *Philosophy of Science* 71(4):425-47.
Teller, P. (2004b) "The Law of Idealization," *Philosophy of Science* 71(5):730-41.
Thomä, H (2000) "Gemeinsamkeiten und Widersprüche zwischen vier Psychoanalytikern," *Psyche-Z Psychoanal.* 54:172–89.

Thomä and Kächele (1975) "Problems of Metascience and Methodology in Clinical Psychoanalysis," *Ann. Psychoanal.* 3:49-119.

Thomä, Grünzig, Böckenförder, and Kächele (1976) "Das Konsensusproblem in der Psychoanalyse,"*Psyche* 30(11):978-1027.

Thompson, M. (2008) *Life and Action: Elementary Structures of Practice and Practical Thought* (Cambridge, Mass.: Harvard UP).

Torrey, E. (1992) *The Freudian Fraud* (New York: Harper Collins).

Toulman, S. (1948) "The Logical Status of Psychoanalysis," *Analysis* 9(2) (reprinted in *Philosophy and Analysis* ed. Margaret Macdonald New York: Philosophical Library, 1954).

Truax, C. (1966) "Reinforcement and Nonreinforcement in Rogerian Psychotherapy," *J. of Abnor. Psych.* 71:1-9.

Tutte, J. (2004) "The Concept of Psychical Trauma: A Bridge in Interdisciplinary Space," *IJP* 85:897-921.

Van der Kolk and Van der Hart (1995) "The Intrusive Past: The Flexibility of Memory and the Engraving of Trauma," in Caruth (ed.) *Trauma: Explorations in Memory* (Baltimore: The Johns Hopkins University Press).

Van Fraassen, B. (1980) *The Scientific Image* (Oxford: Oxford UP).

von Rad, Senf, and Bräutigam (1998) "Psychotherapie und Psychoanalyse in der Krankenversorgung: Ergebnisse des Heidelberger Katamnesenprojektes," *Psychother. Psychosom. med Psychol* 48:88-100.

Waelder, R. (1960) *Basic Theory of Psychoanalysis* (New York: IUP).

Waelder, R. (1962) "Psychoanalysis, Scientific Method, and Philosophy, *JAPA* 10:617-637.

Waelder, R. (1933) "The Psychoanalytic Theory of Play," *PSQ* 2:208-224.

Waldron, S. (1997) "How Can We Study the Efficacy of Psychoanalysis?" *PSQ* LXVI:283-384.

Waldron, Scharf, Hurst, Firestein, and Burton (2004) "What Happens in a Psychoanalysis: A View through the Lens of the Analytic Process Scales (APS)," *IJP* 85:443-466.

Wilkins, W. (1984) "Empirically Equating Psychotherapy and Placebos: Critique and Alternatives," *Journal of Social and Clinical Psychology* 2:289-304.

Wallerstein, R. (1975) *Psychotherapy and Psychoanalysis: Theory, Practice, Research* (New York: IUP).

Wallerstein, R. (1986) *Forty-Two Lives in Treatment: A Study of Psychoanalysis and Psychotherapy* (New York: Guilford Press).

Wallerstein, R. (1988) "One Psychoanalysis or Many," *IJP* 69:5-21.

Wallerstein, R. (ed.) (1992) *The Common Ground of Psychoanalysis* (Northvale, NJ: Jason Aronson) .

Wallerstein, R. (1995) *The Talking Cures and the Psychotherapies* (New Haven: Yale UP).

Wallerstein, R. (1999) *Psychoanalysis: Clinical and Theoretical* (Madison: IUP).

Wallerstein, R. (2000) "Psychoanalytic Research: Where do we Disagree?" in *Clinical and Observational Psychoanalytic Research* (eds.) Sandler, Sandler, and Davies (London: Karnac): 27-31.

Wallerstein, R. (2004) *Psychoanalysis: Education, Research, Science and Profession* (New York: IUP).

Watt, D. (1986) "Transference: A Right Hemisphere Event? An Inquiry into the Boundary Between Psychoanalytic Metapsychology and Neuropsychology," *Psychoanalysis and Contemporary Thought* 9(1):43-77.

Watt, D. (1990) "Higher Cortical Functions and the Ego: The Boundary Between Psychoanalysis, Behavioral Neurology, and Neuropsychology," *Psychoanal. Psychol.* 7(4):487-527.

Watt, D. (1999) "Emotion and Consciousness. Part I. A review of Jaak Pankseep's *Affective Neuroscience*," *J. of Consciousness Studies* 6(7):191-200.

Wampold, B. (2002) *The Great Psychotherapy Debate: Models, Methods, and Findings* (Mahwah: Erlbaum).

Weber, M. (1958) *Max Weber: Essays in Sociology*, trans. Gerth and Mills (New York: Oxford UP).

Weber, Max. (1978) *Economy and Society*, ed. Roth and Wittich (Berkeley: U of California Press).

Weber et al. (1966) "The Application of Ego Strength Scales to Psychoanalytic Clinical Records," in *Developments in Psychoanalysis at Columbia University* (eds.) Goldman and Shapiro (New York: Hafner) :215-281.

Weber, Bachrach, and Solomon (1985) "Factors Associated with the Outcome of Psychoanalysis. Report of the Columbia Psychoanalytic Center Research Project (II)," *IRP* 12:127-141.

Webster, R. (1995) *Why Freud was Wrong* (New York: Harper Collins).

Weinberger and Silverman (1987) "Subliminal Psychodynamic Activation: A Method for Studying Psychoanalytic Dynamic Propositions," in Hogan and Jones (eds.)*Perspectives in Personality Vol. 2* (Greenwich: JAI Press): 251-287.

Weinberger and Silverman (1990) "Testability and Empirical Verification of Psychoanalytic Dynamic Propositions Through Subliminal Psychodynamic Activation," *Psychoanalytic Psychology* 7(3): 299-339.

Werman, D. (1979) "Methodological Problems in the Psychoanalytic Interpretation of Literature: A Review of Studies on Sophocles' Antigone," *J. Am. Psychoan.Assoc.*, 27:451-478.

Westen, D. (1990) "Toward a Revised Theory of Borderline Relations: Contributions of Empirical Research," *IJP* 71:661-693.

Westin, D. (2000) "The Search for Objectivity in the Study of Subjectivity: Reply to Commentary," *Psychoanalytic Dialogues* 12(6):915-920.

Westen and Gabbard (2002) "Developments in Cognitive Neuroscience: II. Implications for Theories of Transference," *Journal of the American Psychoanalytic Association* 50: 99-134.

Westen and Morrison (2001) "A Multidimensional Meta-Analysis of Treatments for Depression, Panic, and Generalized Anxiety Disorder: An Empirical Examination of the Status of Empirically Supported Theories," *J. of Consulting & Clinical Psychol.* 69:875-899.

Westphal, M. (1979) *History & Truth in Hegel's Phenomenology* (Indianapolis: Indiana University Press).

Whitford, M. (1991) *Luce Irigaray: Philosophy in the Feminine* (London: Routledge).

Wilcocks, R. (1994) *Maelzel's Chess Player: Sigmund Freud and the Rhetoric of Deceit* (Lanham: Rowman and Littlefield).

Williams, B. (1998) "The End of Explanation (a Review of *The Last Word*, by T. Nagel)," in *The New York Review of Books* November 19, 1998.

Winnicott, D. (1964 [1950]). "The Deprived Child and How He can be Compensated for Loss of Family Life" in *The Family and Individual Development* (London: Tavistock).

Winnicott, D. W. (1972) *Holding and Interpretation: Fragment of an Analysis* (New York: Grove).

Winnicott, D.W. (1965) *The Maturational Process and the Facilitating Environment* (New York: IUP).

Winnicott, D.W. (1975) *Through Pediatrics to Psycho-analysis* (New York: Basic Books).

Winnicott, D.W. (1996 [1971]) *Playing and Reality* (New York: Basic Books).

Wisdom, J. (1967) "Testing an Interpretation Within a Session," *IJP* 48:44-52.

Wittgenstein, L. (1981) *Tractatus Logico-Philosophicus,* trans. Ogden (London: Routledge).

Wittgenstein, L. (2009) *Philosophical Investigations*, trans. Anscombe, Hacker, and Schulte (New York: Wiley-Blackwell).

Wolff, P. "The Irrelevance of Infant Observations for Psychoanalysis," *JAPA* 44:369-92.

Wolitzky, Klein, and Dworkin (1975) "An Experimental Approach to the Study of Repression," *Psychoanalysis and Contemporary Science* 4:211-233.

Woolf, V. (1976) "Sketch of the Past," in *Moments of Being* (ed.) Schulkind (London: Sheldon Press).

Woozley, A. (1976) *Theory of Knowledge* (London: Hutchinson).

Yorke, C. (1994) "Freud or Klein: Conflict or Compromise," *International Journal of Psychoanalysis* 75: 375-385.

Yovell, Y. (2000) "From Hysteria to Posttraumatic Stress Disorder: Psychoanalysis and Neurobiology of Traumatic Memories," *Journal of Neuropsychoanalysis* (2):171-181.

Yu, C.K. (2001a) "Neuroanatomical Correlates of Dreaming," *Neuropsychoanalysis* 3:47-59.

Yu, C.K. (2001b) "Neuroanatomical Correlates of Dreaming II," *Neuropsychoanalysis* 3:139-201.

Yu, C.K. (2003) "Neuroanatomical Correlates of Dreaming, III: The Frontal Lobe Controversy (Dream Censorship)," *Neuropsychoanalysis* 5:159-169.
Zajonc, R. (1968) "Attitudinal Effects of Mere Exposure," *Journal of Personality Social Psychology Monographs* 9(2)2:1-27.
Zetzel, E. (1970 [1956]) "Therapeutic Alliance in the Analysis of Hysteria," in *The Capacity for Emotional Growth* (New York: IUP): 182-196.

Index

www.ingramcontent.com/pod-product-compliance
Ingram Content Group UK Ltd.
Pitfield, Milton Keynes, MK11 3LW, UK
UKHW020905190926
475560UK00010B/194

9 780739 169513